"When Will These Things Be?" Questions on Eschatology

EDITED BY MARK MAYBERRY
AND KYLE POPE

© **Truth Publications, Inc. 2020.** All rights reserved. No part of this book may be reproduced in any form without prior written permission from the publisher. Printed in the United States of America.

ISBN 10: 1-58427-486-7

ISBN 13: 978-1-58427-486-5

Cover Photos: istockphoto.com

Truth Publications, Inc.
CEI Bookstore
220 S. Marion St., Athens, AL 35611
855-492-6657
sales@truthpublications.com
www.truthbooks.com

Table of Contents

Preface, by Kyle Pope 5
Introduction, by Mark Mayberry 7

Big Questions
    What Is Eternal Life and Why Should It Matter to Me?
        Tommy Peeler. 23
    What Does the Bible Teach about Hell and Who Will Go There?
        Ron Halbrook. 60
    Am I Ready for the End?
        Bobby Graham 109

The Kingdom
    Has the Kingdom of Christ Been Established?
        Joe Price. 123
    Does the Physical Nation of Israel Still Play a Role in God's Final Plans?
        Stephen Russell. 153
    Can Signs Foretell When the End Will Come?
        Allen Dvorak 168

Judgment Day
    What Does the Bible Teach about the Coming of Christ?
        Kevin Kay 185
    What Is the Biblical Teaching on the Resurrection?
        Bruce Reeves. 222
    Does the Bible Teach the "Rapture," the Coming of an Antichrist, and the
        Battle of Armageddon?
        Mark Mayberry 249

Tough Questions
    Does the Bible Teach an End of This Universe?
        Chris Reeves 287
    What Is the Focus of the Mount of Olives Discourse?
        Kyle Pope. 343
    When Was Revelation Written and Why Does It Matter?
        Daniel H. King, Sr. 371

Personal Eschatology: Men's Studies
    Where Are the Dead?
        Jesse Flowers 409
    Does the Bible Teach Purgatory?
        Daniel and Diana Dow 421
    Does the Bible Teach Reincarnation?
        Steve Wallace 435

Personal Eschatology: Women's Studies
    Where Are the Dead?
        Aleta Samford 451
    Does the Bible Teach Purgatory?
        Daniel and Diana Dow 466
    Does the Bible Teach Reincarnation?
        Jennifer Maxey 480

Appendix: General Studies
    Premillennialism
        Mike Willis 507
    Postmillennialism
        David Dann 512
    Amillennialism
        Sean Cavender 518
    The New Heavens and New Earth
        Jim McDonald 522
    The AD 70 Doctrine
        Don McClain 526
    Eco-Eschatology
        Matthew Bassford 530
    What Does the Bible Teach about Hades and Sheol?
        Kyle Pope 534

Preface
By Kyle Pope

> He has made everything beautiful in its time. Also He has put eternity in their hearts, except that no one can find out the work that God does from beginning to end (Eccl. 3:11, NKJV).

Eschatology is the study of "end times" and the biblical events, promises, conditions, and elements associated with them. Man has always been fascinated by the prospect of what the future holds and whether the Bible enables us to discern how and when "the end" will come. At the beginning of Jesus's longest discourse on end-times events, His disciples started the discussion with the words, "Tell us, when will these things be?" (Matt. 24:3a). The essays contained in this book present the reader with similar questions in an effort to look to the Scriptures for answers to the common questions that confront us.

Following an Introduction surveying New Testament teaching on Christ's kingdom, the reader will find five categories of questions: (1) *Big Questions,* considering final reward, punishment, and preparation; (2) *The Kingdom*, its establishment, alleged relationship to modern Israel, and signs of the end; (3) *Judgment Day,* the coming of Christ, resurrection, and denominational notions taught about it; (4) *Tough Questions,* concerning the duration of the universe, scope of Jesus's teachings on "the end," and the timing of John's Apocalypse; then finally (5) *Personal Eschatology,* through separate men's and women's tracks, this section examines the present condition of the dead and various concepts taught about it in Scripture and the religious world. The book ends with an Appendix offering essays that form a virtual expanded glossary summarizing some major eschatological doctrines and false doctrines.

The authors of these essays are all faithful Christians with a sincere love for God and a respect for the authority of Scripture. We firmly believe that the reader will find in this volume a valuable resource to aid in the study of God's revelation on questions about "end times." Its

"When Will These Things Be?" : Questions on Eschatology

format allows it to function as a reference tool the student may consult again and again. Thank you for considering this material. May the Lord be glorified by its use and may the Lord bless you in the study of these important issues.

Introduction
By Mark Mayberry

Although confusion abounds in today's religious world on the subject of the kingdom, this is nothing new. The Jewish people mistakenly thought the Messiah would establish a physical earthly kingdom. Modern millennialists (of the pre- and post- variety) evidence similar erroneous thinking. To help prepare the reader for this series of lessons on eschatology, let us consider what the Bible teaches regarding the kingdom of God, Christ, or heaven.

Essential Kingdom Concepts

Sacred Scripture frequently focuses on kingdom concepts. For additional study, use your digital Bible program to search for the following phrases: "kingdom of God," "the kingdom of heaven," "the kingdom of Christ," "the kingdom of His beloved Son," or verses containing "heavenly" and "kingdom," etc.

Jesus Christ, the Lamb of God and Lion of the tribe of Judah, is "King of kings and Lord of lords" (Rev. 17:14). As those who share in the inheritance of the saints in light, we should be thankful because God "rescued us from the domain of darkness and transferred us into the kingdom of His beloved Son" (Col. 1:12-14).

Definitions

What is a kingdom? A kingdom is a monarchy, i.e., a realm ruled by a king or queen. *The American Heritage Dictionary* says a kingdom is "a political or territorial unit ruled by a sovereign" (AHD). *Collins English Dictionary* defines a "kingdom" as "a territory, state, people, or community ruled or reigned over by a king or queen" (CED).

From the standpoint of Scripture, we need an understanding of two words: king and kingdom.

A king (Greek *basileus*) is "(1) one who rules as possessor of the highest office in a political realm, king, generally of a male ruler who

"When Will These Things Be?" : Questions on Eschatology

has unquestioned authority (exceptions are client rulers who owe their power to the grace of Rome) in a specific area; (2) one who possesses unusual or transcendent power, an extension of meaning #1; (a) of the Messianic king (Matt. 2:2); (b) of God (Matt. 5:35); (c) of a king of spirits in the nether world, Abaddon (Rev. 9:11)" (BDAG).

A kingdom (Greek *basileia*) refers to "kingdom, sovereignty, royal power" (Thomas, 932). BDAG defines it as "(1) the act of ruling; (a) generally, kingship, royal power, royal rule; (b) especially, of God's rule the royal reign of God; (2) territory ruled by a king, kingdom."

Let us consider the kingdom of God, Christ, or heaven, with particular focus on its ruler, subjects, territory, law, internal unity, and the need for militant defense against external threats.

A Kingdom Requires a Ruler

The realm over which God or Christ rules is called "the kingdom of God," "the kingdom of heaven," "the kingdom of Christ," "the kingdom of His beloved Son," or the "heavenly kingdom." During the Christian era, royal rule has been bestowed upon Jesus Christ (1 Tim. 6:13-16; Rev. 17:14; 19:11-16).

A Kingdom Requires Subjects

Faithful disciples of Christ are counted as citizens in the kingdom of God (Eph. 2:19-22). Citizenship is not bestowed by physical birth (as with ancient Israel), but by spiritual birth (i.e., it is reserved for those who make a conscious effort to understand and obey) (John 3:3-5; Heb. 8:10-12). Unrepentant sinners are excluded from the kingdom of Christ and God (Eph. 5:3-10).

A Kingdom Requires a Territory

The territory over which God and Christ rule involves three distinct realms: the world, the heart, and the church. In a broad sense, God rules in the kingdoms of men (Dan. 2:20-22; 4:16-17; 4:34-35). From an individual standpoint, the Father and Son reign in the hearts of those who believe and obey (Rom. 10:8-13; Col. 3:15-17). In a spiritual sense, Jesus Christ is Head of the body, the church, which is His kingdom (Matt. 16:18-19; Eph. 1:18-23; Col. 1:18).

A Kingdom Requires a Law

During His earthly ministry, Jesus went about preaching "the gospel of the kingdom" (Matt. 4:23). As the One who possesses all authority,

Introduction

Christ calls all humanity to discipleship and full submission to His commandments (Matt. 28:18-20). As free moral agents, we may reject His love and light, but we do so at our own peril (John 12:44-50).

A Kingdom Requires Internal Unity

There is internal unity within the Godhead, i.e., the Father, Son, and Holy Spirit function in perfect harmony (John 5:30-32; 10:30; 16:12-15). Recall the Deuteronomic declaration: "Hear, O Israel! The LORD is our God, the LORD is one!" (Deut. 6:4). Based upon this reality, the charge leveled against Jesus by the Pharisees (i.e., "This man casts out demons only by Beelzebul the ruler of the demons") was ludicrous (Matt. 12:22-29). Like the Lord God of Sacred Scripture, followers of Jesus Christ should strive for unity (John 17:20-21; Eph. 4:1-6).

A Kingdom Requires Militant Defense

Satan is the god of this world (2 Cor. 4:3-4). He is the relentless enemy of God, Jesus, the Holy Spirit, the truth, and all who would pursue the paths of righteousness. He brings death and destruction (Rev. 9:7-11). Persistent, unrepentant sin will exclude us from God's eternal kingdom (Matt. 13:36-43). Light and darkness, good and evil, sanctification and sin are mutually exclusive concepts (Eph. 5:11-14). No fellowship can exist between those who accept the rule of Christ and those who reject it (2 Cor. 6:14-18). As soldiers of the cross, let us stand firm against the schemes of the devil (Eph. 6:10-17). Recognizing that conflict is unavoidable (Phil. 1:27-30; 1 Thess. 2:1-2), may we courageously defend the truth, and the church or kingdom of our Lord (John 18:36; 1 Tim. 6:12; 2 Tim. 4:6-8).

The Kingdom in Prophecy, Preaching, and Practice

Next, let us consider the kingdom of God, Christ, or heaven in prophecy, preaching, and practice. Doing so provides historical context and practical benefits.

The Kingdom in Prophecy

Reflect upon Daniel's interpretation of the vision of Nebuchadnezzar. Foreshadowing the establishment of God's kingdom, Daniel said, "In the days of those kings the God of heaven will set up a kingdom which will never be destroyed, and that kingdom will not be left for another people; it will crush and put an end to all these kingdoms, but it will itself endure forever. . ." (Dan. 2:44-45). Ponder Isaiah's prophecy about

"When Will These Things Be?" : Questions on Eschatology

the Messianic king and His kingdom: "For a child will be born to us, a son will be given to us; and the government will rest on His shoulders; and His name will be called Wonderful Counselor, Mighty God, Eternal Father, Prince of Peace. There will be no end to the increase of His government or of peace, on the throne of David and over His kingdom, to establish it and to uphold it with justice and righteousness from then on and forevermore" (Isa. 9:6-7).

The Kingdom in Preaching

Turning to the New Testament, please note the perspectives of John and Jesus, who affirmed, "the kingdom of heaven is at hand" (Matt. 3:2; 4:17; 10:7) or "the kingdom of God is near" (Luke 10:8-11). In the sermon on the mount, Jesus frequently referred to "the kingdom of heaven" (Matt. 5:3, 10, 19-20; 7:21). In His parables, our Lord oft said, "The kingdom of heaven is like. . . ," making comparisons to a mustard seed, leaven, hidden treasure, or a merchant seeking fine pearls, a dragnet cast into the sea, and the wise conduct of the head of a household or landowner (Matt. 13:31, 33, 44, 45, 47, 52; 20:1). In contrast with the four gospels, the perspective of Acts, following the day of Pentecost, is, "The kingdom of heaven is here!" (Acts 1:3, 6-8; 8:12; 14:22; 19:8; 20:25; 28:23, 31). The same is true in the apostolic epistles (Rom. 14:17; 1 Cor. 4:20; 6:9-10; Col. 1:13; 4:11; Heb. 12:28-29; etc.).

The Kingdom in Practice

A King

According to biblical teaching, Jesus is King of kings. Standing before Pilate, Christ affirmed that He was king over a spiritual kingdom (John 18:36-37). Paul referred to Jesus as "He who is the blessed and only Sovereign, the King of kings and Lord of lords" (1 Tim. 6:13-16; cf. Rev. 17:14).

A Territory

Although Jesus is Lord over all the earth, the boundaries of His rule are not measured in miles but in the submissiveness of human hearts (1 John 2:3-6). Like Israel of old (Exod. 19:5-6), if we comply with the conditions of the New Covenant (Heb. 8:8-13), we can be counted as a kingdom of priests and a holy nation (1 Pet. 2:9-10; Rev. 1:6; 5:10).

A Constitution

The kingdom of God or Christ is governed by the Lord's sovereign will. In giving the great commission, Jesus said, "All authority has been

Introduction

given to Me in heaven and on earth. . ." (Matt. 28:18-20). He is seated at the right hand of God, "far above all rule and authority and power and dominion." All things are subject unto Him. He is head of all things to the church (Eph. 1:20-23).

A Citizenship
Entrance into the kingdom of heaven is limited to those who are citizens, i.e., those who have been brought near by the blood of Christ (Eph. 2:11-16). All who walk according to the apostolic pattern enjoy the rights of citizenship (Phil. 3:17-21).

Terms of Admission
How does one enter the kingdom of God, Christ, or heaven? We must be converted and become like children if we are to enter the kingdom of God (Matt. 18:1-4). Men must be born again—of water and the Spirit—to enter the kingdom of God (John 3:3-5).

Blessings and Benefits
What are the blessings and benefits of such citizenship? In this life, we enjoy righteousness and peace and joy in the Holy Spirit (Rom. 14:16-18). In eternity, we will enjoy the blessings of heaven (Matt. 25:34-40).

Duties and Responsibilities
What are the duties and responsibilities? We must walk in a manner worthy of God, who calls us into His own kingdom and glory (1 Thess. 2:10-12). Otherwise, we will hear those fateful words, "Depart from Me. . ." (Matt. 7:21-23).

The Kingdom: When and Where? INTRODUCTION

When and where would the kingdom of God be established? The perspective of the questioner affects the answer. Was the question asked from an Old Testament perspective? Was the question posed during the days of John the Baptist, or while Jesus Christ walked the earth? Is the query offered from a New Testament perspective, i.e., during the gospel age, or Christian dispensation? Finally, is there a sense in which certain aspects of kingdom prophecies anticipate eternity?

How do devoted Bible students distinguish between these different perspectives? A key element in understanding kingdom prophecies is to recognize the chronological distinction between "in that day," "at hand," "already," and "not yet." The prophets of old foreshadowed the coming of

"When Will These Things Be?" : Questions on Eschatology

Christ, describing events that would occur "in that day." Both John the Baptist and Jesus repeatedly said, "Repent for the kingdom of heaven is at hand." Some of Jesus's parables, and various apostolic statements, refer to the kingdom as a present reality, bringing blessings and enjoining responsibilities. Some of Jesus's parables, and various apostolic prophecies, refer to the Second Coming of Christ as the time at which the kingdom prophecies will be fully realized.

In Sacred Scripture, "the kingdom of God" or "heaven" is identified in four ways: (1) From an Old Testament perspective, it will occur "in that day"; (2) During the ministries of John and Jesus, it was "at hand"; (3) From Pentecost onward, the kingdom is counted as a present reality; (4) Nonetheless, some kingdom prophecies have not yet been fulfilled.

The Kingdom: When and Where? IN THAT DAY

Old Testament prophets foreshadowed future events—some near at hand and others more distant, some relating to the captivity and restoration of Israel and Judah, others predicting the coming of Christ and the messianic age. In reading such prophecies, note the overlapping occurrences of two phrases: "In the last days. . ." and ". . .in that day. . . ."

Isaiah and Micah famously predicted the coming of Christ, the establishment of the church, and the peaceful nature of the Messianic kingdom—all of which would occur "in the last days" (Isa. 2:2-4; Micah 4:1-5). As these two prophets continue describing related events, both use the phrase "in that day" (Isa. 2:12, 17-18; Micah 4:6-7). "In that day" also portends the coming of "the Branch of the Lord" (Isa. 4:1-6), employing unmistakably Messianic language (Isa. 11:1-5; 53:2; Jer. 23:5; 33:15; Zech. 3:8-10; 6:12).

When Micah specified that Bethlehem would be the birthplace of the Messiah (Micah 5:1:2), the prophet adds that "He will arise and shepherd His flock." Moreover, "He will be great to the ends of the earth. This One will be our peace" (vv. 4-5). After subsequent struggles and successes (vv. 5-6), the remnant of Jacob will be like dew and showers, bringing divine blessings (v. 7), and like a devouring beast, executing divine wrath (v. 8). All their enemies will be cut off (v. 9). "It will be in that day," declares the Lord . . . God will cut off horses and chariots, cities and fortifications so that His people will learn to trust in Him. He will cut off sorceries and fortune-tellers so that His people will learn to listen to Him. He will cut

Introduction

off carved images, sacred pillars, and the Asherim so that His people will learn to worship Him. He concludes by saying, "I will execute vengeance in anger and wrath on the nations which have not obeyed" (vv. 10-15).

A point of clarification is in order. While Old Testament prophets used the language mentioned above in talking about the establishment of the Messianic kingdom, which occurred on Pentecost, we should recognize that Jesus, in the Olivet Discourse (Matt. 24; Mark 13; Luke 21), addresses two distinct subjects: (1) the destruction of Jerusalem which occurred in AD 70, and (2) and the future return of the Lord in final judgment. Concerning the Second Coming, Jesus said, "But of that day and hour no one knows, not even the angels of heaven, nor the Son, but the Father alone" (Matt. 24:36; cf. Mark 13:32).

The Kingdom: When and Where? AT HAND

Both John the Baptist and Jesus Christ commanded their audiences, saying, "Repent for the kingdom of heaven is at hand" (Matt. 3:2; 4:17; 10:7; Mark 1:14-15). What relevant lessons can we draw from such preaching?

The Need for Repentance

The pronouncements of John and Jesus emphasized the need for repentance. Both exhorted their hearers, "Repent for the kingdom of heaven is at hand."

Consider the broader statement concerning John (Matt. 3:1-3) and the prophecy from which it is derived (Isa. 40:3-8). What is the application? Let's remove any obstacle that stands between God and us, so that we can see His glory.

Consider the broader statement concerning Jesus (Matt. 4:12-17) and the prophecy from which it is derived (Isa. 9:1-7). What is the application? We must turn from darkness and despair to the light, and from oppression to freedom, order, and righteousness.

What does it mean to repent? Repentance is a change of heart followed by a change of life—requiring that we turn away from sin (Ezek. 14:6) and turn to God (Acts 26:19-20). The preaching of John had a dramatic impact: "Then Jerusalem was going out to him, and all Judea and all the district around the Jordan; and they were being baptized by him in the Jordan River, as they confessed their sins." While some scoffed, many obeyed (Matt. 3:4-12; Luke 3:7-14). The crowds were questioning John, saying, "Then what shall we do?" He identified specific areas of application. As we examine John's warnings to the religious hierarchy, the crowds, the tax collectors and soldiers, we find the following admonitions:

Stated Positively	Stated Negatively
Be Content	Don't Be Greedy
Be Fruitful	Don't Be Barren
Be Generous	Don't Be Selfish
Be Honest	Don't Cheat
Be Sincere	Don't Pretend

These concepts are fundamental and applicable to every age group: children, young adults, married couples, parents, the elderly. They should be applied in every relationship: the home, the church, the workplace, the neighborhood, etc. These principles guide us at work and play, and also during times of worship.

The Need for Full Assurance

The preaching of John and Jesus emphasized the need for full assurance. John confidently asserted, "Behold, the Lamb of God who takes away the sin of the world!" (John 1:29-34). Jesus boldly declared, "I am the bread of life" (John 6:35), "I am the Light of the world" (8:12), "I am the door of the sheep" (10:7), "I am the good shepherd" (10:11), "I am the resurrection and the life" (11:25), "I am the way, and the truth, and the life; no one comes to the Father but through Me" (14:6), etc.

The Greek word *plērophoria*, derived from *plērophoreō* (to bring in full measure, to fulfill), refers to "full assurance." BDAG defines it as a "state of complete certainty, full assurance, certainty." This word occurs four times in the New Testament (Col. 2:2; 1 Thess. 1:5; Heb. 6:11; 10:22). In the NASB, it is rendered "conviction" (1x) and "full assurance" (3x). Delivered by the Holy Spirit and endowed with divine power, the gospel is capable of producing full conviction (1 Thess. 1:5). We should search the Scriptures and grow in knowledge so that we might have a full assurance of understanding (Col. 2:2), hope (Heb. 6:11), and faith (Heb. 10:22).

Let us recognize the danger of doubt. The Greek word *distazō* generally means "to be uncertain, to have second thoughts about a matter."

Introduction

Specifically, it means "(1) to have doubts concerning something, doubt, waver; (2) to be uncertain about taking a particular course of action, hesitate in doubt" (BDAG). This word occurs twice in the New Testament (Matt. 14:31; 28:17). It is used of Peter, who (while walking to Jesus on the water) noticed the winds and the waves, and began to sink (Matt. 14:28-33, esp. v. 31). What was the solution? Keep your eyes upon Jesus! It is also used of the disciples who (after the resurrection) worshiped Jesus on the mountain, but some were doubtful (Matt. 28:16-20, esp. v. 17). What was the solution? Remember the Lord's absolute authority.

The Need for Conviction

The miracles of Jesus provided evidence that the kingdom prophecies were being fulfilled: "If I cast out demons by the Spirit of God, then the kingdom of God has come upon you" (Matt. 12:22-29; Luke 11:14-23; cf. 1 John 3:7-8). Does doubt cloud your conviction? Then reconsider the evidence, openly and honestly, as Jesus encouraged John to do when he needed reassurance (Luke 7:18-23; cf. Isa. 35:1-10). Even after the resurrection, fear and doubt continued to trouble the disciples. Appearing to them, Jesus said, "See My hands and My feet, that it is I Myself; touch Me and see, for a spirit does not have flesh and bones as you see that I have. . ." (Luke 24:36-43). In other words, "Look at the evidence."

The Need for Clarification

A point of clarification is in order. The Apocalypse foreshadows judgments that were at hand and also more distant. Doom would befall Rome in the relatively near future: "the time is near" (Rev. 1:3). The same was true of the unrepentant churches (Rev. 3:3, 11). Similar language is also used of the future, final judgment of all humankind: "Behold, I am coming quickly, and My reward is with Me, to render to every man according to what he has done" (Rev. 22:12). Again, "He who testifies to these things says, 'Yes, I am coming quickly.' Amen. Come, Lord Jesus" (Rev. 22:20).

The Kingdom: When and Where? NOW

Examining this issue from a New Testament perspective, we learn that the kingdom is a current reality. Citizenship in the kingdom of God, Christ, or heaven demands that we manifest proper attitudes and actions.

Current Reality

In promising to build His church, Jesus gave the keys of the kingdom unto Simon Peter (Matt. 16:13-19). He also spoke of the imminent ar-

"When Will These Things Be?" : Questions on Eschatology

rival of the kingdom: "Truly I say to you, there are some of those who are standing here who will not taste death until they see the kingdom of God after it has come with power" (Mark 9:1; cf. Luke 9:27).

After His resurrection, Jesus instructed the disciples to remain in Jerusalem until they were clothed with the power of the Holy Spirit (Luke 24:44-49; Acts 1:4-8). The apostles were subsequently baptized with the Holy Spirit on the day of Pentecost (Acts 2:1-4). Three thousand men responded obediently to the preaching of the gospel (Acts 2:37-42). From that point forward, their numbers grew daily: "The Lord was adding to their number day by day those who were being saved" (Acts 2:46-47). After the events that are recorded in Acts 2, the church is described as a present reality (Acts 5:11; 8:1; 9:31; 13:1; etc.), as with the kingdom (Col. 1:13-14; Heb. 12:28; Rev. 1:6, 9; 5:10).

Current Attitudes

Those who seek citizenship in the kingdom of heaven must have a Christ-like disposition. Disciples of Christ should manifest humility (Matt. 5:3; 19:23-24) and trust (Matt. 19:13-15; Mark 10:13-16).

The phrase, "the kingdom of heaven is like," occurs seven times in seven verses, all of which appear in the gospel of Matthew—communicating lessons about growth (Matt. 13:31–33), labor (Matt. 20:1–16), separation (Matt. 13:47–50), and value (Matt. 13:44-45, 52).

Current Actions

Those who seek citizenship in the kingdom of heaven must accept the rule of Christ in their lives. All who would enjoy this blessed state must readily receive the word (Acts 19:8; 28:23, 31), and be baptized (John 3:3, 5; Acts 8:12). As believers, they must be mindful (Mark 14:22-25), active (Col 4:11), and steadfast (Acts 14:22; 2 Thess. 1:5). As brethren, they must be harmonious (Rom. 14:15-17). As those who bear the image of Christ, they must be transformed (1 Cor. 6:9-11; Gal 5:19-26).

The Kingdom: When and Where? NOT YET

Finally, let us recognize that specific biblical prophecies about the kingdom of God, Christ, or heaven await eternity. In his second (and final) epistle to Timothy, written shortly before his death, Paul spoke of a future reward, and an ultimate manifestation of the kingdom (2 Tim. 4:1-8). Although the aged apostle did not expect to be rescued out of the lion's mouth a second time, yet he was assured of ultimate victory: "The

Introduction

Lord will rescue me from every evil deed, and will bring me safely to His heavenly kingdom; to Him be the glory forever" (2 Tim. 4:16-18). Faithful disciples enjoy many blessings in this life and long for the day when God will provide a glorious entrance into the eternal kingdom of our Lord and Savior Jesus Christ (2 Pet. 1:10-11). While those who obey the gospel are added to the church and enjoy citizenship in the kingdom of God and Christ, specific promises still await future fulfillment.

Replacement

Paul affirmed, "Flesh and blood cannot inherit the kingdom of God." Saints have not yet received a body suitable for dwelling in the presence of God for all eternity: "this perishable must put on the imperishable, and this mortal must put on immortality" (1 Cor. 15:50-58). Consider the significance of the descriptive terms used in this context: "imperishable" and "immortality." Occurring seven times in seven verses, the Greek word *aphtharsia* signifies "the state of not being subject to decay/dissolution/interruption, incorruptibility, immortality" (BDAG). It describes the body we will inhabit in eternity (1 Cor. 15:42, 50, 53-54), the love that we must manifest (Eph. 6:24), and a state for which we diligently strive (2 Tim. 1:10)—all of which are made possible through the gospel of Jesus Christ (Rom. 2:7). The Greek word *athanasia*, a compound of the negative prefix and *thanatos* (death), signifying an existence beyond the reach of death. Rendered "immortality," it occurs three times in three verses and describes our heavenly bodies (1 Cor. 15:53-54), and in a unique sense, God: while we have the promise of life beyond the grave, death cannot touch deity (1 Tim. 6:16).

Reward

Matthew 25 contains two parables emphasizing the need for preparation. It begins by saying, "Then the kingdom of heaven will be comparable to ten virgins, who took their lamps and went out to meet the bridegroom. Five of them were foolish, and five were prudent" (vv. 1-2). In the parable of the talents, Christ proceeds to a parallel illustration: "For it is just like a man about to go on a journey who called his own slaves and entrusted his possessions to them. To one he gave five talents, to another, two, and to another, one, each according to his own ability; and he went on his journey" (vv. 14-15). The chapter concludes with a portrayal of the judgment: "But when the Son of Man comes in His glory, and all the angels with Him, then He will sit on His glorious throne.

"When Will These Things Be?" : Questions on Eschatology

All the nations will be gathered before Him; and He will separate them from one another, as the shepherd separates the sheep from the goats; and He will put the sheep on His right, and the goats on the left" (vv. 31-33). Faithful servants of the Lord will receive an eternal reward—an inheritance beyond measure—for services rendered: "Come, you who are blessed of My Father, inherit the kingdom prepared for you from the foundation of the world..." (v. 34).

Recognition

We have a longing for recognition. Sometimes, we only want someone to say, "Good job!" In the final day of judgment, faithful servants of the Lord will hear words of praise and commendation: "Well done, good and faithful slave. You were faithful with a few things, I will put you in charge of many things; enter into the joy of your master" (Matt. 25:14-30, esp. vv. 21, 23).

Rest

In contrast with the wicked (who experience eternal torment and have no rest), those who have suffered for the cause of Christ will be granted rest (Rev. 14:9-13). Present diligence is demanded if we hope to enjoy that realm of promised rest: "So there remains a Sabbath rest for the people of God. For the one who has entered His rest has himself also rested from his works, as God did from His. Therefore let us be diligent to enter that rest, so that no one will fall, through following the same example of disobedience" (Heb. 4:9-11).

Responsibility

Jesus said, "You who have followed Me, in the regeneration when the Son of Man will sit on His glorious throne, you also shall sit upon twelve thrones, judging the twelve tribes of Israel..." (Matt. 19:27-30). He made a similar promise to those who had stood by Him in His trials (cf. Luke 22:24-30). He extends this promise to saints who suffered martyrdom during the persecutions described in the Apocalypse (Rev. 20:1-5).

Re-Organization

In coming to this earth, Jesus Christ relinquished the glory that He formerly enjoyed in heaven (Phil. 2:5-8). After completing His mission, Christ returned to the Father and was seated at the right hand of God (Heb. 1:3-4). Christ currently possesses all authority (Matt. 28:18-20), but in the end, He will return ruling authority to the Father (1 Cor. 15:20-28).

Introduction

Conclusion

Considering the benefits and blessings that are reserved for the faithful, how could any right-thinking individual reject the kingdom of Christ and God?

May we engage in honest self-examination: Are you prepared to receive the kingdom? Let us understand the demands of faith. Faith is foundational, leading us to obedience and bringing untold blessings. Faith is essential (Heb. 11:1-6). Are you plagued by doubt? Is your faith on unstable footing? Dig deeper! Search the Scripture. Rightly divide the word of truth. Consider the evidence!

Recognize the demands of repentance (i.e., a change of heart followed by change of conduct). While cases of human cruelty and natural calamity capture the public's attention, even greater spiritual catastrophe awaits all of us unless we repent and obey God (Luke 13:1-9).

When the Lord Jesus Christ returns in glory, the saints will undergo bodily replacement, receive a reward and recognition, enjoy rest, be entrusted with responsibility, and observe a divine re-organization. Consider the implications of each of these concepts and the obligations they carry. When Christ returns, it will be too late to prepare. Today is the day of salvation.

Have you (and I) complied with the kingdom's terms of admission, and thus, gained access to its blessings and benefits? Are you (and I) fulfilling the obligations and responsibilities of citizens within the kingdom? If not, are you (am I) mindful of the perils and punishments that await? Do not delay. Accept the rule of God in your life. Submit to the King of kings and Lord of lords. By obeying the gospel message, and being baptized for the remission of sins, you will be added to the church and granted citizenship in the kingdom of God's dear Son. Live in hope of eternity.

Bibliography

American Heritage Dictionary of the English Language, 5th ed. Boston, MA: Houghton Mifflin Harcourt Publishing Company, 2016.

BDAG=Bauer, Walter, Frederick W. Danker, William Arndt, and F. Wilbur Gingrich. *A Greek-English Lexicon of the New Testament and Other Early Christian Literature.* 3rd ed. Chicago, IL: University of Chicago Press, 2000.

"When Will These Things Be?" : Questions on Eschatology

Collins English Dictionary—Complete and Unabridged, 12th ed. New York: Harper Collins Publishers, 2014.

NASB=New American Standard Bible: 1995 Update. La Habra, CA: The Lockman Foundation, 1995. Unless otherwise noted, all Bible quotations come from the NASB.

Thomas, Robert L. *New American Standard Hebrew-Aramaic and Greek Dictionaries: Updated Edition.* Anaheim, CA: Foundation Publications, Inc., 1998.

Big Questions

What Is Eternal Life and Why Should It Matter to Me?
   Tommy Peeler

What Does the Bible Teach about Hell and Who Will Go There?
   Ron Halbrook

Am I Ready for the End?
   Bobby Graham

"When Will These Things Be?"
Questions on Eschatology

What Is Eternal Life and Why Should It Matter to Me?

By Tommy Peeler

Introduction

The word *heaven* is used in different ways in Scripture. The first time it is used is in the first verse of the Bible. "God created the heavens and the earth" (Gen. 1:1).[1] The phrase "heaven and earth" refers to the totality of God's creation.[2] (Deut. 4:26; 30:19; 31:28; 32:1; Pss. 121:2; 124:8; 134:3; 146:6; Isa. 1:2; Jer. 23:24; Mark 13:31; Acts 17:24; 1 Cor. 8:5). In this sense, the heavens themselves tremble at the wrath of God (2 Sam. 22:8). These heavens and earth will pass away (Isa. 34:4; Matt. 24:35; Mark 13:31; Luke 21:33; 2 Pet. 3:10; Rev. 21:1).

Heaven is also the dwelling place of God. God is our Father in heaven or heavenly Father (Matt. 5:16, 45, 48; 6:1, 9, 14, 26; 7:11, 21, 21; 12:50; 18:10, 14; 23:9). Paul tells masters to watch how they treat slaves because

---

[1] In Hebrew the term for heaven is plural, but it is generally translated in the LXX by a singular.

[2] Mitchell G. Reddish, "Heaven," in the *Anchor Bible Dictionary*, Vol. 3, 90-91.

Tommy Peeler was born and raised in Dickson, TN. He was blessed to be raised in the home of Christians, Sanders and Peggy Peeler. He and his wife, Christi (formerly Sellers), married in June of 1984. They are blessed with three sons: Josiah, Nathan, and Isaiah. Tommy has been blessed to preach and teach the Bible and he presently preaches at the Brandon church of Christ in Brandon, FL and teaches at Florida College. He can be reached at christipeeler@yahoo.com.

"When Will These Things Be?" : Questions on Eschatology

their Master and yours is in heaven (Eph. 6:9; Col. 4:1). When we speak of the dwelling place of God, heaven is not a part of this creation (Heb. 9:11, 24).

Heaven is also the final home of God's people, where God brings us home to Himself. Jesus pronounced a blessing upon the persecuted, "Rejoice and be glad, for your reward in heaven is great" (Matt. 5:12; Luke 6:23). Jesus exhorts the rich young ruler to follow Him with the hope of treasure in heaven (Matt. 19:21; Mark 10:21; Luke 18:22). Paul wrote of "the hope laid up for you in heaven" (Col. 1:5). Peter talks of an inheritance "reserved in heaven for you" (2 Pet. 1:4).[3]

The truths about resurrection and eternal life are more clearly revealed in the NT (2 Tim. 1:10). God's people throughout time have been motivated by a hope of eternal life, dwelling with God, or heaven. Hebrews 11, the Biblical Faith Hall of Fame, describes the career of some Old Testament characters who walked by faith. In Abraham's time, the area of Mesopotamia was at the top of the list among the most advanced and sophisticated places in the world. However, when God called him to leave, he left, not even knowing where he was going (8). God promised him Canaan as an inheritance (8). He lived as an alien in this promised land (9). At the time he died (Gen. 25:7-11), the only part of the land he owned was the cave of Machpelah to bury Sarah (Gen. 23). Abraham, Sarah, Isaac, and Jacob were "strangers and exiles" on earth (13). Notice the use of words connected with sight in this section on Abraham. Abraham was "looking for the city. . ." (10)[4] and having "seen" the promises of God (13). This ties to the definition of faith given in Hebrews 11:1. Faith believes God's promises even though they remain unseen. Abraham's belief that God was "faithful who had promised" (11) leads him to "see" that he and his descendants would inherit the land. Abraham trusts the promises of God that he would receive the land, but this trust is ultimately about more than seeking Canaan. It shows that "he was looking

---

[3] In the course of this study, passages will be used that do not specifically mention the word "heaven." However, I include them because I believe they contain the same idea.

[4] The word "city" is in Hebrews 11:10,16 and "country" is in verse 14.

What Is Eternal Life and Why Should It Matter to Me?

for the city which has foundations, whose architect and builder is God" (10).[5] It is about his desire for a heavenly city (16).

Abraham's circumstances in Hebrews 11 in some ways parallel our situation. He was an "alien" (9), a "stranger and exile" (13), as we are (2 Pet. 2:11). He was an heir of God's promises (9)[6] as are we (Rom. 8:17; Heb. 1:13-14). He was promised a great inheritance (8) as we also are (1 Cor. 15:50; 1 Pet. 1:3-4). He was looking for something more than this world had to offer (13-16). We do the same. "For here we do not have a lasting city, but we are seeking the city which is to come" (Heb. 13:14). Abraham did not see the full realization of God's promises, but he believed they were true (13) because He believed that God is faithful (11). We are in the same situation trusting God as reliable and trustworthy (Heb. 6:12-20).

What We Believe about Eschatology Affects How We Live

In 2 Peter 3, scoffers are asking, "Where is the promise of His coming?" (3:3-4).[7] This is not the first time mockers denied prophetic words of judgment. In Ezekiel 12, the people were claiming that every vision fails (v. 22) or that at least it will be a long time in coming (v. 27). The same kind of mockery was hurled at Jeremiah the prophet: "Where is the word of the LORD? Let it come now" (Jer. 17:15). When mockers say all things continue as they have from the beginning of creation (3:4), they overlook the fact that God destroyed the world with the flood (3:5-6). All things have not continued as they were from the beginning. The same God who destroyed the world by a flood now reserves the present heavens and earth for the day of judgment for the ungodly (3:7). The delay is not because God does not keep His promises, but it is because He wants to give people an opportunity to repent (3:8-9). He does not want any to perish, but He desires that all repent (Ezek. 18:23; 32; 33:11).

---

[5] In Hebrews for something to be built by God or built without hands is important (Heb. 8:2; 9:11, 24). In the whole Bible we see the importance of things not made with hands (Dan. 2:34-35, 45; Mark 14:58; 2 Cor. 5:1; Col. 2:11).

[6] The word *promise* is a key word in Hebrews 11:8-16 appearing in vv. 9, 11, 13.

[7] If the Biblical book is not mentioned in this paragraph, the references are to 2 Peter.

"When Will These Things Be?" : Questions on Eschatology

The day of the LORD will come like a thief[8], and the present heavens and earth will be destroyed (3:10-12). God will bring a new heavens and a new earth where righteousness dwells (3:13). This anticipation about the future changes the way we live right here and now. Eschatology affects our ethics. It motivates us to live lives of "holy conduct and godliness" (3:11). We live righteously, anticipating a new environment where righteousness dwells (3:13).[9]

Eschatology also inspires hope. 1 John 3:1-3 tells us that we are presently God's sons. When He appears, then we will be like Him because we shall see Him as He is. This hope that we will be like Him encourages us to be pure as He is pure. Hope can motivate us to bear the unbearable and to withstand overwhelming difficulties. Our hope for Jesus's return sustains us in dark times. It encourages us to a purity of life so that we may have confidence before Him and not shrink away from Him at His coming (1 John 2:28).

Our Citizenship Is in Heaven

> For our citizenship is in heaven, from which we eagerly wait for a Savior, the Lord Jesus Christ; who will transform the body of our humble state into conformity with the body of His glory, by the exertion of the power that He has even to subject all things to Himself (Phil. 3:20-21).

The Philippians were very proud of their Roman citizenship. Antony and Octavian defeated Brutus and Cassius at the battle of Philippi in 42 BC.[10] Many military veterans settled there, and Philippi was "a little Rome, Rome away from home."[11] In Acts 16:20-21, the masters of the slave girl assert Paul and Silas are causing great trouble in the city. They explain their opposition by saying they are Jews and accusing them of "proclaiming customs which it is not lawful for us to accept or observe *being Romans*" (Italics indicates my emphasis.) This leads to Paul and

---

[8] The picture of the LORD coming as a thief in the night is common in the New Testament (Matt. 24:42-43; Luke 12:39-40; 1 Thess. 5:2, 4; Rev. 3:3; 16:15). The phrase seems to indicate how many will be unprepared for His coming.

[9] The warning that "Bad company corrupts good morals" (1 Cor. 15:33) comes in the midst of some who denied the resurrection of the dead. This highlights the link between eschatology and ethics.

[10] Everett Ferguson, *Backgrounds of Early Christianity*, 3rd ed., 25-26.

[11] Ibid., 41.

What Is Eternal Life and Why Should It Matter to Me?

Silas being beaten with rods and placed in stocks (Acts 16:22-24). When Paul is being released, he reveals that he, too, is a Roman citizen and has been beaten in public with no trial (Acts 16:37).[12] Paul, a Roman citizen, writes to remind those who boasted in their Roman citizenship that their real citizenship is in heaven.

What does it mean that our citizenship is in heaven? One thing it means is that we live by a different standard from those around us. While all the world is accountable to God (Rom. 14:10-12; 2 Cor. 5:10), many in the world are oblivious to that fact. Being citizens of the kingdom of God, we are conscious of the fact we are accountable to Him and that we live by another standard (Matt. 5:3-12). We seek to live in a way consistent with God's values. While seeking to respect rulers (2 Pet. 2:13-17), we are "aliens and strangers" on this earth (2 Pet. 2:11-12). These values seem strange to our world, and they, therefore, do not understand our actions (2 Pet. 4:3-4). As citizens of heaven, we grieve over what makes God grieve, and we rejoice in the things that make God rejoice.

As citizens of heaven, we are tormented by the behavior of our world. In reading Genesis, I do not have a high estimation of Lot. He does show hospitality to visitors (Gen. 19:2-3; Heb. 13:2). He also seeks to talk the men of Sodom out of their plans of homosexual rape (Gen. 19:4-8). However, he seems to choose selfishly (Gen. 13:8-13). He makes a foolish offer of his own daughters to the men at his door (Gen. 19:8). He hesitates when the time bomb of God's judgment is ticking (Gen. 19:16-22). He even engages in drunkenness and incest (Gen. 19:30-38). However, 2 Peter 2:6-8 provides a little more positive insight into Lot. The word *oppressed* used in 2 Peter 2:7 is *kataponoumenon* (καταπονούμενον), and this word is used only one other time in the New Testament. In Acts 7:24, it is used of Moses seeing the Egyptian mistreating a Hebrew slave. That Hebrew slave is described as "the oppressed." The same word used to describe the oppression of a slave is used to describe the response of Lot to his ungodly world. The word *tormented, ebasanizen* (ἐβασάνιζεν) in 2 Peter 2:8, is used some twelve other times in the New Testament.[13] It

---

[12] The only times in Acts that Paul directly refers to his Roman citizenship are in Acts 16:37 and 22:25-29. In Acts 25:8-12, his appeal to Caesar assumes this.

[13] The passages that use this word are Matthew 8:6, 29; 14:24; Mark 5:7; 6:48; Luke 8:28; 2 Pet. 2:8; Rev. 9:5; 11:10; 12:2; 14:10; 20:10.

"When Will These Things Be?" : Questions on Eschatology

described the torment of a paralyzed servant (Matt. 8:6), one controlled by a demon (Mark 5:7), and even the torment of hell (Rev. 14:10; 20:10). This is the word used to describe Lot's response to the sins of Sodom. He was oppressed and tormented by the lives of those in Sodom. Is this our response to the values and standards of our world? Do we sigh and groan over all the abominations which are committed in our world (Ezek. 9:4)? May the LORD help us to be citizens of heaven to such a degree that we find the values of this world oppressive and tormenting. Being shocked at the sin of the world must lead us to avoid sin in our own lives and to seek the LORD, who alone provides forgiveness and healing from sin. It should motivate us to rescue as many as we can from this world (Jas. 5:19-20; Jude 22-23).

We Lay Up Treasures in Heaven

Matthew 6:19-21 teaches us that our goal is not the accumulation of riches here on the earth but in heaven. Treasures upon earth are prone to destruction and corruption (19; Jas. 5:2-3). Treasures in heaven are not subject to destruction or thieves (20). Treasures in heaven are more real and permanent than any treasures upon earth can be. If we make our treasure there, our hearts will follow (21). Sometimes we say that if our hearts are right, then we will give properly. I do not deny that point, for it is also made in the Bible. Paul talks of the generous giving of the Macedonians and states that it is because "they first gave themselves to the LORD" (2 Cor. 8:5). Their giving demonstrated that their hearts were right and that they had given their hearts to the LORD. However, the Bible also approaches this same subject from the other direction. If we put our treasure in heaven, then our hearts will be sure to follow.[14]

Luke 12:33-34 is very similar to Matthew 6:19-21. The context of this statement in Luke is instructive and helpful. Luke 12:13-21 informs us of the one in the crowd who calls upon Jesus to divide the family inheritance with him. Jesus instead warns the man against covetousness or greed, stressing that life is not about our possessions (Luke 12:13-15). Jesus gives the parable of the man we speak of as the rich fool. The man's

---

[14] The Bible does this with other subjects. We cannot claim to love God if we do not love our brother (1 John 4:20-21). Our love of God is proved by love for our brother, but love for God is also proof we love our brother (1 John 5:1-3).

What Is Eternal Life and Why Should It Matter to Me?

crops brought forth abundantly (Luke 12:16),[15] but he thought only of himself and his wants (Luke 12:17-19). The rich man expresses no dependence on God or concern for his fellowman. He acts as if he will live forever.[16] God calls such a man a fool (Luke 12:20). Sometimes in the Old Testament, the word *fool* describes a person who lives as if there is no God (Ps. 14:1; 53:1).[17]

Jesus's teaching in Luke 12:22-34 is a call to check our priorities.[18] It is a call to make God our highest priority. While all the world pursues what they will eat and drink, Jesus calls His people to seek His kingdom (29-31). The God who provides for the birds and even the grass is the God who provides for His people. He is worthy of our trust in Him (24, 27-28). Freeing ourselves from worry about these things leaves us free to pursue a higher and nobler matter, His kingdom. Rather than being occupied with the buildup of treasures with an eye to self-security in this life (21), disciples need to be concerned with ensuring that they possess treasures in heaven. Therefore, seeking the kingdom (31) is tantamount to setting one's treasure in heaven (34).[19]

Numerous vocabulary connections can be made between Luke 12:13-21 and Luke 12:22-34. Luke 12:13-21 has no parallel outside the gospel of Luke. Notice the word *treasure* in verse 21 also appears in verses 33-34. The rich man of 12:13-21 "stores up treasure for himself and

---

[15] While some in the Bible obtained their wealth by cheating and mistreating the poor (Jer. 22:13-19; Amos 2:6-7; 4:1; 5:10-13; 6:1-7; 8:4-6) such is not always the case. Abraham is an example of a rich man (Gen. 13:2) who did justice and righteousness (Gen. 18:19). Even the wicked man of Luke 12 does not seem to have sinned in his attainment of wealth, but because of his attitudes and actions in the use of his wealth.

[16] Psalm 49:11 says, "Their inner thought is that their houses are forever and that their dwelling places to all generations."

[17] The person under discussion in Psalm 14:1 and 53:1 would probably not deny God's existence, but the existence of God makes no difference in his thoughts and behavior. The principle problem of this man is "his failure to account for God in his plans" (Green, 487).

[18] The verses referred to in this paragraph are from Luke 12.

[19] Joel B. Green. *The Gospel of Luke*. Grand Rapids: Eerdmans, 1997, 495. I have only slightly altered Green's wording here.

"When Will These Things Be?" : Questions on Eschatology

is not rich for God." His security was in his wealth and not in God. The rich man seems to be the prime illustration of what it means to lay up treasures upon the earth. However, in contrast, Jesus calls us to "make yourselves money belts which do not wear out, an unfailing treasure in heaven," and "where your treasure is, there your heart will be also." The word *soul* in verses 19, 20 is the same Greek word translated *life* in verses 22-23. The terms *eat* and *drink* are used by the rich man in verse 19 and verses 22, 29 as well. While the rich man speaks to his soul (19) and says, "eat, drink, and be merry," Jesus says our soul[20] is about more than eating and drinking (22-23). We should not merely seek physical sustenance; instead, He calls us to seek God's kingdom earnestly (29-31). The words *barn* and *barns* appear in verses 18 and 24. While the rich man is planning to tear down his barns and build bigger ones to store all his crops (18), God provides for the ravens though they have no barns (24). The word *possessions* in verse 15 is also used in verse 33. Jesus warns the man worried about his inheritance that life does not consist of the abundance of possessions (15), and Jesus encourages His disciples to "sell your possessions and give to charity" (33). The man questioning Jesus about his inheritance (13) has concerns that Jesus says are just not a priority for His disciples. These key words demonstrate the complete contrast in the way the rich man lives and the way that Jesus calls His disciples to live.[21] Are we living more as the rich fool than as Jesus teaches? Are we laying up our treasures in heaven?

In Luke 16:1-13, Jesus gives the parable often described as the Parable of the Unjust Manager. The unjust manager was about to lose his job (2) and wanted to act in such a way that others would receive him into their homes after his job was finished (3-4). One point of the parable seems to be that we must use the resources that we are given so that when "the mammon of unrighteousness" fails, we will be received into eternal dwellings (9).[22] We must use what God has given us so that we will be welcomed into eternal dwellings. Yet, the world sometimes puts forth

---

[20] Greek word *psychē* (ψυχή).

[21] Similar points are made by Green, 486-487.

[22] The Greek word *dechomai* (δέχομαι) is used both in Luke 16:4 and 9 though it is translated "will welcome" in v. 4 and "will receive" in v. 9 in the NASB. In both cases even the same form of the verb is used.

What Is Eternal Life and Why Should It Matter to Me?

more energy and exerts more wisdom in obtaining temporary housing than we do in seeking an eternal abode (8). We must be faithful in the use of money that God has given us; if not, "who will entrust the true riches to us?" (11). This passage promises that those who are faithful to God will possess true riches (11) and that which is their own (12) in the sense that we cannot know in this world. This passage calls upon each of us to use what God has given to His glorify and to prepare for our eternal home. It an exhortation to lay up treasure in heaven.

While Luke 16:1-13 teaches us to use our wealth so we will be welcomed into eternal dwellings, Luke 16:19-31 shows us one who ended up in torment for not using his wealth properly. The rich man of this account was obviously Jewish. He called Abraham father (24, 27, 30), and Abraham referred to him as child (25). However, he ended up in torment begging for mercy (23-24).[23] He ended up here because he did not listen to Moses and the prophets (29, 31), and specifically, he did not listen to what Moses and the prophets said about caring for the poor (20-21).[24] This is a warning to us all. If we do not use our money as God has guided us, why do we think we would do better if we were eyewitnesses of the resurrection? (30-31).

The rich young ruler wanted to know what to do to receive eternal life (Luke 18:18-30). When Jesus quotes the Ten Commandments, He does not specifically refer to the first four commandments, which focus more directly upon God. He also does not initially quote the tenth commandment, which prohibits covetousness (20). While the young man is confident that he has kept these commandments (21), Jesus makes a great demand. The young man must sell all and distribute to the poor, and then he shall have treasure in heaven (22). Sadly, this ruler chose

---

[23] The rich man of Luke 16:19-31 epitomizes the warning of John the Baptist in Luke 3:8 "Do not begin to say to yourselves, 'We have Abraham for our father,' for I say that from these stones God is able to raise up children to Abraham."

[24] The law and the prophets had plenty to say about the proper treatment of the poor. A few of the passages that fall into that category are Exodus 22:21-27; Lev. 19:9-10; Deut. 15:1-11; 24:19-22; Prov. 14:31; 17:5; 19:17; 22:22-23.

fleeting riches instead of eternal life (23).[25] However, unique these demands, Jesus draws a general conclusion that is quite shocking. It is hard for the wealthy to enter the kingdom of God (24-25). The Bible reveals to us that wealth can be a curse as well as a blessing. Riches can and often do lead us to forget our total dependence upon God (Deut. 6:10-12; 8:10-20). Sometimes the pursuit of wealth interrupts the pursuit of God (Luke 8:14; 14:18-19). Sometimes the acquisition of wealth makes our need for God seem less urgent. When our wealth multiplies, then our hearts may become proud, and we may forget the LORD our God to whom we owe everything (Deut. 8:13-14). Israel's story was that often when they did prosper, they forgot God (Deut. 32:15; Hos. 10:1; 13:6) or even attributed their prosperity to other gods (Hos. 2:5; Jer. 44:17-18). The writer of Proverbs 30 requested "neither poverty nor riches" (30:8). He does not want riches because he may "be full and deny You and say, 'Who is the LORD?'" (30:9). Wealth can dull our senses to our desperate need for God.[26]

1 Timothy 6:17-19 warns the rich in this present world not to put their trust in riches. While I understand that we might not even be aware that these words apply to us, most of us are rich compared to the first-century world. We are cautioned not to put our trust in the "uncertainty of riches." If there is anything certain about riches, it is that they are uncertain (Prov. 23:4-5; 27:24; Matt. 6:20). We are not to fix our hope on riches, but we fix our hope on God (1 Tim. 5:5). God is the source of all

---

[25] This seems to demonstrate the man's violation of the commandment against covetousness and the command to have no other gods since covetousness is idolatry (Eph. 5:5; Col. 3:5). The linking of covetousness and idolatry is also done in Job 31:24-28 and Matthew 6:24.

[26] Luke is the gospel that puts the most emphasis on the proper use of material possessions. Much of what Jesus taught about the use of possessions in Luke is lived out in Acts by the early church. The early church was a community of love and concern for each other as demonstrated in their use of their possessions (Acts 2:42, 44-45; 4:32, 34-35, 36-37). We also see some who made great financial sacrifices for their love of God (Acts 19:19). A big emphasis in the NT is the making of Jews and Gentiles into one new man in Christ (Eph. 2:11-22), and one way this was done was by Gentile Christians giving to their poor Jewish brothers in Jerusalem (Acts 11:27-30; 24:17). We also see in Acts that covetousness is the downfall of many (Acts 1:18; 8:18-23) and the fear of the loss of riches results in hostility to the gospel (Acts 16:16-21; 19:24-28).

What Is Eternal Life and Why Should It Matter to Me?

our blessings as He "richly supplies us with all things to enjoy" (6:17). As we do good, are rich in good works, generous and ready to share (6:18), then we are laying up for ourselves a treasure of a good foundation for the future (6:19).

Sometimes the persecution of early Christians was the seizure of their wealth (Heb. 10:32-34). "For you showed sympathy to the prisoners and accepted the seizure of your property joyfully, knowing that you have for yourselves a better possession and a lasting one" (10:34). The world may take our wealth, but we have riches that the world cannot take away. We have something better and more lasting than anything the government can seize. Martin Luther wrote, "Let goods and kindred go, this mortal life also." The early Christians lived all of these. Many Christians around the world experience the same challenges today. Job said, "Naked I came from my mother's womb, and naked I shall return there. The LORD gave and the LORD has taken away. Blessed be the name of the LORD" (Job 1:21).

God has prepared riches for His people that are beyond any the world can provide. May this inspire us to lay up our treasure in heaven. "Earth holds no treasures but perish with using, however precious they be. But there's a country to which I am going, Heaven holds all to me. Heaven holds all to me, Brighter it's glories will be. Joy beyond measure will be my treasure. Heaven holds all to me."[27]

Any Suffering Endured to Attain the Goal of Heaven Is Small by Comparison

Heaven is so glorious that any suffering we endure on the way to the goal is small. Second Corinthians 4:17 speaks of a "momentary, light affliction." Would you describe Paul's affliction as light? Notice some other things Paul says in 2 Corinthians 4 about his afflictions. In this context, Paul speaks of being "afflicted in every way" and "perplexed" (4:8). He is "persecuted" and "struck down" and "always carrying about in the body the dying of Jesus" (4:9-10). He says that "we are constantly delivered over to death for Jesus's sake" (4:11) and that "death works in us" (4:12).

No epistle of Paul gives as much detail about what he suffered in his ministry as 2 Corinthians. The same suffering described in 2 Corinthians

---

[27] Tillet S. Tiddlie, "Heaven Holds All to Me."

"When Will These Things Be?" : Questions on Eschatology

4 repeatedly appears throughout the whole epistle. In 1:8, Paul says we were "burdened excessively, beyond our strength, so that we despaired even of life." In 1:9, he says, "We had the sentence of death within ourselves." When Paul was in the middle of this, he may have had trouble speaking of his afflictions as light. Look at the lists of things Paul endured in 6:4-5, 11:23-28, and 12:10. For Paul to speak of his afflictions as "light and momentary" is possible only if they are being compared to something far greater. His sufferings can only be said to be light and momentary in light of the eternal weight of glory, which is far beyond all comparison. Paul uses the same terms to describe this glory (*hyperbolē* [ὑπερβολὴ], "beyond all measure"; *ebarēthēmen* [ἐβαρήθημεν], "we are weighed down") that he used to describe his sufferings in 1:8. In Asia, Paul says that he was *burdened excessively* (1:8; *hyperbolē* [ὑπερβολὴ], 'beyond all measure;' *ebarēthēmen* [ἐβαρήθημεν], "we were weighed down.') "He now evaluates that affliction and all his afflictions differently" (Garland, *2 Corinthians*, 243). That affliction beyond all measure is small compared to the glory beyond all measure. What does this say about the glory to come? How great must it be if it makes his intense sufferings seem light?

2 Corinthians 4:17 contrasts what is momentary and what is eternal. Some experiences on earth are great, but even these last only for a moment. Here we are forever chasing after the wind. However, the blessings of heaven will be eternal. This emphasis continues in 2 Corinthians 5, which says that we have a building from God "eternal in the heavens" (1) and "what is mortal will be swallowed up by life." (4). In the context of 2 Corinthians 5:7, what does it mean that we live by faith and not by sight? It deals with looking away from the present sufferings, which can be seen to the eternal glory, which cannot be seen (4:18).

Notice, too, that 2 Corinthians 4:17 says this light momentary affliction is actually working or producing this eternal glory. The same word translated *producing* in 4:17 is translated "prepared" in 5:5.[28] The suffering is not just to be endured, but it somehow prepares us for eternal glory. In the context of 2 Corinthians, this may be that our afflictions lead us to see our limitations and show us not to put trust in ourselves but to put our trust in God, who raises the dead (1:9). When we recognize our weakness,

---

[28] From the form *katergazomai* (κατεργάζομαι).

What Is Eternal Life and Why Should It Matter to Me?

then we lean on God's strength (12:10). Far from stopping us from obtaining our goal, hardships, adversity, and persecution may actually strengthen us and help us in our journey to heaven (Rom. 5:3-5; Jas. 1:2-4).

O LORD, I believe, help my unbelief.

All of this motivates us not to give up hope. "Therefore we do not lose heart" (2 Cor. 4:16).[29] Ephesians 3:13 uses the same word, "Therefore I ask you not to lost heart at my tribulations on your behalf, for they are for your glory." May the LORD help us keep our eye on His eternal glory so that we do not give up in the difficulties of the present.

We understand that a glorious and victorious ending may transform our views of the struggles along the way. We understand that in sports, politics, or economic matters. In 2 Corinthians 4:16-5:10 Paul's goal is "not to answer speculative questions about the life to come and when we receive the spiritual body, but to show how the assurance of the life to come changes everything for the Christian in the present" (Garland, *2 Corinthians*, 246).

Suffering is woven all through 1 Peter.[30] Suffering is mentioned in every chapter in this epistle. Christians are being slandered in 2:12, 15; 3:16, maligned in 4:4 and reviled in 4:14. The Christians are "distressed by various trials" and "tested by fire" (1:6-7). In 4:12, "Beloved, do not be surprised at the fiery ordeal among you, which comes upon you for your testing, as though some strange thing were happening to you." While they are not to suffer as criminals, if they suffer as Christians, they are not to be ashamed but to glorify God (4:15-16). The brethren are encouraged that other brothers are going through the same experiences of suffering (5:8-9). In the context of 5:8-9, it is through persecution that the devil is seeking to devour them. Peter discusses the possibility of suffering unjustly and encourages believers to imitate Jesus, the ultimate example of One who suffered unjustly (2:18-25).

---

[29] The word translated "lost heart" is *ekkakeō* (ἐκκακέω) and it is also used in Luke 18:1; 2 Corinthians 4:1; Galatians 6:9; Ephesians 3:13; 2 Thessalonians 3:13. All of these passages are encouraging us not to give up in specific circumstances.

[30] All the passages in this paragraph are from 1 Peter.

"When Will These Things Be?" : Questions on Eschatology

How can we overcome suffering? First, we must remember the sacrifice of Christ. 1 Peter constantly calls attention to Christ's suffering for us (1:11; 2:4, 7, 21; 3:18; 4:1, 13; 5:1). Jesus was rejected, mocked, tortured, and murdered. Yes, He demands much of us. However, our Lord has first blazed the trail for us and asks nothing of us that He has not done Himself. He suffered intensely and has shown us how to act in the midst of it. Second, sharing the sufferings of Christ means that we will rejoice in His glory at His revelation, and we will be blessed (4:13-14). Third, the trials are but for a moment, and the glory is eternal. Suffering for a little while is contrasted with eternal glory in 5:10. While the various trials of 1:6-7 are for a "little while," the hope of heaven is for an inheritance that is "imperishable," "undefiled," and unfading (1:3-4).

The principle that events in the life of Christ transform Scripture is shown by the birth of Christ. Micah 5:2 says, "But as for you, Bethlehem Ephrathah, *too little to be among the clans of Judah*, from you One will go forth for Me to be ruler in Israel. His goings forth are from long ago, from the days of eternity" (NASB). Notice the italicized part, which I have added for emphasis. When Herod gathers the chief priests and scribes and asks where the Messiah was to be born, they answer him in Bethlehem of Judea and quote from Micah 5:2. Notice how they quote the passage: "And you Bethlehem, land of Judah, *are by no means least among the leaders of Judah*; For out of you shall come forth a ruler who will shepherd My people Israel" (Matt. 2:5-6; italics mine). Notice the difference in the italicized parts. While the prophecy originally states that Bethlehem is "too little to be among the clans of Judah," the quotation of it stresses that you are "by no means least among the leaders of Judah." This difference has no basis in either the Hebrew text nor the Septuagint.[31] "Bethlehem was insignificant by worldly standards, but once it was graced with the birth of the Messiah, it was no longer insignificant, at least not by God's standards."[32] The Messiah's birth here "has brought the city greatness."[33] The events of the life of the Messiah have transformed even the wording of Scripture.

---

[31] W.D. Davies and Dale C. Allison, Jr., *The Gospel According to Saint Matthew*, T and T Clark, Reprinted 2003, 242.

[32] Craig L. Blomberg, "Matthew," in *Commentary on the New Testament Use of the Old Testament*, 6.

[33] Davies and Allison, 242.

What Is Eternal Life and Why Should It Matter to Me?

Notice how this same principle applies to the death and resurrection of Jesus. Romans 8:36 quotes from Psalm 44:22, which says, "For your sake, we are being put to death all day long; we are considered as sheep to be slaughtered." The case here is not that its wording is altered like the comparison between Micah 5:2 and Matthew 2:5-6, but the difference in the context of Psalm 44 and Romans 8 is striking. In the Old Testament, Psalm 44 is a national or community lament. It is filled with first-person plural pronouns. The psalm begins by dealing with Israel's glorious past (1-8). Some of the victories they won are enumerated. They defeated the Canaanites (2-3) and other foes (5-6). These victories were not by their power but by God's (3, 4-5, 7-8). However, 9-16 transitions from Israel's glorious past to her miserable present. The LORD who saved them (7) has rejected them (9); He put to shame those who hate them (7), but now He has brought Israel to dishonor (9). While God previously pushed back Israel's adversaries (5), now He causes Israel to turn back before the adversary (10). They are a reproach and derision among the nations (13-15). The psalm protests that Israel has boasted in God "all day long" (8), but they have been humiliated and dishonored "all day long" (15). The lament then protests the innocence of God's people (17-22). Though God had turned back Israel (10), Israel has not turned back from Him (18). One writer says, "No other Psalm makes such claims of national fidelity to God."[34] Yet, despite Israel's loyalty to God, they are "killed all day long" (22). Finally, the lament contains a plea for help from God (23-26). Israel has not forgotten God (17, 20), but they ask why God has forgotten their affliction and oppression (24). The God who favored His people with His presence (3) has now hidden His face from them (24). They wonder why God is asleep while His people suffer so.

In contrast to Psalm 44, Romans 8 is filled with hope. Romans 8:18 stresses the same truths as 2 Corinthians 4:16-17. "For I consider the sufferings of this present time are not worthy to be compared with the glory that is to be revealed to us." The worst of disasters like tribulation, distress, persecution, famine, nakedness, peril, sword, height, depth, or even death is unable to separate us from the love of God which is in Christ (Rom. 8:35, 38-39). "Death, the dreaded separator of loved ones, had for most of the OT period been thought even by the people of God to separate men from God's fellowship (cf., Pss. 6:5; 30:9; 88:5, 10-12;

---

[34] "Psalms" in *Wycliffe Bible Commentary*, Moody Press, 1962, 511.

"When Will These Things Be?" : Questions on Eschatology

115:17; Isa. 38:18)."[35] It is noteworthy this national lament is quoted in one of the most hopeful and encouraging passages of the New Testament. In the context of Romans 8, the death and resurrection of Christ have changed everything (34). These events have even transformed the laments of Scripture into praise (36). It is not that the pain of suffering is removed, but the death and resurrection of Jesus show us that we are conquering through the experiences of suffering. The fact that Jesus has died and risen from the dead transforms this psalm from words of hopelessness to words of hope.

Hosea 13:14 is quoted in 1 Corinthians 15:55-57. The context of Hosea 13:14 stresses judgment though the Septuagint (LXX) translates this more positively.[36] However, statements of judgment surround the context of Hosea 13:14. The context speaks of God's anger and wrath (Hos. 13:11) and Israel's destruction (Hos. 13:9), their iniquity and sin (Hos. 13:12), and lack of wisdom (Hos. 13:13). An east wind will blast destructive winds against them (Hos. 13:15), and Samaria will be held guilty and experience horrific calamity (Hos. 13:16). The context leads me to conclude that Hosea 13:14 is not a statement of hope but one of despair. However, Paul takes this statement and weaves it into one of the most hopeful texts of the NT. "Paul projects an eschatological vision of a single death precisely because Jesus Christ has himself absorbed the sting on the basis of how his death and resurrection addresses the problem of human sin and the law (vv. 55-57)."[37]

Why do I include this explanation of these passages here? The use of Psalm 44:22 in Romans 8 and Hosea 13:14 in 1 Corinthians 15 demonstrates that God may turn the most desperate passages and fill them with hope. If God can do that with these words, can He not also do so with the events of our lives?

Moses is given as an example of faith to the Hebrews in Hebrews 11:23-29. Moses chose to endure ill-treatment with the people of God

---

[35] C.E.B. Cranfield, *Romans*, vol. 1, chaps 1-8, T and T Clark: Edinburgh, 441.

[36] This is one of several passages from the OT that was translated in a more hopeful way in the Septuagint (LXX).

[37] Anthony C. Thiselton, *The First Epistle to the Corinthians*, Grand Rapids: Eerdmans, 2000.

What Is Eternal Life and Why Should It Matter to Me?

rather than to enjoy the passing pleasures of sin (25).[38] Moses chose "poverty, contempt, and affliction; for Israel at this time was a nation of slaves, groaning under its heavy load, with broken spirits and vanished hopes, hemmed in by daily abuse."[39] He chose the reproach of Christ rather than the riches of Egypt. He chose the more difficult path than a life of affluence and ease, "for he was looking for the reward" (26). He was seeing Him who is unseen (27). The treasures of heaven made all the sacrifices and sufferings of life worthwhile.

We can, therefore, rejoice in sufferings because we stand in a noble line of succession: "for in the same way they persecuted the prophets who were before you" (Matt. 5:12; Luke 6:23). We have a great reward: "Rejoice and be glad, for your reward in heaven is great" (Matt. 5:12; Luke 6:23). The seventy (or seventy-two) returned and said even the demons are subject to us in Your name (Luke 10:17). Jesus told them, "Do not rejoice in this, that the spirts are subject to you, but rejoice that your names are written in heaven" (Luke 10:20).

An athlete will put himself through grueling training and exercise incredible self-disciple to have a chance to be the one who will be awarded a perishable wreath. Should not their examples give us a powerful object lesson of what we should do to finish the race and obtain an imperishable wreath (1 Cor. 9:24-27)?[40]

We long to be in heaven because it is the dwelling place of God. In Solomon's prayer of dedication for the temple in Jerusalem, he often emphasizes that God is in heaven (1 Kings 8:30, 32, 34, 36, 39, 43, 45, 49, 54). The point of these repeated references to God being in heaven stresses that no earthly place, even the temple, is adequate as a dwelling place for God (1 Kings 8:27; Isa. 66:1-2). God is our Father in heaven or heavenly Father (Matt. 5:16, 45, 48; 6:1, 9, 14, 26; 7:11, 21, 21; 12:50; 18:10,

---

[38] The word *ill-treated* is also used in Hebrews 11:37 and 13:3. In 13:3 it refers to some of the experiences of their brothers in Christ.

[39] Neil Lightfoot, *Hebrews*, 216.

[40] The text in 1 Corinthians 9:24-27 is in the context of encouraging Christians to forego their liberties so that others may reach the goal. We should forego our rights that make our brothers stumble (1 Cor. 8:7-13). Since heaven is worth any sacrifice we make to reach the goal, then it is also worth making sacrifices that others may reach it as well.

14; 23:9). Heaven is so identified with God that sometimes "heaven" is used as a metonymy for God's name. Daniel tells Nebuchadnezzar that his kingdom would be restored to him when he recognized that "heaven" rules (Dan. 4:26). The prodigal son acknowledged, "I have sinned against heaven and in your sight" (Luke 15:18, 21). Jesus asked the religious leaders if the baptism of John was "from heaven or from man" (Matt. 21:25; Mark 11:30; Luke 20:4). John the Baptist said, "A man can receive nothing unless it has been given him from heaven" (John 3:27). This is also seen in Matthew's use of the phrase "kingdom of heaven," where Mark and Luke use the phrase the "kingdom of God" (cf. Matt. 3:2 with Mark 1:15; Matt. 19:23 with Mark 10:23; Luke 18:24).[41] Heaven is so identified with God that the words can be used interchangeably. We long to be there because the God we love is there.

Repeatedly in the New Testament, our eternal reward is to be with God and Christ. On the night before the crucifixion, the disciples are troubled that Jesus is leaving them (John 13:33, 36-37). Jesus promises, "I will come again and receive you to Myself, that where I am, there you may be also" (John 14:3). Paul prefers "to be absent from the body and to be at home with the LORD" (2 Cor. 5:8). Paul writes that he has the desire to depart this life "and be with Christ" (Phil. 1:23). The Thessalonians were tempted to grieve as the world that does not have hope, and the apostle says, we will "be caught up in the clouds to meet the Lord in the air, and so we shall always be with the Lord" (1 Thess. 4:13, 17).

Revelation 21-22

John sees a new heaven and earth for the first heaven and earth have passed away (Matt. 5:18; Mark 13:31; 1 Cor. 7:31; 1 John 2:17). There is no more sea (21:1). Why does the verse emphasize there being no sea? In Revelation, the sea is the place from which the dreadful beast arises (13:1-10; cf. Dan. 7:1-8). The great harlot sits on many waters (17:1). Those who trade with her make their living on the seas (18: 17, 19). The sea is forced to give up its dead (20:13).[42] In 4:6, the sea may separate

---

[41] Matthew uses the phrase "kingdom of heaven" 33 times, but the phrase appears only in Matthew.

[42] Ideas suggested by G.K. Beale, *The Book of Revelation*, 1041-42.

What Is Eternal Life and Why Should It Matter to Me?

mankind from the presence of God.[43] In the world of Israel's neighbors, the sea was pictured as a chaos monster who must be subdued by the gods of the peoples. While the "gods" of the nations subdued the sea with great difficulty, God does so with ease (Job 38:8-11; Prov. 8:29; Jer. 5:22). The LORD dries up the waters (Isa. 1:2; 19:5; Jer. 51:36; Ezek. 30:12; Nah. 1:4; Ps. 18:16; Job 12:15) and rebukes the seas (Isa. 1:2; Nah. 1:4; Hab. 3:8; Pss. 18:6; 29:3).[44]

The holy city descends from heaven (21:2; 3:12) and is made ready like a bride adorned for her husband (21:2; 19:7-8). The words about the holy city descending out of heaven are repeated in verse 10. Revelation 21:1-2 may be a heading to the more detailed description in 21:9-22:5.[45] The holy city adorned beautifully as a bride occurs in Isaiah 52:1 and 61:10. A loud voice (16:17; 19:5) announces from the throne that the tabernacle is among men and that God has come to dwell among men (21:3).[46] The idea of God as being our God and our being His people is used repeatedly in the Bible. Here the statement is slightly altered, and "people" in the NASB is actually plural, "peoples."[47] This word stresses the idea that God's people are from every tribe, tongue, people, and nation (Rev. 5:9; 7:9). The key concept is "the intimate communion that God and His people will have with one another."[48] God will wipe away every tear from their eyes (21:4; 7:17). This condition is a complete contrast to those who are thrown into outer darkness. They will experience weeping and gnashing of teeth (Matt. 13:42, 50; 22:13; 24:51; 25:30). There will be no end to their tears or grief.

There will no longer be any death. Since sin has been atoned for by the death of Christ (Rev. 1:5; 5:6, 9, 12; 7:13-14; 12:11), death, the com-

---

[43] Ray Summers, *Worthy is the Lamb*, Nashville: Broadman, 212. Robert Harkrider, *Truth Commentaries: Revelation*, Bowling Green, KY: Truth Publications Inc., 239.

[44] Ideas suggested by Aune, 1119-1120.

[45] Aune, 1120.

[46] The verb *skēnoō* (σκηνόω) is used in the NT in John 1:14; Revelation 7:15; 12:12; 13:6; 21:3. This word is used in the Septuagint for the tent of meeting.

[47] All nations are flowing into this new Jerusalem along the lines of Isaiah 2:2-4.

[48] Beale, *The Book of Revelation*, 1046. Hailey, 407, writes "The development of God's presence among His people now reaches its zenith as He dwells or tabernacles with them in His heavenly fellowship."

"When Will These Things Be?" : Questions on Eschatology

panion of sin, is defeated as well (Rom. 1:32; 5:12; 6:23). "There will no longer be any death; there will no longer be any mourning, or crying, or pain." The language of 21:4 picks up the wording of Isaiah 25:8 "He will swallow up death for all time, and the Lord God will wipe tears away from faces." Isaiah 65:17 and 66:22 promise a new heaven and a new earth. God promises, "For the youth will die at the age of one hundred and the one who does not reach the age of one hundred shall be thought accursed" (Isa. 65:20). As great as the promise of Isaiah 65:20 is, it does not compare to Revelation 21:4. Instead of living to be one hundred, the complete cessation of death is God's promise.[49]

God promises to make all things new, proclaiming that He is the Alpha and Omega, the beginning and the end (21:5-6; 1:8; 22:13; Isa. 41:4; 43:10; 44:6; 48:12). This is only the second time that God has directly spoken in the book.[50] "The point of the title is that the God who transcends time guides the entire course of history because He stands as sovereign over its beginning and end."[51] The readers are assured that just as God brought the first creation into being, so He will bring history to its triumphant conclusion.[52] God promises the overcomer (2:7, 11, 17, 26; 3:5, 12, 21) that He will be his God, and the overcomer will be God's Son and will inherit[53] all things (21:7). "One difference between v. 3 and v. 7 is that the saints now are each referred to individually as 'son' instead of collectively as 'people.'"[54] The glory of this occasion exceeds our ability to describe it with words. The opposite fate is experienced by those who will be cast into the "lake that burns with fire and brimstone." This phrase is also used in Revelation 19:20; 20:10, 14, 14, 15, as well as here in 21:8. The second death appears in 2:11; 20:6, 14; 21:6.

Revelation 21:9-22:5 seems to expand on the ideas introduced in 21:1-8. The next verses focus on the bride, the wife of the Lamb (9), and the city (10). John is carried away in the Spirit to see the mountain and the

---

[49] Aune, 1124.

[50] The first occasion was in Revelation 1:8.

[51] Beale, *The Book of Revelation*, 1055.

[52] Beale, *The Book of Revelation*, 1055. I have slightly altered Beale's words.

[53] Matthew 19:29; 25:34; Heb. 1:14.

[54] Beale, *The Book of Revelation*, 1058

What Is Eternal Life and Why Should It Matter to Me?

city (10; similar to 1:10; 4:2; 17:3). Ezekiel had a similar experience (Ezek. 40:2). The city shines with the glory of God (11; Isa. 60:1). The city had the brilliance of jasper (4:3). The city has a great and high wall and twelve gates with three facing in each direction and twelve foundation stones (12-14). The gates are named for the twelve tribes, as are the twelve gates of the ideal Jerusalem in Ezekiel 48:31-35. The twelve gates also have twelve angels at the gates. Are the angels serving as watchmen for the city? (Isa. 62:6). The twelve foundation stones have the twelve names of the apostles (14). The number twelve is used six times in verses 12-14. The angel who spoke with John had a gold rod to measure the city (15). The city was a square with its length, width, and height being equal (16). Ezekiel pictures the ideal temple and city (48:20) like a square. The walls of the city were 72 yards (17). The foundation stones of the building are given in verses 19-20. These stones echo the words of Isaiah 54:11-12. The gates were of twelve pearls, and the street of the city was pure gold, like transparent glass (21). Pearls were viewed as of great value (Matt. 7:6; 13:46; 1 Tim. 2:9).

In Revelation 21:22-27, there is no temple in this city. The temple was, in a special way, the dwelling place of God. The presence of God and the Lamb are direct, and there is no temple (21:22).[55] [56] Ezekiel's vision of an ideal temple in Ezekiel 40-48 finds fulfillment in the presence of God and the Lamb. There is no sun or moon in the city, for it is illumined by the glory of God (21:23; 22:5). The nations will walk in its light, and the kings will bring their glory and honor into it (21:24, 26).[57] "The glory and

---

[55] The temple was also a place where sins were forgiven. In 1 Kings 8 the prayer at the dedication of the temple asks for forgiveness (1 Kings 8:30, 34, 36, 39, 50). Sacrifices were offered here, and they are connected with forgiveness: Burnt offerings (Lev. 1:4; Job 1:5; 42:7-9), sin offerings (Lev. 4:20, 26, 31, 35; 5:6, 10, 13), trespass offerings (Lev. 5:16, 18; 6:7) are all connected with forgiveness of sins in these verses. Full forgiveness will be ours and therefore no need of a temple.

[56] The fact that there is no temple in the New Jerusalem distinguished John from many Jewish apocalyptic writers. See Beale, *Revelation*, 1092. No teaching of Jesus seems to make the religious establishment any angrier than His teaching that the temple will be destroyed (John 2:19-22; Mark 14:58; 15:29). Beasley-Murray, 325-326.

[57] The kings of the earth in 17:2; 18:3, 9 committed acts of immorality with the harlot. In 19:19 they make war against the Lamb, and in 6:15 they are

honor" appears elsewhere in this book in 4:9, 11; 5:12, 13. These verses refer to the praise of God and the Lamb.[58] These nations are giving all glory, honor, and praise to God and the Lamb. In the day, the gates of the city will never be closed (21:25). There is absolute security in the city, and there is no need to close the gates that guard and protect the inhabitants of the city. There is no night in this city (21:25; 22:5). All that is unclean, and those who practice abominations, do not enter the gate of the city (21:27; 22:15). Only those whose names are written in the Lamb's Book of Life will enter there (21:27).[59]

What is Indicated by the Description of This City?

The description emphasizes the breath-taking beauty of the city (21:11, 18-21). It stresses the spaciousness of the city (21:16). The size of the city emphasizes its spaciousness. A point is being made about the accessibility of this city (21:21). Notice the abundance of entry points for the city. Most ancient cities had one gate that was closed at night. The security of the city is indicated (21:25, 27; 22:15). The wall excludes those on the outside of the city (Rev. 22:15). Walls distinguished cities from smaller settlements. The walls of the city emphasize the protection of the city (Isa. 26:1; Zech. 2:4ff.), the home of all God's redeemed people. This description shows the unity of God's people under the Old and New covenants by mentioning the twelve tribes and twelve apostles (21:12-14). Most of all, God and the Lamb (21:22-23) are in the city. None of the beauty and grandeur of the city would make it heaven if they were not there.

Revelation 22:1-5 pictures a river of the water of life flowing from the throne of God and the Lamb (1). The water is as clear as crystal. Compare this clear water with the words of Revelation 4:6 and contrast the words with Revelation 8:10-11 and 16:4-7. On either side of the river was the tree of life (2). Ezekiel 47:1-12 pictures a trickle of water

---

terrified at the wrath of the Lamb. But here they are bringing their glory and honor into the new Jerusalem. In Revelation 21:22-27 the picture of all nations streaming to God's city from Isaiah 2:2-4 and Micah 4:1-3 with all nations worshiping the LORD in Revelation 15:4 find fulfillment.

[58] Beale, *Revelation*, 1095.

[59] The book of life in Revelation is also mentioned in 3:5; 13:8; 17:8; 20:12, 15. Elsewhere in the NT it is only mentioned in Philippians 4:3.

What Is Eternal Life and Why Should It Matter to Me?

flowing from the temple that gets stronger as it goes and gives life to everything it touches. The same picture is alluded to in Joel 3:18 and Zechariah 14:8. Notice the emphasis on "life" in these verses 1 and 2, "the water of life and the tree of life." There will be no more curse (3). Curses have come into the world because of sin and wickedness (Gen. 3:14, 17; 4:11; Deut. 27:15-26; 28:15-68). Yet, for God's servants, sin has been defeated, and the curse has been removed (Zech. 14:11). They will serve Him (3). Revelation 7:15 says that we "serve Him day and night in His temple." They will see His face, and His name will be upon their forehead (4). When Moses asked to see God's glory, he was told, "You cannot see My face, for no man can see Me and live" (Exod. 33:18-20). Philip asked, "Lord, show us the Father, and it enough for us" (John 14:8). When our bodies are transformed into the likeness of His body (Phil. 3:21; 1 John 3:1-2), then we will see His face. "Just one glimpse of Him in glory will the toils of life repay."[60] His name will be on our foreheads (4).[61] The text says there is no night[62] and that we will reign forever (5).[63] This verse shows the ultimate fulfillment of the promise of Revelation 3:12. What greater blessings could there be than these?

Notice the emphasis on God and the Lamb in 22:1-5. The "throne of God and of the Lamb" is mentioned in 22:1, 3. The Lord God will illuminate the city (5), and we will see His face (4). The picture of heaven given in Revelation is God-centered. Even with the street of gold and the gates of pearl, heaven would not be heaven if God were not there.

---

[60] This line is from the hymn by Eliza E. Hewitt, "When We All Get to Heaven."

[61] The sealing of these servants on their forehead is also found in Revelation 7:3; 14:1. In Revelation 3:12 God's people have the name of my God and the city of God written on them. This contrasts with those who have the mark of the beast on their right hand and their forehead in Revelation 13:16.

[62] Night and darkness are sometimes a picture of evil and wickedness in Scripture. Examples are so plentiful as to almost not need examples. However, a few examples of this are in Ephesians 5:8-11; 1 John 1:7; 2:9-11. The references may also be a reminder that all wickedness is banished from this place.

[63] Exodus 19:5-6 says Israel was to be a royal priesthood. These promises to Israel are also made to the church in 1 Peter 2:9-10; Rev. 1:6; 5:10, but they will be fulfilled in a deeper way in eternity.

"When Will These Things Be?" : Questions on Eschatology

Is Revelation 21-22 speaking of our present experience as Christians or to what God has prepared for us in eternity? I have no difficulty saying that these chapters describe the blessings of God that we begin to experience in this life. Perhaps the closest parallel we have in the New Testament to the language of Revelation 21:1, 5 is found in 2 Corinthians 5:17. In 2 Corinthians 5:17, Paul speaks of the old things that have "passed away" and "new" things as Revelation 21:1 speaks of the first heaven and the first earth "passed away" and a "new" heaven and earth. "In Paul's view the new creation came into being in the death and resurrection of Christ, so that to step into fellowship with Christ is to participate in that new world."[64] Obviously, there is a fulfillment of this right here and now. The phrase *Inaugurated Eschatology* applies to this concept.[65] However, the fulfillment of this here and now does not eliminate a greater fulfillment yet to come. The greatest fulfillment is in the days to come, eternity. While we "see" God in a sense here and now (1 John 3:6; 3 John 11), there is a sense in which we do not and cannot (Exod. 33:18-23; 1 Tim. 6:16). However, then we will see His face (Rev. 22:4). There will be depth and richness to these blessings that we can scarcely conceive now. We have begun to experience God's blessings, but for the child of God, the best is yet to come.

Heaven Will Be the Ultimate Fulfillment of All Scripture

God will be with His people forever in heaven. This perfect union between God and His people will make heaven the ultimate fulfillment of all of Scripture and all of human history. Speaking of Revelation 21-22, one said, "The vision, therefore, may be viewed as the climax not only of the book of Revelation but of the whole story of salvation embodied in the Bible."

The Answer to Man's Problem

Heaven will be the answer to the problem of sin that was introduced into the world in Genesis 3. The curse of Genesis 3 is completely removed, and eternity is described in terms of the garden of Eden. At the end of the Bible, man is, by God's grace, given what He lost at the beginning of the Bible. The overcomers in Ephesus are promised that they will

---

[64] Beasley-Murray, 308.

[65] My first introduction to the phrase was in the book by Anthony A. Hoekema, *The Bible and the Future*, Grand Rapids: Eerdmans, 1979.

What Is Eternal Life and Why Should It Matter to Me?

eat of the tree of life, which is in the midst of the paradise of God in Revelation 2:7. The language of Revelation 22:1-5 seems to invoke the language of Genesis 2-3 intentionally. The mention of the tree of life (Gen. 2:9; 3:22), the river (Gen. 2:10-14)[66], and the curse (Gen. 3:14, 17) call the garden of Eden to our attention. The perfect environment that was lost to man in the beginning because of his sin has been provided again by the Lamb that was slain. "Heaven is the place of perfect fellowship, perfect protection, perfect provision of needs, perfect service to God."[67] Paradise Lost is now paradise Regained.[68] The beginning of the Bible is perfectly answered by the ending of the Bible.

The statement "I will be his God and he will be My son" in Revelation 21:7 is the essence of a phrase that is used of man's relationship with God throughout Scripture. The key character of the Scripture is God, and the second key character is mankind. The problem of the Bible is sin, and the theme of the Bible is God bringing man back into fellowship with Him after man's sin. There is no phrase that better summarizes the theme of the Bible than the phrase, "I will be their God and they will be My people." In Genesis 17:7, as God is describing His covenant with Abraham, He said that His purpose is "to be God to you and to your descendants after you." When God promises to deliver Israel from Egypt, He says, "Then I will take you for My people, and I will be your God" (Exod. 6:7). As Moses describes the blessings of the covenant to Israel, He says, "I will also walk among you and be your God, and you shall be My people" (Lev. 26:12). After God invokes captivity, which is the ultimate curse of the covenant, He still does not give up on His people. Jeremiah and Ezekiel preach that the city of Jerusalem will be destroyed, the temple will be burned, and the people will go into captivity. However, they also stress there is a bright future for the people of God and use the phrase "I will be their God and they will be My people" to drive home this point (Jer. 24:7; 30:22; 31:1, 33; 32:38; Ezek. 34:30; 36:28; 37:23, 27; Zech. 8:8; 13:9). This

---

[66] That the garden in some way is reflected by the city of Jerusalem may be indicated by the fact that the Gihon is one of the rivers of the garden (Gen. 2:13), and the only other times that Gihon is mentioned in the Bible are in reference to the spring that flows in the city of Jerusalem (1 Kings 1:33, 38, 45; 2 Chron. 32:30; 33:14).

[67] Summers, 215.

[68] This borrows a phrase from John Milton.

"When Will These Things Be?" : Questions on Eschatology

phrase "And I will be a father to you, and you shall be sons and daughters to Me" is used to describe Christians in 2 Corinthians 6:18. The same idea, but not the exact phrasing, is used in Romans 9:25-26 and 1 Peter 2:10. This phrase describes God's relationship with His people throughout time. He will be our God, and we will be His people on a deeper level than we can experience here and now.

The Fulfillment of God's Promises

Heaven will be the ultimate fulfillment of promises God made to Abraham and his offspring. God promised Abraham to give him the land of Canaan in Genesis 12:7, saying, "To you and your descendants, I will give this land." These promises to Israel dominate much of the rest of the book of Genesis[69] and the Pentateuch.[70] God gave Israel the land even though the people in the land were stronger and mightier than they were (Deut. 7:1-4). God kept His promises to the forefathers to give them the land of Canaan (Josh. 21:43-45; 23:14). However, the book of Joshua ends with the funerals of Joshua and Eleazer and the burial of Joseph's bones (Josh. 24:29-33). Though God's people had the land, this was not their ultimate rest. Hebrews 11:8-16 compares Abraham's journey to Canaan in Genesis 12:1-3 to a quest for the heavenly city as already discussed. Hebrews 3:7-4:11 show the Promised Land of Canaan as a foreshadowing of the ultimate land of rest and promise. Heaven will be the ultimate home that God's people have longed for throughout time.

Heaven will be the ultimate fulfillment of the promises to Abraham to bless all nations through him (Gen. 12:3; 22:18). Those who are saved in Revelation are from "every tribe and tongue and people and nation" (Rev. 5:9; 7:9; 14:6). "The nations will walk by its light, and the kings of the earth will bring their glory into it" (Rev. 21:24). These will bring "the glory and honor of the nations into it" (Rev. 21:26).

The Fulfillment of the Exodus from Egypt

Heaven will be the ultimate fulfillment of the Exodus from Egypt. The book of Revelation abounds in Exodus imagery. The seven trumpets of Revelation 8:1-11:19 and the bowls of wrath in Revelation 16 are patterned after the plagues of Egypt from Exodus 7-11. The first trumpet (Rev. 8:7) and the seventh bowl of wrath (Rev. 16:17-21) describe hail

---

[69] Genesis 13:14-18; 15:7-21; 48:21-22; 49:28-33; 50:22-26.

[70] Exodus 3:8, 17; 6:8; 12:25; 13:5; 33:2-3; Numbers 13-14; Deut. 1:19-46.

What Is Eternal Life and Why Should It Matter to Me?

and remind the reader of the plague God used against the Egyptians (Exod. 9:13-35). In the second trumpet (Rev. 8:8-9) and the second bowl (Rev. 16:3), the waters become blood (Exod. 7:14-24). Darkness is the result of the fourth trumpet (Rev. 8:12) and the fifth bowl (Rev. 16:10-11), which is the ninth plague (Exod. 10:21-29). The fifth trumpet (Rev. 9:1-12) deals with locusts just as the eight plague does (Exod. 10:1-20). The sixth trumpet in Revelation 9:13-21 sounds much like the plague of the firstborn in Exodus 11-12. Just as a defiant ruler oppressed God's people in the book of Exodus, so the same was happening in the book of Revelation.[71] The judgments God poured out on His enemies in the plagues foreshadow the judgments that will come on all who defy Him and mistreat His people throughout history.

The salvation of the book of Revelation is also described in terms of the Exodus. In Revelation 15:2-3, those who have been victorious over the beast are standing on the sea of glass and singing "the song of Moses" and "the Lamb." The sea seems like "a kind of heavenly Red Sea."[72] At the Exodus, the Israelites sang, celebrating their deliverance (Exod. 15:1-18). Those who are victorious over the beast sing and celebrate their deliverance in the same way. There is no more important event in Israel's history than the Exodus. It was the act of salvation in the Old Testament. It also becomes a foreshadowing of salvation for God's people throughout history. The return from the Babylonian captivity is described as an exodus in Isaiah 43:16-20; 48:21-22. Also notice Ezra 1:5-6 as compared to Exodus 3:21-22; 11:2-3; 12:35-36. In a sense, the return from Babylonian captivity even eclipses the Exodus (Jer. 16:14-15; 23:7-8). At the transfiguration, Jesus talked to Moses and Elijah about His exodus (Luke 9:31). Jesus's death gives deliverance from the greater foes of sin and death.[73]

---

[71] G.R. Beasley-Murray, *Revelation*, 155, words this much more eloquently than I have.

[72] Ibid., 235.

[73] All through the Old Testament the great oppressors of God's people are a picture of the greatest foes of sin and death. The wording of Nahum 1:15 and in Isaiah 52:7 provides the background of Romans 10:15. In Nahum 1:15 the enemy is Assyria and in Isaiah 52:7 the enemy is Babylon, but the deliverance from these enemies is a picture of deliverance from the greatest of all foes, sin itself. "Because of the broader redemptive-historical structure of Scripture, this deliverance from Assyria's oppression may be perceived

"When Will These Things Be?" : Questions on Eschatology

The final fulfillment of the Exodus will be in heaven. "The parallel to the Exodus narrative in the Old Testament is not accidental but conscious and deliberate."[74] Heaven will be the fulfillment of the desire of God to create a holy environment that is stressed in Leviticus and Numbers (Rev. 21:27; 22:15).

The Fulfillment of God's Promise to David

Heaven will be the ultimate fulfillment of God's promises to David. The language of Revelation 21:7, "I will be his God and he will be My son" seems to be worded in a way to call attention to the promises made to David in 2 Samuel 7:14. In 2 Samuel 7:14, God promises David, "I will be a father to him and he will be a Son to Me." The Father/Son relationship between God and the king is also mentioned in Psalm 2:7: "You are My Son, Today I have begotten you."[75] [76]Psalm 2:8-9 also says this King will ask of God, and God will give the nations as an inheritance and the ends of the earth as a possession. The King will rule with a rod of iron and break them as a fragile piece of pottery.[77] These words about the coming King's ruling the nations with a rod of iron are applied to Christ in Revelation 12:5 and 19:15.[78] Interestingly, these words about ruling with a rod of iron are promised to overcoming Christians in Thyatira in Revelation 2:26-27. We will share in Christ's reign. Revelation 3:21

---

    as a microcosmic depiction of deliverance from all oppression that comes as a consequence of sin, Satan, and death." Palmer, *Nahum, Habbakuk and Zephaniah*, 83.

[74] Beasley-Murray, 155.

[75] This passage is quoted and applied to Christ at His baptism (Matt. 3:17; Mark 1:11; Luke 3:22), His transfiguration (Matt. 17:5; Mark 9:7; Luke 9:35), and His resurrection (Acts 13:33). Hebrews 1:5; 5:5 also quotes the verse and applies it to Jesus. In Hebrews 1:5, 2 Samuel 7:14 is quoted as well as Psalm 2:7 and applied to Christ.

[76] Psalm 89:26-27 says the king will be the "firstborn" and "the highest of the kings of the earth," and the king will cry to God, "You are my Father."

[77] Psalms 2, 45, 72, 89, 101, 110, 132, 144 are among the Psalms generally labeled as royal psalms. These psalms focus on the king.

[78] Jesus is shown to be the fulfillment of the promises to David from the first verse of the New Testament (Matt. 1:1) and throughout the rest of the New Testament as well (Matt. 9:27; 12:23; 15:22; 20:30-31; 21:9, 15; 22:41-46; Acts 2:29-36; 13:23-37; Rom. 1:2-3; 2 Tim. 2:8; Rev. 3:7; 5:5; 22:16).

What Is Eternal Life and Why Should It Matter to Me?

promises that the one who overcomes in Laodicea will sit with Christ on His throne as He overcame and sat with the Father on His throne.[79] In Revelation 21:7, we will inherit all things, which inheritance is a fulfillment of the words of Psalm 2:8. We will ultimately share in those blessings promised to the Messianic King.

The Fulfillment of God's Choice of Jerusalem

Heaven is the ultimate fulfillment of God's choice of Jerusalem. Deuteronomy emphasizes the place the LORD would choose for a dwelling for His name (Deut. 12:5, 11, 14, 21, 26). The city which the LORD chose was Jerusalem (1 Kings 11:13, 32, 36; Zion Psalms 46, 48). Psalm 78 is a historical psalm that celebrates God's choice of David (Ps. 78:70) and His choice of Mount Zion (Ps. 78:68). A person's attitude toward Jerusalem was indicative of his attitude toward God Himself (Ps. 137:5-6). Mount Zion is the place of salvation and deliverance in Scripture (Joel 2:32; Obad. 21), and the fulfillment is pictured in Revelation 14:1. The earthly Jerusalem was to be a city of righteousness and faithfulness, but it rarely lived up to those expectations (Isa. 1:21, 26). The context of Isaiah 1:21 tells us how the city for which God had such high designs became a harlot.[80] Silver coins minted with the words "Jerusalem the holy" are found on Jewish coins minted in the Jewish revolt of 66-70 AD.[81] However, the "holy city" was full of sin, and it received judgment. Even in the book of Revelation, that is the case. The "holy city" of Revelation 11:2 was more related to Egypt and Sodom than it was to a holy city, and it was one with Sodom and Egypt who crucified the LORD (Rev. 11:8). Jerusalem failed to live up to God's high ideals for the city. The earthly city was a foreshadowing of a city that was to come (Gal. 4:26; Heb. 12:22). John sees the holy city from a great and high mountain (Rev. 21:10). This wording about a high mountain recalls the wording of Isaiah 2:2-4 and Micah 4:1-4 with all nations coming to God's mountain to learn His ways and to walk in His path (Zech. 8:3, 15; 14:21). This is not to suggest a fulfillment in the literal earthly city. Instead, it is to emphasize that all

---

[79] 2 Timothy 2:11-13; Rev. 5:9 speak of believers sharing in the reign of their Savior.

[80] Jerusalem or Israel is referred to as a harlot in Ezekiel 16:15-34; Hos. 2:2-13; Jer. 2:1-2; 3:1.

[81] David E. Aune, *Revelation 17-22*, Nashville: Thomas Nelson Publishers, 1121.

"When Will These Things Be?" : Questions on Eschatology

these passages about a holy city will be fulfilled in the city described in Revelation 21-22.

The Fulfillment of Isaiah's Prophecy

Heaven will be the ultimate fulfillment of the promises Isaiah makes in the latter part of his book about the return from captivity and the rebuilding of the city of Jerusalem. Isaiah wrote around 740-680 BC. (Isa. 1:1). His call took place around 740, in the year King Uzziah died (Isa. 6:1). He records the death of Sennacherib at the hand of his sons, which happened in 681 (Isa. 37:37-38). Though Isaiah lived and preached at this time, in Isaiah 40-66, his prophecies assume the Babylonian captivity he warned of in Isaiah 39. His emphasis, though, is not on the captivity itself, but his emphasis in Isaiah 40-66 is on the return from captivity and the rebuilding of Jerusalem. Isaiah even mentions Cyrus by name many years before he was born as God's anointed who would decree the rebuilding of the city and the temple (Isa. 44:28; 45:1). Notice the abundance of references to Isaiah in Revelation 21. Revelation 21:1 speaks of a "new heavens and a new earth" (Isa. 65:17; 66:22). Revelation 21:2 mentions "the holy city" (Isa. 52:1). Revelation 21:2 describes a bride adorned for her husband (Isa. 61:10). In Revelation 21:6, God speaks of drinking "the spring of the water of life without cost" (Isa. 55:1). Revelation 21:11 talks of the city's reflecting "the glory of God" (Isa. 60:1). Revelation 21:23 tells us that the city will have no need of the sun or the moon (Isa. 60:19-20). The nations will walk in the glory of the city (Rev. 21:24; Isa. 60: 3, 5) and bring their glory into the city (Rev. 21:26; Isa. 60:11). Even the description of God and Christ as the "Alpha and Omega, the first and the last, and the beginning and the end" in Revelation 21:6; 22:13 go back to the book of Isaiah (41:4; 44:6; 48:12). The whole contrast between Babylon the harlot and Jerusalem the bride is also found in the book of Isaiah

The Answer to Life's Emptiness

Heaven will be the answer to the emptiness of life found in Ecclesiastes.[82] From the beginning of Ecclesiastes (1:2) until its end (12:8), the word *vanity* sounds loudly.[83] Ecclesiastes stresses that the days of our life

---

[82] The same Greek word used in the LXX to translate "vanity" in the book of Ecclesiastes is used in Romans 8:20.

[83] The word *vanity* is used 32 times outside of Ecclesiastes and 35 times within the book. In the OT the word refers to something that is fleeting and im-

What Is Eternal Life and Why Should It Matter to Me?

are few (2:3; 5:18; 9:9; 11:10) and death is the certain end regardless of what we do (2:12-17, 18-23; 3:19-21; 5:15-16; 7:1-2; 9:2-6). This fact of death renders meaningless any accomplishments we are able to attain. While wisdom excels folly, the wise man will die just like the fool, so what, therefore, is the advantage of being wise (2:12-17)? If we are able to save some money, all of it must be left behind (5:15-16), and no one knows whether the one we leave it to will be wise or foolish (2:18-23). Ecclesiastes is not Messianic in the sense that it makes direct prophecies of Christ. Instead, it is Messianic in the sense that it raises questions and presents problems of human existence that only Jesus can answer. While Ecclesiastes laments that everything we do will be forgotten (1:9-11; 2:16; 8:10; 9:5), in heaven, God remembers and rewards even the smallest acts of service (Matt. 10:42; 25:40; Mark 9:41; Heb. 6:10). Praise God that through His resurrection, Jesus has conquered death (John 11:25-26; 1 Cor. 15:25-26), and in heaven, there will be no more death (Rev. 21:4).

The Perfect Marriage between God and His People

Heaven will be the perfect marriage between God and His people. Men and women were created for intimacy with each other (Gen. 2:18-25). Even more, however, we were created for intimacy with God. The history of marriages made in time will find its fulfillment in the perfect marriage between the Lamb and His people in eternity.[84] It will be a love stronger and more fulfilling than anything we read about in the Song of Solomon. The relationship between God and Israel is described in terms of a marriage in Isaiah 54:5; Jeremiah 3:1-11; Hosea 1-3. In the New Testament this image is used in Mark 2:19-22; Matthew 22:1-14; 25:1-13;

---

permanent—Job 7:16; Ps. 38:6; 62:10; 78:33; 144:4; Prov. 13:11; 21:6. Vanity refers to something vain, empty, and pointless—Job 9:29; 21:34; 27:12; 35:16; Ps. 39:7; 62:10; 94:11; Prov. 31:30; Lamentations 4:17; Isa. 30:7; 49:4; Jer. 10:3, 15; 16:19; 23:16; 51:18; Zech. 10:2. The word also refers to the emptiness and futility of idols—Deuteronomy 32:12; 1 Kings 16:13, 26; 2 Kings 17:15; Ps. 31:7; 62:11; Jer. 2:5; 8:19; 10:18; 14:22; Jonah 2:9. In the book of Ecclesiastes maybe the best ideas is that the word means something is in vain and fails to achieve their purpose—2:1-2, 15-16; 3:19; 5:6; 6:2, 4, 11-12; 7:6. Eric Ortlund, *Journal of the Evangelical Theological Society* (2013), 700-701.

[84] Matthew 22:30; Mark 12:25; Luke 20:35-36 tells us in our relationships with our fellow human beings that in the resurrection there is no marriage or is there giving in marriage.

"When Will These Things Be?" : Questions on Eschatology

John 3:29; 2 Corinthians 11:2; Ephesians 5:25. The relationship between God and His people is described as a marriage in the book of Revelation (19:7-9; 21:2, 9). The end of the book of Revelation presents a tale of two cities. The contrast is strong between Babylon, the harlot, and Jerusalem, the bride. Babylon has in her hand a golden cup full of abominations and the unclean things of her immorality (Rev. 17:4). While Babylon offers a cup of abomination, the bride offers the cup of invitation (Rev. 22:17). All that marriage was ever intended to be, and more will be fulfilled in the marriage between God and His people.

The Fulfillment of the Temple

Heaven will be the ultimate fulfillment of the temple. The tabernacle and the temple emphasize the presence of God. Revelation 21:3 says, "Behold, the tabernacle of God is among men, and He will dwell among them, and they shall be His people, and God Himself will be among them." The idea of God's dwelling[85] with man is a key idea throughout Scripture. In the garden of Eden, the Lord God was walking in the garden among the trees of the garden (Gen. 3:8). The Hebrew Hithpael form of God walking back and forth in a garden is used to describe God's presence in the temple (Lev. 26:12; Deut. 23:14; 2 Sam. 7:6-7; Ezek. 28:14). [86] The purpose of the tabernacle God instructs Israel to build is that God may dwell among His people. "Let them construct a sanctuary for Me, that I may dwell among them" (Exod. 25:8, similar wording is in Exod. 29:45-46). When the tabernacle was completed, the cloud covered the tent of meeting, and it is stated twice that the glory of the LORD filled the tabernacle (Exod. 40:34-35). The temple was a permanent version of the tabernacle. The similarity between 1 Kings 8:10-13 and Exodus 40:34-35 is very clear and straightforward.[87] The brilliance of God's glory glowing on Mount Sinai (Exod. 24:16), on the tabernacle (Exod. 40:34-35), and in the temple (1 Kings 8:11) now radiates through all of God's city (Rev. 21:11). God's dwelling among men takes a new form in the person of Christ. John 1:14 says, "The word became flesh, and dwelt among us, and

---

[85] The Greek word is the same as the one used in John 1:14.

[86] G.K. Beale, *A New Testament Biblical Theology*, Grand Rapids: Baker, 2011, 617. See both this page and footnote 8 on this point.

[87] Ibid, 617-622. Beale points out other comparisons between the garden, the tabernacle, and the temple.

What Is Eternal Life and Why Should It Matter to Me?

we saw His glory, glory as of the only begotten from the Father, full of grace and truth." In the person of Jesus, God was dwelling[88] with men. Jesus is the fulfillment of all the tabernacle and temple were intended to be (John 2:19-22; 4:19-24). Often individual Christians and the church, the people of God collectively, are spoken of as the temple (1 Cor. 3:16; 6:18-20; 2 Cor. 6:16; Eph. 2:19-22; 1 Pet. 2:4-5).[89] The experiences of God's dwelling with man in time only foreshadow the ultimate reality of God's dwelling with man in eternity. He will dwell among us more intimately than we ever experience here.

What is the purpose for the mention of the twenty-four thrones and the twenty-four elders in Revelation 4:4, 10? The twenty-four elders are often said to be the names of the twelve tribes and the twelve apostles. There is certainly some biblical basis for the identification (Rev. 21:12-14). However, the number *twenty-four* may have another significance. 1 Chronicles 22-29 records David's work of preparation of the temple, which is not recorded elsewhere. In 1 Chronicles 24, David divided the descendants of Aaron, the priests, who were to serve in the temple, into twenty-four families. 1 Chronicles 25 divides the Levites that served as temple singers into twenty-four families. The prominence of the number twenty-four in temple worship may indicate that the *twenty-four* elders of Revelation 4 picture heaven as the perfect temple of which the Jerusalem temple was a dim reflection. Heaven is the perfect temple where the perfect worship is rendered.

Is there a tabernacle or temple in heaven? In addition to Revelation 21:3, chapter 7 and verse 15 says, "He who sits on the throne will spread His tabernacle over them." The city is laid out as a square (Rev. 21:16) like the holy of holies (1 Kings 6:20). In these ways, heaven is the ideal temple where the ultimate worship of the true God takes place. However, the Bible also says, "I saw no temple in it, for the Lord God the Almighty and the Lamb are its temple. And the city has no need of the sun or the moon to shine on it, for the glory of God has illumined it, and the lamp is the Lamb" (Rev. 21:22-23). Some passages point to a tabernacle or temple in

---

[88] This is the verb form of the word *tabernacle*.

[89] Everett Ferguson, *The Church of Christ: A Biblical Ecclesiology for Today*, Grand Rapids: Eerdmans, 1996. On pages 124-129 he deals with this picture of the church as the temple.

"When Will These Things Be?" : Questions on Eschatology

heaven, and some say there is none. Both of these ideas point to the same reality—both point to the presence of God.

Heaven will be the ultimate fulfillment of Ezekiel's ideal temple in Ezekiel 40-48. Notice how much of the language of Ezekiel 40-48 is used in Revelation 21. John says he was carried away in the Spirit to a great and high mountain (Rev. 21:10; Ezek. 40:2). Revelation 21:11 speaks of the glory of God in a similar way to Ezekiel 43:2. Revelation 21:12-14 mentions the twelve gates of the city with the names of the twelve tribes, which is an obvious reference to Ezekiel 48:31-34. Revelation 21:15 describes a measuring rod to measure the city like what we see in Ezekiel 40:3. Revelation 21:16 describes the square of the city like the city in Ezekiel 48:15-20. Revelation 21:27 speaks of nothing unclean entering the city, and the same idea is found in Ezekiel 44:9. The description of the river that flows through the city and the tree of life in Revelation 22:1-5 are also in Ezekiel 47:1-12. While the promises of Ezekiel 40-48 may have some level of fulfillment in the temple built after the captivity, its final fulfillment will be in the "perfect temple" of heaven.

The Fulfillment of God's Promises to Victors

Heaven will be the ultimate fulfillment of the promises to the overcomers of the seven churches of Asia. Heaven is a fulfillment of the New Testament as well as the Old Testament. This truth can be illustrated by the promises to the seven churches of Asia. "He who overcomes will inherit these things" (Rev. 21:7). "The promises to the conquerors, declared in the seven letters of chapters 2-3, therefore find their summary expression at this point."[90] G.K. Beale says it well:

> The multiple inheritance is underscored by citation at the end of the Apocalypse of some of the promises to the overcomers from the letters: "the tree of life which is in the paradise of God" (2:7; 22:2), inclusion in the new temple (3:12; 21:22ff.), participation in "the new Jerusalem, which comes down out of heaven from God" (3:12; 21:2, 10), the name of God on one's person (3:12; 22:4), one's "name written in the book of life" (3:5; 21:27), bright garments (3:5; 21:2, 9ff; 19:7-8), a bright stone and luminary (2:17, 28; 21:11, 18-21, 23; 22:5, 16), consummate reigning with Christ (2:26-27; 3:21; 22:5), and exclusion from the "second death" (2:11; 21:7-8).[91]

---

[90] Beasley-Murray, 313.

[91] Beale, *The Book of Revelation*, 1058.

What Is Eternal Life and Why Should It Matter to Me?

The Fulfillment of Jesus's Teaching

Heaven is the ultimate fulfillment of Jesus's teachings. In John, Jesus is the good Shepherd (John 10:1-18). He is the fulfillment of all that is said of the LORD in Psalm 23. Revelation 7:17 says, "The Lamb in the center of the throne will be their Shepherd." Jesus also reveals Himself as the living water that can forever satisfy our thirst (John 4:10, 13-14). He is the bread of life who satisfies our hunger and thirst (John 6:35). The Lamb "will guide them to the springs of the water of life" and "They will hunger no more, nor thirst anymore" (Rev. 7:16-17). God says in heaven that He "will give to the one who thirsts from the spring of the water of life without cost (Rev. 21:6; 22:17). The good Shepherd will forever lead His people to the green pastures and quiet waters. While this point could be expanded much further, heaven will be the ultimate fulfillment of Jesus's words.

Why did God create man? Why did God create man in light of all the pain that our disobedience brings Him (Gen. 6:5-7; Eph. 4:30)? God knew that most would be lost (Matt. 7:13-14; Luke 13:22-24). He knew all that people whom He loved would suffer throughout time and eternity. He knew all the suffering that innocent people throughout history would experience. Job (Job 3:1-10) and Jeremiah (Jer. 20:14-18) experienced enough pain that they wished they had never been born. There must be something so glorious and so thrilling about heaven and God's dwelling with His people forever that it was worth all the pain in time and eternity to create man. Heaven must be great to be worth it all!

Bibliography

Aune, David E. *Revelation 17-22*. Nashville: Thomas Nelson Publishers, 1998.

Beale, G.K. *A New Testament Biblical Theology: The Unfolding of the Old Testament in the New*. Grand Rapids, MI: Baker, 2011.

———. *The Book of Revelation*. The New International Commentary on the Greek New Testament. Grand Rapids, MI: Eerdmans, 1999.

Beale, G.K. and D.A. Carson, eds. and D.A. Carson, eds. *Commentary on the New Testament Use of the Old Testament*. G.K. Beale and D.A. Carson, eds. Grand Rapids: Baker, 2007.

"When Will These Things Be?" : Questions on Eschatology

Beasley-Murray, G.R. *Revelation*. The New Century Bible. Grand Rapids, MI: Eerdmans, 1974.

Bock, Darrell L. *Luke 1:1-9:50: Baker Exegetical Commentary on the New Testament*. Grand Rapids, MI: Baker Academic, 1994.

———. *Luke 9:51-24:53: Baker Exegetical Commentary on the New Testament*. Grand Rapids, MI: Baker Academic, 1996.

Cranfield, C.B.E. *Romans 1-8*. International Critical Commentary Series, Edinburgh: T and T Clark, 1975.

Curry, Melvin. *Truth Commentaries: 2 Corinthians*. Bowling Green, KY: Guardian of Truth, 2008.

Davies, W.D. and Dale C. Allison, Jr. *The Gospel According to Saint Matthew*. T and T Clark. Reprinted 2003.

Ferguson, Everett. *Backgrounds of Early Christianity*, 3rd ed. Grand Rapids, MI: Wm. B. Eerdmans Publishing Co., 2003.

———. *The Church of Christ: A Biblical Ecclesiology for Today*. Grand Rapids, MI: Erdmans, 1996.

Garland, David. *2 Corinthians*. New American Bible Commentary. Nashville: B and H Publishing Group, 1999.

Green, Joel B. *The Gospel of Luke*. New International Commentary on the New Testament. Grand Rapids: Eerdmans, 1997.

Hailey, Homer. *Revelation*. Grand Rapids: Baker, 1979.

Harkrider, Robert. *Truth Commentaries: Revelation*. Bowling Green, KY: Guardian of Truth, 2008.

Hoekema, Anthony A. *The Bible and the Future*. Grand Rapids: Eerdmans, 1979.

Kidner, Derek. *The Message of Ecclesiastes*. Downers Grove, IL: InterVarsity Press, 1976.

Lightfoot, Neil. *Jesus Christ for Today: A Commentary on Hebrews*. Grand Rapids, MI: Baker Book House, 1976.

Ortlund, Eric. "The Gospel in the Book of Ecclesiastes." *Journal of the Evangelical Theological Society* 56 (Dec. 2013): 697-706.

What Is Eternal Life and Why Should It Matter to Me?

Palmer, O. Robertson. *The Books of Nahum, Habakkuk, and Zephaniah.* The New International Commentary on the Old Testament. Grand Rapids, MI: Eerdmans, 1990.

Reddish, Mitchell G. "Heaven." *Anchor Bible Dictionary*, Vol. 3, 90-91. David Noel Freedman, ed. New York: Doubleday, 1992.

Roberts, J.W. *The Revelation to John.* Austin, TX: Sweet Publishing Co., 1974.

Summers, Ray. *Worthy Is the Lamb.* Nashville: Broadman, 1951.

Schoonhoven, C.R. "Heaven." *International Standard Bible Encyclopedia*, Vol. 2, 654-655. Geoffrey W. Bromiley, ed. Grand Rapids, MI: Eerdmans, 1982.

Thompson, James. *The Second Letter of Paul to the Corinthians.* Austin, TX: Sweet Publishing Co., 1970.

Thiselton, Anthony C. *The First Epistle to the Corinthians.* Grand Rapids, MI: Eerdmans, 2000.

What Does the Bible Teach about Hell and Who Will Go There?

By Ron Halbrook

The Bible teaches in Matthew 13:41-42 that Christ will sentence the wicked to eternal torment on the Last Great Day:

> The Son of man shall send forth his angels, and they shall gather out of his kingdom all things that offend, and them which do iniquity; And shall cast them into a furnace of fire: there shall be wailing and gnashing of teeth.[1]

No one has ever lived who is more qualified to warn about the reality and dangers of hell than Jesus Christ, the Son of God. God sent many warnings through His prophets about hell throughout Old Testament history, but no teacher recorded in Scripture spoke as often or as graphically about hell as Jesus did. He is the last great prophet sent by God to all

---

[1] All Scripture quotations are from the King James Version unless otherwise noted.

Ron Halbrook was born in Indianola, MS in 1946, moved to Belle Glade, FL in 1951, and grew up and graduated from high school there. He preached for the Southside Church of Christ in Belle Glade in the summer of 1964. During his years at Florida College (1964-67), his preaching continued with the Central congregation near Live Oak, FL (fall 1965), the West Sixth St. church in Pine Bluff, AR (summer 1966), and the Hercules Ave. church in Clearwater, FL (1966-67).

During 1967-73, Ron labored with the Wooley Springs church near Athens, AL, taught high school at Athens Bible School and finished a degree in history at Athens College (1969). He labored with the Broadmoor church in Nashville,

What Does the Bible Teach about Hell and Who Will Go There?

humanity "in these last days" (Heb. 1:1-2). The apostles through whom Jesus Christ gave His final revelation to all mankind fervently affirmed the reality of hell and warned men to flee from it.

Hell's Reality Demanded by God's Love and Justice

God has warned man about hell from the beginning of time until this very moment. The Bible records such warnings from Genesis to Revelation. Hell must exist and does exist because God and Satan *cannot* unite. Sin and righteousness *cannot* mix. Truth and lies *cannot* compromise. Saints and sinners *cannot* coalesce. Oil and water naturally inevitably separate. Once man's inner character has been crystallized and hardened by sin, it can *never* be in harmony with God's pure loving character. Where can such a man with such a heart abide forever?

God's loving character forbids Satan, sin, and sinners to enter heaven to soil and spoil it with rebellion and chaos. God is unalterably holy. God's love and holiness are innately intolerant of the malice and impu-

---

TN 1973-78 (and completed a master's degree in church history at Vanderbilt University, 1979), the Knollwood church in Xenia, OH 1978-82 (with Mike Willis in a two-preacher arrangement), the church in Midfield, AL 1982-84, and the West Columbia, TX church in 1984-97. In August of 1997, he began working in a two-preacher arrangement with Andy Alexander at the Hebron Lane Church of Christ in Shepherdsville, KY. Andy moved to Bowling Green, KY in 2003 and Steven Deaton took his place at Hebron Lane in June 2004, followed by David Dann in April 2017. This arrangement allows Ron to hold several gospel meetings and make four trips to the Philippines each year. He has made seventy-seven trips to the Philippines since 1995 and also preached in New Zealand, Australia, England, and France. Ron's articles have appeared in such religious journals as *Truth Magazine*, *Searching the Scriptures*, and *The Preceptor*. Other writing includes tracts (*Unity with Christ and Christians; Honorable Marriage; The Original Church of Christ; Is Mark 16:15-16 Genuine Scripture?*), booklets (*Trends Pointing toward a New Apostasy; Understanding the Controversy, The Authority of Christ*), workbooks (*Leadership in the Church*), and books (*The Doctrine of Christ and Unity of the Saints; Halbrook-Freeman Debate on Marriage, Divorce, and Remarriage*). Ron has served on the staff of *Truth Magazine* since 1974 and the board of Truth Publications since 1977.

Ron married Donna Bell in 1967. They have three children: Jonathan (married Tanya Bryant; children: Payton, Cole, Paige, Abbie), David (married Starla Page; children: Joel, Esther, Eliel), and Deborah (married Jamie Williams; children: Timothy, Seth, Arabelle). He can be reached at halbrook@twc.com.

"When Will These Things Be?" : Questions on Eschatology

rity of all forms of sin and rebellion. His divine nature *must separate* "the righteous" and "the wicked" as Abraham affirmed with the rhetorical question, "Shall not the Judge of all the earth do right?" (Gen. 18:23, 25).

Indeed, God's character as reflected in His word is "perfect," "sure," "right," "pure," "clean," and "true and righteous altogether" (Ps. 19:7-9). God will not allow Satan and his followers to mar, degrade, and disgrace heaven as they have the affairs of earth life. God's love as well as His wrath *must* and *will* banish Satan and his followers to hell forever.

The Bible reveals the character of God as perfect both in love and in justice. God declared His nature to Moses to be taught to Israel:

> And the LORD passed by before him, and proclaimed, The LORD, The LORD God, merciful and gracious, longsuffering, and abundant in goodness and truth, Keeping mercy for thousands, forgiving iniquity and transgression and sin, and that will by no means clear the guilty; visiting the iniquity of the fathers upon the children, and upon the children's children, unto the third and to the fourth generation (Exod. 34:6-7).

Before his death Moses taught Israel a song which includes praise of His perfect divine nature:

> I will proclaim the name of the LORD. Oh, praise the greatness of our God! He is the Rock, his works are perfect, and all his ways are just. A faithful God who does no wrong, upright and just is he (Deut. 32:3-4, NIV).

Israel was repeatedly warned to be faithful to God because His perfect justice will surely punish sin: "For the LORD thy God is a consuming fire, even a jealous God" (Deut. 4:24).

> Know therefore that the LORD thy God, he is God, the faithful God, which keepeth covenant and mercy with them that love him and keep his commandments to a thousand generations; And repayeth them that hate him to their face, to destroy them: he will not be slack to him that hateth him, he will repay him to his face (Deut. 7:9-10).

To deny the Bible's teaching about hell is to deny the very love and justice which characterize the true God revealed in Scripture, and thus to deny His very essence and existence. Such a denial does nothing to exonerate God and make Him more palatable to modern man but only reveals the depths to which sin corrupts and depraves human hearts. The sinner's feeble wicked objections to eternal punishment in hell as

What Does the Bible Teach about Hell and Who Will Go There?

somehow unjust will not withstand "the day of God's wrath, when his righteous judgment will be revealed" (Rom. 2:5).[2]

Yet, all the teaching revealed and preserved by God in Scripture about hell and who will go there has been adamantly denied by Satan and by self-willed men unwilling to face responsibility for their sins. All the lies of Satan designed to convince us to sin rest on two great pillars of deception: (1) *Sin is a blessing wrongfully denied to man by God*, and (2) *sin will not be punished, most certainly not by conscious eternal torment in hell*. Satan's brazen subtlety is introduced in Genesis 3:4-5:

> And the serpent said unto the woman, Ye shall not surely die: For God doth know that in the day ye eat thereof, then your eyes shall be opened, and ye shall be as gods, knowing good and evil.

On these two lies hang all unbelief and disobedience.

Satan has been diligently maintaining these two pillars from the first time he invaded the Garden of Eden until this very hour. He cannot delude us into rebelling against God our Creator and Sustainer, and he cannot rob our souls of the blessings of fellowship with God, unless he convinces us of these two great lies. Our chaotic, sin-cursed world testifies loudly to Satan's skill in honing and polishing these great pillars of deception.

Despite Satan's diligence and persistence in hiding the horrors of hell, God's love and justice demand its reality. Let us "fear, lest by any means, as the serpent beguiled Eve through his subtilty, so your minds should be corrupted from the simplicity that is in Christ," "for we are not ignorant of his devices" (2 Cor. 11:3; 2:11).

---

[2] Some men such as Edward Fudge have taught that hell must involve annihilation because the doctrine of hell as eternal torment makes God "a sadist" (Fudge, *The Fire That Consumes*, 431) and is "a gross slander against the heavenly Father" (Fudge and Peterson, *Two Views of Hell*, 20). It is well known that atheists, skeptics, infidels, and universalists of all stripes make exactly the same argument in rejecting hell whether viewed as eternal torment or as annihilation. Carol Meyer rejects all versions of hell with the question, "How could such cruelty and sadism be consistent with a God of love?" (Meyer, "Debunking the myth of hell").

"When Will These Things Be?" : Questions on Eschatology

The Existence of Hell Is Clear in Genesis 1-3

The battle lines in the war between God and Satan for our souls were drawn in the events recorded in Genesis 1-3. God created man in His own image, referring not to the fleshly form of the body but to the spirit which inhabits and animates the body. The spirit or soul made in God's image gives life to the body first in the womb, later exits the body at the point of physical death, and finally re-enters the body in the resurrection.[3] But the spirit never ceases to exist.

It is clear from the beginning of time that God created man to live in perfect fellowship with Him, not to die!

Man was created to live in a paradise of physical blessings in the Garden of Eden in the beginning of time and in a spiritual paradise of fellowship with God extending beyond time into eternity. God intended our companionship with Him to continue into eternity without the pain and suffering of physical death as can be seen in the case of Enoch who "walked with God" 365 years and was taken from earth without experiencing death (Gen. 5:23-24).[4]

---

[3] James argues that as faith animates obedience, the spirit animates the body, but "the body without the spirit is dead" (Jas. 2:26). Thayer explains that the Greek words for "spirit" (*pneuma*) and "soul" (*psuchē*) are generally synonyms "used indiscriminately" whereas "body" (*soma*) and "soul" are "put in contrast." Furthermore, he explains it is the spirit which is "possessed of the power of knowing, desiring, deciding, and acting" (see entry on *pneuma*, Thayer, 520).

When Jacob died "and was gathered unto his people," it refers to his spirit not his body because 40 days of embalming and 70 days of mourning passed before Joseph requested permission from Pharaoh to take Jacob's body to Canaan for burial (Gen. 49:33-50:13, see 49:33).

The spirits of the rich man, Lazarus, and even Jesus entered the hadean realm at death (Luke 16:19-31; 23:46; Acts 2:25-31). Hebrews 12:23 refers to the righteous dead as "the spirits of just men made perfect," i.e., their spirits live in the hadean realm awaiting the resurrection. (For more study on hades, see the essay "What Does the Bible Say about Sheol and Hades?" by Kyle Pope in the Appendix).

The resurrection refers to spirits re-entering their bodies at the call of Christ (John 5:28-29). The part of man made in God's image does not cease to exist.

[4] The genealogy from Adam to Lamech recorded in Genesis 5 follows a pat-

What Does the Bible Teach about Hell and Who Will Go There?

God warned Adam against the consequences of sin when He said, "For in the day that thou eatest thereof thou shalt surely die" (Gen. 2:17). As surely as physical death severs our ties with our earthly companions, spiritual death bereaves us of our spiritual fellowship with God. Our first parents experienced death in both ways.

Unless there should be some means of forgiving sin, the sentence of spiritual death must continue into eternity since the spirit never ceases to exist. For that reason hell, "the lake which burneth with fire and brimstone," was prepared as the everlasting abode of all who experience "the second death" (Rev. 21:8). That some such place must exist is positively implied by the context of the events in Genesis 1-3.

Men Destined to Hell in Patriarchal and Mosaic Ages

The Bible clearly teaches that men who rebelled against God in the Patriarchal and Mosaic Ages are destined to spend eternity in hell.

In Genesis 6, God found the human family was filled with wickedness, evil, corruption, and violence. He called on Noah, "a preacher of righteousness," to build an ark and to preach that men must repent lest they perish in a terrible flood. His patience was extended for 120 years while Noah was building the ark and preaching repentance (Gen. 6:1-13; 2 Pet. 2:5). All men and animals perished in the Flood except those in the ark with Noah (Gen. 7:21-23).

The people who drowned in the Flood did not cease to exist. In 1 Peter 3:19-20 Peter speaks of their souls being held by God "in prison" in his time. Christ through the Spirit used Noah "and preached unto the spirits in prison; Which sometime were disobedient, when once the longsuffering of God waited in the days of Noah." Peter says the angels who sinned are likewise cast down into this hadean realm of torment called "*tartarus*," "into chains of darkness, to be reserved unto judgment"

---

tern. Each man "lived," then the text says, "and he died" (vv. 3, 5, 6, 8, 10, 11, 12, 14, 15, 17, 18, 20, 25, 27, 28, 31), with the exception of Enoch. Enoch "lived," then twice the text says, "he walked with God," then, "and he was not; for God took him" (vv. 21-24). The repeated words "and he died" emphasize the certainty of the consequences God had pronounced against sin in Genesis 2:17 in conjunction with God expelling Adam and Eve from the Garden wherein stood the tree of life (3:22-24).

(2 Pet. 2:4).[5] These angels and the spirits of men who died in the Flood are clearly alive, not annihilated, and they all are being held in view of the Final Judgment when the wicked will be cast into hell.

No stronger evidence for the reality of hell can be found in the Old Testament than God's fiery destruction of Sodom. God utterly destroyed the cities, people, animals, and surrounding vegetation in the Valley of Siddim as a symbol of the power of His righteous wrath against sin for all future generations. "Then the Lord rained upon Sodom and upon Gomorrah brimstone and fire from the Lord out of heaven; and he overthrew those cities, and all the plain, and all the inhabitants of the cities, and that which grew upon the ground" (Gen. 19:24-25).

The souls of these sinners were not incinerated like their bodies were, but the wrath of God's fiery punishment pursued them beyond this life. By the time of Moses the region was called the Salt Sea—meaning the Dead Sea—and he warned Israel that they too would become a wasteland if they broke His covenant and worshiped other gods (Gen. 14:3; Deut. 29:23; 32:32). The prophets repeatedly used Sodom as a reminder of God's power to destroy nations and to punish sinners (Isa. 1:9-10; 3:9; Jer. 49:17-18; 50:35-40). Jesus verified the historicity of God's wrath against Sodom and made it clear its inhabitants are in "hades" awaiting the final "day of judgment" along with other men who have rebelled against Him (Matt. 10:15; 11:23-24).

---

[5] *Tartarus* appears as "hell" in the KJV and most other translations, but the Greek word for hell is *gehenna*. The question becomes is *tartarus* a synonym for torment in hades, for hell, or both? "Cast them down to hell" is *tartarōsas*, a verb which could be translated "consigning to tartarus" (Hamilton, 123). Sinful spirits are held captive in *tartarus* awaiting their final judgment or sentence to be cast into gehenna. The Anglicized term "tartarus" appears in 2 Peter 2:4 in Alfred Marshall's *Interlinear Greek-English New Testament* (1960), Alexander Campbell's *The Living Oracles* (1826), H.T. Anderson's *The New Testament Translated from the Original Greek* (1864), *The New Testament, Confraternity Version*, (Catholic, 1967), and *The New American Bible* (Catholic, 1976), whereas "hades" appears in J.B. Rotherham's *The Emphasized Bible* (1897). Jude 6 which is parallel to 2 Peter 2:4 does not use *tartarus* but simply says the wicked angels are "reserved in everlasting chains under darkness unto the judgment of the great day." This confirms that however other Greek and Jewish writers may have used *tartarus*, Scripture uses it as a temporary realm for the wicked awaiting Final Judgment.

What Does the Bible Teach about Hell and Who Will Go There?

Both Jude and Peter continue the same train of thought and teaching. Jude warned, "Even as Sodom and Gomorrah, and the cities about them in like manner, giving themselves over to fornication, and going after strange flesh, are set forth for an example, suffering the vengeance of eternal fire" (v. 7). "Suffering" is a "present active participle" in Greek which means that the inhabitants of "Sodom and Gomorrah are currently . . . undergoing punishment" (Hamilton, 439).

Warning against false teachers and the judgment to come, Peter wrote, "And turning the cities of Sodom and Gomorrah into ashes condemned them with an overthrow, making them an example unto those that after should live ungodly" (2 Pet. 2:6). Both of these writers demonstrate continuity and consistency in what the Bible teaches about the destiny of the wicked:

> When God rained "brimstone and fire" upon Sodom, He literally turned the city "into ashes" (Gen. 19:24; 2 Pet. 2:6). He did it in such a fashion as to demonstrate that this fire came *from God*, not from man. Whether men like it or not, God destroyed Sodom in such a way as to memorialize for all time *His hatred of immorality, especially homosexuality*. Furthermore, He sent such a horrible, unrelenting, unquenchable fire as to necessarily imply "the vengeance of eternal fire" (Jude 7). *The fire of God's anger pursued the Sodomites on earth, still torments them in hades, and will punish them throughout all eternity"* (Halbrook, "Sodom and Gomorrah," 596).

John saw a vision of faithful martyrs lying "in the street of the great city, which spiritually is called Sodom and Egypt, where also our Lord was crucified" (Rev. 11: 8). Rome was immoral and obstinate like Sodom, binding people in sin as Egypt enslaved the Jews, yet the martyrs and the cause of truth were ultimately victorious. "*The last book of the Bible reminds us of the symbol given in the first book. The spirit of Sodom is doomed to utter and eternal defeat*" (ibid.).

In dramatic ways God displayed His wrath against sin and rebellion to Israel as they journeyed from Egypt to Canaan. God executed Nabab and Abihu, sons of the High Priest, by raining fire down upon them when they used "unauthorized fire" to burn incense (Lev. 10:1-3, ESV, NIV). When Korah, Dathan, and Abiram challenged the authority of Moses and demanded the priesthood, the earth opened and they

"When Will These Things Be?" : Questions on Eschatology

"went down alive into sheol"[6]—separating them from Israel and from Israel's God for time and eternity (Num. 16:33, ASV, ESV). Fire consumed their 250 confederates and a plague took another 14,700 who murmured against God's justice (Num. 16:35, 49).

Many Israelites who later complained against their diet of manna died from poisonous snakes, and another 24,000 died of a plague for their immorality and idolatry (Num. 21:6; 25:9). All of these souls were God's chosen people who became separated from God for time and eternity by their sinful attitudes and deeds. Paul said by divine inspiration, "Now all these things happened unto them for ensamples: and they are written for our admonition, upon whom the ends of the world are come. Wherefore let him that thinketh he standeth take heed lest he fall" (1 Cor. 10:11-12).

Hell in the Psalms: Multiplied Sorrows

The Psalms cultivate and celebrate both the hope of the righteous to live in fellowship with God forever and the reality of the everlasting defeat, separation, and punishment of His enemies. The presence of the Lord "at my right hand" gives man "hope" beyond the grave: "For thou wilt not leave my soul in hell [sheol, ASV, ESV]; neither wilt thou suffer thine Holy One to see corruption. Thou wilt shew me the path of life: in thy presence is fulness of joy; at thy right hand there are pleasures for evermore" (Ps. 16:8-11). While Christ fulfilled the ultimate meaning of this passage in His resurrection, it gives hope to all who die with faith in the God of "pleasures for evermore" in His presence—"at thy right hand."[7] In contrast, "Their sorrows shall be multiplied that hasten after another god" (v. 4). The text says "their sorrows shall be multiplied," not extinguished at some point by the annihilation of the sinner.

---

[6] *Sheol* is the Hebrew term for hades, the realm where the spirits of the dead await the resurrection and Final Judgment. For more study on *sheol*, see "What Does the Bible Say about Sheol and Hades?" by Kyle Pope in the Appendix.

[7] Both Peter and Paul apply this Psalm to the resurrection of Jesus (Acts 2:25-31; 13:29-37). The righteous will share His victory over death and dwell in God's presence forever as is made clear throughout the Bible, especially in passages such as 1 Corinthians 15 and Revelation 21:1-22:5. "And these blessings are not for the Son only. All those who believe in Him and obey Him have eternal life in Him (John 3:15-16, 36; 10:28; Rom. 2:7; 6:23; 1 John 2:17) and enter into the joy of their Lord (Matt. 25:21, 23; 1 Pet. 4:13)" (Blackmore, 219).

What Does the Bible Teach about Hell and Who Will Go There?

Since God enthroned David over Israel, David's enemies are God's enemies. In praying for God's help, David expressed his faith in God's righteous judgment against His enemies in the past:

> Thou hast rebuked the nations, thou hast destroyed the wicked; Thou hast blotted out their name for ever and ever. The enemy are come to an end, they are desolate for ever; And the cities which thou hast overthrown, The very remembrance of them is perished (Ps. 9:5-6, ASV).[8]

New enemies have now risen against David and God will in like manner cast them into "sheol, even all the nations that forget God" (v. 17, ASV). Thus, the wicked are erased from God's "record of those who are to live," "and God's judgment on them is no temporary thing; it has been imposed **for ever and ever** ([Heb.] *l'wlm w'd*, stressing the length of the doom by stating it in two different ways. . .)" (Blackmore, 173). Their desolation is perpetual or "for ever," "the same Hebrew word that is applied to the bliss of the righteous one in 16:11" (ibid., 174).

Likewise, Psalm 49 contrasts the destiny of "the upright" who obtain victory "in the morning"[9] and the wicked who oppress the righteous—they do not escape the darkness and defeat of sheol. While the wicked suffer "in sheol, with no place to dwell," the righteous do not fear: "But God will ransom my soul from the power of sheol, for he will receive me" (vv. 14-15, ESV). Sheol here does not refer merely to death or the grave to which all men yield, but to the exclusive and eternal torment of the wicked who can never enter God's presence. From torment in sheol they pass to torment in hell.

The horrible fate of the wicked is clearly presented in Psalm 73. Asaph almost stumbled when he saw "the prosperity of the wicked" (v. 3). Later while contemplating their lot in God's sanctuary, "then I understood their final destiny. Surely you place them on slippery ground; you cast them down to ruin. How suddenly are they destroyed, completely

---

[8] Both the Old and New Testaments testify to God having a book of life and those whose names are not recorded in it are destined for eternal doom. "Add iniquity to their iniquity, And may they not come into Your righteousness. May they be blotted out of the book of life And may they not be recorded with the righteous" (Ps. 69:27-28, NASB; cf. Phil. 4:3; Rev. 20:12, 15).

[9] "The morning is the time when troubles are put right: 'Weeping may endure for a night, but joy cometh in the morning' (Ps. 30:5. . .)" (Blackmore, 521).

"When Will These Things Be?" : Questions on Eschatology

swept away by terrors! . . . Those who are far from you will perish; you destroy all who are unfaithful to you" (vv. 17-19, 27, NIV). Asaph is not saying all rich people lose their riches before death, because that is not true. He does not mean simply all rich people die, because he already knew all people die. The reality of their condition separated from God *after* death is what came into focus. "Their final destiny" is "ruin," destruction, "terrors," and to "perish" because they lived and died far from God—and remain forever in that terrible condition.

Hell in the Prophets: No Peace to the Wicked

Isaiah warned hypocrites in Israel that they cannot escape "the devouring fire" of God's "everlasting burnings," i.e., the pain and punishment of God's wrath will pursue them relentlessly (Isa. 33:14). When His chastened people return from Babylonian captivity, they will learn that He provides rivers of blessings to His redeemed but, "There is no peace, saith the Lord, to the wicked" (48:20-22). The righteous die "and enter into peace," and God offers the peace of His presence to all who humble themselves before Him, "but the wicked are like the troubled sea, when it cannot rest, whose waters cast up mire and dirt. There is no peace, saith my God, to the wicked" (Isa. 57:1-2, 15, 19-21). Night and day, for time and eternity, the righteous rest in peace with God which the wicked cannot find. There is *no end of peace* for the righteous, for it is eternal, and *no end of trouble* for the wicked, for it is likewise eternal.

God promised through Isaiah to be with His people in the Messianic Age. This fellowship of God and His saints is pictured by such analogies as the creation of a "new heavens and new earth," a new Jerusalem, a new temple, and a new ingathering of worshipers from all nations "to my holy mountain" (Isa. 65:17-25; 66:7-23).[10] The care, peace, and comfort

---

[10] "Isaiah uses images from his age to paint a magnificent poetic picture to describe the joys of the world to come" in delivering "an oracle describing the messianic era" (note on Isa. 65:17-25 in *ESV Study Bible*, 1359). This is teaching by the use of analogy. The prophets themselves, not to mention the Jews who lived after their time, "enquired and searched diligently" to understand when and how their prophecies would be fulfilled. "Unto whom it was revealed, that not unto themselves, but unto us they did minister the things, which are now reported unto you by them that have preached the gospel unto you with the Holy Ghost sent down from heaven; which things the angels desire to look into" (1 Pet. 2:10-12).

What Does the Bible Teach about Hell and Who Will Go There?

of God for His people are blessings that know no end, just as His anger against the wicked knows no end. "And they shall go forth, and look upon the carcases of the men that have transgressed against me: for their worm shall not die, neither shall their fire be quenched; and they shall be an abhorring unto all flesh" (Isa. 66:24). "Isaiah over and over depicts the salvation that is to be made available in the Lord Jesus Christ, the Messiah . . . . But, the prophet ends his inspired writing. . . after giving the solemn warning concerning the eternal destiny of those who transgress against the Lord and rebel against him" (Humphries, 624).

The Valley of Hinnom outside Jerusalem was also called Tophet or the fiery pit in Isaiah's and Jeremiah's time where infants were sacrificed to Molech (Isa. 30:33; Jer. 7:30-33; 19:1-6). God promised to rename this "fire pit" the Valley of Slaughter as the graveyard where the bodies of Assyria's king and of Judah's rebels would rot and burn: "the breath of the Lord, like a stream of burning sulfur, sets it ablaze" (Isa. 30:33, NIV). The king of Assyria and all of the sinners in Judah were never literally cast into that valley, but the prophecy of their rotting burning bodies represented God's wrath punishing sinners *after their death*. This fire of God's wrath means they would be separated from His love, presence, and fellowship forever in the world to come.[11]

The prophets often teach effectively by using analogies based on well known facts and truths.[12] Ezekiel made the resurrection of the human body and the restoration of Israel from Babylonian captivity analogous (Ezek. 37:11-14). Similarly, Daniel made the resurrection to eternal life or eternal punishment analogous to the fate of Jews who were faithful or unfaithful especially during the trials imposed by Antiochus IV Epiphanes (175-164 BC) while awaiting the arrival of the Messianic kingdom. Many were martyred but others yielded to pagan pressures. Daniel

---

[11] It was shameful to die without a proper burial, but the punishment signified here goes far beyond that cultural concept. The picture is this: God sets "the fire pit" or Valley of Slaughter ablaze with fire and brimstone and it can never be extinguished—the shame and pain reach beyond this world. Made in the image of God, the soul is never extinguished, nor is the fire.

[12] Teaching by analogy is found throughout Scripture. Baptism is made analogous to the death, burial, and resurrection of Jesus in Romans 6:4. Israel passing through the Red Sea is made analogous to our baptism in 1 Corinthians 10:3.

"When Will These Things Be?" : Questions on Eschatology

prophesied that the faith of the martyrs would be vindicated and victorious while the apostates would be exposed as wicked by the rule of the Messiah: "And many of them that sleep in the dust of the earth shall awake, some to everlasting life, and some to shame and everlasting contempt" (Dan. 12:2).[13] Though this analogy found fulfillment in the rise of the Messianic kingdom, it reveals the rock solid conviction of God's people that the Final Judgment Day will result in eternal life for the righteous and eternal punishment for the wicked.

Though Old Testament revelation was not as complete as the New, the Jews in the intertestamental era and beyond continued to maintain the doctrine of the eternal punishment of the wicked. Their extra-canonical literature such as 1 Enoch, 2 (or Slavonic) Enoch, 2 Baruch, 4 Ezra, and 2 Maccabees prove "that belief in resurrection for both righteous and wicked had become general during the last two centuries BC and the first two centuries AD" including " the idea of physical torment for the wicked" (Hooke, 276, 273). Josephus confirms that all Jewish sects except the Sadducees affirmed the immortality of the soul (*Wars*, 2. 8).

Men Destined to Hell in the Gospel Age

During the Gospel Age Jesus and His apostles urgently warned that the wicked will be punished eternally in hell. Jesus referred directly to hell (*gehenna* in Greek) no less than eleven times, far more than any other teacher recorded in Scripture. This is altogether fitting because He more than anyone who has ever lived on this earth knew that the place is real, that many precious souls will go there, and that His mission was to prevent as many as possible from going there!

By the first century AD *gehenna* was a "technical term for unending torment" and "is associated with fire as the source of torment" (Tenny, 347; Orr, 2:1183). The Greek word comes from the Hebrew term for the Valley of Hinnom outside the walls of Jerusalem. "The valley became notorious for its evil associations: the burning of children in worship to Molech (2 Chron. 28:3; 33:6), defilement with dead men's bones by King Josiah in order to stop Molech worship (2 Kings 23:10-14), and the use

---

[13] Daniel 12:1-2 "portrays the cause of the righteous dead during the persecution of Antiochus as being vindicated in the time of 'the end' (the deliverance of Israel from oppression) and the cause of the faithless apostates as ultimately in defeat and spiritual humiliation" (King, *Truth Commentaries: Daniel*, 752).

What Does the Bible Teach about Hell and Who Will Go There?

of its name as a symbol for divine punishment (Jer. 7:32)" (Halbrook, "Eternal Punishment," 123). In the time of Jesus, Hinnom was a common dump for discarding and burning the dead bodies of criminals, animals, "and every other kind of filth" (McClintock, 6:764). "Maggots, an acrid odor, and smoldering fire characterized the place" (King, *Truth Commentaries: James*, 318). Kyle Pope notes "this place of sin and *fire*" had become a fitting symbol of "God's final punishment of sin *in fire*" (emph. orig., Pope, *Truth Commentaries: Matthew*, 328).[14]

What Jesus Personally Taught about Hell

Jesus firmly established and defended three prerequisites to the truth of the doctrine of hell as eternal punishment. First, *the spirit survives the death of the body.* In debating the Sadducees who denied this foundational truth, Jesus focused on how God referred to Himself in speaking to Moses at the burning bush in Exodus 3. Jesus asked, "Have ye not read that which was spoken to you by God saying, I am the God of Abraham, and the God of Isaac, and the God of Jacob?" Then Jesus pointed out the necessary implication of God's statement: "God is not the God of the dead, but of the living" (Matt. 22:31-32). As surely as God was alive in Moses's time, so were Abraham, Isaac, and Jacob.

Second, in Luke 16:19-31 Jesus demonstrated that *the spirits of the dead are alive and conscious in hades.* There "they are either comforted or tormented according to their standing with God . . . . All of this occurs while their bodies are still in the grave and other men still alive on earth, before the resurrection day (vv. 22, 27-31)" (Halbrook, "Eternal Punishment," 123).[15]

Third, *the dead will be raised to a future destiny at the Second Coming of Christ.* Jesus said in John 5:28-29 that "the hour is coming, in the

---

[14] For an excellent discussion of "The *Gehenna* of Fire," see Pope, *Truth Commentaries: Matthew*, 327-329.

[15] The Jehovah's Witnesses sect and others try to escape the force of the account in Luke 16:19-31 by claiming it was only a parable—as if that reduces it to the level of a fable and not a real event. In truth, parables were based on real life events which happen many times in the course of human experience, thus creating immediate common ground for the teacher and the student in conveying the lesson. No Bible parable is based on a fable. Furthermore, the text does not call this account a parable and no parable of Jesus identifies people by their personal names such as Lazarus in Luke 16. Lazarus and the rich man were real people who died and entered hades.

"When Will These Things Be?" : Questions on Eschatology

which all that are in the graves shall hear his voice, And shall come forth; they that have done good, unto the resurrection of life; and they that have done evil, unto the resurrection of damnation."

In dealing directly with hell (*gehenna*) eleven times in His teaching, Jesus never introduced the subject as some theoretical hypothesis for theological debate but always described it as the final punishment for sin from which there is no escape. In announcing the new kingdom of God soon to appear, He contrasted its spiritual nature with the civil nature of the old Israel. The civil penalty for murder under the Law of Moses was execution, but under the rule of God's new kingdom the bitter rash abusive anger which leads to murder will be punished with eternal separation from God in "hell fire" (Matt. 5:22, see vv. 21-26). Christ spoke as the king of the new kingdom by repeating the authoritative clause, "But I say unto you," in contrast to Moses or any other prophet or teacher (Matt. 5:22, 28, 32, 34, 39, 44).

Next, the civil law code under Moses required the death penalty for adultery. Under the reign of Christ, people who purpose and plan to commit adultery will face a far worse penalty: "thy whole body . . . cast into hell" (Matt. 5:27-30). If repentance seemed as difficult as plucking out an eye or cutting off a hand, it was preferable to the punishment for refusing to repent. Jesus is not teaching self-mutilation but effectively uses hyperbole and metonymy to emphasize His point. The eye and the hand are instruments by which sin is committed. Thus, by metonymy these instruments represent the sins themselves which must be severed or eradicated from our lives if we are to avoid spending eternity in hell. To obey Him we must repent of all thoughts and deeds leading to adultery.

After His transfiguration Jesus used the same imagery contrasting the pain of repentance and of the far greater pain of hell to quell the disciples' squabble on the road to Capernaum about positions of pride and power in the new kingdom of God (Matt. 18:1-14; Mark 9:33-50).[16] With the blunt force of this truth, He sought to convince them and us to

---

[16] Jesus had taken Peter, James, and John with Him to the mount of His transfiguration. Perhaps this private attention given by Jesus to the three disciples "started the dispute as to which should hold the highest office in the kingdom" as he led his disciples back to Galilee. "The fires of envy thus set burning were not easily quenched" (McGarvey, *The Fourfold Gospel*, 430).

What Does the Bible Teach about Hell and Who Will Go There?

repent of selfish pride and self-seeking before it is too late, which reveals His underlying love for all men.

Against this backdrop of selfish quarreling, Jesus warned in Matthew 18:5-9 about the sin of causing other people to sin. He described the punishment for such conduct as being worse than a terrifying death by drowning in the ocean with a large millstone tied around the neck.[17]

> Woe to the world because of its stumbling blocks! For it is inevitable that stumbling blocks come; but woe to that man through whom the stumbling block comes! And if your hand or your foot causes you to stumble, cut it off and throw it from you; it is better for you to enter life crippled or lame, than having two hands or two feet, to be cast into the eternal fire. And if your eye causes you to stumble, pluck it out, and throw it from you. It is better for you to enter life with one eye, than having two eyes, to be cast into the fiery hell" (vv. 7-9, NASB).

Rather than using our bodies to engage in sin, which in turn leads other people to sin, we should seek to save as many precious souls as possible like a shepherd who rescues lost sheep (vv. 10-14). If we obey Christ in this matter, we will "enter life" which is eternal fellowship with God rather than "being cast into the fiery hell" (literally, the *gehenna* of fire, v. 9) which is "eternal fire" (v. 8)—the painful ruin and misery of eternal separation from God.

In the parallel account in Mark 9, "hell" is graphically described as "the fire that never shall be quenched, where their worm dieth not, and the fire is not quenched" (vv. 42-48). The decaying bodies consumed by maggots and the filthy rubbish consumed by fire in the Valley of Hinnom point to the horrors of eternal punishment away from God's presence.[18] "The

---

[17] It is translated "large millstone" in the NIV because *mulos onikos* is literally "'millstone of a donkey,' i.e., a millstone turned by a donkey—far larger and heavier than the small millstones (24:41) used by women each morning" (note on Matt. 18:6 in *Zondervan NIV Study Bible*, 1497). "Greeks, Romans and Egyptians were punished by such millstone drowning. But the fate of one who, by striving for place, causes others to sin, will be worse than that" (McGarvey, *The Fourfold Gospel*, 432).

[18] God's presence is indicated by entering "into life" or "into the kingdom of God" (vv. 43, 45, 47). "To enter **the kingdom of God** is to enter **life**, the parallel teaches. The reference, in this case, is to the 'eternal kingdom,' an expression used by Peter and alluded to in other passages (see 2 Pet. 1:11; Matt. 25:34; 1 Cor. 6:9; 15:50; Gal. 5:21)" (Stauffer, *Truth Commentaries: Mark*, 218).

"When Will These Things Be?" : Questions on Eschatology

two figures depict hell as a state of decay which is never completed and of burning which does not consume" (McGarvey, *The Fourfold Gospel*, 433).

Knowing His disciples would face bitter opposition as they traveled and taught His word, Jesus urged them to put fidelity to the truth and their mission above personal comfort and safety. "And fear not them which kill the body, but are not able to kill the soul: but rather fear him which is able to destroy both soul and body in hell" (Matt. 10:28). When man kills the body, the soul continues to live, but only God can "destroy both soul and body in hell." To "destroy" *(apollumi)* is to bring to ruin like the Jews in verse 6 who were "lost" *(apollumi)* without a shepherd to guide them. In verse 28, it means to *"give over to eternal misery"* (Thayer, 64).[19] Jesus used this same verb in well known passages such as Luke 13:3 ("except ye repent, ye shall all likewise perish") and John 3:16 (believers do "not perish").

Its cognate "destruction" *(apoleia)* is found in passages such as Philippians 3:19 ("whose end is destruction") and 2 Peter 3:16 ("unto their own destruction") which means *"the loss of eternal life, eternal misery, perdition, the lot of those excluded from the kingdom of God"* (Thayer, 71).

Jesus gave a similar fearful warning of the fate that awaits disciples who sacrifice the truth to save their lives in Luke 12:4-5, "And I say unto you my friends, Be not afraid of them that kill the body, and after that

---

[19] Writers who teach the wicked will be annihilated consider Matthew 10:28 a favorite passage because it says God can "destroy *(apollumi)* both body and soul in hell." For instance, see Fudge, *The Fire That Consumes*, 173-178; Hailey, *God's Judgments and Punishments*, 150; and Smith, *After Life*, 167 which says this passage is "the primary scriptural cornerstone for the case" for annihilation. No standard Greek lexicon defines *apollumi* or its cognates to mean annihilation. "The idea is not extinction but ruin, loss, not of being, but of well-being" (Vine, 1.302). The prodigal son's father said his son "was lost *(apollumi)* and is found" (Luke 15:24). The son had not been annihilated but his fellowship with his father had been lost or destroyed.

In the course of this study, it will become obvious that Hailey once believed that hell meant eternal torment but changed near the end of his life. His commentary on the book of Revelation parallels Matthew 25:46 with forceful statements about eternal torment in Revelation. He said at that time, "There are many who question the eternal duration of this torment, but these must explain away biblical teaching" (Hailey, *Revelation*, 399). His later attempt to "explain away biblical teaching" is puzzling and failed to do so.

What Does the Bible Teach about Hell and Who Will Go There?

have no more that they can do. But I will forewarn you whom ye shall fear: Fear him, which after he hath killed hath power to cast into hell; yea, I say unto you, Fear him." This clearly refers to eternal punishment rather than annihilation. When men "kill the body," there is "no more that they can do," but there is something only God can do: cast them body and soul "into hell." If murder results in the annihilation of a person, and if hell results in the same thing, God can do no more than man.

Hell is not the site where punishment ends in the cessation of being but the place of endless punishment of ceaseless beings.

Jesus gave eight characteristics of a person's character required to enter God's new kingdom at the beginning of his ministry (Matt. 5:3-12). Near the end of it He pronounced judgment against the character of the Jewish leaders reflected in eight of their prominent characteristics which prevented them from entering the kingdom (Matt. 23:13-36).[20] "Blessed" becomes "woe." When they proselyted Gentiles, they perverted the Law and bound their own traditions on them: "Woe unto you, scribes and Pharisees, hypocrites! for ye compass sea and land to make one proselyte, and when he is made, ye make him twofold more the child of hell than yourselves" (v. 15). The zeal of the convert often exceeds the teacher.

While professing to honor the prophets martyred by their fathers, the religious leaders were animated by the same evil attitudes of their fathers and were planning the murder of Jesus. "Woe to you, scribes and Pharisees, hypocrites! . . . Ye serpents, ye generation of vipers, how can ye escape the damnation of hell?" (Matt. 23:29, 33).

These same warnings are desperately needed today! Religious teachers often pervert God's Word, bind their own traditions, and bitterly resent anyone who exposes their error and evil. Jesus yet held out hope to any among His audience who would finally recognize Him as the Messiah, saying, "Blessed is he that cometh in the name of the Lord" (Matt. 23:39). The same door of mercy remains open wide today for anyone who will acknowledge the truth of the gospel and submit to Jesus as the Christ, the Son of the living God.

---

[20] For more on the contrast between Jesus's sermons in Matthew 5 and 23, see Pope, *Truth Commentaries: Matthew*, 790-792.

"When Will These Things Be?" : Questions on Eschatology

Additional Descriptions of Eternal Punishment by Jesus

Numerous times in His ministry Jesus warned against and shed light on the doom of hell without using the term *gehenna*. Having used *gehenna* three times early in the Sermon on the Mount, He referred to the same punishment as "destruction" *(apoleia)* for those who enter the wide gate and follow the broad road of sin (Matt. 7:13). The disciples used this very word when the woman poured expensive ointment on Jesus, and they asked, "To what purpose is this waste *(apoleia)*?" (Matt. 26:8). The ointment was not annihilated, nor is the sinner—but he is brought to utter ruin.

When a Roman centurion asked Jesus to merely speak the word to heal his sick servant, he manifested greater faith than the Jews among whom he lived. Jesus remarked that such Gentiles would sit at the great banquet in God's fellowship, "but the children of the kingdom shall be cast out into outer darkness: there shall be weeping and gnashing of teeth" (Matt. 8:12). The Jews who thought their heritage automatically qualified them to enter heaven would find themselves in hell, a terrifying experience like total darkness, so painful that weeping and gnashing of teeth replace words of anguish. The reward and the punishment Jesus described do not occur on earth but on the day "ye shall see Abraham, and Isaac, and Jacob, and all the prophets, in the kingdom of God" (Luke 13:28). This reminds us of the rich man who could see Abraham and Lazarus in the hadean realm.

Lest we also find ourselves in hell on that Great Day, let us live by obedient faith in Christ rather than trusting in our heritage of religious background, blood, race, family, nationality, education, social standing, financial status, or any other purely human characteristic. Sin cuts across all these boundaries. Nothing but God's grace through Jesus Christ can redeem us from our sins and we receive this amazing gift only through obedient faith in Jesus Christ.

Christ often referred to the torment experienced in hell as "weeping and gnashing of teeth."[21] In the parable of the tares, the righteous (the wheat) and the wicked (the tares or weeds) dwell side by side in the world until Christ comes to separate the wicked by casting them "into a furnace of fire: there shall be weeping and gnashing of teeth" (Matt.

---

[21] The KJV translates *klauthmos* as weep or wail. See Matthew 8:12; 22:13; 24:51; 25:30 and also Luke 13:28.

What Does the Bible Teach about Hell and Who Will Go There?

13:41-42). Likewise, in the parable of the net, all sorts of fish live together in the sea and are caught up together in the fisherman's net, but then the good or edible fish and the bad or useless fish are separated. "So shall it be at the end of the world: the angels shall come forth, and sever the wicked from among the just, And shall cast them into the furnace of fire: there shall be wailing and gnashing of teeth" (vv. 49-50). The parable of the faithful and evil servants shows that the same fate awaits those who do not prepare for our Lord's return (Matt. 24:45-51).

Three times Jesus described hell as the place of "outer darkness" as recorded by Matthew. Darkness is the realm of sin and separation from God throughout Scripture. When Jesus healed the centurion's servant, He spoke of the destiny of unbelieving Jews who would be "cast out into outer darkness: there shall be weeping and gnashing of teeth" (8:12). In the parable of the wedding feast, the man who did not properly prepare by wearing the proper garment represented people who claim to be saved but who do not change their hearts and lives. Such people will be "cast into outer darkness; there shall be weeping and gnashing of teeth" (22:13). The same is said of the man who wasted the money his master entrusted to him in the parable of the talents, a warning to us not to waste the abilities and opportunities given by the Lord to us (25:30).

Total darkness is "often used as a torture technique during wartime" because its effects are disorienting and terrifying to the point that it drives humans to the brink of insanity (Kelly Tatera, "Isolation in the Dark..."). That is why Jesus used darkness as a figure of the torment of hell, a place "where the wailing and gnashing of teeth is heard in the thick blackness of night" (Robertson, I, 65). Pope well observes,

> Jesus here describes the conditions the wicked will experience in eternal punishment as that of **outer** (or perhaps the "outermost") **darkness**. The soul separated from the presence of God is totally cut off from God—who "is light" (1 John 1:5). In such a condition, the lost soul, **weeping** will mourn his or her lost opportunity, with the **gnashing of teeth** from pain, regret, and punishment (Pope, *Truth Commentaries: Matthew*, 751).

It is imperative to understand that such language as used by Jesus to explain hell cannot be satisfied by annihilation. Non-existence is not a condition of separation from God nor of torment but is the absence of all suffering and of any relationship to God whether positive or negative.

"When Will These Things Be?" : Questions on Eschatology

Demons were terrified by the knowledge that Jesus had the power "to destroy" them by consigning them to "torment." Confronted by Jesus, an evil spirit cried out in Mark 1:24, "Let us alone; what have we to do with thee, thou Jesus of Nazareth? art thou come to destroy us? I know thee who thou art, the Holy One of God." On a similar occasion in Matthew 8:29 the demons asked him, "What have we to do with thee, Jesus, thou Son of God? art thou come hither to torment us before the time?" They are fully aware that at an appointed time their destiny is not release from torture as would be provided by annihilation but rather to be cast "into everlasting fire, prepared for the devil and his angels" (Matt. 25:41).

Jesus used this same verb "to destroy" (*apollumi*) both in Matthew 8:29 and Matthew 10:28 to describe the destiny of the wicked. Furthermore, he taught that "wicked men who die foretaste that horrible suffering while awaiting their final sentence. The rich man cried out, 'I am tormented in this flame' (Luke 16:24)" (Halbrook, "Eternal Punishment," 124-125).

In Matthew 25:31-46 Jesus pulled back the curtain to let us see the Final Judgment Day. Two key words announce the opposite destinies of the saved and the lost: "Come," and, "Depart." He will invite those who served Him by serving His brethren to enter the kingdom prepared for the redeemed "before the foundation of the world" (vv. 34-40). He will cast those who did not faithfully serve Him "into everlasting fire, prepared for the devil and his angels" (vv. 40-45). In summary, "And these shall go away into everlasting punishment: but the righteous into life eternal" (v. 46).

The Greek word *aiōnion* is translated "everlasting" or "eternal" and basically "means ageless, without beginning or end as of God (Rom. 16:26), without beginning as in Rom. 16:15, without end as here and often" (Robertson, 1.147). Every standard Greek lexicon confirms that *aiōnion* expresses the essence of duration. The conclusion of philologist Moses Stuart is unassailable: "WE MUST EITHER ADMIT THE **ENDLESS** MISERY OF HELL, OR GIVE UP THE **ENDLESS** HAPPINESS OF HEAVEN" (emph. orig., Stuart, 62). Jesus used *aiōnion* in reference to both in Matthew 25:46: *aiōnion* punishment and *aiōnion* life.

Numerous attempts have been made to somehow diminish the time element when *aiōnion* is applied to divine punishment, such as claiming it refers to an age or quality of punishment terminated by annihilation. "The effort to make it mean '*aeonian*' [an age which ends, R.H.] fire will make

What Does the Bible Teach about Hell and Who Will Go There?

it mean '*aeonian*' life also. If the punishment is limited, *ipso facto* the life is shortened" (Robertson, 1.147). Isaac Errett pointed out, "The contrast in Matt. 25:46 is not between *aiōnion* existence and *aiōnion* non-existence, but between *aiōnion life* and *aiōnion punishment*, both of them implying *aiōnion existence*" (emph. orig., Errett, 18). In short, as Pope concludes, "both the **punishment** (*kolasin*) and the **life** (*zoen*) are 'everlasting' or 'eternal'" (emph. orig., Pope, *Truth Commentaries: Matthew*, 917).

This all comports with what Jesus said in John 3:36, "He that believeth on the Son hath everlasting life: and he that believeth not the Son shall not see life; but the wrath of God abideth on him."[22] As surely as eternal life cannot fail the believer, the sentence of God's wrath abides on the unbeliever. To abide is to permanently remain—God's righteous wrath will punish sinners forever.[23] Predicated on obstinate disobedience, "absolute permanence of wrath is here indicated" (Olshausen, 2:371).

Jesus underscored the reality of hell by frequent warnings about the punishment to be meted out on the Final Judgment Day, especially as recorded by John. Jesus often spoke of His right to "judge" and to pronounce the final "judgment" of the souls of men.[24] He claimed His very

---

[22] The ASV and other modern translations translate "believeth not" as "obeyeth not." "Unbelief itself is here regarded as disobedience, and, indeed, as total disobedience proceeding from the entire man; and being such, is not merely *a* disobedience . . . but *the* disobedience out of which all others arise" (Olshausen, 2:371).

[23] Jesus used the present indicative of *menō*, "to continue to be" (Thayer, 399). The punishment cannot be annihilation because if there is no more "him," then "the wrath of God" can no longer "abide on him." "He who disobeys the Son incurs the worst possible guilt a mortal, sinful being can incur. This at once, by separating him from the Son, cuts him off from life eternal, 'he shall not see life' . . . ,shall not 'have' it and thus in any way experience what it is, now and in the next world. This is infinite loss. This negative result of the disobedience of unbelief involves the corresponding positive result, 'on the contrary . . . , the wrath of God remains upon him'" (Lenski, 295).

[24] John records Jesus affirming His authority as the final judge of all men by using the verb judge (*krinō*) and the noun judgment (*krisis*) for a combined total of 23 times. The verb *krinō* as used by Jesus is translated in the KJV "judge" (5:22, 30; 18:15-16, 50; 12:47 [twice]-48 [twice]; 16:11) and "condemn" (3:17-18 [twice]). Jesus's use of the noun *krisis* is translated "judgment" (5:22, 27, 30;

"When Will These Things Be?" : Questions on Eschatology

presence in the world was a prelude to the Judgment Day because decisions men made to believe in Him or to reject Him irrevocably sealed their opposite destinies on the Final Day.

To the consternation of the Jewish leaders, Jesus healed a lame man on the Sabbath Day, and they were further inflamed when He affirmed He did it in unison with God the Father, "making himself equal with God" (John 5:1-18, see v. 18). Jesus again made Himself equal to the Father by affirming He could raise the dead both *physically and spiritually*. Anyone who believes in Christ now has "everlasting life, and shall not come into condemnation (*krisis*); but is passed from death unto life" (John 5:24). "The Son of God" has power to raise the spiritually dead to life "and authority to execute judgment also, because he is the Son of man," the Messiah.[25] This means He will conduct the Final Judgment when "all that are in the graves shall hear his voice, and shall come forth; they that have done good, unto the resurrection of life; and they that have done evil, unto the resurrection of damnation (*krisis*)" (John 5:25-29). The "condemnation" or "damnation" of which He spoke is a direct reference to eternal torment in hell.

In recording the miracles of Jesus, John presents rock solid evidence that the Son of Man is the Messiah, yea, He is the Son of God, divine, deity. He dispenses life to the spiritually dead now, and will be "the agent of the final resurrection and judgement," which is "the supreme act of Jesus the Son of man" (Barrett, 219).

What Jesus Taught through the Apostles about Hell

Jesus sent the Holy Spirit to guide His apostles "into all truth" (John 16:13). Paul taught sinners to repent in view of "the day of wrath and revelation of the righteous judgment of God" when the righteous receive "eter-

---

8:16; 12:31; 16:8, 11), "damnation" (5:29), and "condemnation" (3:19; 5:24). Once he used *krīmu*, "judgment," the verdict or sentence of condemnation which His presence brought upon men who heard Him and willfully rejected Him. In short, they sealed their own doom by openly revealing their own character ("for judgment I am come into this world," 9:39).

[25] The Jews understood Daniel 7:13-14 to be Messianic. "There . . . a Son of man appears before the throne of the Ancient, in order to be formally invested with all might and dominion. In allusion to this, it is now said . . . he is also Judge, for everything is delivered into His hands" (Olshousen, 2:398).

What Does the Bible Teach about Hell and Who Will Go There?

nal life" but the wicked "indignation and wrath, tribulation and anguish"—they "perish" (*apollumi*) (Rom. 2:5, 8-9, 12). We are saved from this coming wrath by the blood of Jesus (Rom. 5:9). Twice in the Ephesian letter Paul identifies "the children of disobedience" as "the children of wrath," a theme often echoed in his epistles (Eph. 2:2-3; 5:6; Col. 3:6; 1 Thess. 1:9; 2:16; 5:9).

Stubborn carnal minded men have protested God's anger through the ages, even in biblical times.[26] Rationalists "have assailed 'the wrath of God' as being an impossibility" and even a justification for atheism as they caricature God's wrath as "cruel, bloodthirsty, etc." Lenski responds,

> God's wrath is the inevitable reaction of his righteousness and holiness against all sin and guilt . . . when God is challenged by human sin and unbelief, God in accord with His very being must cast far from Him those who persist in this desperate challenge. A holy and righteous God must come to a final issue with all those who reject Him and His saving grace in the Son. They who will not have life by that very fact remain in death" (Lenski, 295-296).

Merrill C. Tenney put it this way: "God is neither easily angered nor vindictive. But by His very nature He is unalterably committed to opposing and judging all disobedience" (King, *Truth Commentaries: John*, 69). Men complaining against the righteous judgments of God simply confirm their own obstinacy and persistence in sin and rebellion against God, thus confirming the justice of His judgment!

Instead of complaining against God's wrath, the apostles were motivated by it to proclaim salvation in Jesus Christ. In 2 Corinthians 5 Paul affirmed that "we must all appear before the judgment seat of Christ," and added, "Knowing therefore the terror of the Lord, we persuade men." He explained "that God was in Christ, not imputing their trespasses unto them," and then he pled, "Now then we are ambassadors for Christ, as though God did beseech you by us: we pray you in Christ's stead, be ye reconciled to God" (2 Cor. 5:10-11, 19-20). Men will not be lost in hell because God is vindictive and bloodthirsty but only because they resist and refuse His forgiveness in spite of all He has done to save them. They defy His warnings and His wrath, and accuse God of evil, thus judging themselves "unworthy of everlasting life" (Acts 13:46).

---

[26] Israel's complaints against Moses and Aaron when God punished rebellion in the camp were actually directed at God Himself (Num. 16:11, 41).

"When Will These Things Be?" : Questions on Eschatology

The New Testament often uses the words die (*apothnēskō*), dead (*nekros*), and death (*thanatos*) in the spiritual sense of separation from God both in this life and the life to come. "Death is the opposite of life; it never denotes non-existence. As spiritual life is 'conscious existence in communion with God,' so spiritual death is 'conscious existence in separation from God'" (Vine, 1.276). Jesus warned unbelievers "if ye believe not that I am he, ye shall die in your sins" (John 8:24), i.e., they will "remain in eternal separation from God" (Vine, 1.309).

Paul explained how he personally became accountable for sin in Romans 7:9, "Once I was alive apart from the law; but when the commandment came, sin sprang to life and I died" (NIV). Five times in Romans 5:12-21 Paul contrasts the reign of sin and "death" over men with the reign of God's grace which brings "eternal life" to all who submit to Christ (vv. 12 [twice], 14, 17, 21). Death here comprises "*all the miseries arising from sin*" in this world "*to be followed by wretchedness in the lower world*" opposite to eternal life (entry on *thanatos*, Thayer, 283).

Men who have not submitted by faith in Christ to baptism are described by Paul as "dead in trespasses and sins," or "children of disobedience" destined to face God's "wrath" (Eph. 2:1-3; cf. 2:5; 5:14; Col. 3:12-13 where the "dead" who had been baptized had been "forgiven").

Sin in the Garden of Eden unleashed the horrific power of death both physically (the body separated from the soul) and spiritually (the soul separated from God). Paul rejoices that God's grace has been manifested "by the appearing of our Savior Jesus Christ, who abolished death, and brought life and immortality to light through the gospel" (2 Tim. 1:10). The work of Christ "abolished" (*katargeō*) death—death was "*utterly defeated, put out of commission, rendered ineffective*" (Hendricksen, 233). Death was defeated in both its spiritual and physical dimensions by His perfect sacrifice and by His victory over the grave. This death pertained to the physical body "with the implied idea of future misery in the state beyond" (entry on *thanatos*, Thayer, 283). In this passage as in Romans 6:23 "spiritual death merges into ... eternal death" (entry on *thanatos*, Arndt and Gingrich, 352).[27]

---

[27] It is important to notice in 2 Timothy 1:10 that "death" is put opposite, not merely to physical resurrection, but rather to "life and immortality." "As a result of Christ's Atonement, for the believer *eternal death* no longer exists.

What Does the Bible Teach about Hell and Who Will Go There?

In 2 Thessalonians 1:4-10 Paul taught that people who afflict and trouble the saints of God will themselves receive affliction and trouble by "the righteous judgment of God" (v. 5). Divine justice demands that God afflict unbelievers who afflicted His saints with many afflictions (vv. 4, 6-7). Thayer (291) says the verb afflict or trouble (*thilbō*) and the corresponding noun (*thilipsis*) involve "*affliction, tribulation, distress*," i.e., they refer to infliction of pain and suffering. The righteous will be relieved from all suffering when Christ returns in His glory, but the wicked will be immersed in suffering from which they will never escape. He will come "in flaming fire taking vengeance on them that know not God, and that obey not the gospel of our Lord Jesus Christ: Who shall be punished with everlasting destruction from the presence of the Lord, and from the glory of his power" (vv. 8-9). Far from annihilation, the "destruction" or ruin continues for all eternity as "banishment and separation from the presence of the Lord with all its joys" (McGarvey, *Thessalonians*, 32).

Satan continues to contend it will not be so in the voice of the sinner who protests a just God cannot render such judgment. The truth is that the sinner's "repeated choice of godlessness ends in a settled character of godlessness . . . . *Exclusion from the presence of the Lord* is what he has

---

Spiritual death is vanquished more and more in this life and completely at the moment when the soul departs from its physical enclosure. And *physical death* has been robbed of its curse and has been turned into gain (John 11:26; then Phil. 3:7-14; then 1 Cor. 15:26, 42-44, 54-57). *That* He did *on the one hand*; and *on the other hand* He *brought to light* . . . life and incorruptibility . . . The two concepts 'life and incorruptibility' probably constitute a hendiadys; hence, *incorruptible* (or imperishable) *life*" (Hendricksen, 233). If "life and immortality" are a hendiadys where two words are joined by "and" to convey an idea with emphasis, the meaning here is simply "eternal life" as found in some translations (God's Word Translation; Names of God Bible; "everlasting life," Worldwide English; "the life that is eternal," Phillips New Testament; "life that never dies," Contemporary English Version, New Life Version; "immortal life," Good News Translation, The Passion Translation; "life that cannot be destroyed," Easy-to-Read Version, International Children's Bible). Dozens of translations retain "life and immortality." In any case, by contrasting "death" with "life and immorality" or "eternal life" the passage shows that *Christ rolled back all the ill effects of "death" for the saved, not merely its physical effect*. The wicked will escape physical death at the resurrection but not spiritual death.

been seeking all of his days. Now he has it" (Ronald A. Ward, *A Commentary on 1 and 2 Thessalonians*, 147 as quoted by Weaver, 433). Some will insist they are following the Lord while they reject and twist His teaching to suit their own desires, which in fact is just another way to reject Christ Himself (John 12:48; Matt. 7:21-23).

In 2 Thessalonians 2:1-12 Paul personifies all false teachers as "the man of sin" who serves Satan by deceiving people (vv. 3, 9-10). Professing to be a child of God, he is actually "the son of perdition" or destruction (*apoleia*, v. 3). This lawless man and work would multiply and spread until he would be fully exposed: "And then shall that Wicked be revealed, whom the Lord shall consume with the spirit of his mouth, and shall destroy with the brightness of his coming" (v. 8). "Consume" (*analiskō*) means to slay or defeat, as in Galatians 5:15 where saints are warned not to consume each other. It is parallel here in verse 8 to "destroy" (*katargeō*), meaning literally "to reduce to inactivity," i.e., to utterly defeat and render ineffective (Vine, 1.13-14). Both words are parallel to the fate of the followers of false teachers in verses 10 and 12: to "perish" (*apollumi*, verb form of noun in v. 3) and to be "damned" (*krinō*), "judged" (ASV), or "condemned" (NIV).

The five words pointing to the fate of sinners in this passage are obviously equivalent. All refer to eternal punishment in hell, not to annihilation, extinction, or non-existence. In defining *apollumi*, Vine says, "The idea is not extinction but ruin, loss, not of being, but of well-being" (1:302).

Hell in Hebrews and James: A Raging Fire

The Hebrew writer urged Christians to grow beyond the level of milk or basic principles such as the "eternal judgment" (*krima*). This term for judgment is typically used of a judge's decree of condemnation which renders the sentence of the guilty party. God's final "decision is valid *eternally*," "eternally in force," or "timeless and endless" (respectively Arndt and Gingrich, 451; Thayer, 360; Robertson, 5.374). In order for the sentence and its enforcement to be timeless, the sinner must be likewise timeless.

Paul explained that "as it is appointed unto men once to die, but after this the judgment (*krisis*)," even so Jesus offered one perfect sacrifice and will never need to die again (Heb. 9:27-28). This simple truth precludes

What Does the Bible Teach about Hell and Who Will Go There?

reincarnation, or multiple resurrections offering a second chance for salvation, or a person performing rituals to save souls in hades, or any other hope for the dead to change their status before the Final Judgment! "Every person has but a single life before eternal **judgment**" (entry on 9:27-28, *English Standard Version Study Bible*, 2376).

Hebrews 10:26-31 sheds more light on that Final Judgment. Christians who return to a life of sin consign themselves to a future "of judgment (*krisis*) and of raging fire that will consume the enemies of God" (v. 27, NIV). This furious fire, literally "zeal of fire," is pictured as "a living thing, its flames seething to consume these enemies of Christ" (King, *Truth Commentaries: Hebrews*, 335). This fire perpetually consumes, devours, or eats up (literal meaning of *esthiō*) the enemies of Christ as when an animal devours its prey. The Law of Moses executed rebels by stoning, but the Son of God will exact "much sorer punishment" or "much worse punishment" (v. 29, KJV, NKJV), the equivalent of "perdition" or "destruction" (*apoleia*, v. 39; indicating "loss of well-being, not of being," Vine, 1.303). If the spirit of man does not survive the death of the body, the warning of a punishment worse than execution in verse 29 is nullified and meaningless.

James twice identifies eternal punishment in hell as "death" which is also "the wages of sin" in Romans 6:23. God has no desire or plan to lure men to sin, but using conception and birth as metaphors, James explains what happens when men harbor sin in their hearts by their own choice: "Then when lust hath conceived, it bringeth forth sin: and sin, when it is finished, bringeth forth death" (1:13-15). If we convert a sinner, we "save a soul from death" (5:20). These passages cannot refer to physical death because all men die physically, and many die before the age of accountability. Furthermore, saving "a soul" points to "that eternal aspect of man at times referred to as 'the spirit' or 'the eternal soul' which survives beyond physical death and goes back to God (Eccl. 12:7)" and "**death** points not to physical extinction but to the eternal consequence of living a life in **error**" (King, *Truth Commentaries: James*, 488).

In warning against using the tongue as an instrument of sin, James compares it to a raging destructive fire which "sets a person's entire life on fire with flames that come from hell itself" (3:6, Contemporary English Version). Here hell "stands for the powers of darkness, whose characteristics and destiny are those of hell" (Vine, 2.213). The person using his tongue to sin is doing Satan's work and will share Satan's destiny.

"When Will These Things Be?" : Questions on Eschatology

Also, James paints a vivid picture of the destiny of those who oppress the poor and hoard wealth. They will "weep and howl" in manifold "miseries" when their ill-gotten gain "will be evidence against you and will eat your flesh like fire" because they have gorged themselves like cattle for "a day of slaughter" (5:1, 3, 5, ESV). "These things will not only be lost forever but will be **evidence** at their final trial before God and will feed the very flames of the lake of **fire**, where they will spend eternity" (entry on James 5:2-3, *English Standard Version Study Bible*, 2398). The saints must faithfully wait for "the coming of the Lord" lest they too "be condemned" (*krinō*) because at all times "the judge standeth before the door" ready to come (5:7-9).

Hell in Peter's and Jude's Epistles: None Escape Their Final Judgment

Both Peter and Jude warn that fallen angels along with false teachers and their followers face "swift destruction" (*apoleia*) for which they are reserved "unto the day of judgment to be punished" (2 Pet. 2:1-10, see vv. 1, 3-4, 9; cf. 3:7). Peter even argues the state of apostates will be worse than their state if they had never known and obeyed the truth, a contrast which collapses if annihilation is the punishment for men in both states (2:20-21). Are there two different states of non-existence, one worse than the other?

Jude's warning of "the judgment of the great day" spotlights the inhabitants of Sodom who "are set forth for an example, suffering the vengeance of eternal fire" (vv. 6-7). When God rained down literal fire on them, the result was not the relief of extinction but was the foretaste of torment in hades at death followed by torment in hell as a result of the Final Judgment. What a graphic picture of the eternal fire of God's wrath against Satan, sin, and sinners!

Hell in the Book of Revelation: Fire and Brimstone for Ever and Ever

In the book of Revelation God showed John visions of the warfare between the Roman Empire and the saints, ultimately between God and Satan, including pictures of the defeat and eternal punishment of His enemies. Faithful martyrs will receive a victory "crown of life" and will not suffer "the second death," eternal separation from God "in the lake which burneth with fire and brimstone" (Rev. 2:10-11; 20:6, 14; 21:8).

Spiritual death is a state of miserable ruin in separation from God, not a state of non-existence. Paul said the wicked woman who "liveth in

What Does the Bible Teach about Hell and Who Will Go There?

pleasure is dead while she liveth" (1 Tim. 5:6). The second death figuratively expresses spiritual separation from God just as the first or physical death separates body and soul. The second death is the extension and intensification of the state of suffering in eternal separation from God—it is specifically *"the miserable state of the wicked in hell"* (entry on *thanatos*, Thayer, 283). The doctrine of annihilation nullifies the second death because extinction is the absence of any relationship to God, good or bad, the absence of both rewards and punishment.

In Revelation 2-3 special messages are addressed to seven churches in Asia pointing out their strengths and weaknesses to prepare them for the storm of trials they faced as Rome began to enforce emperor worship. A self-styled prophetess in the church at Thyatira was stigmatized by the Lord with the evil name Jezebel. Like her namesake she was guilty of spiritual adultery because she taught God's people to compromise with idol worship by participating in feasts held in pagan temples to honor the gods.[28]

Just as the original Jezebel was cast down from a window to her painful death in 1 Kings 9:33, even so Christ would cast the wicked adulteress and her followers "into a bed" where all of them would suffer "great tribulation" and "death" (Rev. 2:21-22). This was not the threat of annihilation but of great "tribulation" (*thlipsis*, "trouble, affliction, distress," Monce, 743)— also called "death" (*thanatos*), spiritual separation from God extending into eternity. 2 Thessalonians 1:6 and 9 identify the "tribulation" meted out by the Lord as "everlasting destruction from the presence of the Lord." The powerful picture of spiritual rejection and severance from the fellowship of Christ announced to Jezebel is not unlike His warning to the lukewarm Laodiceans, "I will vomit you out of My mouth" (Rev. 3:16, NKJV).

Revelation 6-20 records visions John saw revealing the course of divine punishment which would fall on the Roman Empire for its evil persecution and execution of Christians. The story is told three times, or

---

[28] The name Jezebel "is used figuratively like that of 'Balaam' to describe those who thought only of their covetous, selfish desires" (Harkrider, 41). This wicked queen "led her husband Ahab to serve Baal (I Kings 16:31). She cut off the prophets of Jehovah (I Kings 18:4) and encouraged idolatry by feeding the prophets of Baal and the Asherah (I Kings 18:19). Her sins were summed up as 'the whoredoms and witchcrafts' of Jezebel (2 Kings 9:22)" (Hailey, *Revelation*, 137).

"When Will These Things Be?" : Questions on Eschatology

recapitulated, utilizing different figures and symbols each time. The story is told first by the opening of seven sealed messages, then the sounding of seven trumpet warnings, and then the pouring out of seven bowls of divine wrath. Each cycle points directly or indirectly to the Final Judgment when God rewards His faithful saints and punishes the wicked.

Seven messages in a scroll with seven seals are announced by Christ as He breaks each seal (6:1-8:1). With the breaking of the fifth seal (6:9-11), John sees the souls of martyred saints crying out to God, "How long, O Lord, holy and true, does thou not judge and avenge our blood on them that dwell on the earth?" This scene teaches neither "soul sleep" nor "soul extinction" but rather "the conscious existence of the soul after death" (King, *I Saw the Heaven Opened,* 186). In asking God to "judge" (*krinō*) and "avenge" (*ekdikeō*), the martyrs are not asking for vengeance as petty personal retaliation "but for a vindication of their death and the cause for which they had died" (Hailey, *Revelation*, 195). Jesus used this very same word *ekdikeō* when He promised God would "give justice to" or "vindicate his elect" when the Son of man comes to judge the world (Luke 18:7-8, NASB, RSV). The visions which follow clearly show that this vindication of the cause of truth upheld by the martyrs requires the eternal punishment of God's enemies in hell.

The opening of the sixth seal in Revelation 6:12-17 confirms that the destiny of the wicked is not annihilation and extinction but that they would prefer such an end to the wrath which awaits them! They will wish to die in an avalanche rather than face "him that sitteth on the throne, and . . . the wrath of the Lamb" (v. 16). In answer to the question, "Who shall be able to stand?" there is a vision of faithful saints first "on the earth" and then in their final victory "before the throne, and before the Lamb" (6:17; 7:1, 3, 9).

The opening of the seventh seal pictured a time of awesome silence in heaven. Next, the sounding of seven trumpet warnings recapitulates the story of God's chastisements ending with the Final Judgment (8:2-11:19). The seventh trumpet announces the Final Judgment when men of all nations acknowledge the royal authority of Christ. On this day, "the time has come for judging the dead," a time for rewarding the faithful and "for destroying those who destroy the earth" (11:15-19, see v. 18). When divine destruction falls on those who destroy, this verb (*diaphtheirō*) means to bring to ruin like a moth ruins cloth in Luke 12:33 and a false teacher corrupts his mind in 1 Timothy 6:5, not to annihilate cloth or minds or sinners.

What Does the Bible Teach about Hell and Who Will Go There?

A vision of the ferocious battle between God with His saints and Satan with his Roman agents includes pictures of the martyred saints resting from their labors in the hadean realm while all who succumbed to emperor worship find no rest (12:1-14:20).

> The same shall drink of the wine of the wrath of God, which is poured out without mixture into the cup of his indignation; and he shall be tormented with fire and brimstone in the presence of the holy angels, and in the presence of the Lamb: And the smoke of their torment ascendeth up for ever and ever: and they have no rest day nor night, who worship the beast and his image, and whosoever receiveth the mark of his name (14:10-11).

Their torment is not relieved by extinction but extends from hades into hell for eternity. "As the day of the righteous is a glorious, eternal day, the night of the wicked is a dreadful, eternal night; the two abide side by side, continuing simultaneously. What a terrible price to pay for rejecting Christ and bowing to Caesar as Lord!" (Hailey, *Revelation*, 310).

In the next vision seven bowls of divine wrath are poured out upon the Empire (15:1-16:21). A series of partial judgments against Rome leads up to the last bowl when "God now gives to her 'the cup of the wine of the fierceness of his wrath,' that is, the hot burning anger of His wrath" in 16:16-21 (see v. 19, Hailey, *Revelation*, 339). This evil empire will never rise again when God says, "It is finished" (v. 17). Like the fire that engulfed Sodom's inhabitants and pursued them even beyond the grave in Jude 7, the wrath of God against His enemies in the Roman Empire would pursue them beyond the grave, as Revelation makes very clear.

Rome is portrayed in a vision in chapters 17-18 as a whore sitting on a vile beast and her name is called Babylon (17:3, 5, 10). "As the beast portrays the state's power to coerce religious conformity through violence, so the prostitute symbolizes the seductive appeal of a worldly economic system driven by the quest of affluence and pleasure" (entry on 17:4, *English Standard Version Study Bible*, 2487). This evil alliance is judged and defeated by Jesus Christ, pictured as a conquering King who cast them into the ocean to sink forever like a huge millstone and who "treadeth the winepress of the fierceness and wrath of Almighty God" (18:20-21; 19:11-21). The beast and his false prophet are both to be "cast alive into a lake of fire burning with brimstone" and all their followers and cohorts are slain as well (19:20-21).

"When Will These Things Be?" : Questions on Eschatology

The judgment depicted is not the mere physical destruction of buildings, possessions, and armaments belonging to the Roman Empire but is *the eternal punishment of persons* from the highest rank to the lowest position who embraced and perpetrated the evil principles and powers of that era. These verses picture "the final overthrow of the principles of evil of which Rome was the immediate, visible, and temporary manifestation" (Raymond Calkins,163). Hailey observes that "in this defeat and destruction is revealed the destiny of all such powers that should ever arise to fight against God and His kingdom" (Hailey, *Revelation*, 388).

A new vision of three scenes pictured in chapter 20 depict God's judgment for time and eternity on Satan, the instigator of the evils of the mighty Roman Empire and of all ages of man. In *verses 1-6* souls of the faithful martyrs who died at the hand of Rome experience a resurrection or complete victory of their cause as they "reigned with Christ a thousand years" (vv. 4-5).[29] While the saints share this perfect victory figuratively expressed as 1,000 years, Satan is bound and cast into the Abyss or "bottomless pit" so that his defeated cause represented by the Roman Empire cannot be resurrected. He is not rendered wholly inactive but is bereft of the power he exercised through Rome.[30]

---

[29] It is not the purpose of this lesson to give a detailed review of premillennial theories, but I will note here two fundamental errors of all such systems. They claim that the 1,000 years are a literal number of years on the calendar, and that this defines the period of Jesus's reign. First, we should understand, "The thousand years during which Satan is bound must be interpreted symbolically, as are other numbers in the book. This number is a complete number which stands for an indeterminate but full period of time (cf. Job 9:3; 33:23; Ps. 50:10; Eccl. 6:6; 7:28; 2 Pet. 3:8)" (Hailey, *Revelation*, 391). Second, "this passage is not about the reign of Christ, but about the reign of the martyrs . . . . Jesus is said to be reigning over His people in literal contexts throughout the New Testament (Eph. 1:20-22; Phil. 2:9-11; Col. 1.15-18; 1 Tim. 1:16, 17; Rev. 1:5, 6; 17:14; 19:16)" (King, "*I Saw the Heaven Opened*," 319). Christ reigned with the Father all along as is evident in chapter 5. Now that Rome has fallen, the martyrs reign *with Him* as the reward of their fidelity in chapter 20.

[30] "Though Satan has continued to use various methods to turn disciples away from the Lord, the church has not suffered the severe oppression of a world dominion as in the days of the Roman empire" (Harkrider, 227).

What Does the Bible Teach about Hell and Who Will Go There?

In *verses 7-10* Satan is permitted to rally all of the evil forces at his disposal for one last malicious attempt to defeat God's redemptive plan, but it ends with him being "cast into the lake of fire and brimstone . . . and . . . tormented day and night for ever and ever" (v. 10). As Ezekiel 38-39 referred to the grand alliance of the enemies of God's people as Gog and Magog, "Revelation employs these symbols again to represent all of the world's spiritual pagan forces that Satan can marshall [*sic*] in one last attempt to overthrow God's spiritual kingdom . . . . This battle will not be a physical conflict, but a moral and spiritual one" (Harkrider, 232).[31] Satan is finally vanquished to hell for ever, never to rise again, but what of the great masses of humanity who have followed him?

In *verses 11-15* the heavens and the earth are no more as all the dead stand before God who sits on "a great white throne" to pronounce His final judgment on all men "according to their works." All people whose names were not written in the book of life were "cast into the lake of fire," also called "the second death," from which there is no escape. "They will experience the same punishment prepared for the devil and his angels (Matt. 25:41; Rev. 20:10)" (Harkrider, 237). Homer Hailey's explanation of the eternal nature of this punishment is especially powerful and irrefutable:

> There are many who question the eternal duration of this torment, but these must explain away biblical teaching. Jesus said that at the judgment those on His left hand would be told, "Depart from me, ye cursed, into the eternal fire prepared for the devil and his angels . . . and these shall go away into eternal punishment; but the righteous into eternal life" (Matt. 25:41, 46). Both the punishment and the life are eternal. In Revelation it is said of these two groups that those before the throne "serve him day and night" (7:15), and the wicked "have no rest day or night" (14:11), and that with the devil they are tormented (25:41, 46), a torment which is "day and night, for ever and ever." There is no day there, for it is "outer darkness" (Matt. 22:13; 25:30). Since the day is in heaven and the night in hell, and since the one group serves Him day and night while the other group is tormented night and day, it follows that the night endures as long as the day. But since God is the light of the eternal day, the day (and, consequently, the night) will never end.

---

[31] "According to Ezekiel, God uses sword (38:21), fire (39:6), and burning sulfur (38:22) to execute judgment against Gog and Magog. John also employs these same instruments of divine judgment in his vision to describe their downfall (vv. 9-10)" (King, *"I Saw the Heavens Opened,"* 324).

"When Will These Things Be?" : Questions on Eschatology

> The period of this torment, "for ever and ever," is the same in duration as God, for He lives "for ever and ever" (4:9) (Hailey, *Revelation*, 399).

Satan's defeat for time and eternity is sealed by Revelation 20.

The last two chapters, 21-22, emphasize the eternal fellowship of the saints with God in heaven while echoing the defeat of Satan and his followers. The final reward of the faithful is pictured in 21:1-22:5, but sinners "shall have their part in the lake which burneth with fire and brimstone: which is the second death" (21:8).

The fate of God's faithful servants and of Satan's evil followers is determined by the character developed by each person in the course of life's attitudes, decisions, and actions. "He that is unjust, let him be unjust still: and he which is filthy, let him be filthy still: and he that is righteous, let him be righteous still: and he that is holy, let him be holy still" (22:11). Vine notes that the adverb "still" (*eti*) here "indicates the permanent character, condition and destiny" of saints and sinners (Vine, 4.74). The existence and character of *both* the righteous and the wicked extend beyond the grave which positively necessitates "their separation to different locations in eternity" (King, *"I Saw the Heaven Opened,"* 355). This precludes the theory of annihilation, "the doctrine of universal salvation," and various claims of "a second chance in eternity" (ibid.).

John is told that all who are washed in the blood of the Lamb will enter the gates into the city of God, but sinners remain "outside" (22:15, ESV). If they remain outside, they exist. If they were annihilated, they would be neither inside nor outside. To be outside the city of God means to be bereft of the presence and fellowship of God forever, a horrible fate indeed!

In concluding the book of Revelation, the Lord warns against tampering with this great book of prophecy. Anyone who perverts "this book" by adding to it will suffer "the plagues that are written in this book," and anyone who removes any part of these words will be barred from "the holy city" (vv. 18-19). The need for this warning is made abundantly clear by numerous rationales and explanations of men who attempt to mitigate or entirely remove the doctrine of the eternal torment of the wicked in hell from this book and from the entire Bible!

Denials of the Bible's Teaching on Hell

Satan, the father of lies, was the first to deny God's warning against hell in the course of convincing Eve to sin when he said, "Ye shall not

What Does the Bible Teach about Hell and Who Will Go There?

surely die" (Gen. 3:4). This lie echoes throughout human history as men have sought to ease their minds regarding the consequences of sin. Speaking from a heart "full of the fury of the Lord," Jeremiah said of false teachers in Israel, "They have healed also the hurt of the daughter of my people slightly, saying, Peace, peace; when there is no peace" (Jer. 6:11, 14). Or as the New Living Translation says, "They offer superficial treatments for my people's mortal wound. They give assurances of peace when there is no peace."

The main lines of thought in opposition to eternal torment in hell are universalism (all will be saved) and annihilation. Different theories and twists lead to those options, but they are the only options to the Bible doctrine of hell. Annihilation is embraced by secularists who believe there is no existence beyond earth life. It is embraced by pagan religions such as Hinduism and Buddhism which teach annihilation of personal existence is the highest good and ultimate goal of all life after many recurring reincarnations. It is also embraced by professed Christians who claim it is the final punishment of the wicked.

Advocates of universalism and of extinction routinely make superficial subjective appeals to the love and justice of God. They claim eternal punishment in hell is unloving and unfair, and thus inconsistent with the divine nature of God. "Yet ye say, The way of the Lord is not equal. Hear now, O house of Israel; Is not my way equal? are not your ways unequal?" (Ezek. 18:25).

Hell manifests both the love and the justice of God. No man can conceive of higher standards of true love and justice for man made in God's image than God Himself manifests. God's perfect love and perfect justice are manifested in the perfect sacrifice of Jesus Christ for our sins, His victory over death, and His offer of forgiveness to all sinners through the gospel (Rom. 3:23-26; 5:8-10; Mark 16:15-16). His love of truth, purity, and holiness requires that people who embrace sin and rebellion in rejecting the gospel be separated from Him and that their corruption must not corrupt heaven. His justice requires eternal torment because sin is an infinite injustice and hearts characterized by the love of sin at death will not change in eternity (Rev. 22:11). The God who "is love" is the same God who "is a consuming fire" (1 John 4:8; Heb. 12:29). It is not God who lacks love and justice in punishing sin, but men who lack love and justice by embracing sin and denying hell in rebellion against God's love and justice.

"When Will These Things Be?" : Questions on Eschatology

Annihilationists labor long and hard to refute the premise that the soul survives the death of the body and will exist for eternity. In debate with the Sadducees over this very premise, Jesus defended the eternal or immortal nature of man's spirit. He said that "God is not the God of the dead, but of the living" in direct reference to Abraham, Isaac, and Jacob being very much alive in the time of Jesus and his contemporaries ("that which was spoken unto you," Matt. 22:31-32). They, like Lazarus, existed in the hadean realm very much alive and conscious, awaiting the resurrection of both the righteous and the wicked (Luke 16:19-31; John 5:28-29).

God alone exists as immortal from everlasting to everlasting, and thus He alone is "the Father of our spirits," but He also created man "in his image" as an immortal being who exists forever (Ps. 90:2; 1 Tim. 1:17; 6:15-16; Heb. 12:9; Gen. 1:26-27).[32] Though the expression "immortal soul" or "eternal spirit" is not found in Scripture, the immortal or eternal essence of man created in God's image is clearly taught.

Denying that the spirit of man survives the death of his body, annihilationists claim death results in annihilation for all men. Next will come the resurrection, but since that which does not exist cannot be resurrected, it really means a total re-creation of the person. Then, the wicked are cast into hell with the end result of annihilation, *again*.

If death is annihilation and non-existence is punishment, let us consider the consequences of such teaching.

1. All people are punished before conception because they do not exist.

2. Both the righteous and the wicked are punished when they die.

3. Babies suffer the same fate as Hitler when they die because both are annihilated.

4. Animals are punished by death because their lives are extinct and annihilation is punishment.

---

[32] God is said to be "the only Potentate" and "who only hath immortality" in 1 Timothy 6:15-16 because He is the origin or source of all rule and of immortality (*athanasia* formed from *a*, privative meaning "not" or "absence," plus *thanatos*, death, thus deathlessness, unceasing, or unending life; see Greek lexicons). All rule is derived from God, as is the immortality of the soul. (Kyle Pope prefers to use eternal rather than immortal in reference to the soul; see Pope, "'Immortal' and 'Incorruptible.'")

What Does the Bible Teach about Hell and Who Will Go There?

5. Death removes Christians from the love of Christ and of God because they no longer exist (Rom. 8:35, 38).

6. Punishment by God is no sorer than by man because annihilation is the result in both cases (Matt. 10:28; Heb. 10:28-29).

7. Jesus was wrong in saying it had been better for Judas "if he had not been born" (Matt. 26:24). If he had not been born, he would have never existed and when he is punished in hell (if hell is annihilation) his condition will be as if he had never existed.

8. Peter was wrong in teaching that the apostate's end will be worse than if he had not known the truth (2 Pet. 2:20)—in either case his end is extinction.[33]

9. The bodies of the wicked must die twice which contradicts Hebrews 9:27: "it is appointed unto men once to die."

10. The biblical punishment of hell is identical to the heaven or Nirvana of Buddhism and Hinduism: extinction of personal identity and consciousness.

11. When Jesus died, he was thus annihilated, obliterated, and extinct. Edward Fudge devoted a whole chapter of his book *The Fire That Consumes* to affirm this very thing with a subsection entitled "Jesus' Death Involved Total Destruction" continuing for seven pages. Fudge grants that "we naturally recoil from such a thought" but nonetheless insists it is true (231). Blinded by his devotion to the annihilation theory, Fudge did not see that he contradicted the claim of Jesus, "Before Abraham was, I am" (John 8:58; cf. Exod. 3:14).[34] Barrett, a Greek scholar,

---

[33] These first eight points are found in abbreviated form in my lecture on "Eternal Punishment" on page 132.

[34] "His use of 'I am' brought to their minds a profusion of texts from the Hebrew Scriptures, beginning with God's description of Himself as 'I AM' in the narrative of Moses's commission (Exod. 3:14), through the 'I AM HE' passages in Isaiah (41:4; 43:11-13; 44:6; 45:6, 18, 21; 48:17). One and all, they are an assertion of timeless deity" (King, *Truth Commentaries: John*, 180). "The words 'I am' in Greek use the same expression (*Ego eimi*) found in the Septuagint in the first half of God's self-identification in Exod. 3:14, 'I AM WHO I AM.' Jesus is thus claiming not only to be eternal but also to be

"When Will These Things Be?" : Questions on Eschatology

explains the significance of "I am" (*ego eimi*) as "a properly continuous tense, implying neither beginning nor end of existence." Thus Jesus affirmed, "Before Abraham came into being, I eternally was, as now I am, and ever continue to be" (283, 292). Yet, the annihilation theory insists that Jesus's death was the end of His existence as with all others who die.

Actually, the state of non-existence is neither a state of reward nor punishment—non-existence is the absence of both.

Jesus Himself precluded universalism and annihilationism in words too simple to be misunderstood. Neither the character nor the final state of men can be changed at death. When He spoke of the status of Lazarus and the rich man in hades awaiting the resurrection, He affirmed they were separated by a great gulf or chasm which could not be crossed (Luke 16: 26). Next, He affirmed that He will raise all the dead, "they that have done good, unto the resurrection of life; and they that have done evil, unto the resurrection of damnation" (John 5:28-29).

And, finally, He affirmed that He will separate them forever: "And these shall go away into everlasting punishment: but the righteous into life eternal" (Matt. 25:46). The wicked are cast "into hell, into the fire that never shall be quenched" (Mark 9:43-48). The wicked can by no means be saved after death nor will they be exterminated—they will suffer eternal torment in hell.

Advocates of the AD 70 doctrine or realized eschatology are at pains to explain all of the final events to occur at the end of time in terms of the passing away of the old Jewish order and the establishment of the church of Christ as the new kingdom of God. This includes the resurrection, the Judgment, and entrance into heaven or hell—all of these events occurred with the fall of Jerusalem and the removal of the Mosaic system. By the time they explain such simple passages as John 5:28-29, Mark 9:43-48, and Matthew 25:46 regarding the fate of sinners as nothing more than the end of Judaism, the Bible doctrine of hell vanishes from view.[35] No

---

the God who appeared to Moses at the burning bush" (note on John 5:58, *English Standard Version Study Bible*, 2041).

[35] The father of this heresy among churches of Christ was Max King. He claimed all such expressions as the second death, everlasting destruction, outer darkness, and the furnace of fire are metaphors which refer to the kingdom being "completely taken" from the Jews "and given to Abraham's spiritual seed," which was fulfilled "through the dissolution of Judaism"

passage teaches the wicked will be raised body and soul to be cast into the fires of hell. All we know is that they simply die in their sins and nothing is revealed about their eternal state. This is nothing less than Satan's sleight of hand at work again!

Annihilation Shipwrecks on the Rock of Matthew 25:46

No passage of inspired Scripture gives the slightest hint of support for annihilationism, but one simple statement of the Savior brings the theory to wreck and ruin: Matthew 25:46. Summarizing the final outcome of the Judgment Day, Jesus said, "And these shall go away into everlasting punishment: but the righteous into life eternal." Moses Stuart's assessment is unassailable: "WE MUST EITHER ADMIT THE **ENDLESS** MISERY OF HELL, OR GIVE UP THE **ENDLESS** HAPPINESS OF HEAVEN" (emph. orig., Stuart, 62).

Edward Fudge's 500 page tome *The Fire That Consumes* asserts the annihilation of the wicked but flounders on this simple passage. He is more willing to yield "some billions of aeons of bliss" in heaven than to accept eternal punishment as unending but finally concedes eternal means eternal (Fudge, 195ff). He argues eternal punishment means an extended period of suffering followed by extinction (ibid., 47-48, 192-202). If that be the case, eternal life *must be* an extended period of bliss followed by extinction. Buddhism salutes that flag. As Gerstner observes in refuting Fudge, his view reduces hell to a temporal punishment with the eternal effect of non-existence, i.e., "no further punishing ever in gehenna. Gehenna's fire is quenched and its worms die" (Gerstner, 129).

Homer Hailey's book attempting to prove that "those who suffer the punishment of eternal fire are to exist no more" is filled with hundreds of Scripture references but only once refers to Matthew 25:46 with no explanation of it (Hailey, *God's Judgements and Punishments*, 142, 153). The clos-

---

(King, *The Spirit of Prophecy*, 351, 356). King denied that passages such as 1 Corinthians 15 or John 5:28-29 refer to the future coming of Christ and the future resurrection of our physical bodies because "Christ came in AD 70; therefore, the resurrection occurred then also," i.e. resurrection is a metaphor for the full establishment of the church (King in *The McGuiggen-King Debate*, 243). King taught that without a bodily resurrection saints receive their full and final reward with Christ at death, but he offers no passage which confirms this claim, nor does he offer any passages which address the eternal punishment of the wicked (ibid., 249).

"When Will These Things Be?" : Questions on Eschatology

est he came is a brief reference to the Judgment scene in Matthew 25 where he comments, "The verdict will be **eternal** punishment itself, or eternal life with God; neither is referred to as simply eternal existence" (emph. orig., ibid. 134). This statement is true, but it is also true that eternal existence is a necessary predicate to eternal life with God or eternal punishment.

LaGard Smith in his 334 page *After Life* argues "the soul and its resurrection body" will be annihilated in hell "sooner or later."[36] He attempts to deal with Matthew 25:46 by postulating that the term "eternal" refers to the nature of the punishment but not the duration, and yet he falls back to duration by claiming the punishment has "eternal, lasting, never-ending repercussions"—i.e., extinction (Smith, 174-175). In which case, we must explain eternal life as a blissful experience which also fulfills its meaning in eternal, lasting, never-ending extinction—again, the Buddhist's Nirvana.

Sinners facing eternal suffering would find the promise of "non-existence" to be "rather a Favor" than a threat because it would "totally release them from those Torments" (Horbery, 104). As Jonathan Edwards put it, "Is it possible that God should threaten them with putting an end to their miseries?" (McClintock, 1:236). Simply put, the cessation of punishment is *not* punishment.

Every attempt to remove duration from eternal punishment in Matthew 25:46 ultimately destroys both God and man. "Those who argue for 'eternal' as a spiritual quality rather than as duration must soon find themselves holding a sword which cuts in every direction; this sword annihilates the eternal God, heaven, hell, and thus the swordsman as well!!!" (Halbrook, "Eternal Life," 553).

Indeed, many modern biblical scholars such as Bart D. Ehrman have lost all sense of the eternal.[37] His recent book on *Heaven and Hell: A History of the Afterlife* claims Jesus taught that good ethical people would live again

---

[36] "At some point—sooner or later—hell will mean the everlasting destruction of the soul and its resurrection body" (Smith, 164). On this same page Smith insists that eternal punishment will not continue "throughout an endless eternity."

[37] "Ehrman is a professor of religious studies at the University of North Carolina, and a leading authority on the New Testament and the history of early Christianity" who has written or edited over thirty books (Ehrman, 327).

What Does the Bible Teach about Hell and Who Will Go There?

soon in "God's utopian kingdom . . . on earth" while bad people would be "exterminated out of existence" at death according to Matthew 25:46 (Ehrman, 154, 160). That hope failed and Ehrman is left with nothing:

> I certainly don't think the notion of a happy afterlife is as irrational as the fires of hell; at least it does not contradict the notion of a benevolent creative force behind the universe . . . . But I have to say that at the end of the day I really don't believe it either. My sense is that this life is all there is (Ehrman, 294).

Such men as Ehrman have lost all sense of the eternal in reference to God, heaven, hell, or man. His answer is there is no answer: "I have no way of knowing. And neither does anyone else" (Ehrman, 294). Brethren who deny eternal torment in hell are starting down the wrong road—a road to nowhere.

Vital Lessons Emphasized by the Reality of Hell

The reality of hell emphasizes and underscores *the awful sinfulness of sin* as nothing else can. Eternal torment in hell is the only just penalty for the infinite and eternal crime of sinning against God. Man was created not merely to exist (animals exist) but preeminently to live in fellowship with God, which is true life. Jesus said, "And this is life eternal, that they might know thee the only true God, and Jesus Christ, whom thou hast sent" (John 17:3). To walk in the light of God's truth is to walk in fellowship with Him, to know the life which is eternal life (1 John 1:5-7; 5:7). We receive the fulness of that gift in heaven (Titus 1:2).

Men who exist but live in sin are dead while they live (1 Tim. 5:6). Adam and Eve committed one sin and thus came under the pall of death —first, spiritual death, then physical death (Gen. 2:17; 3:8, 19, 24). Every sin of every man is a heinous insult to God and rebellion against God which cannot be rolled back—it stands in infamy for eternity. Eternal punishment in hell, the second death, is the only just punishment (Rev. 21:8).

A second lesson we must learn from the reality of hell is that *God will punish sin*. God warned Adam and Eve, "for in the day that thou eatest thereof thou shalt surely die" (Gen. 2:17). The reality of death did not sink into their souls until it was too late. The truth that God punishes sin was confirmed by the Flood of Noah's day and by the fiery destruction of Sodom. The rich man who neglected Lazarus learned too late as he cried out, "I am tormented in this flame" (Luke 16:24). Paul wrote by divine in-

"When Will These Things Be?" : Questions on Eschatology

spiration, "For the wages of sin is death" (Rom. 6:23). Christ said through John that sinners "shall have their part in the lake which burneth with fire and brimstone: which is the second death" (Rev. 21:8). We must take these warnings seriously before it is too late.

God's super-abundant grace is the third lesson to be learned from the reality of hell. The Law of Moses was designed to give the Jews deeper insight into sin's horrendous violation of God's sovereignty, holiness, love, and justice (Rom. 7:12-13). Sin utterly and irrevocably destroys man's fellowship with God, and thus man's highest purpose and happiness. This should have convinced every Jew of man's desperate need for a Savior. And thus Paul cried out in Romans 7:24, "O wretched man that I am! who shall deliver me from the body of this death?" Man is truly helpless and hopeless in sin, but Paul explained that "where sin abounded, grace did much more abound: That as sin hath reigned unto death, even so might grace reign through righteousness unto eternal life by Jesus Christ our Lord" (Rom. 5:20-21). Hell reminds us to praise God because His grace is greater than our sins!

Who Will Be Cast into Hell?

The Bible is clear that all who live and die in sin will be cast into hell. Hell is a prepared place for a prepared people. Hell was prepared for Satan with all of his angels and demonic spirits (Matt. 25:41; 8:28-29; 2 Pet. 2:4). Men who have the capacity to know right and wrong will be lost because of their sins, "For all have sinned, and come short of the glory of God" (Rom. 3:23). It is sometimes suggested that men are lost because they have not heard the gospel, but the truth is that they are lost because they have sinned. It is also true they cannot be saved until they hear the gospel (John 6:45).

All men "that know not God, and that obey not the gospel of our Lord Jesus Christ" will be lost in hell (2 Thess. 1:7-10). This includes men who are ignorant of God and who refuse to seek Him—their ignorance is culpable because the evidence of God surrounds every person (Ps. 19:1-6; Rom. 1:29; 2 Pet. 3:5). "He is not far from each one of us" (Acts 17:27, NIV). Secular minded people who attempt to push God out of His universe and who convince themselves that death means simply "the lights go out" will be shocked to find themselves in the lake of fire.

Most people will be cast into hell because they take the course of least resistance in life by walking in the broad way "that leadeth to destruction" (Matt. 7:13-14). Carnal minded people freely following "the

What Does the Bible Teach about Hell and Who Will Go There?

lust of the flesh, and the lust of the eyes, and the pride of life" are destined to suffer the torments of hell (1 John 2:15; Gal. 5:19-21). "The coming of the Son of man" will find people "eating and drinking, marrying and giving in marriage" unprepared to face the wrath of God (Matt. 24:37-39).

The lost will include multitudes that are content or even confident in their practice of false religions and traditions (Matt. 7:21-23; Rom. 10:1-3). Many religious leaders who see themselves as guiding and leading people to the paradise of God do not know their efforts are "vain," their work "shall be rooted up," and they with their followers "shall fall into the ditch" (Matt. 15:8-14). Addressing such leaders and teachers who deceive and take advantage of people for gain, Jesus said, "Ye serpents, ye generation of vipers, how can ye escape the damnation of hell?" (Matt. 23:33).

Halfhearted, neglectful, hypocritical, and apostate Christians who think they hold tickets which guarantee their entrance into heaven will be terrified to learn their names have been removed from the book of life. Simon was told to "repent" or "perish" with his money (Acts 8:20-22). In the parable of the wedding feast, those who entered unprepared were "cast into outer darkness" (Matt. 22:11-13). Those who obey the gospel and then abandon the truth will find "the latter end is worse with them than the beginning" because they will be tormented by knowing their names were once written in the book of life (2 Pet. 2:20). Christ warned lukewarm Christians at Laodicea, "I will vomit you out of My mouth" (Rev. 3:16, NKJV). With Paul, let us say, "But we are not of them who draw back unto perdition; but of them that believe to the saving of the soul" (Heb. 10:39).

There is no reason for even one soul to be lost in hell when God sent Jesus Christ to be "the atoning sacrifice for our sins, and not only for ours but also for the sins of the whole world" (1 John 2:2, NIV). He came from heaven to be "the way, the truth, and the life" who opens the way to heaven (John 14:1-6). Jesus has given us a stern warning about a clear and present danger of being cast into hell in John 8:24, "I said therefore unto you, that ye shall die in your sins: for if ye believe not that I am he, ye shall die in your sins." The same Jesus promised in John 5:24 to deliver us from the torment of eternal separation from the fellowship of God which is the second death: "Verily, verily, I say unto you, He that heareth my word, and believeth on him that sent me, hath everlasting life, and shall not come into condemnation; but is passed from death unto life."

"When Will These Things Be?" : Questions on Eschatology

All men must know the Savior has come and offers salvation now before He returns for the Final Judgment Day. "And he said unto them, Go ye into all the world, and preach the gospel to every creature. He that believeth and is baptized shall be saved; but he that believeth not shall be damned" (Mark 16:15-16). Among the last words Christ gave John on the Isle of Patmos was this beautiful invitation to the weary sinner, "And the Spirit and the bride say, Come. And let him that heareth say, Come. And let him that is athirst come. And whosoever will, let him take the water of life freely" (Rev. 22:17).

Bibliography

Arndt, William F. and F. Wilbur Gingrich. *A Greek-English Lexicon of the New Testament and Other Early Christian Literature. A translation and adaptation of Walter Bauer's Griechisch-Deutsches Worterbuch zu den Schriften des Neuen Testaments und der ubrigen urchristlichen Literatur.* 4th revised and augmented edition, 1952. Chicago, IL: The University of Chicago Press, 1957.

Barrett, C.K. *The Gospel According to St. John: An Introduction with Commentary and Notes on the Greek Text.* London: SPCK, 1960.

Blackmore, Evan and Marie. *Truth Commentaries: Psalms (1): Psalms 1-72.* Mike Willis, ed. Athens, AL: Truth Publications, 2017.

Calkins, Raymond. *The Social Message of the Book of Revelation.* New York: The Womans Press, 1920.

Ehrman, Bart D. *Heaven and Hell: A History of the Afterlife.* New York: Simon and Schuster, 2020.

———. "What Jesus Really Said about Heaven and Hell." TimeNewsLetters, May 11, 2020. https://time.com/5822598/jesus-really-said-heaven-hell/?utm_source=newsletter&utm_medium=email&utm_campaign=the-brief&utm_content. Accessed by Ron Halbrook, 5-11-2020.

English Standard Version Study Bible. Wheaton, IL: Crossway, 2008.

Errett, Issac. "Review of a Lecture by Moses E. Lard on Endless Punishment." Cincinnati: Standard Publications Co., 1879.

What Does the Bible Teach about Hell and Who Will Go There?

Fudge, Edward William. *The Fire That Consumes: A Biblical and Historical Study of Final Punishment.* Fallbrook, CA: Verdict Publications, 1982.

———and Robert A. Peterson. *Two Views of Hell: A Biblical and Theological Dialogue.* Downers Grove, IL: InterVarsity Press, 2000.

Gerstner, John H. *Repent or Perish (With a Special Reference to the Conservative Attack on Hell).* Ligonier, PA: Soli Deo Gloria Publications, 1990.

Hailey, Homer. *God's Judgements and Punishments: Nations and Individuals.* Las Vegas, NV: Nevada Publications, 2003.

———. *Revelation: An Introduction and Commentary.* Grand Rapids, MI: Baker Book House, 1979.

Halbrook, Ron. "Eternal Life, 1-3." *Truth Magazine.* 19.35-37 (July 17-31, 1975): 550-553, 572-574, 585-590.

———. "Eternal Punishment." *The Doctrine of Last Things*, 114-137. Melvin D. Curry, ed. Temple Terrace, FL: Florida College Bookstore, 1986.

———. "Sodom and Gomorrah: A Sign of Eternal Torment." *Guardian of Truth* 35.19 (October 3, 1991): 594-596.

Hamilton, Clinton D. *Truth Commentaries: 2 Peter and Jude.* Mike Willis, ed. Bowling Green, KY: Guardian of Truth Foundation, 1995.

Harkrider, Robert. *Truth Commentaries: Revelation.* Mike Willis, ed. Bowling Green, KY: Guardian of Truth Foundation, 1997.

Hendricksen, William. *New Testament Commentary: Exposition of the Pastoral Epistles.* Grand Rapids, MI: Baker Book House, 1965.

Horbery, Matthew. *An Enquiry into the Scripture Doctrine Concerning the Duration of Future Punishment.* 1774. Reprint. London: Wesleyan Conference Office, 1878.

Hooke, S.H. "Life After Death: V. Israel and the After Life," and "VI. The Extra-Canonical Literature." *The Expository Times* 76 (1965): 236-239 and 273-276.

Humphries, John A. *Truth Commentaries: Isaiah*. Mike Willis, ed. Athens, AL: Truth Publications, 2019.

King, Daniel H., Sr. *"I Saw the Heaven Opened": A Commentary on Revelation*. Athens, AL: Truth Publications, 2018.

———. *Truth Commentaries: Daniel*. Mike Willis, ed. Athens, AL: Guardian of Truth Foundation, 2012.

———. *Truth Commentaries: James*. Mike Willis, ed. Athens, AL: Guardian of Truth Foundation, 2015.

———. *Truth Commentaries: John*. Mike Willis, ed. Bowling Green, KY: Guardian of Truth Foundation, 1998.

King, Max. *The Spirit of Prophecy*. Warren, OH: Parkman Road Church of Christ, 1971.

Lenski, R.C.H. *Interpretation of St. John's Gospel*. Columbus, OH: The Wartburg Press, 1942.

Lyons, Eric and Kyle Butt. "The Eternality of Hell [Part 1]" and [Part 2]." Apologetics Press, 2005. http://apologeticspress.org/apPubPage.aspx?pub=1&issue=561 and https://apologeticspress.org/apcontent.aspx?category=11&article=1475 respectively. Accessed by Ron Halbrook, 3-9-2020.

McClintock, John and James Strong. *Cyclopedia of Biblical, Theological, and Ecclesiastical Literature*. Harper and Bros., 1870; reprint. Grand Rapids, MI: Baker Book House, 1969.

McGarvey, J.W. "The Destiny of the Wicked." *Lard's Quarterly* 2 (July 1855): 424-442.

———. *Sermons*. Guide Printing and Publications Co., 1894. Reprint. Nashville: Gospel Advocate Co., 1958.

——— and Philip Y. Pendleton. *The Fourfold Gospel or A Harmony of the Four Gospels*. Cincinnati: Standard Publications Co., 1914. Reprint Marion, IN: Cogdill Foundation, 1978.

———. *Thessalonians, Corinthians, Galatians and Romans*. Cincinnati: Standard Publications Co., 1916.

What Does the Bible Teach about Hell and Who Will Go There?

McGuiggan, Jim and Max R. King. *The McGuiggan-King Debate*. Warren, OH: Parkman Road Church of Christ, 1975.

Meyer, Carol. "Debunking the myth of hell." EarthBeat column, blog Eco Catholic Feb. 3, 2011 in National Catholic Reporter. https://www.ncronline.org/blogs/earthbeat/eco-catholic/debunking-myth-hell. Accessed by Ron Halbrook, 6-10-2020.

Morey, Robert A. *Death and the Afterlife*. Minneapolis, MN: Bethany House Publications, 1984.

Mounce, William D., General editor. *Mounce's Complete Expository Dictionary of Old and New Testament Words*. D. Matthew Smith and Miles V. Van Pelt, assoc. eds. Grand Rapids, MI: Zondervan, 2006.

Olshausen, Hermann. *Biblical Commentary on the New Testament*. 6 Vols. Revised by A.C. Kendrick. New York: Sheldon, Blakeman and Co., 1857-58. Reprint. Bowling Green, KY: Guardian of Truth Foundation, 2005.

Orr, James, General editor. *International Standard Bible Encyclopaedia*. Chicago: Howard-Severance Co., 1915.

Pope, Kyle. "'Immortal' and 'Incorruptible.'" *Biblical Insights* 3.12 (Dec. 2003): 11.

_____. *Truth Commentaries: Matthew*. Mike Willis, ed. Athens, AL: Guardian of Truth Foundation, 2013.

Robertson, A.T. *Words Pictures of the New Testament*. 6 Vols. Nashville, TN: Broadman Press, 1930.

Shedd, William G.T. *The Doctrine of Endless Punishment*. New York: Charles Scribners Sons, 1886. Reprint. Minneapolis: Klock and Klock, 1980.

Smith, F. LaGard. *After Life: A Glimpse of Eternity Beyond Death's Door*. Nashville, TN: Cotswold Publications, 2003.

Stauffer, L.A. *Truth Commentaries: Mark*. Mike Willis, ed. Bowling Green, KY: Guardian of Truth Foundation, 1999.

Stuart, Moses. *Exegetical Essays on Several Words Relating to Future Punishment*. 1830. Reprint. Rosemead, CA: Old Paths Book Club, 1954.

Tatera, Kelly. "Isolation in the Dark Drives Humans to Brink of Insanity, Studies Find." *The Science Explorer*, Nov. 19, 2015. http://thescience-explorer.com/brain-and-body/isolation-dark-drives-humans-brink-insanity-studies-find. Accessed by Ron Halbrook, May 15, 2020.

Tenny, Merrill C., General editor. *Zondervan Pictorial Bible Dictionary*. Grand Rapids, MI: Zondervan Publications House, 1963.

Thayer, Joseph Henry. *Greek-English Lexicon of the New Testament*. Marshallton, DE: National Foundation for Christian Education, n.d.

Vine, W.E. *An Expository Dictionary of New Testament Words*. 4 Vols. Westwood, NJ: Fleming H. Revell Company, 1940.

Weaver, Walton. *Truth Commentaries: 1 and 2 Thessalonians*. Mike Willis, ed. Athens, AL: Guardian of Truth Foundation, 2013.

Whiston, William, trans.. *Josephus: Complete Works*. Grand Rapids, MI: Kregel Publications, 1960.

Willis, Mike. *Then Comes the End*. Bowling Green, KY: Guardian of Truth Foundation, 1997.

Zondervan New International Version Study Bible, Fully Revised. Kenneth L. Barker, General editor. Grand Rapids, MI: Zondervan, 2002.

Am I Ready for the End?
By Bobby Graham

In a much earlier time and in a society that stood for something, I was a Boy Scout. We regularly said the Boy Scout Pledge: "On my honor, I will do my best to do my duty to God and my country and to obey the Scout Law; To help other people at all times; To keep myself physically strong, mentally awake, and morally straight." Our motto was, "Be Prepared." We frequently engaged in a variety of learning experiences to prepare ourselves for whatever might confront us in the world. Recent fundamental changes in this organization have rendered its leaders void of the moral preparation to help anybody in the truest sense of the

---

Bobby L. Graham was born August 30, 1946 to Mary and Leon Graham. He spent most of his teenage years under the preaching of Curtis Flatt and Franklin T. Puckett. Bobby graduated from Coffee High School in 1964; attended Florida College and graduated with a B.A. in History from Athens College and finished his Master's Degree in Education at Virginia Commonwealth University. He began preaching in 1962 while still in high school. He married Karen Ruth Hodge in November, 1967; they have three children: Richard, Mary Katherine (Darren Winland), and Laura Ruth (Jeremy Paschall). He has two grandchildren. Bobby has preached for several congregations in Alabama, Virginia, and is presently preaching at Old Moulton Road in Decatur, AL. He wrote for *Gospel Guide* for 33 years and has written for most journals published by brethren over the last 50 years, including the "Question and Answer Column" for *Truth Magazine* for over a decade. He has made many trips to Northeastern and New England states, preached much in the mountains of Virginia and Kentucky, preached in some Western states, and made nineteen preaching trips to Belize. He may be reached at: bobbylgraham@pclnet.net.

"When Will These Things Be?" : Questions on Eschatology

word, leaving the boys morally "helpless" compared to earlier times. The concept of readiness is again stressed in the United States Coast Guard's motto *Semper Paratus*, a Latin phrase meaning "Always Ready." Surely readiness about physical things is important, but far more significant is our spiritual preparedness.

The New Testament theme of readiness is one that now commands our attention. There has never been a time when the Lord's people did not need to prepare themselves for His coming at the end of time. It is little wonder that the New Testament emphasizes preparation. The lessons in this book have dealt with the different occasions, which constituted the end for certain people; in each case, the Lord encouraged their readiness. Both death and the Second Coming of Jesus Christ face us as real eventualities. Am I ready to die? Am I ready for the Lord to return? Are you ready to face the Lord in judgment?

We frequently and appropriately urge preparation for important events in life—walking, talking, starting school, graduation, becoming a Christian, seeking a job, starting a family, buying or selling a house, rearing one's children, etc. As important as the world thinks most of them to be, none measures up to the gravity of being ready for the end, whether it be death or the Lord's coming. Other measures are sometimes available to compensate for our unreadiness in physical matters. Still, there is nothing that can make up for our lack of spiritual preparation for the end. Have we made ourselves ready, or have we dawdled? Are you ready?

At the other end of the spectrum of extremes from the nonchalant are the date setters. According to Jesus Christ in Matthew 24:36, no human knows the time of the end. However, all can know what the Lord has revealed about the end of this world, and about the importance of being prepared. To that end, we seek the information provided by the Bible. There is no excuse for not being ready!

The Reality of the End

Who can forget the fearful warnings about the change of the calendar to January 1, 2000 [(1/1/2000), i.e., "Y2K"] more than twenty years ago, especially during 1999? How many gave heed? How many made changes? How many computers underwent special preparation? As the end of the year passed and the new year began, nothing happened! Then we knew what many anticipated, but many others denied: *It was all hype.*

Am I Ready for the End?

Those who spoke the most about it knew the least. Many so-called *experts* became what they had been all along, *ex spurts,* or "drips under pressure." Were they ready for their end?

God is the real expert in the case of the end. He alone knows when it will happen. The end is just as real as God's word is reliable. If divine promises are trustworthy, then the end is coming at a time we do not know! The approach of one's death is often more detectable, as health and age signals appear. There are no signs or signals of the end of time, or the Lord's coming. Those who would deny the reality of the Second Coming, the general resurrection, and the judgment are not the experts; they are the "drips under pressure." With their elite viewpoint gained by a "superior" hermeneutic, which amounts to nonsense, they have gained a small following. When the Lord comes back, He will show them in their true colors. When those in the graves come forth, they will call them liars. When the judgment takes place as God intends, they will then appear as a fearful lot of deniers and nay-sayers. Long past will be any idea that they were merely harmless theoreticians of the wonky type who fed their grist to the credulous and gullible masses. Are they ready for their end?

All must choose whom they will hear and heed—the God of time and creation who planned its end or the deniers of God's word on this matter. The choice each one makes will influence his readiness for the coming end. When the dead arise, it is the voice of the Son of God that will beckon them forth from their tombs (John 5:28). Preparation must involve hearing His voice now so we can be ready then (Matt. 17:5). Are you ready?

What End Do We Mean?

Our theme connecting all lessons in this series relates to "Questions on Eschatology." Different writers have already paid ample attention to the various "ends" relevant to the theme and matters pertaining to them. Consideration has been paid to the following issues related to the end:

- Eternal life
- Hell
- The so-called end (which amounts to no end) of realized eschatology(the AD 70 Doctrine)
- Israel's role in the end
- Signs about the end

"When Will These Things Be?": Questions on Eschatology

- Whether Jesus Christ will actually return since Jerusalem has been destroyed
- Whether there will really be a resurrection of the dead
- The reality or fable of the rapture
- The destruction or renovation of our universe
- Our Lord's Matthew 24-25 prophecy's relevance to the end of this world
- The relevance of the book of Revelation to the end
- The current status of the dead
- The fictions of purgatory and reincarnation

Different ends have come before us in our study. Which is the end taught in the New Testament? The end of Jerusalem, which took place in AD 70 and is supposed by some to be the end? The end of Judaism or the emergence of the church? The end of the final judgment coming only after the rapture? The end of the 1940s, when Jesus supposedly came? The renovation of this universe? The Second Coming of Jesus Christ at the End of the World to raise and judge all? Surely all of our studies have led us to this point of focusing upon the end, which makes all the difference in the world! The Bible holds the answer!

> Then comes the end, when He delivers the kingdom to God the Father when He puts an end to all rule and all authority and power. For He must reign till He has put all enemies under His feet. The last enemy that will be destroyed is death. For "He has put all things under His feet." But when He says, "all things are put under Him," it is evident that He who put all things under Him is excepted. Now when all things are made subject to Him, then the Son Himself will also be subject to Him who put all things under Him, that God may be all in all (1 Cor. 15:24-28).

The Bible Speaks of the Last Day

Much has been said and written concerning the last day, both by God and by men. The same could also be said about the first day, but God has told us more about the last day than about the first day. Men have often speculated and guessed in a hurtful way about the end of time, but God has simply affirmed truth by disclosing His plans to us. What He has revealed concerning that day at the end of time should inform and motivate us to be ready for it.

Am I Ready for the End?

The expression "last day" implies other days, even a continuum of days filling the "time" part of duration or eternity. Someone once said that time is a parenthesis between two eternities. God was there before time and will be there after time. While time is measured by days, weeks, months, years, and centuries, eternity is unmeasured and unmarked by such time markers. Peter did not define a day or 1,000 years when he wrote 2 Peter 3:9, but he was presenting God's way of viewing that eternal duration, which includes the parenthesis or interval of time. An eternal God does not perceive of different measures of time the same as finite man. He simply is not bound by time!!

Many think of the last day as consisting of 1,000 years, just as others assert that the first day lasted millions of years. Both groups err in that they say what God does not reveal. The First and Last both share the attribute of being another is a series of days—in their cases, the initial and the terminal days in time. They are the same kind as the others and have the same duration as the rest, i.e., twenty-four hours. It is not denied "day" sometimes is used figuratively to denote a period, as in 2 Corinthians 6:2. No such instance of this word is found in the Bible when an adjective such as "first," "second," or "last" modifies it. The last day is simply the final period of twenty-four hours' duration. Because it will be the last, there will be no others after it!

What Does the Bible Say about the Last Day?

Certainly, the Bible presents the last day as an eventful time; it will be busy as men would describe it. Significant events, all related to divine warnings about the last day, will fill that time.

1. The Dead Will Be Raised. Are You Ready?

And this is the will of Him who sent Me, that everyone who sees the Son and believes in Him may have everlasting life; and I will raise him up at the last day.... No one can come to Me unless the Father who sent Me draws him; and I will raise him up at the last day (John 6:40, 44).

Both the good and the bad will arise in the same hour. Jesus said, "Do not marvel at this; for the hour is coming in which all who are in the graves will hear His voice and come forth—those who have done good, to the resurrection of life, and those who have done evil, to the resurrection of condemnation" (John 5:28-29).

"When Will These Things Be?" : Questions on Eschatology

2. All the Living Will Be Changed. Are You Ready?

> Then comes the end, when He delivers the kingdom to God the Father, when He puts an end to all rule and all authority and power. For He must reign till He has put all enemies under His feet. The last enemy that will be destroyed is death . . . . Now this I say, brethren, that flesh and blood cannot inherit the kingdom of God; nor does corruption inherit incorruption. Behold, I tell you a mystery: We shall not all sleep, but we shall all be changed—in a moment, in the twinkling of an eye, at the last trumpet. For the trumpet will sound, and the dead will be raised incorruptible, and we shall be changed (1 Cor. 15:24-26, 50-52).

The resurrection of the wicked will not follow that of the righteous 1,000 years later, though some misinterpret 1 Thessalonians 4:16 to mean such. If such were true, then the resurrection of the wicked would not be in the same hour, but 365,000 days after the last day.

3. Jesus Will Come Back. Are You Ready?

1 Thessalonians 4:13-17 makes it clear that the general resurrection will accompany His coming. Are you ready?

> But I do not want you to be ignorant, brethren, concerning those who have fallen asleep, lest you sorrow as others who have no hope. For if we believe that Jesus died and rose again, even so God will bring with Him those who sleep in Jesus. For this we say to you by the word of the Lord, that we who are alive and remain until the coming of the Lord will by no means precede those who are asleep. For the Lord Himself will descend from heaven with a shout, with the voice of an archangel, and with the trumpet of God. And the dead in Christ will rise first. Then we who are alive and remain shall be caught up together with them in the clouds to meet the Lord in the air. And thus we shall always be with the Lord.

> Finally, there is laid up for me the crown of righteousness, which the Lord, the righteous Judge, will give to me on that Day, and not to me only but also to all who have loved His appearing (2 Tim. 4:8).

> And now, little children, abide in Him, that when He appears, we may have confidence and not be ashamed before Him at His coming (1 John 2:18).

> For whoever is ashamed of Me and My words in this adulterous and sinful generation, of him the Son of Man also will be ashamed when He comes in the glory of His Father with the holy angels (Mark 8:38).

Am I Ready for the End?

4. The Final Judgment Will Take Place. Are You Ready?
Matthew 25:31-32 pictures Jesus coming again to judge all nations.

> When the Son of Man comes in His glory, and all the holy angels with Him, then He will sit on the throne of His glory. All the nations will be gathered before Him, and He will separate them one from another, as a shepherd divides his sheep from the goats.

The people of Nineveh will be there (Matt. 12:41).

The Queen of the South will be there (Matt. 12:42).

The people of Tyre, Sidon, and Sodom will be there (Matt. 11:20-24).

The wicked and the righteous will be there and will receive their eternal rewards (2 Thess. 1:6-10; Matt. 25:46).

You will be there to be doomed or blessed (2 Cor. 5:10)! Are you ready?

5. All Things Temporal Will Be Destroyed. Are You Ready?
Our present order, designated as "the heavens and the earth which now exist," will be kept by the divine word until fire overwhelms it all at the time of "the day of judgment and perdition of ungodly men" (2 Pet. 3:7). Such expressions as "pass away," "melt," "burned up," "dissolved," do not describe any remodeling job I have ever seen. Are you ready?

> But the day of the Lord will come as a thief in the night, in which the heavens will pass away with a great noise, and the elements will melt with fervent heat; both the earth and the works that are in it will be burned up. Therefore, since all these things will be dissolved, what manner of persons ought you to be in holy conduct and godliness, looking for and hastening the coming of the day of God, because of which the heavens will be dissolved, being on fire, and the elements will melt with fervent heat? Nevertheless, we, according to His promise, look for new heavens and a new earth in which righteousness dwells (2 Pet. 3:10-13).

6. Christ's Mediatorial Reign over the Kingdom Will End. ARE YOU READY?

> Then comes the end, when He delivers the kingdom to God the Father, when He puts an end to all rule and all authority and power. For He must reign till He has put all enemies under His feet. The last enemy that will be destroyed is death (1 Cor. 15:24-26).

"When Will These Things Be?" : Questions on Eschatology

By this time, Jesus Christ will have completed His work as a mediator between God and man (1 Tim. 2:5; Heb. 9:15). The redemption secured by the blood of His cross is attainable by all, thus precluding any further mediatorial role for Him. He will not cease being divine or possessing His divine authority, but He will cease His work as Prophet, Priest, and King.

Ready or Not, Here I Come!

Jesus Christ will consult no one about the time of His return. No surveys or polls will influence His decision. No advance troops will indicate His nearness. No harbinger will herald His arrival. No signs will alert anyone that the Son of God will soon descend. He will simply arrive, as promised in the Scriptures. Faith in these promises will distinguish believers from unbelievers. The willingness to trust and obey will distinguish the prepared from the unprepared. As most of us know from the childhood game called "Hide and Seek," the person seeking the others says, "Ready or not, here I come." So it will be when the Lord returns at the end of all things.

> But of that day and hour no one knows, not even the angels of heaven, but My Father only. But as the days of Noah were, so also will the coming of the Son of Man be. For as in the days before the flood, they were eating and drinking, marrying and giving in marriage, until the day that Noah entered the ark, and did not know until the flood came and took them all away, so also will the coming of the Son of Man be. Then two men will be in the field: one will be taken and the other left. Two women will be grinding at the mill: one will be taken and the other left. Watch therefore, for you do not know what hour your Lord is coming (Matt. 24:36-42).

Ordinary, legitimate concerns of life have been, and will again be, distractions. The unprepared will not be claimed by the Lord, but those ready will be His. The important word is *watch*.

> But concerning the times and the seasons, brethren, you have no need that I should write to you. For you yourselves know perfectly that the day of the Lord so comes as a thief in the night. For when they say, "Peace and safety!" then sudden destruction comes upon them, as labor pains upon a pregnant woman. And they shall not escape. But you, brethren, are not in darkness, so that this Day should overtake you as a thief. You are all sons of light and sons of the day. We are not of the night nor of darkness. Therefore let us not sleep, as others do, but let us watch and be sober. For those who sleep, sleep at night, and those who

get drunk are drunk at night. But let us who are of the day be sober, putting on the breastplate of faith and love, and as a helmet the hope of salvation (1 Thess. 5:1-8).

As unexpected as the thief's coming at night or the labor pains of an expectant mother, so shall the sudden destruction of the Lord's coming interrupt the peace and safety of the unprepared. Escape will not be an option! Sober watching—not climbing on housetops in white garments to gaze upward at the sky—is here explained to mean manning the armor of a soldier. It encompasses faith in God and love for both God and man (Heb. 11:6; Matt. 22:37-40). This is what it means to prepare for the Lord's coming. Are you ready?

Are You Ready?

To protect the vital organs, soldiers wore a breastplate. A helmet was the most conspicuous part of the advancing soldier's armor, as it secured his mind and heart (1 Thess. 5:8). Faith, hope, and love are combined here by Paul to form a defense against our Satanic adversary and all of his minions as they try to devour us (1 Pet. 5:8-9). These active virtues must energize us to fight for our souls, thus mounting a vigorous defense to ensure our readiness when the Lord comes. Are you fighting?

When God unleashed the fountains of the great deep and opened the windows of heaven, most people were not ready because they failed to believe God and to love God, as well as their neighbors. They trusted in themselves, not in the living God. They were wrapped up in themselves, failing to love God and others. Therefore, they joined the opposition instead of fighting against it. They compromised when they should have stood fast for God and right. They blended in when they could have stood out as God's own special people. Most were so focused upon "every imagination of the thoughts of his heart" that it repented God He had made man, but man did not repent. Few were concerned enough about their neighbors to join hands with Noah, who was proclaiming righteousness to warn all who would listen. Is it any different with us? Are we ready, or are we loaded down with sin?

Remember that faith, hope, and love must also combine in our lives to motivate and guide us to be ready. Faith in God's very existence and in His plan to reward us must form a principal part of our lives, according to Hebrews 11:6. Hope for what we do not see must be strong to motivate us

"When Will These Things Be?": Questions on Eschatology

to follow God's leading because hope causes us to wait patiently for the reward (Rom. 8:24-25). Love also must be there, because love is the bond of perfectness to connect loving God and loving all whom God loves (Col. 3:14). Are we characterized by the faith, hope, and love which God urges?

Are you ready for the reward to be given to the righteous, or for the doom that will torment the wicked (Matt. 25:31-46)? Are you ready for the everlasting peace of the heavenly city, or the eternal fire of hell? Are you watching and praying, or are you slouching along in slovenly fashion, intending sometime to do better (Matt. 26:38, 41)? Have you been washed in the blood of Calvary's Lamb, or will you stand in the shame of your sins (Acts 22:16)? Are you giving to the Lord the faithful, fervent, and fruitful service He deserves, or are you denying Him the honor you owe Him (1 Cor. 15:58)? Are you ready?

Prepare to Meet Your God!

Therefore thus will I do to you, O Israel; Because I will do this to you, Prepare to meet your God, O Israel (Amos 4:12)!

The Lord mercifully warned His people about their waywardness, lest His judgment come upon them when they were not ready. Jesus similarly warned the Israelites of His day that Jerusalem's end was near lest they be taken unexpectedly by that catastrophe (Matt. 24). The suffering Savior warned the disciples of the impending shaking of their faith lest they be overcome by temptation (Matt. 26:38, 41). Our God has not failed to warn us also of the coming of the Lord when time shall be no more.

Why would people claiming to believe in God and to love God continue carelessly on their way of life, heedless to divine warnings? The end of the antediluvian world, the end of the Northern or Southern Kingdom, and the end of Jerusalem and the Jewish Nation were ends earlier marked. Here is a profound difference, friend: The end coming upon the world when He comes again will be the last one, the end that will end all endings. No one will have another way or time to be ready! Are we ready?

Judgment Must Begin at the House of God

For the time has come for judgment to begin at the house of God; and if it begins with us first, what will be the end of those who do not obey the gospel of God? Now "If the righteous one is scarcely saved, Where will the ungodly and the sinner appear?" Therefore let those who suffer according to the will of God commit their souls to Him in doing good, as to a faithful Creator (1 Pet. 4:17-19).

Peter earlier warned about the "end of all things" in 1 Peter 4:7, possibly referring to the end of the world. Clinton Hamilton offers a lengthy and helpful explanation that terms like "at hand," "near," and "approaching" do not always convey the idea of being immediate or imminent (224-233). It is, therefore, not conclusive that the apostle here referred to the end of the temple and Jerusalem in AD 70. Because Peter might have viewed the termination or cessation of all things in God's redemptive plan, the next and last of which remains at the end of time, this is the view which I here take.

God's judgment in the sense of His verdict or conclusion reached concerning His people, constituting His house or temple (1 Pet. 2:5; 4:17), is that they are His righteous saints or Christians. For this, they are suffering the fiery trail like Christ's sufferings (4:12-13). Their faithful endurance (i.e. committing their souls to Him) in doing good (4:16, 19) destines them to share in His glory and gladness with exceeding joy and in being saved (13, 18). Their "scarcely" being saved does not imply they barely get by or in, but the difficulty of the trials which they have withstood (4:18, 12, 16). The same wrath of God, which will bring everlasting judgment to the wicked persecutors, will not encompass the righteous.

It is a righteous thing for God to punish the guilty; it accords with God's righteous judgment.

> We are bound to thank God always for you, brethren, as it is fitting because your faith grows exceedingly, and the love of every one of you all abounds toward each other, so that we ourselves boast of you among the churches of God for your patience and faith in all your persecutions and tribulations that you endure, which is manifest evidence of the righteous judgment of God, that you may be counted worthy of the kingdom of God, for which you also suffer; since it is a righteous thing with God to repay with tribulation those who trouble you, and to give you who are troubled rest with us when the Lord Jesus is revealed from heaven with His mighty angels, in flaming fire taking vengeance on those who do not know God, and on those who do not obey the gospel of our Lord Jesus Christ. These shall be punished with everlasting destruction from the presence of the Lord and from the glory of His power, when He comes, in that Day, to be glorified in His saints and

"When Will These Things Be?" : Questions on Eschatology

to be admired among all those who believe, because our testimony among you was believed (2 Thess. 1:3-10).

Faith on the part of the saved and unbelief on the part of the damned vindicate God's justice. All received the same offer of pardon in Jesus Christ (Mark 16:15-16). When the sinner refuses the offer of mercy in the Lord, he invites God's judgment.

In 1 Peter, we find another appeal which should warn us about being ready. The difference lies in obeying the gospel of God (4:17). Peter's audience had obeyed it when it was earlier preached to them. By it, they had been begotten, born again, and have purified their souls (1:22-25). Their opponents, on the other hand, had not obeyed the gospel (4:17). The New Testament teaches that people can and must obey the gospel (Rom. 1:5; 6:17; 10:16; 16:26; every example of conversion in Acts). Who is ready? The obedient or disobedient? Are you ready?

Bibliography

Hamilton, Clinton D. *Truth Commentaries: 1 Peter*. Bowling Green, KY: Guardian of Truth Foundation, 1995.

The Kingdom

Has the Kingdom of Christ Been Established?
   Joe Price

Does the Physical Nation of Israel Still Play a Role in God's Final Plans?
   Stephen Russell

Can Signs Foretell When the End Will Come?
   Allen Dvorak

"When Will These Things Be?"
Questions on Eschatology

Has the Kingdom of Christ Been Established?

By Joe Price

Introduction

The Old Testament contains the record of God's prophets foretelling of a future, insurmountable kingdom. Anticipated by Israel for centuries, the approach of this kingdom was privately announced by an angel to Mary in the obscure village of Nazareth—far from Jerusalem, where kings had once ruled the nation. The angel Gabriel told Mary the Lord God would give her child "the throne of His father David. And He will reign over the house of Jacob forever, and of His kingdom there will be no end" (Luke 1:32-33, NKJV, throughout unless otherwise noted). Not only would this king be the son of David, but He would also be the Son of God (Luke 1:35; Rom. 1:3-4).

Joe R. Price was born on October 16, 1957, in Paris, TX. He grew up in nearby Delta County, where he heard and obeyed the gospel in July 1974 in Cooper, TX. He and his wife Debbie were married on January 5, 1979, and they have four children and two grandchildren. Joe began preaching the gospel in 1978, working with churches in Colorado, Texas, and Utah, in addition to his current work in Bellingham, WA, where he has worked as an evangelist with the Mt. Baker church since 1996. He writes a weekly bulletin, *The Spirit's Sword*, as well as daily *Sword Tips*. His sermons and articles are available on the Bible Answers website (bibleanswer.com). Joe has made annual preaching trips to India since 2006, where he teaches preacher training classes along with visiting and preaching for local churches. He can be reached at: joerprice@mail.com.

"When Will These Things Be?" : Questions on Eschatology

Additionally, an angel told Joseph the child would save His people from their sins and fulfill Isaiah's prophecy of Immanuel (Matt. 1:20-23; Isa. 7:14). Zacharias, the father of John, spoke wondrous things of this Messiah, who was bringing deliverance from their enemies and "salvation to His people by the remission of sins" (Luke 1:67-79, esp. v. 77). Wonderful expectations, indeed, which are now fully realized in Jesus Christ (Acts 2:32-41).

Jesus fulfilled His ministry by going throughout Galilee "preaching the gospel of the kingdom" (Matt. 4:23; 9:35). He preached, "it is your Father's good pleasure to give you the kingdom" (Luke 12:32). He explained that people were pressing toward the kingdom since the days of John, the Messiah's forerunner (Luke 16:16). Jesus even claimed some who were listening to him preach would not die until they saw the kingdom come with power (Mark 9:1). Either the kingdom came with power during their lifetime, or Jesus is a false prophet unworthy or our faith and allegiance (Acts 3:22-26).

Nevertheless, many refuse to believe Christ established His kingdom in the days of the New Testament, nor do they think it exists today. For instance, premillennialism says God dramatically altered His program, withdrew the kingdom promise, and substituted the church age in its place. (All of this, they say, was due to the Jews' rejection of Christ.) A well-known advocate of this view argues that following the Jews' rejection of Jesus, "a definite movement may be traced in the withdrawal of the offer of the kingdom" and for "the period of the King's absence" Jesus "announces the inception of an entirely new, unheralded, unexpected program—the church" (Pentecost, 463-464). Thus, many view the kingdom of Christ and the church of Christ as separate entities rather than two terms describing the same assembly of redeemed souls (Matt. 16:18-19; Heb. 12:22-25).

Consequently, questions arise over whether Jesus is reigning today as King over His kingdom. What is His kingdom? Was His kingdom established in the first century? If so, when? If not, when will it be established? Is Jesus reigning as King today, or is He only a promissory King? Was the prophetic kingdom postponed? Was a lesser, inferior arrangement (the church) established in its place between God and His people? That is, did the church replace the promised and anticipated kingdom?

Has the Kingdom of Christ Been Established?

Or, is the church of Christ the kingdom of Christ? How can Jesus be a reigning King today without His kingdom also existing today? These are just some of the questions generated when one concludes the kingdom of Christ has not been established.

All have failed who try to calculate the return of Jesus and the establishment of His kingdom here on earth. The doctrine of premillennialism lends itself to such vain speculations by anticipating the future establishment of Christ's prophetic kingdom. Other teachings, such as realized eschatology (RE), which is also called the AD 70 doctrine, miss the mark regarding the timing and completeness of the kingdom's establishment. This doctrine holds that the kingdom was established gradually from AD 30 to 70 and that the eternal days of the kingdom began when Jerusalem was destroyed by the Roman army.

We reject both of these denials concerning when the Messiah's kingdom was fully established. The Scriptures teach the kingdom prophecies were fulfilled in the days of the apostles beginning in Acts 2, and that the establishment of the kingdom and the church are two ways of looking at the same event (Acts 3:24-26).

Pilate's rhetorical flourish, "What is truth?" ought to be given serious attention concerning the establishment of the kingdom? As questions arise over the kingdom's nature and establishment, they are answered in the word of God. So, with the apostle, we will ask, "What does the Scripture say?" (Rom. 4:3).

To know God's answer to whether the kingdom has been established, we will examine some of the significant kingdom prophecies in the Old Testament and the inspired accounts of their fulfillment in the New Testament. By doing so, it will become increasingly apparent that the church of Christ is the kingdom of prophecy. We will demonstrate that Christ not only described the nature of His kingdom, He and His apostles repeatedly taught its imminent appearance and establishment, even pinpointing the time of its arrival. We will intermingle this analysis with pertinent references to false doctrines that twist and undermine Bible teaching regarding the kingdom. The Scriptures teach the kingdom of Christ was established entirely on Pentecost, some fifty days after the death of Jesus Christ, and that His kingdom is the church of Christ.

"When Will These Things Be?" : Questions on Eschatology

Defining Terms

A kingdom is the realm of a king's dominion, populated by a citizenry and ruled over by the exercise of the king's sovereign authority and power.

The Hebrew word translated "kingdom" almost 900 times in the Old Testament (as in 2 Sam. 7:12-13) is *mamlâkâh* (from *mâlak*, "to reign," "to ascend the throne"), and means "dominion, i.e., (abstr.) the estate (*rule*) or (concr.) the country (*realm*):—kingdom, king's, reign, royal" (Strong, H4467). It signifies a "kingdom, sovereignty, dominion, reign" (BDB, 575).

The Greek word translated "kingdom" in the New Testament is *basileia*, "prop. *royalty*, i.e., (abstr.) *rule*, or (concr.) a realm (lit. or fig.):—kingdom, + reign" (Strong, G932). Again, "*royal power, kingship, dominion, rule*: Luke 1:33; 19:12, 15; 22:29; John 18:36; Acts 1:6; Heb. 1:8; 1 Cor. 15:24; Rev. 17:12; of the royal power of Jesus as the triumphant Messiah . . . i. e., to come in his kingship, clothed with this power: Matt. 16:28; Luke 23:42" (Thayer, 96).

God's Old Testament prophets anticipated a King who would be a great Deliverer (a Savior), whose dominion would be perpetual, and whose power would be unmatched. Isaiah wrote,

> For unto us a Child is born, unto us a Son is given; And the government will be upon His shoulder. And His name will be called Wonderful, Counselor, Mighty God, Everlasting Father, Prince of Peace. Of the increase of His government and peace there will be no end, upon the throne of David and over His kingdom, to order it and establish it with judgment and justice from that time forward, even forever. The zeal of the Lord of hosts will perform this (Isa. 9:6-7).

Christ's New Testament apostles and prophets wrote of a King who is now on His throne as God's anointed King, reigning in righteousness over His kingdom:

> But to the Son He says: "Your throne, O God, Is forever and ever; A scepter of righteousness is the scepter of Your kingdom. You have loved righteousness and hated lawlessness; Therefore God, Your God, has anointed You with the oil of gladness more than Your companions" (Heb. 1:8-9).

Has the Kingdom of Christ Been Established?

> Therefore, since we are receiving a kingdom which cannot be shaken, let us have grace, by which we may serve God acceptably with reverence and godly fear (Heb. 12:28).

The inspired Scriptures identify the King as Jesus, His kingdom as presently existing, and His subjects as those who "serve God acceptably" (i.e., Christians).

1. *The prophesied King is Jesus Christ, the Son of God (2 Sam. 7:12-14; Luke 1:32-33).* Jesus declared this good confession to Pilate when he said, "Are You a king then?" Jesus answered, "You say rightly that I am a king. For this cause I was born, and for this cause I have come into the world, that I should bear witness to the truth. Everyone who is of the truth hears My voice" (John 18:37; cf. 1 Tim. 6:13).

2. *The prophesied kingdom is the church of Christ.* Jesus used "church" and "kingdom" interchangeably in Matthew 16:18-19. In a night vision, Daniel saw

> . . . One like the Son of Man, coming with the clouds of heaven! He came to the Ancient of Days, and they brought Him near before Him. Then to Him was given dominion and glory and a kingdom, that all peoples, nations, and languages should serve Him. His dominion is an everlasting dominion, which shall not pass away, and His kingdom the one which shall not be destroyed (Dan. 7:13-14).

The fulfillment of Daniel's vision is unmistakable in this inspired description of God's mighty power,

> Which He worked in Christ when He raised Him from the dead and seated Him at His right hand in the heavenly places, far above all principality and power and might and dominion, and every name that is named, not only in this age but also in that which is to come. And He put all things under His feet, and gave Him to be head over all things to the church, which is His body, the fullness of Him who fills all in all (Eph. 1:20-23).

Separating the establishment of the kingdom from the beginning of the church is a tortuous misuse of the Scriptures.

3. *The citizens of Christ's kingdom are Christians.* These are the ones who volunteer themselves to Christ "in the day of (His) power," when the Lord Jesus sits at the right hand of God and rules in the midst of His enemies (Psa. 110:1-3). Those redeemed by the blood of Christ are citizens of the kingdom, having been delivered by the Father "from the power of darkness and conveyed us into the kingdom of the Son of His love" (Col. 1:13-14). The sinner's salvation ("delivered from the power of darkness") and the kingdom's establishment ("conveyed into the kingdom of the Son of His love") are inextricably connected.

An Overview of the Kingdom's Approach, Establishment, and Identity

Jesus preached the good news of a kingdom, the establishment of which was "at hand" (Mark 1:14-15). Its citizens are "not of this world," because the kingdom He came into the world to rule as King is "not of this world" (John 18:36-37). Through the saving power of the gospel, the Father "has delivered us from the power of darkness and conveyed us into the kingdom of the Son of His love" (Col. 1:13). Today, and since the gospel went out from Jerusalem, Christians populate and participate in the Son's kingdom.

What is the kingdom Jesus preached? What is the kingdom into which saved people are transferred? Does this kingdom exist today? Or, is it yet to be established and its blessings fully realized? Is kingdom citizenship prospective or actual?

Scripture confirms the kingdom of Old Testament prophecy is the church Jesus built and to which saved souls are added. The kingdom of Christ is the church of Christ (Matt. 16:18-19; Acts 2:47).

Old Testament prophets saw the Messiah's kingdom through eyes of faith and recorded divinely inspired messages of its nature, its coming, its King, and its citizens. The New Testament apostles and prophets openly declared the fulfillment of these kingdom prophecies (Ps. 2 in Acts 13:32-33; Isa. 2 in Luke 24:47; Joel 2 in Acts 2:16-21; Dan. 2 in Mark 9:1, among many others). Luke noted that Christ explained the "things pertaining to the kingdom of God" to His apostles by "opening their understanding" of the prophecies and His fulfillment of them (Acts 1:2-3; Luke 24:44-47).

John, the Messiah's messenger, then Jesus and His disciples, preached the kingdom was "at hand" and "near" (Matt. 3:2; 10:7; Mark 1:14-15; Luke 10:9). Indeed, "The law and the prophets were until John. Since that time the kingdom of God has been preached, and everyone is pressing into it" (Luke 16:16). Jesus said the coming of the kingdom of God is not "with observation" (visibly, JRP) of invading armies and glorious fanfare. Instead,

Has the Kingdom of Christ Been Established?

in line with its spiritual nature, the kingdom is "within you" (Luke 17:20-21). Many were hoping for a king bringing military power and objectives watch Jesus enter Jerusalem on the foal of a donkey, not upon a mighty steed (Zech. 9:9; Matt. 21:1-11). Their hopes were being dashed, even as God's will was being fulfilled. Just days after shouts of "Hosanna to the Son of David," the crowd's enthusiasm degenerated into "Let him be crucified!" (Matt. 27:20-23). Nevertheless, death did not prevail against God's purposes. The Son of God was raised from the dead, and His kingdom came with power, just as Jesus said it would (Mark 9:1; Acts 2:1-4).

Great commission preaching proclaimed that Jesus fulfilled the prophecies of a King and His kingdom. Samaritans heard and believed Philip preaching "the things concerning the kingdom of God" (Acts 8:12). In an Ephesian synagogue, Paul "spoke boldly for three months, reasoning and persuading concerning the things of the kingdom of God." Kingdom preaching—"the word of the Lord Jesus"—produced disciples even as others became hardened against "the Way" (Acts 19:8-10).

Years did not dilute Paul's enthusiastic kingdom message. To a gathering of Jews in Rome, he "explained and solemnly testified of the kingdom of God, persuading them concerning Jesus from both the Law of Moses and the Prophets, from morning till evening" (Acts 28:23). Significantly, "the salvation of God" that was "sent to the Gentiles" included "preaching the kingdom of God and teaching the things concerning the Lord Jesus Christ" (Acts 28:28, 30). Repeatedly in the apostles' preaching, there is a link between salvation from sins and the presence of the kingdom.

The New Testament testifies of neither a complete absence nor of a transitional establishment of the kingdom of God. Instead, it bears witness to a robust and powerful spiritual kingdom, with the disciples of Christ inhabiting heavenly places with the King who is reigning on God's "holy hill of Zion" (an expression that typifies the rule of the Messiah over God's people, Psa. 2:6-7; Heb. 12:22; Eph. 1:3; 2:4-6).

Jesus now reigns at the right hand of God as King of His kingdom, the head of His church (Dan. 7:13-14; Acts 2:32-36; Eph. 1:20-23). Christians share in kingdom blessings now, while anticipating the reward of eternal life in the eternal kingdom (Eph. 1:3; Phil. 3:20; Rev. 1:9; 2 Pet. 1:10-11).

"When Will These Things Be?" : Questions on Eschatology

Old Testament Kingdom Prophecies and Their New Testament Fulfillment

The New Testament repeatedly announces the fulfillment of the Old Testament kingdom prophecies. Consider the following kingdom prophecies and their New Testament fulfillment.

1. *2 Samuel 7:11-17: A promised son would be King over God's house.* The king demanded by Israel in the days of Samuel was not the intent and will of God. Israel was rejecting God as their king (1 Sam. 8:4-22). In David, God chose a man after His own heart to be king and commander over His people (1 Sam. 13:14; Acts 13:22).

When King David's rule was secure, he planned to build a house for the ark of God (2 Sam. 7:1-3). God sent the prophet Nathan to David with the message that his son, not David, would build God's house. Instead, God promised to establish David's house (i.e., rule; cf. 2 Sam. 7:11). God's prophet explained:

> When your days are fulfilled and you rest with your fathers, I will set up your seed after you, who will come from your body, and I will establish his kingdom. He shall build a house for My name, and I will establish the throne of his kingdom forever. I will be his Father, and he shall be My son. If he commits iniquity, I will chasten him with the rod of men and with the blows of the sons of men (2 Sam. 7:12-14).

Solomon, David's son, was chosen by God to sit on the Lord's throne over Israel and to build His house in Jerusalem. If Solomon would steadfastly observe God's commands, God would establish his kingdom as promised (2 Chron. 28:5-7; 1 Kings 8:12-21). Yet, God had much greater plans for His King, His kingdom, and His people than building a house made with human hands (1 Kings 8:27; Psa. 103:19; Acts 7:47-50).

The angel Gabriel saw in Mary's Son, Jesus, the fulfillment of God's promise to David: "He will be great, and will be called the Son of the Highest; and the Lord God will give Him the throne of His father David. And He will reign over the house of Jacob forever, and of His kingdom there will be no end" (Luke 1:32-33). Jesus is God's Son, and He is sitting on David's throne, ruling over Israel (the people of God, Gal. 6:16; Rom. 2:28-29; 9:5-6) until the end of the age.

The New Testament reveals the fulfillment of Nathan's prophesy about the son of David and Gabriel's announcement about the Son of

Has the Kingdom of Christ Been Established?

God in the resurrection, ascension, and coronation of Jesus at God's right hand (Psa. 89:3-4, 34-37; 110:1-2; Jer. 23:5-6; Rom. 1:3-4; Acts 2:30-36). On Pentecost following the ascension of Jesus, the apostle Peter noted that God "has made" (aorist, i.e., it has already occurred in time) Jesus "both Lord and Christ" at His right hand (Acts 2:36). Peter said Jesus had been King since He sat down at God's right hand. Necessarily then, His kingdom was established (and continues to exist) since that momentous event. (Jesus is not a King without a kingdom.)

Nathan's prophecy of God's promised Son and King is applied to Jesus in Hebrews 1:5 ("I will be to Him a Father, and He shall be to Me a Son") *after* He "sat down at the right hand of the Majesty on high" (Heb. 1:3-4). The kingdom was established when the King sat down on His throne at God's right hand. From that moment forward, Jesus has reigned over His kingdom. The establishment of the Son's kingdom is not set in our future when Christ returns (1 Cor. 15:23-24). Nor did the early saints live through a forty-year transitional period until the kingdom was fully established or possessed in AD 70 (Max King, 239, 154; Gibson, 10-11).

God rebuilt David's house (ruling monarchy) when Jesus built His church, composed of those who call on the name of the Lord (Amos 9:11-12; Acts 15:16-17). It is this house of God, the church of Christ, that is the kingdom of heaven (Matt. 16:18-19). Today, Jesus is the Son over the house of God, "whose house we are. . ." (Heb. 3:6).

2. *Psalm 2: God's Anointed is installed as King and announced as His Son.* This Messianic psalm is often quoted in the New Testament, where its content is applied to Jesus in Acts 4:25-28; 13:32-33; Hebrews 1:5; 5:5; and Revelation 2:26-27; 12:5; 19:15-16. In this psalm, the futility of man's rebellion against the Lord and His Anointed (the Messiah, Christ) is portrayed poetically (vv. 1-3), followed by the Lord's triumphant reply (vv. 4-6). The exaltation of God's Son is inevitable, and the extent of His power is complete (vv. 7-9). Therefore, kings and judges are admonished to embrace and honor the Son to be blessed and to avoid His wrath (vv. 10-12).

This grand psalm outlines the coming of Christ to the earth and His rejection by men. Man's futile attempts to destroy God's Anointed were overwhelmed by God (Acts 4:25-28). Jesus was declared to be the Son

"When Will These Things Be?" : Questions on Eschatology

of God by His resurrection, thus fulfilling God's promise to install His Anointed King on His holy hill of Zion (Acts 13:32-33; Rom. 1:4). This picturesque view of Christ's reign is fulfilled in Jesus enthroned at God's right hand (Psa. 110:1-2; Acts 2:33-36). There, the "scepter of righteousness is the scepter of (His) kingdom" (Heb. 1:5, 8; Psa. 45:6-7; Isa. 11:1-4; Jer. 23:5-6). God's King, Jesus Christ, rules today in righteousness with all authority, putting the wicked under His wrath and blessing those who honor Him (Psa. 2:10-12).

The attempts to deny Jesus is now King reigning over His kingdom are just as futile as the attempts to prevent God from installing Christ as King. One cannot successfully recognize Jesus Christ to be the Son of God without simultaneously bowing before Him as "the blessed and only Potentate, the King of kings and Lord of lords" (1 Tim. 6:15). Denying Jesus is King over His kingdom today denies the fulfillment of the second psalm.

3. Isaiah 2: *The kingdom to be established and inhabited in the latter days.* Isaiah lifted the gaze of his prophetic eyes beyond Jerusalem's mountain to catch a glimpse of the Messiah's kingdom—Mt. Zion, the heavenly Jerusalem (Heb. 12:22). Micah joined Isaiah in describing this wondrous kingdom and its inhabitants, who would "walk in the name of the Lord our God forever and ever" (Mic. 4:1-4, 5). They wrote of the "latter days" as they looked beyond their time to a future when "the mountain of the Lord's house" would be exalted above the mountain tops. Then, "all nations" would inhabit Zion, going "up to the mountain of the Lord, to the house of the God of Jacob" (Isa. 2:2-3). At that time, the word of the Lord would go forth from Jerusalem, judging the nations and bringing peace—as "they shall beat their swords into plowshares, and their spears into pruning hooks; Nation shall not lift up sword against nation, neither shall they learn war anymore" (Isa. 2:4).

Many conclude that since this kingdom scene of world peace has not happened, surely this prophecy has not yet been fulfilled. However, this prophetic peace is available now through the Prince of peace. Paul said Jesus "is our peace," not that He "will be our peace" (Eph. 2:14-18). By him, sinners are now reconciled with God and with one another. When Jesus came preaching the kingdom, he was preaching peace to all humanity (Matt. 4:23; Eph. 2:17). The establishment and the advancement of Isaiah's prophetic kingdom are fulfilled in the preaching and planting

Has the Kingdom of Christ Been Established?

of the gospel of the kingdom into the hearts and lives of previous enemies, "thus making peace" (Isa. 2:3-4; Eph. 2:15).

The "mountain of the Lord's house" signifies the seat and power of government (Isa. 2:2; Jer. 51:25). Isaiah would also foretell of the Son upon whose shoulders the government would rest (Isa. 9:6). "Of the increase of His government and peace there will be no end, upon the throne of David and over His kingdom, to order it and establish it with judgment and justice from that time and forward, even forever. The zeal of the Lord of hosts will perform this" (Isa. 9:7). According to Isaiah, the Son is on the throne of David ruling over His kingdom when the government of God's house is on His shoulders. Authority over heaven and earth has already been given to Christ (Matt. 28:18). The government is now on His shoulders. Therefore, Jesus is now on His throne, ruling God's house.

Zechariah confirmed the same in predicting the Lord's return to Zion to dwell in Jerusalem, the "City of Truth" and the "Mountain of the Lord of hosts, the Holy Mountain" (Zech. 8:3). The King who came to Jerusalem with salvation and peace was Jesus, and He "speaks peace to the nations" (Zech. 9:9-10; Eph. 2:14-22). This peace is in Christ now, not in a future, idyll kingdom on earth.

Isaiah said his prophecy concerning the kingdom would "come to pass in the latter days" (Isa. 2:2). That is, days that followed, a latter time in contrast to the former (Deut. 4:30). Isaiah's "latter days" corresponds to "these last times" when Christ was revealed to redeem the world (1 Pet. 1:20). Isaiah's "latter days" are "these last days" in which God speaks to us "by His Son" and in which the Hebrews writer lived (Heb. 1:1-2). Peter's use of Joel 2:28 confirms the prophetic "latter days" as the days of the gospel age (Acts 2:16-17). Furthermore, Jesus said the spread of the gospel from Jerusalem is the fulfillment of Isaiah, Micah, and the other Old Testament prophets who wrote of Him and His kingdom (Luke 24:44-47; Acts 1:3, 8).

Consider this summary as we close our comments on Isaiah 2: "Isaiah is often called the Messianic prophet. Isaiah not only foretold the death of Christ in chapter 53, but he also foreshadowed the establishment of the church (Isa. 2:1-4). Isaiah prophesied that the church would be established in the last dispensation of time, the Messianic or Christian

"When Will These Things Be?" : Questions on Eschatology

age (v. 2; Heb. 1:1-2; Acts 2:16-17). He prophesied that the church would have its beginning in Jerusalem or Zion (v. 3; Luke 24:46-47; Acts 2:1-4). All nations and peoples would have access to the Lord's house, thus foreshadowing the universal scope of the gospel's call (v. 2-3; Mark 16:15-16; Col. 1:23). The church would be judged and governed by Christ (v. 4; Matt. 28:18; John 12:48). Finally, Isaiah prophesied that this would be a peaceful and prosperous kingdom (v. 4; Matt. 5:9; Rom. 8:6)" (Mayberry).

4. *Joel 2: A kingdom in which spiritual blessings abound.* Joel lifted Israel's hope of receiving abundant spiritual blessings from the Spirit of God. These blessings would be universal ("all flesh") and not for Israel only. The central message of Joel's prophecy in Joel 2:28-32 is the blessed salvation made possible by the work of the Spirit. The Holy Spirit would reveal the mind of God (2:28-29; John 16:8-13). The Spirit's revelation would be confirmed in God's decisive judgment against Jerusalem ("the great and awesome day of the Lord," 2:30-31; cf. Matt. 24:3-34, esp. v. 29). By His Spirit, God would announce salvation (deliverance from condemnation) to be given to "whoever calls on the name of the Lord" (2:32). These universal spiritual blessings of salvation would be obtained "in Mount Zion and in Jerusalem" (2:32).

After His resurrection, Jesus spoke to His apostles about the kingdom of God (Acts 1:3). In the course of these instructions, He commanded them to wait in Jerusalem for the Father's promise of Holy Spirit baptism, which they would soon receive (Acts 1:4-5). Their kingdom anticipation was evident as they asked whether this was the time the Lord would restore the kingdom to Israel (Acts 1:6-7). While assuring them the Father would attend to the timing of that event, Jesus reiterated the power they would receive and the work they would do when the Holy Spirit came upon them. They would be His witnesses by preaching the gospel to the world (Acts 1:8; Mark 16:15-20).

We cannot miss a significant point concerning the kingdom in Acts 1:3-8. The presence of the Spirit, His blessings, and His work testify to the establishment of the kingdom of God. Without His work, the kingdom is not present. Yet, through His work, the kingdom exists. The kingdom came into existence when the Holy Spirit was poured out.

Has the Kingdom of Christ Been Established?

The day of Pentecost soon arrived, and the Holy Spirit came upon the apostles with great power (Acts 2:1-4). They miraculously spoke in foreign languages as they preached the gospel of Christ to Jews "from every nation under heaven" (Acts 2:5-13). While some who heard them mockingly said they were drunk, Peter explained, "This is what was spoken by the prophet Joel," and then quoted Joel 2:28-32 (Acts 2:14-16, 17-21). This event was fulfilling Joel's prophecy, as the Spirit began to be poured out on all flesh (Jews and Gentiles). The gospel was preached through the Spirit and brought salvation to all who call on the name of the Lord—beginning in Jerusalem (Acts 2:21; 1:8). That gospel proclaims the King is seated at God's right hand, and that in His kingdom salvation, the remission of sins, is obtained (Acts 2:32-37, 38-41, 47).

The Spirit would continue to spread universal blessings of salvation as he came upon Cornelius and his household to bear witness that Gentiles, as well as Jews, are saved by faith (Acts 10:44-48; 11:15-18; 15:7-11). As Isaiah said, the nations began flowing to Mount Zion (i.e., the mountain of the Lord) for salvation. The kingdom had come, and salvation was being offered to all. It is still being offered. Since the day of Pentecost (Acts 2), the Lord has been adding the saved to His church (Acts 2:47). Since the day of Pentecost (Acts 2), God has delivered sinners "out of the kingdom of darkness and conveyed us into the kingdom of the Son of His love" (Col. 1:13). Joel's prophecy of kingdom blessings is fulfilled in Christ and His church. The kingdom has been established. Salvation in the kingdom continues to be preached to the world. Kingdom salvation is received by all who call on the name of the Lord.

5. *Daniel 2: When God's kingdom would be established, and its superiority over the kingdoms of men.* Daniel interpreted King Nebuchadnezzar's dream of a great image made of gold, silver, bronze, iron, and clay being overwhelmed by a stone that filled the earth (Dan. 2:32-35). The events of this dream told of "what will happen in the latter days" (Dan. 2:28). Daniel's explanation identified the "latter days" when God would set up His kingdom.

Daniel explained the image depicted four kingdoms, with Nebuchadnezzar and his kingdom of Babylon as the head of gold (Dan. 2:36-38). Babylon was defeated by the Medes and Persians (the chest and arms of silver), who were in turn conquered by Greece (the belly and thighs of bronze) under Alexander the Great (Dan. 2:39). The Roman Empire

"When Will These Things Be?" : Questions on Eschatology

was the fourth kingdom (the legs of iron and feet mingled with iron and clay). It existed from about 60 BC to the fifth century AD. Rome's dominion was powerful (typified by the image's legs of iron), vast, and diverse (typified by feet of iron and clay). Its diversity of peoples and cultures eventually contributed to its demise (Dan. 2:40-43).

Nebuchadnezzar also saw a stone that did not originate with man, but was "cut out without hands," 2:34). That stone struck the feet of the great image, completely obliterating it (i.e., the kingdoms the image represented). In turn, the stone became a great mountain that filled the whole earth (Dan. 2:34-35). The interpretation is certain and sure: God would set up His kingdom during the reign of the kings of Rome (the fourth world kingdom). God's kingdom would be more powerful and more enduring than the kingdoms of men (Dan. 2:44-45).

Daniel foresaw the establishment of the kingdom, the church. During the Roman kings, God sent His Son into the world to be a King (Luke 2:1-7; 3:1-3; Gal. 4:4; John 18:37). People had been anxiously looking for the kingdom since the days of John (Luke 16:16). As Jesus preached the gospel of the kingdom, He was saying, "The time is fulfilled, and the kingdom of God is at hand. Repent, and believe in the gospel" (Mark 1:14-15). The time had arrived for God to set up His kingdom.

Daniel prophesied when the kingdom would be established: "In the days of these kings" (of the fourth kingdom). Daniel prophesied what God would do: "The God of heaven will set up a kingdom." Daniel prophesied the power of the kingdom: "It shall break in pieces and consume all these kingdoms." Daniel prophesied the nature of the kingdom: It is eternal. "It shall stand forever" (Dan. 2:44).

The kingdom of God is of divine origin. It was set up by God during the Roman Empire, and like a great mountain, it fills the earth. Its preeminence, its power, and its prominence are proclaimed and sustained by God and the King He has installed, Jesus the Christ (Col. 1:13-14, 18).

Many other Old Testament prophecies speak of a coming King and His kingdom, and they are all fulfilled in Jesus (Luke 24:44-48; Acts 3:24-26). The prophecies concerning Christ and His kingdom are linked inseparably to the gospel and the salvation of those who compose the

Has the Kingdom of Christ Been Established?

Lord's church. Here are additional prophecies of the King ruling in His kingdom with their New Testament fulfillment:

a. **Psalm 110**: The announcement of the Messiah's reign and His installment as King. (See its fulfillment in Matt. 21:41-45; Acts 2:34-36; Heb. 5:4-6; 6:20; 7:17-21).

b. **Isaiah 9:6-7**: A Son who is the Prince of Peace and rules on the throne of David over His kingdom. (See its fulfillment in Gal. 4:4; Matt. 16:13-19; 28:18; Acts 2:30-36; 5:30-31).

c. **Isaiah 11**: The king's righteous rule of peace. (See its fulfillment in Eph. 2:13-22; Rom. 15:8-13).

d. **Daniel 7:13-14**: The coronation of the king. (See its fulfillment in Eph. 1:20-23; Acts 2:33).

e. **Zechariah 6:12-13**: The Branch, who would build God's temple and be a priest on his throne. (See its fulfillment in Matt. 16:18; Eph. 2:19-22; 1 Tim. 6:15; Heb. 1:3-4; 8:2).

f. **Zechariah 9:9-10**: The lowly king arrives with salvation and a message of peace to the nations. (See its fulfillment in Matt. 21:1-11).

To deny the kingdom's existence today is to deny the power of God, the purposes of God, and the fulfilled prophecies of the word of God. To deny the kingdom is an established and present reality is to deny Jesus is the King of His kingdom and the head of His church (Acts 2:33-36; Eph. 1:20-23). To reject the kingdom's existence is to reject salvation and the spiritual blessings obtained by its citizens (Psa. 110:3; Col. 1:13-14; Phil. 3:20).

Yes, the kingdom has been established.

Jesus Announced the Approach of the Kingdom

Jesus "witnessed the good confession before Pontius Pilate" when the Roman governor asked him, "'Are You a king then?' Jesus answered, 'You say rightly that I am a king. For this cause I was born, and for this cause I have come into the world, that I should bear witness to the truth. Everyone who is of the truth hears My voice'" (John 18:37). Jesus was born into the world to be a King. During His earthly ministry, He testified of His authority as King and of the approach of His kingdom. Christ identified His kingdom as His church. The following Scriptural evidence

"When Will These Things Be?" : Questions on Eschatology

compels the conclusion of faith that Jesus is now King ruling His kingdom. His birth into this world to be a king has been accomplished. His kingdom has been established.

Jesus said the time for the kingdom was approaching. The time for the kingdom's arrival was near when Jesus began His earthly ministry. As He preached the gospel of the kingdom of God in Galilee, He said, "The time is fulfilled, and the kingdom of God is at hand. Repent, and believe in the gospel" (Mark 1:14-15). The time was right to establish the kingdom. The kingdom was "at hand" ("to make near, approach" [Strong, G1448]). Jesus used the nearness of the kingdom as an incentive to repent and to be prepared for its arrival. If the kingdom was not near, the incentive He used is disingenuous and deceptive. We choose to believe it was just as Jesus said, namely, the kingdom was ready to be set in place.

If the kingdom was postponed as premillennialism teaches, then how was Jesus so mistaken? How can we possibly put confidence in anything Jesus said if what He taught about the nearness of the kingdom was so wrong? In truth, it is the unscriptural notion that God substituted the church for the kingdom due to Israel's rejection of Jesus that is so wrong. This error assails the credibility of Jesus Christ, who is "the Truth" (John 14:6).

Jesus said people had been approaching the kingdom since the days of John. "The law and the prophets were until John. Since that time the kingdom of God has been preached, and everyone is pressing into it" (Luke 16:16). John's message and baptism of repentance prepared the way for the Messiah's arrival (Luke 3:3-6). Just as rocks were removed from a roadway to make the passage of the king smooth and unimpeded, John's call to repent and be baptized for the remission of sins removed the obstacles of sin from the hearts of people to prepare them for the Messiah's arrival. People were becoming increasingly disposed to repent and reform their lives as they anticipated the approaching King and His kingdom.

Jesus taught people to pray, "Your kingdom come" (Matt. 6:10). He told one man, "You are not far from the kingdom of God" (Mark 12:34). To others, he said, "Do not fear, little flock, for it is your Father's good pleasure to give you the kingdom" (Luke 12:32). Was all the preparation and anticipation of the kingdom in vain? Did God direct John and Jesus to stir up the people about a coming kingdom, knowing He would delay

Has the Kingdom of Christ Been Established?

its full establishment, as the AD 70 doctrine opines? Or, as premillennialism teaches, did God withdraw the kingdom promise all together? These doctrines indict God and His Christ of misleading and deceiving the people.

On the contrary, John's preaching prepared hearts for the Messiah and His kingdom, which was near. Jesus, the Messiah, explained kingdom citizenship to hearts ready and willing to receive its gospel (Matt. 4:23; 5:1-7:29; 13:18-23). The kingdom was about to arrive.

Jesus said the presence of the Spirit of God showed the kingdom's approach. The miracles of Jesus demonstrated the presence of God's power over Satan and testified that "the kingdom of God has come upon you" (Matt. 12:28; Luke 11:20). Just as Isaiah and Joel linked the Spirit of God with the King and His kingdom, Jesus identified Himself as the King coming with His kingdom (Isa. 42:1-4; 61:1-3; Luke 4:18-21; Joel 2:28-32; Acts 2:16-17).

Jesus identified His church as the kingdom of heaven. Jesus assured Peter and the other apostles that the strength of death ("the gates of hades") would not prevent Him from establishing His church. He would do so upon the solid foundation that He is "the Christ, the Son of the living God" (Matt. 16:16-18; 1 Cor. 3:11). The resurrection of Jesus Christ confirmed Him as the Son of God and enabled Him to sit on David's throne and rule the kingdom of God (Psa. 16:8-11; Acts 2:24-36; Rom. 1:4).

It is not coincidental that Jesus used "kingdom" as a synonym for "church" in Matthew 16:18-19, ". . . on this rock, I will build My church, and the gates of hades shall not prevail against it. And I will give you the keys of the kingdom of heaven, and whatever you bind on earth will be bound in heaven, and whatever you loose on earth will be loosed in heaven." When the apostles preached the gospel on Pentecost, access to the kingdom was given to all who believed it, repented, and were baptized in the name of Jesus Christ (Acts 2:36-41, 47). The kingdom came into existence that day. Those whom Jesus saved from their sins did not enter a non-existent kingdom. The Lord added souls to His church as they were being saved (Acts 2:47). They were transferred into the kingdom of the Son as they were being redeemed (Col. 1:13-14). The church and the kingdom are two descriptions of saved souls. The church is composed of those called out of sin by the gospel, the assembly of the saved (Heb. 12:23).

"When Will These Things Be?" : Questions on Eschatology

The kingdom is composed of the same people, redeemed, and counted as citizens of heaven (Col. 1:13-14; Phil. 3:20). Doctrines that separate the kingdom and the church and identify them as separate groups of saints—whether by forty years (as per the AD 70 doctrine) or by thousands of years (as per premillennial teaching)—pervert the gospel of Christ (Gal. 1:6-9).

Premillennialism attempts to make a distinction between the kingdom of God and the kingdom of heaven (Johnson). However, no such difference exists in the Scriptures. The kingdom is called "the kingdom of heaven" because it belongs to heaven. Its source, its nature, and its citizenship are heavenly. It is a heavenly kingdom that is not of this world (John 18:36; Phil. 3:20). The kingdom is called the "kingdom of God" because it belongs to God, not men. The kingdom is of divine origin and is not the work of human wisdom and human hands (Dan. 2:34, 45). Jesus used the "kingdom of heaven" and the "kingdom of God" interchangeably, as seen in the parallel passages of Matthew 13:11 with Mark 4:11, and Matthew 13:31-32 with Mark 4:30-31. Premillennialism makes a distinction between the kingdom and the church without a difference to prop up its faulty interpretation of prophecy.

The kingdom of prophecy is the church of Christ. Therefore, when Christ established His church, His kingdom was necessarily established (Acts 2:41, 47; Col. 1:13).

Jesus said the kingdom would come with power during the lives of those who heard Him teach. Jesus taught the people and His disciples that some of them would not die until they saw the kingdom present with power. "And He said to them, 'Assuredly, I say to you that there are some standing here who will not taste death till they see the kingdom of God present with power'" (Mark 9:1). They would witness the powerful reality and presence of the kingdom. Simply put, the kingdom would come in their lifetime.

The kingdom came with power on Pentecost when the apostles were baptized with the Holy Spirit. Jesus spoke to His apostles during the forty days between His resurrection and ascension about "the things concerning the kingdom of God" (Acts 1:3). Before His ascension, Jesus told them to remain in Jerusalem to be "endued with power from on high" in fulfillment of the Father's promise to send them the Holy Spirit (Luke

Has the Kingdom of Christ Been Established?

24:48-49). They questioned Jesus whether "not many days from now" (when they would be baptized with the Holy Spirit) was when He would "restore the kingdom to Israel" (Acts 1:4-6). Jesus said that information and action were under the sovereign will of the Father. It was enough for them to know they would "receive power when the Holy Spirit" came upon them, thus enabling them to be His witnesses to the world (Acts 1:7-8; John 14:26; 15:26-27; 16:8-13).

The apostles received power from heaven when they were baptized with the Holy Spirit just ten days later on the day of Pentecost, (Acts 2:1-4). On that day, the apostles preached Jesus Christ is at God's right hand, sitting on the throne of David and ruling by the might of His power (Acts 2:30-36; Psa. 110:1-2). On Pentecost, Christ's power over sin was announced and applied as sinners believed, repented, and were baptized for the remission of sins (Acts 2:37-41). On Pentecost, sinners were delivered "from the power of darkness and conveyed into the kingdom of the Son" (Col. 1:13). On Pentecost, the kingdom came with power from heaven as the Holy Spirit baptized the apostles of Christ, empowering them to preach the gospel. The heavenly power they received revealed the gospel, inspired its preaching, and miraculously certified its content (Acts 2:1-7, 14-22; Gal. 1:11). On Pentecost, heavenly power established the Messiah's kingdom, His church (Acts 2:39-41). From Pentecost onward, the Lord continues to add every saved soul to the church (i.e., the kingdom, Acts 2:47; Heb. 12:28).

Jesus is a false prophet if the establishment of the promised kingdom is postponed to a time beyond the death of Jesus's contemporaries (Deut. 18:20; Mark 9:1). This consequence must be faced by doctrines that deny the kingdom's arrival (premillennialism), or that describe the kingdom's appearance as a gradual transition out of the seedbed of Judaism (as per the AD 70 doctrine).

Jesus preached the imminent arrival of the kingdom of God. At no time did Jesus retract His announcement of its coming. At no time did He make disclaimers to change the time of the kingdom's arrival. What Jesus predicted concerning the power and presence of the kingdom was fulfilled on Pentecost and recorded in Acts 2. At the right hand of God, Jesus, the seed of David, now reigns on David's throne in fulfillment of the Davidic promise (Pss. 89:26-27; 132:11-18). From Pentecost onward, His subjects offer themselves to Him willingly (Acts 2:40-41; Psa. 110:3).

"When Will These Things Be?" : Questions on Eschatology

The kingdom Jesus predicted exists today. It is His church, the kingdom of heaven (Matt. 16:18-19). Yes, the kingdom has been established.

Jesus Announced the Nature of the Kingdom

The Old Testament prophets anticipated a kingdom of righteousness, mercy, peace, and the fullness of blessings from the Lord God. When questioned by Pilate, Jesus told the governor he was born to be a King, but that His kingdom "is not of this world" (John 18:36-37). The church Jesus established is the kingdom of prophecy. In every way, His kingdom is not of this world.

The kingdom of Christ is not militaristic. Military conquest did not establish it. Neither is it defended by military power. Earlier in His Galilean ministry, "when Jesus perceived that they were about to come and take Him by force to make Him king, He departed again to the mountain by Himself alone" (John 6:15). The Messiah's kingdom would not appear through military triumph over occupying rulers, but by conquering hearts ruled by sin. Indeed, "the kingdom of God is within you" (Luke 17:20-21; Rom. 6:17-18).

The kingdom of Christ is not political and nationalistic. His kingdom is not of the same sort as Caesar's realm. Give Caesar his taxes and give Christ your heart and life (Matt. 22:15-22). One can submit "to every ordinance of man for the Lord's sake" while fearing God and keeping His commands as a citizen of the kingdom of heaven because Christ's kingdom is a spiritual realm that is not of this world (1 Pet. 2:13-17).

The kingdom of Christ is not tribal. One's race and ethnic origin do not determine citizenship in God's kingdom (Rom. 2:28-29; 9:6-8). The church is "the Israel of God," not the nation of Israel in the Middle East. In Christ, there is "neither Jew nor Greek, there is neither slave nor free, there is neither male nor female; for you are all one in Christ Jesus" (Gal. 3:28; Col. 3:11).

Physical borders do not identify the kingdom of Christ. Lines on a map do not designate the limits of Christ's reign since heaven and earth are under His power (Matt. 28:18). Christians compose His kingdom and submit willingly to His rule regardless of where they live on this planet.

The kingdom of Christ endures while the kingdoms of men fall. The kingdom of God outlasts the kingdoms of men because its nature is spiri-

Has the Kingdom of Christ Been Established?

tual, not earthly, and eternal, not temporal (1 Cor. 15:23-24; 2 Pet. 1:10-11; Matt. 25:34-40). The kingdom has existed from Pentecost onward, much more than the one thousand years promoted by premillennial error. Indeed, the kingdom of God "shall stand forever," undefeated by the powers of sin and death (Dan. 2:44).

Yes, the kingdom has been established.

Christians Currently Participate in the Kingdom

The New Testament shows first-century Christians were full participants in the kingdom. Therefore, we conclude that Christ established His kingdom in their day and that it continues to exist today (Dan. 2:44).

Salvation from sins is in the kingdom of God. The presence of gospel salvation and the existence of the kingdom are inseparable. Acts 28:28-31 makes this clear. There, preaching "the salvation of God" (v. 28) to the Gentiles is equivalent to "preaching the kingdom of God and teaching the things which concern the Lord Jesus Christ" (v. 31). Like Philip before him, when preaching salvation to the lost, Paul proclaimed "the things concerning the kingdom of God" (Acts 8:12).

The Redeemer who saves us is also the King into whose kingdom the Father transfers us when He redeems us through the blood of Christ (Col. 1:13-14). Jesus said it was the Father's "good pleasure to give you the kingdom" (Luke 12:32). That is precisely what the Father does since the kingdom exists (Heb. 12:28).

Christians are priests in the kingdom of God. Without dispute, Christians are "living stones" who form a "spiritual house, a holy priesthood, to offer up spiritual sacrifices acceptable to God through Jesus Christ" (1 Pet. 2:5). The church is a "royal priesthood" (1 Pet. 2:9). "Royal" translates the Greek word *basileion*, meaning "kingly (in nature)" (Strong, G934). This word refers to a king's court in Luke 7:25. As Herbst notes, its use echoes Exodus 19:6 ("And you shall be to Me a kingdom of priests and a holy nation"), and "describes something as relating to a king or belonging to a king" (Herbst). Hence, the church is a royal realm (kingdom) of priests that belongs to the King. If the kingdom does not exist, neither does the "royal" priesthood. Yet, because Christ established His church (i.e., His kingdom), John could say Jesus Christ "has made us kings and priests to His God and Father" (Rev. 1:5-6). Heavenly praise is sung to the Lamb of God because He "made them a kingdom and priests

"When Will These Things Be?" : Questions on Eschatology

to our God, and they shall reign on the earth" (Rev. 5:10, ESV). Today, Christians reign triumphantly over sin and death in Christ's kingdom, serving as priests in His house, the church. "If we endure, we shall also reign with Him" in the eternal kingdom (2 Tim. 2:12; 2 Pet. 1:10-11).

In the first century, the apostles and Christians were co-participants in the kingdom. The apostle John wrote, "I, John, both your brother and companion in the tribulation and kingdom and patience of Jesus Christ, was on the island that is called Patmos for the word of God and for the testimony of Jesus Christ" (Rev. 1:9). "Companion" translates *synkoinonos*, i.e., "one who participates with another in some enterprise or matter of joint concern—'partner, associate, one who joins in with'" (Louw-Nida, 34.6). Their footnote cites the emphatic use of the word as focusing "upon the joint nature of participation" (ibid). Simply put, the apostle John participated in the kingdom with other Christians. Their participation as companions in the kingdom would be impossible if the kingdom did not exist when he wrote the Revelation. The truth is, the kingdom existed then (and now), and we continue to be companions who participate in the kingdom as we serve our King, Jesus Christ.

Christians eat the Lord's Supper in the kingdom. Jesus placed His supper in the kingdom by saying, "But I say to you, I will not drink of this fruit of the vine from now on until that day when I drink it new with you in My Father's kingdom" (Matt. 26:29). Christians have communion with Christ by eating the Lord's Supper, and this occurs in the kingdom (1 Cor. 10:16-17).

Christians regularly ate the Lord's Supper beginning in Acts 2:42. This fact leads to the inescapable conclusion that the kingdom existed at the same time. That means Jesus participated in the supper with His disciples (Matt. 26:29). The practice of the Lord's Supper in the early church is a problem for those who believe the kingdom does not yet exist. Without the kingdom, there is no communion with Jesus in the Lord's Supper. Yet, since the Lord's Supper was present in the early church, the kingdom was necessarily present. If the kingdom does not exist yet, then why do premillennialists eat the Lord's Supper outside of the kingdom? If the kingdom does not exist, Jesus does not commune with His disciples in it. The fact that Christians have eaten this memorial supper from Pentecost to this moment affirms the kingdom's existence from the first century onward.

Has the Kingdom of Christ Been Established?

The Lord's Supper in the early church is also a problem for those who believe the kingdom gradually developed until being completely established in AD 70. If the kingdom did not altogether exist until AD 70, then there was no complete communion with Christ in the supper from AD 30-70. Yet, Christians came together on the first day of the week to break bread long before AD 70 (Acts 2:42; 20:7). By doing so, Christ had complete fellowship with them when they communed with His blood and body (1 Cor. 10:16-17). The fact that the Lord's Supper was eaten for forty years before AD 70 proves the kingdom also existed during that time. Ever since then, Christ communes with His disciples in the kingdom when they eat His supper.

Christians are citizens of the heavenly kingdom and live according to the gospel of the kingdom. The Sermon on the Mount teaches how to be citizens of the kingdom that now exists (Matt. 5-7). The teachings of this sermon find application today as they describe the lives of Christians, whose "citizenship is in heaven" (Phil. 3:20). Jesus preached the gospel of the kingdom, teaching His disciples how to live in the kingdom now, not in a future paradisiacal kingdom on earth (Matt. 4:23; 5:1-12; 13-16; 6:24-34; 7:24-29). Christians are not kingdom citizens in prospect. Christians are citizens of the kingdom that has existed since Christ's exaltation at the right hand of God (Acts 2:32-36).

Sinners "see the kingdom of God" by being born again (John 3:3). "See" is translated from *eidon*, which means "to *know*:—be aware, behold... perceive... understand" (Strong, G1492). Jesus went on to explain that "unless one is born of water and the Spirit, he cannot enter the kingdom of God" (John 3:5). The point of salvation is when sinners gain entrance into the kingdom, further confirming that the kingdom has been established and presently exists. That salvation is the entry point into the kingdom harmonizes with being conveyed into the kingdom of the Son when sins are forgiven (Col. 1:13-14). Those who are born again enter the kingdom of Christ, His church (1 Pet. 1:22-23; Acts 2:47).

If Christ did not establish the kingdom of God, then no one can be born again—"see" and "enter" the kingdom—until he does. The fact that sinners are born again proves the kingdom is seen and entered. It has been established.

"When Will These Things Be?" : Questions on Eschatology

Christians compose the kingdom Christ will deliver to God the Father on the day He returns and raises the dead. Christ foretold that "all who are in the graves will hear His voice and come forth—those who have done good, to the resurrection of life, and those who have done evil, to the resurrection of condemnation" (John 5:28-29). Jesus was not describing a multi-phased resurrection of the righteous and the wicked (demanded by premillennialism and its 1,000-year earthly kingdom prediction).

When Christ returns, the resurrection of the dead will be bodily ("in the graves"), it will be at the same time ("the hour," the "last day," John 6:39-40, 54), and it will be general ("all"). When Christ comes and raises the dead, "Then comes the end, when He delivers the kingdom to God the Father when He puts an end to all rule and all authority and power. For He must reign till He has put all enemies under His feet. The last enemy that will be destroyed is death" (1 Cor. 15:24-26).

Death will be abolished when Christ comes and raises the dead. Then, He will deliver the kingdom to the Father. This demands the kingdom already exists when Christ returns. He is not coming to establish the kingdom but to give it to the Father. "Delivers" in 1 Corinthians 15:24 means "to surrender, i.e., yield up, interest, transmit" (Strong, G3860). It means to "hand over, give (over), deliver, entrust" (BDAG, 761). Instead of establishing the kingdom when He returns, Christ will entrust the kingdom (over which He presently reigns) to the Father for its eternal care and preservation (1 Cor. 15:27-28; Acts 2:3-36; Eph. 1:22-23).

Christians compose the kingdom. We are citizens of the kingdom. We participate in the kingdom, and we have fellowship with Jesus in the kingdom. The inescapable conclusion to draw from Scripture is the kingdom has been established and continues to exist. Sinners enter the kingdom when they are born again (John 3:3, 5). In the kingdom, Christians are priests who offer God spiritual sacrifices of service (1 Pet. 2:5, 9). Christians participate together in the spiritual blessings of the kingdom, including their triumph over sin and death in Christ (Rev. 1:6, 9; 5:8-10; 17:14). Christ communes with Christians in the kingdom when we eat the Lord's Supper (Matt. 26:29; 1 Cor. 10:16-17). Christ will deliver His kingdom to God the Father when He comes on the great day of resurrection and judgment (1 Cor. 15:24-26).

Yes, the kingdom has been established.

Has the Kingdom of Christ Been Established?

Gospel Preaching Is Kingdom Preaching

The gospel is God's power to save believers as it reveals how God justifies sinners by faith (Rom. 1:16-17; 3:21-26). When the apostles fulfilled their commission to preach the gospel to every creature, they announced the authority Jesus Christ possesses in heaven and on earth (Mark 16:15-16; Matt. 28:18-20). His authority is complete, which is entirely consistent with the truth that Christ is now "King of kings and Lord of lords" (1 Tim. 6:15; Rev. 17:14).

Jesus is not a figurehead king. He has the power to give life and to execute judgment (John 5:21-22). As King, Christ has "all authority" to do so. As Isaiah prophesied, so it is that the government is on His shoulders (Isa. 9:6). His authority exists now as He sits on the throne of David—not in the prospect of a future, millennial reign—but in fulfillment of God's promised King and His kingdom (Isa. 9:7).

Preaching Christ's gospel involves preaching His authority and His kingdom. "All should honor the Son just as they honor the Father. He who does not honor the Son does not honor the Father who sent Him" (John 5:23). By denying the establishment of the kingdom on Pentecost (Acts 2), one denies the full, complete, and functional authority of Christ. By doing so, one dishonors the Son and the Father, who told Jesus to "sit at My right hand, till I make Your enemies Your footstool" (Psa. 110:1; Acts 2:34-35).

Consider the link between preaching the fullness of the gospel and preaching the fullness of the kingdom.

The apostles and prophets of Christ preached the kingdom when they preached the gospel. Peter and the apostles preached the enthronement of the King on Pentecost (Acts 2:30-31, 33-36). Sitting at the right hand of God signifies the supreme place of honor and power. Inspired Scripture describes his coronation at the right hand of God in:

> . . . Which He worked in Christ when He raised Him from the dead and seated Him at His right hand in the heavenly places, far above all principality and power and might and dominion, and every name that is named, not only in this age but also in that which is to come. And He put all things under His feet, and gave Him to be head over all things to the church, which is His body, the fullness of Him who fills all in all (Eph. 1:20-23).

"When Will These Things Be?": Questions on Eschatology

As God's anointed and crowned King, Jesus now has the preeminent position of power and honor. This power includes being the head of His body, the church (which Jesus identified as the kingdom of heaven, Matt. 16:18-19). As preeminent sovereign, Christ Jesus rules the nations and His people (Psa. 110:2-3). One cannot possess and exercise sovereign rule without a realm (i.e., a kingdom) over which that authority exists and is applied. That kingdom is the church, and Jesus now reigns as King and serves as High Priest on His throne (Zech. 6:12-13; Heb. 5:5-6; 8:1).

Jesus Christ is not a King without a kingdom (which premillennialism is forced to admit if it is true). Nor was Christ given a transitional reign from AD 30-AD 70 (as realized eschatology asserts).

When Philip preached Christ to the city of Samaria, he "preached the things concerning the kingdom of God" (Acts 8:12). His preaching included "the name of Jesus Christ" (i.e., the power and authority of Christ, the King). Those who believed the gospel Philip preached were baptized. They were born again of "water and the Spirit" and entered the kingdom of God (John 3:5). By the power of the King, these Samaritans were saved and added to the church (Acts 2:47). Being born again, they entered the kingdom (John 3:5; Col. 1:13).

The enemies of the gospel knew it proclaimed Jesus is King. When Paul taught the gospel in the Thessalonian synagogue, he used the Scriptures to explain and show that Christ had to suffer and rise from the dead. Then, he testified, "This Jesus whom I preach to you is the Christ" (Acts 17:2-3).

This gospel preaching provoked the envious Jews of Thessalonica to assault Jason and other brethren, whom they brought before the rulers of the city and said, "These who have turned the world upside down have come here too. Jason has harbored them, and these are all acting contrary to the decrees of Caesar, saying there is another king—Jesus" (Acts 17:7).

These enemies of the gospel knew that preaching Jesus is the Christ meant Jesus is a King. By distorting the nature of the King and His kingdom, they falsely accused the brethren. These enemies of the cross of Christ understood Paul was setting forth Jesus as a King. (They left out the part that this King's kingdom is "not of this world," John 18:36.) Premillennial error has convinced millions that Jesus is a monarch without

Has the Kingdom of Christ Been Established?

a realm, a King without a kingdom. Yet, a King without a kingdom posed no threat to Caesar. Even Pilate acknowledged this by finding no crime in Jesus (John 18:36-38). Their distortion of the King and His kingdom was a lie, but their conclusion that Paul preached Jesus as King was accurate. Those who distort the nature of the King and His kingdom today join hands with the unbelieving, envious Jews of Thessalonica.

The apostle Paul preached the kingdom of God when he persuaded a Jewish audience about Jesus. What he preached to the Jews in Rome was what he had taught years earlier to the Thessalonian Jews:

> So when they had appointed him a day, many came to him at his lodging, to whom he explained and solemnly testified of the kingdom of God, persuading them concerning Jesus from both the Law of Moses and the Prophets, from morning till evening (Acts 28:23).

Preaching the gospel to a Jewish audience meant preaching the kingdom over which Christ rules in fulfillment of Old Testament prophecy (Psa. 2:6-7; Jer. 23:5-6). Jews and Gentiles who believe and obey the gospel are saved by Christ and enter His kingdom (John 3:5). Isaiah and Micah prophetically described people entering the kingdom as going up to the mountain of the Lord's house (Isa. 2:2-3; 35:8-10; Mic. 4:1-2). Souls persuaded and saved by the gospel of the kingdom are among those who offer themselves willingly in the day of the king's power (Acts 28:24; Isa. 2:2-3; Psa. 110:3). Paul did not preach a postponed, prospective, or transitional kingdom. Gospel preaching brings the lost into the kingdom of God today, just as it did in Rome through the preaching of Paul, the apostle (Acts 28:24).

Preaching the salvation of God is preaching the kingdom of God. Paul told the unbelieving Jews in Rome "that the salvation of God has been sent to the Gentiles, and they will hear it" (Acts 28:28). Luke records how Paul preached salvation to the Gentiles. Paul was "preaching the kingdom of God and teaching the things which concern the Lord Jesus Christ with all confidence, no one forbidding him" (Acts 28:31). If God postponed the kingdom, then salvation was also delayed. If the kingdom does not exist today, neither does salvation. If the establishment of the kingdom was transitional until AD 70, then salvation was also transitional. Yet, salvation has been fully available to the whole world since the apostles spread the gospel to the world, beginning in Jerusalem (Acts 1:8; 2:22-41). That is when the kingdom of Christ came

"When Will These Things Be?" : Questions on Eschatology

into existence. The rule and reign of Jesus Christ and His salvation has existed ever since.

New Testament writers testify to the establishment of the kingdom. From Pentecost to this moment, sinners are conveyed into the Son's kingdom when they are redeemed (Col. 1:13-14).

Jesus now rules on His throne, where the "scepter of righteousness is the scepter of Your kingdom" (Heb. 1:8-9; Psa. 45:6-7). A king wields the scepter of His kingdom (the symbol of His power or authority) because His kingdom exists. Without a kingdom, any symbol of authority becomes meaningless. If there is no present kingdom, then Jesus has no current authority. However, since Christ has "all authority," His kingdom exists, and righteousness is the standard of His rule (Isa. 11:3-5).

Christians are receiving an unshakeable kingdom through the blessed will of God (Heb. 12:28). We have "come to Mount Zion," to the "heavenly Jerusalem," and to the "general assembly and church of the firstborn who are registered in heaven" (Heb. 12:22-23). God's word removes every kingdom of men and every force that stands against His sovereign will (Heb. 12:25-27). The kingdom of God remains unshakeable and endures forever (Heb. 12:28; Dan. 2:44).

Gospel preaching demands kingdom preaching. The King is Jesus, His kingdom is the church, and His willing subjects are Christians. Whenever salvation is preached and received, the King (Christ) and His kingdom (the church) are present. That has been true since the apostles preached the gospel of the kingdom on Pentecost in Acts 2.

Yes, the kingdom has been established.

Conclusion

Has the kingdom of Christ been established? Yes, it has. The Old Testament kingdom prophecies are fulfilled in the New Testament age by Jesus Christ (Acts 3:20-26). At the right hand of God, Jesus Christ now rules His kingdom and offers His salvation to the world through His gospel. The word of the Lord has gone out from Jerusalem to the ends of the earth. The gospel continues to call the lost to come and "go to the mountain of the Lord, to the house of the God of Jacob," to learn "His ways" and to "walk in His paths" of salvation's peace and safety (Isa. 2:3-4).

Has the Kingdom of Christ Been Established?

In signaling the triumph of Christ over Satan in the great spiritual battle for the souls of men and women, John:

> Heard a loud voice saying in heaven, "Now salvation, and strength, and the kingdom of our God, and the power of His Christ have come, for the accuser of our brethren, who accused them before our God day and night, has been cast down" (Rev. 12:10).

This great scene depicts Christ's triumphant redemptive work that gives sinners victory over sin (Rev. 12:9; John 12:31-33; Heb. 2:14-15).

The voice John heard said, "Now. . . the kingdom of our God" has come. When did the kingdom come? The kingdom came when salvation, strength, and the power of Christ did. The kingdom came when the accuser (Satan) was defeated. Christ cast out Satan (with his mastery of sin and death) by His death on the cross and His resurrection from the dead (John 12:31). When victory over sin and death was declared is when the kingdom came. The day of salvation now exists (2 Cor. 6:2). We now have strength in the Lord and in the power of His might (Eph. 6:10). Even so, the kingdom of our God has now come (Mark 9:1; Col. 1:13).

The kingdom of Christ is not of this world. It is divine in its origin, heavenly in its nature, redemptive in its purpose, and superior to the kingdoms of men. Jesus is its crowned, exalted, and reigning King, and Christians are His loyal subjects. On the day of His return, Christ will deliver the kingdom to God, the Father, and the kingdom of heaven will endure eternally.

Praise be to God. Yes, His kingdom has been established.

Bibliography

Arndt, W., Danker, F. W., & Bauer, W. *A Greek-English Lexicon of the New Testament and Other Early Christian Literature*. 3rd ed. Chicago: University of Chicago Press, 2000.

Brown, F., Driver, S. R., & Briggs, C. A. *Enhanced Brown-Driver-Briggs Hebrew and English Lexicon*. Oxford: Clarendon Press, 1977.

Gibson, Marc W. "The AD 70 Doctrine Examined." *A Study of the AD 70 Doctrine: Realized Eschatology*. Mike Willis, ed., 5-24. Bowling Green, KY: Guardian of Truth Foundation, 2006.

Herbst, J. W. "Kingship." *Lexham Theological Wordbook*. D. Mangum, D. R. Brown, R. Klippenstein, and R. Hurst eds. Bellingham, WA: Lexham Press, 2014.

The Holy Bible: English Standard Version. Wheaton, IL: Crossway Bibles, 2016.

Johnson, Gaines R. "Kingdom of Heaven and Kingdom of God: The Doctrinal Differences." *The Bible, Genesis and Geology*. https://kjvbible.org/thekingdoms.html.

Louw, J. P., & Nida, E. A. *Greek-English Lexicon of The New Testament: Based on Semantic Domains* (electronic version of the 2nd ed.). New York: United Bible Societies, 1996.

King, Max R. *The Spirit of Prophecy*. Warren, OH: Parkman Road Church of Christ, 1983.

Mayberry, Mark. "Premillennialism: The Kingdom of God." *Watchman Magazine* 7.3 (June, 2004) http://www.watchmanmag.com/0706/070617.htm.

The New King James Version. Nashville: Thomas Nelson, 1982.

Pentecost, J. Dwight. *Things to Come: A Study in Biblical Eschatology*. Grand Rapids, MI: Zondervan, 1958.

Strong, James. *A Concise Dictionary of the Words in the Greek Testament and the Hebrew Bible*. Bellingham, WA: Logos Bible Software, 2009.

Thayer, James. *A Greek-English Lexicon of the New Testament*. New York: Harper and Brothers, 1889.

Does the Physical Nation of Israel Still Play a Role in God's Final Plans?

By Stephen Russell

Introduction

Premillennialism is a view that I grew up hearing preached about but rarely espoused by my friends. As I got older, I heard more of it, especially as it intertwined with politics. Now, as I survey the religious horizon, I see that it is a robust doctrine with champions from across the spectrum of liberal and conservative theologians alike.

Historically, it is not a doctrine that filled the writings of early church fathers. In fact, during a period of waning fascination with premillennialism, one proponent of the doctrine suggested that conservatives opposing it "found refuge in the ancient creeds, which for the most part say nothing about the millennium" (Walvoord[1], "The Millennial Issue").

---

[1] John Walvoord served at the president of Dallas Theological Seminary from 1952-1986. He was a prolific writer on the subject of premillennialism and a scholarly defender of the doctrine even before it gained wider popularity.

Stephen Russell is a native of Birmingham, Alabama. He began preaching in 2000, working as an intern under brother Raymond Harville at the Elgin Hills congregation in Killen, AL. Following his studies there he worked with the congregation in Pleasant Grove, AL (2001-2006), and then with the Southeast Church of Christ in Montgomery, AL (2006-2015). While in Montgomery, he studied at Troy University. Stephen currently works with the Pepper Road Church of Christ in Athens, AL, where he lives with his wife, Amy, and two daughters, Emma and Anna. He can be reached at: stephendrussell@gmail.com

"When Will These Things Be?" : Questions on Eschatology

Many premillennialists struggle to find the tiniest snippets of support from historical sources up until the late seventeenth century. Even then, they find their support more among postmillennialists than actual premillennialists. This observation is only offered to suggest that the doctrine is a relatively new concept, at least in its modern iteration. Yet, of course, if it is found in the pages of Scripture, it does not matter if the world forgot about it for a thousand years. It would still be true. We will look to God's word to establish our case.

But our task is not to take on the subject of premillennialism in its entirety. Rather we take our aim at its core. Our subject for this hour is the question of the role of the physical nation of Israel in God's ongoing plans and particularly His final plans. That such is the core of premillennialism is suggested by some of the doctrine's greatest advocates:

> The crucial issues in relation to premillennialism are two-fold: (1) Does the Abrahamic covenant promise Israel a permanent existence as a nation? If it does, then the church is not fulfilling Israel's promises, and (2) Does the Abrahamic covenant promise Israel permanent possession of the promised land? If it does, then Israel must yet come into possession of the promised land, for she has never fully possessed it in her history (Ryrie, 53-56).

> The Abrahamic covenant required that Israel continue as a nation forever in order to fulfill the everlasting covenant (Gen. 17:7) and in order to have the land as an everlasting possession (Gen. 17:8). All the facts. . . that Israel continues as a nation, is not disinherited, is not supplanted by the church, and that Israel's basic covenants are dependent upon God's faithfulness alone for fulfillment, combine to require Israel's restoration after these centuries of dispersion and chastening (Walvoord, *The Millennial Kingdom,* 184).

The doctrine of premillennialism is rooted and grounded in the question of what we make of physical Israel today. Proponents of the doctrine must stand on the notion that every promise and prophecy made concerning Israel is literal and physical and that those promises remain unfulfilled to this day. Many notions arise from this view, but it is this

---

> Unlike some of the more radical proponents of premillennialism, Walvoord offers a methodical and careful defense. While I obviously disagree with his conclusions, his writings made it easier to define the issues at hand and so I have quoted him several times throughout this manuscript.

Does the Physical Nation of Israel Still Play a Role in God's Final Plans?

view that feeds so many other consequences. Therefore, let us take aim at the question at hand and see if we can find what clarity God offers us on the subject.

"Literal" Interpretation

Do you take the Bible literally? That is the question often posed by premillennialists. It is certainly admirable when people want to take the words of Scripture "at face value." We all understand the danger of turning every passage into figurative, ambiguous generalities. Scripture indeed has concrete meaning. However, the question is not whether we take every phrase literally, rather do we take it at its meaning?

When it suits him, the premillennialist cries out that we should simply take the Bible at its word, then conveniently sidesteps when it does not suit him. John MacArthur, for example, marches through Matthew 24, pointing out how literal all the various elements are. Still, when he comes down to the simplest and most straightforward of phrases in verse 34 ("Truly I say to you, this generation will not pass away until all these things take place.²"), he dances around the obvious meaning: "But if verse 34 is to be understood with such wooden literalness, the rest of the Olivet Discourse must be spiritualized or otherwise interpreted figuratively in order to explain how Christ's prophecies could all have been fulfilled by AD 70 without His returning bodily to earth" (MacArthur, *The Second Coming*, 80). He takes the imagery and uses it to explain away the plain statements of fact. This is upside down.

Not only do we need to distinguish between the usage of literal and figurative language, but we must allow the New Testament to guide us in those distinctions. This is another point of contention with premillennialists. They believe that the Old Testament can be, indeed should be, completely interpreted without aid from the New Testament. Again, MacArthur notes:

> It is not legitimate to say that the Old Testament is this oblique, mysterious, hidden book with all kinds of things that you can't know about apart from the New Testament—that is, to give the primacy of interpretation to the New Testament. This is what Walter Kaiser—great scholar—says is having a canon within a canon, having a rule within a

---

2   All Scripture quotations taken from the *New American Standard Bible*, La Habra, CA: The Lockman Foundation, 1995. Used by permission.

"When Will These Things Be?" : Questions on Eschatology

rule. This, then, means that the Old Testament cannot be interpreted on its own; that people who are writing it and reading it can't have any idea what it is that they're writing and reading (MacArthur, "Why Every Calvinist Should Be a Premillennnialist, Part 2").

Not legitimate to say the Old Testament is mysterious?!? That is exactly what Paul says it is (Col. 1:25-27). Peter says that the ones writing were, in fact, not able to fully understand what they wrote (1 Pet. 1:10-12). Do MacArthur and other premillennialists suppose that anyone in Israel understood that the rock in the wilderness represented Christ (1 Cor. 10:1-4)? The New Testament does indeed take primacy. The Old Testament is an incomplete revelation. It is like saying the end of the book can't explain what happens in any of the previous chapters.

So we see that we have a fundamental difference in how we interpret Scripture. This is at the heart of so many doctrinal disagreements, is it not? Let us receive communication from God's word, like any other communication. It will be full of figurative and literal language, and we will have to use discernment to understand the difference just like we do in conversations with one another. And let us take the authoritative interpretation of the New Testament as the final revelation from God. It is the piece that completes the puzzle. Without it, we cannot see the full picture.

The Promises Fulfilled

We will answer our title question in three parts. To begin, we will consider the promises made to Israel. As we have already suggested, the promises to Israel and their fulfillment (or lack thereof) are at the heart of our question. These promises we are speaking of are delivered first to Abraham in Genesis 12:1-3. God goes on to reiterate and give more detail concerning these promises subsequent revelations to Abraham (Gen. 13:16; 15:5, 18; 17:4-5). Additionally, these promises were passed down to the succeeding generations, to Isaac (Gen. 26:5) and then to Jacob (Gen. 28:1-5). These promises can be briefly summed up as the three promises: land, nation, and seed.

The land promise is first described by God as "this land" when Abraham comes into the land of Canaan (Gen. 12:7). In another meeting, God defines the promise with the boundaries of the "river of Egypt" to the "river Euphrates" (Gen. 15:18). The contention of premillennialists

Does the Physical Nation of Israel Still Play a Role in God's Final Plans?

is that Israel has never enjoyed the fulfillment of this promise as they have never fully inhabited the land, nor have they ever fully driven out all other peoples and solely possessed the land. Moreover, they also hold that even if Israel had possessed the land, the promise is eternal, and so they must still possess it (cf. Gen. 17:7-8).

The second promise is that Abraham would be made into a great nation (Gen. 12:2). Of the fulfillment of this promise, there is little debate. The only question concerned here is whether or not that promise must remain true today. Of course, if one believes that the land promise must be maintained forever, then it holds that the nation which possesses the land must exist forever. However, defenders of premillennialism, in general, do not suggest that the nation promise remains unfulfilled.

Finally, there was the promise that all the nations of the earth would be blessed through Abraham's seed: "And in you, all the families of the earth will be blessed" (Gen. 12:3). Even here, we find disagreement as to the fulfillment of the promise. That Christ fulfills this promise is not denied, but *how* He fulfills it is at issue. Walvoord makes clear that Jesus only fulfills it in the same physical way that Abraham himself was a blessing to all nations:

> As a general promise it is probably intended to have a general fulfillment. Abraham himself has certainly been a blessing to all nations and has the distinction of being honored alike by Jew, Mohammedan, and Christian. The seed of Abraham or the nation of Israel itself has been a great blessing as the channel of divine revelation and the historic illustration of God's dealings with men. The seed of Abraham, the Lord Jesus Christ Himself, has also been a blessing to all nations. The blessing bestowed includes not only the salvation of many but the revelation of God, the revelation of moral law, and the many by-products of Biblical Judaism and Christianity (Walvoord, "The Millennial Issue").

Premillennialists, then, conclude that Jesus does not fulfill this specifically through redemption but through the general blessings he brought in His life as a whole. Thus, the promises to Abraham are neatly made entirely physical.

Let us take each promise in its course and note what God's word has to say about the fulfillment of them in turn.

"When Will These Things Be?" : Questions on Eschatology

The Land Promise

Obviously, the promise of land was not fulfilled in Abraham's day. Stephen makes special note of this in his address to the Jewish audience in Acts 7:5. Yet, we do have a time marker given with the land promise beginning in Genesis 15:13:

> Know for certain that your descendants will be strangers in a land that is not theirs, where they will be enslaved and oppressed four hundred years. But I will also judge the nation whom they will serve, and afterward, they will come out with many possessions. As for you, you shall go to your fathers in peace; you will be buried at a good old age. Then in the fourth generation, they will return here, for the iniquity of the Amorite is not yet complete (Gen. 15:13-16).

This does not nail down the land promise to that time, but in the context of telling Abraham that the promise will be to his descendants, God indicates the time frame that those descendants would come into the land. It would be a strange inclusion if God meant that the promise would actually be fulfilled several thousand years beyond that time.

One more time marker should be noted. Fast-forward to the time of Israel's bondage in Egypt. When God visited Moses through the burning bush, He promised to deliver the children of Israel from Egyptian bondage: "So I have come down to deliver them from the power of the Egyptians, and to bring them up from that land to a good and spacious land, to a land flowing with milk and honey, to the place of the Canaanite and the Hittite and the Amorite and the Perizzite and the Hivite and the Jebusite" (Exod. 3:8). In this reiteration of the land promise, notice the circumstances: Israel will leave Egyptian captivity and come to the land possessed by specific peoples. Are we to understand that Israel will go back into Egyptian captivity, and the peoples mentioned will somehow reappear in Canaan? Or is that part of the promise not to be fulfilled?

Let us come then to the point of inheritance of the land. That inheritance is indeed pronounced in no uncertain terms during the days of Joshua. After he led the people to invade and conquer the land, it is proclaimed that God has delivered on all that He had promised: "So the LORD gave Israel all the land which He had sworn to give to their fathers, and they possessed it and lived in it" (Josh. 21:43). Of this passage, Walvoord says it cannot be taken at face value (ironic coming from the

Does the Physical Nation of Israel Still Play a Role in God's Final Plans?

fellow telling me to take all prophecy at face value) because there are peoples listed who remain unconquered. He concludes, ". . . the statement of Joshua 21:43-45 must be understood as teaching that God on His part was faithful, but that the children of Israel did not enter into their possession" (Walvoord, "Chapter IV"). So the result is that Joshua says God was faithful in fulfilling, but premillennialists maintain their own definition of "fulfilled."

Conditional Promises

There is another point brought up by this last observation from Walvoord. He says that the problem is that God was faithful, but the people were not. This is "the rub" when it comes to an understanding of the promises to Israel. The premillennialist believes that God's promises are unconditional and will be fulfilled no matter what. In fact, MacArthur notes that this is what makes premillennialism so compatible with Calvinism.

> Now they make perfect amillennialists. That's a perfect setup for them. God doesn't choose you; you choose Him. You can choose Him and then not choose Him, and then choose Him again and then not choose Him. You make the decision and so all of the promises of God are conditional on you. Amillennialism really seems to fit them. But not us who live and breathe the rarified air of sovereign grace and election. . . It makes sense for their theology. Israel sinned, you're out. Israel sinned; the promises cancelled. Israel disobeyed the Law, you're done. Israel crucifies the Messiah, that's it. You forfeit everything and God gives it to somebody else, namely the church (MacArthur, "Why Every Calvinist Should Be a Premillennialist, Part 1").

So confident is MacArthur about this that he goes on to say in a follow-up sermon, "You will not find a statement about Israel's disobedience, apostasy, rejection of Christ, bringing about the forfeiture of their salvation and the Kingdom of Christ" (MacArthur, "Why Every Calvinist Should Be a Premillennialist, Part 2"). In Deuteronomy 30:15-20, God says they will prosper in the land if they obey, but will be destroyed if they do not. In Joshua 23:14-16, Joshua repeats the warnings and assures them that God will keep all of His promises for good and for ill. In succeeding generations, the prophets pick up these warnings again and again as they are coming true, all the way up to the destruction of Jerusalem during Jeremiah's days. Reading in Ezekiel and Jeremiah Israel's rejections of

"When Will These Things Be?" : Questions on Eschatology

God's warnings that He would cut off His people, one hears echoes of the modern premillennialists, who refuse to believe He did so. Finally, Jesus Himself speaks clearly about the rejection of Israel as a nation. "Jerusalem, Jerusalem, who kills the prophets and stones those who are sent to her! How often I wanted to gather your children together, the way a hen gathers her chicks under her wings, and you were unwilling. Behold, your house is being left to you desolate" (Matt. 23:37-38)!

The Seed Promise

We will address the nation promise more fully in another section, looking at this point in detail at the seed promise. We have frequently identified this third promise as "the spiritual promise." Perhaps, though, we should not hastily dismiss the fact that there is a physical element to God's third promise to Abraham and his descendants.

As we trace this particular promise, we find it is also reiterated to both Isaac and Jacob. Unlike the land and nation promises, the seed promise is bestowed exclusively to Jacob's son, Judah (Gen. 49:10). A later prophecy identifies David as the one through whom the promise would be fulfilled (2 Sam. 7:12-13). Hence, a descendant of David will rule as king and build a house for God. Enter Solomon.

When Solomon comes to the throne, he comes as the "prince of peace" (the literal meaning of his name). He comes as the seed of David. He sits on the throne in Jerusalem and builds the house for the name of God. When Solomon dedicates that house, he says some interesting things. In the first place, he borrows the language of 2 Samuel 7 and applies it to himself (1 Kings 8:19-20). Later, he declares that God has fulfilled all that was promised through Moses (1 Kings 8:56). Thus, we can conclude that Solomon is affirming that all of the promises to Abraham have been fulfilled.

The objection some might pose here is that the apostle Paul attests that the seed promise refers to Jesus (Gal. 3:16). Yet, consider that, while Solomon fulfilled God's promise to David in 2 Samuel 7:12-13, the ultimate fulfillment in a spiritual sense rests in Jesus. It is no contradiction to see a complete fulfillment of all the *physical* promises as the climax of Israel's history while yet expecting a future spiritual fulfillment. We often point to the seed promise as *the* spiritual promise, but both the nation and land promises include spiritual elements as well. The church

Does the Physical Nation of Israel Still Play a Role in God's Final Plans?

constitutes a spiritual nation from Abraham's seed (1 Pet. 2:9). Similarly, we look toward a land of promise. If we accept Solomon's word, Israel received a physical fulfillment of land, nation, *and* seed promises at the zenith of her existence, the point at which David's heir completed a physical house for God.

The Law Fulfilled

Another less prominent notion among premillennialists is that once Israel is restored to power, the Law of Moses will once again be the law of the land. I found little from current scholars pressing this aspect of the millennial kingdom, but it indeed remains a tenet among some. Hal Lindsey, at one time among the most famous proponents of premillennialism, wrote:

> The main points are these: first, there will be a reinstitution of the Jewish worship according to the Law of Moses with sacrifices, and oblations in the general time of Christ's return. . . We must conclude that a third Temple will be rebuilt upon its ancient site in Old Jerusalem. . . Jerusalem will be the spiritual center of the entire world and. . . all the people of the earth will come annually to worship Jesus who will rule there (Lindsey, 45, 46, 165).

Others try to build a case that the Jews remained under the Law while only Gentiles were called to Christ. In either case, we find that these notions ignore the purpose of the Law as it is explained to us in the New Testament.

Often, we spend our time in proving that the Old Testament has been "replaced" by the New Testament. We use passages like Colossians 2:14 and Hebrews 8:13 or 10:9 to show that the covenant of Moses has passed away, and the covenant of Christ is raised up in its place. Though there is no doubt on this point, it does not give us the complete picture nor the best answer to what premillennialists are teaching.

It is not that the Old Law has merely passed away; it has actually been *fulfilled*. Jesus emphasizes this point in answer to the supposed charge that He had disregarded the Law (Matt. 5:17). How did He fulfill the Law? He fulfilled it in every way imaginable.

Consider the book of Leviticus, for example. It begins with descriptions of sacrifices. They are made for atonement, thanksgiving, petition, communion, and more. Christ has fulfilled the purposes of all of those

"When Will These Things Be?" : Questions on Eschatology

sacrifices in His one sacrifice (Heb. 10:10). Imagine all the effort that went into the various sacrifices offered from the time of Leviticus until Jesus. Now He comes and does not just set those sacrifices aside, He provides for every advantage of those sacrifices but even more overwhelmingly. Those sacrifices were place holders for the one true sacrifice.

Next, Leviticus tells us about the priesthood. Christ comes not merely setting aside the priesthood but fulfilling it by becoming the perfect High Priest (Heb. 7:26-28). We are now all priests under that high priesthood (Rev. 1:6). Again, the priesthood under Moses pointed to a greater priesthood under Christ.

Leviticus goes on to define holiness. It does so by pointing to physical uncleanness to illustrate spiritual uncleanness and then by pointing to actual moral impurity. Christ demonstrates the beauty of holiness when He comes and lives a pure and sinless life. The physical illustrations of the Law of Moses, when used as pictures in teaching children, illuminate greater truths. The greater truth of holy living remains, and the schoolhouse illustrations fall away (Gal. 3:24-25).

Finally, Leviticus points to our relationship with our fellow man: "You shall love your neighbor as yourself; I am the LORD" (Lev. 19:18). Consider Romans 12. After Paul has made his case against the physical nation of Israel (we will address this later), he comes at last to some application. In verse 1, he tells them to offer sacrifice so that they would be acceptable (note the similar language in Lev. 1:4). Then in verse 2, Paul calls them to holiness or separateness from the world (the pattern of Leviticus). Then he goes into the particular point that so many Jews struggled with—the love of one's neighbor. Perhaps you think this is not a tight connection, but if you follow all the way into Romans 13, you see that Paul quotes the Law, disclosing that the summation of all is "you shall love your neighbor as yourself" (Rom. 13:9). Further still, "love fulfills the Law" (Rom. 13:10).

To the Jews, who adamantly maintained that they would follow the Law no matter what, Jesus explained that if they listened to Moses, they would follow Him (John 5:45-46). Paul's instructions to the Christians in Rome did not differ from what the Law required; instead, he demanded that they follow the Law to its conclusion, that is, to Christ.

Does the Physical Nation of Israel Still Play a Role in God's Final Plans?

Why would someone follow the Law to where it leads, its culmination, only to go back to the beginning? When you have the real thing, why settle for the place holder? Don't give me the shadow; I want the substance.

The Nation Fulfilled

Finally, to clarify biblical teaching on the role of the nation of Israel, we must consider the New Testament references to the nation of Israel.

By my count, the name Israel occurs seventy-five times in the New Testament. Many of these references, though not all of them, are to the literal nation of Israel. Paul leaves no question regarding what is meant by "physical Israel." Concerning his right to be called a Jew according to the flesh, he wrote, ". . . although I myself might have confidence even in the flesh. If anyone else has a mind to put confidence in the flesh, I far more: circumcised the eighth day, of the nation of Israel, of the tribe of Benjamin, a Hebrew of Hebrews; as to the Law, a Pharisee" (Phil. 3:4-5). Notice the key indicators of his citizenship as a Jew: he was born of the tribe of Benjamin, and he was circumcised on the eighth day. Of course, being a Benjamite was not required, but being of one of the twelve tribes was a necessity to be a Jew. To say it more broadly, to be considered a Jew, one had to descend from Abraham. Additionally, circumcision was a key indicator of Jewish identity.

Besides references to literal Israel, the New Testament alludes to "Israel" or to "children" of Abraham who neither descended physically from him nor had they experienced physical circumcision (Rom. 9:6-8). In Galatians 3:29, Paul describes the Christian's relationship to Abraham. Writing to Gentiles who had become Christians but were now being taught that they also needed to put on the trappings of the Law of Moses, namely circumcision, Paul clearly states that those who put on Christ are "Abraham's descendants." As he carries the argument into chapter four, he elaborates, using the story of Sarah and Hagar, and their respective sons, to illustrate his point. Allegorically, Hagar and Ishmael represent those who are of the "present Jerusalem" (physical Jerusalem), while Sarah and Isaac symbolize those of the "Jerusalem above" (spiritual Jerusalem). Ishmael's only connection to Abraham was through the flesh. Likewise, faithless Israel, who had rejected the fulfillment of the Law in Christ, had only a physical connection to Abraham. In contrast, those who put on Christ are related to Abraham through the work of God, just

"When Will These Things Be?" : Questions on Eschatology

as Isaac had come only through God's promise. Can you imagine being a Jew and hearing that the real children of Abraham are the ones who may not even be physically descended from him? What a shock! This idea is so unfathomable that some today cannot seem to grasp it. "For they are not all Israel who are *descended* from Israel" (Rom. 9:6).

Concerning circumcision, we find similar statements. Paul describes circumcision as, on the one hand, no longer carrying any great significance. "For in Christ Jesus neither circumcision nor uncircumcision means anything, but faith working through love" (Gal. 5:6). On the other hand, circumcision is redefined in distinctly spiritual terms. "For he is not a Jew who is one outwardly, nor is circumcision that which is outward in the flesh. But he is a Jew who is one inwardly; and circumcision is that which is of the heart, by the Spirit, not by the letter; and his praise is not from men, but from God" (Rom. 2:28-29). The apostle goes so far as to designate this spiritual circumcision the "true" circumcision (Phil. 3:3).

Undeniably, the physical promises and the physical aspects of the nation of Israel now have been made spiritual. Some think this concept is too "simple." Speaking of the book of Zechariah and whether its prophecies point to the church, John Piper contends, "It is too simple to say that since the time of Christ the church has replaced Israel as God's chosen people, even though that is true, in a sense" ("There Shall Be a Fountain Opened"). John MacArthur refers to this interpretation as "replacement theology," suggesting that it is simplistic to inject the church in the place of Israel ("Why Every Calvinist Should Be a Premillennialist, Part 2"). The idea is widely expressed that there must be something more.

Premillennialists it seems, espouse a decidedly base view of the church. They regard the bride of Christ and demand, "Is that it?" In Zechariah 4:10, the prophet asks Zerubbabel, "Who has despised the day of small things?" Premillennialists have done just that when they look at the church.

God has not identified the church as a replacement for Israel. He certainly has not said she is a backup plan for Israel, nor a placeholder. If anything, Israel was a placeholder for the church. When premillennialists speak dismissively of taking the promises spiritually, they ignore a magnificent truth of the New Testament. To say God's promises have a

Does the Physical Nation of Israel Still Play a Role in God's Final Plans?

spiritual application does not weaken their substance, but instead makes them a more substantial reality. Too often, we speak of spiritual reality as somehow less real. "Oh, you mean only in a spiritual sense." Only? Notice the way the Hebrew writer speaks concerning the physical tabernacle versus the spiritual one. He calls the physical tabernacle the "copy" and the "shadow" of things to come (Heb. 8:5). The spiritual tabernacle, he proclaims, is the "true" one—one that is "more perfect" than the physical (Heb. 8:2; 9:11). The thing you could touch with your hands, the law that was so physical in its instruction, is the "mere shadow," while "the substance" is found in Christ (Col. 2:17). Without the guidance of divine revelation, we would indeed find this illogical. Spiritual appears to us as inferior to something physical. However, God reveals that the physical is subordinate to the spiritual. Though the church is a less tangible version of Israel, it is considerably more substantive than the physical nation that foreshadowed it.

But What about Romans 11:26?

One of the most quoted passages from premillennialists concerning Israel is Romans 11:26, "and so all Israel will be saved." What does Paul mean here?

Let us begin by tracking the arguments of the letter as a whole. Paul begins in the first chapter by showing that the Gentile world has sinned and is therefore justly condemned. He quickly moves on in chapter two to his main target, the Jews, who also have sinned. Accordingly, Paul concludes are all in the same boat (Rom. 3:23). Chapter four says faith is the only thing that will save any of us. In fact, faith is the only thing that has ever saved man. In the fifth chapter, Paul gives us a choice: follow Adam to damnation or Christ to salvation. Chapter 6 points to baptism and the commitment to Christ that comes with it. In Romans 7, Paul offers a comparison of life under the Law of Moses with life in Christ, followed in chapter 8 by a description of the blessed assurance of the one who has put on Christ. Then he drops the hammer. In Romans 9, Paul presents the case against Israel. If it had not been for God's plans to bring a Redeemer through Israel, they would have been destroyed a long time before just like Edom and so many other unrighteous nations had been. Having served their purpose as a nation, since they refuse to be used as vessels of honor, they will be fashioned into vessels of dishonor. God has opened the gates to all who will draw near to Him, even those who were once not His people (Rom. 9:24-26). Answering the objection that Israel did not know better, Paul asserts that they had preachers and had ignored them. Further, the Gentiles, who had not previously had access to God's special revelation, had heard and responded (Rom. 10). As chapter 11 opens, none of the preceding discussion suggests that Paul is preparing to argue that physical Israel will be saved no matter what. On the contrary, he declares that Israel is lost.

Does this mean all of Israel is lost? Paul denies this. He is a Jew and is not lost. Just as there were 7,000 faithful Israelites in the days of Elijah, so there remained faithful Jews in the days of Paul. He uses the illustration of a tree, comparing Jews and Gentiles to natural and wild branches. Paul cautions in 11:19 that the Jews were broken off because of their unbelief, a warning to Gentiles who will be broken off if they fall into unbelief. While the Israelites rejected God and were broken off, the Gentiles believed and were ingrafted. In the same way, physical descendants of Abraham may return to God by being grafted in as well (11:23). In verse twenty-five, Paul contends that Israel has been partially hardened so that the fullness of the Gentiles could come in. Verse twenty-six explains, ". . . and so [likewise, in the same way] all Israel will be saved." In the same way as to what? In the same way that the Gentiles came in, all Israel will be saved. If any confusion remains, the source of salvation for the Jews is not left shrouded in mystery. It will be the "Deliverer from Zion" of whom Isaiah prophesied. R. L. Whiteside observes a similarity to the connection Peter makes in Acts 15:11, "But we believe that we are saved through the grace of the Lord Jesus, in the same way as they also are" (Whiteside, 241). The "we" in this context is the Jews and the "they," the Gentiles, all saved the same way, through the same Savior. To suggest that some future salvation is coming for Israel is to suggest they will be saved in some way distinct from the Gentiles, which is the very point Paul argues against throughout the letter to the Romans.

Conclusion

Does the physical nation of Israel still play a role in God's final plans? God's plans for Israel all pointed to Christ. The physical nation of Israel today has as much significance as physical circumcision. "For neither is circumcision anything, nor uncircumcision, but a new creation" (Gal. 6:15).

Does the Physical Nation of Israel Still Play a Role in God's Final Plans?

Bibliography

Lindsey, Hal. *The Late Great Planet Earth*. Grand Rapids, MI: Zondervan, 1971.

MacArthur, John. *The Second Coming: Signs of Christ's Return and the End of the Age*. Wheaton, IL: Crossway Books, 2003.

———. "Why Every Calvinist Should Be a Premillennialist, Part 1." *Grace to You*. March 25, 2007. https://www.gty.org/library/sermons-library/90-334/why-every-calvinist-should-be-a-premillennialist-part-1.

———. "Why Every Calvinist Should Be a Premillennialist, Part 2." *Grace to You*. April 1, 2007. https://www.gty.org/library/sermons-library/90-335/why-every-calvinist-should-be-a-premillennialist-part-2.

Piper, John. "There Shall Be a Fountain Opened." *Desiring God*. December 5, 1982. *https://www.desiringgod.org/messages/there-shall-be-a-fountain-opened*.

Ryrie, Charles Caldwell. *The Basis of the Premillennial Faith*. Dubuque, IA: ECS Ministries, 2005.

Walvoord, John. "Millennial Series: Part 1: The Millennial Issue in Modern Theology." *Walvoord.com*. https://walvoord.com/article/38. Accessed March 27, 2020.

———. "Millennial Series: Part 12: The Abrahamic Covenant and Premillennialism." *Walvoord.com*. https://walvoord.com/article/49. Accessed March 27, 2020.

———. "Chapter IV: The Promise of the Land to Israel." *Walvoord.com*. https://walvoord.com/article/285. Accessed March 27, 2020.

———. *The Millennial Kingdom: A Basic Text in Premillennial Theology*. Grand Rapids, MI: Zondervan, 1994.

Whiteside, Robertson L. *A New Commentary on Paul's Letter to the Saints at Rome*. Denton, TX: Miss Inys Whiteside, 1961.

Can Signs Foretell When the End Will Come?

By Allen Dvorak

Introduction

This world will end. "The heavens will pass away with a roar, and the heavenly bodies will be burned and dissolved" (2 Peter 3:10a).[1] A day like no other day. Who would not want to know when that day will occur? Who would not want to know when the end of the world will happen?

The thought of having such knowledge is tempting fruit. Because people want to know what the future holds for them, the claim to have special knowledge of the end of the world is often a means of amassing power and influence, not to mention monetary profit.

---

[1] Unless otherwise indicated, quotations from Scripture are from the ESV.

Allen Dvorak was born in 1959 and grew up in Illinois. He married Debbie (Nunn), whom he met at Florida College, in 1980 and they have two sons, David (Lauren Dvorak née Nerland) and Jonathan (Katie Dvorak née Picogna) and four grandchildren. He has a Bachelor's Degree in Public Speaking from Lamar University. Allen has been preaching since 1980, working with congregations in Illinois (Benton area), Ohio (Cincinnati area), Texas (Corpus Christi; Groves), Brazil (São Paulo) and Alabama. Fluent in Portuguese, he continues to make occasional trips to Brazil. Allen also served as one of the editors of *Biblical Insights* from 2012-2015. After working with the Gooch Lane congregation in Madison, Alabama for 8½ years, he helped start the Kelly Spring Road congregation in Harvest, Alabama in 2006 and serves as both preacher and an elder for that congregation. The congregation's website is www.spreadingtruth.org. He can be reached at allen.dvorak@reagan.com.

Can Signs Foretell When the End Will Come?

It is not surprising then that historically predictions of the end of the world have abounded. And they are not confined to modern day psychics and self-styled prophets. One website lists predictions of the end of the world from ancient times all the way to the present ("A Brief History of the Apocalypse"). Historian David Montaigne recently claimed, based on alleged biblical clues, that the end of the world would occur in December of 2019 (http://endtimesand2019.webs.com).

Any large-scale catastrophe is seen by some as a sign of Christ's final coming and the end of the world. The underlying premise seems to be that the end of the world will be heralded by such global catastrophes, and so it only remains for us to recognize these "signs."

Is it possible to know just when Jesus will return, signaling the end of the world? Does the Bible actually provide us with signs that will allow us to identify the time of Jesus's Second Coming?

As already noted, there are plenty of individuals who have predicted the end of the world. Some of these predictions have nothing to do with religion or the Bible. A conventional theory among scientists is that as the sun ages and becomes a "red giant" (a type of star), it will expand and consume the inner planets of the solar system (Morris). Of course, scientists predict that this event will happen somewhere between one and five billion years in the future, so go ahead and send in your mortgage payment this month! Some environmentalists have predicted the destruction of the planet a few years in the future, based on what they perceive to be humanity's destructive behavior.

Our study focuses on predictions regarding the end of the world that are based on supposed biblical signs. Claiming to read the "tea leaves" of current events, some religious prognosticators attempt to connect those events with biblical statements or prophecies.

Some religious groups seem to specialize in setting dates for the end of the world. The Jehovah's Witnesses, for example, have a penchant for declaring that such and such date is of biblical significance in the fulfillment of prophecy. The Jehovah's Witnesses have their roots in the Adventist teaching of a man named William Miller. Miller claimed that Jesus's Second Coming would be no later than April 18, 1844. When that day passed with no visible coming of the Lord, many of Miller's followers rejected his teaching, but some believed that Miller was simply wrong about the date

"When Will These Things Be?" : Questions on Eschatology

and character of the Lord's coming. A man by the name of Charles Russell came into contact with individuals of this second group. Eventually, he became the leader of a religious group later known as the Jehovah's Witnesses. Along with another leading individual named N. H. Barbour, Russell taught that the invisible coming of the Lord took place in 1874, beginning a 40-year period of "harvest."[2] The end of the harvest would be 1914.

Beginning in the mid-1880s, Charles Russell wrote a 7-volume series of doctrinal studies originally titled *Millennial Dawn* and later known as *Studies in the Scriptures*. In those publications, Russell made some bold and broad predictions about what would happen in 1914. Note the following quotations from these books:

> Truly, it is expecting great things to claim, as we do, that within the coming twenty-six years all present governments will be overthrown and dissolved; but we are living in a special and peculiar time, the "Day of Jehovah," in which matters culminate quickly; and it is written, "A short work will the Lord make upon the earth" ("The Time Is at Hand," 98-99).

> Be not surprised, then, when in subsequent chapters we present proofs that the setting up of the Kingdom of God is already begun, that it is pointed out in prophecy as due to begin the exercise of power in AD 1878, and that the "battle of the great day of God Almighty" (Rev. 16:14), which will end in AD 1915, with the complete overthrow of earth's present rulership, is already commenced ("The Time Is at Hand" 101).

> All this is in harmony with the Scriptural declaration that the Kingdom of God must first be set up before its influence and work will result in the complete destruction of "the powers that be" of "this present evil world"—political, financial, ecclesiastical—about the close

---

[2] The 40-year harvest is derived from the period of time from the ministry of Jesus to the time of the Roman destruction of Jerusalem. The harvest at the end of the world will supposedly be parallel. As Barnett notes (14), Russell calculated the 40-year period to be 1874-1914, but J. F. Rutherford, Russell's successor at the helm of the organization, calculated 1878-1918, allowing for the period of time of Jesus's public ministry, i.e., approximately 3.5 years. Such differences (and even the selection of 1874 as the time of Jesus's invisible return, His "presence") illustrate the imaginative and arbitrary use of "biblical mathematics." The year 1874 was supposedly 6,000 years after creation, according to some calculations of the time of creation, and the 6,000 years is equal to six days, according to the reckoning of time by Deity (2 Pet. 3:8—one day equals 1,000 years).

Can Signs Foretell When the End Will Come?

> of the "Times of the Gentiles," October AD 1914 ("The Battle of Armageddon," 622).
>
> The beginning of the earthly phase of the Kingdom in the end of AD 1914 will, we understand, consist wholly of the resurrected holy ones of olden time,—from John the Baptizer back to Abel;—"Abraham, Isaac, Jacob and all the holy prophets" ("The Battle of Armageddon," 625).

Continuing to describe conditions in the millennial kingdom of God, begun in the year 1914, Russell wrote:

> Moral reforms will be instituted along all lines; financial, social and religious questions will all be recast in harmony with both Justice and Love... How much this will signify as regards the suppression of all lines of business which tempt humanity by alluring and seducing through the weaknesses of their fallen natures and the unbalance of mental and moral qualities! The distillery, the brewery, the saloon, the brothel, the poolroom, all time-killing and character-depraving businesses will be stopped; and their servants will be given something to do that will be beneficial to themselves and others.
>
> Similarly, the building of war-vessels, the manufacture of munitions of war and defense will cease, and armies will be disbanded. The new kingdom will have no need of these . . .
>
> The banking and brokerage businesses, and other like employments, very useful under present conditions, will no longer have a place. . . ("The Battle of Armageddon," 632-633).

In the Publishers' Foreword to Volume 2 of *Studies in the Scriptures*, the following text is found:

> While THE TIME IS AS HAND [the title of the second volume—ASD] was first published twenty-five years prior to 1914, yet it pointed out that date as marking the end of "Gentile Times," therefore, the time when we could expect to witness the overthrow of Gentile Governments. No one can justly discredit the author simply because at that early period in which he wrote, he did not clearly see the length of time that would be required, following 1914, for the complete dissolution of the old-world order. In his own Foreword, written in 1916, he acknowledges the error of some of his deductions concerning 1914. We republish that Foreword, beginning on the next page, and recommend that it be carefully read.
>
> Today, the year 1914 stands out as one of the most important in all human history; for now it is clearly recognized by students of history

"When Will These Things Be?" : Questions on Eschatology

and world economics, that it marked the end of a world. Many of the kingdoms that flourished prior to that date have now been destroyed; and the only people who know what the world of tomorrow is to be, are those who understand something of the vision presented in the prophecies of the Bible. This book helps one to see that vision.

A couple of observations beg to be made. First, when one compares Russell's predictions for 1914 with what actually happened, it is evident that he was just flat wrong in his predictions! Yet, the Watchtower Organization (Jehovah's Witnesses) claims that no one can "justly discredit" him simply because he didn't "see clearly." Although the publishers try to downplay his failure by claiming that the year 1914 was so significant in human history that it "marked the end of a world," there is no way to hide the fact that Russell made some rather detailed predictions that did not come to pass. Second, the claim is made for superior knowledge possessed by some who correctly understand the prophecies of the Bible.

A study of the history of the Jehovah's Witnesses reveals that they have repeatedly been wrong in their predictions of dates/events surrounding the final coming of the Lord. I have cited Russell's predictions concerning 1914 in some detail to illustrate a pattern that I have observed in the teaching of the Jehovah's Witnesses and other date-setting religious groups/persons. When the original predictions do not come to pass, either it is suggested that the date was "not quite accurate" or that the date was accurate, but its significance was slightly different than originally predicted. In either case, the failure of these prophecy experts does not cause them to stop setting dates for the end of time and the coming of the Lord and provides an opportunity for atheists to scoff at the gullibility of "religious people."

But we must ask the question, "Is the failure of such predictions simply the result of not understanding biblical prophecies correctly, or has God not given us adequate information to predict the time of the Lord's return with certainty?"

The God Who Knows the Future

When the Old Testament prophets wished to contrast Jehovah, the true and living God, with useless idols, they emphasized God's creative power and His ability to predict the future. Isaiah wrote:

> Remember this and stand firm, recall it to mind, you transgressors, remember the former things of old; for I am God, and there is no

Can Signs Foretell When the End Will Come?

other; I am God, and there is none like me, declaring the end from the beginning and from ancient times things not yet done, saying, "My counsel shall stand, and I will accomplish all my purpose" (46:8-10).

and

Thus says the Lord, the King of Israel and his Redeemer, the Lord of hosts: "I am the first and I am the last; besides me there is no god. Who is like me? Let him proclaim it. Let him declare and set it before me, since I appointed an ancient people. Let them declare what is to come, and what will happen. Fear not, nor be afraid; have I not told you from of old and declared it? And you are my witnesses! Is there a God besides me? There is no Rock; I know not any" (44:6-8).

and

The former things I declared of old; they went out from my mouth, and I announced them; then suddenly I did them, and they came to pass. Because I know that you are obstinate, and your neck is an iron sinew and your forehead brass, I declared them to you from of old, before they came to pass I announced them to you, lest you should say, "My idol did them, my carved image and my metal image commanded them" (48:3-5).

God did give signs on occasion to indicate that some event or judgment was at hand. During the last week of the public ministry of Jesus, He predicted the complete destruction of the temple complex (Matt. 24:1-2; Mark 13:1-2; Luke 21:5-6). His disciples asked when this would happen, what would be the sign of His coming in judgment? In response, Jesus gave the disciples some "signs" that they could recognize, indications that the destruction of Jerusalem was near. For example,

So when you see the abomination of desolation spoken of by the prophet Daniel, standing in the holy place (let the reader understand), then let those who are in Judea flee to the mountains (Matt. 24:15-16).

But when you see Jerusalem surrounded by armies, then know that its desolation has come near. Then let those who are in Judea flee to the mountains, and let those who are inside the city depart, and let not those who are out in the country enter it (Luke 21:20-21).

Jesus gave these "signs" for the express purpose of helping Christians avoid the physical judgment coming upon the Jewish nation in general and Jerusalem in particular. If Jesus could provide such warning signs

"When Will These Things Be?" : Questions on Eschatology

to identify the general time of the destruction of Jerusalem, surely He can "signal" the time of the end of the world with definitive signs! Why, then, has He not done this? Or has He? Many believe that the Scriptures contain the clues that reveal the "time of the end," if one has the ability to interpret the clues.

The Book of Revelation

For those who try to "nail down" the precise time of Jesus's Second Coming, the book of Revelation is a favorite playground. The vivid figures of the book stir the imagination and stimulate many theories regarding their meaning. The book also speaks of the "coming" of Jesus (e.g., 1:7; 22:7, 12, 20), leading many readers to look for information regarding the timing of His Second Coming.

It is important to understand that Revelation is an example of a type of literature known as *apocalyptic*. Apocalyptic literature employs signs, symbols and visions to convey information. By the use of such figurative language, apocalyptic literature both "covers" and "uncovers," revealing information to those who understand the significance of the figures, but hiding the message from those who do not. It is like looking at a message written in code; if you do not know the key to the code, it does not make much sense. To say that many people do not really understand the message of Revelation is certainly an understatement!

The storyline of Revelation, particularly as detailed in the second half of the book, involves a dragon, a beast that rises from the sea, a beast that rises out of the earth and a prostitute who is referred to as "Babylon the great" (chapters 13 and 17). As a prophetic book (1:3), Revelation predicted the divine judgment against the prostitute, who was a persecutor of Christians, although God's judgment of the sea beast and the false prophet (chapter 19) was also predicted.

Believing that Revelation contains prophecies of "the end of the world" and events in close proximity, chronologically speaking, many Bible students have identified the great prostitute with various evil men, the Roman Catholic Church and even the United States. Attempts are made to relate current events, political alliances and persons to details and figures in Revelation for the purpose of predicting the future and, in particular, the Second Coming of the Lord.

Can Signs Foretell When the End Will Come?

Revelation does indeed refer to a "coming" of the Lord (e.g., 1:7; 3:11; 16:15; 22:7, 12, 20; et. al.) and there are many theories about the nature of that coming. It is worth noting that sometimes a "coming" of the Lord is a reference to a temporal judgment (e.g., Micah 1:3; Matt. 16:28; 24:30; 26:64; Luke 21:27), but it is clear from Scripture that Christ will "come" again at the end of time (2 Pet. 3:1-10; Heb. 9:28). The context and content of a passage determine which "coming" is under consideration.

The judgment that the apostle John saw in Revelation 20:11-15 is considered by many to be a prophetic description of the final judgment at the end of time. Death and hades were thrown into the lake of fire (v. 14). Writing to the Corinthians, the apostle Paul connected the destruction of death with "the end." He wrote:

> Then comes the end, when he delivers the kingdom to God the Father after destroying every rule and every authority and power. For he must reign until he has put all his enemies under his feet. The last enemy to be destroyed is death. (1 Cor. 15:24–26)

But when will the judgment that John saw occur? Earlier in Revelation 20, there is mention of a 1,000-year period during which Satan would be bound, i.e., prevented from deceiving the nations as he had previously done (vv. 1-3). After the thousand years, Satan would be released for a little while and would return to his previous strategy, but he would be defeated and thrown into the lake of fire, consigned to eternal torment (vv. 7-10; cf. Matt. 25:41).

Many have tried to calculate the time of the end of the world and the final judgment by identifying the period of human history that corresponds to the millennium mentioned in Revelation 20. However, it is critical that we remember that Revelation is apocalyptic literature, a book of symbols and signs. Is the millennium a literal period of time or is it just an extended, but undefined period of time? The Scriptures sometimes use the number "thousand" to indicate a large, but not exact quantity (e.g., Psa. 50:10; 84:10; 2 Pet. 3:8). Even if the millennium is a literal time period, when did it start? Has it started yet?

There is a sense in which these questions regarding the millennium are irrelevant. A basic principle for the interpretation of biblical passages is to interpret the "hard" passages in light of the "easy" passages. That principle is an application of the harmony of truth. One passage in Scripture

"When Will These Things Be?" : Questions on Eschatology

may supplement the information in other passages, but will not contradict them. Passages difficult to understand because of figurative language or their cryptic nature will not contradict other clear, literal passages. Nothing revealed in the book of Revelation on a particular subject will contradict other biblical passages that address the same subject. As will be subsequently noted in this study, an examination of other passages that speak of the final coming of Christ reveals that His coming will be "as a thief in the night" (1 Thess. 5:1-3; 2 Pet. 3:10). It would be a contradiction of those passages for Revelation to provide signs that pinpoint the time of His coming.

Matthew 24

The synoptic Gospels record a conversation concerning the temple that Jesus had with His disciples. Jesus was in the temple and lamented the unwillingness of "Jerusalem" to accept God's efforts to nurture the nation. He said, "See, your house is left to you desolate" (Matt. 23:38). Interestingly, Matthew 24 indicates that Jesus "left the temple and was going away, when his disciples came to point out to him the buildings of the temple" (v. 1, ESV). It seems odd that the disciples were "pointing out to him," the buildings of the temple since Jesus would have been quite familiar with Herod's temple. I suspect that the disciples may have had difficulty understanding Jesus's comment about the "desolate" house in light of the magnificence of the Jerusalem temple.

If the disciples had difficulty with Jesus's previous comments, His prediction about the buildings of the temple must have been truly shocking! "You see all these, do you not? Truly, I say to you, there will not be left here one stone upon another that will not be thrown down" (Matt. 24:2). His prediction of the destruction of the temple prompted the later questions by the disciples as He sat on the Mount of Olives.

The Olivet Discourse, as Jesus's teaching on this occasion has been called, has generated a great deal of controversy among Bible students, principally for several reasons. The breadth of the questions asked by the disciples, the type of language used by Jesus in His response to those questions, and the mention of the Lord's "coming" (v. 30) have caused many to wonder if Jesus was talking about the destruction of Jerusalem, the end of the world, or both. Since there is another study in this series that will address Matthew 24 in detail, I will confine my discussion to a couple of salient points for the focus of this study.

Can Signs Foretell When the End Will Come?

As already noted, the context of the disciples' questions would suggest, at the very least, that they were asking about the destruction of the temple. Some argue, based on Mark's wording of these questions, that they were also asking about the end of the world (age). Matthew 24:36 ("But concerning that day and hour. . .") is suggested as the transition in focus from the destruction of Jerusalem (and the temple) to the final coming of Jesus and the end of the world.

Jesus employed apocalyptic language similar to that in the book of Revelation, language which might seem at first blush to refer to cataclysmic events at the end of the world:

> Immediately after the tribulation of those days the sun will be darkened, and the moon will not give its light, and the stars will fall from heaven, and the powers of the heavens will be shaken (Matt. 24:29).

Such language, however, was employed in the Old Testament to describe God's temporal judgments against the nations. For example, the prophet Isaiah used apocalyptic language to describe God's temporal judgment against Babylon.

> The oracle concerning Babylon which Isaiah the son of Amoz saw. . . Behold, the day of the Lord comes, cruel, with wrath and fierce anger, to make the land a desolation and to destroy its sinners from it. For the stars of the heavens and their constellations will not give their light; the sun will be dark at its rising, and the moon will not shed its light. . . Therefore I will make the heavens tremble, and the earth will be shaken out of its place, at the wrath of the Lord of hosts in the day of his fierce anger (Isa. 13:1, 9-10, 13).

Regardless of how "cataclysmic" such language sounds, passages like Isaiah 13 indicate we cannot conclude that it concerns the end of the world without contextual evidence. In the case of Matthew 24, it is also important to note that Jesus gave a "chronological marker" for the fulfillment of the things He was predicting.

> Truly, I say to you, this generation will not pass away until all these things take place (Matt. 24:34).

"All things" must at least include the matters already discussed in Matthew 24. Jesus gave signs by which disciples could know that the destruction of the temple (and Jerusalem) was "near" (Luke 21:20), but even such signs did not pinpoint in advance the exact time of the destruction.

"When Will These Things Be?": Questions on Eschatology

What about the remainder of the chapter, verses 36-51? Even if these verses are speaking of the final coming of the Lord, those looking for signs are going to be disappointed. Consider these statements:

> But concerning that day and hour no one knows, not even the angels of heaven, nor the Son, but the Father only. . . Therefore, stay awake, for you do not know on what day your Lord is coming. . . Therefore you also must be ready, for the Son of Man is coming at an hour you do not expect (Matt. 24:36, 42, 44).

Jesus specifically said that His "coming" under consideration in this passage would be "at an hour you do not expect." His comment would apply to whichever coming(s) one sees in the passage!

The Thessalonians

Paul wrote two letters to the church at Thessalonica not long after the congregation was established. It appears that some had misunderstood his teaching about the return of the Lord and were concerned that Christians who died prior would not be raised from the dead. In his first letter, the apostle responded to this misapprehension by noting that, when "the Lord Himself will descend from heaven. . . the dead in Christ will rise first" (1 Thess. 4:16). Paul continued his discussion of the coming of the Lord (4:15) in chapter five, noting that the "day of the Lord will come like a thief in the night" (5:2). His point in describing the Lord's coming this way, especially in light of the "noise" in 4:16, is not that the coming of the Lord would be a silent coming, but rather that it would be unexpected and a surprise to many (5:4). Paul wrote of his confidence in the Thessalonians that they would be sober and watchful, not surprised by the day (5:4-8). A people aware of the certainty of His coming and constantly prepared for it will not be surprised by it—even without signs!

It is obvious from Paul's second letter to the Thessalonians that not all misunderstandings or controversies regarding the final coming of Jesus had subsided. It appears that the Thessalonians had likely received some verbal message or letter purporting to be from the apostle, "to the effect that the day of the Lord [had] come" (2:2). The "day of the Lord" mentioned in chapter two clearly seems to be the final coming of the Lord in light of the context; Paul had referenced the end of the world in chapter one (cf. vv. 5-12). The substance of what Paul wrote to the Thessalonians is that the "coming of our Lord Jesus Christ" would not be

Can Signs Foretell When the End Will Come?

immediate. Some things that would happen first, namely, a rebellion and the revealing of the man of lawlessness (2:3).[3]

Paul wrote that he had taught the Thessalonians about these things (2:5), and so his references are not detailed ("and you know what is restraining him now" (v. 6). There is much speculation about these events, i.e., the rebellion and the identity of the man of lawlessness, but Paul's description makes any identification very difficult. Also, our understanding of Paul's comments must be harmonized with what is written about the Lord's return in other passages.

Luke 12

As previously noted, not every mention of a "coming" of the Lord necessarily refers to the final coming of the Lord at the end of the world. Context and content are the determinates for which coming of the Lord (temporal judgment or end of the world) is under consideration, but sometimes the context does not supply much in the way of clues. For example, consider Luke 12:35-40, which says,

> Stay dressed for action and keep your lamps burning, and be like men who are waiting for their master to come home from the wedding feast, so that they may open the door to him at once when he comes and knocks. Blessed are those servants whom the master finds awake when he comes. Truly, I say to you, he will dress himself for service and have them recline at table, and he will come and serve them. If he comes in the second watch, or in the third, and finds them awake, blessed are those servants! But know this, that if the master of the house had known at what hour the thief was coming, he would not have left his house to be broken into. You also must be ready, for the Son of Man is coming at an hour you do not expect.

---

[3] Some identify the "man of lawlessness" ("the man of sin" and "the son of perdition," NKJV) with "the" Antichrist. In premillennial theory, the Antichrist is an individual who opposes Jesus Christ during the "end times." Often the supposed actions of the Antichrist are drawn from the text of Revelation. A couple of observations: (1) the term "antichrist" never appears in the book of Revelation; it only appears in the general epistles of John (1 John 2:18, 22; 4:3; 2 John 7) and (2) the term "antichrist" is used in the plural in 1 John 2:18, suggesting that a particular type of individual is being considered rather than one specific individual, and *they* were already present in John's day.

"When Will These Things Be?" : Questions on Eschatology

Even if Luke 12:35-40 is about the final coming, the statement of verse 40 indicates that we will not be able to anticipate the exact time that the Son of Man is coming. The implication of this truth is that there will not be signs of the coming of the Son of Man!

Hebrews 10:25

On the other hand, sometimes context, even the general context of an entire book, can help with specific statements that appear to refer to the coming of the Lord. For example, the author of Hebrews encouraged his readers not to neglect the practice of assembling together but to encourage one another, "and all the more as you see the Day drawing near" (10:25).

There are several possibilities for the meaning of the "day" in this passage, including the day of one's death, the time of the destruction of Jerusalem, and the day of the Lord's final coming. Whatever the "day" is in this passage, the readers could see it drawing near.

To identify the "day" with the day of one's death seems unlikely to me, since that day is usually not known with certainty. To argue that one draws inexorably nearer to the day of one's death is true, but does not help; the text does not just indicate that the day is getting nearer, but that the readers could "see" the day getting nearer. I do not believe the writer was simply stating a truism.

Other passages have noted that the day of the Lord will come like a thief in the night with the apparent emphasis on the fact that it will be unexpected (cf. 1 Thess. 5:2; 2 Pet. 3:10). If such is the day of the Lord's final coming, how will any of us "see" it drawing near? The author of Hebrews does not give any "signs" to help his readers "see" when that day is getting near. Considering the teaching of other passages on the final coming of the Lord, it seems unlikely that this is the meaning of "day" in Hebrews 10:25.

The book of Hebrews was written to Jewish Christians, some of whom were considering a return to Judaism. The fact that the author of the book does not mention the destruction of the temple seems to be critical information for determining the date of authorship. Anyone making the argument that the Old Testament sacrificial system had been changed would very likely mention the destruction of the temple in AD 70, and yet there is no mention of that event in the book. It seems more

Can Signs Foretell When the End Will Come?

likely to me that the "day" of Hebrews 10:25 is a reference to the coming of the Lord in temporal judgment against Jerusalem.

2 Peter 3

In his second epistle, the apostle Peter warned about scoffers who would express doubts regarding the certainty of the Lord's coming. "They will say, 'Where is the promise of his coming?'" (2 Pet. 3:4). In the context of this chapter, it is evident that the Lord's final coming is under consideration. The "day of the Lord" would be accompanied by the destruction of the heavens and earth by fire (vv. 7, 10, 12). Even though the apostle Peter affirmed the certainty of the Lord's coming, he also indicated that the day of the Lord will "come like a thief," i.e., unexpectedly (v. 10). This is the same thing that Paul affirmed in 1 Thessalonians 5:2.

Conclusion

It is worth noting that Charles Russell did not claim to be inspired (miraculously guided by the Holy Spirit) in his interpretation of biblical prophecy.[4] He believed that he had a clear understanding of future events based on revelation already delivered. There are many, however, who would claim progressive revelation, informing them of future events, including the timing of the final coming of Jesus and the end of the world. When Russell's predictions for 1914 did not come to pass, many legitimately concluded that his understanding of biblical prophecy was *not* clear! But when individuals claim to know the time of the end through revelation given specifically to them and their predictions fail, they are false prophets! Under the Old Testament dispensation, false prophets were to be punished with death (Deut. 18:20), thus illustrating the Lord's attitude toward those who falsely claim divine inspiration.

Moses noted that some things are "secret," not revealed to man, and those things "belong" to the Lord our God (Deut. 29:29). The time of the final coming of the Lord and the end of the world is in the category of "secret things." The conclusion of this study is that, since God has not revealed signs that foretell the end of time, the coming of the Lord will be as a thief in the night.

Collective experience demonstrates that men tend to procrastinate in their preparation for events that are forecast for the distant future. The

---

[4] At least according to the Foreword of his second volume in the *Studies in the Scriptures* series!

young person just beginning a career may not see the need to plan or save for retirement because it is far off into the future. If God had given signs so that men could know precisely when the Lord and Judge of all mankind would return, how many would perhaps wait until the last moment to prepare for that day?

As already noted, the apostle Peter affirmed the certainty of the Lord's coming and the end of the world, even though he did not give any signs of when that would occur. In light of that certainty, he encouraged his readers to live holy and godly lives, to "be diligent to be found by him without spot or blemish, and at peace" (2 Pet. 3:11, 14). That is good counsel for every generation.

Bibliography

Barnett, Maurice. *Jehovah's Witnesses.* Vol. 1. Cullman, AL: Printing Service, n.d.

The Holy Bible: English Standard Version (ESV). Wheaton, IL: Crossway Bibles, 2016. (Unless otherwise indicated, quotations from Scripture are from the ESV).

Russell, Charles T. "The Time Is at Hand." *Studies in the Scriptures*, Vol. 2. East Rutherford, New Jersey, n.d. (originally published in 1889)

———. "The Battle of Armageddon." *Studies in the Scriptures*, Vol. 4. East Rutherford, New Jersey, n.d. (originally published in 1897).

Montaigne, David. *End Times and 2019.* Kempton, IL: Adventures Unlimited Press, 2013. http://endtimesand2019.webs.com.

Morris, Ian. "End of the World: Biblical Prophecy Predicts Rapture in 2019." *Mirror.* https://www.mirror.co.uk/science/end-world-biblical-prophecy-predicts-13799960.

Nelson, Chris. "A Brief History of the Apocalypse." *abhota.info.* http://www.abhota.info/end1.htm#top.

Judgment Day

What Does the Bible Teach about the Coming of Christ?
   Kevin Kay

What Is the Biblical Teaching on the Resurrection?
   Bruce Reeves

Does the Bible Teach the "Rapture," the Coming of an Antichrist, and the Battle of Armageddon?
   Mark Mayberry

"When Will These Things Be?"
Questions on Eschatology

What Does the Bible Teach about the Coming of Christ?

By Kevin Kay

Introduction

Verse 1: It may be at morn, when the day is awaking,
When sunlight through darkness and shadow is breaking,
That Jesus will come in the fullness of glory
To receive from the world "His own."

Verse 2: It may be at midday, it may be at twilight,
It may be, perchance, that the blackness of midnight
Will burst into light in the blaze of His glory,
When Jesus receives "His own."

Kevin Scott Kay was born September 27, 1957 in San Francisco, CA. He is married to Kathy (Stevens). He received his formal education at Florida College (A.A., 1977) and the University of South Florida (B.A., communications and English, 1979). Brother Kay's preaching work has enabled him to work with churches in Crandall, IN (1980–84); Ray's Branch in Bowling Green, KY (1984–91); Wallisville Road in Highlands, TX (1991–97); Brookmead in Johnson City, TN (1997–2015); East Columbus in Columbus, MS (2015-2018); and Courtland Ave. in Kokomo, IN (2020-present). Several of his articles have been published in religious journals. He was a contributor to *Is It Lawful? : A Comprehensive Study of Divorce*, ed. Dennis Allen and Gary Fisher (1989). He has done evangelistic work in Bratislava, Slovakia (1996) and Mariupal, Ukraine (2007). He has hosted the annual *Studies in the Scriptures Conference* since 2000. He can be reached at: kevinskay@gmail.com.

"When Will These Things Be?" : Questions on Eschatology

Verse 3: While hosts cry Hosanna, from heaven descending,
With glorified saints and the angels attending,
With grace on His brow, like a halo of glory,
Will Jesus receive "His own."

Verse 4: Oh, joy! oh, delight! should we go without dying,
No sickness, no sadness, no dread and no crying;
Caught up through the clouds with our Lord into glory,
When Jesus receives "His own."

Refrain: O Lord Jesus, how long, how long
Ere we shout the glad song—
Christ returneth! Hallelujah!
Hallelujah! Amen.
Hallelujah! Amen.

—*Christ Returneth,* by H.L. Turner

The writer of Hebrews declares that just as Jesus "appeared to put away sin by the sacrifice of Himself," so "He will *appear a second time, apart from sin, for salvation*" (Italics added, Heb. 9:26-28). Like the death, burial, and resurrection of our Lord, the Second Coming of Jesus is a cardinal doctrine that is repeatedly affirmed throughout the NT.[1] On the night of His betrayal, Jesus promised His apostles that He would return with these soul-stirring words: "Let not your heart be troubled; you believe in God, believe also in Me. In My Father's house are many mansions; if it were not so, I would have told you. I go to prepare a place for you. And if I go and prepare a place for you, *I will come again and receive you to Myself;* that where I am, there you may be also. And where I go you know, and the way you know" (Italics added, John 14:1-3). Jesus also alluded to His Second Coming in several of His parables: the parables of the tares (Matt. 13:24-30, 36-43), the dragnet (Matt. 13:47-50) the ten virgins (Matt. 25:1, 5-6, 10, 13), the talents (Matt. 25:14-15, 19, 27), the expectant steward (Luke 12:35-48), and the pounds (Luke 19:12-13, 15,

---

[1] "It is claimed that *one out of every thirty verses in the Bible mentions this doctrine*; to every one mention of the first coming the Second Coming is mentioned eight times; *318 references to it are made in 216 chapters*; whole books (1 and 2 Thess., e. g.) and chapters (Matt. 24; Mark 13; Luke 21, e. g.) are devoted to it" (Italics added, Evans and Coder, 236). Note: The Olivet Discourse (Matt. 24; Mark 13; Luke 21) is devoted to both the Second Coming and the destruction of Jerusalem in AD 70.

What Does the Bible Teach about the Coming of Christ?

23). When the apostles witnessed Jesus's ascension to heaven, two angels promised that He would return (Acts 1:9-11).

Repeatedly throughout the NT, the Second Coming is briefly mentioned or alluded to by several NT writers: Peter (Acts 13:19-20; 1 Pet. 1:7, 13; 5:4), Paul (1 Cor. 1:7-8; 4:5; 11:26; Col. 3:4; 1 Tim. 6:14; 2 Tim. 4:1, 8; Titus 2:13), the writer of Hebrews (Heb. 9:27-28), John (1 John 2:28; 3:2), and Jude (Jude 14-15). Then, in addition to these brief references, extensive and detailed discussions of the Second Coming are found in the writings of Paul (1 Cor. 15; 1 and 2 Thess.) and Peter (2 Pet. 3).

The Second Coming is certainly a major theme in Paul's letters to the Thessalonians. References to the Second Coming are scattered throughout 1 Thessalonians—at the end of each chapter in our modern versions (1 Thess. 1:10; 2:19-20; 3:11-13; 4:13-18; 5:23-24), and then Paul addresses the subject in detail in one lengthy passage (1 Thess. 4:13-5:11). He also addresses the subject at length once again in his second letter to the Thessalonians (1:6-10; 2:1-12).[2]

Four key terms are used by NT writers to refer to the Second Coming. While these terms do not always refer to that event, they indeed refer to it in many contexts.

"Coming" or **"Presence"** (*parousia*) is used twenty-four times in the NT to refer to:

- A physical coming of men (1 Cor. 16:17; 2 Cor. 7:6-7; Phil. 1:26)
- Physical presence (2 Cor. 10:10; Phil. 2:12)
- The Incarnation (2 Pet. 1:16)
- The coming of Christ in AD 70 to destroy Jerusalem (Matt. 24:3, 27; Jas. 5:7-8)[3]

---

[2] "[O]ver a quarter of 1 Thessalonians and nearly half of 2 Thessalonians deal with problems and issues regarding the *parousia* or coming of Christ from heaven" (Wanamaker, 10).

[3] I have classified the two statements in Matthew (Matt. 24:3, 27) in this way because they occur in the Olivet Discourse before Jesus said: "Assuredly, I say to you, *this generation* will by no means *pass away* till *all these things take place.*" (Italics added, Matt. 24:34). I have also classified James's statement in this way because he refers to a coming that was "at hand." However, the disciples may have been thinking about the "Second Coming" and mis-

"When Will These Things Be?" : Questions on Eschatology

- The Second Coming (Matt. 24:37, 39; 1 Cor. 15:23; 1 Thess. 2:19; 3:13; 4:15; 5:23; 2 Thess. 2:1, 8; 2 Pet. 3:4, 12; 1 John 2:28)
- The coming of the lawless one (2 Thess. 2:9)[4]

"Revelation" (*apokalupsis*) is used eighteen times in the NT to refer to:

- The revelation of God's word (Luke 2:32; Rom. 16:25; 1 Cor. 14:6, 26; Gal. 1:12; 2:2; Eph. 3:3; Rev. 1:1)
- Paul's vision of paradise (2 Cor. 12:1, 7)
- The Second Coming (Rom. 2:5; 8:19; 1 Cor. 1:7; 2 Thess. 1:7; 1 Pet. 1:7, 13; 4:13)[5]

"Appearing" or **"Brightness"** (*epiphaneia*) is used six times in the NT to refer to:

- The Incarnation (2 Tim. 1:10)
- The Second Coming (2 Thess. 2:8; 1 Tim. 6:14; 2 Tim. 4:1, 8; Titus 2:13)[6]

---

takenly equated it with the destruction of Jerusalem (Matt. 27:3), and Jesus may be contrasting His "Second Coming" (Matt. 24:27) with the coming of false christs (Matt. 24:24-26). Also the expression "at hand" does not always imply imminence (cf. Deut. 32:34-35; Isa. 13:6; 46:13; 51:5; 56:1; Joel 1:15; 2:1; Obad. 15). For a detailed argument of a different interpretation of *parousia*, see Kyle Pope's study "What Is the Focus of the Mount of Olives Discourse?" later in this book.

[4] "The word rendered 'coming' is *parousia*, lit., a presence, *para*, with, and *ousia*, being (from *eimi*, to be) and denotes both an arrival and a consequent presence with" (Vine, *Collected Writings*, n.p.).

[5] "The coming of Christ will also be an *apokálypsis*, an 'unveiling' or 'disclosure.' The power and glory that are now His by virtue of His exaltation and heavenly session must be disclosed to the world. Christ has already been elevated by His resurrection and exaltation to the right hand of God, where He has been given sovereignty over all spiritual foes (Eph. 1:20-23). He now bears the name that is above every name; He is now the exalted Lord (Phil. 2:9). He is now reigning as king at God's right hand (1 Cor. 15:25). However, His reign and His lordship are not evident to the world. His *apokálypsis* will be the revealing to the world of the glory and power that are now His (2 Thess. 1:7; 1 Cor. 1:7; cf. 1 Pet. 1:7, 13)" (Ladd, 2:139).

[6] "A third term, *epipháneia*, 'appearing,' indicates the visibility of Christ's return. Although this term is limited largely to the Pastoral Epistles, Paul tells

What Does the Bible Teach about the Coming of Christ?

"**Appearance**" (*phaneroō*) is used in the NT to refer to:

- The Incarnation (1 Tim. 3:16; 2 Tim. 1:9-10; Heb. 9:26; 1 Pet. 1:20; 1 John 1:2; 3:5, 8)
- Jesus's revelation to Israel (John 1:31)
- Post-resurrection appearances (Mark 16:12, 14; John 21:1, 14)
- The Second Coming (1 Cor. 4:5; Col. 3:4; 1 Pet. 5:4; 1 John 2:28; 3:2)[7]

The Second Coming is described as a *day of manifestation*. It will be that great "last day" (John 6:39-40, 44, 54; 11:24; 12:48) when deity manifests itself in the glorious return of the Christ; so, it is described as:

- "The day of God" (2 Pet. 3:12)
- "The day of the Lord" (1 Thess. 5:2; 2 Pet. 3:10)
- "The day of the Lord Jesus" (1 Cor. 5:5; 2 Cor. 1:14)
- "The day of our Lord Jesus Christ" (1 Cor. 1:8)
- "The day of Jesus Christ" (Phil. 1:6)
- "The day of Christ" (Phil. 1:10; 2:16; 2 Thess. 2:2)
- "The revelation of our Lord Jesus Christ" (1 Cor. 1:7)
- "The revelation of Jesus Christ" (1 Pet. 1:7, 13)
- "His [Jesus's] coming" (1 Cor. 15:23; 1 Thess. 2:19; 2 Thess. 2:8; 2 Pet. 3:4; 1 John 2:28)

The Second Coming is a *day of visitation* when deity intervenes to reward the righteous and punish the wicked; so, it is described as:

- "The day of visitation" (1 Pet. 2:12)
- "The day of judgment" (Matt. 10:15; 11:22, 24; 12:36; Mark 6:11; 2 Pet. 2:9; 3:7; 1 John 4:17)
- "The day of judgment and perdition of ungodly men" (2 Pet. 3:7)
- "The day of redemption" (Eph. 4:30; cf. Rom. 8:18-23)
- "The day of wrath" (Rom. 2:5)

---

the Thessalonians that Christ will slay the man of lawlessness by the breath of His mouth and destroy him by the *epipháneia* of His *parousía* (2 Thess. 2:8). The return of the Lord will be no secret hidden event but a breaking into history of the glory of God" (Ladd, 2:139).

[7] *Phaneroō* means "*to make manifest or visible or known* what has been hidden or unknown, *to manifest,* whether by words, or deeds, or in any other way. . ." (Thayer, 648).

"When Will These Things Be?" : Questions on Eschatology

The Second Coming is a *day of significance*. It is so unique and momentous that sometimes it is merely described as:

- "That day" (Matt. 7:22; 24:36; Mark 13:32; Luke 10:12; 21:34; 2 Thess. 1:10; 2:3; 2 Tim. 1:12, 18; 4:8)
- "The great day" (Jude 6)
- "This day" (1 Thess. 5:4)

The OT provides the background for the concept of "the day of the Lord." It does not refer to a particular day as opposed to all others. It is a "type of time" (like our expression "the day of reckoning") involving three basic concepts: (1) Punishment of the unfaithful in Israel; (2) Destruction of the enemy nations; and (3) Deliverance of the righteous (Hab. 3:12-13).[8] There are many "days of the Lord" in Scripture, and all that precedes the final day of the Lord foreshadows that great event:

- For Israel (Hos. 9:7; Amos 5:18, 20; Mic. 7:4)
- For Philistia (Jer. 47:4)
- For Ephraim (Hos. 5:9)
- For Judah (Isa. 2:12; Jer. 18:17; 30:7; Ezek. 7:19; 21:25, 29; Joel 1:15; 2:1-2, 11, 31; Hab. 3:16; Zeph. 1:7-8, 14, 18)
- For Jerusalem in 586 BC (Isa. 10:3; Lam. 1:12; 2:1, 21; Ezek. 22:24)
- For Damascus (Isa. 17:11)
- For Egypt (Jer. 46:10; Ezek. 30:3, 9; 32:10)
- For the nations (Isa. 63:4; Joel 3:14; Zeph. 2:2-3; 3:8; Zech. 14:1)
- For Edom (Isa. 34:8; Obad. 15)
- For Amon (Ezek. 21:29; Amos 1:14)
- For Tyre (Ezek. 26:18; 27:27)
- For Babylon (Isa. 13:6, 9; Jer. 50:27, 31; 51:2)
- For Gog (Ezek. 39:13)
- For Jerusalem in AD 70 (Luke 17:24, 30; 21:20-24; Acts 2:19-20)

---

[8] "The day of the Lord in the Old Testament is a *day of judgment*. Yahweh will *punish the evil within Israel* (Amos 5:18-20) on that day, and *the wicked among the nations will face a day of terrible wrath* (Isa 13:6-13; Obad 15). Those who have not repented will face 'destruction from the Almighty' (Joel 1:13-15). Yet the punishment of the evil is at the same time *the deliverance of the righteous* (Joel 2:31-32; Zech 14:1-21; Mal 4:5)" (Italics added, Martin, 33:158-159).

What Does the Bible Teach about the Coming of Christ?

- For the Earth-dwellers (Rev. 6:17)
- For the Beast, the False Prophet, and the Kings of the Earth (Rev. 16:14)
- For Angels That Kept Not Their Own Principality (Jude 6)
- For All Men (Matt. 11:22, 24; 12:36; Luke 10:12, 14; Rom. 2:5; 1 Cor. 1:8; 5:5; 2 Cor. 1:14; Eph. 4:30; Phil. 1:6, 10; 2:16; 1 Thess. 5:2, 4; 2 Thess. 1:10; 2:1-2; 2 Tim. 1:12; 4:8; 2 Pet. 2:9; 3:7, 10, 12)

Unfortunately, there is a great deal of misunderstanding and false teaching in the religious world today concerning The Second Coming. So, in this study, I hope to tell you what you really need to know about the Second Coming in ten words. These are ten key words that encapsulate the NT's teaching on this subject, and if you can remember these ten words, you will: (1) Have a good understanding of what the NT teaches about the Second Coming of Christ; (2) Be able to recognize and answer false teaching on this subject; and (3) Be reminded and encouraged to live a godly life. All the ten words that I have chosen end with a certain similarity in sound, and I have done that intentionally to help you remember them hopefully.

New Testament Teaching about the Second Coming
The Second Coming Will Be *Personal*.

To properly understand The Second Coming, we need to realize that the NT speaks of many different "comings" of the Lord. Many of these are what we might call figurative, representative, or impersonal comings. For example, when Jesus promised to send the Holy Spirit to the apostles as their Helper, He told them, "I will not leave you orphans, *I will come to you*" (Italics added, John 14:16-18). Thus, the guidance of the Holy Spirit was a "coming" of the Lord, but it was not the Second Coming. Paul told the Ephesians, "And *He* [Jesus] *came and preached peace to you who were afar off and to those who were near*" (Italics added, Eph. 2:17). Jesus preached peace to the Gentiles, not during His Personal Ministry (Matt. 15:24), but through the preaching of the apostles. Once again, this was a "coming" of the Lord, but it was not The Second Coming. There are other "comings" of the Lord that are not The Second Coming, as well.[9]

---

[9] The "comings" of the Lord include: (1) The Incarnation (John 1:11; 3:31; Acts 7:51-52; 1 Tim. 1:15; 2 Tim. 1:10; Heb. 9:26); (2) The Giving of the Holy Spirit (John 14:16-18, 28); (3) The Indwelling of Deity (John 14:23); (4) The Ascension (Dan. 7:13-14); (5) The Coming in His Kingdom (Matt. 16:27-28; cf. Mark 8:38; 9:1; Luke 9:26-27); (6) The Preaching of the Gospel to the Gen-

"When Will These Things Be?" : Questions on Eschatology

However, the Second Coming, or the final coming, will not be a figurative or representative coming, but a literal and personal coming of Jesus Christ. Jesus promised on more than one occasion that He would return personally. Shortly before His Transfiguration, Jesus told His disciples, "for *the Son of Man* will come in the glory of His Father with His angels, and then He will reward each according to his works" (Italics added, Matt. 16:27; Mark 8:38; Luke 9:26). On the night of His betrayal, Jesus told His apostles that He was going away to the Father, and that He would come again. He said, "And if *I go* and prepare a place for you, *I will come again* and receive you to Myself; that where I am, there you may be also" (Italics added, John 14:3). He also told them, "You have heard Me say to you, '*I am going away and coming back to you.*' If you loved Me, you would rejoice because I said, 'I am going to the Father,' for My Father is greater than I" (Italics added, John 14:28).

The apostles taught that Jesus would return personally. Peter told a Jewish audience, presumably not long after Pentecost, to repent and turn from their sins "so that times of refreshing may come from the presence of the Lord, and that He may send *Jesus Christ*, who was preached to you before whom heaven must receive until the times of restoration of all things. . ." (Italics added, Acts 3:19-20). Paul told the Philippians, "For our citizenship is in heaven, from which we also eagerly wait for *the Savior, the Lord Jesus Christ*, who will transform our lowly body that it may be conformed to *His glorious body*, according to the working by which He is able even to subdue all things to Himself" (Italics added, Phil. 3:20-21). He told the Colossians, "When *Christ who is our life appears*, then you also will appear with *Him* in glory" (Italics added, Col. 3:4). He told the Thessalonians, "For *the Lord Himself* will descend from heaven (Italics added, 1 Thess. 4:16). He told Timothy to "keep this commandment without spot, blameless until *our Lord Jesus Christ's ap-*

---

tiles (Eph. 2:17); (7) The Punishment or Blessing of Churches (Rev. 2:5, 16, 25; 3:3, 11, 20; 16:15; 22:7, 12, 20); (8) The Destruction of Jerusalem in AD 70 (Mal. 4:1, 5; Matt. 10:23; 23:37-39; 24:3, 27, 30; 26:64; Mark 13:26; Luke 21:27; Heb. 10:37; Jas. 5:7-8) [see footnote 3]; (9) The Judgment on the Beasts and Babylon (Rev. 1:7; 11:16-18; 14:14-20; 16:4-7; 19:1-2, 11-16, 19-21); and (10) The Final Coming (Matt. 24:42-44; 25:31-33; Luke 18:6-8; John 14:1-3; 21:22-23; Acts 1:9-11; 1 Cor. 15:23; 1 Thess. 3:11-13; 4:13-18; 5:23; 2 Thess. 1:6-10; 2:1-3; 1 Tim. 6:13-16; 2 Tim. 4:1; Heb. 9:28; 2 Pet. 3:10-13).

What Does the Bible Teach about the Coming of Christ?

pearing" (Italics added, 1 Tim. 6:14). He told Titus that Christians should be "looking for the blessed hope and glorious appearing of *our great God and Savior Jesus Christ"* (Italics added, Titus 2:13). The writer of Hebrews says, "To those who eagerly wait for Him *He* will appear a *second time*, apart from sin, for salvation" (Italics added, Heb. 9:28).

According to these passages, the Jesus who will one day return is the Jesus who first came into the world in the incarnation (Heb. 9:28), who gave Himself for our sins (Titus 2:13-14; Heb. 9:28), who was raised from the dead (1 Thess. 1:10), who was preached to the Jews (Acts 3:19-21), who ascended to the Father (John 14:3, 28; Acts 3:19-21), and who was received by heaven (Acts 3:19-21). When Jesus returns in the Second Coming, He will not send someone else as His proxy. He will come in the majesty of His own personal presence.

The Second Coming Will Be *Visible*.

As the apostles watched Jesus ascend into heaven, two angels spoke to them and said, "Men of Galilee, why do you stand gazing up into heaven? *This same Jesus*, who was taken up from you into heaven, will *so come in like manner* as you saw Him go into heaven" (Italics added, Acts 1:9-11). Paul told the Colossians, "When Christ who is our life *appears*, then you also *will appear* with Him in glory" (Italics added, Col. 3:4; cf. 1 Tim. 6:14-15; 1 John 2:28). The original word that Paul uses (*phaneroō*) means "1. To cause to become visible, *reveal, expose publicly"* (BDAG, 1048). John told his readers: "Beloved, now we are children of God; and it has not yet been revealed what we shall be, but we know that when He is *revealed*, we shall be like Him, for *we shall see Him as He is"* (Italics added, 1 John 3:2). The Second Coming of our Savior will be a revelation (1 Cor. 1:7; 1 Pet. 1:7, 13). The original word (*apokalupsis*) means "*an uncovering*; (1) prop. *a laying bare, making naked. . ."* (Thayer, 62). John told the seven churches of Asia, "Behold, He is coming with clouds, and *every eye will see Him*, even they who pierced Him. And all the tribes of the earth will mourn because of Him. Even so, Amen" (Italics added, Rev. 1:7).[10] When Jesus returns, mankind will see Him come in the clouds (Acts 1:9-11), in His glory (Matt. 25:31; Mark 8:38; Luke 9:26),

---

10 Rather than an allusion to the Second Coming, this could be an allusion to Jesus's coming in judgment on Jerusalem in AD 70 (if the book was written before that event) or His coming in judgment on Rome (if the book was written later).

"When Will These Things Be?" : Questions on Eschatology

with His angels (Matt. 25:31; 2 Thess. 1:7; Jude 14-15), and in flaming fire (2 Thess. 1:7). His first advent was as a baby in a manger and a humble servant (Luke 2:7; Phil. 2:5-8). His second advent will be as a glorious King (Matt. 25:34).

The Second Coming Will Be *Audible.*

Paul told the Thessalonians: "For the Lord Himself will descend from heaven with a *shout*, with the *voice* of an archangel, and with the *trumpet* of God. . ." (Italics added, 1 Thess. 4:16). When Jesus returns, there will be no uncertainty about what is happening. With the reverberation of this shout, the archangel's voice, and the trumpet of God, all the world will know that the end has come.[11]

The Second Coming Is *Unpredictable.*

A great many speculations have been made down throughout the centuries concerning the time of Christ's Second Coming. "From Hippolytus to the present day there has been a continuous succession of these calculations, arbitrary enough in both their point of departure and their method of reckoning. The early church fathers most commonly looked for the second advent at the end of 6,000 years of the world's history; and many definite dates have been confidently announced" (Jackson, 7:376).

Yet, despite a plethora of these speculations, the NT does not reveal the time of Christ's Second Coming. In fact, it teaches that the timing of Christ's Second Advent is unknowable (Matt. 24:36, 42; 25:13; Mark 13:32-33, 35) and unpredictable. Jesus will return like a thief in the night (1 Thess. 5:1-2; 2 Pet. 3:10), and that means He will return "at an hour you do not expect" (Matt. 24:44, 50; Luke 12:40). Have you ever been burglarized? I have, and those thieves came without warning or

---

[11] "Used in conjunction the voice of the archangel and the shout of command and the trumpet depict a grand fanfare. No one will be able to miss the event. No one will fail to realize that something remarkable is about to occur" (Martin, 33:151). "The *loud command (keleusma)* is used of the cry of the charioteer to his horses or the hunter to his hounds; it is the shout of the ship's master to the rowers, or of the commander to his soldiers. Always there is the ring of authority and the note of urgency. It is not said who will utter the *command*, but it may well be the Lord (cf. John 5:25, 28). If not, then the *command*, the *voice* and the *trumpet call* may all be ways of referring to the same thing (Rev. 1:10 has 'a loud voice like a trumpet')" (Morris, *1 and 2 Thessalonians*, 13:91).

What Does the Bible Teach about the Coming of Christ?

announcement when I least expected it. Jesus promised that His return would be like the coming of the flood in the days of Noah when "they were *eating* and *drinking*, *marrying* and *giving in marriage*, until the day that Noah entered the ark" (Italics added, Matt. 24:37-39). In other words, it will be "business as usual" when Jesus returns. Jesus says, "But *of that day and hour no one knows*, not even the angels of heaven, but *My Father only*" (Matt. 24:36). The apostle Paul tells us that Jesus will return when the wicked are thinking that all is "peace and safety" (1 Thess. 5:3).

Despite this clear NT teaching, men have been predicting when the Lord would return virtually since the time of the apostles. Many vague, general predictions have been made, asserting that the Second Coming would occur in the near future. For example, in 1920, the Watchtower Society published a booklet by J. F. Rutherford entitled "Millions Now Living Will Never Die." A Christadelphian pamphlet entitled "Not As Foolish As You May Think" says, "The Second Coming . . . will *probably happen in your lifetime*" (Italics added, quoted by Tolle, 9). In the Seventh-Day Adventist publication *Present Truth*, we are told: "Christ has made it plain that *his return is to take place in the present generation. It will occur in our time*" (Italics added, Jan. 1, 1942, 3, quoted in Tolle, 9).

In addition to these vague, general predictions, several have been so bold as to predict specific years (or even days) for Jesus's return. Some well-known examples are as follows:

- 1843 (William Miller)
- Mar. 21, 1844 (William Miller)
- Oct. 22, 1844 (William Miller)
- 1914 (Charles Taze Russell)
- 1918 (Charles Taze Russell)
- 1925 (Judge Rutherford)
- 1975 (Jehovah's Witnesses)
- June 28, 1981 (Bill Maupin)
- Sept. 13, 1988 (Edgar C. Whisenant)
- 1988 (Hal Lindsey)
- 1989 (Edgar C. Whisenant)[12]

---

[12] For more detailed information concerning failed Second Coming predic-

"When Will These Things Be?" : Questions on Eschatology

All of these dates have come and gone, and Christ has not returned. Therefore, since all these predictions have failed, we can know that these "date setters" were false prophets (Deut. 18:20-21). Let us never forget that Jehovah hates those who preach a lying vision (Jer. 14:14; 23:16, 23-32).

While we may shake our heads at such foolish speculation, what about us? Since the NT clearly teaches that the timing of our Lord's return is unknowable and unpredictable, should we sing "It Won't Be Very Long" and "Jesus Is Coming Soon"? Have you looked closely at the words of those songs? Can we really supply book, chapter, and verse for what they actually say? Would it be permissible for me to preach what we sing in these hymns?[13] If it might be very long, how can we sing it won't be very long? Oh, I believe there is a place for "poetic license" in our hymns, but just how far can it be stretched? The NT teaches that no one knows the day or the hour of our Lord's return. It teaches that Christ will not return until men have been given every opportunity to repent (2 Pet. 3:9-10), until the times of restitution of all things (Acts 3:21), and until the day that God has appointed arrives (Acts 17:30-31). That means "It Might Be Very Long" and "Jesus Might Not Be Coming Soon." Brethren, we say that we should speak where the Bible speaks and remain silent where the Bible is silent, but are we really doing that when we sing these hymns? It is foolish and presumptuous for us to speculate where God has not revealed. The "secret things" belong unto God (Deut. 29:29). If it were important for us to know the time of the Second Coming, God would have told us. In fact, I believe it is important that we do not know, so we will get ready and stay ready rather than postpone our obedience to the Lord.

The Second Coming Is *Inevitable*.

No matter how long the Lord delays His return, no matter how long man waits, no matter how many times the end-time prognosticators fail

---

tions, see Beck, 32:5:142-143, 149; Beck, 32.6.166-167; Lewis, 12:2:57; Lewis, 13:1;25; Martin, "Date Setters," 32.10.17-19; Mayberry, "Date Setters," 32:24:752-754; Predictions and claims for the Second Coming of Christ https://en.wikipedia.org/wiki/Predictions_and_claims_for_the_Second_Coming_of_Christ.

[13] In the August 19, 1998 edition of the *Albuquerque Journal* there was a paid advertisement entitled "Christ Is Coming Very, Very Soon" (Thetford, 1). If you would object to that statement, how can you sing "Jesus Is Coming Soon"?

What Does the Bible Teach about the Coming of Christ?

in their predictions concerning the time of the Second Coming, Peter says "the day of the Lord *will come* as a thief in the night" (Italics added, 2 Pet. 3:10). Sadly, the longer the Lord delays His return, the greater the temptation to doubt His coming (2 Pet. 3:3-4) and neglect our proper preparation (Luke 12:42-48). Do not let that happen to you! There is a reason for the Lord's delay, and that is the longsuffering of God. He wants to give everyone every opportunity to be saved (2 Pet. 3:9).

The Second Coming Will Be *Inescapable*.

"What a spectacle that will be!" writes Perry Cotham, "all the children of men will be there: the living, the multitudinous hosts of the dead, from every place and of every age of the world from the time of Adam to that of the Lord's return. The small and the great, the good and the bad, the rich and the poor, the wise and the simple, all races and all tongues, will appear before the great white throne" (15-16). All nations will be assembled before Jesus for judgment (Matt. 25:31-32), and He will judge all (2 Cor. 5:10), the world (Acts 17:30-31), the living and the dead (2 Tim. 4:1).

The Second Coming and the judgment to follow will be inescapable (1 Thess. 5:3). If O. J. didn't do it, whoever did escaped the judgment of men, and if O. J. did do it, he escaped the judgment of men (at least criminal conviction for that violent crime). However, when the Lord returns, His judgment will be inescapable.

The Second Coming Will Be *Eschatological*.

That is a word we do not use very often, but we shouldn't be intimidated by it. The term "eschatology" simply means "the study of last things." So, when I say that the Second Coming will be eschatological, I mean that the Second Coming of Jesus will "wind up" this earthly scene (1 Cor. 15:20-24).

The chronology of the last day will run something like this. First, Jesus will return unexpectedly like a thief in the night (Matt. 24:36, 42-44; 1 Thess. 5:1-6). Second, when He comes with His angels (Matt. 16:27; 25:31; 2 Thess. 1:7), He will descend from heaven in glory with a shout, with the voice of the archangel, and with the trump of God (1 Thess. 4:16). Third, the lawless one will be destroyed (2 Thess. 2:1-8). Fourth, all the dead, both the righteous and the wicked, will be raised at the same hour (John 5:28-29; Acts 24:15; cf. 2 Thess. 1:6-10) with incorruptible bodies (1 Cor. 15:35-49) on the last day (John 6:39-40,

"When Will These Things Be?" : Questions on Eschatology

44, 54; 11:24).[14] Jesus's Parable of the Tares indicates that there will be no separation between the righteous and the wicked until the end (Matt. 13:24-30, 36-43). We can also know that all the dead will be raised at the same time because the NT reveals that the unsaved will be judged on the same day that the saved are resurrected. Please consider the following syllogism:

- *Major Premise:* Those who accept Christ will be raised on the last day (John 6:39-40, 44, 54; 11:24).
- *Minor Premise:* Those who reject Christ will be judged on the last day (John 12:48).
- *Conclusion:* Therefore, the resurrection of the righteous and the resurrection of the wicked will occur at the same time.

Fifth, those who are still living when Christ returns will be changed in a moment, in the twinkling of an eye (1 Cor. 15:47-52; cf. 2 Cor. 5:1-8; Phil. 3:20-21; 1 John 3:2). Just as our physical body bears the image of the first man, Adam, so our spiritual (resurrection) body will bear the image of the last Adam, Christ (Phil. 3:20-21). Sixth, Jesus will be "glorified

---

[14] This one resurrection of both the righteous and the wicked will result in two different destinies: life for the righteous and condemnation for the wicked. In 1 Thessalonians 4:13-18, only the resurrection of the righteous is under consideration, because Paul is specifically dealing with their questions concerning those who die in Christ before He comes again. The contrast in this passage is between the righteous dead and the righteous living, not between the righteous dead and the unrighteous dead, as premillennialists argue. "It is clear also that both groups—the survivors and the dead (or those fallen asleep)—are *believers*. Anyone can see at once that the apostle is not drawing a contrast between believers and unbelievers, as if, for example, believers would rise first, and unbelievers a thousand years later. He states: '"And *the dead* in Christ will rise first; then *we who are alive, who are left* shall be caught up together with them in clouds...'. *Both* groups ascend to meet the Lord. *Both* consist of nothing but believers" (Hendriksen, 115).

What Does the Bible Teach about the Coming of Christ?

in His saints"[15] and "admired among all those who believe"[16] (2 Thess. 1:9-10). Seventh, all the righteous will be caught up to meet the Lord in the air (1 Thess. 4:13-17) and be glorified (Col. 3:4). Eighth, Jesus will sit on the throne of His glory to judge the world in righteousness (Matt. 25:31; Acts 17:30-31). Ninth, all men will be gathered before Him to give an account of the deeds done in the body (Rom. 14:10-12; 2 Cor. 5:10), and they, along with wicked angels (2 Pet. 2:4; Jude 6), will be judged by the word of Christ on the last day (John 12:48). Tenth, Jesus will make a separation between the righteous and the wicked and pronounce the eternal destinies of each (Matt. 25:31-46), acknowledging the righteous and denying the wicked before the angels (Luke 12:8-9) and God (Matt. 10:32-33). Eleventh, with the resurrection of the dead and the final judgment, death, the last enemy, will be destroyed (1 Cor. 15:20-26, 54-57). Twelfth, the heavens and the earth will be destroyed (2 Pet. 3:7, 10-12). Thirteenth, the creation will be delivered from bondage (Rom. 8:19-22). Fourteenth, Jesus will deliver up the kingdom to God, and He will again be subjected to the Father (1 Cor. 15:24-28).[17] Finally, the righteous will

---

[15] Three different explanations of this glorification are possible: (1) Jesus will be glorified *by* His saints; (2) Jesus will be glorified *among* or *in the midst* of His saints; and (3) Jesus glory will be *reflected in* His saints. "The issue centers on the meaning of the preposition *en* ('in'), which could be instrumental (Christ is glorified by or through believers), causal (believers are the cause or reason for Christ to be glorified), or locative (Christ's glorification takes place in the presence of believers). Although a case can be made for each option, the locative sense is supported by three factors... The locative meaning (1) agrees with the meaning of *en* in Ps. 88:8 LXX, (2) matches the parallel phrase 'to be marveled at in all who believe,' and (3) contrasts well the fate of the Thessalonians' tormentors, who will be excluded 'from the presence of the Lord' (1:9)" (Carson and Beale, 885).

[16] "As with the opening half, here too Paul's language echoes the OT, this time Psalm 67:36 LXX (68:35 ET): 'God will be marveled at in the presence of his holy ones.'... Once again we see how Paul takes an OT text that originally refers to God and applies it to Christ" (Carson and Beale, 884-885).

[17] Although it is true that Christ will take the church (His people) to be with God the father (1 Thess. 4:13-18), I do not believe that is what Paul is saying here. I believe he is saying that Jesus will relinquish His Messianic authority back to God the Father. Also, please note that Jesus will not return to "set up" His kingdom, as premillennialists tell us, but rather "deliver up" His kingdom. Christ's

enjoy the new heavens and the new earth for eternity (2 Pet. 3:12-13),[18] and the wicked will be tormented in hell (Matt. 25:46; 2 Thess. 1:6-10).[19]

The Second Coming Will Be *Judicial*.

When Jesus came into the world the first time, He did not come as a Judge; He came as a Savior (John 3:16-17). However, when He returns, He will come as the Judge of all mankind (Acts 17:30-31; 2 Tim. 4:1). We can be assured that this judgment will come because God raised Jesus from the dead. When Jesus sits on the throne of His judgment, all men will stand before Him (Matt. 25:31-32a), and every man will give an account for the things done in his body, whether good or bad (2 Cor. 5:10). In that last great tribunal, Jesus will judge our words (Matt. 12:36-37), our works (Eccl. 12:14; Rom. 2:6), and even the secrets of our hearts (Eccl. 12:14; Rom. 2:16; 1 Cor. 4:5). Each of us will be judged by the standard of Christ's words (John 12:48). All will bow before Him and confess (Rom. 14:10-12; Phil. 2:9-11), but for the wicked, it will then be too late. Every man will be rewarded according to his deeds (Rom. 2:5-11). The righteous will hear His words of welcome and will be ushered into eternal life, and the wicked will hear His words of rejection and will be banished into eternal punishment (Matt. 25:34-46).

---

kingdom was established when He ascended to the right hand of God (Mark 16:19; Acts 2:33; 5:31; Eph. 1:20; Col. 3:1; Heb. 1:3; 8:1; 10:12; 12:2; 1 Pet. 3:22), and then His kingship was publicly proclaimed on Pentecost (Acts 2:30-36).

[18] Will the eternal abode of the righteous be in heaven or in the new heavens and the new earth (i.e., a recreated universe)? Many believe that the expression "new heavens and a new earth" (2 Pet. 3:13; Rev. 21:1) is just a periphrastic reference to heaven, and there are several passages that apparently indicate that the final abode of the righteous will be in heaven, where God is now (cf. Matt. 5:3, 12; Phil. 3:20; Heb. 10:34; 1 Pet. 1:4; *et al.*). On the other hand, some believe that heaven will come down to the new earth (cf. Rev. 21:1-4), and this new earth will be the final abode of the righteous. This view makes it much easier to explain two apparently contradictory passages (Rom. 8:18-23 & 2 Pet. 3:10-13). However, it is certainly a "sticky wicket" to know how literally the symbolism in the book of Revelation should be interpreted. Whichever view is correct, the righteous will be with God, wherever He is, and that is really the important thing.

[19] The exact chronological order of some of the eschatological events is difficult, if not impossible to determine.

What Does the Bible Teach about the Coming of Christ?

The Second Coming Is *Potential*.

By that, I mean that the Second Coming of our Lord could occur at any moment (Matt. 24:45-51). While the Lord might delay His coming for another five years or another 500 years or another 5000 years or for that matter even longer, He could come in the next five minutes. He could come in the next 5 seconds. While we know this and believe this, do we live like believers in this regard? To emphasize my point, let me ask you some penetrating questions. How real to you is the possibility that Jesus could come in your lifetime? How often in an average week do you think about the Second Coming? When you wake up in the morning, do you ever think that this could be the day when Jesus returns? How often do you remember that Christ could come *today*? I'm trying to help you realize that we not only need to know that Christ will come someday, and He could come any day, but we also need to live with the consciousness that Christ could come *today*!

The Second Coming Should Be *Motivational*.

After Peter responds to the scoffers who deny the Second Coming (2 Pet. 3:1-9), after he declares, "But the day of the Lord *will come*. . ." (Italics added, 2 Pet. 3:10), and after he describes what will happen on that great day (2 Pet. 3:10), he asks, "what manner of persons ought you to be.. .?" (2 Pet. 3:11). Because of the momentous things that will take place at the Second Coming and because it could occur at just any moment, the Second Coming of Jesus is intended to motivate us to godly living (2 Pet. 3:14-18).

Christians should be an *expectant* people. Paul says that Christians should be "*looking for* the blessed hope and glorious appearing of our great God and Savior Jesus Christ" (Italics added, Titus 2:13). Peter tells us that we should be "*looking for*. . . the coming of the day of God" and "*look[ing] for* new heavens and a new earth in which righteousness dwells" (Italics added, 2 Pet. 3:12-13). Although Christ's Second Coming will be unannounced and unexpected, like the coming of a thief (1 Thess. 5:1-3; 2 Pet. 3:10), faithful Christians will not be surprised by it, not because they know when He will return, but because they are looking and longing for that great day to come (1 Thess. 5:4-8; 2 Tim. 4:8). Along with the apostle Paul, we should be saying, "O Lord, come!" (1 Cor. 16:22).

Christians should be a *hopeful* people. Peter tells us that we have a living hope for several reasons. First, we have an inheritance awaiting us that is incorruptible, undefiled, unfading, and reserved for us. Second, we are

"When Will These Things Be?" : Questions on Eschatology

kept by God's power through our faith for a salvation that is ready to be revealed in the last time. Third, we know that our various trials in this life can prove the genuineness of our faith. Fourth, we know that praise, honor, and glory await us at the revelation of Jesus Christ (1 Pet. 1:3-7). When faithful Christians die, we sorrow as did those who mourned Tabitha's passing (Acts 9:36-39), but not as those who have no hope because we know that when Jesus returns, the dead will be raised, the living will be changed, and the faithful will be with the Lord forever (1 Thess. 4:13-18).

Christians should be a *joyful* people. We can rejoice, even amid our trials (1 Pet. 1:6-7), because just as we partake of Christ's sufferings, we will partake of His glory when He returns (1 Pet. 4:12-14; 5:10). Peter's words remind me of that grand old hymn "Glory for Me," by Charles H. Gabriel:

> Verse 1: When all my labors and trials are o'er,
> And I am safe on that beautiful shore,
> Just to be near the dear Lord I adore,
> Will through the ages be glory for me.
>
> Chorus: Oh, that will be glory for me,
> Glory for me, glory for me,
> When by His grace I shall look on His face,
> That will be glory, be glory for me.

Christians should be a *patient* people. James says, "therefore, *be patient*, brethren, until the coming of the Lord (Italics added, Jas. 5:7-11). The original word (*makrothumeō*) means "(1) to remain tranquil while waiting, *have patience, wait*. . . (2) to bear up under provocation without complaint, *be patient, forbearing*. . ." (BDAG, 612). Like a farmer who must wait, after he has sown, watered, and weeded, to reap the harvest, we must "not grow weary while doing good, for in due season we shall reap *if we do not lose heart*" (Italics added, Gal. 6:9).

Christians should be a *persevering* people. The writer of Hebrews says:

> For you have need of *endurance*, so that after you have done the will of God, you may receive the promise: 'For yet a little while, And He who is coming will come and will not tarry. Now the just shall live by faith; But if anyone draws back, My soul has no pleasure in him.' But we are not of those who draw back to perdition, but of those who believe to the saving of the soul (Italics added, Heb. 10:36-39).

What Does the Bible Teach about the Coming of Christ?

Those who believe to the saving of the soul will persevere to the end no matter what. It is not those who start the race who receive the prize but those who finish. The words of Adlai Stevenson should serve as a warning to us all when he said, "On the plains of hesitation lie the blackened bones of countless millions, who, at the dawn of victory, sat down to rest, and resting—died!"

Christians should be a *fearful* people. Peter says:

> And if you call on the Father, who without partiality judges according to each one's work, conduct yourselves throughout the time of your stay here in *fear*; knowing that you were not redeemed with corruptible things, like silver or gold, from your aimless conduct received by tradition from your fathers, but with the precious blood of Christ, as of a lamb without blemish and without spot (Italics added, 1 Pet. 1:17-19).

Knowing that one day God will judge us, through His Son (Acts 17:30-31; Rom. 2:16), and knowing that we have been redeemed by the priceless, precious blood of the Lamb, we should be filled with awe, reverence, and yes, fear (Heb. 10:26-31). I loved my earthly father dearly. I was never afraid of him, but I feared his anger and his punishment when I did something wrong. So, it should be with our heavenly Father. We should love Him dearly and not be afraid of Him, but we should greatly fear His wrath and punishment.

Christians should be a *prepared* people. If the Parable of the Ten Virgins (Matt. 25:1-13) teaches anything, it teaches that we need to be ready for the return of our Lord. Since the timing of His return is unknowable, the only way to be prepared is to get prepared and stay prepared (Matt. 24:42-51; Luke 12:35-48). "There's a great day coming, are you ready for that day to come?"

Christians should be a *pure* people. Peter says:

> Therefore gird up the loins of your mind, be sober, and rest your hope fully upon the grace that is to be brought to you at the revelation of Jesus Christ; as *obedient children*, not conforming yourselves to the former lusts, as in your ignorance; but as He who called you is holy, *you also be holy in all your conduct*, because it is written, 'Be holy, for I am holy'" (Italics added, 1 Pet. 1:13-16).

He also tells us that we should be living our lives in "*holy conduct* and *godliness*" and that we should "be diligent to be found by Him in peace, *without spot* and *blameless*" (Italics added, 2 Pet. 3:10-14). John says that everyone who has the hope of seeing Jesus as He is "*purifies himself*, just as He is pure" (Italics added, 1 John 3:2-3). In light of "the blessed hope and

"When Will These Things Be?" : Questions on Eschatology

glorious appearing of our great God and Savior Jesus Christ," we should be "denying *ungodliness* and *worldly lusts*," and we should "live *soberly, righteously*, and *godly* in the present age" (Italics added, Titus 2:11-14). Every Christian should regularly ask himself this question: "Would I want Christ to find me doing what I'm doing right now when He returns?"

Christians should be a *working* people. While we watch and wait for our Lord's return, we need to be working. Now is not the time to quit our jobs, sell our possessions, dress in white robes, ascend a mountaintop somewhere, and look longingly into the distance, as some have done when they thought that the Second Coming was imminent. Paul told the Thessalonians that they were to "*serve* the living God" while they waited for His Son (Italics added, 1 Thess. 1:9-10).

After Jesus told the Parable of the Expectant Steward (Luke 12:35-40), Peter asked, "Lord, do You speak this parable only to us, or to all people?" (Luke 12:41). Jesus replied:

> Who then is that faithful and wise steward, whom his master will make ruler over his household, to give them their portion of food in due season? *Blessed is that servant whom his master will find so doing when he comes.* Truly, I say to you that he will make him ruler over all that he has (Italics added, Luke 12:42-44).

"So doing" what? Obviously, whatever the master has instructed him to do. Paul ended his great exhortation about the resurrection of the dead with these words: "Therefore, my beloved brethren, be steadfast, immovable, *always abounding in the work of the Lord*, knowing that *your labor is not in vain in the Lord*" (Italics added, 1 Cor. 15:58).

Christians should be a *faithful* people. Paul tells us that we will be presented "*holy*, and *blameless*, and *above reproach* in His sight—*if indeed you continue in the faith*, grounded and steadfast, and are *not moved away* from the hope of the gospel. . ." (Italics added, Col. 1:21-23). The writer of Hebrews explains that we are members of Christ's house (i.e., family) "*if we hold fast* the confidence and the rejoicing of the hope firm to the end." We will remain "partakers of Christ *if we hold* the beginning of our confidence steadfast to the end" (Italics added, Heb. 3:6, 14). Jesus exhorted the persecuted church in Smyrna to "*be faithful unto death*, and I will give you the crown of life" (Italics added, Rev. 2:10, ASV). I don't think Jesus merely meant until you die; I believe He meant "to the point of death" (CSB; NIV).

What Does the Bible Teach about the Coming of Christ?

New Testament Teaching about the Second Coming Refutes Religious Error

There is a great deal of error that is taught about the Second Coming. Although this study cannot address every erroneous idea, I want to describe and then briefly respond to three false doctrines.[20] The Jehovah's Witnesses teach that Jesus came invisibly in 1914 to all but the elect (i.e., only the elect witnessed this coming).[21] The dispensationalists teach that the Second Coming will be in two stages. They tell us that the first stage is the "rapture," when Jesus returns *for* the righteous (i.e., the *parousia* = "the day of Christ"), and the second stage is the "Revelation" (i.e., the *apokalupsis* = the *epiphaneia* = "the day of the Lord") which takes place seven years later after the "Tribulation,"[22] when Jesus returns *with* the righteous.[23] Realized Eschatologists[24] teach that the Second Coming oc-

---

[20] Responding in detail to these false doctrines is beyond the scope of my assignment.

[21] "So AD 1914 marks the time of *Christ's invisible return in spirit*" (Italics added, *This Means Everlasting Life*, 221). "This second presence (*par-ou-si'a*) of Christ the Messiah was to be *invisible* and the unmistakable sign he gave shows conclusively that *this return of Christ began in the year 1914*. Since that time Christ has turned His attention toward earth's affairs and is dividing the people and educating the true Christians in preparation for their survival during the great storm of Armageddon . . . ." (Italics added, *Make Sure of All Things*, 320).

[22] Premillennialists are divided as to the time sequence of the rapture and the tribulation. Pre-tribulationists (most dispensationalists) believe that the rapture will occur *before* the tribulation begins. Mid-tribulationists believe that the rapture will occur in the *middle* of the tribulation. Post-tribulationists (historic premillennialists) believe that the rapture will occur *after* the tribulation ends. According to dispensationalists, after the rapture has occurred, there will be no children of God on earth.

[23] "Christ will come *for* His saints (the rapture, the parousia, or presence); afterwards, He will come *with* His saints (the revelation, epiphany, or appearing of Christ)" (Ludwigson, *A Survey of Bible Prophecy*, 134, quoted in Curry, xiii). "From thence Christ will descend to the air to *receive His saints* at the *Rapture*, 1 Thess. 4:16; Phil. 3:20, 21, and will subsequently *come with His saints* and with His holy angels at *His second advent*, Matt. 24:30; 2 Thess. 1:7. (Italics added, Vine, Unger, and White, 2:298)

[24] Realized eschatology is also known as covenant eschatology, fulfilled es-

"When Will These Things Be?" : Questions on Eschatology

curred in AD 70 when Jesus came in judgment on Jerusalem; therefore, they tell us there will be no future Second Coming, bodily resurrection of the dead, day of judgment, or end of the world.[25]

NT teaching concerning the Second Coming refutes Jehovah's Witnesses' doctrine. Obviously, if the Second Coming will be personal, visible, audible, unpredictable, eschatological, and judicial, as the NT teaches, then He did not return invisibly in 1914 as the JW's claim, because that so-called coming did not fulfill these criteria.

NT teaching concerning the Second Coming refutes dispensational premillennialism. There will be only a one-time, "Second Coming." The writer of Hebrews says that Jesus "will *appear* a second time" (Italics added, Heb. 9:28). NT writers say nothing about a two-stage return: first at the "rapture" and then, after a seven-year "tribulation" period, once again at the "Revelation."

While dispensationalists make a distinction between the "rapture" and the "revelation," the various terms, used in the NT to refer to the Second Coming are used interchangeably to describe the same event. Jesus used the terms *parousia* and *erchomai* in the same context to refer to the same event:

> But as the days of Noah were, so also will the *coming (parousia)* of the Son of Man be. For as in the days before the flood, they were eating and drinking, marrying and giving in marriage, until the day that Noah entered the ark, and did not know until the flood came and took them all away, so also will the *coming (parousia)* of the Son of Man be. Then two men will be in the field: one will be taken and the other left. Two women will be grinding at the mill: one will be taken and the other left. Watch therefore, for you do not know what hour your Lord is *coming (erchomai)*. But know this, that if the master of the house had known what hour the thief would come, he would have watched and not allowed his house to be broken into. Therefore you also be ready, for the Son of Man is *coming (erchomai)* at an hour you do not expect. (Italics added, Matt. 24:37-44).

---

chatology, consistent eschatology, transmillennialism, covenant theology, (hyper) preterism, and the AD 70 doctrine.

[25] Max King: "The Holy Scriptures teach the Second Coming of Christ, including the establishment of the eternal kingdom, the day of judgment, the end of the world, and the resurrection of the dead, occurred with the fall of Judaism in 70 AD" (*The Nichols-King Debate*, 1).

What Does the Bible Teach about the Coming of Christ?

Paul used the terms *apocalypsis*, *erchomai*, *parousia*, and *epiphaneia* in the same context to refer to the same event:

> Since *it is* a righteous thing with God to repay with tribulation those who trouble you, and to give you who are troubled rest with us when the Lord Jesus is *revealed* (*apokalypsis*) from heaven with His mighty angels, in flaming fire taking vengeance on those who do not know God, and on those who do not obey the gospel of our Lord Jesus Christ. These shall be punished with everlasting destruction from the presence of the Lord and from the glory of His power, when He *comes* (*erchomai*), in that Day, to be glorified in His saints and to be admired among all those who believe, because our testimony among you was believed (Italics added, 2 Thess. 1:6-10).

> Now, brethren, concerning the *coming* (*parousia*) of our Lord Jesus Christ and our gathering together to Him, we ask you not to be soon shaken in mind or troubled, either by spirit or by word or by letter, as if from us, as though the *day of Christ* had come . . . . And then the lawless one will be revealed, whom the Lord will consume with the breath of His mouth and destroy with the *brightness* (*epiphanea*) of His *coming* (*parousia*) (Italics added, 2 Thess. 2:1-2, 8).

If one reads this extended passage, without any preconceived ideas, it is obvious that there is no change of subject in this context. Paul is describing what will occur at the Second Coming of our Lord, and he uses all these various terms interchangeably.

John used the terms *parousia* and *phaneroō* in the same context to refer to the same event:

> And now, little children, abide in Him, that when He *appears* (*phaneroō*), we may have confidence and not be ashamed before Him at His *coming* (*parousia*). If you know that He is righteous, you know that everyone who practices righteousness is born of Him. Behold what manner of love the Father has bestowed on us, that we should be called children of God! Therefore the world does not know us, because it did not know Him. Beloved, now we are children of God; and it has not yet been *revealed* (*phaneroō*) what we shall be, but we know that when He is *revealed* (*phaneroō*), we shall be like Him, for we shall see Him as He is (Italics added, 1 John 2:28-3:2).

Furthermore, not only are these various terms used interchangeably, but many of these terms are associated with the same happenings (as seen in the appendix at the end of this study).

"When Will These Things Be?" : Questions on Eschatology

NT writers use the same terms to refer to different events in the dispensational scheme of eschatology. For example, Paul uses the term *parousia* to refer to what dispensationalists call the "rapture" (1 Thess. 4:15) and the "revelation" (1 Thess. 3:13; 2 Thess. 2:8). He uses the term *apokalupsis* to refer to what dispensationalists call the "rapture" (1 Cor. 1:7) and the "revelation" (2 Thess. 1:7-8). He also uses the term *epiphaneia* to refer to what dispensationalists call the "rapture" (1 Tim. 6:14) and the "revelation" (2 Thess. 2:8).[26]

There will be no secret, mysterious "rapture" of the saints. While it is true that the righteous dead who are raised and the righteous living who are transformed will together be "caught up"[27] to meet Christ when He returns (1 Thess. 4:13-18), Paul's teaching about this event is very different from what dispensationalist teach about their so-called "rapture" and "revelation."

Dispensationalism vs. The New Testament	
The "Rapture"	**The Resurrection**
Invisible Coming	*Visible* Coming (1 Thess. 4:16; Acts 1:11)
Secret Coming	*Public* Coming (1 Thess. 4:16)
Christ Comes *for* His Saints	Christ Comes *for* (1 Thess. 4:14) and *with* His Saints to God (1 Thess. 3:13)
Righteous Dead Raised before *Unrighteous Dead*	Righteous Dead Raised before *Righteous Living* Changed (1 Cor. 15:51-53; 1 Thess. 4:16-17)
Only *Righteous* Resurrected[28]	Resurrection of *All Men*: Righteous and Wicked (John 5:28-29[29]; Acts 24:15)

---

[26] See Hoekema, 165-166.

[27] "Though the word *rapture* does not occur in our English translations of the Bible, it is derived from the Vulgate rendering of the verb 'caught up' (*harpagēsometha*) in 1 Thessalonians 4:17, *rapiemur*" (Hoekema, 164, n. 3).

[28] "The understanding of three major (mass) resurrections to which the pre-tribulation pre-millennial position leads are: first, saints deceased at the time of Jesus's coming—which includes the rapture (1 Cor 15:23, 52); second, Israel and tribulation believers at the end of the tribulation (Dan 12:13; Rev 20:4); third, the final resurrection which will include all the unredeemed and those who died during the millennium, whether redeemed or unredeemed (Rev 20:5)" (Mills, n.p.).

[29] The fact that Jesus says, "*all* who are in the graves will hear His voice and come forth" (Italics added, John 5:28) contradicts dispensational doctrine.

What Does the Bible Teach about the Coming of Christ?

Dispensationalism vs. The New Testament	
The "Rapture"	The Resurrection
Righteous Raised *1,007* Years before the Last Day[30]	Righteous Raised on the *Last Day* (John 6:39-40, 44, 54; 11:24)
Wicked Left Behind[31]	*None* Left Behind (Matt. 13:24-30, 36-43, 47-50)
Only *Righteous* Rewarded[32]	*Righteous* Rewarded (1 Thess. 4:15-18) and *Wicked* Punished (2 Thess. 1:6-10)
Marriage Supper In Heaven for Saints and Tribulation on Earth for Wicked	*Final Judgment* for all (Heb. 9:27; 2 Tim. 4:1-2)
Death *Continues*	Death *Conquered* (1 Cor. 15:25-26)
Three Comings (Incarnation, "Rapture," and "Revelation")	*Second* Coming (Heb. 9:26-28)
Three Resurrections: (1) Righteous; (2) Tribulation & OT Saints and (3) Wicked	*One* Resurrection: Righteous and Wicked (John 5:28-29)

Dispensationalism vs. The New Testament	
The "Revelation"	The Resurrection
Seven Years after Rapture	*Same Time* As Rapture
Christ Comes *with* His Saints	Christ Comes *for and with* His Saints (1 Thess. 3:13; 4:14)
Resurrection of Tribulation *Saints and OT Saints*	Resurrection of *All Men*: Righteous and Wicked (John 5:28-29; Acts 24:15)
Christ *Sets Up* His Kingdom	Christ *Delivers up* His Kingdom (1 Cor. 15:24)
Death *Continues*	Death *Conquered* (1 Cor. 15:25-26)

Dispensationalists tell us that at the "Rapture," church-age saints hear, but not the wicked or OT saints; at the "Revelation," Tribulation and OT saints hear, but not the wicked; and at the end of the Millennium, the wicked hear, but not the righteous.

[30] Dispensationalists argue that the "last day" is a long period of time.

[31] If the Second Coming will be personal, visible, audible, eschatological, and judicial, as the NT teaches, it will not leave anyone "left behind," scratching their heads and wondering why all the good folks have suddenly disappeared, as dispensationalists claim.

[32] "This position [dispensationalism] also concludes that there will be at least three judgments: first, the rewarding of believers (2 Cor 5:10) during the wedding feast of the Lamb—which will occur simultaneously with the tribulation; second, the rewarding of Israel and deceased tribulation saints

"When Will These Things Be?" : Questions on Eschatology

While dispensationalists posit a silent, mysterious, and secret rapture of the church, the two key passages they cite to "prove" this doctrine describe something very different. Paul says:

> But I do not want you to be ignorant, brethren, concerning those who have fallen asleep, lest you sorrow as others who have no hope. For if we believe that Jesus died and rose again, even so God will bring with Him those who sleep in Jesus. For this we say to you by the word of the Lord, that we who are alive and remain until the *coming* of the Lord will by no means precede those who are asleep. For the Lord Himself will descend from heaven with a *shout*, with the *voice* of an archangel, and with the *trumpet* of God. And the dead in Christ will rise first. Then we who are alive and remain shall be caught up together with them in the clouds to meet the Lord in the air. And thus we shall always be with the Lord. Therefore comfort one another with these words (Italics added, 1 Thess. 4:13-18).

> But concerning the times and the seasons, brethren, you have no need that I should write to you. For you yourselves know perfectly that the *day of the Lord* so comes as a *thief* in the night. For when they say, "Peace and safety!" then *sudden destruction* comes upon them, as labor pains upon a pregnant woman. And they shall not escape. But you, brethren, are not in *darkness*, so that this Day should overtake you as a thief (Italics added, 1 Thess. 5:1-4).

> But now Christ is risen from the dead, and has become the firstfruits of those who have fallen asleep. For since by man came death, by Man also came the resurrection of the dead. For as in Adam all die, even so in Christ all shall be made alive. But each one in his own order: Christ the firstfruits, afterward those who are Christ's at His *coming*. Then comes *the end*, when He *delivers the kingdom to God the Father*, when He *puts an end to all rule and all authority and power*. For He must reign till He has put all enemies under His feet. The *last enemy* that will be destroyed is *death*. . . . Behold, I tell you a mystery: We shall not all *sleep*, but we shall all be *changed*—in a moment, in the twinkling of an eye, at the *last trumpet*. For the trumpet will sound, and *the dead will be raised incorruptible*, and *we shall be changed* (Italics added, 1 Cor. 15:20-26, 51-52).

The first passage does not describe a secret, mysterious, silent return of the Lord nor a mysterious disappearance of the saints. As we

---

at the end of the tribulation (Dan 12:13); and finally, the judgment of all the rest of mankind, whether redeemed or unredeemed, at the end of the millennium (Rev 20:11-15)" (Mills, n.p.)

What Does the Bible Teach about the Coming of Christ?

have already noted, when Jesus returns, it will be personal, visible, and audible—a return that all will see and hear. The righteous will see Him (1 John 3:2), but He will also be "revealed" to the wicked as well (2 Thess. 1:7; cf. Rev. 1:7). Furthermore, when Jesus returns and the righteous are "caught up," at that same time (not 1,007 years later), the wicked will be overtaken and destroyed (2 Thess. 1:6-10). The second passage teaches that when Jesus returns and the righteous dead are raised, and the righteous living are changed, "then comes the end" of all rule, authority, power, and death (not 7 years of "Tribulation" with more death followed by 1,000 years of the "Millennium"). When Jesus returns, according to this passage, Jesus will "deliver up" (not set up) His kingdom.

The happenings on the "last day" also demonstrate that the Second Coming is a one-time event. On the "last day" the righteous will be resurrected (John 6:39-40, 44, 54; 11:24) and the wicked will be judged (John 12:48); therefore, the righteous and the wicked must be raised at the same time. This is precisely what Jesus says, "Do not marvel at this; for *the hour* is coming in which *all* who are in the graves will *hear* His voice and *come forth*—those who have *done good*, to the *resurrection of life*, and those who have *done evil*, to the *resurrection of condemnation*" (Italics added, John 5:28-29). Jesus speaks of one resurrection with two different results. Paul says the same thing, "I have hope in God, which they themselves also accept, that there will be *a* resurrection of the dead, both of *the just* and *the unjust*" (Italics added, Acts 24:15). Notice it is "a" resurrection of both the just and the unjust, not two resurrections separated by 1007 years (the tribulation + the millennium), as dispensationalists claim.

Since the righteous dead are raised on the "last day" and the righteous living are changed (1 Cor. 15:50-52; 1 Thess. 4:15-17), and all this occurs at the *parousia* (1 Cor. 15:20-23; 1 Thess. 4:15-16), and the wicked are judged on the "last day" (John 12:48), and the living and the dead are judged by Jesus at the *Epiphanea* (2 Tim. 4:1), and the righteous receive rest and the wicked receive punishment at the *apokalupsis* (2 Thess. 1:6-9), these three terms must refer to the same event—the one-time Second Coming of our Lord. Since the old heavens and earth are destroyed at the *parousia* (2 Pet. 3:10-12), and the creation is delivered from the bondage

"When Will These Things Be?" : Questions on Eschatology

of corruption at the *apokalupsis* (Rom. 8:20-21), those two terms must refer to the same thing.[33]

NT teaching refutes realized eschatology (i.e., the AD 70 doctrine). Realized eschatologists (RE) teach that the Second Coming occurred in AD 70 primarily because the NT describes an imminent coming of the Lord (Matt. 10:23; 16:28; Heb. 10:37; Jas. 5:7-8) and this imminent coming, they tell us, could only be Jesus's coming in judgment on Jerusalem in AD 70. This coming is indeed predicted in both the OT and the NT (Mal. 4:1, 5; Matt. 23:37-39; 24:3, 27, 30; 26:64; Mark 13:26; Luke 21:32) and it was imminent. It was to occur before that contemporary generation passed away (Matt. 24:34; Mark 13:30; Luke 21:32). However, none of this proves realized eschatology for several reasons.

First, Jesus's coming in judgment on Jerusalem is not the only coming of the Lord. The NT refers to many "comings of the Lord."[34] Of course, this means if there are many different comings of the Lord, then there could be a future coming of the Lord after AD 70. We must not immediately and automatically assume that a particular passage is talking about Jesus's coming in judgment on Jerusalem in AD 70, or for that matter, the Second Coming. We must determine which coming is under consideration based upon the context. Furthermore, RE's must prove, not just assume and assert, that any particular coming of the Lord refers to His coming in judgment on Jerusalem in AD 70.

Second, although RE's argue for an imminent coming based upon the definition of the Greek word *mellō*, this word can indicate either imminence or inevitability (BDAG, 627-628; Thayer, 396-397; Vine, 2:4). In fact, the RE "proof texts" that are referred to in Greek lexicons are said to indicate inevitability rather than imminence, and this fact is also reflected in the way this term is translated in our standard English versions. Furthermore, the Greek word *mellō* simply cannot mean imminence in several passages. John the Baptist was the "Elijah who is to come" (Matt.

---

[33] "Though earlier pretribulationists used to call the first phase of the Second Coming the *parousia* and the second phase the *revelation* or the *appearing*, most contemporary pretribulationists now acknowledge that the three words are used indiscriminately in the New Testament for what they regard as the two phases of Christ's return (see Gundry, *The Church and the Tribulation*, 158)" (Hoekema, 166, n. 8).

[34] See footnote 9.

What Does the Bible Teach about the Coming of Christ?

11:14),[35] yet Malachi prophesied that "Elijah" would come 400+ years before John the Baptist was born (Mal. 4:5-6). The prophets and Moses foretold that Christ's suffering, resurrection, and preaching to Jews and Gentiles *"would* come" (Acts 26:22-23), yet Moses prophesied of Jesus (cf. Deut. 18:18; cf. Acts 3:22-26) 1400+ years before His birth. Adam was a type of "Him *who was to come*" (Rom. 5:14), yet thousands of years intervened between the time of Adam and Jesus. The Jews were kept under guard by the law for the faith that *"would afterward* be revealed" (Gal. 3:23), yet the OT was written between 1400-400 BC. That is at least 400 years before the faith was revealed. The Jewish feasts, new moons, and Sabbaths were "a shadow of things to *come*" (Col. 2:16-17), yet these Jewish rituals were observed 1400+ years before Christ. Paul was a pattern to those who are going to believe (1 Tim. 1:16), and he is still that pattern today. The law was a shadow of the good things *to come* (Heb. 10:1), yet the law was given at Mt. Sinai ca. 1445 BC and the new covenant came into effect ca. AD 30. Abraham went out to the "place which he *would* receive as an inheritance" (Heb. 11:8), yet although Abraham never received this inheritance personally (Acts 7:5; Heb. 11:9-10, 13), he did inherit the promised land through his descendants (Gen. 28:4; Ezek. 33:23-24) 400 years after the promise (Gen. 15:13-16; Acts 7:6-7). Isaac blessed Jacob and Esau "concerning *things to come*" (Heb. 11:20). This included the coming of "Shiloh" (Gen. 49:10), the Messiah. Moreover, the contexts of RE "proof texts" do not demand immediacy. In fact, the connotation of imminence is absurd in some RE "proof texts." How would a so-called imminent judgment (Acts 17:30-31) on the Jews in Jerusalem in AD 70 be a motivation for Gentiles in Athens to repent of their sins? The Gentiles in Athens would have been on the side of the Romans who destroyed Jerusalem! Why would Felix, a Roman, be terrified (Acts 24:24-25) by a judgment on the Jews in Jerusalem in AD 70?

Third, Jesus's coming in judgment on Jerusalem is not the only imminent coming of the Lord. The NT refers to imminent comings of the Lord that could not be the destruction of Jerusalem. Jesus came representatively through the Holy Spirit (John 14:16-18, 28). On the night of His betrayal, Jesus promised to send the Holy Spirit to the apostles. There is no good reason to believe that Jesus's words "I will come to you" refer

---

[35] Although the term *mellō* is untranslated in our English versions, it is present in the Greek text.

"When Will These Things Be?" : Questions on Eschatology

to anything else but this. Then before His ascension, Jesus promised the apostles Holy Spirit baptism "not many days from now" (Acts 1:4-5), and the apostles received Holy Spirit baptism on Pentecost ten days later (Acts 2:1-4). Therefore, this was an imminent coming of the Lord that was not the destruction of Jerusalem. Jesus's coming to punish or bless the seven churches of Asia was imminent; He promised to come quickly (Rev. 2:5, 16; 3:11; 22:7, 12, 20). However, His coming to punish or bless was dependent on their repentance or faithfulness (Rev. 2:5, 16; 3:3, 11, 19-20). So once again, these were imminent comings of the Lord that had nothing to do with Jesus's coming in judgment on Jerusalem. So, if there are imminent comings of the Lord that cannot refer to the destruction of Jerusalem, RE's must prove, and not just assume and assert, that any particular imminent coming refers to the destruction of Jerusalem.

Fourth, the NT also speaks of a delayed coming of the Lord that was not imminent. Jesus said that there would be a coming of the Son of Man that would be like the coming of the flood (Matt. 24:36-39), and Peter says, "the Divine longsuffering *waited* in the days of Noah, while the ark was being prepared" (Italics added, 1 Pet. 3:20), evidently for about 120 years (Gen. 6:3). Several of Jesus's parables that obviously allude to a coming of the Lord speak of a delay. In the Parable of the Faithful and Evil Servant, the master delayed his return (Matt. 24:48-51). In the Parable of the Ten Virgins, the bridegroom delayed His coming (Matt. 25:5). In the Parable of the Talents, the lord returned "after a long time" to settle accounts (Matt. 25:19). Paul told the Thessalonians that the coming of the Lord would not occur until there was a falling away, and the man of sin would be revealed (2 Thess. 2:1-5). Peter reminded his readers that scoffers were asking, "Where is the promise of His coming?" (2 Pet. 3:4). So, if there is a delayed coming, that coming must be different than Jesus's imminent coming in judgment on Jerusalem in AD 70.

Fifth, there is a coming of the Lord in Scripture that just does not "fit" the destruction of Jerusalem. There is a coming of the Lord like the ascension (Acts 1:9-11). Jesus ascended bodily and visibly in a literal ascension. What would the apostles have understood the angels to mean when they said, "*This same Jesus*, who was taken up from you into heaven, will so come *in like manner* as you saw Him go into heaven" (Acts 1:11)? Jesus did not come bodily and visibly and literally (in the sense that the apostles would have understood the angels' language) in the destruction of Jerusa-

What Does the Bible Teach about the Coming of Christ?

lem in AD 70. The expression "in like manner" modifies "will so come," not "this same Jesus."[36] We can state this objection in the form of a syllogism:

- *Major Premise*: Jesus will return bodily and visible (Acts 1:9-11; 1 Thess. 4:13-18).
- *Minor Premise*: Jesus did not return bodily and visibly in AD 70.
- *Conclusion*: Therefore, Jesus will return bodily and visibly at some future time.

"When the plain sense makes good sense, any other sense is nonsense." There is a coming of the Lord that is personal, audible, and visible (1 Thess. 4:13-18). Nothing like this occurred in AD 70. There is a coming of the Lord to judge all nations (Matt. 25:31-33). Were all nations judged in AD 70? There is a coming to punish the ungodly (Jude 14-15; 2 Pet. 3:7; John 12:48; 2 Thess. 1:7-10), but there was no universal punishment of the ungodly in AD 70. There is a coming to destroy the heavens and the earth (2 Pet. 3:3-13), and this did not happen when Jerusalem was destroyed in AD 70. In the O. J. Simpson trial, when the bloody gloves apparently did not fit, O. J.'s attorney, Johnny Cochran, said, "If it doesn't fit, you must acquit." In like manner, if there is a "coming" that does not "fit" AD 70, we must conclude that there is another and different coming that is yet to occur.

Finally, if the "Second Coming" (Heb. 9:28) occurred in AD 70, as RE's claim, two significant questions beg for an answer. First, should we continue to observe the Lord's Supper today? Paul told the Corinthians that in the Lord's Supper, we "proclaim the Lord's death *till He comes*" (Italics added, 1 Cor. 11:23-26). If Jesus came in AD 70, and He is not coming again, as RE's claim: (1) Does the Lord's Supper no longer proclaim Christ's death? or (2) Is the Lord's Supper no longer applicable today? Second, why is realized eschatology "unrealized" in early post-

---

[36] "The Greek *hon tropon* literally means 'what manner.' The Greek phrase 'never indicates mere certainty or vague resemblance; but wherever it occurs in the New Testament, denotes identity of mode or manner' (A. Alexander, Acts, ad loc.). Consequently, we have express biblical warrant to expect a visible, bodily, glorious return of Christ paralleling in kind the ascension" (Gentry, n.p.). "*In the same way* refers to the manner of the Lord's return, that is, on the clouds of heaven, as is depicted in other passages of the New Testament. This may be rendered in some languages as 'just like he went'" (Newman, 21).

apostolic writings?[37] Those early writers believed: (1) The last days were continuing (Ignatius, Eph. 11; Barnabas 4) (2) There would be a future coming of Christ (2 Clement 17; Didache, 166); (3) There would be a future resurrection of the dead (Polycarp, Phil. 2, 7; Martyrdom, 14) and (4) There would be a future day of judgment (Polycarp, Phil. 7; Martyrdom, 11; Clement, 2 Clem. 9, 16). There is not a hint of "realized eschatology" from their pens.

Conclusion

Christ first came to earth as a babe in a manger (Luke 2:7). He will return as the King of kings (Rev. 17:14). He came in the likeness of men (John 1:14; Phil. 2:5-8). He will return in the glory of God (Mark 8:38). He came as the servant of servants (Matt. 20:28). He will return as the Lord of lords (Rev. 17:14). He first came in a body of flesh to save (Heb. 2:14-15). He will return in His glorified body to judge (2 Tim. 4:1). "There's a great day coming, are you ready for that day to come?"

Bibliography

Beck, David. "Latter Day Prophets: How Accurate Are They? (1)." *Guardian of Truth* 32.5 (March 3, 1988):142-143, 149.

———. "Latter Day Prophets: How Accurate Are They? (2)." *Guardian Of Truth* 32.6 (March 17, 1988):166-167.

Carson, D. A. and G. K. Beale. *Commentary on the New Testament Use of the Old Testament*. Grand Rapids: Baker Academic, 2007.

Coffman, John C. "The Second Coming of Christ and Judgment." *Great Bible Doctrines*. Bible Faculty of the Florida College, eds. Florida College Annual Lectures, 241-257 Marion, IN: Cogdill Foundation Publications, 1975.

Cotham, Perry. "The Second Coming" (tract).

Curry, Melvin D., ed. *The Doctrine of Last Things*. Florida College Annual Lectures. Temple Terrace, FL: Florida College Bookstore, 1986.

Danker, Frederick William, ed. *A Greek-English Lexicon of the New Testament and Other Early Christian Literature*. 3rd ed. Chicago: The University of Chicago Press, 2000.

---

[37] See Almon Williams, "AD 70: The End?" *The Doctrine of Last Things*, 1986, 216-219, and W. Terry Varner, *Studies in Biblical Eschatology*, 1:78-97.

What Does the Bible Teach about the Coming of Christ?

Elwell, Walter A., and Barry J. Beitzel. "Second Coming of Christ." *Baker Encyclopedia of the Bible*. Grand Rapids, MI: Baker Book House, 1988.

Evans, William, and S. Maxwell Coder. *The Great Doctrines of the Bible*. Chicago: Moody Press, 1974.

Gentry, Kenneth. "A Brief Analysis of Full Preterism or Hyper Preterism." *Fide-o.com*. http://fide-o.com/2009/05/full-preterism/.

Hendriksen, William. *New Testament Commentary: Exposition of Thessalonians*. Grand Rapids: Baker Books, 1955.

Hoekema, Anthony A. *The Bible and the Future*. Grand Rapids, MI: William B. Eerdmans Publishing Company, 1994.

Jackson, Samuel Macauley, ed. *The New Schaff-Herzog Encyclopedia of Religious Knowledge: Embracing Biblical, Historical, Doctrinal, and Practical Theology and Biblical, Theological, and Ecclesiastical Biography from the Earliest Times to the Present Day*. New York; London: Funk and Wagnalls, 1908–1914.

Ladd, G. E. "Eschatology." Geoffrey W. Bromiley, ed. *The International Standard Bible Encyclopedia, Revised*. Grand Rapids, MI: Wm. B. Eerdmans, 1979-1988.

Lewis, Brent. "For Building up: Those Who Don't Know Enough to Know They Don't Know." *Christianity Magazine* 12.2 (Feb. 1995): 57.

———. "For Building up: 1996 Is the Year—Or Is It?" *Christianity Magazine* 13.1 (Jan. 1996): 25.

Make Sure of All Things. Brooklyn, NY: Watchtower Bible and Tract Society, Inc. International Bible Students Association, 1957.

Martin, D. Michael. *1, 2 Thessalonians*. E. Ray Clendenen, ed. *The New American Commentary*, Vol. 33. Nashville: Broadman and Holman Publishers, 1995.

Martin, Luther. "Date Setters." *Guardian of Truth* 38.18 (Sept. 15, 1994): 17-19.

Mayberry, Mark. "Date Setters." *Guardian of Truth* 32.24 (Dec. 15, 1988): 752-754.

McGuiggan, Jim. *The Kingdom of God and the Planet Earth*. Lubbock: Montex Publishing Co., 1978.

"When Will These Things Be?" : Questions on Eschatology

Miller, Rodney M. *The Lion and the Lamb on Planet Earth*. Orlando, FL: Miller Publications, 1981.

Mills, M. S. *The Life of Christ: A Study Guide to the Gospel Record*. Dallas, TX: 3E Ministries, 1999.

Morris, Leon. *1 and 2 Thessalonians*. Leon Morris, ed. Tyndale New Testament Commentaries. Downers Grove, IL: InterVarsity Press, 1984.

Morris, L. "Parousia." Geoffrey W. Bromiley, ed. *The International Standard Bible Encyclopedia, Revised*. Wm. B. Eerdmans, 1979-1988.

Newman, Barclay Moon, and Eugene Albert Nida. *A Handbook on the Acts of the Apostles*. UBS Handbook Series. New York: United Bible Societies, 1972.

"Predictions and claims for the Second Coming of Christ." *Wikipedia.org*. https://en.wikipedia.org/wiki/Predictions_and_claims_for_the_Second_Coming_of_Christ.

Thayer, Joseph Henry. *A Greek-English Lexicon of the New Testament: Being Grimm's Wilke's Clavis Novi Testamenti*. New York: Harper and Brothers., 1889.

Thetford, Richie. "Christ Is Coming Very, Very Soon?" *Rio Grande Valley Bulletin*. November 1, 1998.

This Means Everlasting Life. Brooklin, NY: Watchtower Bible and Tract Society, Inc. International Bible Students Association, 1950.

Tolle, James M. "The Second Coming." Tolle Publishing. (tract).

Vine, W. E. *Vine's Complete Expository Dictionary Of Old And New Testament Words*. William White, Jr. and Merrill F. Unger, eds. Nashville: Thomas Nelson Publishers, n.d.

———. *Collected Writings of W.E. Vine*. Nashville, TN: Thomas Nelson, 1996.

Wanamaker, Charles, *The Epistles to the Thessalonians: A Commentary on the Greek Text*. The New International Greek Testament Commentary. Grand Rapids: William B. Eerdmans Publishing Co., 1990.

Welch, Robert C. "Resurrection of the Dead and 'The Rapture.'" *Great Bible Doctrines*. Bible Faculty of the Florida College, eds. Florida College Annual Lectures, 225-240. Marion, IN: Cogdill Foundation Publications, 1975.

What Does the Bible Teach about the Coming of Christ?

Appendix: Events Associated with the Second Coming

	Coming *Parousia*[38]	Revelation *Apokalupsis*	Appearing *Epiphaneia*	Appears *Phaneroō*	Comes/Coming *Erchomai*
Unpredictable coming	Matt. 24:36-39; 1 Thess. 4:15 & 5:2; 2 Pet. 3:4 & 10				Matt. 24:42-44, 50; 25:10-13; Mark 13:35-37; Luke 12:35-40; 1 Thess. 5:1-2; Rev. 16:15
Coming of the Lord	1 Thess. 2:19; 4:15-16; Jas. 5:7-8; 1 John 2:28	1 Cor. 1:7; 1 Pet. 1:7	1 Tim. 6:14	1 John 2:28; 3:2	John 14:3; 1 Cor. 11:26
Coming on clouds					Acts 1:9-11; Rev. 1:7
Coming with angels		2 Thess. 1:7			Matt. 16:27; 25:31; Mark 8:38; Luke 9:26; Jude 14[39]
Appearing in glory		1 Pet. 4:13	Titus 2:13	Col. 3:4	Matt. 16:27; Mark 8:38; Luke 9:26; 2 Thess. 1:10
Lawless one destroyed	2 Thess. 2:1, 8	2 Thess. 2:8	2 Thess. 2:8		
Righteous dead raised with spiritual bodies	1 Cor. 15:20-23; 1 Thess. 4:15-16				John 5:28-29
Righteous living changed	1 Cor. 15:50-52; 1 Thess. 4:15-17				
Redemption of saints' bodies		Rom. 8:19, 23		1 John 3:2	
Rapture[40] of the saints	1 Thess. 2:19; 4:17; 5:23; 2 Thess. 2:1			Col. 3:4	

"When Will These Things Be?" : Questions on Eschatology

	Coming *Parousia*	Revelation *Apokalupsis*	Appearing *Epiphaneia*	Appears *Phaneroō*	Comes/Coming *Erchomai*
Saints appear before God	1 Thess. 3:13				John 14:6
Universe destroyed	2 Pet. 3:10-12				
Creation delivered from bondage		Rom. 8:19-22			
New heavens and new earth	2 Pet. 3:13				
Judgment of all men			2 Tim. 4:1	1 Cor. 4:5; 2 Cor. 5:10	Matt. 25:31-33; 1 Cor. 4:5
Reward for righteous		Rom. 2:5-11; 2 Thess. 1:6-7; 1 Pet. 1:7	2 Tim. 4:8	1 Pet. 5:4	Matt. 16:27; 24:45-47; 25:34, 46; Luke 12:42-44
Punishment for wicked	Matt. 24:37-39	Rom. 2:5-11; 2 Thess. 1:6-10			Matt. 16:27; 24:48-51; 25:41, 46; Luke 12:45-48; Col. 3:6; 1 Thess. 1:1
Jesus delivers kingdom to God	1 Cor. 15:24				
Death is destroyed	1 Cor. 15:25-26				
Jesus subjects Himself to God	1 Cor. 15:28				

What Does the Bible Teach about the Coming of Christ?

---

[38] Reading each row of this chart horizontally will reveal the key terms that are associated with each happening. Reading each column of this chart vertically will reveal all the various happenings that are associated with each key term. Reading the chart as a whole will indicate that all of these key terms and all of these events are associated with one another.

[39] While the Olivet Discourse refers to the Son of Man coming on the clouds with His angels (Matt. 24:30-31 = Mark 13:26-27 = Luke 21:27), this is not a reference to the Second Coming, but rather His coming in judgment on Jerusalem (cf. Isa. 19:1). This must be the case since Jesus said, "Assuredly, I say to you, *this generation* will by no means *pass away* till *all these things take place*" (Italics added, Matt. 24:34 = Mark 13:30 = Luke 21:32). All these things are the things that Jesus had just previously mentioned, including His coming on the clouds. Furthermore, the expression "this generation" as it is used in the NT, always refers to Jesus's contemporary generation (cf. Matt. 11:16-17 = Luke 7:31-32; Matt. 12:41-42, 45; Mark 8:12, 38; Luke 11:29-32, 49-51; Luke 17:25; Matt. 23:36; Matt. 24:34 = Mark 13:30 = Luke 21:32; Acts 2:40).

[40] I am using the term "Rapture" here, not as dispensationalists use it, but as Paul speaks of the saints being "caught up" in the clouds to meet the Lord (1 Thess. 4:17).

What Is the Biblical Teaching on the Resurrection?

By Bruce Reeves

Introduction

Job asked the most foundational question anyone could ask, "If a man dies, will he live again?" (Job 14:14). Early on in Scripture, we see that the God who created life is the same God who promises the hope of resurrection for His people (Matt. 22:29-32; cf. Exod. 3:6). As we move into the New Testament, we read of Jesus's suffering and resurrection from the dead (Luke 24:45-47; John 2:22; 12:16; 20:9). Nonetheless, some Bible students are more comfortable discussing the resurrection of Christ than they are the general resurrection at the end of time. Interestingly, it is in the future resurrection of humanity that we find a theological category for the resurrection of Christ (Acts 23:6; 24:14-15, 21; 26:6-8; 1 Cor. 15: 1-4, 20-22). Devoted followers of Christ have always understood

---

Bruce Reeves was born in Blytheville, AR, October 13, 1974, the son of Carl and Carolyn Reeves. He and his wife Rachel have been married for twenty years and have one son, Connor. Bruce received a BA degree from Hendrix College and a Bachelor of Ministry degree from Harding University. Bruce has been working with the Highway 65 church of Christ in Conway, AR for the past nineteen years. He has held numerous gospel meetings across the nation and has written for several religious journals among brethren as well. Bruce is active in apologetics in the public forum. Two of the nine formal religious discussions in which he has participated have been published: The *Reeves-Scheel Debate on the Godhead and Baptismal Formula* and the *Reeves-Cook Debate on Baptism*. He enjoys spending time with his family and reading. He can be reached at brochuck1@aol.com.

What Is the Biblical Teaching on the Resurrection?

the resurrection to be central to the gospel (John 5:28-29; 11:24; Rom. 8:23; 1 Cor. 15:1-58; Phil. 3:20-21; 1 John 3:1-2).

Yet, some have gone to great lengths to dismiss the truth of the resurrection by redefining and distorting significant biblical teaching on the subject, having deemed the concept as unreasonable and unbelievable. However, as Christians, we do not believe in the annihilation of modernism, the materialism of atheism, or the reincarnation of false religions; instead, we affirm the resurrection gospel of the risen Christ!

Sadly, even among professing believers, some adamantly deny a future, bodily resurrection for the righteous and wicked. Erroneous and unbiblical eschatological doctrines concerning the subject of the future resurrection are not harmless. The underpinnings and consequences of such denials of God's word are riveting and destructive to the faith of Christ (2 Tim. 2:16-18).

Defining Resurrection

The concept of what constitutes resurrection needs to be clarified at the very beginning because the word can be used figuratively, spiritually, or literally. The term "resurrection" is used figuratively to describe the resurrection of a cause among God's people in several passages. For instance, Ezekiel's vision of a valley filled with dry bones is expressing the hopeless feelings of Jewish exiles and God's purpose to restore them to life as "the whole house of Israel" (Ezek. 37:1-11). They were not literally dead or in their graves, but God promised to restore them to life "in their own land" (Ezek. 37:14). John's visions in the book of Revelation similarly describe souls who had been slain for the testimony of Jesus (Rev. 6:9-11) as reigning with Christ for a thousand years (Rev. 20:5-6). This resurrection is not speaking of a literal resurrection, but of a figurative resurrection in their vindication after the Lord brought judgment on Rome.

We also read of our spiritual resurrection when we obey the gospel of Christ. Paul often identifies our spiritual transformation with Jesus's bodily death, burial, and resurrection. The apostle speaks of our conversion in such terms as "crucifixion," "death," "burial" and "resurrection" when he writes,

> Therefore we have been buried with Him through baptism into death, so that as Christ was raised from the dead through the glory of the Father, so we too might walk in newness of life. For if we have become

united with Him in the likeness of His death, certainly we shall also be in the likeness of His resurrection, knowing this, that our old self was crucified with Him, in order that our body of sin might be done away with, so that we would no longer be slaves to sin (Rom. 6:4-6).

For through the Law I died to the Law, so that I might live to God. I have been crucified with Christ; and it is no longer I who live, but Christ lives in me; and the life, which I now live in the flesh I live by faith in the Son of God, who loved me and gave Himself up for me (Gal. 2:20).

And in Him you were also circumcised with a circumcision made without hands, in the removal of the body of the flesh by the circumcision of Christ; having been buried with Him in baptism, in which you were also raised up with Him through faith in the working of God, who raised Him from the dead (Col. 2:12).

"Resurrection" is used literally regarding the resurrection of Christ from the grave and the future resurrection of humanity on the last day. This resurrection is the bodily raising from the dead of a person to a qualitatively different type of life in which death and decay no longer have any effect. It is a transformation of the whole person—body and soul—into being fit for God's eternal presence.

Although we read of resurrections in the Bible before Christ, in reality, they might be better understood as miraculous resuscitations. Although people were brought back from the dead, they would have to die again and were not transformed, as will be the case in the general resurrection (1 Kings 17:17-24; 2 Kings 4:32-37; 13:20-21; Matt. 27:52-53; Mark 5:35-43; Luke 7:11-17; John 11:39-44; Acts 9:40; 20:9-10). Jesus is the only one who was raised never to die again and, therefore, serves as the "first fruits" of the future harvest of the final resurrection (Acts 26:23; 1 Cor. 15:21-23; Rev. 1:18).

Figures of Speech Demand a Literal Reality

It is important to recognize that the figurative usages of terms such as "resurrection," "coming," and "judgment" are grounded in the literal reality of such concepts. If there was never going to be a worldwide judgment, future resurrection, or actual personal and visible coming of Christ, how could such terms be used in a figurative sense? When the biblical writers use these figures, the implication is that the literal reality serves as the foundation for their meaning. For example, the figurative

What Is the Biblical Teaching on the Resurrection?

usage of "resurrection" by Ezekiel concerning Israel (Ezek. 37:1-14), Isaiah regarding Judah (Isa. 26:14, 19), Paul regarding his Jewish kinsmen (Rom. 11:15), or John regarding faithful Christians (Rev. 20:4-6) would be meaningless if there was never to be a resurrection (John 5:28-29). Yet, since there is to be a future bodily resurrection, one can see the significance of the figures of speech. Dan King writes,

> ... A whole host of Old Testament passages are suggestive of the future life, future rewards, and punishments, a judgment after this life, resurrection of the dead, etc. But it is a given in Old Testament research that the fuller revelation of these important doctrines of eschatology await the coming of the Messiah Jesus and His matter-of-fact pronouncements detailing what the future is to be like (King, 773).

Resurrection in the Old Testament

Some argue that a general bodily resurrection is never mentioned or alluded to in the Old Testament, but nothing could be further from the truth. Although we know that the New Testament provides more clarity regarding eschatological issues, it is noteworthy that the Jewish people were already familiar with the concept of resurrection during the days of the prophets.

The Sadducees, who denied the resurrection, questioned Christ with a hypothetical scenario concerning a woman who had been married to seven different men by asking, "Which one's wife shall she be?" (Luke 20:27-33). Jesus answered their argument by emphasizing the distinction between "this age" and "the age to come" (Luke 20:34-35). While humanity in "this age" will marry and die, those in the "age to come" will not marry or die because "they are like angels and are sons of God, being sons of the resurrection" (Luke 20:35-36). The Sadducees' argument was without merit since physical relationships are not a concern in eternity. This passage is speaking of an actual bodily resurrection, or this section would have no bearing on the marital relationship.[1] Jesus does not agree with the view of the Sadducees but defends the truth of the resurrection.

---

[1] Some realized eschatology advocates argue that this passage speaks of Levirate marriage in an attempt to argue that the resurrection of this context was fulfilled in AD 70 when Jesus figuratively returned. This interpretation indicates a desperate attempt to reframe a passage that explicitly contradicts Covenant Eschatology (Don K. Preston, Holger Neubauer).

"When Will These Things Be?" : Questions on Eschatology

The Lord appealed to the Pentateuch in His quotation of Exodus 3:6 declaring that it proves "concerning the dead, that they rise" (Mark 12:26; cf. Matt. 22:31; Luke 20:37). Christ did not side with those who deny that the Old Testament supports the doctrine of the future bodily resurrection. He cites Exodus 3:6, which necessarily infers the resurrection, "But that the dead are raised, even Moses showed, in the passage about the burning bush. . ." (Luke 20:37)

Jesus argues that although Abraham, Isaac, and Jacob had physically died, they were yet presently alive. Since the Lord continues to be their God after their death, this necessarily implies a resurrection. The Scripture says, "I am the God of Abraham, and the God of Isaac, and the God of Jacob" (Luke 20:37) and "God is not the God of the dead but of the living; for all live to Him" (Luke 20:38). Is Jesus saying they were already in a resurrected state? No. Before this He had described conditions in "that age" which did not yet apply to Abraham, Isaac, and Jacob (Luke 20:34-36). He is asserting that the fact of their continued existence infers a future hope. Jesus concludes that our bodies will be resurrected and transformed by our living God. Our Creator is the God of restoration and redemption.

The prophet Hosea likewise introduces the concept of resurrection in his description of the condition of God's people. Amid the Lord's judgment, Hosea offers words of hope to those who would repent. The judgment of the northern kingdom of Israel in this context is a reference to 722 BC, not AD 70. There continued to be hope for a remnant that endured in this great judgment upon the nation even though physical death was bearing down on them. It is as if God asks if he should save Israel from death, "'Shall I ransom them from the power of sheol?' 'Shall I redeem them from death?' O Death, where are your thorns? O sheol, where is your sting? Compassion shall be hidden from my sight'" (Hos. 13:14).[2] God would restrain His hand no longer, which brings physical death through judgment upon the disobedient. Idolatrous Israel was already spiritually dead (Hos. 13:1-2). Therefore, the grave they stood in danger of was literal, physical death due to their spiritual rebellion (Hos.

---

2   The Hebrew term *nōḥam* is translated as "compassion" or "repentance." The term "repentance (KJV) demonstrates that God would not reverse His promise for both judgment and hope. This translation also changes Hosea's statements from a question to a proclamation.

What Is the Biblical Teaching on the Resurrection?

13:7-14). Their hope was not in avoiding physical death, but in overcoming death through the resurrection if they returned to the Lord.

This hope of the resurrection is why Paul referenced this passage in his treatment of the future bodily resurrection. The apostle would introduce the questions addressed to "death" and "sheol," from Hosea when he gives thanks to Jesus Christ and the cross (1 Cor. 15:56-57).

Peter draws a similar reference from David's words, "For you will not leave my soul in hades, nor will You allow Your Holy One to see corruption" (Acts 2:27; Ps. 16:10). He goes on to explain,

> Therefore, being a prophet, and knowing that God had sworn with an oath to him that of the fruit of his body, according to the flesh, He would raise up Christ to sit on his throne, he, foreseeing this, spoke concerning the resurrection of the Christ, that His soul was not left in hades, nor did His flesh see corruption (Acts 2:30-31).

If these subtle passages infer the resurrection of Christ, how could one deny that Hosea 13:14, which refers to a future bodily resurrection by Paul himself, is revealing such truth? The apostle did not take the verse out of context; instead, he put it into the context of God's grace in the redemption of His people (1 Thess. 5:23).

One of the most explicit passages concerning resurrection in the Old Testament is Daniel 12:2, "Many of those who sleep in the dust of the ground will awake, these to everlasting life, but the others to shame and everlasting contempt." The larger context sets these statements, beginning in chapter 10, which describes the future oppression of the Jewish people by their Greek rulers. This culminated in the violent attacks by Antiochus IV Epiphanes in his endeavors to eliminate all aspects of Jewish religion and culture. He went to great lengths to Hellenize the Jewish population of Palestine, which in turn led to the Maccabean Revolt. The conclusion of chapter 11 refers to the downfall of Antiochus, in contrast to God's vindication for His saints (12:1-3).

The expression "at that time" makes a logical, not a temporal, connection with the description of Antiochus's decline. Daniel's vision through prophetic telescoping reveals the Lord's answer to the terrible persecution of His people in this particular situation. Jeff Wilson writes, "This telescoping is possible because of prophetic reliance upon typol-

"When Will These Things Be?" : Questions on Eschatology

ogy: every enemy of God's people is a type of Satan, every day of the Lord is a type of the eschatological day of the Lord, every deliverance is ultimately a type of God's restoration to *shalom*—life through resurrection" (Wilson, 93).

There are those who doubt that this text is speaking of a future bodily resurrection. They frequently bring up the fact that the word "many" is used in Daniel 12:2. However, this is explained well by John Goldingay:

> The reference to the exposure of the wicked (i.e., 12:2—"others to disgrace and everlasting contempt") brings out how verses 1–3 as a whole are concerned with restoration to life not for its own sake or for the sake of communion with God, but as part of and as a means to vindication. It is for this reason that the seer speaks of many being awakened, not all: those who were faithful but who lost their lives awake for vindication, those who were wicked but who seemed to triumph awake for condemnation. We need to keep in mind that the passage is handling a specific problem (Goldingay, 308).

N.T. Wright also affirms that the term "many" is simply being applied to this particular situation, yet speaks of a future bodily resurrection:

> Those who awake are "many," but not, it appears, all. The passage is not attempting to offer a global theory of the ultimate destination of the whole human race, but simply to affirm that, in a renewed bodily life, God will give everlasting life to some and everlasting contempt to others. In the context there can be little doubt who these persons are: they are the righteous who have suffered martyrdom on the one hand, and their torturers and murderers on the other. The rest—the great majority of humans are simply not mentioned (Wright, 110).

Resurrection is introduced here as God's solution to the suffering of His people. Thus, Jesus declared the universal resurrection for humanity: "Do not marvel at this; for an hour is coming, in which all who are in the tombs will hear his voice, and will come forth; those who did good deeds to a resurrection of life, those who committed evil deeds to a resurrection of judgment" (John 5:20-29). God will reverse the oppression of the wicked, and He will bring about complete victory over sin and all of its effects (2 Cor. 15:57).

The Lord seeks to comfort His faithful servants and encourage their covenant faithfulness in their persecution by appealing to the power of resurrection (Dan. 12:2, 13). Preterists will often argue that the phrase

What Is the Biblical Teaching on the Resurrection?

"holy people" in Daniel 12:7 simply speaks of the nation of Israel. However, it is worthwhile to note that in Daniel 8:23-24, the phrase "holy people" speaks of those who died for their faithfulness to the covenant of God under the persecution of Antiochus (Preston, 342). Likewise, Daniel uses the term "saints" for the faithful of God throughout the book (Dan. 7:18, 21, 25, 27). Daniel 11:35 describes their sacrifice for truth under such oppression, "Some of those who have insight will fall, in order to refine, purge and make them pure until the end of time; because it is still to come at the appointed time" (Dan. 11:35). It is also telling to notice the parallel descriptions between the "holy people" who suffered in Daniel 11:35 and 12:3, thus, indicating that the context describes the same people.

Preterists must find a transition verse, which moves the reader from Antiochus's persecution of faithful Jews to the Roman destruction of Jerusalem in AD 70. However, these assertions are difficult to sustain in the reading of the text.[3] Jim McGuiggan argues for Daniel 11:36 being a transition point (McGuiggan, 205), while Don K. Preston has proposed that Daniel 11:45 is the transition verse.[4] However, it seems more reasonable to understand these final verses as a prophetic description of the end of Antiochus's wicked persecution of the Jewish people.

It is certainly fair to consider what exactly Jesus intends when He identifies the destruction of Jerusalem with the "abomination of desolation" mentioned by the prophet Daniel (Dan. 11:31; 12:11; cf. Matt. 24:15). Because it has been demonstrated that Daniel chapters 11 and 12 are describing Antiochus's abuse of power and persecution of faithful Jews, what was Jesus saying in Matthew 24:15? Christ's application of Daniel's phrase "the abomination of desolation" (Dan. 11:31; 12:11) to the destruction of Jerusalem in AD 70 was intended to reference a well-known and tragic event in Jewish history. In other words, when you see the sort of event that Daniel foretold in his prophecy, then it is time for you to depart from Jerusalem (Matt.

---

[3] Some believe Daniel 11 transitions to the Roman Empire and speaks of a figurative resurrection while rejecting realized eschatology. Advocates of this doctrine must find more than the interpretation under consideration in Daniel 12 to sustain their system. However, it is the perspective of this writer that they cannot find even that view in the reading of the context of Daniel.

[4] https://youtube.com/watch?v=PjOMCLbPhvc.

24:15-16).⁵ R.C.H. Lenski offers the following thoughts concerning Matthew 24:15:

> The moment believers see this (and it is something unmistakable and easy to see) they are to flee the country posthaste. This is the same abomination that was "spoken of". .. through Daniel, the prophet in 11:31 and 12:11 . . . when he prophesied what is recorded in 1 Maccabees 1:20-68, note v. 57. Antiochus Epiphanes erected a pagan altar on top of the great altar of burnt sacrifice before the Sanctuary (Holy and Holy of Holies). Jesus does not say that Daniel prophesied the event that would usher in the destruction of Jerusalem. He says only that the same kind of an abomination with the same kind of an effect would appear in the Temple (Lenski, 938).

The prophecy of Daniel came true in the reign of Antiochus Epiphanes's oppression of God's people and even served as a foreshadowing depiction of what would happen in AD 70 (Matt. 24:15). Daniel was encouraged to have full confidence in his future vindication as Yahweh's prophet through his future resurrection, "But as for you, go your way to the end; then you will enter into rest and rise again for your allotted portion at the end of the age" (Dan. 12:13). Kyle Pope argues that this verse addresses hope of the future resurrection:

> A post-death "inheritance" must describe some provision God grants to Daniel after this life. The fact that he is said to "arise" to his "inheritance" suggests that this is not the resurrection of a cause, or some unseen spiritual vindication of the faithful dead. This is something that will grant an "inheritance" to him personally. This suggests a literal (not a figurative or collective) resurrection. The timing of this is also compelling. It is not simply "the end". . . . Rather, it is at "the end of the days" (Pope, 90).

The Resurrection Gospel: Paul's Treatment of the Bodily Resurrection in 1 Corinthians 15

Paul's teaching regarding the resurrection in 1 Corinthians 15 is the most extensive treatment of the subject in all of the New Testament. Some in Corinth claimed to believe in the resurrection of Christ, while at

---

5   See Kyle Pope's discussion of the relationship of Daniel's usage of the phrase "abomination of desolation" and Jesus's reference to Daniel's description in light of the destruction of Jerusalem in AD 70 as discussed in Matthew 24:15 (*Thinking about AD 70*, Kyle Pope, 83).

What Is the Biblical Teaching on the Resurrection?

the same time denying the future bodily resurrection of humanity. Those who subscribe to realized eschatology must redefine key terms in this context and accept a strained and skewed view of Paul's writings due to their denial of a future bodily resurrection as well.

As we consider the context of 1 Corinthians 15, it is essential to identify what was being denied in Corinth to appreciate the development of the apostle's argumentation. Realized eschatology proponents will argue that the resurrection of this context was both a figurative resurrection of the cause of Christianity and a spiritual gathering of Old Covenant Jewish and Gentile believers together in the body of Christ in AD 70. However, the context reveals that the issue in Corinth was the teaching that denied the future bodily resurrection of humanity.

Paul begins his discussion of the general resurrection by reminding the Corinthians of the foundation of their hope in Christ. They received the gospel of salvation through their faith in the death, burial, and resurrection of Jesus. They were saved through their continued faith in these fundamental facts of the gospel (1 Cor. 15:1-3). The Lord had physically died for their sins, physically been buried, and physically been raised from the dead.[6] The concern was that their rejection of the future bodily resurrection would logically lead to either a diminished view of the resurrection body of Jesus or a denial of His resurrection altogether.

With the realized eschatology perspective in mind, one wonders how a denial of either a figurative resurrection of a cause or a spiritual gathering accomplished 815 miles away from Corinth in the destruction of Jerusalem in AD 70, would lead to a denial of the bodily resurrection of Christ? However, it is reasonable to see that a denial of the general bodily resurrection would remove the categorical foundation upon which one could accept the resurrection of Jesus from the dead (Acts 24:15; 26:8).

---

[6] There have been uncertain sounds from the realized eschatology camp concerning the atoning value of the offering of Jesus's physical life. Their denigration regarding the sufficiency of Christ's blood and death is troubling. Some proponents of realized eschatology have described the blood of Christ as "corruptible" and have paralleled the atonement of Christ to the "Old Testament sacrifices." Additionally, phrases such as "spirit-blood" express the past notions of numerous Christological heresies. These positions are the logical consequence of a denial of a future bodily resurrection, as well as an actual, visible, and personal return of Christ in His glorified body.

"When Will These Things Be?": Questions on Eschatology

Paul affirms that once the Corinthians had confessed faith in the resurrection of Christ, they should have had no objections to believing in the resurrection of humanity. He declares to the Corinthians, "Now if Christ is preached, that He has been raised from the dead, how do some among you say that there is no resurrection of the dead?" (1 Cor. 15:12). The same Jesus that had appeared to James and all of the apostles had also appeared to Paul "as to one untimely born" (1 Cor. 15:8-11; cf. Acts 9:3-8; 22:6-11; 26:12-18). Earlier, the apostle had rhetorically asked the Corinthians, "Am I not free? Am I not an apostle? Have I not seen Jesus our Lord? Are you not my work in the Lord?" (1 Cor. 9:1)

The Corinthians did not deny the resurrection of Christ per se, but they rejected the future, bodily resurrection. Similarly, those who subscribe to an over-realized eschatology affirm their belief in the resurrection of Christ but deny the future resurrection of the righteous and wicked. Paul correlates references to the resurrection of Christ and the general resurrection frequently throughout this chapter (1 Cor. 15:12, 13, 15, 16, 18).

Although some may question how serious the denial of the future resurrection is, one should consider Paul's rebuke of an over-realized eschatology of the first century. He wrote, "But avoid worldly and empty chatter, for it will lead to further ungodliness, and their talk will spread like gangrene. Among them are Hymenaeus and Philetus, men who have gone astray from the truth saying that the resurrection has already taken place, and they upset the faith of some" (2 Tim. 2:16-18). Was the error of which Paul spoke merely a poorly timed eschatology? Their error was not merely a matter of timing; they were also denying the true nature of the resurrection and thus were "making shipwreck of the faith" (2 Tim. 2:18) (P.H. Towner, 95-124). Preterists will counter, "If the resurrection was a general and bodily event, how could anyone have been deceived by thinking it had already past?" The deception was not only regarding the timing of the resurrection, but also the nature of the resurrection, much like the influence of our preterists friends today.

Paul warns that denying an essential element of the gospel will unravel the entire story of salvation. For the apostle, once the theological dominos start falling, there is no stopping point. For instance, when the general resurrection is denied, then the bodily resurrection of Christ will be questioned. Once that occurs, there can be no salvation because the gospel message has been undermined (1 Cor. 15:12-19). Realized escha-

What Is the Biblical Teaching on the Resurrection?

tology impacts not only our view of the end of time, but also our understanding of the redemptive purposes of God, the nature and atonement of Christ, the outworking of salvation, the nature of the church, along with its worship and work, and the biblical teaching concerning the eschatological events of our future.

The Scriptural understanding of the resurrection provided a foundation through which Paul accepted the resurrection of Christ (Acts 24:15; 26:3, 8). Based on the Law and the prophets, the Jews believed in a bodily resurrection of the dead (John 11:24). Therefore, Paul was convicted that God could and would raise the dead and, thus, had raised Jesus from the dead. Therefore, for the Corinthians to deny a future resurrection would remove any reasonable foundation for the resurrection of Christ.

Paul inseparably connects the first fruits of Jesus's resurrection and the harvest of our future bodily resurrection, "But now Christ is risen from the dead, and has become the first fruits of those who have fallen asleep" (1 Cor. 15:20). The first fruits are the first of a kind, and the latter fruits are the same in kind (Pope, 93). First fruits, as the initial product, provide both the guarantee and representation of the same quality or character. Thus, Jesus's bodily resurrection serves as the guarantee or promise of our future bodily resurrection, "But each one in his own order: Christ the first fruits, afterward those who are Christ's at His coming" (1 Cor. 15:23).

The Adam-Christ typology describes the curse of physical death in the sin of Adam and the super-reversal of the sin curse through Christ. He wrote, "For since by man came death, by Man also came the resurrection of the dead. For as in Adam all die, even so in Christ all shall be made alive" (1 Cor. 15:21-22). If these verses were referring to spiritual death, then the logical consequence would be that of universalism since "all shall be made alive." It is true, however, that all men will come forth from the grave, some to eternal life and some to condemnation (John 5:28-29). Just as the sin of Adam brought physical death upon all of mankind (Gen. 3:17-19), so the resurrection of Christ guarantees the bodily resurrection of both the wicked and righteous (John 5:28-29; Acts 24:15). Jesus became incarnate to rescue us from "the fear of death" and the slavery of despair (Heb. 2:9-18).

Many realized eschatology advocates will attempt to redefine the terms of 1 Corinthians 15 to maintain their denial of the personal bodily resurrection. Words such as "death," "resurrection," and "body" are defined to remove the human body, physical death, and bodily resurrection from consideration. In the dictionary of the preterists "death" refers only to spiritual death, "resurrection" refers merely to a figurative resurrection, and the singular term "body" always refers to the spiritual body of Christ in His church.[7] Sam Dawson writes, "We established in the previous chapter of this volume that the resurrection Paul spoke of in 1 Corinthians 15 was not a resurrection of physical bodies out of holes in the ground, but the resurrection of Old Covenant Israel from the death of its fellowship with God" (Dawson, 109). Again he comments, "Who were the 'dead ones?' They were the same Old Covenant dead ones Paul discussed throughout the chapter, the very ones the Gentile Christians in the Paul Party denied the resurrection to" (ibid., 190). The preterists assume and interject their concept that the entire book of 1 Corinthians is about Jewish-Gentile tensions in the same way that epistles of Romans, Ephesians, Colossians, etc. address. Yet, they offer no proof in any way that would legitimize such a perspective. While the doctrine of a future, bodily resurrection was not a problem in the majority consensus of Jewish thought, it was certainly a problem in Platonic pagan thought (Acts 17:32). The idea of a general resurrection at the end of the age is foreign to the Greeks. Interestingly, advocates of preterism accuse others of ignoring the context of 1 Corinthians 15, but then turn around and impose on the chapter a context that does not exist. This approach is not exegesis but rather proof-texting, which this speculative theory demands.

The interpretations of realized eschatologists serve as a significant distortion of the context under consideration. Paul explicitly appeals to the physical death and bodily resurrection of Jesus as the foundation of our hope (1 Cor. 15:3-4, 12-17). He also uses the metaphor of being "asleep" to refer to those who had physically died (1 Cor. 15:6, 18, 20; cf. 12, 16, 21-22, 26, 29, 32, 35, 51). The apostle asks, "Why are we in danger every hour?" He then goes on to say, "I die daily" and "If from

---

[7] The term "body" does refer to the spiritual body of Christ in many contexts in the New Testament. Yet, it would be irresponsible biblically to demand that such is the case in every usage. Such an interpretation would lead to absurd conclusions. This is especially evident when Preterists argue that even the phrase "our body" refers to the spiritual body of Christ. There is no sense in which the church of Christ is "our body."

What Is the Biblical Teaching on the Resurrection?

human motives I fought with wild beasts in Ephesus, what does it profit me?" (1 Cor. 15:30-32). He then reaches to his rhetorical peak when he proclaims, "If the dead are not raised, 'Let us eat and drink, for tomorrow we die.'" In other words, why do I jeopardize my physical life for Christ if there is no resurrection? Why would Paul use such reasoning if physical death was not under consideration? Some who wish to defend realized eschatology have gone so far as to deny that physical death is a consequence of sin or that the personal, bodily resurrection is even addressed in 1 Corinthians 15. Yet, there is no doubt that the plain reading of the text deals with physical death as a curse of sin and the future resurrection as the redemption of the body (Rom. 8:23).

It is worthy of note that Paul presents the Adam-Christ typology to include all of humanity in his discussion (1 Cor. 15:21-23). By way of contrast, he does not appeal to *Moses* for those only "under the Law;" instead, he appeals to Adam to include both Jews and Gentiles in the promise of resurrection. Although, in the book of Romans, Paul uses this typology to emphasize the universal problem of sin in spiritual death "because all have sinned" (Rom. 5:12), in 1 Corinthians 15 he uses the typology to describe physical death as a consequence of Adam's sin. God's purpose is that His people enjoy victory over sin and all of its effects through Jesus Christ.

Jesus will reign until He has "abolished" all "rule," "authority," and "power" and, therefore, conquers all of God's "enemies under his feet," including "death" (1 Cor. 15:24-26). At the "end," Christ will "hand over the kingdom to God" and will Himself be subject to His Father that "God may be all in all" (1 Cor. 15:24-28). This subjection does not deny His divinity, but it does emphasize the diversity of function in the Godhead and the sacrifice of the Son (1 Cor. 8:6; 11:1-3; Phil. 2:6-11). At this point, every vestige effect of sin will have been abolished, and the ultimate conquering of death will have occurred in the bodily resurrection, destruction of the world, and the return of Christ (2 Pet. 3:1-18).

The argument in this context is that the denial of the general resurrection leads to the rejection of the Lordship of Christ and His salvific purposes (1 Cor. 15:28). Any view that minimizes the absolute and total victory over sin and death accomplished in the bodily resurrection undermines the foundation of our hope in Christ. Although some question how eschatological teachings really affect our everyday living, Paul responds by emphasizing that our moral standards are grounded in our

"When Will These Things Be?" : Questions on Eschatology

faith regarding what Christ has done and promised us. He stated, "Do not be deceived: 'Bad company corrupts good morals.' Become sober-minded as you ought, and stop sinning, for some have no knowledge of God. I speak this to your shame" (1 Cor. 15:33-34).

Paul Addresses the Corinthian's Questions and Arguments

We are now introduced to the argumentative questions that were being foisted upon the minds of the Christians in Corinth. Paul writes, "But someone will say, 'How are the dead raised? And with what kind of body do they come?'"(1 Cor. 15:35) The false teachers at Corinth were asking these questions to assert that a bodily resurrection would be impossible. Yet, Paul appeals to the sovereign power of God as Creator. He also appeals to the laws of nature that were observable on a daily basis.

From an agricultural standpoint, every time a seed, which had the God-given germ of life, was put into the ground, it died, decayed, and decomposed, and then life came forth from death. We read, "You fool! That which you sow does not come to life unless it dies; and that which you sow, you do not sow the body, which is to be, but a bare grain, perhaps of wheat or of something else" (1 Cor. 15:36-37). A natural analogy is given, which expresses an evident truth: a seed dies, is planted, and life comes forth from that seed in a different form. Paul is not arguing for a resurrection into a corruptible, perishable body, but that our bodies will be changed and transformed by the power of God (1 Cor. 15:36-37; cf. Matt. 22:29-32; Phil. 3:20-21).

Many scholars have referred to the continuity between our present body and our resurrection body as a "somatic union" (Barclay, 505). Although our glorified body will be distinct from our present bodies, we should not think of the process as an exchange, but rather a transformation. Matthew Bates writes, "The bodily resurrection suggests an analogy. Our present bodies are like kernels of wheat, but our resurrected bodies will be like the full plant. . ." (Bates, 146).

To question the ability of God to perform His will when He has promised to do so is unbelief, not faith (Phil. 3:20-21). If God made us, He can raise us! As our God has created various forms for His creatures so they may exist in the natural realm, so He will transform our bodies to function in the spiritual realm:

What Is the Biblical Teaching on the Resurrection?

> But God gives it a body just as He wished, and to each of the seeds a body of its own. All flesh is not the same flesh, but there is one flesh of men, and another flesh of beasts, and another flesh of birds, and another of fish. There are also heavenly bodies and earthly bodies, but the glory of the heavenly is one, and the glory of the earthly is another. There is one glory of the sun and another glory of the moon, and another glory of the stars; for star differs from star in glory (1 Cor. 15: 38-41).

Just as God gave a body to each of His creations suiting their needs and His glorious plans, so He will provide the type of body necessary for us to function in the spiritual realm throughout eternity. The apostle Paul now brings the Holy Spirit's application home to us, "So also is the resurrection of the dead. It is sown a perishable body, it is raised an imperishable body; it is sown in dishonor, it is raised in glory; it is sown in weakness, it is raised in power; it is sown a natural body, it is raised a spiritual body. If there is a natural body, there is also a spiritual body" (1 Cor. 15:42-44). Interestingly, there is both continuity and discontinuity between the pre-resurrection body and the post-resurrection body. The term "it" refers to our physical body, i.e., that which is sown is that which is raised albeit transformed. The transformed body will not be subject to decay, corruption, or death, for death will have been absolutely and finally conquered.

Jesus's mortal body was sown as a "perishable," "dishonorable," "weak," and "natural" body. But His resurrection body was raised as an "imperishable," "glorious," "powerful," and "spiritual" body. Likewise, our mortal body is described as that which is "perishable," "dishonorable," "weak," and "natural." Whereas our resurrection body will be raised "imperishable," "glorious," "powerful," and "spiritual." Indeed, Christ's resurrection body serves as the first fruits of our future resurrection (1 Cor. 15:20-23).

The "natural body" is designed to function in the natural realm, whereas the "spiritual body" is transformed to function in the spiritual realm. The phrase "spiritual body" is not equivalent to a bodiless spirit because that would be a denial of the very phrase itself. A spiritual body is an incorruptible, imperishable, powerful, and glorified body. Those who mock the notion of a future resurrection body will inevitably diminish and even deny the resurrection body of our Lord. The contrast is not between us having form versus having no form. A spiritual body is as

"When Will These Things Be?" : Questions on Eschatology

tangible as was Christ's resurrection body (Luke 24:39). The term "spiritual" modifies the word "body," but it does not replace it (Rom. 8:11, 23, 24; Phil. 3:20-21). Michael Gorman insightfully comments,

> We must stress here one key point that contemporary Christians often fail to understand or try to avoid: that Christ's resurrection was a bodily resurrection. Paul was a Pharisee, not a Platonist, and he did not believe in the mortality of a body-less soul. Bodily resurrection does not simply mean the resuscitation of a corpse, but neither is it merely symbolic language for Christ's ongoing existence in the church as His body, or something similar. The resurrection is a mystery . . . the resurrection is a bodily experience (Gorman, 258).

Defenders of realized eschatology frequently argue that the "body" described in 1 Corinthians 15 is the corporate body of Christ. This interpretation radically changes the reading of not only this context but also the entire New Testament. Holger Neubauer, a Full Preterist, explains his view of the problem at Corinth, "If you do not believe that the Old Testament saints, (Abraham, Noah, Moses, Daniel, etc.), will be granted spiritual life in AD 70 when Jerusalem is destroyed—then Christ has not been raised . . . and our preaching is vain and your faith is vain" (Neubauer, "There Is One 'The Body'").

He again comments, "The question revolved around the idea that the Old Jewish saints could not be raised in a new body of Christ that comprised of both Jew and Gentile. . ." (Neubauer, "The Resurrection of 1 Corinthians 15"). Speaking of 1 Corinthians 15:48 Neubauer writes, "The 'they' refers to those who were becoming 'heavenly' during the transition period as the church was stripping off its layers of Judaism. . ." (Neubauer, ibid.) The consequences of this perspective are drastic and concerning. This view drastically distorts the context and background of 1 Corinthians 15. Realized eschatology argues that: (1) there were two bodies in the one church prior to AD 70; (2) believers were not "fully forgiven until AD 70;" (3) Christians were not actually spiritually alive until AD 70; which (4) logically implies that the church was corruptible and dying until AD 70 (Williams, 233-238).

Paul continues to apply the Adam-Christ typology to the resurrection, "So also it is written, 'The first man, Adam, became a living soul.' The last Adam became a life-giving spirit. However, the spiritual is not first, but the natural; then the spiritual" (1 Cor. 15:45-46). Adam was the

What Is the Biblical Teaching on the Resurrection?

first natural human being, i.e., a "living soul," (*soma psychikon*), whereas Christ as the "last Adam became a live-giving spirit" (*soma pneumatikon*) in the resurrection. Mike Willis comments, "We receive a 'living soul' (a body fitted for life in this world) from Adam; we receive a quickening spirit or 'life-giving spirit' (a body fitted for life in the world to come) from Christ" (Willis, 464).

As we have "borne the image of the earthy, we will also bear the image of the heavenly" (1 Cor. 15:49). The NET Bible offers the following text-critical note regarding 1 Corinthians 15:49:

> Paul wrote to combat an over-realized eschatology in which some of the Corinthians evidently believed they were experiencing all the benefits of the resurrection body in the present, and thus that their behavior did not matter. If the subjunctive is the correct reading, it seems Paul makes two points: (1) that the resurrection is a bodily one, as distinct from an out-of-body experience, and (2) that one's behavior in the interim does make a difference (see 15:32-34, 58).

John writes, "Beloved, now we are children of God, and it has not appeared as yet what we will be. We know that when He appears, we will be like Him, because we will see Him just as He is" (1 John 3:2). Even though we all have our questions about the resurrection, this passage is not teaching us that we cannot understand the nature of the resurrection body. Rather, the apostle is emphasizing that we have not "actually been manifested" or "shown forth in actuality" in our glorified condition as the children of God (King, 88). Our resurrection body will be like Jesus's resurrection body (Willis, "Resurrection!," 127).

For us to enjoy an eternal existence in the spiritual realm, our bodies must be changed. Paul writes, "Now I say this, brethren, that flesh and blood cannot inherit the kingdom of God; nor does the perishable inherit the imperishable. Behold, I tell you a mystery; we will not all sleep, but we will all be changed" (1 Cor. 15:50-51). The phrase "flesh and blood" does not negate a resurrection body, but it does exclude a corruptible, natural, and perishable body from receiving the heavenly reward. The expression "flesh and blood" refers to the current bodily state of the Christians to whom Paul is writing (Matt. 16:17; Gal. 1:16; Eph. 6:12; Heb. 2:14). The brethren at Corinth were spiritually alive before AD 70 (1 Cor. 1:1-2; 12:13). Therefore, the transformation Paul is speaking of is a bodily resurrection (1 Cor. 15:51-53).

"When Will These Things Be?" : Questions on Eschatology

Paul explains that not all men will die, but all will be changed. This change will occur in a "moment, in the twinkling of an eye, at the last trumpet; for the trumpet will sound, and the dead will be raised imperishable, and we will be changed" (1 Cor. 15:51-52). The term "moment" refers to a particle of time so small that it cannot be divided (Vine, 823). The "moment" is so brief that it is described as the "twinkling of an eye." This is the only time the phrase is used in the NT, but the idiom literally means in the "blinking of an eye." In a moment, "the dead will be raised imperishable and we will be changed." Just as "it" will be "sown" and "it" will be "raised," so "this perishable must put on imperishable, and this mortal must put on immortality" (1 Cor. 15:52-54). Paul penned similar concepts to the Philippians, "For our citizenship is in heaven, from which also we eagerly wait for a Savior, the Lord Jesus Christ; who will transform the body of our humble state into conformity with the body of His glory, by the exertion of the power that He has even to subject all things to Himself" (Phil. 3:20-21).[8]

The believer's body will be changed from being "perishable" and "subject to death" to be in a condition in which it is not subject to death any longer. What is "mortal is swallowed up of life" (2 Cor. 5:4). In victorious language, Paul, under the inspiration of the Holy Spirit, references Isaiah 25:8 and Hosea 13:14 as he offers Jesus Christ as the answer to the curse of sin and death (1 Cor. 15:54-55). Israel deserved the punishment of God, which would include physical death, "Shall I ransom them from the power of sheol? Shall I redeem them from death? O Death, where are your thorns? O sheol, where is your sting? Compassion will be hidden from My sight" (Hos. 13:14). Paul provides the quotation of Hosea's writings and incorporates the Spirit's revelation of the gospel—victory is in Jesus! No one has the right to redefine Paul's words in a way that departs from the plain meaning of the context. Those who deny that Hosea's writ-

---

[8] The notion that this verse is speaking of a change in the church in the "stripping away of the layers of Judaism" is based on various misunderstandings of realized eschatology and offers a contradictory and absurd reading of this verse in light of the context. One should notice that Christians prior to AD 70 enjoyed a "heavenly citizenship" thus the term "body" in this context is not speaking of the corporate body, but the believer's corporeal body and his or her hope of a future bodily resurrection when Christ returns. One may ask, "When is the church of Christ described as being vile?" "When is the church of Christ ever described as 'our body'"?

What Is the Biblical Teaching on the Resurrection?

ings can be applied to the future bodily resurrection misunderstand both Hosea and the apostle Paul. The New Testament writers often help us see the fullness of the writings of the prophets, so why should this verse not be another example of such (Ps. 16:9-10; Acts 2:26-27; 13:35-36; Isa. 55:3; Acts 13:34-35). What a beautiful story of salvation is seen in the contrast between the phrases, "compassion will be hidden from My sight" (Hos. 13:14) and "thanks be to God, who gives us the victory through our Lord Jesus Christ" (1 Cor. 15:57). Our conviction concerning the future resurrection will lead us to be "steadfast, immovable, always abounding in the work of the Lord" thanks to our assurance in Christ (1 Cor. 15:58).

The Resurrection and Moral Purity

The Corinthians were encouraged to pursue sexual purity in light of their future resurrection, "Food is for the stomach and the stomach is for food, but God will do away with both of them. Yet the body is not for sexual immorality, but for the Lord, and the Lord is for the body" (1 Cor. 6:13). The apostle does not share the notion that God is indifferent toward either the use or purpose of our bodies. Preterists frequently argue that the use of the singular term "body" in Scripture uniformly refers to the corporate body of Christ, but this argument breaks down quickly in several New Testament texts, and this is one of them. Our body is not to be used for sexual immorality because it will be raised for God's glory. Paul writes, "Yet the body is not for immorality, but for the Lord, and the Lord is for the body. Now God has not only raised the Lord, but will also raise us up through His power" (1 Cor. 6:13–14). This resurrection cannot be describing a future spiritual resurrection because they had already been "washed, sanctified, and justified" in the name of "Jesus Christ" (1 Cor. 6:9-11). Paul's argument is only sensible if he believes in the somatic union between our present body and our future resurrection body.

Paul goes on to write, "Do you not know that your bodies are members of Christ? Shall I then take away the members of Christ and make them members of a prostitute? May it never be! Or do you not know that one who joins himself to a prostitute is one body with her? For He says, 'The two shall become one flesh'" (1 Cor. 6:15-16). Note that the plural term "bodies" (1 Cor. 6:15) is equivalent to the singular term "body" (1 Cor. 6:18) in this context. Sexual sin is a sin against one's own body, and this is the body that will be changed and raised by the power of God. We read, "But the one who joins himself to the Lord is one spirit with Him. Flee sexual immorality. Every other sin that a man commits is outside the body, but the sexually immoral man sins against his own body" (1 Cor. 6:17-18).

There is no doubt that we are stewards of our bodies and must use them for the Lord's purpose. The view that God is indifferent about the physical body sounds more like paganism than Christianity and entirely misses the significance of the resurrection. Paul said, "Or do you not know that your body is a temple of the Holy Spirit who is in you, whom you have from God, and that you are not your own? For you have been bought with a price: therefore glorify God in your body" (1 Cor. 6:19-20). Paul also exhorts the Thessalonians along the same lines, "Now may the God of peace Himself sanctify you entirely; and may your spirit and soul and body be preserved complete, without blame at the coming of our Lord Jesus Christ" (1 Thess. 5:23). Is he simply saying, "Use your bodies for God's glory until the destruction of Jerusalem in AD 70?" Certainly not! He is encouraging us to sanctification in light of the full benefits of the redemption of our spirit, soul, and body at Christ's final coming at the end of time.

Some of the Corinthians had such a low view of the physical body that they reasoned it had no bearing on their spiritual wisdom and standing. Yet, Paul corrects a distinctive dualism between the body and soul of man that was characteristic of paganism (Rom. 12:1-2). While the appetite and food are for each other, sexual immorality and the body are not. Paul argues that our "bodies" are "members of Christ," therefore, when we use our bodies to sin, we are actually dismembering, pulling apart, and taking back the very "members of Christ" in our conduct. Paul declares, "May it never be!" Every Christian is to be God's temple (1 Cor. 6:19). Like the community as a whole (1 Cor. 3:16), each believer is to be "a temple of the Holy Spirit" (1 Cor. 6:19). If we as disciples use our bodies to participate in sin, we are guilty of idolatry. We are to use our lives and bodies as a channel for the praise of God and the gospel of Christ. It is no wonder Paul uses the future bodily resurrection as a powerful admonition for the purity of believers, "For you have been bought with a price: therefore glorify God in your body" (1 Cor. 6:20).

The Hope of the Resurrection (2 Corinthians 4:1-5:11)

The hope of the resurrection offers us tremendous motivation to live for Christ even under the most intense trials of this life (2 Cor. 4:1-6). Even though Christians can face the threat of physical death, we still live

What Is the Biblical Teaching on the Resurrection?

in the hope of our future reward, "Therefore we do not lose heart, but though our outer man is decaying, yet our inner man is being renewed day by day" (2 Cor. 4:16). Paul's hope in God's power enabled him to endure suffering, pain, and even physical death, knowing that he would be resurrected to life just as Jesus was raised (2 Cor. 4:7-11). What is the foundation for such a hope? Paul answers the question powerfully, "Knowing that He who raised the Lord Jesus will raise us up also with you" (2 Cor. 4:14).

The epistle to the Romans similarly points us toward the hope of the children of God by appealing to our future resurrection, "But if the Spirit of Him who raised Jesus from the dead dwells in you, He who raised Christ Jesus from the dead will also give life to your mortal bodies through His Spirit who dwells in you" (Rom. 8:11). It is noteworthy that Paul mentions three resurrections in this verse: Jesus's resurrection, our spiritual resurrection in Christ, and the resurrection of our bodies. This verse presents a real problem for those who deny that there will be a bodily resurrection. Neubauer posits the following explanation of this verse, "When Paul says, 'will also give life to your mortal bodies through His Holy Spirit who dwells in you' (8:11), he is not speaking of individual bodies, but corporate bodies comprised of both Jew and Gentile. . . The 'one body' is the church and it is that body that is Paul's focus in the scheme of redemption" (Neubauer, "There Is One 'The Body.'"). This line of argumentation not only leads to the conclusions that there were two bodies prior to AD 70 in the church, but also that these two bodies were "mortal" and that the one body of Christ did not exist until AD 70. This argument also denies the explicit promise for Christians today concerning their future hope.

As children of God, we are presently "heirs of God" and "fellow heirs with Christ" with an incomparable hope that is to be revealed in our glorification (Rom. 8:17-18). Not only have we presently experienced the redemption of our souls, but we will also experience the "redemption of our bodies" (Rom. 8:23-25). Has this hope already been realized, or is it yet to come? In Romans 8:23 and Philippians 3:21, the phrase "our body" emphasizes the nature of our future resurrection. To attempt to interpret the phrase as the corporate body of Christ does not fit the context at all. The body of Christ is never described as "our body," for it does not belong to us (Rom. 8:23; 2 Cor. 4:10; Phil. 3:21).

"When Will These Things Be?" : Questions on Eschatology

With 2 Corinthians 4 and Romans 8 in the background of our discussion, we will now consider 2 Corinthians 5:1-11. Paul assures the Corinthian believers of their hope despite suffering, "For we know that if the earthly tent which is our house is torn down, we have a building from God, a house not made with hands, eternal in the heavens. For indeed in this house we groan, longing to be clothed with our dwelling from heaven, inasmuch as we, having put it on will not be found naked" (2 Cor. 5:1-3). Paul denounces disembodied immortality as being "naked" and anticipates a powerful resurrection.

Are we to believe that the apostle is describing a contrast between the Old Covenant and New Covenant? Is his phrase "earthly tent" really a reference to Judaism? Does this harmonize with this context? The reference to being "in this tent" refers to the physical body (2 Pet. 1:13-14). These Christians were no longer in the tent of Judaism (Rom. 7:1-5; Gal. 3:22-28; Eph. 2:12-22; Col. 2:14-16), but they were in the tent of their bodies (2 Cor. 4:7-11). Do not Christians today still "groan" in their longing for their resurrection?

> For indeed while we are in this tent, we groan, being burdened because we do not want to be unclothed but to be clothed, so that what is mortal will be swallowed up by life. For indeed while we are in this tent, we groan, being burdened, because we do not want to be unclothed but to be clothed, so that what is mortal will be swallowed up by life. Therefore, being always of good courage, and knowing that while we are at home in the body we are absent from the Lord—for we walk by faith, not by sight—we are of good courage, I say, and prefer rather to be absent from the body and to be at home with the Lord. Therefore we also have as our ambition, whether at home or absent, to be pleasing to Him. For we must all appear before the judgment seat of Christ, so that each one may be recompensed for his deeds in the body, according to what he has done, whether good or bad (2 Cor. 5: 1-4).

Max King asserts that the "earthly tent" of 2 Corinthians 5:1 and the phrase "at home in the body" of 2 Corinthians 5:6 refers to solidarity with the Old Covenant, whereas to be "absent from the body" is to be in the completed New Covenant (King, 597-603). This interpretation is an extremely strained reading of this section of Scripture, to say the very least. Being "at home in the body" is to be "absent from the Lord" and to be "absent from the body" is to be "at home with the Lord" (2 Cor. 5:6, 8). Yet, in either state, whether in or out of the body, we are to be "pleasing to

What Is the Biblical Teaching on the Resurrection?

the Lord." Would Paul have said viewing Judaism as still binding after the cross and Pentecost would have been "pleasing to the Lord"? Of course not! One cannot please God "in the flesh" (Rom. 7:6; 8:8), in spiritual adultery (Rom. 7:1-6), nor can one live in the Spirit and in the flesh at the same time (Rom. 8:1-9). The "body" of 2 Corinthians 5 cannot be the Old Covenant body but must be our physical body.

When Paul warns Christians that they will be judged for the "deeds done in the body," he is referring to our actual physical bodies, not merely Jews living under the Old Covenant. This verse applies as much to us today as it did to the Corinthians in the first century. The text uses varied phrases which all speak of our corporeal bodies, "earthen vessels" (2 Cor. 4:7), "our body" (2 Cor. 4:10), "mortal flesh" (2 Cor. 4:11), "outer man" (2 Cor. 4:16), "earthly tent" (2 Cor. 5:1), "our house" (2 Cor. 5:1), "this house" (2 Cor. 5:2), "this tent" (2 Cor. 5:4), "what is mortal" (2 Cor. 5:4), and "the body" (2 Cor. 5:6, 8, 10). Although we are relationally with the Lord right now (Eph. 2:6), there is a sense in which we are absent from Him and look forward to coming into His presence in eternity (2 Cor. 5:6, 8; Phil. 1:21-23). We are not yet "at home with the Lord," or else we would be walking by sight rather than faith (2 Cor. 5:7-8).

"Comfort One Another with These Words" (1 Thessalonians)

The church at Thessalonica was zealous for the Lord (1 Thess. 1:1-10), but still needed teaching concerning the final resurrection and the Second Coming of Christ (1 Thess. 4:13). There was a Jewish element in the congregation to be sure (Acts 17:1-10). However, there are at least three factors which indicate a Gentile element as well: first, they had turned from serving idols to serving the living God (1 Thess. 1:8-10), Gentiles were especially struggling with sexual immorality as a result of past paganism (1 Thess. 4:1-6), and 1 Thessalonians focuses on issues confronting Gentile believers (1 Thess. 2:14; 4:3, 5). Paul's reference to the resurrection does not refer to the destruction of Jerusalem in AD 70 for several reasons: Gentile believers did not need to be rescued from the destruction of Jerusalem (1 Thess. 1:10); the destruction of Jerusalem would not cause Gentile Christians to be shaken, seeing that it was 918 miles away (2 Thess. 2:1-2); the Thessalonians were already spiritually living with the Lord (1 Thess. 1:3, 6; 5:10); and it would be absurd for Paul to promise these Gentile Christians that their "spirit, soul and

"When Will These Things Be?" : Questions on Eschatology

body" would be "preserved complete, without blame" because Jerusalem would be destroyed (1 Thess. 5:23; cf. 2:19-20; 3:13).

Apparently, there were Thessalonian Christians who were under the impression that believers had to be alive when Jesus returned to be saved. He writes, "But we do not want you to be uninformed, brethren, about those who are asleep, so that you will not grieve as do the rest who have no hope" (1 Thess. 4:13). The contrast is between those who are physically alive and physically dead. Paul is encouraging Thessalonian believers, whether Jewish or Gentile, regarding the hope for those who had died, lest they "grieve as those who have no hope" (1 Thess. 4:19; cf. 1 Cor. 15:19).

Paul clarifies that those who "have fallen asleep in Jesus" are secure thanks to the death and resurrection of Christ, "For if we believe that Jesus died and rose again, even so God will bring with Him those who have fallen asleep in Jesus" (1 Thess. 4:14). They had a future hope of a bodily resurrection because Jesus, Himself, had been raised bodily as the first fruits of a future harvest in the general resurrection (1 Thess. 4:14; cf. 1 Cor. 15:20-23). Those physically alive when Jesus comes again will be changed (1 Cor. 15:51-54), but will not "precede those who have fallen asleep" (1 Thess. 4:15). The teaching that the "dead in Christ will rise first" has to be speaking of a bodily resurrection because these brethren were already spiritually alive (Eph. 2:4-8; Col. 2:11-13).

Those saints who are physically alive, whoever they are, will be "caught up together" (1 Thess. 4:17).[9] This gathering is not their initial uniting (Eph. 2:12-22), but a reuniting when the resurrection and Second Coming of the Lord occur (Heb. 9:26-28). To attempt to explain away literal passages by laying figurative passages over them is hermeneutically flawed. The reason this language can be used figuratively is that it is grounded in reality, and it is that very reality that is being discussed in this context.

---

[9] Full Preterists will argue that the "gathering" described in Scripture is uniformly speaking of Jews and Gentiles being unified in AD 70. However this expression does not always, if ever, refer to the destruction of Jerusalem in AD 70 (Gen. 49:10; Psa. 102:22; Isa. 2:2-3; 11:12; 40:11; Jer. 31:11; Ez. 34:11; 37:21-22; Hos. 1:10; Mic. 2:12). If these passages are Messianic, they refer to the results of the cross of Christ in the establishment of Christ's church and the unity of believers before AD 70 (Eph. 2:11-22). 1 Thessalonians 4:17 does not speak of the unity of Christians because that was already a reality; therefore, it is speaking of the reuniting of Christians when Jesus returns for His people.

What Is the Biblical Teaching on the Resurrection?

We have believed in the resurrection gospel! It is a message that proclaims the resurrection of Christ (Rom. 10:9-10), the resurrection of the new man in righteousness (Col. 3:11-12), and the future bodily resurrection. When we consider the pains of death we remember the grace of Christ; when we contemplate the anguish of loss, we remember the comfort of the Holy Spirit; when we experience the terrors of death, we hear the sounds of victory; and when we shed the tears of agony, we see the faithful Savior as He holds us safely in His arms and promises us the resurrection morning is coming. Let us hear the beautiful words of the devoted apostle Paul, "But thanks be to God, who gives us the victory through our Lord Jesus Christ. Therefore, my beloved brethren, be steadfast, immovable, always abound in the work of the Lord, knowing that your toil is not in vain in the Lord" (1 Cor. 15:57-58).

Bibliography

Goldingay, John E. *Daniel.* Word Biblical Commentary 30. Dallas: Word Books, 1989.

Gorman, Michael J. *Participating in Christ: Explorations in Paul's Theology and Spirituality.* Grand Rapids, MI: Baker Academic, 2019.

King, Daniel H. *Truth Commentaries: Daniel.* Bowling Green, KY: Guardian of Truth Publishing Co., 2012

———. *Truth Commentaries: First John.* Bowling Green, KY: Guardian of Truth Publishing Co., 2004

King, Max R. *The Cross and the Parousia of Christ: The Two Dimensions Of One Age- Changing Eschaton.* Warren, OH: Parkman Road Church of Christ, 1987.

Lenski, R.C.H. *The Interpretation of St. Matthew's Gospel.* Minneapolis: Augsburg Publishing House, 1964.

McGuiggan, Jim. *The Book of Daniel.* Lubbock, TX: International Biblical Resources, 1978.

Neubauer, Holger "There Is One 'The Body.'" *DonKPreston.com.* August 8, 2016. https://donkpreston.com/guest-article-there-is-one-the-body-by-holger-neubauer.

———. "The Resurrection of 1 Corinthians 15." *DonKPreston.com.* August 8, 2016. https://donkpreston.com/the-resurrection-of-1-corinthians-15-article-9-by-holger-neubauer.

Pope, Kyle. *Thinking about AD 70: Challenging Realized Eschatology.* Athens, AL: Truth Publications, Inc., 2019.

Preston, Don K. *We Shall Meet Him in the Air: The Wedding of the King of Kings.* Ardmore, OK: JaDon Management Inc., 2009.

Towner, P.H. "Gnosis and Realized Eschatology in Ephesus (of the Pastoral Epistles) and the Corinthian Enthusiasm." *Journal for the Study of the New Testament* 31 (1987): 95-124.

Willis, Mike. "Resurrection!" *A Study of the AD 70 Doctrine: Realized Eschatology.* Mike Willis ed., 126-129. Bowling Green, KY: Guardian of Truth, Publishing Co., 2006.

———. *Truth Commentaries: 1 Corinthians.* Bowling Green: Guardian of Truth Publishing Co., 1994.

Wilson, Jeff. "To Fulfill the Scriptures: Testimony for the Resurrection from the Rest of the Old Testament." *Of First Importance He Was Raised and Appeared: Studies in the Resurrection.* Dan Petty, ed., 128-159. Temple Terrace: Florida College Press, 2013.

Wright, N.T. *The Resurrection of the Son of God.* Christian Origins and the Question of God 3. Minneapolis: Fortress Press, 2003.

Does the Bible Teach the "Rapture," the Coming of an Antichrist, and the Battle of Armageddon?

By Mark Mayberry

Introduction

Christ will come again! While Christians eagerly anticipate the Lord's Second Coming (John 14:1-3; 1 Cor. 16:22; 1 Thess. 5:1-6), this does not mean that we accept the tenets of premillennialism?

Defining the Doctrine

Premillennialism affirms that Christ will return before the start of His 1,000-year earthly reign. *Merriam-Webster's Collegiate Dictionary* defines "premillennialism" as "the view that Christ's return will usher in a future millennium of Messianic rule mentioned in Revelation." This word came into common usage circa AD 1883, a time of intense speculation about biblical eschatology.

Mark Mayberry (1957—), the son of Donald Mayberry and Ruth Hutcheson Mayberry, was born in Nashville and raised in Middle Tennessee. He spent most of his childhood in Clarksville, where he obeyed the gospel and was a member of the South Clarksville congregation. He met Sherelyn Finley while attending Florida College, and they were married in June of 1978. After moving to Texas, the Mayberrys lived in Groveton (79–81), Tyler (81–86), and Cooper (86–91), laboring with faithful brethren in each community. In 1991, they moved to Clarksville, TN, and spent seven years working with the Warfield Boulevard congregation. The family returned to Texas in 1998, to the city of Alvin, located south of Houston,

"When Will These Things Be?": Questions on Eschatology

Postmillennialism is the doctrine that the Second Coming of Christ will occur after the millennium. Premillennialism is the view that Christ's return will usher in a future millennium of Messianic rule mentioned in Revelation." In contrast, amillennialism affirms a symbolic and non-literal understanding of the 1,000-year reign of Christ, which began on the day of Pentecost and will continue until Jesus returns. Many religious groups advocate this doctrine: "Bible" churches, Southern Baptists, Jehovah's Witnesses, Assemblies of God, and various other Pentecostal bodies. Promoters among the denominations include William Miller, Charles T. Russell, Cyrus Scofield, Billy Graham, and, most recently, Tim LaHaye. Past proponents among brethren were R. H. Boll and his followers.

Note the following discussion of "Premillennialism" that comes from "Salvation Belongs to the Lord: An Introduction to Systematic Theology," by John M. Frame:

> There are two forms of premillennialism, one usually called *classical* or *historic* and the other called *dispensational*. Both view the millennium as yet future, beginning after the Lord returns to earth.
>
> The classical form of premillennialism is a very ancient view that goes back to some of the earliest church fathers. They taught that at the end of the present age Jesus will come and raise believers to be with Him. Then He will reign upon the earth for a thousand years or some other long period of time. During this time (and not until then) Satan is bound in the bottomless pit. At the end of this time, God will release Satan, and at his instigation some on earth will rebel against Jesus (Rev. 20:3, 7, 8). But the Lord will put down the revolt and raise all the dead for final judgment. Then come the new heavens and new earth.

---

which remains their home. They work and worship with the Lord's church that assembles at Adoue Street, where he also serves as an elder, along with Darin Henry and Paul Linden. His Bible Study website is http://markmayberry.net and his personal blog is http://markmayberry.org. The church website is http://www.ascoc.org. He and Sherelyn are blessed with two wonderful sons: Nathan and Ryan; two lovely daughters-in-law: Sarah and Emilee; and two precious grandchildren: Kaelyn and Jackson. They have been encouraged by good brethren in each place where they have lived, and are also thankful for their extended physical families, most of whom are loving, faithful Christians. Mark has written extensively over the years on a wide variety of biblical and religious topics. He is the Secretary of Truth Publications, Inc. and serves as a Board Member. He is the current editor of *Truth Magazine* and can be reached at mark@truthpublications.com.

Does the Bible Teach "Rapture," an Antichrist, and Armageddon?

The dispensational form of premillennialism is more recent (nineteenth century) and more complicated. The key to understanding the dispensational view is the idea that Jesus actually returns twice, which makes a total of three times that Jesus comes to earth. His first coming was, of course, His conception in the womb of Mary two thousand years ago. At His Second Coming, at the end of this age, He comes secretly and raptures believers to be with Him. The rapture is described in 1 Thessalonians 4:16-17, where Paul says, "For the Lord Himself will descend from heaven with a cry of command, with the voice of an archangel, and with the sound of the trumpet of God. And the dead in Christ will rise first. Then we who are alive, who are left, will be caught up together with them in the clouds to meet the Lord in the air, and so we will always be with the Lord" (v. 16). The rapture is the Lord's taking His people to be with Him in the air. All Christians believe in the rapture. What is unique to dispensationalism is the view that the rapture is invisible and secret. This is the picture presented in the *Left Behind* novels and movies: believers mysteriously disappear from offices, streets, airplanes, and so on, with nobody knowing where they are.

Then, according to the dispensational premillennialist, comes a seven-year period of satanic dominance, which gets much worse in the last three and one-half years (these figures come from Dan. 7:25; 9:27; 12:7, Rev. 12:14). The seven-year period is called *the great tribulation*. Most dispensationalists believe that Jesus's secret coming to rapture His saints takes place *before* the great tribulation. So, their view of Jesus's return is not only premillennial but also pretribulational, "pretrib," as we say. There are some dispensationalists, however, who hold that the rapture is midtribulational (that is, three and one-half years into the great tribulation, before the worst part of it) or posttribulational. On the majority pretribulational view, of course, believers do not have to endure the great tribulation at all. Jesus rescues them from it.

After the great tribulation, Jesus returns again—His second, Second Coming, or His third coming. In the earlier (secret) coming, Jesus comes *for* His saints; in the visible third coming, he comes *with* His saints. This coming is public. He then reigns on earth for one thousand years, which may or may not be a literal number. This is the millennium described in Revelation 20:1-6. At the end of this time, there is another apostasy, a period in which Satan is loosed. Then comes the final judgment and the new heavens and new earth.

For the dispensational premillennialist, the millennium is a time in which God fulfills promises He made specifically to the Jews. In the dispensational view, there are two distinct people of God, the Jews and the church of Christ (which contains both Jews and Gentiles). God has promised that the Jews will rule in an expanded land of Palestine, which will literally take place in the millennium. Nondispensationalists believe that the promise of land to Israel is fulfilled in the promise to all Christian believers of a new heaven and new earth. For the nondispensationalist, there is only one people of God: that olive tree of Romans 11 from which some branches have been removed (unbelieving Jews) and others (believing Gentiles) have been grafted in (Frame, 304-305).

Refuting the Doctrine

There are as many variations of premillennialism as there are proclaimers of this theory. However, several common themes remain constant. Premillennial teachers say that Jesus came to establish an earthly kingdom, but He was surprisingly and unexpectedly rejected. Therefore, He returned unto the Father and, as an afterthought or substitute measure, set up the church instead. Nevertheless, Christ will establish His millennial kingdom at His Second Coming. One of the fundamental tenets of premillennialism is that the kingdom and the church are not the same, but are distinct from one another. Advocates of this view say the Old Testament prophets foreshadowed the personal ministry of Christ and also the kingdom, but not the church. They did not anticipate "the church in the valley." However, this doctrine is refuted in the Bible. Let us realize that premillennialism is not taught in the Bible. Instead, it is based on human speculation. Those who promote this doctrine systematically twist and pervert the Scriptures to fit their views. Let us review some of the central tenets of this doctrine, and compare them to the word of God.

The Church Was Not an Afterthought

Premillennialists erroneously argue that the church is an afterthought. In contrast, inspired writers of the New Testament state that the church is a manifestation of God's eternal purpose (Eph. 3:8-11; cf. Heb. 12:22-24). The church is composed of the saved; the saved are the church. After the church was established on the day of Pentecost, "The Lord was adding to their number day by day those who were being saved" (Acts 2:47). It is composed of those who are called according to His purpose (Rom. 8:28-30). It is committed to the promotion and support of everlasting truth (1 Tim. 3:14-15).

Does the Bible Teach "Rapture," an Antichrist, and Armageddon?

Jesus Was Not Surprisingly Rejected

Based upon a misreading of Old Testament prophecies, many first-century Jews expected the Messiah to be an earthly king. Some wanted to make Jesus into such a king, but He refused (John 6:14-15; cf. also 12:12-13). Premillennialists erroneously teach that Jesus came to establish an earthly, physical kingdom, but was surprisingly rejected.

Consider the implications of such a position: If a small band of His enemies could stop the Lord from accomplishing His purpose, then His power is, indeed, limited and inadequate. Yet, the Scriptures affirm that Jesus Christ possesses all power and authority, being King of kings and Lord of lords (Matt. 28:18-20; Eph. 1:18-23; Col. 1:16-17; 2:9-10).

The Lord's rejection and death were foretold by the prophets (Isa. 53:3-5). God planned that the Messiah should die (Acts 2:22-23; 3:18). He was delivered up because of our offenses and raised for our justification (Rom. 4:25). We were redeemed with the precious blood of Christ, foreknown before the foundation of the world, and He appeared in these last times for our sake (1 Pet. 1:18-20). Apart from Jesus's death, burial, and resurrection, we have no hope (1 Cor. 15: 1-5, 17-22).

The "Church" and "Kingdom" Are Equivalent

Premillennialists make a false distinction between the church and the kingdom. In reality, they are the same. When Simon Peter made the good confession, affirming that Jesus was the Christ, our Lord said, "Upon this rock, I will build My church, and the gates of hades shall not prevail against it." The very next verse says, "I will give you the keys of the kingdom of heaven . . ." (Matt. 16:16-19). The church and the kingdom are equivalent, referring to the same entity.

The church or kingdom was established during the first century. John the Baptist affirmed the nearness of the kingdom (Matt. 3:1-2). So also did Jesus (Matt. 4:17; Mark 1:14-15; cf. Matt. 4:23; 16:28 Mark 9:1; Luke 11:20), the twelve apostles (Matt. 10:5-7), and the seventy who were sent to the house of Israel (Luke 10:8-11).

Immediately before returning to the Father, Jesus spoke of things concerning the kingdom of God, suggesting the fulfillment of God's promises was imminent (Acts 1:3-5). Evidencing a continued misunderstanding of the spiritual nature of the kingdom, the disciples asked,

"When Will These Things Be?" : Questions on Eschatology

"Lord, is it at this time you are restoring the kingdom to Israel?" Jesus pointed to Pentecost: "You will receive power (and understanding) when the Holy Spirit has come upon you" (Acts 1:6-8; cf. John 16:12-13). These promises came to fruition on the day of Pentecost (Acts 2:1-4).

Afterward, as the gospel spread forth from Jerusalem (Acts 1:8; 8:4-5), Philip preached the good news about the kingdom of God (Acts 8:12). Paul proclaimed the same message (Acts 19:8; 28:23, 31). Apostolic associates were called "fellow-workers for the kingdom of God" (Col. 4:10-11).

The church and the kingdom are composed of the same individuals (Acts 20:28; 1 Pet. 1:18-19; Rev. 5:9-10). Both realms are accessed through baptism (John 3:1-5; Acts 2:38-40, 46-47; 1 Cor. 12:13; Gal. 3:27-29). The spiritual communion of the Lord's Supper, which believers share each Lord's day, occurs only within a kingdom context (Acts 2:42; 20:7; 1 Cor. 10:16-17; 11:23-26).

God's Kingdom Is Spiritual

Although premillennialists mistakenly teach that Jesus came to establish an earthly kingdom, the Bible affirms that His kingdom is spiritual in nature (Luke 17:20-21; John 18:36-37; Rom. 14:16-17). The kingdom of God is a demonstration of divine power (1 Cor. 4:18-21; cf. 1 Cor. 2:1-5; Rom. 1:16-17).

Moreover, the Scriptures reveal that God's kingdom is currently in existence (Col. 1:13-18; 1 Thess. 2:11-12; Heb. 12:28-29; Rev. 1:6, 9). Christ reigns presently as King over His kingdom (Luke 1:31-33; Heb. 1:8; 2:9; cf. Eph. 2:19-22).

The Kingdom Prophesies Were Fulfilled

Premillennialism ignores the fact that the kingdom prophecies of the Old Testament were fulfilled. Miraculous signs and wonders occurred on Pentecost:

> When the day of Pentecost had come, they were all together in one place. And suddenly there came from heaven a noise like a violent rushing wind, and it filled the whole house where they were sitting. And there appeared to them tongues as of fire distributing themselves, and they rested on each one of them. And they were all filled with the Holy Spirit and began to speak with other tongues, as the Spirit was giving them utterance (Acts 2:1-4).

Does the Bible Teach "Rapture," an Antichrist, and Armageddon?

As the apostles preached the gospel, many were amazed and perplexed ("We hear them in our own tongues speaking of the mighty deeds of God" [vv. 7-12]), while others were mockingly dismissive ("They are full of sweet wine" [v. 13]). After answering the absurdity of the charge ("These men are not drunk, as you suppose, for it is only the third hour of the day" [v. 15]), Simon Peter affirmed these miracles represented the fulfillment of Old Testament prophecy ("This is what was spoken of through the prophet Joel" [v. 16]).

> "And it shall be in the last days," God says, "That I will pour forth of My Spirit on all mankind; and your sons and your daughters shall prophesy, and your young men shall see visions, and your old men shall dream dreams; Even on My bondslaves, both men and women, I will in those days pour forth of My Spirit and they shall prophesy. And I will grant wonders in the sky above and signs on the earth below, blood, and fire, and vapor of smoke. The sun will be turned into darkness and the moon into blood, before the great and glorious day of the Lord shall come. And it shall be that everyone who calls on the name of the Lord will be saved" (Acts 2:17-21; cf. also Joel 2:28-32).

Joel's prophecy was not the only one that was fulfilled on Pentecost. Psalms 2 anticipates the reign of the Lord's Anointed. Isaiah 2 predicts the establishment of God's house and the proclamation of God's law, beginning in Jerusalem (Mt. Zion). Daniel 2 foreshadows the establishment of God's eternal kingdom during the days of the Roman Empire. These significant events would occur "in the last days." From an Old Testament standpoint, "the last days" anticipates the final dispensation of time, i.e., the Christian era, the gospel age (Isa. 2:2; Jer. 23:20; 49:39; Ezek. 38:16; Hos. 3:5; Micah 4:1; Acts 2:17; Heb. 1:1-2; etc.).

The Messianic kingdom was, indeed, established in the "last days." Peter said, "This is what was spoken of through the prophet Joel." The same thing could be said regarding Psalm 2, Isaiah 2, and Daniel 2. If such did not occur, the word of God has failed, and the kingdom prophecies are made void. The inspired apostles affirm that these prophecies were fulfilled. Uninspired proponents of premillennialism say they were not. Who are you going to believe?

"When Will These Things Be?" : Questions on Eschatology

What about the Rapture?

Introduction

The coming of Jesus Christ is a central theme of the Bible. The Old Testament anticipated the coming of Christ; the Gospels bear witness to the fact that He did come, while the epistles emphasize that He is coming again. Frequently the question arises, "When will Christ return?" The Bible says, "Now as to the times and the epochs, brethren, you have no need of anything to be written to you. For you yourselves know full well that the day of the Lord will come just like a thief in the night" (1 Thess. 5:1-2). In this regard, Jesus said, "But of that day and hour no one knows, not even the angels of heaven, nor the Son, but the Father alone" (Matt. 24:36).

Defined and Explained

Merriam-Webster's Collegiate Dictionary defines "rapture" as "(1a) a state or experience of being carried away by overwhelming emotion; (1b) a mystical experience in which the spirit is exalted to a knowledge of divine things; (2) an expression or manifestation of ecstasy or passion." While this general definition of the word does not directly address the denominational doctrine, note that it describes "a state or experience of being carried away" in an emotional or mystical sense.

Premillennialists use the term to communicate their particular perversion of biblical teaching about the Second Coming of Christ. Dispensational premillennialists argue that the rapture (which they distinguish from the Lord's Second Coming) is affirmed in John 14:1-3, 1 Corinthians 15:51-57, and 1 Thessalonians 4:13-18. Before the so-called seven-year period of tribulation, Jesus will allegedly descend from heaven, snatching up the church to be with Himself. In contrast, dreadful trials will be unleashed upon an unrepentant and unbelieving world. Afterward, the Lord will return to the earth in glory, establish His Messianic kingdom, and reign on the throne of David in Jerusalem for 1,000 years.

The Dictionary of Christianity in America

The Dictionary of Christianity in America summarizes the "Rapture of the Church" as follows:

> A phrase premillennialists use to refer to the "catching up" (from Latin *rapio*) of the church to be with Christ at his Second Coming. All premillennialists trace the doctrine to the same passage (1 Thess. 4:15-17)

Does the Bible Teach "Rapture," an Antichrist, and Armageddon?

but disagree on when it will occur in relation to the tribulation period, which they identify as the "seventieth week" of Daniel 9:24-27. Historically, premillennialists have divided over whether the rapture will happen before, during or after the tribulation (Reid).

Describing the divisions that exist among premillennial proponents regarding the rapture (i.e., pretribulationism, midtribulationism, posttribulationism), Daniel Reid says, "Though such interpretive disagreements may seem inconsequential to outsiders, differences over the timing of the rapture have often produced fierce antagonism among premillennialists, with advocates of one view refusing to associate with those of another." Speculative theories inevitably are polarizing; division always results from unauthorized additions to Sacred Scripture.

The Holman Illustrated Bible Dictionary

Pete Schemm offers the following brief description of the "Rapture" in the *Holman Illustrated Bible Dictionary*. It refers to:

> God's taking the church out of the world instantaneously. The Latin term *rapio*, which means to "snatch away" or "carry off," is the source of the English word. While there are differing views of the millennium (Rev. 20:2-7) in relation to Christ's Second Coming (e.g., premillennial, postmillennial, and amillennial), nevertheless, all evangelicals affirm a literal return of Christ to the earth preceding the eternal state. In premillennialism, however, the distinct event of the rapture is often emphasized.
>
> The main biblical passage for the rapture (Gk. *harpazo*) of the church is 1 Thessalonians 4:15-17. Other texts often used to support the doctrine of the rapture are John 14:1-3 and 1 Corinthians 15:51-52. There are three main approaches to understanding the rapture in premillennialism: (1) In the *pretribulational* view Christ raptures the church before any part of the seven-year tribulation begins (Dan. 9:24-27; Matt. 24:3-28; Rev. 11:2; 12:14). Upon Christ's coming in the air, which is distinct from and that precedes His coming to the earth, believers will be "caught up together . . . in the clouds to meet the Lord in the air" (1 Thess. 4:17 HCSB). In this view believers are delivered "from the coming wrath" (1 Thess. 1:10; Rev. 3:10) by being taken out of the world. (2) A *midtribulational* view also sees the rapture as a distinct event that precedes Christ's Second Coming and delivers believers from the last half of the seven-year period, the "great tribulation" (Matt. 24:15-28; Rev. 16-18). (3) A *posttribulational* view holds that the rapture and the Second Coming occur at the same time. Therefore, the church remains

on earth during "the time of Jacob's distress" (Jer. 30:7 NASB). Unlike the world, however, believers who go through the tribulation will be protected from the devastating outpouring of God's wrath and judgment (1 Thess. 5:9) (Schemm, 1366).

Alleged Proof Texts for the Rapture

Premillennialists turn to Matthew 24:30-31 and 1 Thessalonians 4:16-17 to bolster their doctrine. Other alleged proof texts, such as those offered by James Swanson and Orville Nave in *New Nave's Topical Bible* (i.e., 2 Cor. 12:4; 1 Thess. 4:17; Jude 23; Rev. 12:5) are taken entirely out of context and offer no support for this speculative theory.

Many brethren separate Matthew 24 into two distinct discussions, with the former section dealing with the destruction of Jerusalem (vv. 4-35) and the latter part focusing on the Lord's Second Coming (vv. 36-51). If one operates from this perspective, Jesus's comments in vv. 30-31 have no bearing on the Second Coming and do not foreshadow a future rapture. Brother Kyle Pope offers an alternative approach to the Olivet Discourse, rejecting premillennial dogma while affirming that Jesus intermixes His comments about the destruction of Jerusalem in AD 70, and also foreshadows his future return that will occur at the last day. For an informative discussion of Matthew 24, please see *The Book of Matthew*, by Kyle Pope, which is part of the *Truth Commentaries*. Regarding verses 30-31, he says:

> Some brethren feel compelled to conclude that Jesus is using eschatological language here and in the previous verse in reference to the fall of Jerusalem because of the misapplications premillennialists have made to these Scriptures. As noted above, premillennialists argue that the "abomination of desolation" (24:15) is a future desecration of a rebuilt temple, and the "great tribulation" (24:21) is global in nature, preceding Jesus's coming to establish an earthly millennial reign. We can reject these false conclusions, but still acknowledge when Jesus addresses things that point to final judgment (Pope, 861-862).

Paul's Instruction Concerning the Dead In Christ (1 Thess. 4:13-18)

Addressing the disciples in Thessalonica, Paul offers instruction concerning those who have died in Christ. When faced with death, sinners are often overwhelmed with grief and hopelessness. Yet, believers enjoy confidence and divine consolation. Foreshadowing the glorious day of

Does the Bible Teach "Rapture," an Antichrist, and Armageddon?

Christ's Second Coming, the apostle says these events will occur in order: The Lord will descend from heaven. The dead in Christ will rise first. Those who are alive will be caught up together with them in the clouds to meet the Lord in the air, and shall thus always be with the Lord. Such words offer great comfort when believers walk through the shadowy valley of death. Consider the following familiar translations of this text:

> But I would not have you to be ignorant, brethren, concerning them which are asleep, that ye sorrow not, even as others which have no hope. For if we believe that Jesus died and rose again, even so them also which sleep in Jesus will God bring with him. For this we say unto you by the word of the Lord, that we which are alive and remain unto the coming of the Lord shall not prevent them which are asleep. For the Lord himself shall descend from heaven with a shout, with the voice of the archangel, and with the trump of God: and the dead in Christ shall rise first: Then we which are alive and remain shall be caught up together with them in the clouds, to meet the Lord in the air: and so shall we ever be with the Lord. Wherefore comfort one another with these words (1 Thess. 4:13-18, KJV).

> But I do not want you to be ignorant, brethren, concerning those who have fallen asleep, lest you sorrow as others who have no hope. For if we believe that Jesus died and rose again, even so God will bring with Him those who sleep in Jesus. For this we say to you by the word of the Lord, that we who are alive and remain until the coming of the Lord will by no means precede those who are asleep. For the Lord Himself will descend from heaven with a shout, with the voice of an archangel, and with the trumpet of God. And the dead in Christ will rise first. Then we who are alive and remain shall be caught up together with them in the clouds to meet the Lord in the air. And thus we shall always be with the Lord. Therefore comfort one another with these words (1 Thess. 4:13-18, NKJV).

> But we do not want you to be uninformed, brethren, about those who are asleep, so that you will not grieve as do the rest who have no hope. For if we believe that Jesus died and rose again, even so God will bring with Him those who have fallen asleep in Jesus. For this we say to you by the word of the Lord, that we who are alive and remain until the coming of the Lord, will not precede those who have fallen asleep. For the Lord Himself will descend from heaven with a shout, with the voice of the archangel and with the trumpet of God, and the dead in Christ will rise first. Then we who are alive and remain will be caught up together with them in the clouds to meet the Lord in the air, and so

"When Will These Things Be?" : Questions on Eschatology

> we shall always be with the Lord. Therefore comfort one another with these words (1 Thess. 4:13-18, NASB).
>
> But we do not want you to be uninformed, brothers, about those who are asleep, that you may not grieve as others do who have no hope. For since we believe that Jesus died and rose again, even so, through Jesus, God will bring with him those who have fallen asleep. For this we declare to you by a word from the Lord, that we who are alive, who are left until the coming of the Lord, will not precede those who have fallen asleep. For the Lord himself will descend from heaven with a cry of command, with the voice of an archangel, and with the sound of the trumpet of God. And the dead in Christ will rise first. Then we who are alive, who are left, will be caught up together with them in the clouds to meet the Lord in the air, and so we will always be with the Lord. Therefore encourage one another with these words (1 Thess. 4:13-18, ESV).

As Robert Harkrider points out, premillennialists claim that the rapture is taught in 1 Thessalonians 4:16-17, where "the apostle Paul describes the rapture when all true believers will be caught up to meet the Lord during a silent, secret encounter. All unbelievers and insincere Christians will be 'left behind.' Hal Lindsey, famous author of books on premillennialism, wrote: 'These believers will be removed from the earth before the Great Tribulation—before that period of the most ghastly pestilence, bloodshed, and starvation the world has ever known' (*The Late Great Planet Earth*, 127)" (*The Book of Revelation: Including a Study of Premillennialism*, 3).

Premillennialists are guilty of gross speculation, reading into the text a whole sequence of events that are the product of their imagination. Walton Weaver reminds us of the simple truths communicated in this context:

> Not only will the dead in Christ not be excluded from the glories of this event, but they will go to meet the Lord at the same time the living will be caught up to be with Him. This again raises the question, had the Thessalonians come to believe that the dead would miss this glorious event, or perhaps that they might not share in its honors until a later date? Whatever their apprehensions concerning the dead in Christ may have been, Paul's words assure them that those who are dead will by no means be disadvantaged (Weaver, 297).

Verse 13

Ignorance is not bliss (Acts 17:23, 30). Divine revelation grants knowledge of things that are essential, not speculative (2 Pet. 1:3).

Does the Bible Teach "Rapture," an Antichrist, and Armageddon?

Apparently, some disciples at Thessalonica had passed away. Therefore, Paul addresses the question, "What happens to believers who die before the Lord's return?" Here the apostle affirms the reality of the afterlife. Death is a temporary state, often likened unto "sleep" (John 11:11-14; Acts 7:60; 13:36; 1 Cor. 15:6). Yet, for the faithful, death will give way to life for all eternity (1 Cor. 15:20-22, 51-54).

Faithful Christians maintain hope, even when faced with death (Titus 2:13; Heb. 6:18-19), but unbelievers have no such confidence (Eph. 2:12).

Historians have recorded the last words of famous men. Notice the despair in the following examples compiled by Lockyer:

> **Thomas Hobbes** (1588-1674), noted British political philosopher whose skepticism corrupted many men of his day, said, "If I had the whole world, I would give it to live one day. I shall be glad to find a hole to creep out of the world at. I am about to take a leap in the dark!"
>
> **Edward Gibbon** (1737-1794), the English historian who wrote *The Decline and Fall of the Roman Empire,* was an infidel who died without the comfort of the Gospel. To those at his bedside, he said, "This day may be my last. I will agree that the immortality of the soul is, at times, a very comfortable doctrine. All this is now lost, finally, irrevocably lost. All is dark and doubtful."
>
> **Gabriel Mirabeau** (1749-1791), a great French statesman during the pre-revolutionary period, said, "Give me more laudanum [a solution of opium in alcohol] that I may not think of eternity and of what is to come. I have an age of strength, but not a moment of courage."
>
> **Thomas Paine** (1737-1809), the renowned American author and infidel who exerted considerable influence against belief in God and the Scriptures, came to his last hour a disillusioned and unhappy man. During his final moments on earth, he said: "I would give worlds, if I had them, that *Age of Reason* had not been published. O Lord, help me! Christ, help me! O God, what have I done to suffer so much? But there is no God! But if there should be, what will become of me hereafter? Stay with me, for God's sake! Send even a child to stay with me, for it is hell to be alone. If ever the devil had an agent, I have been that one."

Verse 14

Paul said, "For if we believe that Jesus died and rose again. . . ." No doubt or uncertainty is here expressed. "Since we believe . . ." captures the idea. Our hope of heaven is based upon the fact of Jesus's death, burial, and resurrection (1 Cor. 15:1-4).

Verse 15

The word translated "prevent" or "precede" literally means "to come before (another)." When Christ returns, the dead will be raised first, and then saints yet living will be caught up to meet the Lord in the air. "Those who have fallen asleep" refers to those who have died in Christ Jesus. The Bible knows nothing of the doctrine of "soul sleep." Instead, the dead have a conscious existence beyond the grave (Luke 16:19-31).

Verse 16

Christ's Second Coming will be accompanied by a loud shout, the voice of the archangel, and a blast from the trumpet of God (1 Cor. 15:52; cf. Joel 2:1; 3:16).

Verse 17

Returning to the Father, Jesus ascended into heaven, and a cloud received Him out of their sight (Acts 1:9-11; cf. Dan. 7:13-14). He will come again in like manner as He departed. Saints will meet Him in the clouds. Therefore, when a faithful disciple dies, those who remain behind should not allow themselves to be consumed by grief and despair. Death is but a doorway into a better realm. Such hope sustains us.

What about the Antichrist?

Introduction

Who is the antichrist? *Nelson's New Illustrated Bible Dictionary* offers the standard evangelical answer: The antichrist refers to "a false prophet and evil being who will set himself up against Christ and the people of God in the last days before the Second Coming. The term is used only in the writings of John in the New Testament. It refers to one who stands in opposition to all that Jesus Christ represents (1 John 2:18, 22; 4:3; 2 John 7). John wrote that several antichrists existed already in his day—false teachers who denied the deity and the incarnation of Christ—but that the supreme Antichrist of history would appear at some future time" (s.v., "Antichrist.")

In contrast, the *New Bible Dictionary* supplies a more balanced approach, saying, "The expression *antichristos* is found in the Bible only in

Does the Bible Teach "Rapture," an Antichrist, and Armageddon?

the Johannine Epistles (1 John 2:18, 22; 4:3; 2 John 7), but the idea behind it is widespread. We should probably understand the force of anti as indicating opposition, rather than a false claim, i.e., the antichrist is one who opposes Christ rather than one who claims to be the Christ. If this is so, then we should include under the heading 'antichrist' such OT passages as Daniel 7:7f., 21f., and those in 2 Thessalonians 2 and Revelation which deal with the strong opposition that the forces of evil are to offer Christ in the last days" (Morris, 49).

What is the biblical meaning? The Greek word *antichristos*, a compound of *anti* (against) and *Christos* (the Anointed One, Messiah, Christ), refers to the "antichrist, (one who opposes Christ)" (Thomas, 500). BDAG says it relates to the "antichrist, adversary of the Messiah, to appear in the last days." The word is not found outside Christian circles, but the concept is. For the general idea in the NT without the word, see 2 Thessalonians 2:1-12 and Revelation 12-14." Louw and Nida say the word identifies "one who is opposed to Christ, in the sense of usurping the role of Christ—'antichrist.' The term *antichristos* appears to have become increasingly equivalent to a proper name as the personification of all that was opposed to and contrary to the role and ministry of Christ" (53.83). Strong/Thayer says it refers to "the adversary of the Messiah" (500). This word occurs five times in the NT and only in the epistles of John (1 John 2:18, 22; 4:3; 2 John 7).

> Children, it is the last hour; and just as you heard that **antichrist** is coming, even now many **antichrists** have appeared; from this we know that it is the last hour (1 John 2:18).

> Who is the liar but the one who denies that Jesus is the Christ? This is the **antichrist**, the one who denies the Father and the Son (1 John 2:22).

> Beloved, do not believe every spirit, but test the spirits to see whether they are from God, because many false prophets have gone out into the world. By this you know the Spirit of God: every spirit that confesses that Jesus Christ has come in the flesh is from God; and every spirit that does not confess Jesus is not from God; this is the spirit of the **antichrist**, of which you have heard that it is coming, and now it is already in the world (1 John 4:1-3).

> For many deceivers have gone out into the world, those who do not acknowledge Jesus Christ as coming in the flesh. This is the deceiver and the **antichrist**. Watch yourselves, that you do not lose what we

have accomplished, but that you may receive a full reward. Anyone who goes too far and does not abide in the teaching of Christ does not have God; the one who abides in the teaching, he has both the Father and the Son (2 John 7-9).

Opposition vs. False Claim

The term "antichrist," refers to one who is an adversary of the Messiah and an opponent of God. As L.L. Morris states, "We should probably understand the force of *anti* as indicating opposition, rather than a false claim, i.e., the antichrist is one who opposes Christ rather than one who claims to be the Christ."

The concept of opposing the will of God is as old as religion itself. In the Old Testament, God's foes are often described as "sons of Belial." Because of their innumerable sins (i.e., idolatry, sodomy, rape, drunkenness, blasphemy, disrespect for authority, etc.), the Lord considered such individuals to be base and worthless.

Intertestamental Example

Daniel foretold the rise of the tyrant Antiochus Epiphanes, who became king of Syria in 168 BC. He made a relentless effort to wipe out Jewish culture and religion. After invading Jerusalem, Antiochus killed thousands and sold countless other Jews into slavery. He erected an altar to Zeus in the courts of the temple and sacrificed swine's flesh upon it. Antiochus came to personify the forces of evil arrayed against God and His people.

New Testament Examples

The New Testament also contains many references to those who oppose the will of God. The disciples are warned of false christs who would attempt to deceive even the elect (Matt. 24:5, 24). In the parable of the tares, the devil opposed the work of Christ by sowing weeds amidst the wheat (Matt. 13:37-39). Paul warned the Ephesian elders of the danger of treacherous leaders (Acts 20:29-30).

Speculation vs. Scripture

Many view the antichrist as an apocalyptic figure, the last great opponent of Christ whose might is manifested in the end times but is ultimately judged and destroyed. Many equate him with "the man of sin" in 2 Thessalonians 2 and sometimes with "the beast" of Revelation. Those promoting a futuristic interpretation of Revelation say the antichrist is

Does the Bible Teach "Rapture," an Antichrist, and Armageddon?

a mighty and wicked ruler who will arise just before the second advent of Christ. This view also calls for the restoration of the Jewish nation, rebuilding of the temple, and restoring Levitical sacrifices and rituals. Afterward, the antichrist will break his covenant with the Jews, ushering in the great period of tribulation.

Although premillennialism is widely accepted in the religious world, it violates clear New Testament teaching. Furthermore, such an interpretation would have offered no comfort to John's readers who were suffering persecution from the Roman emperor Domitian. John wrote, not to fuel speculation regarding events thousands of years in the future, but to encourage first-century saints who were facing persecution.

Those who take a symbolic view of Revelation assert that the antichrist is "an ageless personification of evil, not identifiable with one nation, institution, or individual" (Hubbard) This idea is supported in the epistles of John. It emphasizes the constant struggle between the forces of God and the allies of Satan (Eph. 6:10-13; 1 Pet. 5:8).

What does John mean when he speaks of the antichrist? According to Thayer, the apostle employed this word to describe that "corrupt power and influence hostile to Christian interests, especially which is at work in false teachers who have come from the bosom of the church and are engaged in disseminating error" (Thayer, #500).

John taught that the spirit of the antichrist was already at work (1 John 2:18). The antichrist denies the deity and Sonship of Christ (1 John 2:22). Moreover, he also denies that Jesus Christ came in the flesh (1 John 4:3; 2 John 7). Since salvation was made possible through the life, death, and resurrection of Jesus (John 3:16; 1 John 4:9-10), the Gnostic creed undercuts the foundation of Christian hope.

John did not conceive of the antichrist as one single individual; rather, this word represents the danger posed by false teachers. Just as the Holy Spirit inspired the true apostles and prophets, the devil provokes false teachers and false prophets to distort truth and lead men astray (2 Cor. 11:13-15; 1 John 4:1).

When we realize that this is a battle, not for land and territory, but the human mind, this discussion becomes all the more significant. The spirit of the antichrist was struggling with the Spirit of God for the possession and control of man's allegiance. This same conflict continues today.

Identifying the Antichrist

Who is the antichrist, the man of sin and lawlessness? Are there many antichrists, or are the ones from John's time only a reflection of the great one to come? Many different and conflicting interpretations have been offered. Some say Nero, others Domitian, or one of the later emperors was the antichrist.

Gregory I, leader of the Catholic Church from AD 590-604, taught that anyone who assumed the title of "universal bishop" was the forerunner of the antichrist. During Medieval times, monks transformed the names of their enemies into a shape resembling the number 666. Gregory IX (AD c1143-1241) claimed that his great antagonist, Fredrick II, king of Germany and emperor of the Holy Roman Empire from AD 1215-1250, was "the beast coming up out of the sea."

At the time of the Reformation, Protestants equated the antichrist with the papacy, arguing that the Pope was the man of sin who takes his seat in the temple of God, proclaiming himself to be God. In contrast, Roman Catholic scholars retaliated, branding Luther, Calvin and the reformers as the antichrist.

Futuristic interpreters of Revelation have identified the antichrist as Napoleon III, Mussolini, Hitler, Stalin, Saddam, presidents Clinton, Bush, Obama, Trump, etc., etc. However, any attempt to precisely identify the antichrist misses the point. "The fact is that antichrist is not so much a person as a principle, the principle which is actively opposed to God and which may well be thought of as incarnating itself in those men in every generation who have seemed to be the blatant opponents of God" (Barclay, *The Letters of John and Jude*, 63).

Does the Bible Teach "Rapture," an Antichrist, and Armageddon?

What about the Battle of Armageddon?

Introduction

The word "Armageddon" only appears in Revelation 16:16. It is the rallying-place of the kings of the whole world, who led by the unclean spirits issuing from the mouth of the dragon, the beast and the false prophet, assemble for "the war of the great day of God, the Almighty." The battle of Armageddon is anticipated in Revelation 16 but is not fought until chapter 19. First, the stage is set for a decisive conflict between Christ and the evil powers persecuting the infant church (Rev. 16:13-16). Then the outcome of the great battle of Armageddon is described where the Son of God is victorious over the forces of evil (Rev. 19:11-21).

The battle of Armageddon is the source of much sensational speculation. The far-fetched views and misconceptions which people have on this subject are truly amazing to consider. Much of the problem lies with the erroneous system of premillennialism. It asserts that universal conflict will soon engulf the nations of the world. The final, catastrophic battle will occur on the plains of Megiddo in northern Palestine. The conflict described in Revelation is viewed as a literal battle, a bloody holocaust such as the world has never known. It is argued that conflicts are now developing that will lead to Armageddon. It supposedly will take place after the seven years of tribulation, and just before the second advent of Christ. Does all this harmonize with the Bible? Is it Scriptural? In a word, "No."

Definition

Armageddon is the combination of two Hebrew words: *har* (mountain) and *Megiddo* (a place in Manasseh). Thus *Har-Mageddon* refers to the "mountain of Megiddo." BDAG says it refers to "Armageddon, a mythical place-name, said to be Hebrew in Revelation 16:16; it has been identified with Megiddo and Jerusalem, but its interpretation is beset with difficulties that have not yet been surmounted."

Where exactly is Har-Mageddon, the mountain of Megiddo? There is no literal Mt. Megiddo, at least in the traditional sense. Reference is either to the hills that surrounded the plains of Esdraelon, or possibly to the large mound of Megiddo itself. "The fact that the tell of Megiddo was about 21 meters high (i.e., approx. 70 feet) in John's day, and was in the vicinity of Carmel Range, justifies the use of Heb. *har*, used loosely in the OT for "hill" and "hill country" (Sheriffs, 81).

The city of Megiddo, which means "a place of troops," was located in the Carmel mountain range in north-central Palestine, overlooking the plain of Jezreel. This valley, also known as the plain of Esdraelon, was some twenty miles long and six miles wide. Megiddo was situated on a major highway that linked Egypt and Mesopotamia. All significant north-south traffic running through Palestine passed by Megiddo, making it a strategic military stronghold.

Megiddo has been the sight of extensive archaeological work. The first city, built at this site around 3500 BC, was surrounded by a massive wall that was thirteen feet thick and later was buttressed to twice that size. A brick wall and gate dating from 1880 BC have also been uncovered. Thutmose III of Egypt captured the city in 1468 BC, and held it for a brief time (Unger, s.v. "Megiddo").

Megiddo was controlled by the Canaanites until they were defeated by the invading Israelites. Megiddo is first mentioned in the Old Testament in the account of the 31 kings conquered by Joshua (Josh. 12:21). When the land of Canaan was divided among the twelve tribes of Israel, Megiddo was awarded to Manasseh. However, the Israelites were unable to completely drive out the native inhabitants (Josh. 17:11-12; Judg. 1:27). Nonetheless, in time the Israelites subdued and possessed the city (1 Chron. 7:28-29).

The city was included in the fifth administrative district of Solomon (1 Kings 4:12). During his reign, Megiddo was reconstructed as a military stronghold. Along with Hazor, Gezer, Lower Beth Horon, Baalath, and Tamar, Megiddo was fortified and established as a chariot city for the armies of King Solomon (1 Kings 9:15-19; 10:26-29).

Symbolism

Waterloo

A place can become symbolic because of some historical event with which it is associated. For example, many are familiar with the saying, "He met his Waterloo!" Waterloo was a small town in central Belgium where Napoleon was finally defeated in 1815. The expression has come to represent a disastrous defeat.

Does the Bible Teach "Rapture," an Antichrist, and Armageddon?

The Alamo
Consider the words "Remember the Alamo!" In that battle, a small group of men stood bravely against impossible odds. This small mission in San Antonio represents the spirit of courage and sacrifice and is a proud part of the heritage of Texas.

Megiddo
So it is with Megiddo. Many important battles in Old Testament times were fought in and around Megiddo. It was the scene of so many decisive battles that it came to stand for battle itself. "These low hills around Megiddo, with their outlook over the plain of Esdraelon, have witnessed perhaps a greater number of bloody encounters than have ever stained a like area of the world's surface" (ISBE, s.v. "Har-Magedon.").

"The 'waters of Megiddo' (Judg. 5:19) and the 'valley-plain of Megiddo' (2 Chron. 35:22) have witnessed important battles, from one fought by Tuthmosis III in 1468 BC to that of Lord Allenby of Megiddo in 1917" (Sheriffs, 81). Over the long history of Israel, Megiddo was the scene of never-to-be-forgotten conflicts. It was famous for two great victories. Here Deborah and Barak overthrew Sisera and the army of the Canaanites (Judg. 4:1-24; 5:19-21). Against overwhelming odds, Gideon and his 300 defeated the Midianites (Judg. 6:33-35; 7:1-25). It was also famous for two great disasters. Here wicked King Saul, who had been rejected by God, was defeated by the Philistines (1 Sam. 31:1-7). Later, King Josiah was killed when he tried to prevent Pharaoh-Necho of Egypt from going to the aid of Assyria (2 Kings 23:29-30; 2 Chron. 35:20-24).

In the Jewish mind, Megiddo was a place of great slaughter and represented God's terrible judgment upon the wicked. Thomas says Armageddon refers to "a mountain of uncertain location." BDAG says Armageddon refers to "a mythical place-name, said to be Hebrew in Revelation 16:16; it has been identified with Megiddo and Jerusalem, but its interpretation is beset with difficulties that have not yet been surmounted." Similarly, Joseph Henry Thayer describes Armageddon as the "proper name of an imaginary place." Over time Armageddon has become a poetic expression for terrible and decisive conflict. It represents the place where those who oppose Christ will be destroyed with a slaughter like those who defied God's will in ancient days.

"When Will These Things Be?" : Questions on Eschatology

Significance

What is the message of Revelation when it speaks of the battle of Armageddon? This book was written during a time of severe and widespread persecution. Christianity appeared to be on the brink of extinction. This was an hour of desperate need. John wrote to reassure disciples that the forces of evil would be completely overthrown, and the cause of Christ would triumph victoriously. The book of Revelation is a message of victory.

Thomas defines *nikaō* as derived from *nikē* (victory), meaning "conquer, prevail" (3528). BDAG says it means to "(1) to win in the face of obstacles, be victor, conquer, overcome, prevail; (2) to overcome someone, vanquish, overcome;(3) to surpass in ability, outstrip, excel." The Greek word *nikaō* occurs a total of twenty-eight times in the NT, of which seventeen are found in the book of Revelation (Luke 11:22; John 16:33; Rom. 3:4; 12:21 (2x); 1 John 2:13, 14; 4:4 (2x); 5:5; Rev. 2:7, 11, 17, 26; 3:5, 12, 21 (2x); 5:5; 6:2 (2x); 11:7; 12:11; 13:7; 15:2; 17:14; 21:7).

John wrote concerning things that would "shortly come to pass" (Rev. 1:1; 22:6). Those who take a futuristic and literal interpretation of Revelation fail to grasp the true message of the book. No interpretation of the book as a whole or this battle, in particular, can have any significance unless it has application to those first-century Christians to whom the book was addressed.

Revelation is an apocalyptic book, filled with signs, visions, and highly symbolic language. Any interpretation that seeks to literalize its images is doomed to absolute failure. This is the cardinal sin of the premillennialists. Those who would view Armageddon literally are very selective in their approach. The context speaks of three frogs, a great red dragon, a sea beast, and an earth beast. If one expects a literal battle, he should expect the army to be headed by three frogs. Both figures are symbolic; neither are literal. There is no reason for making one literal and the other symbolic. If the battle is literal, why not the other symbols as well?

The context speaks of God pouring out His wrath upon the evil forces that opposed the early church. The first angel poured out his bowl on the earth, and men were afflicted with grievous sores. The second angel poured out his bowl on the sea, and the waters turned to blood, and

Does the Bible Teach "Rapture," an Antichrist, and Armageddon?

everything died. The third angel poured out his bowl upon the rivers and streams, with similar effects. The fourth angel poured out his bowl on the sun, and it scorched men with fire. The fifth angel poured out his bowl on the throne of the beast; the kingdom was darkened, and men gnawed their tongues in pain. The sixth angel poured out his bowl on the Euphrates, and it dried up; the way was now prepared for the enemies of the north to make war against the empire. At this point, an interlude occurs in Rev. 16:13-16. The forces of evil gathered together to fight against God at the place called "Har-Mageddon." Then finally, the seventh angel poured out his bowl on the air, resulting in thunder, lightning, earthquakes, and hailstones. Then a voice proclaimed, "It is done!"

What is the biblical meaning? The symbolism is obvious: Even though all the forces of evil might be gathered together as one in their conflict against God, they will be overwhelmed by His decisive and unrelenting judgment. Early Christians were being persecuted by the Roman Empire. The book of Revelation affirms that Christ would come to the aid of His people. Armageddon thus is a vivid symbolic representation of Christ's victory over the forces of evil. The cause of righteousness would triumph over the beast, the false prophet, and their allies. The idolatrous religion and godless government of Rome would fall, but Christianity would continue to grow and prosper. This message of victory is not only the overriding theme of Revelation but is also echoed in Daniel's prophecy (Dan. 2:31-45).

By using the figure of Armageddon, the apostle John does not refer to any particular locality. Ultimately, Armageddon cannot be located on the maps of the earth; its geographical location is unimportant. In Revelation, the battle of Armageddon represents the decisive conflict between good and evil. It symbolizes occasions when righteousness and evil are engaged in deadly combat. However strong the forces of darkness may appear, and however hopeless the righteous may feel, God will ultimately win the victory! How comforting this message must have been to those early Christians who were suffering under the heavy-handed Roman Empire. The whole thrust of the Apocalypse is to assure the saints of this victory and urge them to avoid compromising with error, idolatry, and sin.

Conclusion

Failed Predictions

Attempting to reveal the time of Christ's Second Coming becomes an obsession with some men. Predictions have been made countless times in the last 2,000 years, but none have come to pass. You would think that folks would learn after a while, but the prognostication continues. Consider some members of "The Date Setter's Hall of Shame."

William Miller

William Miller (1782-1849) was one of the founders of the 7th Day Adventist movement. Based on a detailed examination of the Bible, especially the books of Daniel and Revelation, Miller predicted first that March 21, 1844, and later that October 22, 1844, would be the date when Christ would return in glory and the earth would be cleansed by fire, ushering in the millennium. His preaching caused great excitement, and many believed his message. Many Millerites, clad in "ascension robes," mounted chimneys and hilltops to await the Lord's return. Great disappointment ensued when the appointed dates passed without event. Many of his followers drifted away. At this point, a young woman named Ellen G. White (1827-1915) entered the picture. She claimed a vision in which she saw the followers of the Adventist faith being ushered into heaven, providing the movement a much-needed boost of morale. Then she re-interpreted Miller's predictions by saying that he was right on the date but wrong on the event. According to Mrs. White, on October 22, 1844, the Lord went into the most holy place of the heavenly sanctuary. There He began to judge and investigate the lives of the believers. When Jesus finishes this "investigative judgment," He will return to the earth, ushering in the millennium. By putting a new spin on Miller's prophecies, this young woman saved his movement and became the leader of the Seventh Day Adventist Church.

Charles T. Russell

Charles T. Russell, the founder of the Jehovah's Witnesses, was also a famous date setter. Down through the years, either he or his organization has said the Lord would return in 1874, 1914, 1925, 1975, etc. They have been repeatedly disappointed. The Watchtower Society tried to save face by redefining predictions that did not come to pass. When nothing happened in 1914, they revised the projection, asserting that the Lord returned to earth, but in an invisible state.

Does the Bible Teach "Rapture," an Antichrist, and Armageddon?

In 1920, Joseph F. Rutherford wrote,

> As we have heretofore stated, the great jubilee cycle is due to begin in 1925. At that time the earthly phase of the kingdom shall be recognized. The apostle Paul in the eleventh chapter of Hebrews names a long list of faithful men who died before the crucifixion of the Lord and before the beginning of the selection of the church. These can never be a part of the heavenly class; they had no heavenly hopes; but God has in store something good for them. They are to be resurrected as perfect men and constitute the princes or rulers in the earth, according to His promise. (Psalm 45:16; Isaiah 32:1; Matthew 8:11) Therefore we may confidently expect that 1925 will mark the return of Abraham, Isaac, Jacob and the faithful prophets of old, particularly those named by the apostle in Hebrews chapter eleven, to the condition of human perfection (*Millions Now Living Will Never Die*, 89-90).

So where were Abraham, Isaac, Jacob, and all the other faithful ones of old back in 1925? Well, I can tell you where they were not: they weren't on this earth as the Watchtower Society predicted.

Herbert W. Armstrong

In 1956, Herbert W. Armstrong, founder of the Worldwide Church of God, published a booklet called *1975 in Prophecy*, in which he predicted that Christ would return in 1975. Furthermore, he claimed the Bible prophesied that one-third of the population of America, the British nations, and the democracies of northwest Europe would die of famine and disease by the middle 1970s. Another third of the people would die in World War III at the hands of a German-dominated European dictatorship. The remaining third of the population would be transported like cattle as slaves to Europe and South America. Herbert W. Armstrong has now gone on to meet his maker. None of the things that he prophesied ever came to pass.

Hal Lindsey

Hal Lindsey, a graduate of the Dallas Theological Seminary, made himself a wealthy man by popularizing the doctrine of premillennialism in a series of best-selling books in the late 1970s. His most prominent work, *The Late Great Planet Earth*, has sold an estimated 15 million copies. This book, and the subsequent movie of the same name, attempted to offer a blueprint of the end of time by applying various Bible prophecies to the 20th century. By playing loose with the facts and with numerous

"When Will These Things Be?" : Questions on Eschatology

fantastic leaps in reasoning, Lindsey argued that current events signal the end of the world. He said that the problem with pollution, world hunger, and the contemporary Middle East conflicts all were foretold in the Bible. Although Mr. Lindsey was more cautious than some in setting dates for the Second Coming of Christ, he dropped broad hints that 1988 would be a significant year.[1]

Willie Day Smith

Willie Day Smith of Irving, TX, announced that the Lord would rapture His saints on April 1, 1980. A Texas Tech graduate with a chemical engineering degree, Smith based his calculations on a study of Bible prophecy and what he called "Hebrew numerics." Shortly before the target date, he said, "It's interesting that April 1 is April Fools' Day, and the Bible talks about being fools for Christ." When the date passed without event, journalists visiting his home found the doors locked, shades drawn, and two cars in the driveway. One wag wrote that it could not be determined if the latter-day prophet had indeed been raptured, but it appeared that he was simply ignoring visitors. Willie Day Smith was the one who was fooled.[2]

Ted Kresge

In St. Petersburg, Florida, a 41-year-old karate instructor named Ted Kresge kicked off a massive advertising campaign in 1981, declaring that the end was near. He took out full-page ads in more than forty newspapers across the country, claiming that he had "absolute proof" that all born-again Christians would be "raptured" to heaven on Saturday, June 20th, 1981. This would trigger a seven-year period of tribulation, including global famine, natural disaster, economic collapse, world war, and the emergence of the antichrist. Near the close of that epoch, he argued that Christ would return to earth and defeat the evildoers in the climactic battle of Armageddon. Afterward, the earth would enjoy a millennium of peace and prosperity.[3] Yet, as usual, nothing happened. The only people who were "raptured" were the accountants for the newspaper ad departments.

---

[1] *Tampa Tribune*, February 19, 1979, 3D; *Houston Post*, June 14, 1981, 7A.

[2] *Houston Post*, April 2, 1980, Sec. 1, p. 3.

[3] *Houston Post*, June 14, 1981, 7A.

Does the Bible Teach "Rapture," an Antichrist, and Armageddon?

Bill Maupin

Bill Maupin of Tucson, Arizona, leader of the *Lighthouse Gospel Tract Foundation*, predicted that the rapture would occur on Sunday, June 28, 1981. Maupin, who claims that God first began speaking to him in 1965, predicted that a seven-year tribulation period would follow. The antichrist would appear in 1984 and rule the earth until the battle of Armageddon on May 14, 1988. At this point, Maupin believed, the Lord and His followers would return to Earth to establish His kingdom, bringing about 1,000 years of peace.[4] Some of his forty to fifty disciples quit their jobs, sold their homes and cars, or declined to renew their apartment leases. On the appointed day, Maupin went to the desert and waited for Jesus to appear and take him to heaven.[5] After the deadline passed, Maupin admitted that he must have "missed the date." "It's not God's fault. People can blame me," he said.[6]

Edgar Whisenant

In the mid-1980s, a 56-year-old former NASA Rocket Engineer named Edgar Whisenant proclaimed the Lord would return on Tuesday, September 13th, 1988. In his book, *88 Reasons Why the Rapture will be in 1988*, Whisenant affirmed that the saints would be raptured during the 48 hours of this Jewish New Year (Rosh Hashanah, September 11-13). This date was significant because it fell 40 years and 120 days after Israel became a nation on May 14, 1948. He also forecast various other events: Israel would sign a peace treaty with an unnamed antichrist on September 21, 1988. World War III would start on October 4, 1988, and the climactic battle of Armageddon would be fought seven years later in 1995. The final battle with Satan will occur on March 17, AD 2999, and eternity will commence January 1, AD 3000.

The World Bible Society of Nashville, TN, printed over 2,000,000 copies of this book. They sold many booklets but gave away over 700,000 free copies. Reaction varied around the country. Multitudes responded with skepticism, but great excitement was generated in cer-

---

[4] Sam Heilner, *Boston Globe*, June 15, 1981. Downloaded from KI: News 13 Database.

[5] *Houston Post*, June 29, 1981, 5A.

[6] Associated Press, *Boston Globe*, June 30, 1981. Downloaded from KI: News 13 Database.

"When Will These Things Be?" : Questions on Eschatology

tain quarters of the religious community. "Rapture parties" were held where people gathered for prayer, Bible reading, and discussion about the Lord's Second Coming. Costly efforts were made by various individuals to inform the public of the Lord's impending return. A retired Ohio fire-fighter named Ed Koval paid $3,700 to purchase a full-page advertisement in a Toledo newspaper to inform people that the day of reckoning was at hand. A couple in Pensacola, FL, paid $5,000 to put up a dozen billboards announcing the Lord's arrival in September. Once again, these self-appointed harbingers have been revealed to be false prophets.[7]

Elizabeth Clare Prophet

Elizabeth Clare Prophet, head of the Church Universal and Triumphant, said that Armageddon would occur by the end of 1990. Mrs. Prophet, known by church members as Guru Ma (and by skeptics as "Clear Profit"), based her auguries on periodic communiqués from sundry "ascended masters," including Jesus, Merlin, Buddha, and King Arthur. Her church, which was started in 1958, had an estimated 10,000 to 25,000 members and is active in over 100 U.S. cities. She set December 31 as the deadline for natural catastrophe, nuclear holocaust, and worldwide economic ruin. Her faithful followers would escape this dire fate on her 33,000-acre Montana ranch north of Yellowstone Park.[8] Her church can best be described as a New Age movement survivalist cult. Residents became alarmed when church members began coming to her ranch, armed with rifles and handguns. Two church leaders were convicted in 1989 on charges of using false names to buy $150,000 worth of assault weapons and ammunition.

Jerry Falwell

One recent manifestation of Millennial Madness is the effort of some to link so-called biblical prophecies of the end of the world with the Y2K problem. In the period preceding the arrival of January 1, 2000, it was thought that many computers and many software programs would not be able to recognize the 00 of the year 2000. This is sometimes called

---

[7] *Dallas Morning News*, September 3, 1988, p. 45A; *The Paris News*, September 12, 1988, p. 3A; Various other UPI Wire Stories.

[8] Curt Suplee, "Apocalypse Now; The Coming Doom Boom," *The Washington Post*, December 17, 1989. Downloaded from KI: Washington Post Online.

Does the Bible Teach "Rapture," an Antichrist, and Armageddon?

the Y2K or the millennium bug. Nevertheless, fundamentalist Christian broadcaster Jerry Falwell produced a videotape suggesting that Y2K might be God's instrument to help end the world. Entitled "Y2K: A Christian's Guide to the Millennium Bug," this videotape purports to answer the following questions: What is Y2K? Does Y2K threaten the world? Does Y2K fulfill prophesy? What will be affected? What can we do? Falwell said that if the Y2K problem struck with full force, Social Security checks would be stopped, bank funds would be inaccessible, credit cards would be rejected, airplanes would be grounded, military defense systems would fail, along with emergency communications and the power grid, etc. However, for only $25 plus $3 shipping/handling, you could hear Mr. Falwell analyze the problem, and suggest a course of action for dealing with the impending computer crisis. As we know, the Y2K threat was vastly overblown. Planes did not fall from the sky. The economy and infrastructure remained functional. Christ did not return to save the world from the prophesied failure of computer programmers.

Harold Camping

Harold Camping, the 89-year-old religious broadcaster and president of Family Radio, caused a commotion by predicting the rapture would occur at 6 p.m. on May 21, 2011. We're still here. Followers of Mr. Camping were, no doubt, disappointed, but others were gleeful. *The Drudge Report* led with the headline, "World Ends, Film at Eleven!" Those who reject Christ and mock His message have used the failed and false prophecies of Camping and others of his ilk to blaspheme (2 Pet. 3:3-7).

Summary

The Old Testament provides a proper formula for distinguishing between a true and a false prophet: If the words of a prophet do not harmonize with previously revealed truth, he must be rejected as one who counsels rebellion against the Lord's commandments (Deut. 13:1-5). Moreover, if the words of a prophet do not come to pass, he has spoken presumptuously and must be rejected (Deut. 18:15-22).

Divine Truth Leads Us to the Light

The Lord God is a God of truth, and His word is tested (Ps. 31:5; Prov. 30:5). In contrast with Satan, who is the father of lies (John 8:44), Jesus is the very personification of truth (John 14:6), and His word is truth (John 8:31-32). In contrast, apostasy occurs when men fall away

"When Will These Things Be?" : Questions on Eschatology

from the faith, paying attention to deceitful spirits and the doctrine of demons (1 Tim. 4:1-3). False teachers engage in deception (2 John 7-11). Some unstable souls are easily manipulated, ever learning but never able to come to the knowledge of the truth (2 Tim. 3:6-7; 2 Pet. 2:14).

Doctrinal Error Leaves Us in Darkness

Why are people so quick to believe such flawed and unfounded predictions? Why are some folks so gullible? Many who feel anxious and vulnerable with the precipitous state of world affairs find comfort in the premillennial faith. Every crisis becomes a fulfillment of Bible prophecy, providing a semblance of order in disorder, giving meaning to a world filled with madness. During troubled and tumultuous times, such as the years preceding the destruction of Jerusalem in AD 70, many are easily misled by false christs and false prophets (Matt. 24:5, 11, 24).

> For many will come in My name, saying, "I am the Christ," and will mislead many (Matt. 24:5).

> Many false prophets will arise and will mislead many (Matt. 24:11).

> For false christs and false prophets will arise and will show great signs and wonders, so as to mislead, if possible, even the elect (Matt. 24:24).

Why are religious leaders so quick to jump on the bandwagon? Why are some so exploitive? Many attempt to capitalize on the excitement and interest generated by such predictions. Their prime objective is evangelism. If one seeks converts at any cost, the end justifies the means.

The Staunton Street Apostolic Church in Huntington, WV, ran a full-page newspaper ad announcing that Jesus would return on September 13, 1988. After the ad ran, 165 people showed up at the church to be baptized. "We're not trying to be alarmist, but if it does happen, it would be crazy not to prepare your heart," said Edwin Harper, minister of the church.[9]

Billie Friel, pastor of the First Baptist Church in Mount Juliet, TN, said, "This has become something of a spiritual phenomenon . . . I think this book has caused people to go back to the Bible." Friel said that nearly 400 people gathered at his church one Sunday afternoon for a two-hour discussion of Edgar Whisenant's predictions. "About seventy people gave testimonies of how this has changed their lives," he said. "A deadline is

---

[9]   June Preston, *UPI Wire Story*, September 14, 1988.

Does the Bible Teach "Rapture," an Antichrist, and Armageddon?

a great motivator, and this deadline has people studying the Bible," Friel said. "It shakes people up when a deadline is put on something like this."[10]

Nevertheless, there is a downside that cannot be ignored. The use of such predictions to gain converts is crass and exploitative. In the long run, it creates skepticism and disbelief. Many who are unlearned will put their faith in these predictions rather than in the Bible. When such prophecies inevitably fail, the faith of many will be destroyed. They become permanently "turned off" to religion. Recall the fearful warnings of Jeremiah against those who would scatter God's flock (Jer. 23:1-2). Having considered these examples, we should also ponder the words of Moses when he pointed out the difference between a true prophet and a false prophet (Deut. 18:21-22).

> "Woe to the shepherds who are destroying and scattering the sheep of My pasture!" declares the Lord. Therefore thus says the Lord God of Israel concerning the shepherds who are tending My people: "You have scattered My flock and driven them away, and have not attended to them; behold, I am about to attend to you for the evil of your deeds," declares the Lord (Jer. 23:1-2).

> You may say in your heart, "How will we know the word which the Lord has not spoken?" When a prophet speaks in the name of the Lord, if the thing does not come about or come true, that is the thing which the Lord has not spoken. The prophet has spoken it presumptuously; you shall not be afraid of him. (Deut. 18:21-22).

Such an approach is flagrantly manipulative and doomed to backfire. On December 6, 2017, U.S. President Donald Trump announced the United States recognition of Jerusalem as the capital of Israel and ordered the planning of the relocation of the U.S. Embassy in Israel from Tel Aviv to Jerusalem. A few months later, Josiah Hesse wrote an article that appeared in *The Guardian*, entitled, "In U.S. Evangelical Capital, a New Progressiveness and Differing Views on Israel." Surveying attitudes among evangelicals in Colorado Springs, Colorado. He said, "For many on the Christian right, the state of Israel has been seen as a key to fulfilling prophecy. A new generation has other ideas." After

---

[10] Frances Meeker, "Christians Prepare To Meet Jesus," *The Nashville Banner*, September, 1988, A-8.

"When Will These Things Be?" : Questions on Eschatology

reviewing premillennialism's fascination with doomsday predictions/books/movies, etc., Hesse notes that many millennials are moving away from the belief system of their parents, in part because of all the failed prophecies.

> "We've been through all this before," said Bruce McCluggage, a former evangelical who now identifies as a "follower of Christ." Throughout his youth, in the 1970s and 80s, McCluggage was part of the Christian movement that interpreted the signs of Israel as evidence of the last days. But for McCluggage, after a slow-burn of things not coming to pass, that conviction slowly faded.

> "It was a classic tool used to witness to people," he recalled. "We'd ask: 'If Jesus returned today, would you go to heaven?' It was kind of a threat . . . and we thought, with Israel coming together, we could hasten the return of Jesus."

> This "post-evangelical" generation was raised on a steady diet of low-budget movies and pulp novels that injected a potent fear of the coming Rapture, a dynamic most eloquently described by the late Billy Graham. "I pick up the Bible in one hand," he said, "and I pick up the newspaper in the other. And I read almost the same words in the newspaper as I read in the Bible. It's being fulfilled every day round about us."

> In the 1990s, Christopher Stroop was one such evangelical. He has now abandoned his faith and leads a social media campaign seeking to galvanize "exvangelicals" with hashtags like #emptythepews and #rapture-anxiety. He said he had "definitely seen a lot of ex-evangelicals talking about being triggered by the Jerusalem news."

In other words, the fruit of failed predictions is skepticism and unbelief, causing people to abandon their faith, and become opponents of Christianity. Instead of filling the pews, the misapplication of biblical prophecy has lead to an emptying of the benches.

In Summary

The word of God contains many fulfilled prophecies. These primarily focus upon the unfolding scheme of redemption, existing in the mind of God before creation, anticipated in the Garden, promised to the patriarchs, realized through the nation of Israel, and fulfilled in the person of Jesus Christ. Prophecies also focus upon the nations and the time and circumstances of the first coming of Christ.

Does the Bible Teach "Rapture," an Antichrist, and Armageddon?

Exposing its impotence and ineffectiveness, God challenges practitioners of idolatry to relate the former things of the past and accurately reveal the unseen things of the future. Jehovah alone can do such things (Isa. 41:21-24; 43:9-13; 44:6-8). Fulfilled prophecy demonstrates the inspiration and authority of Sacred Scripture (John 13:17-19; 14:25-31; 2 Pet. 1:19-21; cf. also Heb. 2:1-4).

While abundant prophecies were connected with Christ's first coming, relatively few are connected with His second advent. A contrast may be observed in Matthew 24 (and its parallel passages) where Jesus discusses the destruction of Jerusalem, which would be accompanied by various signs, and the ultimate end of the world, which will come like a thief (Matt. 24:36-51; Mark 13:32-37). Not knowing the time of the Lord's return, we should be alert and watchful (Luke 12:39-40; 1 Thess. 5:1-11; 2 Pet. 3:10-13; etc.). Even the end-times prophecy of Revelation 20 provides little specifics, except that things will get much worse before they get much better (Rev. 20:7-10).

Let us never forget that we are at war with Satan and his forces (Eph. 6:11-17). We must fight the good fight of faith (1 Tim. 1:18; 6:12), offering an aggressive defense of the truth (Jude 3). Rome was the evil force when John wrote Revelation, but the principle is timeless. God and His cause will be victorious in the end! The battle will be fierce, the foe is frightening, but victory is ours if we will only remain faithful (1 John 5:4; Rev. 2:10). Ultimately all wickedness and evil will be overthrown by the great power of the Almighty God (Rev. 20:10-15).

Let us rightly divide the word of truth (2 Tim. 2:14-15; 2 Pet. 3:14-16). Let us correctly understand apocalyptic language (Matt. 24:15-16; Rev. 13:18). Let us obey the commands of Scripture (Acts 2:37-38, 46-47; Rev. 7:13-17).

The doctrine of premillennialism has no basis in fact or Scripture. Let us not be swept away in fanciful or fictitious notions. Instead, let us remain faithful to the old paths and not stray from God's word. We do not know when Christ is coming back. Therefore we should always be ready. Our prayer and petition should be that of the apostle: Maranatha! Even so, "Come, Lord Jesus!" Are you prepared to face Christ in judgment?

Bibliography

Barclay, William. *The Letters to John and Jude.* Rev. ed. Philadelphia: Westminster Press, 1976.

BDAG=Bauer, Walter, Frederick W. Danker, William Arndt, and F. Wilbur Gingrich. *A Greek-English Lexicon of the New Testament and Other Early Christian Literature.* 3rd ed. Chicago, IL: University of Chicago Press, 2000.

ESV=The Holy Bible: English Standard Version. Wheaton, IL: Crossway Bibles, 2016.

Frame, John M. *Salvation Belongs to the Lord: An Introduction to Systematic Theology.* Phillipsburg, NJ: P&R Publishing, 2006.

Harkrider, Robert. *The Book of Revelation: Including a Study of Premillennialism.* Athens, AL: Truth Publications Inc., 2014.

Hesse, Josiah. "In US Evangelical Capital, a New Progressiveness and Differing Views on Israel." *The Guardian.* May 19, 2018. https://www.theguardian.com/world/2018/may/19/evangelicals-israel-usa-end-times.

Hubbard, David A. "Antichrist." *Baker's Dictionary of Theology.* Everett F. Harrison and Geoffrey W. Bromiley, editors. Grand Rapids, MI: Baker Publishing Group, 1987.

KJV=The Holy Bible: King James Version. Electronic ed. of the 1769 edition of the 1611 Authorized Version. Bellingham, WA: Logos Research Systems, Inc., 1995.

Lockyer, Herbert. *All the Last Words of Saints and Sinners.* Grand Rapids, MI: Kregel Publications, 1969.

Louw, Johannes P., and Eugene Albert Nida. *Greek-English Lexicon of the New Testament: Based on Semantic Domains.* New York: United Bible Societies, 1996.

Merriam-Webster's Collegiate Dictionary. Springfield, MA: Merriam-Webster, 1996.

Morris, L. L. "Antichrist." *New Bible Dictionary.* Ed. by D. R. W. Wood et al. Leicester, England; Downers Grove, IL: InterVarsity Press, 1996.

Does the Bible Teach "Rapture," an Antichrist, and Armageddon?

NASB=New American Standard Bible: 1995 Update. La Habra, CA: The Lockman Foundation, 1995. Unless otherwise noted, all Bible quotations come from the NASB.

NBD=*The New Bible Dictionary*. J. D. Douglas, ed. Grand Rapids, MI: Wm. B. Eerdmans Publishing Co., 1965.

NKJV=The New King James Version. Nashville: Thomas Nelson, 1982.

Pope, Kyle M. *Truth Commentaries: Matthew.* Mike Willis, ed. Athens, AL: Guardian of Truth, 2013.

Reid, Daniel G. et al. *Dictionary of Christianity in America* Downers Grove, IL: InterVarsity Press, 1990.

Schemm, Pete. "Rapture." *Holman Illustrated Bible Dictionary.* Ed. Chad Brand et al. Nashville, TN: Holman Bible Publishers, 2003.

Sheriffs, R. J. A. "Armageddon." *New Bible Dictionary.* 3rd ed. D. R. W. Wood, ed. Downers Grove, IL: InterVarsity Press, 1996.

Swanson, James, and Orville Nave. *New Nave's Topical Bible.* Oak Harbor, WA: Logos Research Systems, 1994.

The International Standard Bible Encyclopedia (ISBE), 1915 Edition. James Orr, ed. Chicago: Howard-Severance Company, 1915.

Thomas, Robert L. *New American Standard Hebrew-Aramaic and Greek Dictionaries:* Updated Edition. Anaheim, CA: Foundation Publications, Inc., 1998.

Unger, Merrill F. and R.K. Harrison, eds. *The New Unger's Bible Dictionary.* Chicago: Moody Press, 1988.

Weaver, Walton. *Truth Commentaries: The Books of 1 and 2 Thessalonians.* Mike Willis, ed. Athens, AL: Truth Publications Inc., 2013.

Youngblood, Ronald, F. F. Bruce, and R. K. Harrison, eds. *Nelson's New Illustrated Bible Dictionary.* Nashville, TN: Thomas Nelson, Inc., 1995.

Tough Questions

Does the Bible Teach an End of This Universe?
    Chris Reeves

What Is the Focus of the Mount of Olives Discourse?
    Kyle Pope

When Was Revelation Written and Why Does It Matter?
    Daniel H. King, Sr.

"When Will These Things Be?"
Questions on Eschatology

Does the Bible Teach an End of This Universe?

By Chris Reeves

Recent surveys reveal that approximately 75% of Americans still believe in some form of the afterlife.[1] However, *where* we will spend that afterlife and *what* we will be doing there are questions of much debate. Will the afterlife be in heaven, will it be on a restored earth, or will it be somewhere else? Will it even be in a place, or will it be just a state of mind? If in a place, will this place be physical in nature,

---

[1] Maggie Fox, "Fewer Americans Believe in God—Yet They Still Believe in Afterlife." Caryle Murphy, "Most Americans believe in heaven... and hell."

Chris Reeves was born October 20, 1965 in San Antonio, TX to Bill and Twilah Reeves. He attended Florida College from 1984 to 1988 and received a Bible Certificate. He was awarded a B.A. in Biblical Studies from Florida College in 2000. Chris began preaching regularly in 1984 and worked full-time with the McRae Road church of Christ in Camden, SC (1988-1990) and the Highway 9 church of Christ in Corpus Christi, TX (1991-1995). He worked with the Memorial Blvd. church of Christ in Springfield, TN for twenty-one years (1995-2016) and now he is currently working with the Warfield Blvd. church of Christ in Clarksville, TN (2017 to present). Chris has done preaching work outside the country in Mexico, Spain, the Philippines, and Germany. Chris married Cheri Goodall (daughter of Charles and Vernita Goodall) in 1988 and they have four children, Jessica Chapman, Jacob, Mason and Carlin. He writes articles regularly for *Truth Magazine*. Chris has written a commentary on Micah in the *Truth Commentary* series and a workbook on Ephesians in the Bible Text Books series. His book on the New Hermeneutic, *"Out with the Old and in with the New,"* is also published by Truth Publications. He can be reached at chrisreevesmail@gmail.com.

"When Will These Things Be?" : Questions on Eschatology

spiritual, or both? Also, *what* will we be doing in the afterlife? Will we be doing what we are doing now just in a glorified state, or something completely different, or both? For centuries, these questions have been on the minds of many, especially believers. Let us turn to the Scriptures for the answers.

The Biblical View of the Afterlife

My assignment in this lecture is to answer the question: "Does the Bible teach an end of this universe?" This question deals with the nature and location of the final state of the righteous. The answer to this question will vary depending upon whom you ask. Our primary focus is, of course, "What the Scriptures teach?" not the latest opinion of biblical "scholars" or even our brethren might think.

What does the Bible say in answer to this question? Yes, the Bible teaches an end of this universe. God created the heavens and the earth *ex nihilo* (from nothing) and He will one day reduce them *ad nihilum* (to nothing) (Feldman, 56). In this lecture, I want to examine three Bible truths that give an affirmative answer to this question. First, the physical heavens and earth that we now know will one day "pass away." They will come to an end and not remain. Second, the eternal reward of the righteous is "in heaven," not on earth. The reward of the righteous is "heavenly," not earthly. Third, the righteous will dwell in a "new heaven and a new earth." This new heaven and new earth are not a restored version of the heaven and earth that we now dwell in, but it replaces the physical heaven and earth that will pass away. Let us now examine these three biblical arguments in closer detail.

1. Heaven and Earth Will "Pass Away"

The Bible teaches an end of this universe because Jesus said: "Verily I say unto you, This generation shall not pass away, till all these things be accomplished. Heaven and earth shall pass away, but my words shall not pass away" (Matt. 24:35).[2] Peter also wrote: "But the day of the Lord will come as a thief; in the which the heavens shall pass away with a great noise, and the elements shall be dissolved with fervent heat, and the earth and the works that are therein shall be burned up" (2 Pet. 3:10). "Pass away" in these two passages comes from the Greek word

---

[2] All scripture quotations in this lecture are taken from the American Standard Version (1901) unless otherwise noted.

Does the Bible Teach an End of This Universe?

parerchomai (παρέρχομαι) and has the meaning, "come to an end, disappear" (BAGD, 626)[3], or "perish" (Thayer, 488). Our present, physical heavens and earth will one day "pass away"[4] and "disappear" (NIV, NLB, CEV, etc.).

Add to this biblical testimony the following verses that indirectly teach a destruction of our present world:

> While the earth remaineth, seedtime and harvest, and cold and heat, and summer and winter, and day and night shall not cease (Gen. 8:22).

> For verily I say unto you, Till heaven and earth pass away, one jot or one tittle shall in no wise pass away from the law, till all things be accomplished (Matt. 5:18).

> . . . While we look not at the things which are seen, but at the things which are not seen: for the things which are seen are temporal; but the things which are not seen are eternal (2 Cor. 4:18).[5]

> And, Thou, Lord, in the beginning didst lay the foundation of the earth, and the heavens are the works of thy hands: They shall perish; but thou continuest: and they all shall wax old as doth a garment; and as a mantle shalt thou roll them up, as a garment, and they shall be changed: But thou art the same, and thy years shall not fail (Heb. 1:10-12).[6]

Before leaving this point, let me address one matter involving 2 Peter 3:10. The Jehovah's Witnesses and some contemporary Bible scholars argue that the English translation "will be found," "discovered," or "laid bare" in verse 10 is better than "burned up." They say the ancient manuscript evidence is better for *heurethēsetai* (εὑρεθήσεται— "found," "discovered" [New World Translation], "laid bare" [NIV], or "exposed" [ESV]) than for *katakaēsetai* (κατακαήσεται—"burned up" [KJV, NKJV,

---

[3] See Matt. 5:18; Mark 13:30-31; Luke 16:17; 21:32-33; 2 Cor. 5:17; and Jas. 1:10.

[4] By contrast, Jesus's words and God's everlasting kingdom *"shall not pass away"* (Dan. 7:14). Henry C. Thiessen suggests that "pass away" does not mean non-existence, only transition (402). But, he offers no linguistic or lexical support for this opinion.

[5] The adjective "temporary" comes from the Greek word *proschairos* (πρόσκαιρος) meaning "enduring only for a while" (Thayer, 546).

[6] A quote from Psalm 102:25-27.

ASV, NASV, RSV, etc.]). Thus, according to them, the earth and its works will be "discovered" or "laid bare" for renovation and restoration. The earth will not be "burned up" or annihilated, it will be renovated. Limited time and space here do not permit me to deal with all the issues involved in the textual criticism of this verse. The textual problems associated with the choice of words in this verse are admittedly difficult. However, a few brief comments can be made.

First, the translators of several major committee versions retained the word *katakaēsetai* in verse 10 and translated it "burned up." They did so because of the presence of this word in some ancient manuscripts and because the immediate context of verses 10-12 uses language associated with literal fire and burning.[7]

Second, even if the manuscript evidence is better for *heurethēsetai* ("found," "discovered," or "laid bare"),[8] it is not a necessary conclusion that our present earth will be "found," "laid bare," or "discovered" for the purpose of renovation and restoration. If Peter, in fact, used *heurethēsetai*, then his point in this context would be that the earth and works will be discovered, laid bare, or exposed to God's judgment of fire (vv. 7, 10, 12). The earth and its works will have been discovered, laid bare, and exposed to God's fiery judgment when everything melts away and is dissolved and destroyed. J.H. Thayer commented on this word this way: "γῆ καί τά ἐν αὐτῇ ἔργα εὑρεθήσεται *shall be found* namely, for destruction, i.e., will be unable to hide themselves from the doom decreed them by God, 2 Peter 3:10" (*A Greek-English Lexicon of the New Testament*, 261). "Laid bare" for destruction better fits the immediate context of verses 7, 10-12,

---

[7] The verb *katakaiō* (κατακαίω) can be found in Matt. 3:12; 13:30, 40; Luke 3:17; Acts 19:19; 1 Cor. 3:15; Heb. 13:11; Rev. 8:7; 17:16; and 18:8.

[8] This is the oldest reading according to Metzger (636). Peter actually uses a form of this same word in verse 14: *heurethēnai* (εὑρεθῆναι—"to be found"). This may point to some internal evidence for the use of *heurethēsetai* in verse 10.

Does the Bible Teach an End of This Universe?

than "laid bare" for renovation.[9] Whatever is made of the meaning of *heurethēsetai*, it must not contradict the plain meaning of "pass away" in the same verse.

Third, even if *katakaēsetai* ("burned up") is removed from the text, the idea of burning up is still expressed in the words, "with fervent heat," occurring twice in the text (vv. 10, 12). The words "with fervent heat" come from the Greek *kausoumena* (καυσούμενα) meaning "be consumed by heat, burn up. Destroyed by burning, 2 Peter 3:10" (BDAG, 425).

2. The Eternal Reward of the Righteous Is "in Heaven" (Heavenly), Not on Earth (Earthly)

The Bible teaches an end of this universe because heaven, not earth, will be the eternal abode of the righteous. "Heaven" (*ouranos*)[10], in the Bible, can refer to the sky above the earth (Luke 12:56), where the birds fly (Matt. 6:26),[11] the weather is formed (Matt. 16:2-3),[12] the lightning strikes (Luke 17:24), and where the clouds (Matt. 24:30)[13] and rain (Luke 4:25)[14] appear (see Matt. 24:31 and Mark 13:27). "Heaven" can also refer to space above the sky where the sun, moon, and stars are found (Matt. 24:29).[15] Finally, "heaven" can refer to a place above the sky and space

---

[9] For those wanting to study this issue further, you will want to take note that the latest 28th edition of the Nestle-Aland's *Novum Testamentum Graece* reads: οὐκ εὑρεθήσεται, "will not be found." If this is the original reading, then the matter is closed. There will be no earth or works therein found after God's judgment of fire. We also have a parallel in Revelation 20:11 where there it reads οὐκ εὑρέθη, not found.

[10] Time and space does not permit me to cover the OT Hebrew words for heaven. The Heb. שָׁמַיִם (*shamayim*) is equivalent in meaning to the Greek *ouranoi* (οὐρανοί). For the root meaning of *ouranos* (οὐρανὸς), see Vine, "Probably akin to *ornumi*, "to lift, to heave. . ." (298); and, Thayer, "to cover, encompass" (464).

[11] See Matthew 8:20; 13:32; Mark 4:4, 32; Luke 8:5; 9:58; 13:19; and Acts 10:12.

[12] See Luke 12:56; 17:29; and Revelation 16:21.

[13] See Mark 14:62.

[14] See James 5:18 and Revelation 11:6.

[15] See Mark 13:25; Acts 2:19-20; Hebrews 11:12; Revelation 6:13; 8:10; 9:1; and 12:4. Uranus, the seventh planet from the sun derives its name from the Greek word for heaven.

"When Will These Things Be?" : Questions on Eschatology

where God (Matt. 5:16),[16] His angels (Matt. 18:10),[17] and Jesus (1 Pet. 3:22)[18] dwell.[19]

After the judgment day, heaven (God's dwelling place)[20], not the earth, will be the eternal abode of the righteous.[21] Consider the following Bible truths. If the righteous are faithful to the end of their life, or when Jesus returns, their:

---

[16] See Matt. 5:45; 6:1, 9; 7:11, 21, 10:32-33; 12:50; 16:17; 18:10, 14, 19; Mark 11:25-26; and Luke 11:2.

Because God is "in heaven," the spiritual "kingdom of heaven" is a kingdom that is *from* God and *by* God's will. It is a kingdom that is "of heavenly or divine origin and nature" (Thayer). It is a kingdom of people now on earth that will one day reside "in heaven" (2 Tim. 4:18). Additionally, all sin is "against heaven" (Luke 15:18, 21), because it is against God who is "in heaven." Authority (Mark 11:30-31) and signs (Luke 11:16; 21:11, 26) are "from heaven," because God is "in heaven." The one who "swears by heaven," swears by God Himself (Matt. 23:22). In these cases, heaven is synonymous with God.

For "kingdom of heaven" (found only in the book of Matthew), see Matthew 3:2; 4:17; 5:3, 10, 19, 20; 7:21; 8:11; 10:7; 11:11-12; 13:11, 24, 31, 33, 44-45, 47, 52; 16:19, 18:1, 3-4, 23; 19:12, 14, 23; 20:1; 22:2; 23:13; 25:1.

For "heavenly father," see Matthew 5:48; 6:14, 26, 32; 15:13; 18:35; and Luke 11:13. See also Matthew 23:9.

For the "God of heaven," see Revelation 11:13 and 16:11 and for "Lord of heaven and earth," see Matthew 11:25..

[17] See Matthew 22:30; 24:36; Mark 12:25; 13:32; Luke 2:15; 22:43; and Revelation 5:13.

[18] See John 3:13; Romans 10:6; Ephesians 4:10; 6:9; 1 Thessalonians 1:10; Hebrews 4:14; 7:26; 8:1; and 9:24.

[19] This is likely the "third heaven" (paradise) that Paul writes about in 2 Corinthians 12:2. See 1 Kings 8:30.

[20] The Scriptures teach that God is in this space, but certainly not confined to it (1 Kings 8:27).

[21] The Scriptures teach that the righteous enter into the paradise portion of hades when they die (Luke 16:23; Rev. 20:13) and then enter into heaven itself after the Judgment Day. The question "Where are the dead?" now and a study of the Hadean realm ("intermediate state") is the subject of another lecture in this book.

Does the Bible Teach an End of This Universe?

- Reward is great "in heaven," not on earth (Matt. 5:12).[22]
- Treasures are laid up "in heaven," not on earth (Matt. 6:19-20).[23]
- Names are written "in heaven," not on earth (Luke 10:20).
- Resurrected body will be "heavenly," not earthly (1 Cor. 15:48-49).
- House (resurrected body) will be eternal "in the heavens" and "from heaven," not on the earth (2 Cor. 5:1-2).
- Citizenship is "in heaven," not on earth (Phil. 3:20).
- Hope is laid up "in the heavens," not on the earth (Col. 1:5).[24]
- Salvation is unto a "heavenly" kingdom, not an earthly kingdom (2 Tim. 4:18).[25]
- Calling is "heavenly," not earthly (Heb. 3:1).[26]
- Gift is "heavenly," not earthly (Heb. 6:4).
- Better [country] is "heavenly," not earthly (Heb. 11:16).[27]
- City will be the "heavenly" Jerusalem, not the earthly Jerusalem (Heb. 12:22).[28]
- Names are enrolled "in heaven," not on earth (Heb. 12:23).
- Inheritance is reserved "in heaven," not on earth (1 Pet. 1:4).

---

[22] See Luke 6:23.

[23] See Matthew 19:21; Mark 10:21; Luke 12:33 ("in the heavens"); and 18:22. The "treasure in heaven" of Matthew 19:21 is the "eternal life" of Matthew 19:29. The "treasure in heaven" of Mark 10:21 is "the world to come" of Mark 10:30. Paul makes the same point when he writes: "Set your minds on the things that are above, not on the things that are upon the earth" (Col. 3:2).

[24] See Hebrews 6:19-20 and 7:19.

[25] See Matthew 25:34 and 2 Peter 1:11. Traub, commenting on "heavenly" in 2 Timothy 4:18, wrote: "This kingdom is not only in Christ but with Him in heaven" (541).

[26] See Philippians 3:14.

[27] "In heaven" (Heb. 10:34) is found in the KJV and NKJV, but not in other standard versions.

[28] See Galatians 4:26; Hebrews 11:10; and 13:14. The "heavenly" Jerusalem is described figuratively in greater detail in Revelation 21:9-27. Traub, commenting on "heavenly" in Hebrews 11:16 and 12:22, wrote: "This characterizes them as the final aim for God's community" (541).

"When Will These Things Be?" : Questions on Eschatology

- Eternal worship, praise, and service to God will be around His throne "in heaven," not on earth (Rev. 7:15; 14:3; 22:3).[29]

When you examine the many "heaven" or "heavenly" passages in the NT (a little over 300 times),[30] several valuable lessons related to our topic can be learned.

First, the eternal afterlife of the righteous will be "in heaven" or "heavenly." Nowhere in Scripture are we told that the eternal abode of the righteous is on a restored earth. Earth (*gē*), mentioned over 250 times in the NT, is never said to be the final resting place of the righteous.[31]

---

[29] Cottrell writes: "One advantage we will have over His angels is that the resurrected Christ, the Lamb of God, will no longer sit on God's throne in their presence, but will move to the new throne room on our new earth" (571). However, the "throne" of God in the book of Revelation (and the rest of Scripture) is always pictured in heaven and never on earth (Rev. 1:4; 3:21; 4:2-6, 9-10; 5:1, 6, 7, 11, 13; 6:16; 7:9, 11, 15, 17; 8:3; 11:16; 12:5; 14:3; 16:17; 19:4-5; 20:11-12; 21:3, 5; 22:1, 3). Nowhere in Scripture are we told that God's throne leaves heaven and comes to earth. See also 1 Kings 22:19 (2 Chron. 18:18); Psalms 11:4; 103:19; and Hebrews 8:1. The reward of the righteous portrayed in the book of Revelation is clearly set in heaven. They will sit and reign on "thrones" (3:21; 20:4) in heaven, not on earth. The book of Revelation has a heavenly outlook from beginning to end. Jesus is coming in judgment from heaven (1:7). The rewards of Christians are set in heaven (2:7; 3:12; 3:21). God and Jesus are around a throne in heaven (4-5). The martyred saints are under the altar in heaven (6:9). The great multitude of the saved are around the throne in heaven (7:9-17). Divine judgment comes from heaven (8:10; 9:1). God's prophetic message comes from heaven (10:1). The faithful witnesses enter into heaven (11:12). There is spiritual warfare in heaven (12:7). The beast blasphemes those who dwell in heaven (13:6). The 144,000 followers of the Lamb are in heaven (14:1-5) and judgment comes from heaven (14:17-18). The plagues of divine judgment come from heaven (15:5-8). The message of complete judgment comes from heaven (16:17). An angel with great authority comes from heaven (18:1). The voice of a great multitude praising God is heard in heaven (19:1-8) and more divine judgment comes from heaven (19:11). After some time, divine judgment upon the nations comes from heaven (20:9). Lastly, God will dwell with His people in a "new" heaven (21:1-7) and God's servants will serve Him and reign with Him in heaven (22:1-5). Revelation is a book about heaven!

[30] See Appendix 2.

[31] Augustus H. Strong made this candid admission in his *Systematic Theology*: "Is this earth to be the heaven of the saints?" He answered: "First, that the

Does the Bible Teach an End of This Universe?

The many "heaven" or "heavenly" passages just examined above simply do not make sense if heaven is on earth. The speakers and writers of the passages just examined had the opportunity to mention earth as the final destination of the righteous, but they chose not to do so. Why? Earth is not the final destination of the righteous.

"Heavenly" (*ouranios*) means "belonging to heaven, coming from or living in heaven" (BAGD, 593); "what pertains to or is in heaven" (Zodhiates, 1075).[32] What reputable lexicon is there that defines "heavenly" (*ouranios*) as "earthly"? If the Bible writers wanted to say that the eternal reward of the righteous was "earthly," they could have used the Greek word *epigeios* meaning "on the earth" or "belonging to the earth."[33] They did not use this word; instead, they used the word "heavenly" (*ouranios*).

Today, many advocates of a restored earth use the words "heaven" and "heavenly" to describe the eternal abode of the righteous, but they really mean a restored earth.[34] This is misleading on their part. They want you to think about the familiar setting of heaven that you have read about in your Bible and sung about many times while they talk about a restored earth. This is tantamount to a theological "sleight of hand" or "bait and switch."[35]

---

earth is to be purified by fire, and perhaps prepared to be the abode of the saints, although this last is not rendered certain by the Scriptures" (1032).

[32] Vine: "heavenly, what pertains to, or is in, heaven (*epi*, in the sense of 'pertaining to,' not here, 'above')" (298).

[33] See the use of *epigeios* in John 3:12; 1 Corinthians 15:40; 2 Corinthians 5:1; Philippians 2:10; 3:19; and James 3:15.

[34] Grudem, 1162. This doctrine is not new, but it has been given renewed interest among evangelicals in the past 40 years. Some of our brethren have adopted this doctrine in the past 10 years.

[35] Consider the following examples:

J. Richard Middleton: "He hammers home the point that he fully expects 'not to be naked' (5:3), that he does 'not wish to be unclothed' (5:4); instead he longs to be clothed with his *heavenly dwelling* (5:2). In other words, Paul's explicit hope is not for existence as a 'naked' soul or spirit (presumably in heaven), but for eternal embodied life (*on earth*)" (93; emphasis mine).

Jack Cottrell: "The only thing different about life *on the new earth* (i.e., "*in heaven*") is the time will never end. . ." (566) and "The fact that God will

"When Will These Things Be?" : Questions on Eschatology

Restored earth advocates also try to explain away the many "heaven" or "heavenly" passages by saying they merely point to a heavenly *origin* or *source*[36] for these blessings, not where these blessings will actually be *experienced*. According to them, heaven is where our blessings are being *prepared*, but not where they will be *realized*. Earth is where they will be realized.[37] My response: "Nice try." Read these verses again. The words

---

manifest His presence *on the new earth* is that reason why we call it *heaven*" (571; emphasis mine).

Hoekema: ". . .we shall continue to be *in heaven* while we are *on a new earth*" (274; emphasis mine).

[36] Bob Wilkin, commenting on Hebrews 11:13-16, wrote the following: The reference to a "heavenly country" may seem to contradict the idea of the New Earth. It does not. The word *country* is not in the Greek. Abraham and Sarah desired a heavenly *homeland* (compare verse 14). The homeland they sought would be heavenly *in origin, not in location*. The Lord has prepared the New Jerusalem (John 14:1-3; Rev. 21). That city, according to Revelation 21, will be on the New Earth, not in the third heaven.

(Likewise, the Lord commanded us to lay up treasure "in heaven" in Matt 6:19-21. That is where the treasure is *sourced*. But that treasure will be enjoyed on the Millennial Earth and then the New Earth.) https://faithalone.org/blog/does-hebrews-1113-16-contradict-the-new-earth/.

[37] It is popular for New Creation Eschatology (hereafter, NCE) advocates to talk about their supposed "eschatological pattern" or "apocalyptic pattern" throughout the Bible where they say the eternal blessings are *prepared* in heaven now and then *revealed* upon a restored earth in the future (Middleton, 220-221). Consider this quote by N.T. Wright:

". . .Heaven is the place where *God's purposes for the future are stored up*. It isn't where they are meant to stay so that one would need to go to heaven to enjoy them; it is where they are kept safe against the day when they will become a reality on earth. If I say to a friend, 'I've kept some beer in the fridge for you,' that doesn't mean that he has to climb into the fridge in order to drink the beer. God's future inheritance, the incorruptible new world and the new bodies that we are to inhabit that world, are already kept safe, waiting for us, not so that we can go to heaven and put them on there but so that they can be brought to birth in this world or rather in the new heavens and new earth, the renewed world of which I spoke earlier" (151-152).

There is a problem with Wright's beer-in-the-fridge example. It is true that a person does not climb into the fridge to drink the beer. But, neither does Wright have any plans of bringing the fridge to his friend. When was the

Does the Bible Teach an End of This Universe?

"in heaven" and "heavenly" speak to the *place* or *location* (see "place" in John 14:2-3), where these blessings will be enjoyed. "Heavenly" speaks to the idea of locale or locality. What reputable lexicon is there that defines "heavenly" (*ouranios*) as "sourced in heaven, but located on the earth" or "prepared in heaven, but realized on earth"?[38] You will not find one. The eternal blessing for the righteous are "laid up," "prepared," and "kept" in heaven, and that is where they will stay.[39]

Just like there are beings "in heaven" now (God, Jesus, angels),[40] just like there are things that take place "in heaven" now (God's will, answered prayers), just like there are things "in heaven" now (joy, peace, or a sanctuary),[41] so there will be a "heavenly kingdom" that will exist "in heaven" in the future. This is not difficult to understand. Faithful Christians right now have "every spiritual blessing in the heavenly places in Christ" (Eph. 1:3).[42] This refers to our spiritual blessings that we have

---

last time you went to a friend's house and you ask for a non-alcoholic drink out the fridge and he brought the fridge to you? That's what would have to happen for this example to be parallel with Jesus bringing heaven down to us. What proves too much, proves too little.

[38] Other restored-earthers like Jack Cottrell have the righteous going to heaven when they die, coming back to the earth when Jesus returns, going back to heaven for the Judgment Day (at which time God is restoring the earth), and coming back again to live eternally on a restored earth. Up to heaven, down to earth, up to heaven, down to earth—whew! See Cottrell (563).

[39] Traub wrote: "These blessings are in heaven, which means with God or Christ, but with the God or Christ with whom believers will also be, or already are in faith. Heaven here is like a place, but there can be no asking where it is situated, for such a question is opposed to the whole concept" (532).

[40] The KJV of 1 John 5:7 reads: "three that bear record in heaven." See Rev. 12:12; 13:6; 19:1; and 19:14.

[41] See Revelation 14:17; 15:5; and 16:17.

[42] "In the heavenlies" (Gr. ἐν τοῖς ἐπουρανίοις) is used in the NT only by Paul in Ephesians 1:3, 20; 2:6; 3:10; and 6:12. "In the heavenly places" is an actual spiritual realm, place, or location implied by the words "seated Him at His right hand" (Eph. 1:20) and "seated us with Him" (Eph. 2:6). Traub wrote: "ἐπ- here does not denote 'upon' but 'at', i.e., 'in heaven'" (538). See the lecture by Wayne Goff.

"When Will These Things Be?" : Questions on Eschatology

in Christ now in the church, like forgiveness of sins or answered prayer. One day these faithful Christians can look forward to actually being in the "heavenly kingdom" itself (2 Tim. 4:18).

Second, heaven (the dwelling place of God) is a place, not just a subjective state of mind that people enjoy now and in the future. Heaven is a place, a location. God is "in heaven." Jesus came "from" heaven ("from above" in John 3:31)[43] and ascended[44] back "into heaven" (Mark 16:19; Luke 24:51; Acts 1:11).[45] The Son of Man is "in heaven" (John 3:13). When Jesus ascended back into heaven, he went "where he was before" (John 6:62). He has "gone into heaven" (1 Pet. 3:22). Jesus looked up "to heaven" when He prayed.[46] Stephen "looked up steadfastly into heaven, and saw the glory of God. . ." (Acts 7:56). Peter heard a voice "out of heaven" (Acts 11:9). Jesus ascended into "heaven itself" before "the face of God" (Heb. 9:24).[47] The righteous will be in heaven, and the rest will not be able to "enter" (Rev. 21:27); they are "without" (Rev. 22:15). All of these passages imply that there is a location for heaven, though no passage of Scripture is specific about the exact location of it relative to the earth. However, from man's perspective on earth, heaven is "up" (Matt. 14:19).[48]

---

[43] "From above" is used synonymously of heaven in John 3:31; 8:23; 19:11; James 1:17; 3:15 and 3:17. See also John 6:31-33, 38, 41-42, 50-51, 58.

[44] For Jesus's ascension into heaven, see the passages of Scripture that contain the Greek verb *anabainō* (ἀναβαίνω).

[45] Various things and beings are said to come "from" heaven or "from the heavens." See the following Scriptures: 1) ἀπ' (from)—Matthew 24:29, 31; Mark 8:11; Luke 9:54; 17:29; 21:11; 22:43; John 6:38; Romans 1:18; 1 Thess.alonians 4:16; 2 Thessalonians 1:7; Hebrews 12:25; 1 Peter 1:12; and, 2) ἐκ (out of)—Matthew 3:17; 16:1; 21:25 [2x]; 28:2; Mark 1:11; 11:30-31; 13;25; Luke 3:22; 10:18; 11:13, 16; 17:24; 20:4-5; John 1:32; 3:13, 27; 31; 6:31, 32 [2x], 33, 41-42, 50-51, 58; 12:28; Acts 2:2; 9:3; 11:5, 9; 22:6; 1 Corinthians 15:47; 2 Corinthians 5:2; Galatians 1:8; 1 Thessalonians 1:10; 2 Peter 1:18; Revelation 3:12; 8:10; 9:1; 10:1, 4, 8; 11:12; 13:13; 14:2, 13; 16:21; 18:1, 4; 20:1, 9; 21:2, 10.

[46] See Matthew 14:19; Mark 6:41; 7:34; Luke 9:16; 18:13; and John 17:1. The angel in Revelation 10:5 lifted up his right hand "to heaven."

[47] See Revelation 11:12.

[48] See Mark 6:41; Luke 9:16; and 2 Corinthians 12:2. "Exalted unto heaven" in Matthew 11:23 also implies an upward direction of heaven. "Down from heaven" is found in 1 Peter 1:12, Revelation 10:1, 18:1, and 20:1.

Does the Bible Teach an End of This Universe?

Additionally, Jesus's words in John 14:2-3 are important to our study. [49] Jesus said, "And if I go and prepare a place for you, I come again, and will receive you unto myself; that *where I am, there ye may be also*" (emphasis mine). Jesus was leaving to go back to His Father, who was in heaven (John 14:12, 28; 16:5, 28; 17:1). The place He was going to prepare was in His Father's house.[50] And, when He returns a second time, He will

---

[49] When NCE advocates get done with this verse, they have Jesus saying the opposite of what He said. Matthew Benfield wrote: "It is not that He will go to prepare a place for us and then take us to that place, rather, He will prepare a place for us and then reveal that place at His coming" (*A New Heaven*, 42).

[50] Some Bible students understand these verses to say that Jesus is returning to heaven to prepare the church. They say that heaven is already prepared when Jesus says these words, but the church is not. And, the "Father's house" is a reference to the church which is the "house of God." However, I do not take this position for the following reasons. First, Jesus spoke of "my Father's house" in the present tense. The "Father's house" was already in existence in heaven when Jesus said these words, but the church would not be present until days later on Pentecost. (For heaven as God's "habitation," see Psa. 11:4; 33:13-14; and Isa. 63:15). Second, Jesus said He was going to "go" to His Father to prepare a place and that He would come again and "receive" them "unto Myself." All of this activity is heavenward, not focused on the earth. Jesus never said that what He was going to "prepare" would then be brought to the earth. The church is a relationship that is experienced here on the earth. Jesus didn't "prepare" the church in heaven and then bring it to earth. What he left this earth to prepare was in heaven, it stays there, and He receives His disciples to Himself there. Jesus is our "forerunner" into heaven (Heb. 6:20). Third, Jesus was going to return for the purpose of receiving the disciples and taking them to His Father (see also 12:26). The coming of Jesus and the receiving the disciples unto Himself occur at the same time. Jesus wants His disciples to be with Himself ("Myself) and He wants them to come to His Father (vv. 4-6). (Paul wrote, "and so shall we ever be with the Lord," 1 Thess. 4:17.) Once Jesus returned to the Father, both He and the Father were in heaven together. Jesus and the Father in heaven together, not the church, is a focus of this passage and this focus is found throughout John 13-17. Fourth, Jesus said that His disciples already knew the way where Jesus was going (v. 4). They knew the way to the Father in heaven was through Jesus. He had already taught them that principle (see 5:19ff; 6:32ff; 7:37ff; 10:7, 9; 11:25; 12:26, 32ff). They would not have already known the way to the church. For these reasons, I believe that John 14:2-3 teaches that Jesus is going to prepare a place in heaven, not that He is going to prepare the church.

"When Will These Things Be?" : Questions on Eschatology

receive His disciples to Himself where He is (John 13:36). Jesus said, "be with me where I am" in John 17:24. The words "where I am" refer to Jesus in heaven, not on earth (see also 12:26). The focus of Jesus's words is on heaven, not on a restored earth. Jesus is not going to be living for eternity with His disciples on earth.[51] John 14:2-3 is simple to understand.[52]

Third, heaven (the dwelling place of God) and earth are two separate places. Heaven will not become earth. This should go without saying, but it is good to remind us of this important fact. Heaven (God's dwelling place) and earth are two separate places and they are never joined in Scripture. Heaven is the throne of God, and earth is the footstool of His feet (Matt. 5:34-35).[53] All authority has been given to Jesus in heaven and on earth (Matt. 28:18). Heaven and earth are two different places, not the same place, and they will not become the same place in the future.[54]

Additionally, heaven (God's dwelling place) is never said to come to earth or be "joined to a renewed earth" (Grudem, 1160). There will not be a "unification of heaven and earth" or a "joining of heaven and earth" (Grudem, 1158-1159). Heaven and earth will not be "joined together" (Wright, 19, 191). All this scholarly mumbo-jumbo is not in the Bible. Let us, on this topic, "speak where the Bible speaks." Not one time in

---

[51] It is true that Jesus later says the He and the Father will come and abide with the disciples (14:16-18, 23; 15:4-10). This is a different coming that speaks of deity coming to abide in the disciples while they are on the earth through the indwelling of the Holy Spirit, their obedience, and their fruit-bearing.

[52] One way you can tell when a Bible passage is easy to understand is look at the large amount of Scripture twisting that takes place by the errorist to make it say something else. See Middleton on John 14:1-3 (217, 228-229).

[53] See Matthew 23:22; Acts 14:15; 17:24; 1 Corinthians 8:5; 15:47; Ephesians 3:15; Hebrews 12:25-26; Revelation 5:3; and 14:7.

[54] There are 62 passages in the NT mentioning both heaven(s) and earth: Matthew 5:10, 6:10, 11:25; 16:19 [2x]; 18:18-19; 23:9; 24:30, 35; 28:18; Mark 13:27, 31, Luke 4:25; 10:21; 12:56; 16:17; 21:33; John 3:31; Acts 2:19; 4:24; 7:49; 10:11-12; 11:6; 14:15; 17:24; 1 Corinthians 8:5; 15:47; Ephesians 1:10; 3:15; Philippians 2:10; Colossians 1:16, 20; Hebrews 1:10; 12:25- 26; James 5:12, 18; 2 Peter 3:5, 7, 10, 13; Revelation 5:3, 13; 6:13; 8:13; 9:1; 10:5, 6, 8; 11:6; 12:4, 12; 13:13; 14:6-7; 18:1; 20:9, 11; 21:1 [2x].

For passages mentioning heavenly (or heavens) and earthly (or earthy), see: John 3:12; 1 Corinthians 15:47-49; and 2 Corinthians 5:1.

Does the Bible Teach an End of This Universe?

Scripture do we read about heaven coming to earth, heaven on earth, heaven turning into earth,[55] earth turning into heaven, or heaven disappearing and earth remaining.[56] An example of this mindset is found in Russell D. Moore's material on the "new earth":

> The point of the gospel is not that we would go to heaven when we die. Instead, it is that heaven will come down, transforming and renewing the earth and the entire universe. After the millennium, the final judgment, and the condemnation of the lost, John sees a new Jerusalem coming down from the heavens *to earth* (Rev. 21:2). He then describes an eternal order that, consistent with the rest of biblical eschatology, is surprisingly "earthy.". . We lay up treasures in heaven, but the treasure does not stay in heaven. We focus our minds on heaven, but heaven comes down to earth (912-913).

So-called biblical "scholars" today (and some brethren now) speak of heaven (God's dwelling place) "coming to earth," but the Bible never speaks this way. This is pure eisegesis (reading into) of the biblical text. The idea of "heaven on earth" can be found in modern movies and pop-culture songs,[57] but this idea is not found in the Bible. When the righteous get to heaven, they will be singing "a new song" (Rev. 14:3), but I doubt it will be Belinda Carlisle's 1987 "Heaven Is a Place on Earth." Let us practice what we preach to others. Let us "speak where the Bible speaks and be silent where the Bible is silent" and let us "use Bible words in Bible ways."

---

[55] Discussing the "new heavens and new earth" of Revelation 21:1-2, Schoonhoven wrote: "The heavenly order is now subsumed (placed within—CHR) in a terrestrial kingdom where all things are new" (656). Paul Enns wrote: "the new earth becomes part of heaven" (389).

[56] NCE are not agreed on how they should describe the eternal abode of the righteous. Some continue to use the word "heaven," others only "earth," and still others "heaven/earth." The NCE approach actually makes for some novel ideas about heaven. Cottrell, commenting on the abode of the righteous after the Judgment Day writes: "From that point on, then there will actually be *three* "theological" heavens: the divine dimension itself, the divine throne room in the angelic realm, and the divine throne room on the new earth" (571).

[57] See "Heaven on Earth" by the Christian rock band *Stars Go Dim* (2015) and "Heaven on Earth" by Micah Stampley.

"When Will These Things Be?" : Questions on Eschatology

Fourth, when Jesus and others spoke of heaven, they emphasized the spiritual quality of eternal life, not the physical or material life.[58] Heaven is not a material realm on a material earth. Jesus said that things like physical houses and lands are for "now in this time," but in the "world to come," there will be "eternal life" (Mark 10:29-30). The "world to come" is otherworldly, not the world we know on this earth. Also note the argument of the Hebrew writer as he focuses on Jesus ascending back into heaven to carry out His priestly ministry in the "heavenly" tabernacle (Heb. 4:14; 7:26; 8:1, 5; 9:23-24). There is a "heavenly" focus in this argument that must not go unnoticed. Before this section in Hebrews (in 3:1 and 6:4) and after (in 11:16 and 12:22), the author speaks of "heavenly" things for faithful Christians (a heavenly calling, gift, [country], and Jerusalem). These "heavenly" things are *in the same place* where Jesus is now conducting His "heavenly" ministry. These "heavenly" things will not be on a restored earth just as Jesus's "heavenly" ministry is not now (nor will it ever be) on earth. The OT tabernacle did not typify a renewed and restored earth, but the "heavenly" ministry of Jesus (9:23-24). Jesus is our "forerunner" (*prodromos*), leading the way for the faithful "into that which is within the veil," into heaven itself (Heb. 6:20). He goes before the righteous into heaven, and they will follow Him there (see also 12:1-2).[59] He is not leading the faithful to a restored earth.

Many Bible students today are so focused on the material things of a restored earth that I wonder if they are like Nicodemus, who had trouble believing the "heavenly things" that Jesus spoke about (John 3:12-13).[60] One member of the church is even now describing his end-time view as a "materialistic eschatology" (Ashby Camp, "Materiality"). The words of Millard J. Erickson on this point serve as a good reminder concerning our current perspective on heaven:

---

[58] Grudem, referencing Revelation 22:1-2, writes: ". . .it should not strike us as surprising to find that some of the descriptions of life in heaven include features that are very much part of the physical or material creation that God has made" (1161). Later, Grudem writes about "the physical beauty of the heavenly city. . ." (1163).

[59] Thayer defines *prodromos* (πρόδρομος) as follows: "one who comes in advance to a place whither the rest are to follow" (538).

[60] Some evangelicals in the 1980s were focusing on a restored earth to the neglect of heaven which caused Dave Hunt to write a book titled *Whatever Happened to Heaven*.

Does the Bible Teach an End of This Universe?

Sometimes, especially in popular presentations, heaven is depicted as primarily a place of great physical pleasures, a place where everything we have most desired here on earth is fulfilled to the ultimate degree. Thus heaven seems to be merely earthly (and even worldly) conditions amplified. The correct perspective, however, is to see the basic nature of heaven as the presence of God; from His presence, all of the blessings of heaven follow (*Christian Theology*, 1228).

Fifth, when Jesus and others spoke of heaven, they limited their description of life there and did not engage in exaggerated imagination or speculation. Heaven is not what we want it to be. Heaven is what we are told in Scripture. Yes, heaven is described in splendid terms in Scripture.[61] Heaven will be a reward, joy, eternal life, fellowship with the redeemed, home, glory, rest, an inheritance, righteousness, paradise, serving, singing, comfort, no tears, no death, peace, endless, reigning, Jesus face-to-face, God's presence, and more.[62] Heaven will be glorious! Yet, the Bible's description of heaven is still limited.[63]

In contrast, popular authors today like Randy Alcorn and his book titled *Heaven*, encourage imagination about heaven and they write many pages about heaven.[64] They have written much more about heaven than the

---

[61] It is popular to quote 1 Corinthians 2:9 as a reference to heaven, but I do not do so here because that passage is speaking of God's wisdom that was prepared for Paul and revealed to him to preach (see vv. 1-8 and 10-16). It is not a reference to heaven.

[62] See Matthew 5:12; 25:21, 23, 46; Mark 10:30; John 14:2-3; 17:24; Romans 2:7; 2 Corinthians 5:8; Galatians 6:8; 2 Thessalonians 1:7; Titus 1:7; 3:7; Hebrews 4:9-11; 10:34; 1 Peter 1:4; 2 Peter 3:13; Revelation 2:7; 3:12; 7:13-17; 14:1-5, 13; 15:2-3; 19:6-9; 21:1-27; and 22:1-5, 14.

[63] Schoonhoven wrote: "Of great significance is the ambivalent portrayal of heaven given in the biblical materials. The conception of heaven revolves around clouds, harps, and angels, with humanity marching through the Pearly Gates to live a life of bliss. This conception is far removed from the biblical witness" (654). A.A. Hodge, who believed in a restored earth for the righteous, warned against two things: 1) regarding heaven as "too nearly analogous to that of our earthly life" and 2) regarding heaven as "too widely distinguished from that of our present experience" (579).

[64] The references to "imagine," "imagining," or "imagination" are many in the writings of NCE advocates. See Grudem (1162).

"When Will These Things Be?" : Questions on Eschatology

inspired speakers and writers of the NT ever did![65] They mix Bible truths about heaven with their own speculation and imagination about it. They write about animals, music, paintings, architecture, commerce, agriculture, politics, banqueting, and spouses in heaven (Moore, 914-916). Others write about the righteous in heaven having "governmental ministries" (Grider, 542), "judging and ruling," and "authority over cities" (Paul Enns, 390). They write about the righteous building homes, farming, and dining in heaven (ibid., 390-391). Randy Alcorn has probably written more about his imagined life in heaven than anyone. He writes about the possibility of work, cultural developments, dancing, telling stories, art, drama, entertainment, laughing, playing, sports, thrills, crafts, trade, business, technology, machinery, and new modes of travel to other worlds in heaven (Alcorn, 409-443). Bill T. Arnold wrote the following in *Christianity Today*:

> A beautiful sunset—and, yes, perhaps a well-seasoned salad—are glimpses of our blissful enjoyment of Him forever. As far as we know, the pleasures of this life are not obliterated by union with and enjoyment of God in heaven. Rather, it seems likely that all such pleasurable experiences are enjoyed in heaven in a holy way that acknowledges God as their source (*Christianity Today*, 104).

It might be good to remind ourselves at this point that the apostle Paul was caught up to the "third heaven"[66] or "paradise" and heard "unspeakable words, which is not lawful for a man to utter" (2 Cor. 12:2-4). Apparently, no one is stopping Alcorn and others from imagining many things about what heaven will be like and writing volumes about it. Does Alcorn know more about heaven than Jesus, Paul, Peter, or John?

Let us always be content to limit our understanding of heaven to what the Scriptures say. Ray Summers' words serve as an appropriate reminder here:

> It is to life after death that man looks when he begins to consider the nature of life and destiny. His question is always, 'What is that life like?' Man's dreams of what that life will be like have often gone far beyond that which is given by revelation from God. Christians look with disfavor on the sensual views of future survival in some religious systems, but at the same time many so-called Christian concepts come

---

[65] Cottrell, relying on the work of Gilmore, wrote several pages about what he imagines the righteous will be doing in heaven (567-572).

[66] "Third heaven" (τρίτου οὐρανοῦ) is found one time in the NT.

Does the Bible Teach an End of This Universe?

close to the same sensual idea. Islam looks upon man's future life as one in which he shall be married to large-eyed maidens and shall drink of a wine which results in neither headache nor dimmed wits. There are times when a Christian's description of his idea of heaven would be much like that. Knowledge of life after death must be derived from the New Testament (*The Life Beyond*, 196-197).

Sixth, heaven has always been, is now, and will always be where God is. Nowhere in Scripture are we told that God and heaven are coming to a restored earth. The righteous will be with God in heaven. Jesus wanted to ascend unto His Father in heaven. Paul wanted to die and be "with Christ" in heaven (Phil. 1:23). He wanted to be "at home with the Lord" in heaven (2 Cor. 5:8). Being in the very presence of the "glory of God" will be a central feature of one's eternal life in heaven. John wrote: "God himself shall be with them. . ." (Rev. 21:3), "the glory of God did lighten it" (Rev. 22:23), and "they shall see His face. . ." (Rev. 22:4). Now that's heaven!

3. The Righteous Will Dwell in "A New Heavens and a New Earth"

The Bible teaches an end of this universe because the Bible teaches that God will create a "*new* heavens and a *new* earth" (emphasis mine) for the righteous to dwell in.[67] Peter wrote: "But, according to his promise, we look for new heavens and a new earth, wherein dwelleth righteousness" (2 Pet. 3:13), and John wrote: "And I saw a new heaven and a new earth. . ." (Rev. 21:1). Whatever interpretation we give to the new heavens and new earth, it must adhere to the two biblical facts already set forth above. The new heavens and new earth are not our present heaven and earth because these will "pass away," and the new heavens and new earth must be "in heaven" (heavenly), not on earth (earthly).[68] There are three truths I would like to examine regarding

---

[67] The Talmud (*Midrash Rabbah, Genesis 1*) states that the "new heavens and new earth" were created at the end of the creation week in Genesis 1, but there is no biblical evidence for this belief.

[68] The following brief survey of history on this subject was adapted from Gregg R. Allison's chapter on "The New Heavens and New Earth" in *Historical Theology: An Introduction to Christian Doctrine* (723-733). The biblical doctrine of the new heaven and new earth has been interpreted differently by students of the Bible for centuries. Some have emphasized the spiritual nature of this realm while others emphasized the physical. There has been no unified con-

"When Will These Things Be?" : Questions on Eschatology

the new heavens and new earth. First, the new heavens and new earth will follow the complete destruction of the old universe that we now

> sensus about the doctrine after the first-century teaching of Peter and John.
>
> The early "Church Fathers" were divided as to the future state of the present heavens and earth. Some believed that they were to be totally annihilated, while others believed that they would be changed by miraculous divine renewal. For example, Tertullian wrote that the world "shall be consumed in one great flame!" and that "all things which have come from nothing will return ultimately to nothing." Melito of Sardis also believed in the total annihilation of the current heavens and earth. Irenaeus, on the other hand, believed that our present heavens and earth will be transformed. He wrote that "Neither is the substance nor the essence of the creation annihilated. . ." Origen also believed in the transformation of our world and wrote that the passing of the world is "by no means an annihilation or destruction of their material substance. . ." Methodius of Olympus as well believed that the world would be renewed not destroyed.
>
> A few medieval theologians addressed the nature of the eternal state of the righteous. Anselm wrote that "the present physical mass of the universe is to be changed anew into something better" and Thomas Aquinas, writing in is famous *Summa Theologica*, set forth his position that since man is to be renewed so his world will be renewed.
>
> Later, some of the Reformers like John Calvin also addressed the doctrine of the "new heaven and new earth." Calvin believed that the new heavens and new earth of Isaiah 65:17 was to be taken metaphorically of the church. As for his understanding of 2 Peter 3, he believed that the elements of the world are to be "consumed, only that they may be renovated, their substance remaining the same. . ." Some post-Reformation theologians among the Lutherans disagreed with Calvin and set forth their annihilationist perspective; men like John Andrew Quenstedt (1715) and David Hollaz (1707). Others, like William Ames (1634), wrote that "The elements will not be removed but changed. . ."
>
> The understanding of the "new heaven and new earth" in modern biblical scholarship over the past 100 years has been divided just like in previous centuries. However, many denominational scholars have tended to emphasize the physical when writing their systematic theologies. For example, Charles Hodge wrote that the destruction of the world "is not annihilation," and his son, A.A. Hodge, wrote that heaven "must necessarily be thoroughly human in its structures, conditions, and activities." The systematic theologies of Gordon Lewis and Bruce Demarest, and Wayne Grudem also set for the earthly, physical nature of the "new heaven and new earth." In contrast, men like William G.T. Shedd, Donald Guthrie, and Millard J. Erickson, emphasized the spiritual realm of heaven as the place of God.

Does the Bible Teach an End of This Universe?

know. Second, the word "new" points to a completely new realm for the righteous, not a restored universe.[69] Third, the phrase "new heavens and new earth" mentioned by Isaiah, Peter, and John is used by them in a symbolic sense, and this phrase does not describe our physical or material universe renovated.

Evidence for the complete end of the universe is found in the words of both Peter and John. Just before Peter wrote about the new heavens and new earth in 2 Peter 3:13, he wrote these words describing the complete passing of our universe:

> But the day of the Lord will come as a thief; in the which the heavens shall pass away with a great noise, and the elements shall be dissolved with fervent heat, and the earth and the works that are therein shall be burned up. Seeing that these things are thus all to be dissolved, what manner of persons ought ye to be in *all* holy living and godliness, looking for and earnestly desiring the coming of the day of God, by reason of which the heavens being on fire shall be dissolved, and the elements shall melt with fervent heat? (2 Pet. 3:10-12).

Like Peter, John also wrote about the passing of our universe. He wrote: ". . . for the first heaven and the first earth are passed away; and the sea is no more" (Rev. 21:1).[70] "Passed away" in this verse and Revelation 21:4 comes from the Greek word *aperchomai* and has the meaning "depart" (BAGD, 84)[71], or "disappeared" (Zerwick and Grosvenor, 775). Thayer wrote concerning these words "of an evanescent state of things" (57). Evanescent means to pass out of sight, quickly fade or disappear. The *"first heaven and the first earth,"* which we now experience, will one day depart and "go away" (Liddell and Scott, 187).[72]

---

[69] "Recreationists" (those who believe in a completely new heaven and earth) and "renewalist" (those who believe in a restored heaven and earth) are the two popular terms that are being used today in theological circles. See Svigel ("Extreme Makeover").

[70] "First heaven" (πρῶτος οὐρανὸς) is found only here in the NT.

[71] See Revelation 9:12; 11:14.

[72] John uses different words in Revelation 6:14.

"When Will These Things Be?" : Questions on Eschatology

John also wrote: *"the sea is no more."* The "sea" in Revelation represents the realm of mankind now on earth.[73] If the sea is "no more," then life on earth is no more. A few verses earlier in Revelation 20:11, John wrote: "And I saw a great white throne, and him that sat upon it, from whose face the earth and the heaven fled away; and there was found no place for them." Here, John describes in poetic fashion the vanishing and disappearing of our present heaven and earth to make way for the new heavens and new earth.[74] Peter described the passing away in detail and John simply stated the event that would take place.

It is popular for NCE advocates to talk about Revelation 21:2 and say that the new Jerusalem is coming down out of heaven "to earth."[75]

---

[73] See 5:13; 7:1-3; 8:8-9; 10:2, 5, 6, 8; 12:12; 13:1; 14:7; 16:3; 18:17, 19, 21; and 20:8, 13. The exception is the "sea of glass" which is around the throne in heaven (4:6; 15:2). See also Daniel 7.

[74] Compare Revelation 12:6 and 16:20. J. Marcellus Kik commented on Revelation 20:11 this way: "These words teach us the end and annihilation of the material earth and heaven. They fled away and there was no place for their existence in eternity... This is one of the clearest statements in Scripture of the non-eternity of the earth and the heavens" (254). Traub commented on Revelation 20:11 this way: "Heaven and earth are kept for this destruction (2 Pet. 3:7), and both experience the eschatological terror of flight from God's manifestation..." (515). Dave Mathewson commented on Revelation 21:1 this way: "In place of the 'fleeing' heaven and earth are found a new heaven and earth. Thus, reading 21.1 within its broader visionary context, where John reiterates notions of removal, suggests that *at a literary level* John envisions nothing less than the complete removal of the old order to make room for a qualitatively new creative act of God" (38). David J. MacLeod commented on Revelation 21:1 this way: "When John said 'new' (καινος), he probably meant a completely new universe made of new materials and not merely the renovation of the present heavens and earth..." (441). In contrast to this, Heide believes that John is simply saying that "heaven and earth had gone from his sight" (43).

[75] Those scholars who believe in a restored earth take the words "new creature" from 2 Corinthians 5:17 and Galatians 6:15 and apply them to all of creation including the earth. However, in both places, Paul limits his use of this phrase to people who have been converted to Christ. These scholars broaden the meaning of "new creature" to include the earth. See the articles by Moo, Scholz, House, and Beale.

Does the Bible Teach an End of This Universe?

They always add the words "to earth" because this is fundamental to their position.[76] However, according to Revelation 20:11 and 21:1, there is no earth to come down to.[77]

Evidence for the complete end of the universe is also found in the word "new" (*kainos*) that Peter and John used to describe the eternal abode of the righteous. Thayer defined "new" "as respects form; *recently made, fresh, recent, unused, unworn. . . new, which as recently made is superior to what it succeeds*" (317). Arndt and Gingrich say "new" stands "(a) in contrast to something old. . . (b) in the sense that what is old has become obsolete, and should be replaced by what is new. In such a case the new is, as a rule, superior in kind to the old. . ." (394). The word "new" (*kainos*) points to the new kind, nature, or quality of the abode. It will be new in kind, not just another heaven and earth like we now have. It will be altogether new and different.

---

[76] See the article by David L. Turner.

[77] John does not say that the new Jerusalem comes down out of heaven "to earth" (see also 20:10) or "upon earth." Read the text carefully. This is what NCE advocates would like for you to believe, but the text does not say that, either explicitly or implicitly. Neither in this passage nor its parallel in Revelation 3:12 is the New Jerusalem said to come down out of heaven "to earth."

When John wants to make it clear that something is coming down out of heaven *to the earth*, he mentions the earth. He does this in Revelation 10:1-3 with the strong angel, in 13:13 with the earth beast, in 16:21 with the great hail, and in 18:1 with another angel. John does not speak of coming down out of heaven "to earth" when he discusses the new Jerusalem setting. When NCE advocates add "to earth" in Revelation 21:2, they engage in eisegesis (reading into the text that which is not there). The words "out of" heaven in Revelation 21:2 and 21:10 are mentioned to show that John is receiving a vision from heaven. They are not mentioned to give the direction from which the new Jerusalem is travelling to the earth.

Additionally, if the new heaven and new earth of Revelation 21:1 are the heavens and earth restored as some argue, then there are some problems. How can the new heavens and new earth be a physical, restored earth and *also* be the "new Jerusalem" and a "tabernacle"? These are not physical places and things (like much of the rest of the book), but symbols to describe the relationship of God's people to God Himself in heaven.

"When Will These Things Be?": Questions on Eschatology

Heaven will be a completely "new" reality. God's people will be given a "new name" (Rev. 2:17; 3:12)[78] as they sing a "new song" (Rev. 14:3) in the "new heavens and new earth" (2 Pet. 3:13; Rev. 21:1) and the "new Jerusalem" (Rev. 3:12; 21:2),[79] because God makes "all things new" (Rev. 21:5). Note that Peter and John used the word "new" (*kainos*) to describe the eternal dwelling of the righteous, not the word "renew." The words "renew," "renewed," and "renewing" are always used of *persons* in the NT, never of the heavens and earth.[80] Scripture speaks of "new heavens and new earth" (NHNE), not "renewed heavens and renewed earth" (RHRE). "New" and "renew" are two different concepts. We certainly believe in and advocate a NHNE, but not a RHRE. As I admonished us already, let us "speak where the Bible speaks and be silent where the Bible is silent."

Lastly, evidence for the complete end of the universe comes from the way in which Isaiah, Peter, and John all used the expression "new heavens and new earth." All three of these prophets used this phrase in a symbolic way. The words "new heavens and new earth" are a description a new dwelling place—a new age, a new era, a new arrangement of things for God's people. Peter and John used these words in a manner consistent with Isaiah. Isaiah was speaking symbolically of the spiritual realm of Israel's remnant on the earth which culminated in the New Testament church. Peter and John were speaking symbolically of the spiritual realm of the righteous in eternity in heaven.

To understand the words of Peter and John, we must go back to the beginning. The expression "heaven and earth," from beginning to end in Scripture, refers to a dwelling place for mankind. The context will determine the time, location, and nature of this dwelling place. For example, in the beginning, God created the "heavens and the earth" (Gen. 1:1). This obviously is the physical dwelling place of all mankind that we now know upon the earth. Yet, the Scriptures also speak four times of a "new heavens and a new earth," and to this we now turn our attention.

---

[78] Note the similarity with Isaiah 62:2.

[79] See the lecture by Phil Roberts.

[80] See the use of the Greek verb *anakainoō* in 2 Corinthians 4:16 and Colossians 3:10, and the noun *anakainōsis* in Romans 12:2 and Titus 3:5. The Greek verb *ananeoō* is used in Ephesians 4:23 and *anakainizō* is used in Hebrews 6:6.

Does the Bible Teach an End of This Universe?

Isaiah was the first to write about the "new heavens and a (the) new earth" in Isaiah 65:17 and 66:22.[81] After discussing the Lord's judgment upon His rebellious and sinful people (65:1-14) and the reward of the chosen (65:15-16), Isaiah turned his attention to the Lord's new heavens and new earth.[82] Not all of Israel would be destroyed by the Lord's judgment (65:8). There would be a remnant who would return to Israel after the captivity, and the Lord would make a "new" dwelling for them.[83] In other words, there would be hope after judgment. The remnant would be given a "new name" (62:2) and a "new heavens and a new earth" (65:17; 66:22).[84]

Isaiah's new heavens and new earth would be a peaceful and joyous place for Israel's remnant after their time of judgment and trouble. The place would be in the Lord's "holy mountain Jerusalem" (65:9, 18, 19, 25; 66:10, 13, 20). The ones who would benefit from this place are "the chosen" (65:9, 15, 22). They are God's "servants" (65:9, 15; 66:14), "people" (65:10, 18, 19, 22), and "seed" (65:9, 23; 66:22) who have a "contrite spirit" (66:2, 5). The things spoken of here by Isaiah are done so symbolically and applied to Israel's remnant.[85] Israel would be physically living in Palestine (Jerusalem), but their spiritual relationship with God would be like a new heavens and new earth.[86] Because of the wording of Isaiah

---

[81] Many Bible students connect the "new heavens and a new earth" of Isaiah with that of Peter (2 Pet. 3:13) and John (Rev. 21:1) and place it at the end of time. See Grudem (1158); Cottrell (567); and Smith ("Isaiah 65-66"). Others, including many brethren, connect the "new heavens and a new earth" of Isaiah with the NT church. See lectures by Hailey, Harkrider, Payne, and Truex.

82 See also Isaiah 51:6, 16.

83 What Isaiah wrote here is similar to what he had written earlier in the book: "Remember ye not the former things, neither consider the things of old. Behold, I will do a new thing; now shall it spring forth; shall ye not know it? I will even make a way in the wilderness, and rivers in the desert" (43:18-19).

84 The Hebrew word for "new" in these passages is *chadash* (חָדָשׁ).

85 Note the words "as the days of a tree" in 65:22 and "as one whom his mother comforts" in 66:13.

86 Consider 17 spiritual characteristics of this "new" dwelling place found in Isaiah 65:17—66:24: 1.) a place where "new" things for Israel's remnant would

"When Will These Things Be?" : Questions on Eschatology

in 65:25 and 11:6-9 are identical, we know that the spiritual blessings of the new heavens and new earth that begin with Israel's remnant after the captivity extend into the period of the coming Messiah.[87]

Peter and John followed Isaiah in writing about the new heavens and new earth. However, what Peter and John wrote about is not the same new heavens and new earth of Isaiah. Peter and John did not directly connect their prophecies to what Isaiah said. In one sense, the new heavens and new earth of Peter and John are similar to Isaiah. There is symbolic language used by all three, there is a description of something "new" that surpasses the old, and there is a promise of no tears (Isa. 65:19; Rev. 21:4). Yet, in another sense, the new heavens and new earth of Peter and John are completely different than that of Isaiah. Peter and John used the expression as a description of the dwelling place of the righteous in heaven and not of the peaceful dwelling place of Israel's remnant on the earth.[88]

---

exist and the "former things" (Israel with its "former troubles," 65:16) would not be remembered (65:17); 2.) a place of "joy" for the Lord's people, not "weeping" (65:18-19); 3.) a place of lengthy "days" (time) for everyone (65:20, 22); 4.) a place of lengthy prosperity for the Lord's "people" and "chosen" (65:21-22); 5.) a place where the Lord's "seed" will not labor in vain and are blessed (65:23; 66:22); 6.) a place where the Lord's people "call" in prayer and are heard (65:24); 7.) a place of peace in the Lord's "holy mountain" (65:25); 8.) a place for those with a "contrite spirit" who "tremble at my word" (66:1-6); 9.) a place where the tender care and comfort of a "mother" is experienced (66:7-13); 10.) a place where the Lord's servants will "flourish" and the Lord's enemies will experience His "indignation" (66:14); 11.) a place where the "fire" of the Lord's judgment will be executed upon the wicked (66:15-17); 12.) a place where all nations will come and see the Lord's "glory" (66:18-19); 13.) a place for worship in the Lord's "holy mountain Jerusalem" (66:20); 14.) a place "for priests and for Levites" to offer up service and sacrifice (66:21); 15.) a place where the Lord's "seed" and "name" will remain (66:22); 16.) a place where "all flesh" (Jew and Gentile) can worship (66:23); and, 17.) a place where those who have "transgressed" are punished eternally (66:24).

[87] I do not have the time or space in this lecture to tie in all the Messianic prophecies found in Isaiah and other places with the new heavens and new earth.

[88] Consider four important differences between Isaiah, Peter, and John:

1.) In Isaiah's new heavens and new earth, there is still sin (65:20; 66:24) and death (65:20). However, in the final new heavens and new earth of Peter and

Does the Bible Teach an End of This Universe?

The main point we need to understand here is that Isaiah, Peter, and John were speaking about a new dwelling place for God's people, not about a renewal of the old dwelling place. Yet, one final question must be addressed concerning the new heavens and new earth. Why, if our eternal home is "in heaven" as argued above, do Peter and John describe heaven as a "new heavens *and new earth*" (emphasis mine)? Why not just say "heaven" and leave it at that? The answer is found in the fact that there are various descriptions (figures) of heaven given by God for mankind to relate to and understand. God, through the Holy Spirit, uses the language of earthly things that mankind already understands now in the present to describe heavenly realities in the future. God uses language and concepts found in the past (the Old Testament) to describe future realities.

For example, heaven is said to be "new heavens and new earth" to describe heaven (in earthly terms) as a place of complete sustenance (Rev. 21:1). Heaven is said to be "new Jerusalem" to describe heaven (in earthly terms) as a place of permanent protection (Rev. 21:2, 10-27).[89] Heaven is said to be a "tabernacle" to describe heaven (in earthly terms) as a place of close communion (Rev. 21:3-7). Heaven is said to be a "bride"

John there will be no sin, only righteousness (2 Pet. 3:13), and there will be no death (Rev. 21:4; 22:15). Note also the reference to Zion giving birth to children (66:7-9). This figure of birth is not found in Peter or John's description of the new heavens and new earth. Will there be houses (65:21-23), mules and dromedaries in heaven (66:20)?

2.) In Isaiah's new heavens and new earth, there is still a literal heaven and earth that God created (65:16; 66:1-2). God is in heaven separated from man on the earth. However, both Peter and John speak of the passing away of our current heaven and earth (2 Pet. 3:10-12; Rev. 21:1) and God is no longer separated from His people (Rev. 21:3).

3.) In Isaiah's new heavens and new earth, there are still enemies of the Lord remaining (66:6, 15-17). However, in John's new heavens and new earth all enemies have been removed (21:8, 27; 22:15).

4.) In Isaiah's new heavens and new earth, Jerusalem on earth is still in existence (65:18-19; 66:10, 13). However, in John's new heavens and new earth a "new Jerusalem" exists (Rev. 3:12; 21:2). It is the "Jerusalem that is above" (Gal. 4:26).

[89] Gundry argues that the New Jerusalem is not a description of a place, but a description of a people ("The New Jerusalem").

to describe heaven (in earthly terms) as a place of loving relationships (Rev. 21:2, 9; see 19:7-8). Heaven is said to be "paradise" or a "garden" to describe heaven (in earthly terms) as a place of living beauty (22:1-5).[90] These earthly terms (figures); however, that God uses to describe heaven do not mean that heaven will be on a renewed earth. They are figures, no more (Thiselton, 197-203).

The "new earth" part of the new heavens and new earth does not mean that heaven will be on a restored earth.[91] These words are simply a part of the total description of the heavenly dwelling place for the redeemed and righteous of all time. The new heavens and new earth of Peter and John are indeed the height of the eschatological hope of all the righteous. God's revelation comes full circle in the book of Revelation. The Bible begins (Gen. 1:1) and ends (Rev. 21:1) with the creation of a dwelling place (heavens and earth) for His people, first earthly, then heavenly.

Erroneous Views of the Afterlife

There is a strong urge among many people today to make heaven into something of their own liking. For these people, heaven is highly individualistic. Heaven is whatever a person wants to make it. Heaven is whatever you want it to be. Heaven is golfing, fishing, boating, reading, cooking, gardening, sewing, bowling, barbequing, etc. Lisa Miller wrote in *Heaven: Our Enduring Fascination with the Afterlife*, "For many Americans, heaven is the kingdom of ultimate personal fulfillment" (216). Do you remember when Hank Williams Jr. sang: "If heaven ain't a lot like Dixie I don't wanna go. . ."? Kevin Rushby, documenting man's idea about paradise past and present, wrote that "paradise was shaped first by religion, then by secularism" (xv).

Many people today, whether consciously doing it or not, create a vision and version of heaven in their mind and then try to convince others of it.[92] While many Protestant denominationalists place heaven on a restored earth, world religionists turn heaven into something else, and atheists place heaven within each one of us. Let us examine a few of these erroneous and false doctrines about heaven.

---

[90] See the lecture by David Barnes.

[91] Writing about 2 Peter 3:13 and Revelation 21:1, P.S. Johnston wrote: "These texts imply a future life for the people of God not in heaven but on a transformed earth" (542).

[92] See the articles by Ralls, Wesley Smith, Bregman, and Stackhouse Jr.

Does the Bible Teach an End of This Universe?

1. Heaven on a Restored Earth

Various religious groups argue that heaven will be on a restored earth. For example, Jehovah's Witnesses say that a "great multitude" of righteous people will live eternally in paradise on earth, while the "little flock" or 144,000 will live in heaven with God (*You Can Live Forever in Paradise on Earth*, 120-126). The Seventh-Day Adventist Church also believes in a restored earth.[93]

Various millennialists also believe that the righteous will live on a restored earth. There are premillennial (both historic[94] and dispensational[95]), postmillennial, and amillennial[96] advocates who say that the righteous will live in paradise on earth for 1,000 years and even beyond.

Realized eschatologists (preterists) are harder to pin down. Partial preterists, full preterists, and hyper preterists believe that the promises of Jesus's coming in the NT were fulfilled in the past in AD 70 and the destruction of Jerusalem. However, they believe different things about the future. Some say that the earth will continue forever; others say it will cease one day. Some say the righteous go to heaven; others say they do not. Some say that we are in heaven right now.[97] Because they have used up most of the Bible to talk about the past, there are not many Scriptures left they say talk about the future.

When asked about the future afterlife, many of them say, "I just don't know." For example, Max King, who advanced preterism among our brethren in the early 1970s, wrote: "I don't know what the destiny of this physical world is that we're living in." But, on another occasion, he admitted that 2 Peter 3 has "a secondary application" and "I have every reason

---

[93] "So according to the Bible, our future home isn't in some far-flung place called heaven. Its right here on this planet only infinitely better than the world is today. God's plan isn't a new planet. It's a complete restoration of the one we're on now." https://www.adventist.org/articles/an-old-world-made-new/.

[94] George Eldon Ladd, 39.

[95] Herman A. Hoyt, 84, 92 and Craig A. Blaising, 162-164.

[96] Robert B. Strimple (104-107) and Anthony A. Hoekema ("Amillennial," 184-187; and *The Bible and Future*, 274-287).

[97] Tim King: "We live in the new heavens and new earth that is to come." Quoted by Kevin Kay ("Realized Eschatology," 78).

"When Will These Things Be?" : Questions on Eschatology

to believe that someday this physical heaven and earth will melt away."[98] Two preterists still known to our brethren today are Samuel Dawson[99] and Don K. Preston.[100] Both have made the point that the righteous go to heaven when they die, the wicked suffer in hell but eventually cease to exist, and the Christian age will continue on earth for eternity.

New Creation Eschatologists (NCE) from various denominational backgrounds also teach a restored earth. They have taken the older premillennial doctrine of a restored earth for 1,000 years and made it a restored earth for eternity (Hoekema, 275-276). Some of the more contemporary and popular NCE advocates among the "scholars" are N.T. Wright,[101] J. Richard Middeton,[102] and Douglass Moo.[103] Other NCE advocates like Randy Alcorn[104] and Scott McKight[105] write for a popular audience. The focus of NCE afterlife is on a restored earth, although a few of these advocates would allow a place for the righteous in *two different places*—some in a new heaven and others on a new earth.[106] They twist and distort a number of Bible passages to teach that heaven will be on a restored earth.[107] One NCE advocate, J. Richard Middleton, is so bold

---

[98] Quoted by Bill Reeves ("The Preterist View Heresy (V)", 7).

[99] *Essays on Eschatology*, 322-323, 466.

[100] https://donkpreston.com/going-to-heaven-what-does-it-take/ and https://www.preteristarchive.com/Hyper/0000_preston_world-without-end.html.

[101] *Surprised By Hope: Rethinking Heaven, the Resurrection, and the Mission of the Church*. In a way, this book really lives up to its title. The reader will be "surprised" all right; surprised at how little sound biblical exegesis is offered by Wright for his doctrine.

[102] *A New Heaven and a New Earth: Reclaiming Biblical Eschatology*.

[103] "Nature in the New Creation;" etc.

[104] *Heaven*.

[105] *The Heaven Promise: Engaging the Bible's Truth about Life to Come*.

[106] Thiessen wrote: "Some of the redeemed will, no doubt, be at home in the new heaven, but even those who dwell on the new earth will have contact with the new heaven" (402). Strong, quoting a certain Dr. A.C. Kendrick, wrote that the righteous may be at home on a restored earth, but they might travel on excursions throughout the universe.

[107] Matthew 5:5 is twisted to say that the meek will inherit a restored earth. Mat-

Does the Bible Teach an End of This Universe?

as to say that he has repented of using the term "heaven" to describe the eternal abode of the righteous.[108]

Some brethren, both institutional[109] and non-institutional,[110] are now arguing the same NCE position. They are saying that the righteous will come back to live eternally on a renewed, renovated, and restored earth. They are reading from the authors just mentioned above and getting this idea from them. Some brethren are also referencing "restoration preachers" who believed that heaven would be on a restored earth.[111] However, regarding these "restoration preachers," we must keep two things in mind. First, many of them had the misguided hope that Jesus would come again in their lifetime and usher in some sort of millennial reign with the righteous on earth. Their misunderstanding of the millennium led to their misunderstanding of the final destiny of the earth. Second, these men, as spiritually gifted as they proved to be, were still men who

---

thew 19:29 is twisted to say that the "regeneration" includes a restored earth. Acts 3:21 is twisted to say that the "restoration of all things" includes a restored earth. Romans 4:13 is twisted to say that the "world" of Abraham will be fulfilled on a restored earth. Romans 8:21 is twisted to say that the creation will be "delivered from the bondage of corruption" when it turns into a restored earth. 1 Corinthians 15:35-58 is twisted to say that the resurrected body will be suitable for a restored earth. Ephesians 1:10 and Colossians 1:20 are twisted to say that the "all things" includes a restored earth. Philippians 3:20-21 is twisted to say that our heavenly citizenship will be brought to a restored earth. 1 Thessalonians 4:16-17 is twisted to say that the faithful will meet Jesus in the air and then return with Him to a restored earth. 2 Peter 3:5-13 is twisted to say that God will renovate and renew the earth with fire and turn it into a restored earth. Revelation 21:1-2 is twisted to say that the New Jerusalem will coming down out of heaven to a restored earth.

[108] "Therefore, for reasons exegetical, theological, and ethical, I have come to repent of using the term 'heaven' to describe the future God has in store for the faithful. It is my hope that readers of this book would, after thoughtful consideration, join me in this repentance" (*A New Heaven and A New Earth*, 237).

[109] John Mark Hicks, Dan Chambers, Wes McAdams, Daniel Hayes, Matthew Benfield, and Ashby Camp are all on record advocating this position.

[110] I can provide documentation for this point to anyone who is interested.

[111] Men like Alexander Campbell, Moses Lard, and James A. Harding. See the articles posted by John Mark Hicks on his website, johnmarkhicks.com.

"When Will These Things Be?" : Questions on Eschatology

made mistakes. They, at times, retained or returned to the denominational theology that they once left. We base our theology today on NT teaching, not upon the theology of past restoration preachers. Like the restorationists' views of instrumental music, the missionary society, and the office of deaconess, their views of returning to a restored earth were simply in error. Yes, you can find the idea of a restored earth among some restoration preachers and in many religious writings (including the uninspired Apocrypha),[112] but not in the inspired text of the biblical writers.

2. Heaven as Something Else

Many religious people down through time have believed that they will go somewhere after death. That somewhere is not the biblical heaven, but some place of bliss. For example, in the Baha'i faith, the soul of man after death continues in a spiritual progress of spiritual education in the presence of God in the next world. In the religions of Hinduism and Buddhism, a person is reincarnated (*samsara*) over and over until he is released (*moksha*) from his karma on his way to nirvana (extinction), the achievement of ultimate enlightenment. Upon reaching nirvana, the soul (*atman*) merges into the cosmic Brahma (i.e., transcendent godhead). Some forms of Hinduism replace the idea of nirvana with a heaven-like place called the "World of the Fathers" (Vedic Hinduism) or "Abode of Salvation" (Devotional Hinduism).

In contemporary Judaism, a view of the resurrection and heaven is maintained by the Orthodox tradition. According to the Midrash Konen, heaven is a great expanse with fine buildings made of cedar for various classes of the righteous. Reformed Jews do not have any particular view of the afterlife. In Islam, both resurrection and heaven are found in the Koran and the Hadith. Heaven, or "paradise" (*al-Jannah*), is a garden composed of eight levels. It is prepared for the saved with all kinds of delights, including, of course, many "wide-eyed houris" (virgins) for the taking.

---

[112] 1 Enoch 45:4-5 reads: "In that day I will cause my Elect One to dwell in the midst of them; will change [the face of] heaven; will bless it, and illuminate it forever. I will also change [the face of] the earth, will bless it; and cause those whom I have elected to dwell upon it. But those who have committed sin and iniquity shall not inhabit it, for I have marked their proceedings. My righteous ones will I satisfy with peace, placing them before Me; but the condemnation of sinners shall draw near, that I may destroy them from the face of the earth."

Does the Bible Teach an End of This Universe?

3. Heavens on Earth

Unbelievers, skeptics, and atheists do not believe, of course, in an afterlife. They believe they have no hope of living beyond the grave even though they will, in fact, do so. When some of them speak of heaven, then, it is to say that heaven is what we make of our life in the here and now. They would say that we need to make our own "heaven" here on earth by living a fulfilled and happy life. According to them, there are as many "heavens" (note the plural) on earth as there are people who can imagine them. Michael Shermer, the former publisher of *Skeptic Magazine* and a regular contributor to *Scientific American,* wrote the following:

> Maybe the "kingdom" to which Jesus refers is the heaven within ourselves, and the heavenly communities we build here on earth. Heaven is not a paradisiacal state in the next world, but a better life in this world. Heaven is not a place to go to but a way to be. Here. Now. Since no one—not even the devoutly religious—knows for certain what happens after we die, Jews, Christians, and Muslims might as well work toward creating heavens on earth (66).

Before the After

Knowing that one day everything we see around us will "pass away," how are we to be living *before* this day comes? If there is an afterlife, what is our *before-life* supposed to be like as a Christian? Let me address two issues: the care of the physical world around us and the care of the spiritual soul within us.

1. Environmentalism

Environmentalism as a cultural phenomenon in America began in the 1960s.[113] By the 1990s, "Evangelical Christians" had gotten involved with environmentalism (Ronan, 18). Today, those who advocate for a restored earth make a strong argument for global environmentalism. They read environmentalism into passages like Romans 8:21.[114] They believe the earth

---

[113] The environmentalist agenda is backed by different motives. Atheistic unbelievers who are environmentalists are active in their cause because they believe the earth is eternal and they should care for it as long as they can. Evangelical believers who are environmentalists are active in their cause because they believe the earth will be restored and they should care for it as long as they can.

[114] Consider the candid admission of Olson who wrote: "We are all becoming aware today of the devastating effects of human exploitation of nature and disregard for its limited resources. I believe it is perfectly appropriate for us to

"When Will These Things Be?" : Questions on Eschatology

will one day be the restored paradise for the righteous, so we must practice responsible Christian environmentalism now.[115] They believe that the Scriptures demand a "distinctive Christian environmental ethos" (Jonathan Moo,"Continuity"). They preach an "eco-theology" (or "green theology") and "eco-praxis" as they read from their "green Bible." They say, "our present eco-crisis is a spiritual crisis" (Olson, 130). They speak of "creation care" and "eco-justice" (Grizzle, "Evangelicals"). They believe that environmentalism today does not make sense unless our earth will one day be restored. If our planet is to be our heavenly home, they say, we might be more diligent in taking care of it.[116] The question they raise is this: If our earth will one day pass away, why even try to conserve it now?[117]

This is a good question. Yet, there is good reason to conserve things now and make them better even if one day they will be gone. For example, we know that one day the marriage relationship will cease to exist (Matt. 22:30), but that does not keep us from being good stewards of our marriage now (1 Cor. 7:3-5). We know that one day the physical body that we now have will die (1 Cor. 15:35-49), but that does not keep us from being good stewards of our body now (1 Cor. 6:19-20). We do not let our marriage and physical body "go to pot" today because one day these things will be gone. In the same way, we can be good stewards of our physical, earthly environment today, knowing that one day it will be gone. Good stewardship of the physical things that God gives us is both encouraging and beneficial for us today.

---

read this new situation back into the meaning of Paul's description of nature's plight in Romans 8. Part of the fallenness of nature is its *openness* to being raped by humans. The actual rape of nature by humans is another shackle added to its imprisonment and another cause for its groaning" (126).

[115] See the chapter by Moore (922) and the articles by Douglas Moo ("Nature"), Olson ("Resurrection"), and Bullmore ("Biblical Passages").

[116] See also the articles by Spencer, Pitetti, Kearns, Bishop, Dumbrell, and Chryssavgis. The articles by Copeland, Burkholder, and Greene review many recent books written to advocate for "Christian environmentalism."

[117] Gale Z. Heide wrote: "If this earth on which we live is going to be completely destroyed, as many evangelicals believe it is, then we have little more responsibility to it than to act as good stewards of the resources God has given us. But if this world has a future in God's plan, being renewed rather than re-created *ex nihilo*, then perhaps we have a much greater responsibility than to merely act as good managers" (39).

Does the Bible Teach an End of This Universe?

Even though the Bible teaches that our universe one day will pass away, can we still be good stewards of the earth that God has given us? Can we be conservationists, preservationists, and environmentalists? Of course, we can. Mankind's dominion over and subjugation of the creation does not give him the right to abuse and misuse creation (Gen. 1:28-30). I was raised by parents who grew up in the Great Depression (one in a city, the other on a farm), and we (eight children) were taught to conserve and preserve. We had to turn off the lights and water faucets that we were not using. We were not allowed to waste food on our plates. We were not allowed to tear up our shoes or clothes purposely. We were made to respect other people's property. We planted trees. We treated our pets with care. We gardened.

Environmentalism is a good thing because every aspect of God's creation is a "good" thing (Gen. 1:4, 10, 12, 18, 21, 25, 31). Recycle if you can. Work to reduce carbon emissions and clean up air and water pollution. (My son-in-law is an engineer working in the battery plant for the electric operated Nissan Leaf that has zero emissions.) Develop alternative sources of energy like that which comes from solar and wind power. Join the Sierra Club. Plant a tree. Be responsible without being radical.[118]

Environmentalism is not the necessary corollary of a coming restored earth, nor is it the direct admonition of the New Testament Scriptures. Where is the NT passage that plainly orders Christians to take care of the earth? Environmentalism is a solid inference from the consequence of knowing that everything comes from and belongs to God. "The earth is Jehovah's, and the fullness thereof; the world, and they that dwell therein" (Ps. 24:1). Our stewardship of God's earth motivates us to environmentalism.[119] Knowing that we pass this earth on to our children and grandchildren motivates us toward environmentalism. These things still motivate us even though heaven will not be on this earth.

Along similar lines, many people today speak of the world ending one day due to "global warming" or "climate change." Have you heard

---

[118] An example of taking environmentalism too far in my opinion is the "What Would Jesus Drive?" initiative. This campaign was popular among some evangelicals a few years back and encouraged people to stop driving gas-guzzling SUVs by pointing to Jesus.

[119] See the lecture by Tony Mauck.

"When Will These Things Be?" : Questions on Eschatology

lately any presidential candidates or leaders in Washington, D.C., say this?[120] There are those people who claim to have "eco-eschatological" fears, and they suffer from "eco-anxiety" (Nugent, "Terrified"). Well, the world we know will indeed come to an end. However, it will not be man's fire of "global warming." It will be by God's fire of cosmic conflagration (2 Pet. 3:10-12).[121] The ultimate end of the world will be caused by the Lord (after all, it's "the day of the Lord"), not because of what mankind is (or is not) doing to the environment. It is the Lord's prerogative in judgment, not man's, to bring our world to an end.

2. What Manner of Persons Ought You to Be?

In closing, I would also say that the question before us in this lecture is not merely academic or theoretical, but a practical one. That our universe will one day come to an end is certain, but what practical impact should that have on our lives today? The question "Does the Bible teach an end of this universe?" should, in fact, motivate us to obey the gospel and live faithfully for Jesus Christ. This question should lead naturally to a second question: "What manner of persons ought you to be?"

In the same place where Jesus said, "Heaven and earth shall pass away" (Matt. 24:35), He also warned men to "watch" and be "ready" for His coming (Matt. 24:42, 44). In the same place where Paul wrote that our hope is laid up "in the heavens" (Col. 1:5), He also exhorted believers to "seek the things that are above" and "set your minds on the things that are above" (Col. 3:1-2). In the same place where Peter wrote that "the earth and the works that are therein shall be burned up" (2 Pet. 3:10), he also wrote about "holy living and godliness," "looking for and earnestly desiring the coming of the day of God," giving diligence to be "found in peace, without spot and blameless in His sight" (2 Pet. 3:12-14). Peter also wrote "beware" (2 Pet. 3:17) and "grow" (2 Pet. 3:18).

In the same place where John wrote: "the earth and the heaven fled away; and there was found no place for them" (Rev. 20:11), he also wrote about the judgment day when "they were judged every man according to their works". . . "and if any was not found written in the book of life, he

---

[120] Various leaders and law-makers in our nation went on record in 2019 saying that the world will end in 12 years due to climate change.

[121] Carsten Peter Thiede is one of the few contemporary scholars who is willing to defend a "cosmic conflagration" teaching of 2 Peter 3.

Does the Bible Teach an End of This Universe?

was cast into the lake of fire" (Rev. 20:13, 15). In the same place where John wrote "the first heaven and the first earth are passed away; and the sea is no more" (Rev. 21:1), he wrote things like "he that overcomes shall inherit these things" (Rev. 21:7); "the lake that burns with fire and brimstone" (Rev. 21:8); "they that are written in the Lamb's book of life" (21:27); "His servants shall serve Him" (Rev. 22:3); "he that is righteous, let him do righteousness still" (Rev. 22:11); "blessed are they that wash their robes" (Rev. 22:14); and, "Without are the dogs. . ." (Rev. 22:15). The answer to our question in this lecture should then be followed by practical obedience to God's word.

In addition to these biblical admonitions, I would also recommend you read three good past lectures given during the 2016 Truth Lectures titled *"This World Is Not My Home."* The presentations by Jeff May, Jeff Archer, and Mark Mayberry will encourage you to stay focused on your heavenly home as you travel through this world. The book *Heaven: O for a Home with God* by brethren Steve Klein and Jeff May is a good read as well.

Preachers, let me encourage you to keep preaching about heaven. Bible teachers, keep teaching about heaven. Brethren keep reading your Bible (not the scholars) about heaven. Song leaders, keep leading songs about heaven. Let us all continue to raise our voices in praise, singing songs like. . .

Heaven will surely be worth it all. . .
    When we all get to *heaven*. . .
In *heaven* they're singing. . .
    Sing to me of *heaven*. . .
Heaven holds all to me. . .
    No tears in *heaven*. . .
Heavenly sunlight. . .
    Heaven's jubilee. . .

"When Will These Things Be?" : Questions on Eschatology

Appendix 1: 2 Peter 3 and New Creation Eschatology[122]

Peter's words in 2 Peter 3 are being used today to teach that the righteous will come back after the Judgment Day and live on a renovated earth for all eternity. Jehovah's Witnesses have used 2 Peter 3 this way for many years. More recently, those who advocate New Creation Eschatology (NCE) are also using Peter's words in a similar way. Some brethren are even now beginning to use 2 Peter 3 this way. Simply put, will the earth one day be renovated, or will it be annihilated? Let us turn our attention to some of the arguments being made in favor of renovation with a biblical refutation of each one.

Argument #1: God's destruction of the world with water in the past is "parallel" to his destruction of the world with fire in the future. The water of the flood in Noah's day is a "type/antitype" of the fire God will use at the end of time. Just as the water that God used in the flood did not completely annihilate the earth, so the fire will not completely annihilate the earth at the end of time.

Answer: First, we should not speak of things that are "parallel" to the flood without Peter telling us that they are parallel. We should not say, for example, that the flood is a "type/antitype" of the fire unless Peter uses that language (see 1 Pet. 3:21). Anyone can come up with "types" and things that are "parallel" between the flood and the end of time and then insert them into the text, but this is eisegesis (reading into the text), not exegesis. Parallels and type/antitype comparisons are alleged by NCE advocates, but they are not actually supported by the text.

Second, the comparison that Peter is making between the flood and the end of time is in reference to "the word of God" (vv. 5, 7). Yes, we all recognize that Peter mentions three time periods: (1) creation and Noah's day—"heavens from of old" (v. 5); (2) Peter's day—"the heavens that now are" (v. 7); and, (3) a future day—"new heavens and a new earth" (v. 13). Yet, the point of comparison between these three time periods is not what NCE advocates make of it. The comparison that Peter makes concerns God's promised Word that brings judgment. God's

---

[122] This material is a reprint (with some revisions and corrections) of an article I wrote that appeared in *Truth Magazine*, March 2015. It is reprinted here with permission from the editor.

Does the Bible Teach an End of This Universe?

word that created the world and brought about the judgment in the flood of Noah's day (vv. 5-6) is "the same word" (v. 7) that will bring about the judgment of fire and destruction at the end of time. This comparison concerning God's word, and none other, can rightly be established from the text. The purpose and effects of the flood are not the "same" as the purpose and effects of the fire. The condition of the earth after the flood is not the "same" as the condition of the earth after the fire.[123] What is the "same" between Noah's world, today, and the end of time, is the power and promise of God's word. God's word is powerful, and God keeps His promised word. Peter makes this point about God's word in answer to the mockers' question in 2 Peter 3:4: "Where is the promise of His coming?" Peter's response: God's word (v. 7) of promise will be kept (v. 13)!

Third, look at all the material in the Bible about the flood outside of 2 Peter 3. What do you find? We are told about the flood in each Scripture to teach us a lesson about how God judges ungodly men and saves the righteous (see Gen. 6-7; Matt. 24:37-39; Luke 17:26-27; Heb. 11:7; 1 Pet. 3:20-21; 2 Pet. 2:5; 3:4-14). Peter is not making the "parallels" or "type/antitype" comparisons that some NCE advocates think he is making. Peter, in keeping with the rest of the Scripture, tells us about the flood and then the fire to make his point about "the day of judgment and destruction of ungodly men" (v. 7; see also Jude 14-23).

Fourth, the purpose of God in using water in connection with the "world" (*kosmos*) of Noah's day was entirely different from his purpose in using fire in connection with the "earth" (*gē*) at the end-time. These two distinct purposes are not parallel. The purpose of the flood was to "perish" (*apōleto*) the "world" (*kosmos*)—every living thing except Noah and his family and the animals in the ark (Gen. 6:7; 7:4, 21-23; 2 Pet. 2:5). Yet, (and note the "but" beginning in v. 7), the purpose of the fire at the

---

[123] Wolters wrote: "However, just as the 'destruction' wrought by the water did not cause the world to vanish (it continues to be preserved 'by the same word' [3:7]), so the 'destruction' which will be wrought by the fire will presumably not cause the world to vanish either" (408). I base my understanding of this text on a straight forward reading of the text not a "presumably" as Wolters does. Wolters goes on his article to use words like "He seems to have in mind. . ." (409), "it seems. . ." (410), "But we seem to have. . ." (411), "Could it be. . ." and "this hypothesis" (412).

"When Will These Things Be?" : Questions on Eschatology

end of time is to dissolve (*luthēsetai*) the very heavens and "earth" (*gē*) themselves (vv. 10, 12).

Argument #2: The destruction of sin is the main point of Peter, not the destruction of the earth. Verse 7 says that God will destroy ungodly men, not the earth.

Answer: It is true that Peter speaks of "the day of judgment and destruction of ungodly men" (v. 7). The "day of the Lord" (vv. 8-9) certainly involves the destruction of the ungodly men. Peter had already mentioned God's judgment against ungodly men in 2 Peter 2:4-6, and 9. However, the question and argument of the mockers in the immediate context deals with their view of "the creation" (v. 4), not with the sin of man. The mockers had ignored the agency of God's powerful word and His divine intervention. They claimed that "the creation" has always continued, and nothing is going to change that. Peter responds by saying that the creation was made "by the word of God" (v. 5), God's word caused it to be "overflowed with water" (v. 6), and God's word one day will cause it to "pass away" with fire (vv. 7, 10-12). The "day of the Lord" is not just about punishing sinners; it is also about removing all together our present heavens and earth to make way for the new heavens and earth (v. 13). Jesus plainly said, "Heaven and earth shall pass away" (Mark 13:31; Luke 21:33).

Argument #3: The fire of 2 Peter 3:7, 10, 12 is the fire of testing and proving (just like in 1 Peter 1:7 and 4:12). This fire is like the fire of the "smelting process" (Wolters, 408). This fire will not destroy the earth; it will simply test it and prove it. This fire will bring about a "cosmic renewal" of the earth through testing and proving.

Answer: First, we all recognize that there are passages in both the OT (Mal. 3:2-4; 4:1) and NT that speak of God using fire to test His *people*. "Fire" can certainly be used figuratively in the context of testing *people* (1 Cor. 3:13-14; 1 Pet. 1:7; 4:12; etc.). Here, Peter is not talking about fire for *people*, but fire for the heavens and the earth (v. 7). What words in the context of 2 Peter 3 indicate that the fire here is being used for testing? There are no words in 2 Peter 3 mentioning "proving," "testing," or "trial" like in the other passages mentioned above. In fact, read all of 2 Peter, and you will not find one reference to testing, proving, or trial like you do in 1 Peter.

Second, fire for testing is *figurative*, but Peter has been speaking of *literal* water (vv. 5-6) and now of *literal* fire in the dissolving of the earth

Does the Bible Teach an End of This Universe?

(v. 7; see Heb. 6:8). The words Peter actually uses in verses 10-12 are associated with *literal* fire, a fire that burns (the Greek word *pyri* used here is also found in Revelation 21:8 for the fire of hell). Here are Peter's words: "great noise," "dissolved" (3x), "fervent heat" (2x), "burned up," "being on fire," and "melt." Peter's graphic and intense description makes it clear that a world conflagration is meant. The earth that God once "compacted" (v. 5), he will one day destroy by loosing it, releasing it, and dissolving it (*lutheesetai*).

Third, the fire of 2 Peter 3 is not for testing or proving, but for dissolving. The fire is for "the earth and the works that are therein" (v. 10) and for "the heavens" (v. 12). The fire (v. 7) is not for some alleged "cosmic renewal," but is for the dissolving of our present heavens and earth (vv. 10-12). The fire will cause the heavens to "pass away" (see also Matt. 24:35; Rev. 20:11; 21:1) and the elements (*stoicheia*, i.e., the elemental particles or components of the universe)[124] to be "dissolved with fervent heat" (v. 10). God's fire is for the dissolving of the physical heavens and the earth (annihilation), not for their testing, proving, or renovation as some allege. We must be content to use the language of Peter, not the language of contemporary scholars.

Argument #4: The translation "will be found," "discovered," or "laid bare" in verse 10 is better than "burned up." The ancient manuscript evidence is better for *heurethēsetai* (εὑρεθήσεται—"found," "discovered," NWT; "laid bare," NIV, NET) than for *katakaēsetai* (κατακαήσεται—"burned up," KJV, NKJV, ASV, NASV, RSV, etc.). Thus, the earth and its works will be "discovered" or "laid bare" for renovation. The earth will not be "burned up" or annihilated; rather, it will be renovated.

Answer: Limited space here does not permit me to deal with all the issues involved in the textual criticism of this verse. However, a few brief comments can be made.

First, the translators of several important versions (see above) retained the word *katakaēsetai* and translated it "burned up." They did so because of the presence of this word in some ancient manuscripts and the immediate context of verses 10-12, which uses language associated with literal fire and burning (see above).

---

[124] Winters tries to argue that the "elements" refers to the elementary teaching of the false teachers in 2 Peter 2 and 3 ("A Strange Death," 158-161).

"When Will These Things Be?" : Questions on Eschatology

Second, even if the manuscript evidence is better for *heurethēsetai* ("found," "discovered," or "laid bare"), it is not a necessary conclusion that our present earth will be "laid bare" for the purpose of renovation. If Peter in fact used *heurethēsetai*, then his point in this context would be that the earth and works will be discovered and exposed to God's judgment of fire (vv. 7, 10, 12). The earth and its works will have been discovered, laid bare, and exposed to God's fiery judgment when everything melts away and is dissolved. J.H. Thayer comments on this word: "γῆ καί τά ἐν αὐτῇ ἔργα εὑρεθήσεται *shall be found* namely, for destruction, i.e., will be unable to hide themselves from the doom decreed them by God, 2 Pet. 3:10" (*A Greek-English Lexicon of the New Testament*, 261). "Laid bare" for destruction better fits the immediate context of verses 7, 10-12, than "laid bare" for renovation. (Note: For those wanting to study this issue further, you will want to take note that the latest 28th edition of the Nestle-Aland's *Novum Testamentum Graece* reads: οὐκ εὑρεθήσεται, "will not be found." If this is the original reading, then the matter is closed. There will be no earth or works therein found after God's judgment of fire. We also have a parallel in Revelation 20:11 where there it reads οὐκ εὑρεθή, not found.)

Third, even if *katakaēsetai* ("burned up") is removed from the text, the idea of burning up is still expressed in the words, "with fervent heat," found twice in the text (vv. 10, 12). The words "with fervent heat" come from *kausoumena* (καυσούμενα), meaning "be consumed by heat, burn up" (BDAG, 426).

Argument #5: The word "new" in verse 13 is from the Greek word *kainos*, meaning "new in quality." This is not the Greek word *neos*, meaning "new in time." The "new heavens and a new earth" will be the old heavens and earth renovated and given a new quality of existence.

Answer: First, Peter indeed uses the word *kainos* in verse 13, and yes, it does mean "new in quality." However, the word *kainos* also carries with it the idea of something brand new (new in time). New in quality does not necessarily eliminate the idea of new in time or new in substance. For example, the "new" (*kainous*) wineskins in Matthew 9:17 (same word and form as 2 Pet. 3:13) were not old wineskins that were renovated. They were completely new wineskins, which replaced the old ones. The old wineskins were discarded, and "new" (*kainos*) wineskins were made and used.

Does the Bible Teach an End of This Universe?

Second, to argue that *kainos* means that something old is renovated does not hold up elsewhere in the NT. Who among us would argue that the "new" (*kainos*) man of 2 Corinthians 5:17 is simply the old man renovated, the "new" (*kainos*) covenant of Hebrews 8:8, 13 is simply the old covenant renovated, or the "new" (*kainos*) Jerusalem of Revelation 21:2 is simply the old, literal Jerusalem renovated?

Third, the word "but" which begins verse 13, introduces a contrast between two different dwelling places, our physical earth now with ungodly men (v. 7), and that of a future new dwelling place for the righteous only (vv. 13-14). This "new" dwelling place for God's people is in heaven (Matt. 5:12; 6:20; Phil. 3:20; Col. 1:5; 1 Pet. 1:4; Heb. 11:16; 12:22-23; 2 Tim. 4:18), not on a renovated physical earth.

Argument #6: The phrase "new heavens and a new earth" in verse 13 is used literally, not symbolically.

Answer: Peter uses the phrase "new heavens and a new earth" in a fashion consistent with Isaiah (Isa. 65:17 and 66:22) and John (Rev. 21:1). Studying the use of this phrase by Isaiah and by John helps us to understand that Peter is using this phrase symbolically. When you study the context of this phrase used by Isaiah, Peter, and John, you will find that all three use this phrase to mean a new order, realm, or environment for God's people that does not involve a literal, restored earth. What God's people have experienced in the past is now gone (Isa. 65:17-25; 2 Pet. 3:10-12; Rev. 20:11; 21:1, 4) and a "new" order or realm awaits them (Isa. 66:22; 2 Pet. 3:13; Rev. 21:1-3, 5). Isaiah, Peter, and John do not use this phrase to mean a literal, renovated heaven and earth for God's people. The "new heavens and a new earth" is certainly a real, literal place, but it is not our heavens and earth restored.

It is undoubtedly good to answer error and false teaching with God's word as I have hoped to do here, but we must also remember the importance of learning what Peter is actually teaching. Therefore, I would like to close with some practical admonitions concerning the coming Judgment Day of 2 Peter 3. Peter wanted his audience to be stirred up to remember some essential truths concerning the Lord's coming and final judgment (vv. 1-2). They were to remember some things and not to be carried away by the error of the mockers (vv. 3-4, see also v. 17). What did Peter want them to remember?

"When Will These Things Be?" : Questions on Eschatology

First, they were to remember that when God speaks concerning coming judgment, God keeps His promised word. God's word is powerful and sure (vv. 5-7).

Second, they were to remember that a Judgment Day will indeed come, and God is not slack (as the mockers suggested) concerning His promise of that day (vv. 8-9).

Third, they were to remember that God's delay is not a sign of weakness, but in fact, one of strength. God is good and longsuffering. He delays His coming to allow all to come to repentance (v. 9, see also v. 15 and Rom. 2:4).

Fourth, they were to remember that the day of the Lord would come unannounced and unexpected, "as a thief" (v. 10). They must be ready.

Fifth, they were to remember that the heavens and the earth they presently know would one day "pass away" and "be dissolved," it would all be gone (vv. 10-12).

Sixth, they were to remember to maintain "holy living and godliness" while they are waiting for the Lord's coming (v. 11). They must be "found in peace, without spot and blameless in his sight" (v. 14).

Seventh, they were to remember, like Abraham (Heb. 11:10, 16), to "look for" something "new" and heavenly (vv. 12-14).

Finally, they were to remember that some who were "ignorant and unsteadfast" would twist the Scriptures to their own destruction before the Lord comes (v. 16). (Note: This very chapter is being twisted by NCE advocates and others who come to the text with their preconceived idea of a renovated earth. They start with a theology of a renovated earth, twist these verses to make their theology fit, and then end by making Peter say the opposite of what he is really saying. They have the earth remaining in a renovated state when Peter said it would pass away!) They were not to be carried away with the error of the wicked or fall from their own steadfastness (v. 17). Instead, they must remember to grow in grace and knowledge (v. 18).

I desire that we all today be reminded of these same things so that we can be prepared to meet the Lord when He comes in judgment.

Does the Bible Teach an End of This Universe?

Appendix 2: The Use of Words for "Heaven" and "Heavenly" in the New Testament

"Heaven" in its various Greek forms is found 280 times in the NT: οὐρανέ (vocative—"O Heaven!") is found one time (Rev. 18:20), οὐρανῷ (dative, singular—"to, for, [or] from heaven") is found 38 times (Matt. 5:34; 6:10, 20; 18:18 [2x]; 22:30; 23:22; 24:30; 28:18; Mark 10:21; 13:32; Luke 6:23; 11:2; 15:7; 19:38; John 3:13; Acts 2:19; 1 Cor. 8:5; Col. 4:1; 1 John 5:7 [KJV]; Rev. 4:1-2; 5:3, 13; 8:1; 11:15, 19; 12:1, 3, 7-8, 10; 13:6, 14:17; 15:1, 5; 19:1, 14), οὐρανῶν (genitive, plural—"of the heavens") is found 42 times (Matt. 3:2, 17; 4:17; 5:3, 10, 19 [2x], 20; 7:21; 8:11; 10:7; 11:11-12; 13:11, 24, 31, 33, 44-45, 47, 52; 16:19; 18:1, 3-4, 23; 19:12, 14, 23; 20:1; 22:2; 23:13; 24:29, 31, 36; 25:1; Mark 1:11; Luke 21:26; Eph. 4:10; 1 Thess. 1:10; Heb. 7:26; 12:25), οὐρανοί (nominative, plural—"heavens") is found 7 times (Matt. 3:16; Heb. 1:10; 2 Pet. 3:5, 7, 10, 12; Rev. 12:12), οὐρανοῖς (dative, plural— to, for, [or] from heavens") is found 38 times (Matt. 5:12, 16, 45; 6:1, 9; 7:11, 21; 10:32-33; 12:50; 16:17, 19 [2x]; 18:10 [2x], 14, 19; 19:21; Mark 11:25-26; 12:25; 13:25; Luke 10:20; 11:2; 12:33; 18:22; 2 Cor. 5:1; Eph. 1:10; 3:15; 6:9; Phil. 3:20; Col. 1:5, 16, 20; Heb. 8:1; 9:23; 12:23; 1 Pet. 1:4), οὐρανὸν (accusative, singular—"heaven") is found 43 times (Matt. 14:19; Mark 6:41; 7:34; 16:19; Luke 2:15; 3:21; 9:16; 15:18, 21; 16:17; 17:24 [2x]; 18:13; 24:51; John 1:51; 3:13; 17:1; Acts 1:10, 11 [3x]; 2:5, 21; 4:12, 24; 7:55; 10:11, 16; 11:10; 14:15; Rom. 10:6; Col. 1:23; Heb. 9:24; 12:26; Jas. 5:12; 1 Pet. 3:22; Rev. 10:5, 6; 11:6, 12; 14:7; 19:11; 21:1), οὐρανὸς (nominative, singular—"heaven") is found 12 times (Matt. 5:18; 16:2-3; 24:35; Mark 13:31; Luke 4:25; 21:33; Acts 7:49; Jas. 5:18; Rev. 6:14; Rev. 20:11; 21:1), οὐρανοῦ (genitive, singular—"of heaven") is found 92 times (Matt. 6:26; 8:20; 11:23, 25; 13:32; 16:1, 3; 21:25 [2x]; 24:29, 30; 26:64; 28:2; Mark 4:32; 8:11; 11:30-31; 13:25, 27; 14:62; Luke 3:22; 8:5; 9:54, 58; 10:15, 18, 21; Luke 11:13, 16; 12:56; 13:19; 17:29; 20:4-5; 21:11; 22:43; John 1:32; 3:13, 27, 31; 6:31, 32 [2x], 33, 38, 41-42, 50-51, 58; 12:28; Acts 2:2; 7:42; 9:3; 10:12; 11:5-6, 9; 17:24; 22:6; Rom. 1:18; 1 Cor. 15:47; 2 Cor. 5:2; 12:2; Gal. 1:8; 1 Thess. 4:16; 2 Thess. 1:7; Heb. 11:12; 1 Pet. 1:12; 2 Pet. 1:18; Rev. 3:12; 6:13; 8:10; 9:1; 10:1, 4, 8; 11:12-13; 12:4; 13:13; 14:2, 13; 16:11, 21; 18:1, 4, 5; 20:1, 9; 21:2, 10), οὐρανοὺς (accusative, plural—"heavens") is found 5 times (Mark 1:10; Acts 2:34; 7:56; Heb. 4:14; 2 Pet. 3:13), οὐρανόθεν (adverb—"from heaven") is found two times (Acts 14:17; 26:13), and μεσουρανήματι (dative, singular—"to, for [or] from the midst of heaven") appears three times (Rev. 8:13; 14:6; 19:17).

"When Will These Things Be?" : Questions on Eschatology

"Heavenly" in its various Greek forms is found 28 times in the NT: οὐρανίου is found one time (Luke 2:13), οὐράνιος is found 7 times (Matt. 5:48; 6:14, 26, 32; 15:13; 18:35; 23:9), οὐρανίῳ is found one time (Acts 26:19), ἐπουράνια is found three times (John 3:12; 1 Cor. 15:40; Heb. 9:23), ἐπουρανίῳ is found one time (Heb. 12:22), ἐπουρανίων is found three times (1 Cor. 15:40; Phil. 2:10; Heb. 8:5), ἐπουράνιοι is found one time (1 Cor. 15:48), ἐπουρανίοις is found 5 times (Eph. 1:3, 20; 2:6; 3:10; 6:12), ἐπουράνιον is found one time (2 Tim. 4:18), ἐπουράνιος is found one time (1 Cor. 15:48), and ἐπουρανίου is found 4 times (1 Cor. 15:49; Heb. 3:1; 6:4; 11:16).

Bibliography

Alcorn, Randy. *Heaven*. Carol Stream, IL: Tyndale House Publishers, Inc., 2004.

Arnold, Bill T. "Vegetarians in Paradise." *Christianity Today* 48.10 (October 1, 2004): 104.

Allison, Gregg R. *Historical Theology: An Introduction to Christian Doctrine*. Grand Rapids, MI: Zondervan Publishing House, 2011.

Archer, Jeff. "I'm Just a' Passin' Through." *This World Is Not My Home*. Mark Mayberry and Mike Willis, eds., 23-31. Athens, AL: Truth Books, 2016.

Barnes, David. "The New Heavens and the New Earth." *Overcoming with the Lamb: Lessons from the Book of Revelation*. Ferrell Jenkins, ed., 200-211. Temple Terrace, FL: Florida College Bookstore, 1994.

Bauer, Walter, William F. Arndt, F. Wilbur Gingrich, and Frederick W. Danker. *A Greek-English Lexicon of the New Testament and Other Early Christian Literature*. 2nd ed. Chicago, IL: The University of Chicago Press, 1979.

Beale, Gregory K. "Eden, the Temple, and the Church's Mission in the New Creation." *Journal of the Evangelical Theological Society* 48.1 (March 2005): 5-31.

Benfield, Matthew. "A New Heaven and a New Earth: A Study in Biblical Eschatology." *A Thesis. The Sunset International Bible Institute*. Lubbock, TX: December 2017.

Bietenhard, Hans. "Οὐρανός." *The New International Dictionary of New Testament Theology*. Vol. 2. Colin Brown, Ed.. Regency Reference Library. Grand Rapids, MI: Zondervan Publishing House. 1986.

Does the Bible Teach an End of This Universe?

Bishop, Steve. "Green theology and deep ecology: New Age or new creation?" *Themelios* 16.3 (Apr.-May 1991): 8-14.

Blaising, Craig A. "Premillennialism." *Three Views of The Millennium and Beyond*. Stanley N. Gundry and Darrell L. Bock, eds. Grand Rapids, MI: Zondervan, 1999.

———. "The Day of the Lord Will Come: An Exposition of 2 Peter 3:1-18." *Bibliotheca Sacra* 169 (Oct.—Dec. 2012): 387-401.

Boles, Kenny. *The Life to Come: What the Bible Says about the Afterlife*. Joplin, MO: College Press Publishing Co., 2010.

Bregman, Lucy. "Stairways to Heaven." *Christian Century* 119.6 (March 13-20, 2002): 26-29.

Bullmore, Michael A. "The Four Most Important Biblical Passages for a Christian Environmentalism." *Trinity Journal* 19NS (1998): 138-162.

Burkholder, Benjamin J. "Heading toward the Environmental Eclipse of Christian Worldview? A Review of Recent Work in Christian Environmental Ethics." *Religious Studies Review* 42.3 (Sept. 2016): 181-188.

Camp, Ashby. "On the Materiality of the Eternal State." *The Outlet*. http://theoutlet.us/OntheMaterialityoftheEternalState.pdf. Accessed February 26, 2020.

Chryssavgis, John. "A New Heaven and a New Earth: Orthodoxy Theology and an Ecological World View." *The Ecumenical Review* 62.2 (July 2010): 214-222.

Copeland, Rebecca. "Creative Adaptations in an Interdependent World: Recent Studies in Religion and Ecology." *Anglican Theological Review* 98.4 (Fall 2016): 729-743.

Cottrell, Jack. *The Faith Once for All: Bible Doctrine for Today*. Joplin, MO: College Press Publishing Co., 2002.

Danker, Frederick W. "2 Peter 3:10 and Psalm of Solomon 17:10." *Zeitschrift für die neutestamentliche Wissenschaft und die Kunde der älteren Kirche* 53.1-2 (1962): 82-86.

Dawson, Samuel G. Essays on *Eschatology: An Introductory Overview of the Study of Last Things*. 3rd ed. Bowie, TX: SGD Press, 2017.

"When Will These Things Be?" : Questions on Eschatology

deSilva, D.A. "Heaven, New Heavens." *Dictionary of the Later New Testament and Its Developments.* Ralph P. Martin and Peter H. Davids, eds. Downers Grove, IL: InterVarsity Press, 1997.

DeYoung, J.C. "Heavens, New (and Earth, New)." *The Zondervan Pictorial Encyclopedia of the Bible.* Vol. 3. Merrill C. Tenney, ed. Grand Rapids, MI: The Zondervan Corporation, 1975.

Dumbrell, William J. "Genesis 1-3, Ecology, and the Dominion of Man." *Crux* 21.4 (Dec. 1985): 16-26.

Emerson, Matthew Y. "Does God Own a Death Star? The Destruction of the Cosmos in 2 Peter 3:1-13." *Southwestern Journal of Theology* 57.2 (Spring 2015): 281-293.

Enns, Paul. *The Moody Handbook of Theology.* Revised and Expanded. Chicago, IL: Moody Publishers, 2008.

Erickson, Millard J. *Christian Theology.* Grand Rapids, MI: Baker Book House, 1989.

Feldman, Seymour. "The End of the Universe in Medieval Jewish Philosophy." *AJS Review* 11.1 (Spring 1986): 53-77.

Fox, Maggie. "Fewer Americans Believe in God—Yet, They Still Believe in Afterlife." *NBC News.* https://www.nbcnews.com/better/wellness/fewer-americans-believe-god-yet-they-still-believe-afterlife-n542966. Accessed February 17, 2020.

Gibson, Marc W. *In What Sense Will Our Resurrected Bodies Be As They Were before, and in What Sense Will They Be Different?* Unpublished Paper. Alpharetta Bible Study, 2014.

———. "Appendix 3: Another Look at ἡ κτίσις and the Interpretation of Romans 8:18-25" *Short Introductory Survey of the Book of Romans.* Unpublished Paper. Alpharetta Bible Study, 2015.

Goff, Wayne. "The Heavenly Places." *Blessed Be God: Studies in Ephesians, Essays in Honor of C.G. "Colly" Caldwell.* Daniel W. Petty, Ed. Temple Terrace, FL: Florida College Press, 2010.

Gottlieb, Roger S. "Religious Environmentalism: What It Is, Where It's Heading and Why We Should Be Going in the Same Direction." *Journal for the Study of Religion, Nature, and Culture* 1.1 (2007): 81-91.

Gouvea, F.Q. "New Heavens and New Earth." *Evangelical Dictionary of Theology*. Second Edition. Walter A. Elwell, ed. Grand Rapids, MI: Baker Academic, 2001.

Greene, Allison Collis. "Climate Change and Religious History." *Religious Studies Review* 42.2 (June 2016): 87-91.

Grider, J.K. "Heaven." *Evangelical Dictionary of Theology*. 2nd ed. Walter A. Elwell, ed. Grand Rapids, MI: Baker Academic, 2001.

Grizzle, Raymond E., Paule E. Rothbock, and Christopher B. Barrett. "Evangelicals and Environmentalism: Past, Present, and Future." *Trinity Journal* 19NS (1998): 3-27.

Grudem, Wayne. *Systematic Theology: An Introduction to Biblical Doctrine*. Grand Rapids, MI: Zondervan Publishing House, 1994.

Gundry, Robert H. "The New Jerusalem People As Place, Not Place for People." *Novum Testamentum* 29.3 (1987): 254-264.

Hailey, Homer. "The New Heavens and the New Earth." *The Doctrine of Last Things*. Melvin D. Curry, ed. Temple Terrace, FL: Florida College Bookstore, 1986.

Harkrider, Robert. "The New Jerusalem." *Portraits of Isaiah*. Daniel W. Petty, ed. Temple Terrace, FL: Florida College Bookstore, 2006.

Heide, Gale Z. "What Is New about the New Heaven and the New Earth? A Theology of Creation from Revelation 21 and 2 Peter 3." *Journal of the Evangelical Theological Society* 40.1 (March 1997): 37-56.

Hendriksen, William. *The Bible on the Life Hereafter*. Grand Rapids, MI: Baker Book House, 1959.

Hodge, A.A. *Outlines of Theology*. Reprint. Carlisle, PA: The Banner of Truth Trust, 1991.

Hodge, Charles. *Systematic Theology*. Vol. 3. Reprint. Grand Rapids, MI: William B. Eerdmans Publishing Co., 1997.

Hoekema, Anthony A. "Amillennialism." *The Meaning of the Millenium: Four Views*. Robert G. Clouse, ed. Downers Grove, IL: InterVarstiy Press, 1977.

———. *The Bible and the Future*. Grand Rapids, MI: William B. Eerdmans Publishing Co., 1979.

House, H. Wayne. "Creation and Redemption: A Study of Kingdom Interplay." *Journal of the Evangelical Theological Society* 35.1 (March 1992): 3-17.

Hoyt, Herman A. "Dispensational Premillennialism" *The Meaning of the Millennium: Four Views*. Robert G. Clouse, ed. Downers Grove, IL: InterVarstiy Press, 1977.

Hunt, Dave. *Whatever Happened to Heaven*. Eugene, OR: Harvest House Publishers, 1988.

James, Steven L. *New Creation Eschatology and the Land: A Survey of Contemporary Perspectives*. Eugene, OR: Wipf & Stock, 2017.

Johnston, P. S. "Heaven." *New Dictionary of Biblical Theology*. T. Desmond Alexander, Brian S. Rosner, D.A. Carson, Graeme Goldsworthy, eds. Downers Grove, IL: InterVarstiy Press, 2000.

Juza, Ryan P. "Echoes of Sodom and Gomorrah on the Day of the Lord: Intertextuality and Tradition in 2 Peter 3:7-13." *Bulletin for Biblical Research* 24.2 (2014): 227-245.

Kay, Kevin. "Realized Eschatology." *Exploring Current Issues Conference* http://www.eciconference.com/Archives/2011/index.html Accessed March 2, 2020.

Kearns, Laurel. "Saving the Creation: Christian Environmentalism in the United States." *Sociology of Religion* 57.1 (1996): 55-70.

Keizer, Garret. "Faith, Hope and Ecology: A Christian Environmentalism." *The Christian Century* 118.33 (Dec. 5, 2001): 16-21.

Kik, J. Marcellus. *An Eschatology of Victory*. Phillipsburg, NJ: Presbyterian and Reformed Publishing Co., 1971.

King Sr., Daniel H. *"I Saw Heaven Opened": A Commentary on Revelation*. Athens, AL: Truth Publications, Inc., 2018.

Klein, Steve, and Jeff May. *Heaven: O For a Home with God*. Privately Published, 2014.

Does the Bible Teach an End of This Universe?

Kohlenberger III, John R., Edward W. Goodrick, and James A. Swanson. *The Exhaustive Concordance to the Greek New Testament.* Zondervan Publishing House, 1995.

Kreeft, Peter. *Every Thing You Ever Wanted to Know about Heaven.* San Francisco, CA: Ignatius Press, 1990.

Kreider, Glenn R. "The Flood Is As Bad As It Gets: Never Again Will God Destroy the Earth." *Bibliotheca Sacra* 171 (Oct.—Dec. 2014): 418-439.

Ladd, George Eldon. "Historic Premillennialism." *The Meaning of the Millenium: Four Views.* Robert G. Clouse, ed., 17-40. Downers Grove, IL: InterVarstiy Press, 1977.

———. *A Theology of the New Testament.* Grand Rapids, MI: William B. Eerdmans Publishing Co., 1979.

Lewis, James R. *The Death and Afterlife Book: The Encyclopedia of Death, Near Death, and Life After Death.* 2nd ed. Canton, IL: Visible Ink Press, 2001.

Liddell, Henry George, Robert Scott, and Henry Stuart Jones. *A Greek-English Lexicon.* 9th ed. Oxford: Oxford University Press, 1977.

MacLeod, David J. "The Seventh 'Last Thing': The New Heaven and the New Earth (Rev. 21:1-8)." *Bibliotheca Sacra* 157 (Oct.—Dec. 2000): 439-451.

Mare, W. Harold. "New Heavens and New Earth." *Wycliffe Bible Dictionary.* Charles Pfeiffer, Howard Vos, and John Rea, eds. Peabody, MA: Hendrickson, 2003.

Mathewson, David. *A New Heaven and A New Earth: The Meaning and Function of the Old Testament in Revelation 21.1-22.5.* Journal for the Study of the New Testament Supplement Series 238. Stanely E. Porter, Ed. London: Sheffield Academic Press, 2003.

Mauck, Tony. "Dominion: Exercised in Stewardship." *In His Image: The Implication of Creation.* Ferrell Jenkins, ed., 119-132. Temple Terrace, FL: Florida College Bookstore, 1995.

May, Jeff. "This World Is Not My Home." *This World Is Not My Home.* Mark Mayberry and Mike Willis, eds., 13-21. Athens, AL: Truth Books, 2016.

Mayberry, Mark. "New Creation Theology." *Truth Magazine* 59.3 (March 2015): 4-6.

———. "If Heaven's Not My Home. . ." *This World Is Not My Home.* Mark Mayberry and Mike Willis, eds. 33-50. Athens, AL: Truth Books, 2016.

McDannell, Colleen, and Bernhard Lang. *Heaven: A History.* New Haven, CT: Yale University Press, 1988.

McGrath, Alister E. *A Brief History of Heaven.* Malden, MA: Blackwell Publishing, 2003.

McKnight, Scot. *The Heaven Promise: Engaging the Bible's Truth about Life to Come.* Colorado Springs, CO: Waterbrook Press, 2015.

Middleton, J. Richard. *A New Heaven and a New Earth: Reclaiming Biblical Eschatology.* Grand Rapids, MI: Baker Academic, 2014.

Miller, Dave. *Evolution, Environmentalism, and the Deification of Nature.* Montgomery, AL: Apologetics Press, no date.

Miller, Lisa. *Heaven: Our Enduring Fascination with the Afterlife.* New York, NY: Harper Collins, 2010.

Moo, Douglas J. "Nature in the New Creation: New Testament Eschatology and the Environment." *The Journal of the Evangelical Theological Society* 49.3 (September 2006): 449-488.

———. "Creation and New Creation." *Bulletin for Biblical Research* 20.1 (2010): 39-60.

Moo, Jonathan. "Continuity, Discontinuity, and Hope: The Contribution of the New Testament Eschatology to a Distinctive Christian Environmental Ethos." *Tyndale Bulletin* 61.1. (2010): 21-44.

Moore, Russell D. "Personal and Cosmic Eschatology." *A Theology for the Church.* Daniel L. Akin, Ed. Nashville, TN: Broadman and Holman Academic, 2007.

Murphy, Caryle. "Most Americans believe in heaven. . . and hell." *Pew Research* https://www.pewresearch.org/fact tank/2015/11/10/most-americans-believe-in-heaven-and-hell/. Accessed February 17, 2020.

Nugent, Ciara. "Terrified of Climate Change? You Might Have Eco-Anxiety." *Time.com* (November 21, 2019) https://time.com/5735388/climate-change-eco-anxiety/. Accessed February 24, 2020.

Olson, Roger E. "Resurrection, Cosmic Liberation, and Christian Earth Keeping." *Ex Auditu* 9 (1993): 123-132.

Overstreet, R. Larry. "A Study of 2 Peter 3:10-12." *Bibliotheca Sacra* (Oct.—Dec. 1980): 354-371.

Payne, Buddy. "The New Creation." *The Gospel in the Old Testament*. Daniel W. Petty, ed., 37-46. Temple Terrace, FL: Florida College Bookstore, 2003.

Pitetti, Conner. "Responding to Religious Oppositions to Environmentalism." *Journal of Church and State* 57.4 (Aut. 2015): 684-706.

Pope, Kyle. "Laid Bare" or "Burned Up." *Faithful Sayings* 12.2 (January 10, 2010). http://www.olsenpark.com/Bulletins10/FS12.2.pdf. Accessed February 26, 2020.

———. "The New Heavens and New Earth." *Truth Magazine* 59.3 (March 2015): 16-18.

———. *Thinking about AD 70: Challenging Realized Eschatology*. Athens, AL: Truth Publications, Inc., 2019.

Preston, Don K. "Going to Heaven, What Does It Take?" *DonKPreston.com* https://donkpreston.com/going-to-heaven-what-does-it-take/. Accessed February 18, 2020.

———. "World Without End." *PreteristArchive.com* https://www.preteristarchive.com/Hyper/0000_preston_world-without-end.html. Accessed February 18, 2020.

Raabe, Paul. "'Daddy, Will Animals Be in Heaven?' The Future New Earth." *Concordia Journal* 40 (Spring 2014): 148-160.

Ralls, Mark. "Reclaiming Heaven." *Christian Century* 121.25 (Dec. 14, 2004): 34-39.

Reeves, Bill. "The Preterist View Heresy (V)." *Truth Magazine* 17.13 (Feb. 1, 1973): 7-9.

Reeves, Chris. "2 Peter 3 and New Creation Theology." *Truth Magazine* 59.3 (March 2015): 12-14.

Roberts, J.W. "A Note on the Meaning of 2 Peter 3:10d." *Restoration Quarterly* 6.1 (1962): 32-33.

"When Will These Things Be?" : Questions on Eschatology

Roberts, Phil. "The City of God." *The Gospel in the Old Testament.* Daniel W. Petty, ed., 233-254. Temple Terrace, FL: Florida College Bookstore, 2003.

Ronan, Marian E. "The Stewardship Model of Christian Environmentalism." *The Living Pulpit* 15.3 (Jul.-Sept. 2006): 18-19.

Rossing, Barbara R. "'Hastening the Day' When the Earth Will Burn? Warming, Revelation and 2 Peter 3 (Advent 2, Year B)." *Currents in Theology and Missions* 35.5 (Oct. 2008): 363-373.

Rushby, Kevin. *Paradise: A History of the Idea That Rules the World.* London: Constable & Robinson Ltd., 2006.

Russell, Jeffrey Burton. *A History of Heaven: The Singing of Silence.* Princeton, NJ: Princeton University Press, 1997.

Santmire, H. Paul. "The Liberation of Nature: Lynn White's Challenge Anew." *The Christian Century* 102.18 (May 22, 1985): 530-533.

Schoonhoven, C.R. "Heaven." *The International Standard Bible Encyclopedia.* Vol. 2. rev. ed. Geoffrey W. Bromiley, Ed. Grand Rapids, MI: William B. Eerdmans Publishing Co., 1982.

Segal, Alan F. *Life after Death: A History of the Afterlife in the Religions of the West.* New York, NY: Doubleday, 2004.

Shermer, Michael. *Heavens on Earth: The Scientific Search for the Afterlife, Immortality, and Utopia.* New York, NY: Henry Holt and Company, 2018.

Sholz, Vilson. "New Creation in Paul." *Missio Apostolica* 7.2 (Nov. 1999): 87-93.

Smith, F. LaGard. *After Life: A Glimpse of Eternity Beyond Death's Door.* Nashville, TN: Cotwold Publishing, 2003.

Smith, Gary V. "Isaiah 65-66: The Destiny of God's Servants in a New Creation." *Bibliotheca Sacra* 171 (Jan.-Mar. 2014): 42-51.

Smith, Wesley. "Do Pets Go to Heaven?" *Christianity Today* 56.4 (April 2012): 66-67.

Spencer, Andrew J. "Beyond Christian Environmentalism: Ecotheology as an Over-Contextualized Theology." *Themelios* 40.3 (2015): 414-428.

Stackhouse Jr., John G. "Harleys in Heaven." *Christianity Today* 47.6 (June 2003): 38-41.

Does the Bible Teach an End of This Universe?

Strimple, Robert B. "Amillennialism." *Three Views of the Millennium and Beyond.* Stanley N. Gundry and Darrell L. Bock, eds. 83-129. Grand Rapids, MI: Zondervan, 1999.

Strong, Augustus H. *Systematic Theology.* rev. ed. Valley Forge, PA: Judson Press, 1996.

Summers, Ray. *The Life Beyond.* Nashville, TN: Broadman Press, 1959.

Svigel, Michael J. "Extreme Makeover: Heaven and Earth Edition—Will God Annihilate the World and Re-Create It Ex Nihilo?" *Bibliotheca Sacra* 171 (Oct.—Dec. 2014): 401-417.

Thayer, Joseph Henry. *A Greek-English Lexicon of the New Testament.* 4th ed. Grand Rapids, MI: Baker Book House, 1977.

Thiede, Carsten Peter. "A Pagan Reader of 2 Peter: Cosmic Conflagration in 2 Peter 3 and the Octavius of Minucius Felix." *Journal for the Study of the New Testament* 26 (1986): 79-96.

Thiessen, Henry C. *Lectures in Systematic Theology.* rev. ed. Vernon D. Doerksen, ed. Grand Rapids, MI: William B. Eerdmans Publishing Co., 1987.

Thiselton, Anthony C. *Life after Death: A New Approach to the Last Things.* Grand Rapids, MI: William B Eerdmans Publishing Co., 2012.

Thompson, Fred P. *What the Bible Says about Heaven and Hell.* Joplin, MO: College Press Publishing Co., 1983.

Traub, Helmut. Οὐρανὸς. *Theological Dictionary of the New Testament.* Vol. 5. Geoffrey W. Bromiley, Ed. Grand Rapids, MI: William B. Eerdmans Publishing Co., 1967.

Truex, Don. "'The New Heavens and the New Earth': God's Promise of Final Restoration." *"Trembling at My Word": God's Power for Restoration.* Daniel W. Petty, ed., 31-40. Temple Terrace, FL: Florida College Press, 2011.

Turner, David L. "The New Jerusalem in Revelation 21:1-22:5: Consummation of Biblical Continuum." *Dispensationalism, Israel, and the Church: The Search for Definition.* Craig A. Blaising and Darrell L Bock, eds. 264-292. Grand Rapids, MI: Zondervan Publishing House, 1992.

You Can Live Forever in Paradise on Earth. The Watchtower Online Library. Accesses February 18, 2020.

Van Den Heever, G. "In Purifying Fire: World View and 2 Peter 3:10." *Neotestamentica* 27.1 (1993): 107-118.

Vine, W.E. "Heaven, Heavenly (-ies)." *Vine's Complete Expository Dictionary of Old and New Testament Words.* rev. ed. Nashville, TN: Thomas Nelson Publishers, 1985.

Vos, Geerhardus. "Heavens, New (and Earth, New)." *The International Standard Bible Encyclopedia.* Vol. 2. James Orr, ed. Reprint. Grand Rapids, MI: William B. Eerdmans Publishing Company, 1974.

Wilkin, Bob. "Does Hebrews 11:13-16 Contradict the New Earth?" *faithalone.org* https://faithalone.org/blog/does-hebrews-1113-16-contradict-the-new-earth/ Accessed February 26, 2020.

Williams, Michael D. "The Noahic Covenant and the Promise of the *Eschaton.*" *Presbyterion* 44.1 (Spring 2018): 80-97.

Willis, Mike. *"Then Cometh the End. . .": A Study of Eschatology.* Bowling Green, KY: Guardian of Truth Foundation, 1999.

Winters, Clifford T. "A Strange Death: Cosmic Conflagration as Conceptual Metaphor in 2 Peter 3:6-13." *Conversations with the Biblical World* 33 (2013): 147-161.

Wolters, Al. "Worldview and Textual Criticism in 2 Peter 3:10." *Westminster Theological Journal* 49 (1987): 405-413.

Wright, N.T. *Surprised by Hope: Rethinking Heaven, the Resurrection, and the Mission of the Church.* New York, NY: Harper One, 2008.

Zerwick, Max and Mary Grosvenor. *A Grammatical Analysis of the Greek New Testament.* rev. ed. Rome: Biblical Institute Press, 1981.

Zodhiates, Spiros. οὐρανός. *The Complete Words Study Dictionary New Testament.* Chattanooga, TN: AMG Publishers, 1992.

What Is the Focus of the Mount of Olives Discourse?

By Kyle Pope

Introduction

Then Jesus went out and departed from the temple, and His disciples came up to show Him the buildings of the temple. And Jesus said to them, "Do you not see all these things? Assuredly, I say to you, not one stone shall be left here upon another, that shall not be thrown down." Now as He sat on the Mount of Olives, the disciples came to Him privately, saying, "Tell us, when will these things be? And what will be the sign of Your coming, and of the end of the age?" (Matt. 24:1-3, NKJV).

The Mount of Olives Discourse represents the most extensive teaching Jesus offered on the subject of eschatology during His earthly ministry. How we understand it, influences how we understand later New

---

Kyle Pope (1963—) has preached the gospel since 1987 for churches in Missouri, Arkansas, Alabama, Kansas, and Texas. He currently preaches for the Olsen Park church of Christ, in Amarillo, TX. In 1982, he and his wife, Toni, were married. They have three children and six grandchildren. Kyle earned his BA from the University of Alabama (1997) in Humanities and MA from the University of Kansas (2000) in Greek and Latin. Truth Publications has published ten of his books including: *The "Gender-Inclusive" Movement Among Churches of Christ; Hope, the Anchor for the Soul; How Does the Holy Spirit Work in a Christian?; How We Got the Bible; The Matthew Commentary* in the *Truth Commentary* series; *"Ready to Give a Defense"—Answering Our Friends' Religious Questions;* and *Romans* in the Bible Text Book series. His most recent work is entitled *Thinking about AD 70: Challenging Realized Eschatology.* He can be reached at kyle@truthpublications.com.

"When Will These Things Be?" : Questions on Eschatology

Testament teaching and, in some cases, how we interpret Old Testament eschatology.[1] The aim of this study is to determine the focus of the discourse considering the following possibilities:

1. It addressed matters that would come long after the first century culminating in a final universal judgment.
2. It focused only on the judgment brought upon Israel in the destruction of Jerusalem in AD 70. Or, . . .
3. It addressed both the destruction of Jerusalem in AD 70 and a future final universal judgment.

We will make the case in the material that follows that the third possibility is the best conclusion one can draw from the text of Scripture. With regard to this, we will also consider two questions:

1. Does Matthew 24:34 constitute a transition from discussing the destruction of Jerusalem exclusively to teaching exclusively on the final judgment? Or, . . .
2. Does Jesus move back and forth between the subjects of AD 70 and final judgment in order to draw distinctions between the two?

This second view is the conclusion we will draw after looking at the evidence pertinent to these questions.

---

[1] I have been blessed with opportunities to write extensively on the Mount of Olives Discourse. In my commentary on Matthew published by Truth Publications, 178 pages were devoted to the Olivet Discourse (*Truth Commentaries: Matthew,* Athens, AL: Guardian of Truth Foundation, 2013). In my recently published book on the AD 70 Doctrine, 35 pages addressed this important teaching (*Thinking about AD 70: Challenging Realized Eschatology,* Athens, AL: Truth Publications, Inc., 2019). In both works, we included charts that walk the reader through the alternating sections of Matthew 24 which address either the destruction of Jerusalem or Final Judgment. Although not included in this essay, those charts follow the same line of reasoning offered in the present study. While there must unavoidably be some overlap between the material offered here and what I have already written on the subject, it is my aim to avoid unnecessary duplication. We will seek to focus in depth on the key issues addressed in ways that offer the reader fresh additional material. Although that will force us to leave some stones "unturned," the reader is urged to investigate our additional studies if interest in some particular question remains unquenched.

What Is the Focus of the Mount of Olives Discourse?

The Texts

As seen in the chart below, the most extended account of the discourse is preserved in Matthew 24:1–25:46. Mark and Luke both provide abbreviated forms of the discourse (Mark 13:1-37; Luke 21:5-38), but are not led by the Holy Spirit to include some elements preserved in Matthew. These include a comparison of the impending events to the "days of Noah" (Matt. 24:37-44), the Parable of the Faithful Servant (Matt. 24:45-51), the Parable of the Ten Virgins (Matt. 25:1-13), the Parable of the Talents (Matt. 25:14-30), and the sheep and goats Final Judgment scene (Matt. 25:31-46). Luke records some accounts of parallel (or similar) teaching that Jesus offered in contexts different from the Olivet Discourse (Luke 17:26-36; 12:41-46; 12:35-38; 19:11-27).

The Mount of Olives Discourse		
Matthew	**Mark**	**Luke**
Foretelling Destruction of the Temple (24:1-2)	Foretelling Destruction of the Temple (13:1-2)	Foretelling Destruction of the Temple (21:5-6)
Disciples' Question (24:3)	Disciples' Question (13:3-4)	Disciples' Question (21:7)
The Beginning of Birthpangs (24:4-8)	The Beginning of Birthpangs (13:5-8)	The Beginning of Birthpangs (21:8-11)
Coming Persecutions (24:9-14)	Coming Persecutions (13:9-13)	Coming Persecutions (21:12-19)
Abomination of Desolation (24:15-22)	Abomination of Desolation (13:14-20)	Surrounded by Armies (21:20-24)
False Christs and False Prophets (24:23-28)	False Christs and False Prophets (13:21-23)	[Lightning and Eagles Gathering – 17:23-24; 37]
Coming of the Son of Man (24:29-31)	Coming of the Son of Man (13:24-27)	Coming of the Son of Man (21:25-28)
Parable of the Fig Tree (24:32-36)	Parable of the Fig Tree (13:28-32)	Parable of the Fig Tree (21:29-33)
[Watch, man on journey, unknown day and hour – 25:13-15; 24:40]	Watch, man on journey, unknown day and hour (13:33-37)	Watch, unknown hour, "all on the face of the earth" (21:34-36)
As the Days of Noah (24:37-44)		[As the Days of Noah – 17:26-36]
Parable of Faithful Servant (24:45-51)		[Parable of Faithful Servant – 12:41-46]
Parable of the Ten Virgins (25:1-13)		[Lamps burning and knocking – 12:35-38]
Parable of the Talents (25:14-30)		[Parable of the Minas –19:11-27]
Judgment Scene (25:31-46)		

"When Will These Things Be?" : Questions on Eschatology

As with any text in which differences exist between accounts of the same event, great caution must be exercised in conclusions we draw about such differences. First, we must recognize that differing accounts do not constitute erroneous or contradictory accounts. The Holy Spirit leads different writers to emphasize different elements for specific purposes (cf. John's emphasis on the final week of Jesus's life, or Mark's emphasis on His miracles rather than His teaching). Secondly, abbreviated accounts do not demand that we treat extended accounts as synonymous in every detail (cf. the exception clause for divorce in Matthew 19 vs. its omission in Mark 10). A belief in the inspiration of Scripture demands that we view inspired texts as divinely shaped compositions intended to communicate exactly what the Holy Spirit meant to convey even when He leads one writer to emphasize elements that He does not lead another writer to include.

The Context

The discourse itself comes on the Tuesday before Jesus's crucifixion at the close of a long day of teaching within the temple (Matt. 21:23-24:1)[2] It is motivated by His response to the disciples' comments about the beautiful buildings of the temple, which may have been prompted by His praise of the widow's offering (Mark 12:41-44; Luke 21:1-4) and His declaration of a house left "desolate" (Matt. 23:38-39). As Jesus and the disciples return toward Bethany for the evening, on the Mount of Olives, which overlooked the temple, His disciples asked Him about His pronouncement of the temple's future destruction. This was not a public discourse. Mark says, "Peter, James, John, and Andrew asked Him privately" (Mark 13:3). It is unclear if any of the other disciples were then present while Jesus answered their inquiry.

The Questions

Pivotal to understanding the focus of the Discourse is our understanding of the question (or questions) the disciples ask Jesus. The chart below shows how each of the Gospels records this encounter:

---

[2] For a breakdown of the evidence that supports this chronology see my study, "The Chronology of Jesus's Final Ten Days," in *Truth Commentaries: Matthew*, Athens, AL: Guardian of Truth Foundation, 2013, 692-694.

What Is the Focus of the Mount of Olives Discourse?

The Disciples' Question		
Matthew	**Mark**	**Luke**
"Tell us, when will these things be? And what will be the sign of Your coming, and of the end of the age?" (24:3b)	"Tell us, when will these things be? And what will be the sign when all these things will be fulfilled?" (13:4)	"Teacher, but when will these things be? And what sign will there be when these things are about to take place?" (21:5-6)

All of the gospel writers include the words "when will these things be"—the phrase used as the title of this series on eschatology. Within the context, we must conclude that they were specifically referring back to what Jesus had just foretold regarding the stones of the temple being "thrown down" (Matt. 24:2; Mark 13:2; Luke 21:6). Any interpretation of this discourse that would argue it only concerned future events long after the first century must ignore this clear context and rely on an imagined rebuilding and future destruction of the temple. This is a glaring flaw in the false doctrine of premillennial dispensationalism. With the destruction of the temple in AD 70 and nearly 2000 years now having passed without "stone upon stone," we must at the very least acknowledge that some of the focus of this discourse addressed events that would happen less than four decades from the time when Jesus spoke these words.

All of the gospel writers (in the Greek) also include the words "and what [is] the sign (*kai ti to sēmeion*)." The conjunction "and" introducing this phrase demands that we see at least two questions here. Even if we take it as parallelism (i.e., asking the same question in two ways), we must concede that at least two things were asked: (1) "When?" and (2) What "sign"—from the Greek *sēmeion* meaning "sign, mark, token" (Thayer)—could the disciples anticipate?

The gospel writers express the "sign" element of the question in different ways. Luke refers to the sign "when these things are about to take place." So, like the first part of the question, "these things" must at least include the destruction of the temple. In Mark, however, it is "when ALL these things will be fulfilled" (emphasis mine). That may be significant, given that Mark only shortly before beginning the discourse records Jesus's words in the temple promising a "greater condemnation" to some (Mark 12:40) and a time "when they rise from the dead" (Mark 12:25). To interpret the wording of their question in Mark or Luke as only ad-

"When Will These Things Be?" : Questions on Eschatology

dressing the destruction of the temple may ignore the full context of the entire day of teaching Jesus has just concluded before leaving the temple (cf. Mark 12; Luke 20; Matt. 22-23).

In Matthew, the "sign" element is two-fold—the sign (1) "of Your coming?" and (2) "of the end of the age?" Let us start with the second part of this wording. Some have argued that "end of the age" should be understood to refer to the end of the Jewish dispensation (Ogden, 65). However, properly, that happened at the cross, not in AD 70 (Rom. 10:4; Col. 2:14). Matthew himself likely defines this term for us in the way he uses it before and after this passage. The phrase "end of the age (*sunteleias tou aiōnos*)" is used six times in the New Testament, five of which are in Matthew.[3] Earlier in the Gospel, it is used twice in the Parable of the Wheat and Tares (Matt. 13:39, 40) and once in the Parable of the Dragnet (Matt. 13:49). In these cases, it applies to a time when "the Son of Man sends out His angels" (Matt. 13:41), when the "tares" will be "burned in the fire" (Matt. 13:40), and the angels will "separate the wicked from among the just" (Matt. 13:49). While preterists have tried to argue that a sending out of angels and burning in fire was accomplished in the destruction of Jerusalem, the church still continues to live in a world of wickedness. There has been no separation of the "wicked from among the just." Further, at the close of Matthew, Jesus also uses the same phrase promising, "lo, I am with you always, even to the end of the age" (Matt. 28:20). Unless we are prepared to interpret all of these as references to the destruction of Jerusalem, the most reasonable conclusion is that Matthew 24:3 (with the other examples in Matthew) refers to final judgment.

"Your Coming"

The first part of Matthew's two-fold "sign" element may be the more challenging, but I submit to you that it is, in fact, a key to understanding not only their question but the flow and focus of the entire discourse. We will devote significant time to exploring this.

Its challenge comes in accurately understanding the meaning of the word translated "coming." In English, the participle of the word "come"

---

[3] Hebrews 9:26 is one instance outside of Matthew, but it uses the plural, speaking of Christ's sacrifice "once at the end of the ages." Paul uses similar wording in 1 Corinthians 10:11, with two plurals declaring that Christians now live at the "ends of the ages (*telē tōn aiōnōn*)."

What Is the Focus of the Mount of Olives Discourse?

always carries a sense of movement and direction. We can illustrate this from an argument made by R. L. Whiteside. Interpreting all elements of the disciples' questions as synonymously referring to the destruction of Jerusalem, he asks, "How could the disciples have asked about His Second Coming when they did not believe He would be killed?" (*Doctrinal Discourses*, 295). Certainly, they did not yet understand that He would later ascend to heaven and then return in judgment. They may well have imagined that if the temple were destroyed, that would be the same time when condemnation would come, and the dead would be raised. Yet, the Greek word *parousia*, translated "coming," does not bear an inherent sense of movement and direction, but presence and location.

Parousia is a noun formed from the preposition *para* (meaning "beside, alongside") and *ousia* (the present participle of the verb *eimi*, meaning "to be"). Participles are verb forms having characteristics of both verbs and adjectives which express qualities abstractly. In English, they are our "-ing" forms of words. We can say, "I see" or "you see," but "seeing" is the participle form of the verb "to see." So, in Greek *ousia* is not "I am" or "you are," but simply "being." So, when combined with the preposition *para*, it forms a noun that literally means "being beside" someone or something.

This literal sense is well attested in the New Testament. Paul praised the Philippians for their obedience "not as in my presence (*parousia*) only, but now much more in my absence (*apousia*)" (Phil. 2:12). Paul cites his critics who claimed, "his bodily presence (*parousia*) is weak, and his speech is contemptible" (2 Cor. 10:10). Those who had been separated but longed to be reunited were said to await one another's *parousia*. Paul says, "I am glad about the coming (*parousia*) of Stephanas, Fortunatus, and Achaicus" (1 Cor. 16:17). He was comforted "by the coming (*parousia*) of Titus, and not only by his coming (*parousia*) but also by the consolation with which he was comforted in you" (2 Cor. 7:6-7). Paul himself, says he longs to comfort the Philippians by his "coming (*parousia*)" (Phil. 1:26). In each of these instances, while the word "coming" is not a mistranslation, motion and direction are incidental to the real focus. It is the actual "presence" of the one being considered that is addressed in the word *parousia*.

"When Will These Things Be?" : Questions on Eschatology

General Evidence from Greek Literature

This sense of an actual presence is overwhelming when we consider how the Greeks used this word. Thucydides used it of a military force that was actually present, as opposed to forces that were elsewhere (*The Peloponnesian War* 6.86.3). Aeschylus used it of a king protecting his palace by his actual presence (*Persians* 169). Euripides used it in speaking of those present to bury a dead body (*Alcestis* 606). Sophocles used it of the support of friends by their actual presence (*Electra* 948). It could be used of the actual presence of bad things (Euripides, *Hecuba* 227; Aristophanes, *Thesmophoriazusae* 1049) or the actual presence of good things (Plato, *Gorgias* 497e). Misfortune could be described as "visitations" (using the plural of *parousia*) of chance (Demosthenes, *Exordia* 39.2). Still, even then, it was not speaking of a figurative presence of misfortune, but its actual presence in the life of those affected by it.

Like the New Testament, it could be used of one nearby, but whose "presence (*parousia*)" was actually delayed for those who wished to see him and speak to him (Sophocles, *Ajax* 539-540) or of travelers whose "presence (*parousia*)" was anticipated (Sophocles, *Electra* 1104). It could be combined with the infinitive of the verb "to have (or hold)" in the sense of "to hold presence" with someone, carrying a meaning equivalent to the idea "to be present" (LSJ, on Sophocles, *Ajax* 540). It was used of the "arrival" of one announced by servant girls (Euripedes, *Alcestis* 209). And a leader's first arrival in a place was said to be his "first presence (*parousia*)" there, usually inferring (or anticipating) that there would be a second "presence" among them (Thucydides, *The Peloponnesian War* 128.5; cf. Dionysius of Halicarnassus, *Antiquitates Romanae* 1.45).

Why Does This Matter?

We may wonder at this point what difference this literal sense makes—how does this impact our understanding of the focus of the Olivet Discourse? That is important for us to understand before we dig even further. If we interpret the disciples' question as only applying to the destruction of Jerusalem, we must conclude that Matthew uses a word to summarize that question that literally speaks of Christ's actual presence at the fulfillment of those events, but He uses it in a figurative (or representative way). In other words, Jesus came through the Roman general Titus or came in a spiritual sense, but He was never actually *present* in the sense He had been *present* prior to His ascension.

What Is the Focus of the Mount of Olives Discourse?

In addition to this, as we will see later in our study, *parousia* is used three more times in the discourse after their initial question. In each of these instances, Jesus seems to be responding directly to the wording of their question. If Matthew is just summarizing Jesus's words, he is, once again, using a word with a literal sense of presence in a figurative (or representative) way. That does not correspond to the basic meaning of the word.

This is a dilemma which those who conclude that the focus of the Olivet Discourse is only on the destruction of Jerusalem fail to consider adequately. Yet, this is a fundamental premise of the AD 70 Doctrine. For example, at least two books that advocate preterism use the word *parousia* in their title,[4] yet, neither book spends much time addressing the actual meaning of the word *parousia*. What both books do is look at scores of references to various "comings" of the Lord and apply the word *parousia* to all of them.

Let's think about that for a moment. Within the Lord's church, we have long seen how the religious world applies meanings to the word "baptism" that do not reflect its biblical usage or its well-established meaning in ancient Greek. The verb *baptizō* means "to immerse," and the noun *baptisma* means "immersion." It is not sprinkling, pouring, or anointing. Yet, imagine if someone wrote a book on baptism and applied the word "baptism" to every reference to water that we find in the New Testament! That is exactly what these preterist books do with the word *parousia*. Now certainly, there can be times in which the Lord may be said to "come" in which the sense is figurative, spiritual, or representative, yet when the word *parousia* is used, the very meaning of the word precludes interpreting it in that way. To illustrate this further, let us look at a particular way in which this word was used in the ancient world.

Parousia as a Technical Term

In addition to its literal sense, there were two overlapping ways in which *parousia* came to be used as a technical term. One of these, "be-

---

[4] (1) James Stuart Russel, *The Parousia: A Critical Inquiry into the New Testament Doctrine of Our Lord's Second Coming*, London: Daldy, Isbister, & Co., 1878, and (2) Max R. King, *The Cross and the Parousia of Christ: The Two Dimensions of One Age-Changing Eschaton*, Warren, OH: Parkman Road Church of Christ, 1987.

"When Will These Things Be?": Questions on Eschatology

came the official term for a visit of a person of high rank, especially of kings and emperors visiting a province" (BAGD). As early as the Ptolemaic Period (323-30 BC), we have papyri that attest to this use. We can read of contributions being made to purchase a crown in anticipation of the "arrival (*parousia*)" of a king (P. Petr. II.39e.18). Another papyrus describes food preparation being made before the coming of an administrator (P. Grenf. II.14b.2). Another manuscript discusses grain provisions that were imposed in preparation for the "*parousia* of the king" (P. Tebt. 48.14).

This technical usage carried well into the Roman period. Polybius also used it of the arrival of a king (*Histories* 12.19.4; 18.48.4) or military commander (*Histories* 2.27.6-7). Josephus used it of the coming of a king (*Antiquities* 11.328; 19.339; *Wars* 2.617), of elders (*Antiquities* 12.86, 93) or of an ambassador (*Antiquities* 12.160). We should note that when used of an ambassador, it was the ambassador's *parousia* that is described— the king does not make his *parousia* through an ambassador.[5] Interestingly enough, although Josephus actually speaks of the *parousia* of Titus, the Roman general who besieged and destroyed Jerusalem, he does not call it the *parousia* of the Lord (*Wars* 5.410).

In a second technical use of *parousia*, "the word served as a sacred expression for the coming of a hidden divinity, who makes his presence felt by a revelation of his power, or whose presence is celebrated in the cult" (BAGD). In this usage, pagans attributed various occurrences to the "presence" of their false gods in the activities being described (cf. Diodorus Siculus, *Bibliotheca Historica* 3.65.1, et al.). Josephus has two

---

[5] Preterist Samuel G. Dawson, in his book *Essays on Eschatology: An Introductory Overview of the Study of Last Things*, Amarillo, TX: SGD Press, 2009, devotes one paragraph to defining *parousia*, at the end of which he writes, "the word is also used to speak of the visitations of royalty, either personally, or through his chosen representative" (439). Given this author's view of AD 70, I understand why he would want to assert that it can be used in a representative sense, but (with one possible exception we will discuss below) I have found no evidence (and he offers no citations) to support this claim. If, by chance, he or others draw this conclusion from Josephus's references to the *parousia* of an ambassador, I urge them to reexamine this example and recognize exactly whose *parousia* is being described. It is that of the ambassador, not the king through an ambassador.

What Is the Focus of the Mount of Olives Discourse?

examples of this usage in commenting on God's real work in the Old Testament. First, he used *parousia* of the presence of God with the Israelites in the wilderness. He claimed that the thunder and lightning and dew on the tabernacle demonstrated that God was actually "present (*parousia*)" in the tabernacle (*Antiquities* 3.80, 202, 203). Second, he used *parousia* in speaking of the time when God revealed to Elisha and his servant the mountains around them with horses and chariots of fire when the Syrian armies were threatening them (2 Kings 6:17). Josephus claimed that this was done to show the "power and *parousia*" of God (*Antiquities* 9.55).

Josephus's second example here is perhaps the most challenging to the argument we are making about the meaning of *parousia*, but we should consider a few things about it. First, Josephus is not an inspired writer—so, it is not the Holy Spirit who calls this a *parousia* of the Lord. Josephus is merely expressing his opinion of the nature of the event. If 2 Kings 6:17 truly can be considered a *parousia* of the Lord, Josephus's wording is the only example I have found in which *parousia* is used in a representative sense. That does not change the fact that the basic meaning of *parousia* still refers to the actual presence of the one to whom it applies. Second, both Josephus and the biblical text describe 2 Kings 6:17 as an event that involved supernatural activity. All true miracles involve some measure of divine presence in their operation. Yet, to my knowledge, those who interpret AD 70 as the Lord's *parousia* do not argue that it involved supernatural activity. As a result, preterists can find no defense of their position by appealing to Josephus's wording.

We should note, "These two technical expressions can approach each other closely in meaning, can shade off into one another, or even coincide" (BAGD). So, both are ways of expressing the writer's belief in the actual presence of kings or deities in the events being described. Sadly, in pagan audiences, the two were often intertwined. In the second century, the first visit of the Emperor Hadrian in AD 124 became a time marker. An inscription from Tegea dates itself to, "the year 69 of the first *parousia* of the god Hadrian in Greece." Hadrian was not a "god," but this shows how such visits were viewed and how the word *parousia* was understood in the ancient world. Many coins commemorating such visits have survived, including those pictured below in honor of Nero (left) and Hadrian (right). On the reverse, both have the Latin word ADVENTVS, corresponding to the Greek word *parousia*.

"When Will These Things Be?": Questions on Eschatology

Imperial Advent Coins

Significance for the Olivet Discourse

How does this evidence impact our understanding of the Mount of Olives Discourse? We have already seen that any view that interprets the discourse as focusing only on events long after the first century ignores the first part of the disciples' question in which the phrase "these things" refers contextually to what Jesus had just said about the destruction of the temple. What conclusions can be drawn about the last part of the question, as seen in Matthew's wording? First, if "end of the age" is used throughout Matthew to refer to final judgment, we cannot treat it as limited only to AD 70 in their question. Further, if the word *parousia* inherently expressed an actual presence and was applied to official visitations, then it shows that the disciples' reference to "Your coming" was asking Him about when He would officially visit Israel in order to fulfill "all these things" (cf. Mark 13:4). That would include eschatological matters discussed earlier in the temple, such as condemnation and resurrection. They didn't have to understand that He would ascend into heaven and then return. However, they were still speaking of an actual presence He would manifest as He fulfilled eschatological events He had been discussing all day long.

Content and Focus

Having made the argument that the disciples' questions encompass matters related to the destruction of the temple and events that would come about well beyond that time, let us briefly see how this is reflected in Jesus's response to their questions. We will watch for three words that relate directly to their questions: (1) "sign," (2) "coming (i.e., *parousia*)," and (3) "end."

It is sometimes easy to miss the fact that much of what Jesus proceeds to tell His disciples is what they will *not* see, or He explains to them things they *will* see which do not signal the "end" or any type of "sign"

What Is the Focus of the Mount of Olives Discourse?

they might anticipate. These include[6] the rise of false christs (Matt. 24:5), wars (Matt. 24:6-7a), famines, pestilence, and earthquakes (Matt. 24:7b). He emphasizes that these are not "the end" (Matt. 24:6b)—referring for the first time to the specific wording of their question. Rather, they are "the beginning of sorrows" (Matt. 24:8) or "birthpangs" (NASB). This corrects either a misconception they already had regarding "the end," or is offered to prevent a misconception they might draw in the future. We should note that any view which argues that verse 34 constitutes a hard transition from discussing AD 70 to Final Judgment must ignore that in verse 6, Jesus has already referred to "the end" or it must interpret "the end" as a reference to something other than final judgment.

Jesus continues by describing other things that do not signal "the end," focusing on persecution, apostasy, and lawlessness (Matt. 24:9-12) but affirming that the gospel must be preached in all the world (Matt. 24:14a). In this context, twice, He refers once again to "the end." First, "he who endures to the end will be saved" (Matt. 24:13), and second, after the gospel is preached in all the world, "then the end will come" (Matt. 24:14b). If we take either of these as references to final judgment, once again, we cannot view verse 34 as a hard transition. Perhaps we might conclude that verse 13 is "the end" of one's life. The parallel in Luke puts this "by your patience possess your souls" (Luke 21:19). The gospel being "preached in all the world as a witness to all the nations" (Matt. 24:14) is a difficult threshold to identify absolutely. The preterist would argue that this happened before AD 70 (cf. Col. 1:6; Rom. 1:8). Nevertheless, the gospel continues to go throughout the world, just as persecution, apostasy, and lawlessness (Matt. 24:9-12) continued well after AD 70 even to the present. Jesus seems to be saying simply that the word of God will go forth and receive acceptance from some and rejection from others before "the end."

"The Abomination of Desolation"

It is after this that Jesus offers the first identifiable thing He says they will "see." He calls it "the abomination of desolation" (Matt. 24:15) and says when they see it, they must flee from Judea to the mountains (Matt. 24:16)—this establishes a specific location for this, Judea. When they see

---

[6] To keep this as concise as possible we will move through the wording as seen in Matthew, referring to the accounts in Mark and Luke when it becomes significant. The reader is urged to follow the chart at the beginning of the study to locate parallel sections within each Gospel.

"When Will These Things Be?" : Questions on Eschatology

it, He says not to delay retrieving your possessions (Matt. 24:17-18), this will be a time especially hard on pregnant women (Matt. 24:19-20). In fact, He says it will be the worst time that has ever been (Matt. 24:21), but it will be shortened for the sake of the elect (Matt. 24:22). Luke adds, "And they will fall by the edge of the sword, and be led away captive into all nations. And Jerusalem will be trampled by Gentiles until the times of the Gentiles are fulfilled" (Luke 21:24).

Premillennialists try to say that the "abomination of desolation" is something that has not yet happened. We should note, however, that Jesus associates this with what was "spoken of by Daniel the prophet" (Matt. 24:15). In the context of prophesying about the persecutions of faithful Jews under the reign of Antiochus Epiphanes, Daniel twice speaks of the "abomination of desolation" in connection with the defiling of the temple (Dan. 11:31; 12:11). In the historical apocryphal book of Second Maccabees it records that in, "the fifteenth day of the month of Chislev, in the hundred forty and fifth year, they set up the abomination of desolation upon the altar, and builded idol altars throughout the cities of Judah on every side" (1:54, KJV). At least part of this "abomination" involved offering a pagan sacrifice on a pagan altar setup over the altar of God (1 Macc. 1:54, 59; cf. 2 Macc. 6:1-5). This wicked ruler even went further by forcing Greek religion on the Jews and killing those who circumcised their children (1 Macc. 1:57-64). This identification of the fulfillment of Daniel's prophecy during the time of Antiochus Epiphanes was widely known among Jews in New Testament times.

The context of Daniel does not suggest that two "Abominations of Desolation" are being prophesied. Jesus is likely pointing to something that will be like what Daniel promised, which had already been fulfilled before the New Testament. Luke does not use the wording from Daniel, but puts it, "But when you see Jerusalem surrounded by armies, then know that its desolation is near" (Luke 21:20). Jesus is talking about the siege of Jerusalem that would result in its destruction. Eusebius claimed that when Christians saw these events unfolding, in obedience to Jesus's warning, they fled to the Perean city of Pella (*Ecclesiastical History* 3.5.3).

The First Use of *Parousia*

As Jesus had warned them earlier, He warns them again that even in these dark times, they must not believe claims of those who pretend to be the Christ (Matt. 24:23-26). He then offers His first use of *parousia*,

What Is the Focus of the Mount of Olives Discourse?

declaring, "For as the lightning comes from the east and flashes to the west, so also will the coming (*parousia*) of the Son of Man be" (Matt. 24:27). We must not miss the contrast here. False Christs can deceive. The actual *parousia* of Christ will be something that no one will miss, everyone will see it, and it cannot be confused or misunderstood—it will be like lightning filling the entire sky. Even without further considering the meaning of *parousia,* this statement alone shows that AD 70 could not be the *parousia* of Jesus. When it happens, everyone will know it, and Jesus will restate this a few verses later (Matt. 24:30).

We must consider, however, the use of *parousia* here. Those who understand verse 34 as a hard shift to address final judgment are forced to take this as a figurative or representative use of the term. Sadly, that is not demanded by the flow of the discourse or inferred in the meaning of the word. It also unnecessarily lends support to the preterist who would interpret it that way throughout Scripture. Remember what we saw regarding its literal meaning—*para* + *ousia,* literally means "being beside." Remember the contrast here between imagined false and unseen Christs with the true and unmistakable actual presence of Christ. If AD 70 was the "*parousia* of the Son of Man," there would be no doubt. The fact that we debate it today shows it could not have been the *parousia* of Christ!

Eagles and Carcasses

How are we to understand Jesus's statement, "For wherever the carcass is, there the eagles will be gathered together" (Matt. 24:28)? Matthew's placement of this immediately after Jesus's words about His *parousia* and lightning might lead us to see this as another way of expressing the clear and universally evident nature of Jesus's *parousia*. In Luke, however, both statements are recorded in a different discourse with the Pharisees regarding "when the kingdom would come" (Luke 17:20-37). Like Matthew's account of the Olivet Discourse, Luke records Jesus's warning against being deceived (Luke 17:21, 23), adding that they will long to see the "days of the Son of Man" (Luke 17:22)—inferring His future absence. Yet, Luke also contrasts false claims with the evident nature of lightning to illustrate, "so also the Son of Man will be in His day" (Luke 17:24), adding that Jesus must first suffer and "be rejected by this generation" (Luke 17:25). We should note, although Luke does not use *parousia* here, the parallel wording indicates that he is speaking of the same event. However, while Luke records Jesus using further parallels to

"When Will These Things Be?": Questions on Eschatology

the Olivet Discourse in discussion with the Pharisees (Luke 17:26-37), he again speaks of "days of the Son of Man"(Luke 17:26) warning at times of events "in that day" (Luke 17:31) and other times of events "in that night" (Luke 17:34), describing one taken and another left (Luke 17:35-36). At the end of Luke's discourse, Jesus is asked: "Where, Lord?"—likely asking "where" these people would be taken (Luke 17:37a). It is to this question that Jesus responds, "Wherever the body is, there the eagles will be gathered together" (Luke 17:37b)—essentially answering where the *taking* will occur rather than answering where they will *be taken*. The prominent association of the Roman armies with the "eagles" carried on their standards and venerated by their soldiers is likely the figure to which Jesus is appealing. Thus, apostate Jerusalem is likely the "body" or "carcass" of which Jesus is speaking. We judge that in both Matthew and Luke, Jesus applies this terminology to the events of AD 70 rather than to His final judgment.[7]

Cosmological Language

In all three Gospels, the discourse shifts at this point to cosmological references. Matthew records:

> Immediately after the tribulation of those days the sun will be darkened, and the moon will not give its light; the stars will fall from heaven, and the powers of the heavens will be shaken. Then the sign of the Son of Man will appear in heaven, and then all the tribes of the earth will mourn, and they will see the Son of Man coming on the clouds of heaven with power and great glory. And He will send His angels with a great sound of a trumpet, and they will gather together His elect from the four winds, from one end of heaven to the other (Matt. 24:29-31).

Luke introduces this section with the simple words, "and there will be" (Luke 21:25), but both Matthew and Mark place it *after* the events just described—"But in those days, after that tribulation" (Mark 13:24). This is an important point to recognize! Whether this cosmological language is to be understood literally or as figurative eschatological judgment language, it is described as occurring *after* AD 70, and it is not equivalent to it.

---

7   For further explanation of this argument, see my study, "For Wherever the Carcass Is, There the Eagles Will Be Gathered Together," *Focus Magazine Online* (April 30, 2015) http://focusmagazine.org/for-wherever-the-carcassis-there-the-eagles-will-be-gathered-together.php.

What Is the Focus of the Mount of Olives Discourse?

Many of us have seen attempts by premillennialists to interpret astronomical events as signs of their imagined dispensational scenarios. I fear that in reaction to this, many of us have felt compelled to argue that these verses must be taken figuratively in application to the destruction of Jerusalem. Certainly, there are times when the Holy Spirit uses cosmological language in a figurative sense to express the significance of a major act of judgment or divine operation (cf. Joel 2:28-31; Acts 2:16-20). In this text, however, we must ask: (1) Does the flow of the discourse demand that we take it figuratively? (2) Is a figurative interpretation consistent with how the same language is used later in the discourse? And (3) What is verse 34, including in its reference to "all these things"?

Let us first notice the events that are connected together here: (1) Cosmological events—to which Luke adds, "men's hearts failing them from fear and the expectation of those things which are coming on the earth" (Luke 21:26); (2) "All the tribes" of the earth will mourn as "they will see the Son of Man coming on the clouds of heaven with power and great glory;" and (3) The sending out of angels with "a great sound of a trumpet" to gather the elect. Are all of these events figurative? Can all of these events apply to what happened in AD 70? Preterists say yes. Some non-preterists say yes, but still argue that all of these events will one day come to pass literally. Is that consistent?

Later in this same discourse, Jesus introduces the sheep and goats judgment scene with the words, "When the Son of Man comes in His glory, and all the holy angels with Him, then He will sit on the throne of His glory" (Matt. 25:31). Does Jesus use the same wording figuratively of AD 70 then literally of final judgment within the same discourse? Later, in the same Gospel, when Jesus stands before the High Priest, He declares, "hereafter you will see the Son of Man sitting at the right hand of the Power, and coming on the clouds of heaven" (Matt. 26:64). Did Jesus mean this figuratively in the Olivet Discourse, but literally when speaking to Caiaphas? The more reasonable conclusion is that in both cases, Jesus is looking ahead to what will ultimately happen when He returns in the final judgment. Paul's teaching to the Thessalonians reflects this very understanding of the wording from the Olivet Discourse where he connects Jesus coming on clouds, with the angels, the last trumpet, and the final judgment with the *parousia* of Christ (1 Thess. 4:16-17; 2 Thess. 1:7-10). Peter associates cosmological events with the *parousia* of Jesus

"When Will These Things Be?" : Questions on Eschatology

(2 Pet. 3:4-10). John records the promise, "Behold, He is coming with clouds, and every eye will see Him, even they who pierced Him. And all the tribes of the earth will mourn because of Him" (Rev. 1:7). This mirrors the very wording of Matthew 24:30.

"Immediately After"

How then do we explain Jesus speaking of these cosmological events as taking place "immediately after" the tribulation of AD 70? Many understand *eutheōs*, the word translated "immediately" to indicate something that happens in consecutive order with no time interval in between. Certainly, *eutheōs* often has that sense (cf. Matt. 4:20, 22; 8:3; 20:34; 27:48; Mark 1:10; 1:31; 2:12), but the word literally refers to the straightness of something (cf. KJV "straightway," Matt. 14:22; 21:2; Mark 2:2). While it generally involves little or no time interval, that is not always the case. In the Parable of the Sower, the seed that fell on stony soil sprang up "immediately (*eutheōs*)" (Matt. 13:5). Obviously, there would have to be some interval between the sowing, and when the plant began to sprout (cf. 25:15-16). Jesus may be using this term consecutively concerning the subjects under discussion. That is, the destruction of Jerusalem would happen first, but His *parousia* would come next ("straightway") in the order of things with no time actually specified. We might compare this with His words we saw above to the High Priest. He declared, "hereafter (*ap' arti*) you will see the Son of Man sitting at the right hand of the Power, and coming on the clouds of heaven" (26:64). The term translated "hereafter" comes from the Greek words *apo* meaning "from" and *arti* meaning "just now, this moment" (Thayer). The High Priest did not see the things promised "just now" (or at "this moment") when Jesus spoke to him. Yet, with these words, Jesus expressed the pending immediacy of the things that he would see in the future. This may be the same way that Jesus uses the term "immediately (*eutheōs*)" in our text.

"Till All These Things Take Place"

Many who would agree with our argument that the discourse addresses both final judgment and the destruction of Jerusalem would contend that verse 34 is where this transition occurs, moving from the latter to the former. The text reads:

> Assuredly, I say to you, this generation will by no means pass away till all these things take place. Heaven and earth will pass away, but My words will by no means pass away (Matt. 24:34-35).

What Is the Focus of the Mount of Olives Discourse?

The next verse then reads, "But of that day and hour no one knows, not even the angels of heaven, but My Father only" (Matt. 24:36). We would agree that verse 36 is addressing final judgment, but we should remember that as early as verses 6 and 14, Jesus has already referred to "the end," in direct response to their question regarding "the end of the age" (Matt. 24:3c). We have also argued that verse 27, in its use of *parousia*—a term referring to an actual presence also points to final judgment and corresponds to their question concerning "Your coming (*parousia*)" (Matt. 24:3b). Yet, we must consider what Jesus includes within the phrase "all these things," which He says will take place before the present generation passed away.

Before leaving the temple, Jesus had foretold the persecution that the Jews would pour out on His disciples (Matt. 23:34), promising that "all the righteous blood" previously shed would "come upon" them (Matt. 23:35), saying, "Assuredly, I say to you, all these things will come upon this generation" (Matt. 24:36). In that context, "all these things" did not include everything He had said during the full day of teaching (i.e., resurrection, etc., Matt. 22:30-32). He was talking about the destruction of Jerusalem, which they would soon face. Similarly, we must remember that so far in the Olivet Discourse, Jesus has mostly told them things they would *not* see or see that would not signal "the end." The only identifiable thing He said they should expect to see was "the abomination of desolation," which is clearly pointed to the destruction of Jerusalem. We do not have to understand "all these things" as inclusive of His *parousia*, cosmological events, His coming on the clouds, the last trumpet, the sending out the angels, and final judgment. Those things would be seen by "all tribes of the earth" (Matt. 24:30; cf. Rev. 1:7), not merely by "this generation" or "those in Judea" (Matt. 24:16). "All these things," as in His words in the temple, points to the destruction of Jerusalem.

"The Sign of the Son of Man Will Appear in Heaven"

We observed above that all three Gospels include as a part of the disciples' questions the words "and what [is] the sign (*kai ti to sēmeion*)," but we also noted that all three express this sign element of the questions differently. Up to this point in the discourse, as Jesus warned of the rise of false christs, He foretold that they would show "signs (pl.) and wonders" (Matt. 24:24; Mark 13:22). In the context of describing hardships that do not signal "the end," Luke adds, "And great earthquakes shall be in divers

"When Will These Things Be?" : Questions on Eschatology

places, and famines, and pestilences; and fearful sights and great signs (pl.) shall there be from heaven" (Luke 21:11). In describing the cosmological events which are said to come after the "abomination of desolation," Luke writes, "And there shall be signs (pl.) in the sun, and in the moon, and in the stars" (Luke 21:25). Yet, none of these "signs" appear to answer the question the disciples posed at the beginning.

Interestingly enough, although all the Gospels include the "sign" element of the question, Mark and Luke do not record a direct answer to this—only Matthew includes it immediately after Jesus's statement regarding cosmological events. He writes:

> Then the sign of the Son of Man will appear in heaven, and then all the tribes of the earth will mourn, and they will see the Son of Man coming on the clouds of heaven with power and great glory (Matt. 24:30).

We argued above that the last part of this verse— "coming on the clouds"— must be considered in light of later uses of the same language referring to final judgment (cf. Matt. 25:31; 26:64; 1 Thess. 4:16-17; 2 Thess. 1:7-10). We should remember that in Matthew, the "sign" element of the question asked what would be the "sign of Your coming (*parousia*)" (Matt. 24:3). While they might have expected Him to point to events that would signal He was about to make His official divine visitation, the wording in Matthew explains that the "sign" of His coming would, in fact, be His coming itself! Matthew does not use *parusia* here for "coming," but instead, he uses the more generic word *erchomai*. He has just used it three verses earlier of the *parousia* being visible to all like lightning that fills the sky (Matt. 24:27). He will also use it after this of the "coming (*parousia*) of the Son on Man" in the comparisons to the "days of Noah" (Matt. 24:37, 39). If we take it literally in the latter instances, we must reasonably take it literally in its first usage in verse 27, which contextually is also connected to verse 30.

We see then that while Jesus does not make a hard transition in verse 34 from foretelling the destruction of Jerusalem to discussing final judgment, He moves from discussing one subject to the other throughout the discourse in order to distinguish the two. The events surrounding the "abomination of desolation" could be seen, identified, and were intended to motivate His disciples to flee from the coming tribulation. The time of His *parousia* could not be ascertained, since "no one knows," that day, "not even the angels of heaven, but My Father only" (Matt. 24:36).

What Is the Focus of the Mount of Olives Discourse?

The overall lesson was the same—be prepared! This can be seen from the general content in the discourse, such as the Parable of the Fig Tree (24:32-36); the Parable of the Faithful Servant (24:45-51); the Parable of the Ten Virgins (25:1-13); and the Parable of the Talents (25:14-30). All of these could have an application to preparation for either AD 70 or final judgment. The summary at the end of Mark's account expresses this well— "What I say to you, I say to all: Watch!" (Mark 13:37).

Parousia after the Olivet Discourse

If our argument is correct that Jesus's use of *parousia* always speaks to a promise of His actual presence in association with its fulfillment, how does its later use reflect Jesus's teaching from the Mount of Olives? In Paul's letters to the church in Thessalonica, believed to have been his earliest writings, Paul speaks six times of Jesus's *parousia*. First, he tells the saints in Thessalonica that they are his hope, joy, and crown of rejoicing "in the presence of our Lord Jesus Christ at His coming (*parousia*)" (1 Thess. 2:19). Next, he prays for them that God "may establish your hearts blameless in holiness before our God and Father at the coming (*parousia*) of our Lord Jesus Christ with all His saints" (1 Thess. 3:13). In the next two chapters, he writes extensively about events that will occur at the *parousia* of Christ. These things include: (1) bringing with Him those who "sleep in Jesus" (1 Thess. 4:14); (2) "the Lord Himself"—another statement of actual presence—"will descend from heaven with a shout, with the voice of an archangel, and with the trumpet of God" (1 Thess. 4:16a); (3) the dead in Christ will rise first (1 Thess. 4:16b)—a fact Paul will restate in 1 Corinthians 15:23 using *parousia*; (4) the living will be "caught up together with them in the clouds to meet the Lord in the air" (1 Thess. 4:17a); (5) from that point on the saints will "always be with the Lord" (1 Thess. 4:17b); and finally, (6) "the day of the Lord so comes as a thief in the night" (1 Thess. 5:2)—echoing Jesus's wording in the Olivet Discourse (Matt. 24:43). Paul speaks of the Lord's *parousia* in connection with all of these things. He declares, "For this we say to you by the word of the Lord, that we who are alive *and* remain until the coming (*parousia*) of the Lord will by no means precede those who are asleep" (1 Thess. 4:15) and concludes "Now may the God of peace Himself sanctify you completely; and may your whole spirit, soul, and body be preserved blameless at the coming (*parousia*) of our Lord Jesus Christ" (1 Thess. 5:23). Could these characteristics be applied to AD 70? No. These state-

"When Will These Things Be?" : Questions on Eschatology

ments, like the Olivet Discourse, are using *parousia* of final judgment, not the destruction of Jerusalem.

In the second epistle, Paul uses *parousia* three times in his teaching on the "man of sin." He begins:

> Now, brethren, concerning the coming (*parousia*) of our Lord Jesus Christ and our gathering together to Him, we ask you, not to be soon shaken in mind or troubled, either by spirit or by word or by letter, as if from us, as though the day of Christ had come (2 Thess.2:1-2).

This echoes Jesus's warning not to be deceived or think that they had missed the Lord's coming (cf. Matt. 24:23-27). Then, just as Jesus had warned of apostasy (cf. Matt. 24:9-12), Paul warns that a "turning away" must come before the *parousia* (2 Thess. 2:3). However we identify the "man of sin," we should note two things: (1) his "coming (*parousia*)" will be "according to the working of Satan, with all power, signs, and lying wonders" (2 Thess. 2:9), yet, (2) "the Lord will consume" him "with the breath of His mouth and destroy" him "with the brightness of His coming (*parousia*)" (2 Thess. 2:8). Was the *parousia* of the "man of sin" an actual presence, but the *parousia* of the Lord figurative, spiritual, and representative? No. Both are describing the actual presence of Jesus and the actual presence of the "man of sin."

The apostles Peter and John, and the Lord's brother James all speak of Christ's *parousia*, reflecting the same influences from the Olivet Discourse. First, Peter speaks of Jesus's first coming to earth as a *parousia*. He writes, "For we did not follow cunningly devised fables when we made known to you the power and coming (*parousia*) of our Lord Jesus Christ, but were eyewitnesses of His majesty" (2 Pet. 1:16). This must be considered in light of how Peter will later speak of a coming *parousia* of Christ. In the same epistle, he uses it of the mocking words of scoffers, who say, "Where is the promise of His coming (*parousia*)? For since the fathers fell asleep, all things continue as they were from the beginning of creation" (2 Pet. 3:4). Does Peter speak of Christ's first *parousia* as an actual, observable presence but want us to understand a future *parousia* as figurative, spiritual, and representative? No. He speaks of both in the same way. We should notice, the words of the mockers infer that something about the true *parousia* of the Lord was understood to disrupt the continuance of things "as they were from the beginning of creation." The events of AD 70 did not do that. To refute the mockers, Peter compares

What Is the Focus of the Mount of Olives Discourse?

the destruction of the flood to the promised destruction of the heavens and the earth (2 Pet. 3:5-6)—echoing Jesus's comparison in the Olivet Discourse (Matt. 24:37-39). Like Paul, Peter speaks of the day of the Lord coming "as a thief in the night" (2 Pet. 3:9a)—again echoing Jesus's words in the discourse (cf. Matt. 24:43). Then, after describing in detail the destruction of the heavens and earth when this day comes (2 Pet. 3:9b-11), he uses *parousia* (not of Christ specifically) but of the "coming (*parousia*) of the day of God" (2 Pet. 3:12). John writes, "And now, little children, abide in Him, that when He appears, we may have confidence and not be ashamed before Him at His coming (*parousia*)" (1 John 2:28). We note that John speaks of this as a time "when He appears"—echoing the promise of the Olivet Discourse that "ALL the tribes of the earth will mourn, and *they will see* the Son of Man coming on the clouds of heaven with power and great glory" (Matt. 24:30, emphasis mine; cf. Rev. 1:7). Finally, James urges patience, "until the coming (*parousia*) of the Lord" (Jas. 5:7), for the "coming (*parousia*) of the Lord is at hand" (Jas. 5:8)—reminding us of Luke's wording from the discourse, "by your patience possess your souls" (Luke 21:19). All of these examples demonstrate how Jesus's teaching on the Mount of Olives influenced New Testament eschatology and a clear understanding of a future final judgment of the world at the final *parousia* of Christ.

Parousia after the New Testament

This conclusion is further supported when we consider the earliest writings by Christians that have survived immediately after the New Testament. Ignatius, for example, was a bishop from the church in Antioch who died at the beginning of the second century. In an epistle to the church in Philadelphia, he uses *parousia* of Jesus's actual presence in His first coming to earth (*To the Philadelphians* 9.2). A second-century apologetic work known as the *Epistle to Diognetus* in the same section uses *parousia* of Jesus's first coming to earth (7.9), then in the same context declares that God "will send Him as judge, and who will endure His coming (*parousia*)?" (7.6), a quote from Malachi 3:2. Another second-century text known as the *Shepherd of Hermas*, offers a parable similar to Jesus's Parables of the Wheat and Tares (Matt. 13:24-30; 36-43) and the Workers in the Vineyard (Luke 20:9-19) in which a master is delayed. In explaining the parable, it says, "the absence of the Master is the time remaining until His coming (*parousia*)" (58.3 [5.5.3]). Well after AD 70, these texts clearly demonstrate an understanding that Christ's *parousia*

"When Will These Things Be?" : Questions on Eschatology

had not yet come and was expected to be an actual presence similar to that seen in His first *parousia*.

Finally, the second-century apologist Justin makes it undeniably clear that Christians immediately after the New Testament did not interpret AD 70 as the *parousia* of Christ promised within the Mount of Olives Discourse. First, in his *First Apology,* he writes:

> For the prophets have proclaimed two advents (*parousia*) of His: the one, that which is already past, when He came as a dishonored and suffering Man; but the second, when, according to prophecy, He shall come from heaven with glory, accompanied by His angelic host, when also He shall raise the bodies of all men who have lived, and shall clothe those of the worthy with immortality, and shall send those of the wicked, endued with eternal sensibility, into everlasting fire with the wicked devils (52.3).

Like the New Testament, this concept of Jesus's incarnation as His first *parousia* runs throughout the writings of Justin (e.g., *1 Apology* 54.7; 48:2; *Dialogue with Trypho* 36.1; 53.1; 88.2; 118.2; 120.3). Yet, as seen in the quote above, Justin is the first to explicitly call the *parousia* promised in the Olivet Discourse His "second *parousia*." In his *Dialogue with Trypho*, a discussion with a Jew who had come to Ephesus fleeing the Bar Kochba rebellion, Justin tries to persuade him that Jesus is the Messiah promised in the Old Testament. In the dialogue, he repeatedly asserts a first and second *parousia* of the Messiah. In discussing Old Testament prophecy, he first introduces this with the assertion:

> Some have reference to the first advent (*parousia*) of Christ, in which He is preached as inglorious, obscure, and of mortal appearance: but others had reference to His second advent (*parousia*), when He shall appear in glory and above the clouds; and your nation shall see and know Him whom they have pierced, as Hosea, one of the twelve prophets, and Daniel, foretold (14.8)

He then refers back to this assertion throughout the rest of the dialogue (32:2; 40.4; 49.2; 52.4; 110.2, 5; 111.1, 121.3). Although Justin lived well after the destruction of Jerusalem, he does not identify it as Christ's *parousia*. On the contrary, writing in the early to mid-second century, he considered it a future event in which Jesus would "come on the clouds" (31.1), "from heaven with glory" (110.2), to condemn death "at the Second Coming (*parousia*) of the Christ Himself" and send some to eternal

What Is the Focus of the Mount of Olives Discourse?

life and others "to be punished unceasingly" (45.4), when He would act as "Judge of all" (49.2). For Justin, those who believed in Jesus, yet suffered "under a defect of the body" could trust in the hope that "He shall raise him up at His second advent (*parousia*) perfectly sound, after He has made him immortal, and incorruptible, and free from grief" (69.7).

We must note one final example from Justin that illustrates graphically that the meaning of *parousia* as used in the Olivet Discourse and subsequent New Testament passages will not allow it to be understood in a figurative, spiritual, or representative sense. Justin is discussing Jacob's blessing to Judah in Genesis 49:8-12. In discussing the Messianic elements of the blessing, he takes a view common in the early church that washing His garments in the "blood of the grapes" referred to the shedding of Christ's blood. He writes:

> For the Holy Spirit called those who receive remission of sins through Him, His garments; amongst whom He is always present (*pareimi*) in power, but will be manifestly (*enargōs*) present (*pareimi*) at His Second Coming (*parousia*) (54.1-2).

In this text, Justin not only uses the noun *parousia* (lit. "being beside") but he twice uses its verb form—*pareimi*, meaning "to be beside" or "present." In this, he draws a distinction between the regular sense in which Christ is "always present" with His people, and the nature of the "second *parousia*" when He will be "manifestly"—from the Greek adverb *enargōs*, meaning "visible, palpable" (LSJ)—"present" with His people. Justin did not see in the promise of Christ's second *parousia* the possibility of it being spiritual and unseen. It would be visible, palpable, and "manifestly" involve His actual presence.

Conclusion

The private teaching of Jesus to His disciples on the Mount of Olives set forth fundamental eschatological concepts that shape core doctrines of faith in Christ and the hope of eternal salvation. We have seen that its focus can be ascertained by careful analysis of its content, context, and use by Christians in the New Testament and beyond.

Of the three possible foci, we first found that any view which interprets it as only addressing events long after the first century ignores the immediate context of the disciples' question motivated by Jesus's foretelling the destruction of the temple (Matt. 24:1-3; Mark 13:1-4; Luke 21:5-

7). In addition to this, such a view must reject the clear identification of the "abomination of desolation" as something foretold in Daniel, fulfilled in the period between the Old and New Testaments, and paralleled in the Roman siege of Jerusalem (Matt. 24:15-23; Mark 13:14-20; Luke 21:20-24; Dan. 11:29–12:12; 1 Macc. 1:54, 57-64, 59; 2 Macc. 6:1-5). We must reject this view of its focus.

We also found that any view which interprets it as only addressing the destruction of Jerusalem fails to consider the wording of the disciples' questions in all three Gospels and their likely relationship to the content of Jesus's prior eschatological teaching in the temple fully (Matt. 24:3; Mark 13:4; Luke 21:5-6). This view also fails to address the consistent meaning of the word *parousia* as it is used throughout the discourse, the rest of the New Testament, in general usage in the ancient world, and the earliest writing by Christians after the New Testament. It is also forced to ignore the consistent use of parallel wording throughout the New Testament to final judgment. This view, therefore, must also be rejected.

Only a view which interprets the discourse as addressing both final judgment and the destruction of Jerusalem adequately answers to the biblical and linguistic evidence. Of this interpretation, we found that a view which sees in verse 34 a hard transition from AD 70 to final judgment fails to explain Jesus's prior references to "the end" in verses 6 and 14. In addition to this, such a view is also forced to treat *parousia* as figurative in verse 27, but literal in verses 37 and 39—an application inconsistent with ancient Greek, biblical, and early Christian usage. This view must also treat cosmological and eschatological wording applied consistently in other New Testament texts (and even later in the Olivet Discourse) as figurative. Because of these factors, this view must also be rejected.

It is clear that Jesus, in answer to the disciples' question (and likely in order to clarify their confusion), addresses both topics moving back and forth between the two in order to distinguish differences between the two. This is the best interpretation in light of the evidence available to us.

Sadly, although challenges to interpretation brought on by false teachings have often caused many to find the teaching of the Olivet Discourse a daunting puzzle to unravel, the core message of preparation and watchfulness remains as clear today as it was when Jesus first taught it.

What Is the Focus of the Mount of Olives Discourse?

His closing words at the end of the Parable of the Ten Virgins summarizes this well, "Watch therefore, for you know neither the day nor the hour in which the Son of Man is coming" (Matt. 25:13).

Bibliography

BAGD = Walter Bauer, William F. Arndt, F. Wilbur Gingrich, and Fredrick W. Danker. *A Greek-English Lexicon of the New Testament and Other Early Christian Literature*. 2nd ed. Chicago: University of Chicago Press, 1979.

Dawson, Samuel G. *Essays on Eschatology: An Introductory Overview of the Study of Last Things*. Amarillo, TX: SGD Press, 2009.

King, Max R. *The Cross and the Parousia of Christ: The Two Dimensions of One Age-Changing Eschaton*. Warren, OH: Parkman Road Church of Christ, 1987.

LSJ = Liddell, Henry George, Robert Scott. *A Greek-English Lexicon*. Revised and augmented throughout by Sir Henry Stuart Jones. Oxford. Clarendon Press, 1940.

Ogden, Arthur M. *The Avenging of the Apostles and Prophets: A Commentary on Revelation*. Pinson, AL: Ogden Publications, 1985.

Pope, Kyle M. "The Chronology of Jesus's Final Ten Days." *Truth Commentaries: Matthew*. Mike Willis, ed., 692-694. Athens, AL: Guardian of Truth Foundation, 2013.

———. "For Wherever the Carcass Is, There the Eagles Will Be Gathered Together," *Focus Magazine Online* (April 30, 2015) https://focus-magazine.org/for-wherever-the-carcass-is-there-the-eagles-will-be-gathered-together.php.

———. *Thinking about AD 70: Challenging Realized Eschatology*. Athens, AL: Truth Publications, Inc., 2019.

———. *Truth Commentaries: Matthew*. Mike Willis, ed. Athens, AL: Guardian of Truth Foundation, 2013.

Russel, James Stuart. *The Parousia: A Critical Inquiry into the New Testament Doctrine of Our Lord's Second Coming*. London: Daldy, Isbister, and Co., 1878.

Thayer, Joseph H. *Greek-English Lexicon of the New Testament.* Grand Rapids, MI: 1985. Reprinted from 4th ed. *Thayer's Greek-English Lexicon of the New Testament.* T and T Clark, 1901.

Whiteside, Robertson L. *Doctrinal Discourses.* Denton, TX: Miss Inys Whiteside, 1955.

When Was Revelation Written and Why Does It Matter?

By Daniel H. King, Sr.

Why Is This Question Important?

Much is at stake when it comes to the date of the Apocalypse of John. Since the book in the main is composed of images of such things as the Old Testament temple, the Ark of the Covenant, along with references to "the holy city," etc., the meaning of such references must be taken either literally (as would be the case in a dating of the work that places it prior to the destruction of Jerusalem) or else figuratively if written after the fall of the city in AD 70.

Moreover, there is an obvious allusion by the author to a monstrous human being, clearly a political leader of the time, who had evil intentions against the church of Christ. On that account, he represented, pro-

---

Daniel H. King, Sr. was born August 1, 1948 in Union City, TN. He and his wife Donna have two children: Dan Jr. and Jennifer. Dan has preached for churches in Downers Grove, IL and Lakeland, FL, but most of his local work has been in Tennessee. He preached for several years in Memphis, but has spent most of his life in the metropolitan Nashville area. He still lives in Middle Tennessee and is associated with the Locust Street church of Christ in Mount Pleasant, where he serves as the local preacher. He has written extensively in many religious journals, both popular and professional. He has been a writer for *Truth Magazine* for over 40 years, and presently serves on the board of directors for *Truth Publications, Inc.* Dan attended Wayne State University, David Lipscomb College (BA), Harding Graduate School of Religion (MA), and Vanderbilt University (Ph.D.). He served as an adjunct professor at Tennessee State University in

"When Will These Things Be?" : Questions on Eschatology

spectively, an impending danger for Christians everywhere this man's influence extended. Students of the book have posited that this monster pictured in chapter 13 was either Nero or Domitian, once more, depending on how they tended to date the work, whether before or after the fall of the city of Jerusalem. Certainly, he was one or the other of these two figures, but he could not have been both. Too, the identification of the great harlot of chapters 17-18 and the city referred to as "Babylon the Great" are taken completely differently depending upon when the book was written. Essentially, these are the main characters of the work, so failing to understand them properly or misidentifying them takes the reader off in the wrong direction entirely in terms of what the book is about and how it is to be perceived.

Interestingly, one viewpoint (the late date) sees Babylon as another center of pagan worship akin to the previous ancient Babylon. That previous capital city of Old Testament fame was home to so many gods and goddesses of the ancient Near East that it would be difficult to name them all. Rome, the capital city of the Roman Empire, was also filled with shrines and temples dedicated to idols and ancestral superstitions and a panoply of strange religious cults. The other perspective (the early date) sees Babylon as the city of Jerusalem, where virtually no idolatrous worship was permitted at the time of her destruction at the hands of the Romans.

She had once been a center for all sorts of hideous idolatrous practices. The Israelite prophets had been unanimous in condemning her for these transgressions. Since the return of the people from captivity, the nation had been guilty only occasionally of that sort of spiritual adultery. And yet, this is one of the chief accusations lodged against the evil city

---

1976 and at Florida College during 1984–88. He has authored several tracts and a number of books: *Hebrew and Hellenistic Thought in the Book of Wisdom*, *We Have a Right* (with Mike Willis), *Responsibility and Authority in the Spiritual Realm* (with Leon Boyd), *At the Feet of the Master Teacher*, *Commentary on the Gospel of John*, *Commentary on the Epistles of John*, *Commentary on the Book of Hebrews*, *Commentary on the Book of Daniel*, *Commentary on James*, *The Days of Creation*, *Searching for Happiness?*, along with *Daniel, Ezekiel, Hebrews and Revelation* in the Bible Text Book adult workbook series. His most recent publication was *"I Saw the Heaven Opened,"* a thematic commentary on the book of Revelation. He can be reached at: dan@truthpublications.com.

When Was Revelation Written and Why Does It Matter?

of the book of Revelation (17:1, 2, 4; 18:3, 9; 19:2). In the past, Israel had been guilty of such things, but not lately. More recently, Jerusalem was guilty of rejection of the Messiah when He appeared, and they failed to admit the sin by hearing and heeding the good news of His resurrection when it was proclaimed (Luke 23:28-31). That was her chief offense (1 Thess. 2:15, 16), not the sin of idolatry. When she was destroyed, it was on that account, not because of the sin of spiritual adultery. Rome, on the other hand, was noted for her idolatry and pagan rituals throughout the early Christian centuries. If that allegation is made against the pagan city of Rome in the Revelation, then it is a just charge against a guilty party.

A major concern, then, in properly dating the Apocalypse is getting the meaning of its symbols right. If the dating is wrong, the symbols are wrong, because they are taken for something that they were never intended to describe. On the other hand, if the date of the production of the work is correct, then the major symbols of the document are perceived in their historical reality and not in a time a quarter of a century earlier when the Jerusalem temple yet stood, and the sacrificial system persisted. Yet, even more important than this is the open door that it provides to the concepts of radical preterism.

Now, we recognize that there are those who do not buy into full-blown preterism who hold to these notions, and we would not want to be understood as accusing them falsely by what we are saying here. Yet, we would beg them to reconsider their approach to these ideas, on account of where their views have led so many others. Because they have given ground to the preterist perspective in so many areas, this revolutionary reinterpretation of the Bible has gained a foothold in the minds of many untaught people, and the results have been destructive wherever this seed of confusion has been sown.

Treatment of the Lord's Olivet Discourse as a preterist document, fulfilled in its entirety by the fall of Jerusalem and the dissolution of the Jewish economy and state, along with the early dating of the Revelation, have opened the door in the thinking of a good many students of the New Testament to the notion that all of biblical prophecy and prediction was realized at that point in time. It has provided the way forward for this heresy to make inroads into popular thinking. To their way of seeing eschatology, the study of "last things," the Second Coming of Christ occurred, along with the resurrection of the dead, and all the other predic-

"When Will These Things Be?" : Questions on Eschatology

tions and prophecies of the Bible were fulfilled in AD 70 when the Jewish economy was brought to its end.

It represents a completely different perspective on the future and the final things of history from the one that was entertained by the apostles and the early church. Such thinking is without precedent in the church of the Ante-Nicene period. They cannot name a single early church figure who believed what they believe today. That being true, what is the explanation for the fact that no one in the second-century church believed their system? If Jesus and the apostles taught their way of thinking about these matters, why was it forgotten so abruptly by those who were instructed in these doctrines? It is not difficult to answer these questions. This was not what Jesus and the apostles taught about eschatology.

How important is this? We consider it singularly important. In our view, the ramifications of this approach to biblical interpretation are more far-reaching than almost any other in circulation today. In our time, there is no more heretical notion that could be entertained by the mind of one who hopes to please the Lord and do his sovereign will than this one.

If, on the other hand, the words of Jesus and John were intoned in the final years of Emperor Domitian, as the earliest church authorities claimed, and as the majority of the external and internal evidence on the subject seems to indicate, then the whole system of the preterists falls flat on its face. Hence, the hope of the future coming of Jesus and the hope of the resurrection of the dead is still alive and well today: "He who gives witness to these things, says, 'Truly, I come quickly.' Even so come, Lord Jesus!" (Rev. 22:20). Such a proclamation, in that context, is the death knell of radical preterist thinking. Jesus spoke of His coming again in the mid-90s of the first century, and John heartily hoped for it. Therefore, this matter must be studied prayerfully and with all due diligence and honest deliberation. It is not an issue of minor import.

The Evidence from Early Churchmen

The earliest evidence regarding the date of the book of Revelation derives from the pen of the heresy fighter Irenaeus. This great early churchman and relentless enemy of the Gnostics was born about AD 120 and died around 200. He was born to Greek parents in Asia Minor and said that when he was a child, he had heard and seen Polycarp in Smyrna

When Was Revelation Written and Why Does It Matter?

before his martyrdom in 155. In his youth, Polycarp had known John. In real terms, Polycarp was one of the last of the living generation of those who had personally known one of the apostles of Christ. So, timewise he was not far removed from the era when the apostles themselves were alive, and especially the apostle John. Therefore, the information he would have regarding the book of Revelation and its provenance would necessarily be very valuable.

In his writings, he suggests that John "saw the revelation... at the close of Domitian's reign" (Irenaeus, *Against Heresies* 5.30.3). He was not making an argument in defense of a point he was attempting to defend; he was simply making a statement of the facts as he knew them. The early church historian Eusebius also attested to the general truth that the earliest traditions handed down from the time were unanimous in this regard (Eusebius, *Church History* 3.18). There are many other reasons that we consider this time period to be exactly right for the writing of the book, in terms of dating it, but these citations from those so close to the happenings are especially important in placing the book into its proper timeslot.

The way that Irenaeus specifies its time period is particularly noteworthy since it was possible for him to connect the event of the penning of the work to many other special historical events or happenings within the church, which might have been equally illustrious or perhaps even more notable. We suppose that if he had thought the event of the fall of Jerusalem had anything at all to do with what the book was about or perhaps even formed the unique frame of reference that many moderns think it does, that he would have said so. And if this *was* the case, then why did he not say that the work was written immediately prior to the destruction of Jerusalem in AD 70?

The answer to this question, of course, is a simple one. He did not say this because he understood that the book had no connection at all with the fall of Jerusalem or the destruction of the Jewish state. He also knew confidently that it was written toward the end of the life of John and that it was under Domitian's aegis that John was exiled, and after his death that he was freed to return to his newly adopted home in Ephesus. Therefore, he chose specifically to associate it with the close of Emperor Domitian's reign. Clearly, this made sense in more ways than one. It is not surprising that many readers of the work since the time of Irenaeus

"When Will These Things Be?" : Questions on Eschatology

have seen a good reason to believe that this unique moment in time, and its interesting political situation, had significant input into the literature of the book of Revelation. It is our conviction that it is important, and that on this account we ought to have some general grasp of the nature and signal events of the reign of this ignominious ruler.

The Monster Domitian and the Apocalypse

Tertullian of Carthage (ca. AD 160-220) described Domitian as "a man of Nero's type in cruelty" (*Apology* 5). Quoting extensively from John's Revelation in another one of his works, he preserves an otherwise unattested story of a failed attempt to kill John: "John was first plunged, unhurt, into boiling oil, and thence remitted to his island-exile" (*Prescription against Heretics* 36). And, although he does not refer to the ruler who was in office at the time of his being sent into exile, it is clear from his reference to the event that it was punitive and not a mere visit or preaching opportunity that brought him to the place, as is sometimes argued by some students of the book of Revelation.

Also, of importance in this regard, is the testimony of Clement of Alexandria (AD 155-215). He echoes the claim that the apostle was sent to Patmos as a punishment, and noted that John returned from the Isle of Patmos "after the tyrant was dead" (*Who Is the Rich Man?* 42). He does not specify the name of the "tyrant" involved in the incident. Yet, he seems to assume the reader will be aware of who he is talking about. Eusebius notes that the tyrant referred to is Domitian rather than Nero (*Church History* 3.23). Clement further speaks of John at this point in his life as an "old man," which is a noteworthy observation. It would have been an inappropriate descriptive of him in his sixties; but would be entirely proper as a depiction of him in his nineties, especially given that there was a well-known tradition in the church that John lived to extreme old age. So, his evidence is also to be taken as opposed to a date for the book in the 60s of the Common Era.

Eusebius speaks of John as having lived a very long life, even until the reign of the emperor Trajan (AD 98-117). About the delivery of the Apocalypse, he says:

> And all the elders that associated with John the disciple of the Lord in Asia Minor bear witness that John delivered it to them. For he remained among them until the time of Trajan (*Church History* 3.23.3).

When Was Revelation Written and Why Does It Matter?

Furthermore, he explained the fact that John was able to return to his home in Ephesus after the time he spent on Patmos, and once more, it was associated with the conclusion of the reign of Emperor Domitian:

> But after Domitian had reigned fifteen years, and Nerva had succeeded to the empire, the Roman Senate, according to writers that record the history of those days, voted that Domitian's honors should be cancelled, and that those who had been unjustly banished should return to their homes and have their property restored to them. It was at this time that the apostle John returned from his banishment in the island and took up his abode at Ephesus, according to an ancient Christian tradition (*Church History* 3.20.10-11).

Then from the third century, there is the evidence of Victorinus of Pettau (martyred during the persecutions of the Emperor Diocletian, ca. AD 303). This author wrote a commentary on the Apocalypse of John. It was primarily allegorical and showed an interest in arithmology. In his commentary, he wrote that John expected martyrdom as his ending but instead was sent into exile. Once more, it was at the hands of Domitian that he says this was done:

> When John said these things, he was in the Island of Patmos, condemned to the mines by Caesar Domitian. There he saw the Apocalypse; and when at length grown old, he thought that he should receive his release by suffering; but Domitian being killed, all his judgments were discharged. And John being dismissed from the mines, thus subsequently delivered the same Apocalypse, which he had received from God (*Commentary on Revelation* 10:11).

Jerome is also an important witness to the date and circumstance of the book's writing. Eusebius Sophronius Hieronymus (AD 347-420), usually called Jerome, or Saint Jerome by Catholic scholars, in his work entitled, *Lives of Illustrious Men*, said that "In the fourteenth year then after Nero, Domitian having raised up a second persecution, he (John) was banished to the island of Patmos, and wrote the Apocalypse" (9).

It should be noted that none of these early authors was in the least confused about when the book was written. All of them are perfectly clear on the matter, and they are all unanimous in their opinion. It was penned in the time of Emperor Domitian, and very near to the end of his reign. Some later writers suggested that Revelation was written in the reign of the emperor Claudius (AD 41-54). Still, this date is quite impos-

"When Will These Things Be?" : Questions on Eschatology

sible because it is inconsistent with all of the facts of John's life and the early history of the church, so they are not taken seriously by anyone. A belief that the work was produced during the 60s and pertained to the persecution by Nero was not held by any of the early writers of the Christian community. This theory has been of considerably later provenance.

The Life and Times of the Emperor Domitian

Domitian (Titus Flavius Domitianus) was emperor during the period AD 81-96. Born on October 24, AD 51, and ascending to the throne on September 14, 81, he proved to be an able administrator and, it has rightly been observed that he did not ignore the welfare of his people as some of the other emperors did. Moreover, he was not an emperor without accomplishments, even though he has sometimes mistakenly been viewed so.

He was responsible for a reform of the coinage, a massive building program (including restoration of the gutted ruins of many public buildings, including the capitol which had burned in AD 80, built a new temple to Jupiter, a new stadium, a concert hall for musicians and poets, for himself a new Flavian Palace on Palatine Hill for official functions, and to the south, he constructed the Domus Augustana, where he held banquets and receptions), he was responsible for the development of an important "power set" within the administration, it was his (rather than Trajan's) admission of a substantial number of easterners into the Senate, he also made serious efforts to come to terms with the various groups within the Senate, etc.

These were just some of his unique contributions to the common life of the people of the Roman capitol. To ignore these benefactions would be to fail to recognize the full portrait of who he was and what he did for Rome. The lesson we may draw from this is that even bad people sometimes accomplish worthwhile things. Unfortunately, in the wake of their acts of calumny, the good is most often utterly forgotten. Historically, however, we cannot permit that to happen. The good must be reported along with the bad.

It should also be noticed that, despite his own personal lack of internally fixed moral values, he made an effort toward raising the standards of public morality in the city. He did this by forbidding male castration,

When Was Revelation Written and Why Does It Matter?

admonishing senators who practiced homosexuality, and censuring the Vestal Virgins for, among other indiscretions, committing incest. One offender was even buried alive, and her lover was also put to death. By those around him during the early part of his reign, he was viewed as generous, possessing self-restraint, considerate of all his friends, and conscientious when dispensing justice. In these regards, he surpassed many of those who preceded him in his office. Domitian especially enjoyed the public games, and in his own case, he favored the chariot races. In fact, he personally enjoyed public entertainments and, recognizing the appetite of the populace, attempted to satiate the people's appetite for them to the point that their enormous expense took a heavy toll on both his and the empire's finances. So, even though the bills did eventually come due, the people of Rome were very happy with his decisions in this realm of public life during the early years of his administration.

Thus, even though it was eventually engulfed in both fear and paranoia, his reign was generally one of peace and stability for the empire. Earlier generations did not have a full enough grasp of these factors in his life's work, as shown by the meager material found in the biography of Stéphane Gsell in 1894. Since that time a mass of epigraphic and archaeological material has been uncovered and now provides for us a more solid basis for a broader and more detailed picture of the period of Roman history than what was given to us through the writings of the early historians alone (Jones, *The Emperor Domitian*, viiff.).

The writer Suetonius claimed that Domitian was raised in "poverty." Of course, "poverty" is a relative term, subject to various shades of meaning. In this instance, the word is clearly used as an insult to the man and his family, rather than as a definitive word expressing the nature of their true financial position in society. This point is used as damning evidence against him, as though he had brought the temporary misfortunes of the family upon them all. In fact, the family was quite wealthy, although between 51 and 59, it was out of favor with the leadership of the country. They owned several villas and estates. As well, when he fell into political disfavor, his father Vespasian was forced to engage in trade to keep up his position in society.

The ancient historians reveal that Domitian was a well-educated man, able to converse elegantly and to produce memorable comments. He wrote poetry during his early years and had written and published a

"When Will These Things Be?" : Questions on Eschatology

book on baldness (he was extremely vain and thus very self-conscious of his being bald, so this subject was a preoccupation for him). Yet, it is highly unlikely that he was interested in literature for its own sake. More probably he wished to make a name for himself among the aristocracy of Rome, and at various times to be seen as a man of letters rather than merely as an ambitious politician, for it is noted that on his accession to power he abandoned his literary pretensions, limited his reading to Tiberius's commentaries, and devoted his attention to his own stern and rigid ideal of emperorship, re-establishing Augustan standards in money as well as in morals for the empire.

Both Tacitus and Suetonius are convinced of this proposition. They refer to his love of reading and writing poetry and interpret it as politically motivated, to deceive everyone with the notion that his pursuits were literary and innocuous. Most modern scholars share their views. The only seeming gestures in the direction of his previous interests during his administration were the construction of the concert hall in Rome and the expenditure of vast sums of money to restore fully the great library at Alexandria, even sending scribes to copy works that he was unable to purchase for the collection. Yet, even this has been interpreted as being a part of the new imperial image of himself that he wished to put before the Roman people rather than a revelation of his true aspirations and interests.

It is evident from the foregoing that Domitian was not an evil man from the outset of his reign. Yet, it is also clear from what follows that he became so over time. It has been suggested, perhaps rightly, that his personal greed and paranoia over the possibility of being assassinated was what made him so. Several other emperors had been murdered prior to his time, so the danger of this cannot be dismissed. Cassius Dio in the *Roman History* said that he was both bold and quick to anger, so this was already an aspect of his character and personality.

But over time, he also proved to be treacherous and secretive, feeling no affection for anyone except for a few women in his life. As his reign progressed and the pressures of ruling mounted, along with the harsh realities of a profligate spending policy, paranoia seized the emperor, and he came to trust almost no one in his inner circle. To pay for his expenditures and extravagances, he tightened the Jewish tax enacted

When Was Revelation Written and Why Does It Matter?

by his father and seized the fortunes of senators and wealthy Romans. His paranoia even extended to his wife, Domitia Logina. At one point, he accused her of adultery (some accounts claimed she had, in fact, committed the transgression) and planned to put her to death, a common practice at the time. Domitia originally had been married to a senator, Aelius Lamia, but he was convinced to divorce her so she could marry Domitian. Under a cloud of suspicion of adultery by Domitia, Domitian temporarily left his wife to live with his niece Julia, Titus's daughter by his second marriage (whom Domitian had earlier refused to marry), until he was eventually convinced by others to return to his wife. The relationship was clearly a very tentative one.

The emperor's extreme paranoia caused him to take certain extraordinary measures to protect himself against assassination or displacement from his high office. He employed informers to provide him with information about potential enemies and fair-weather friends. And, to obtain information about possible plots against his person or of potential rebellion, he ordered interrogators to cut off the hands or to scorch the genitals of prisoners. He lined the gallery where he took his daily walks with highly polished moonstone so that it reflected everything behind him and made it difficult for a potential assassin to approach him without his knowledge.

In September of AD 87, several senators were involved in a conspiracy to kill him, and upon his discovery of the plot, they were all summarily executed. Also, the governor of Upper Germany, Lucius Antonius Saturninus, led a mutiny against him with the fourteenth and twenty-first Legions, and this also was put down by Domitian's general, Lucius Appius Maximus Norbanus, in AD 89. In the end, however, the conspiratorial spirit which he had created in Rome led to his own demise. The emperor himself was assassinated in the year 96 and was succeeded on the same day by his personal advisor Nerva. He was murdered by a group of conspirators, led by a member of the imperial staff named Stephanus who had been accused of embezzlement and so feared for his own life. In the ensuing incident, he was stabbed at first by Stephanus and then hacked to death by a group of coconspirators. So, it could be said that his fears were not utterly unfounded!

One of the most objectionable aspects of his administration had to do with his own constitutional and ceremonial position in the govern-

"When Will These Things Be?" : Questions on Eschatology

ment. He continued his father's policy of holding frequent consulates. In fact, he was consul *ordinarius* every year from 82 to 88. He became censor for life in 85, giving him control over senatorial membership and general behavior. He wore triumphal dress in the Senate, and he presided, wearing Greek dress and a golden crown, over four yearly games on the Greek model, with his fellow judges wearing crowns bearing his own effigy among effigies of the gods. According to the writer Suetonius, his most serious offense to the traditional order was that he insisted on being addressed as *dominus et deus* ("lord and god"). This was distasteful to the Roman people generally and to the Roman elite, particularly, but a special insult to Jewish and Christian sensitivities. He claimed to be the son of Minerva, his own special tutelary goddess. The Jews, of course, were generally considered a protected minority under Roman law, and so were mostly immune from what this might mean for them, but the Christians did not enjoy this special status. For the people of Rome, even though it was an era of relative peace and tranquility strategically, this became a time of great fear and paranoia.

As his reign progressed and the pressures of ruling the empire pressed down ever more heavily upon him, outrageous paranoia seized control of his already fragile personality. He alienated the Senate, stripping it almost entirely of its powers and making of himself an absolute ruler. Senators and imperial officers were executed for the most trivial of offenses. As mentioned previously, his paranoia even extended to his own wife. She was accused of adultery and came near to being executed. On this account, it is thought that she may have participated in the eventual plan that led to his murder since she still feared for her life and was never sure what her status might be in the future.

The arrogant emperor even renamed two months of the year after himself; Germanicus (September) and Domitianus (October). It was during this reign of terror that the church caught his attention. Regarding this, Dio reported that "Domitian slew, along with many others, Flavius Clemens the consul, although he was a cousin and married to Flavia Domitilla, who was also a relative of the emperor. [It has been theorized that this person may have been Clement of Rome (*Clemens Romanus*), or that some slave or freedman from his family was that writer. A Clement is also mentioned in the *Shepherd of Hermas* (cf. *Vis.* 2.4, 3). He has also been identified with the Clement mentioned by Paul in Philippians 4:3.

When Was Revelation Written and Why Does It Matter?

Certainty on the matter has been elusive]. The charge brought against them both was that of atheism (*atheotēs*), a charge on which many others who drifted into what were considered 'Jewish ways,' were condemned. Some of these were put to death, and the rest were at least deprived of their property. Domitilla was merely banished to Pandateria" (Cassius Dio, *Epitome* 67.4; cf. *Ancient History Encyclopedia*, "Domitian," Donald L. Wasson, www.ancient.eu/domitian/).

E. M. Smallwood and a few others have argued that the two individuals mentioned here were not Christians. Smallwood views them as "god-fearers," living on the fringe of Judaism, who followed Jewish customs to the degree that was deemed sufficient to make them subject to attack from Domitian. She regards the case for seeing them as Christians as resting on a flimsy foundation. Yet, her view should not be taken very seriously since there is no evidence in either the Classical or Jewish writings that Domitian ever attacked Jews by race or that they suffered any at all for their religious preferences during his reign.

The status of Judaism as a *religio licita* continued unaffected, and there are no indications that Jews were forced to commit idolatry while he was the Emperor of Rome. Why, then, ought we to assume that god-fearers or proselytes were treated any differently than circumcised Jews and regarded as "atheists"? There is but a single instance that is quoted to support this notion (Apollonius Molon, an illustrious rhetorician who provided material for Apion; Josephus, *Against Apion* 11, 48) and where this appellation is employed to depict Jews, and it is taken from a first century BC reference and is not really relevant to the reign of Domitian. On the other hand, the fact that Christianity was not a *religio licita* at the time and its followers had the charge of "atheism" commonly leveled against them would appear to support overwhelmingly the interpretation most commonly given to this passage (cf. Barnard, 259, n. 4; Smallwood, 1-13).

The state religion had not turned against Christians formally or legally before Domitian. Nero's raging against the Christians had nothing to do with the cult of the emperor. Yet, under Domitian, who, according to the oriental pattern, claimed divine worship for himself as emperor during his lifetime, persecution of Christians by the state on purely religious grounds took place for the first time. Moreover, as we shall elucidate further later on, in the province of Asia, the cult of the emperor was

"When Will These Things Be?" : Questions on Eschatology

promoted with special zeal; in fact, under Domitian, the city of Ephesus received a new temple to honor the emperor and the imperial cult. And so, precisely in the province of Asia, the classical land of the emperor cult, at the time of Domitian, all prerequisites are given for the severe conflict between Christianity and the state religion, which the Apocalypse delineates (Kümmel, *Introduction to the New Testament*, 327-328). Domitian reigned from AD 81-96, and his persecution against Christians began around the year 89. Thus, the period of persecution under this monster, jealous to be worshipped as a god, lasted for some seven years. Considerable damage was done to the church in that period of seven years (an interestingly fortuitous number, given that it is used repeatedly by the author of Revelation to depict various things in the book).

Further, the testimony of Revelation itself favors an origin for this literature in the province of Asia when the Christians were severely oppressed, a time best conceivable under the repugnant character Domitian and not before his reign. The circumstances of John himself, as depicted in the book, testify to this general situation. The writer describes himself as one who in the later persecutions was termed a "confessor," i.e., when taken before the Roman authorities, he had not denied Jesus Christ and worshipped the emperor; instead, he had maintained "the word of God" (1:9), the Christian message, and had given his "testimony," his personal confession or "witness," that he was indeed and in truth a Christian man and a believer in Jesus of Nazareth.

How Trials of Christians Were Conducted

Thankfully, history has described the procedure to which we make reference, as it was followed at the time. Pliny the Younger, then governor of Bithynia in northern Asia Minor, in a letter to the emperor Trajan (AD 96-117), written between 111 and 113, gives his own version of it. He had the images of the gods, including the emperor, placed in the courtroom. He asked suspected persons if they were Christians. He asked those who confessed that they were such a second and a third time, to ensure that they fully understood the question itself and the ramifications of a positive answer.

If they stubbornly persisted with their confession, they were led away for execution. Others, including some who admitted that they had been Christians when questioned, cursed Christ, and worshipped the statues of the gods and that of the emperor, things which those who are "really

When Was Revelation Written and Why Does It Matter?

Christians" quite simply would never do (Pliny, *Epistles* 10.96). Here is Pliny's inquiry, along with the emperor's response:

Pliny's Inquiry

It is my rule, Sire, to refer to you in matters where I am uncertain. For who can better direct my hesitation or instruct my ignorance? I was never present at any trial of Christians; therefore I do not know what are the customary penalties or investigations, and what limits are observed. I have hesitated a great deal on the question whether there should be any distinction of ages; whether the weak should have the same treatment as the more robust; whether those who recant should be pardoned, or whether a man who has ever been a Christian should gain nothing by ceasing to be such; whether the name itself, even if innocent of crime, should be punished, or only the crimes attaching to that name.

Meanwhile, this is the course that I have adopted in the case of those brought before me as Christians. I ask them if they are Christians. If they admit it I repeat the question a second and a third time, threatening capital punishment; if they persist I sentence them to death. For I do not doubt that, whatever kind of crime it may be to which they have confessed, their pertinacity and inflexible obstinacy should certainly be punished. There were others who displayed a like madness and whom I reserved to be sent to Rome, since they were Roman citizens.

Thereupon the usual result followed, the very fact of my dealing with the question led to a wider spread of the charge, and a great variety of cases were brought before me. An anonymous pamphlet was issued, containing many names. All who denied that they were or had been Christians I considered should be discharged, because they called upon the gods at my dictation and did reverence, with incense and wine, to your image which I had ordered to be brought forward for this purpose, together with the statues of the deities; and especially because they cursed Christ, a thing which, it is said, genuine Christians cannot be induced to do. Others named by the informer first said that they were Christians and then denied it; declaring that they had been but were so no longer, some having recanted three years or more before and one or two as long ago as twenty years. They all worshipped your image and the statues of the gods and cursed Christ. Yet, they declared that the sum of their guilt or error had amounted only to this, that on an appointed day they had been accustomed to meet before daybreak, and to recite a hymn antiphonally to Christ, as to a god, and to bind themselves by an oath not for the commission of any crime

"When Will These Things Be?" : Questions on Eschatology

but to abstain from theft, robbery, adultery, and breach of faith, and not to deny a deposit when it was claimed. After the conclusion of this ceremony it was their custom to depart and meet again to take food; but it was ordinary and harmless food, and they had ceased this practice after my edict in which, in accordance with your orders, I had forbidden secret societies. I thought it the more necessary, therefore, to find out what truth there was in this by applying torture to two maidservants, who were called deaconesses. Yet, I found nothing but a depraved and extravagant superstition, and I therefore postponed my examination and had recourse to you for consultation.

The matter seemed to me to justify my consulting you, especially on account of the number of those imperiled, for many persons of all ages and classes and of both sexes are being put in peril by accusation, and this will go on. The contagion of this superstition has spread not only in the cities, but in the villages and rural districts as well; yet it seems capable of being checked and set right. There is no shadow of doubt that the temples, which have been almost deserted, are beginning to be frequented once more, that the sacred rites which have been long neglected are being renewed, and that the sacrificial victims are for sale everywhere, whereas, till recently a buyer was rarely to be found. From this it is easy to imagine that a host of men could be set right, were they given a chance by recantation.

Trajan's Response

You have taken the right line, my dear Pliny, in examining the cases of those denounced to you as Christians, for no hard and fast rule can be laid down, of universal application. They are not to be sought out; if they are informed against, and the charge is proven, they are to be punished, with this reservation—that if anyone denies that he is a Christian, and actually proves it, that is by worshipping our gods, he shall be pardoned as a result of his recantation, however suspect he may have been with respect to the past. Pamphlets published anonymously should carry no weight in any charge whatsoever. They constitute a very bad precedent; and they are also out of keeping with this age (Bettenson, *Documents*, 5-7).

A similar process was likely used in the region where John was indicted and convicted (probably Ephesus). John, however, was not executed for his confession; instead, he was exiled to the island of Patmos, off the coast of Asia Minor, and only about sixty miles southwest of Ephesus. According to the elder Pliny, it was used at times as a place for the banishment of persons who were not accorded the freedoms of ordinary Ro-

When Was Revelation Written and Why Does It Matter?

man society for some reason or other (Eusebius, *Church History* 3.18.5). There is a cave or grotto on Patmos, now made into a chapel, which since the Middle Ages at least has been associated with the apostle John and his work on Revelation.

Later confessors (as they came to be called), in the tradition of the apostle John, enjoyed great prestige and influence in the early church. Ignatius, a bishop from Antioch who suffered the supreme penalty in Rome ca. 110, is an excellent example of this. While en route from his home city of Antioch to Rome with his Roman guard, he was received with great enthusiasm by the Christians of the cities through which he passed. He was also carefully heeded as an authority figure. This was not on account of his bishopric at Antioch but was due to his courage and eagerness to make the confession of the name of Christ when it was so perilous to do so, and thus to die as a martyr (Rist, *Revelation of St. John*, 373). Ignatius seemed eager to die for the cause of Christ. By his time, martyrdom had become a very desirable outcome for those who were intensely loyal to Jesus. John's Revelation set the stage for this elevation of Christian martyrs. It will be recalled that Revelation set them on thrones: "I saw thrones, and they sat on them, and judgment was given to them; and I saw the souls of those who had been beheaded for the testimony of Jesus, and for the word of God. . ." (20:4).

Plainly the atmosphere of Revelation is in many ways comparable to what we see and hear in the writings of Ignatius as well as of Pliny in his letter to Trajan. It was an era of persecution, governmental oppression, and of Christian martyrdom. In the diminutive open letters of the Apocalypse, persecutions are expected at the hands of the authorities (2:10); the blood of martyrs has already flowed (2:13; 6:9); frightful danger threatens all of Christendom (3:10); in fact, the outbreak of general persecution of Christians by the Roman state seems imminent. In 17:6, John sees the harlot, Babylon-Rome, drunk with the blood of the saints of God and from the blood of the witnesses of Jesus (cf. 18:24; 19:2; 16:6; 6:10). In 20:4 participation in a thousand-year reign of Christ is promised to the martyrs, who for the sake of the testimony of Jesus and for the word of God fell victim to the executioner's ax, and who did not worship the beast and its image and did not receive its mark on their foreheads and their hands, i.e., to those who refused divine worship to the emperor and his genius (13:4, 12ff.; 14:9, 11; 16:2; 19:20). It is grossly

"When Will These Things Be?" : Questions on Eschatology

apparent that Christianity has run head-on against the Roman state and the state's favored religion, the emperor cult. This corresponds precisely with the situation under Domitian and the era afterward, but once again, *not prior to his time*.

Therefore, we must conclude that not only was this book written during the period of the domination of the world by Imperial Rome and that the beastly figure in charge at the time was indeed Emperor Domitian, himself a monster who demanded worship of his supposed deity, but that governmental power and its abusive ways are at the heart of the subject-matter of Revelation. As in the Old Testament book of Daniel, which also deals with the relationship between the reign of God and the governments of men, these identical political realities are very much at the forefront of the author's attention (cf. Dan. 2:20-21, 44; 4: 17, 25b, 32b, etc.). The hated tyrant Domitian had already begun his reign of terror at the time of its inception (ca. AD 96).

His persecutions leveled against all who would not profess his divinity and worship him led to the death of many Christians and heralded an era of much more fierce persecution of the church by the Roman state (1:9; 2:10, 13; 6:9-11; 11:7-10; 13:15; 16:6; 17:6; 18:24; 20:4). Christians saw him as a resurrected Nero (13:3, 12), who in AD 64 had persecuted them on the false charge of burning the city of Rome. In fact, it was more likely Nero himself who set the city alight so that he could rebuild it to greater glory (as many Romans believed when the city burned). Yet, at the time, there existed a small element of society that had no political power at all. They were generally hated by the rest of the people. Others feared and distrusted them because they could not understand their strange ways. And, as unfortunate as it was for them, they became the perfect distraction! The Christians provided him with an easy and convenient means of taking attention away from himself. They were his "scapegoat" to divert the public's attention away from his own guilt in the conflagration that brought a portion of Rome to ruin and brought misery into the lives of so many Roman peasants and small businesses.

Domitian, on the other hand, was the second great persecutor of the Christian faith. His actions against certain Christians, on account of their embrace of Christianity, are well attested. Cassius Dio refers specifically to his putting to death his own cousin, Titus Flavius Clemens, and gives him responsibility for the banishment of Domitilla, Clemens' wife,

When Was Revelation Written and Why Does It Matter?

and Domitian's niece. She was sent away to Pandataria (Ventotene), one of the Pontine Islands in the Tyrrhenian Sea. "Atheism" or "sacrilege" (*atheotēs*) and "Jewish ways" were the formal charges that were leveled against them by the Roman state. A great many others were put to death or else deprived of their property on the same grounds, among them being one Acilius Glabrio, consul in AD 91, who had after his consulship been sent into exile (Dion Cassius, quoted in Ramsay, *Church in the Roman Empire*, 260-261).

It is in this frightening environment, then, that the prophecies of Revelation had their origin. Its concentration upon the subject of the persecution and oppression of the saints is fundamental to an appreciation of apocalyptic literature in general and Revelation in particular. It is critical to understand that this type of material was born in the crucible of religious repression, social tyranny, totalitarian cruelty, and the hostility of the state toward pious believers who needed desperately to have something substantial to hold on to in the face of overwhelming coercive power being employed against them, in this instance by various officials of the Roman state. The corrupt and unjust Roman government was their oppressor, but the eternal and all-powerful God was their ever-present ally. It is this complex of important religious, political, and social realities that provides us with the real context of Revelation theologically and historically.

Points to be Considered against the Early Date Hypothesis

Having considered the external arguments for the late date of Revelation and against the pre-AD 70 approach to the work, we turn our attention to the internal factors that lead us to the same conclusion. In the paragraphs below, it is our plan to consider various points that are made both for and against the theory that places the book of Revelation in the years prior to the fall of Jerusalem and the temple. We take no personal credit for them, except in the special form that they take in the present essay. Biblical scholars throughout many years prior to our own time have formulated them as they considered their relative merits and demerits. We are deeply indebted to them. We have simply drawn them together into the present list. Let us consider them in no particular order of importance:

1. *Mention of the temple and the city of Jerusalem.* Those references (particularly 11:1-2) within the book, which allude to the old Jewish capital and its central shrine, are seen literally by these expositors as still

"When Will These Things Be?" : Questions on Eschatology

standing at the time of the author's writing of the document. It is claimed that these allusions make a date later than this untenable. On the other hand, this assumes a literal reading of one or more of the symbols of the book as they are presented in the context of many other symbols, which these scholars admit are to be taken as purely symbolic and not taken as literal.

This leads us to ask an obvious question. Why should these two symbols be isolated and read as literal when the others in these contexts are not so viewed? In fact, it is seldom noticed by them that the description and measurements of the temple as inscribed by John are based not on the Herodian temple which stood in Jesus's day, as is usually assumed by such readers, but on the eschatological portrait of the temple as depicted in Ezekiel 40-48.

If John was alluding to the Herodian temple that stood in Jerusalem during the reign of Emperor Nero, why did he not describe it as it stood? Why did he not give its measurements? The apostle John had no doubt seen it many times. Why did he not picture what he had seen with his own eyes? Why did the measurements of his visionary temple not match with those of the Herodian structure? Could it be that he intentionally avoided both the description and the measurements of the temple of Herod to put the emphasis where it really belonged, namely upon Ezekiel's eschatological one?

In our view, it is interesting to note that most of these same scholars believe that the temple to which the prophet Ezekiel alluded in his prophecies was not that of Herod. They readily admit that Ezekiel spoke as he did to envisage the church in the church age or of an idealized picture of a restored Israel rather than the temple as built by Herod and destroyed by the Romans in AD 70. On this matter, we deem them to be quite right in their interpretation. Moreover, these same students also believe the Messianic prophesies that picture the city of Jerusalem at several different points in the Old Testament also envisage the new covenant realities such as the church and the heavenly Jerusalem. Again, we consider their interpretation to be precisely on point.

So, once more, why in this former instance do they decide to depart from this consistent approach to the figure as it is employed in the prophetic Scriptures generally unless it is to make a special point with this case, namely, to date Revelation in the age of Nero? In our view, this de-

When Was Revelation Written and Why Does It Matter?

fies defensible logic. It also puts them in contradiction with themselves over these other prophetical allusions.

2. *Reference to "Babylon the Great."* The passage, which is central to this hypothesis, is 11:8, which refers to the location "where their Lord was crucified." This reference is taken as proof positive by these writers that the literal city of Jerusalem was in the mind of the writer when he spoke so vehemently regarding the judgment of God upon some great world capital. In that context, the city in question is called "the great city," and in the chapters that follow "that great city" and "Babylon."

However, seeing the metropolis in question as Jerusalem requires one to stretch the language of these texts beyond their natural limits. The reference to the place of the Lord's crucifixion must be torn from its context to provide for such a reading. In point of fact, the whole of this is given a symbolic significance by the author himself. He says that this is a municipality "which spiritually is called" and then identifies it with Sodom and Egypt. Having said this, he goes on to elaborate with the further explanation: "where their Lord was crucified." Hence, the force of the text itself is to say that the city in question is no more to be identified with literal Jerusalem than it is with literal Babylon, literal Sodom, or literal Egypt! So, the passage should be understood as follows: "And their dead bodies shall lie in the street of the great city (Babylon), which spiritually is called Sodom and Egypt, where also our Lord was crucified (Jerusalem)." The author does refer here to all of these places, only making direct reference to two of them. The other two (Babylon and Jerusalem) are inferred but not mentioned.

Another point that deserves consideration here is the author's own words about the nature of this "great city" that he has in mind. Says John, "The woman whom you saw is the great city that rules over the kings of the earth" (Rev. 17:18). The language that he employs can, in no sense, be understood to describe Jerusalem in the days of Emperor Nero, or even of Domitian, for that matter. In the New Testament era, the city of Jerusalem was a minor player in world politics. Simply put, it did not rule over the kings of the earth. Rome did, however. It was the major player in world politics at the time. Too, Jerusalem was not recognized as among the "great cities" of the world during that period, either in terms of its extent or its political and financial influence. Religiously speaking, it was important, but otherwise, it was not.

"When Will These Things Be?" : Questions on Eschatology

The leading cities in the first century were Rome, Alexandria, Antioch, Ephesus, and Carthage. Tacitus estimated the population of Jerusalem in the days of the Jewish rebellion (in the 60s AD) to be about 600,000. Rome's population is generally estimated to have been about one million people. That is nearly twice the size of Jerusalem, in those terms. In AD 117, its empire was estimated as extending to about 6.5 million square kilometers or 4,038,912 miles, with 50-90 million inhabitants. Jerusalem, at that time, had no empire. It was included in the Roman Province of Syria. Once more, Jerusalem could not, in any sense, be compared with mighty Rome.

Further, Rome was recognized by the whole world as the *princeps urbium*, "the greatest of cities" (Horace, *Carmen Saeculare*, 4.3.13). Aelius Aristides referred to it as *hē megalē polis*, "the great city" (*Orations* 26.3; cf. 26.9). An impressive list of citations is available where language comparable to this was employed among the ancient authors. It is found in the three-volume work, *Neuer Wettstein: Texte zum Neuen Testament aus Griechentum und Hellenismus* (Dio Cassius 76.4.4-5; *Anth. Pal.* 9.236; Dion Periegetes 352-56; Athenaeus 1.208b; 3.98c; Porphyry *De abst.* 2.56.9; Procopius *Goth.* 3.22; Vergil *Aeneid* 1.601-6; 7.272-82; *Eclogues* 1.19-25; Livy 1.16.6-7; Ovid *Fasti* 5.91-100; *Metam.* 15.439-49; Manilius 4.686-95, 773-77; Pliny *Hist. nat.* 3.38; Silius 3.505-10, 582-87; Martial 1.3.1-6; 10.103.7-12; Ammianus Marc. 14.6.5-6; cf. Aune, *Revelation 17-22*, 959). The use of the definite article "the" in so many cases provide definitive evidence that there was only one city in the world during that period that was considered the greatest. Jerusalem was not that city.

3. The coming of Christ in judgment (1:7). Some interpreters read Revelation 1:7 in terms of the Lord's return to judge the Jews for their rejection of Him, which employed the Roman army as the rod of God's judgment. This truth is certainly dealt with elsewhere in the Bible, and in language that is both powerful and frightening (cf. Matt. 24; Luke 17; and Mark 13). In the second part of the verse, there is a citation of Zechariah 12:10, which describes those who mourn as "the house of David and the inhabitants of Jerusalem." Following this line of thought to its natural conclusion, those who are convinced that this is the proper approach to the text reflect that the "earth" in the passage means the land of Israel and the "tribes" of Zechariah 12:12 allude to the various clans of Israel.

When Was Revelation Written and Why Does It Matter?

The major problem with this approach to the question is the fact that the passage quoted from Zechariah does not refer to the judgment of Israel, but to her redemption. Now that is a major obstacle! Moreover, Daniel 7:13 is just as clearly being brought into the thought of the writer by his usage of the language of that text, and yet, once more, that text also relates not to the judgment of the Jewish people but to their redemption. So, again, it frustrates the very purpose for which these interpreters envision John as having utilized the passage.

This approach also ignores the common usage of the expression "tribes of the earth" *(pasai hai phulai tēs gēs)* elsewhere in Holy Scripture. Wherever this phrase (or something kin to it) is used in the Greek Old Testament it always relates to other clans and tribes of Gentile extraction, and never to the Twelve Tribes of Israel (cf. Gen. 12:3; 28:14; Ps. 71:17; Zech. 14:17; see also Rev. 5:9; 7:9). The mourning pictured on the part of those who see the Lord at His coming appears not to have to do with those who literally put him to death but those who have rejected him and made of no effect the crucifixion and sacrificial offering inherent in His death. It pictures those who are alienated from His covenants, unwilling to own Him as their King, and so, simply put, the unsaved and unredeemed of all the earth! This is not a passage that depicts the judgment of the Jewish people. So it has nothing at all to do with AD 70.

4. *The seven hills and the seven kings (17:9-10).* It was well known at the time of writing that the city of Rome sat upon seven hills *(Septem montes Romae)* east of the river Tiber and that these seven hills (named as follows: Aventinus, Caelius, Capitolinus, Esquilinus, Palatinus, Quirinalis, Viminalis) formed the geographical heart of the city even as they do to this day. The Romans themselves referred to Rome as the "City of Seven Hills." In fact, they celebrated an annual festival called the *Septimontium* ("seven hills" or "seven mountains"). Plutarch observed that it was to celebrate the inclusion of a seventh hill into the city limits of Rome, granting it the nickname in Greek *heptalophos* "seven-hilled city" (*Roman Questions* 69), or in Latin *septicollis*. This way of referring to the city is well attested in ancient sources (Virgil, *Aeneid* 6.782-783; *Georgics* 2.535; Martial, *Epigrams* 4.64.11-12; Cicero, *To Atticus* 6.5.2; Horace, *Carmen Saeculare* 7).

In AD 71, the Roman mint issued a bronze coin that was a *sestertius* in value, which was one-quarter of a denarius (a day's wage in New Testa-

"When Will These Things Be?" : Questions on Eschatology

ment times). The front of the coin featured a profile of the Roman Emperor Vespasian, and the verso featured a reclining figure of a woman sitting on seven hills, under which was the Latin word *Roma*, the name of the personified figure of *Dea Roma*, the goddess of Rome. The similarity between this image and John's vision of the harlot on the seven-headed beast is inescapable. If residents of Asia Minor possessed such coins or others like them, the connection with Rome would have been immediate and unquestioned (cf. Kyle Pope, *Thinking about AD 70*, 151). So, this was clearly a not-so-subtle hint to the reader regarding the identification of the city in question.

It is frequently argued that Jerusalem was also founded on seven eminences, even though she is not very frequently referred to this way, and certainly not often enough or early enough to be identified as such [Mount of Olives, Nob, "Mount of Corruption" or "Mount of Offence" (2 Kings 23:13), Mount Zion, Ophel Hill, Fort Antonia, and the southwest hill that in the time of Simon the Hasmonean was called "the new Mount Zion"]. The only reference to Jerusalem as a city of seven hills that we know about is found in the *Pirke-de-Rabbi Eliezer*, an eighth-century Midrashic narrative, stating that "Jerusalem is situated on seven hills" (cited in Bialik and Ravenitzky, *The Book of Legends*, 371, para. 111). This may have been a well-known fact, but we doubt it. Certainly, the proof of that is entirely lacking in literature generally. Moreover, an eighth-century document is not satisfactory as proof of its identification as such in the centuries prior to this.

The greater likelihood is that Jews who had some knowledge of the Italian capital took the notion from allusions to Rome and identified various hills about the city with its foundation even though some of the hills were not inside the city at all. In Scripture, Jerusalem is customarily associated with only one hill, and that is Zion. The references are far too numerous to mention. Anyone with very much acquaintance with the Bible will be aware of this. Josephus claimed it was built on two hills but then went on to describe four hills (*Jewish Wars* 5.4.1-2). If anything, it must be said that he stands as a witness against the idea that in the time of John, it was believed that Jerusalem was a city that sat atop seven hills.

Some have also contended that ancient Babylon itself was set on seven hills, but this is a myth based on a misunderstanding of Revelation 17:9-10. There is no factual basis for this idea. Rome is the only city that

When Was Revelation Written and Why Does It Matter?

has had an unquestioned association with seven hills throughout its history! This is a fact that is not subject to debate.

The notion of the seven kings is more difficult. Those who date the book in the age of Nero cannot identify the first of these "kings" (Roman rulers were not so described) as Augustus, the first official Roman Emperor (which would be the most natural way to read the passage). They cannot do this since Nero falls in line at number five in that schema, but have to connect him with Julius Caesar, who first claimed the title of "Emperor" (*imperator*, originally only a military honorific), even though he is not normally numbered in the listing of the emperors.

Thus they are able to identify the sixth ruler as Nero, while Servius Sulpicius Galba would be the seventh who is said to "continue only a short space" (he ruled for only seven months from 68-69, the first of four emperors who ruled in AD 69, which has come to be known as "the year of the four emperors"). The eighth in this numbering system, who is described by the author as "the beast that was and is not," would be the little-remembered figure Marcus Salvius Otho who reigned only three months from January 15 to April 16 of 69. There is nothing about him or his reign as emperor that would make him important enough for this designation. So, even numbered in this most unnatural way, the only advantage to this approach is to have Nero as the Roman emperor at the time of the writing of the book; the other identifications (seventh and eighth) have little significance at all.

On the other hand, those of us who have confidently dated the book in the reign of emperor Domitian, have taken this list in different ways. Some start the listing with Caligula, being that he was the first of the Roman rulers who served in office after the time of Christ and who shared some of the characteristics of Antiochus Epiphanes as a persecutor and oppressor of the worshippers of the true God (reflecting Daniel's prophecy in Daniel 9:26-27 and Matthew 24:15).

Others begin the list with Tiberius, the emperor under whom Jesus was executed by the Roman procurator, and during whose rule the Jewish persecution of Christians was carried out. One may also begin with the great persecutor, Nero, in which case the seventh ruler is Domitian. Still others begin with the Emperor Augustus, proceeding through Tiberias, Caligula, Claudius, and Nero (the five fallen kings), then Vespa-

"When Will These Things Be?" : Questions on Eschatology

sian (the "one" who "is") and Titus (the other one "who has not come"), though the eighth ruler (v. 11) is sometimes identified as Domitian. Yet, this approach has the difficulty of excluding Galba, Otho, and Vitellius, who reigned only briefly and successively after Nero. Their temporary leadership is an argument for considering them illegitimate, even though some ancient writers saw them as belonging in the line of legitimate emperors (*Sibylline Oracles* and Josephus in his *Wars of the Jews*).

Clearly the theme of persecution and oppression of Christ and His church is the dominant thought considered in each of these approaches. It is worthwhile to note that the writer's intent was at the one and the same time to present a "revelation" of events and subtly "conceal" the details of his methodology and technique. In both these things, he has been very successful. Certainly, the prophecy of the "ten kings," which follows this one, is even more elusive as to its precise meaning. In both instances, in our view, the author intends these listings to be only general in nature and not to be taken as precise historical markers. His choice of the two highly symbolic numbers to designate these listings are seven and ten, which should in and of themselves give the reader pause to reflect as to whether he might have meant them only to be figurative in the first place.

If we are forced to come down at one place in our view of the string of leaders, it would be with those who consider Nero to be the first and Domitian to be the seventh, for Nero was the first to marshal the power of the empire against the disciples of Christ, and Domitian was the seventh in order after him. The eighth, on the other hand, is probably a shadowy future leader, perhaps the last in the line of Roman Emperors to persecute the church (Diocletian) or even the final political leader before the Lord's return. Whichever may be the case, it is certain that he will be no different than anyone who has gone before him. He will be an evil man who will attempt to destroy the saints; he will endure for a short time, and then he will go to perdition. That is the thrust of the author's message to the seven churches of Asia, and that is his lesson for us today. Any man who assays to fight against the eternal purposes of God in the world, no matter his station, will be brought down to hell. The Lord will break in pieces His kingdom and will eternally judge him for his insolence and rebellion against his Creator.

5. *The mysterious number "666."* A good number of writers have contended that the number of the beast's name, which is recorded in

When Was Revelation Written and Why Does It Matter?

13:18 as "666," has the numerical value of the title of *Nero(n) Kaisar* (Nero Caesar) in Hebrew transcription. This view is supported by the unlikely variant reading 616, which also yields the name of Nero when the Latinized spelling is followed. That is certainly one of the possible ways of interpreting this number. It has also been alleged that John was enumerating an abbreviated form in Greek of the full Latin title of Domitian (*Imperator Caesar Domitianus Augustus Germanicus*) and that this is just as likely as the former.

As well, some have argued that the number 616 (another possible reading of the Greek text of the verse) totals the Greek for *Gaios Kaisar* (the name of Caligula). Some others have the initials of all the Roman Emperors from Julius Caesar to Vespasian add up to 666, but to get to this number Otho and Vitellius must be excluded from the total. Obviously, coming to a consensus on this question is not a simple matter. However, it must also be noted that early interpreters (less than one hundred years after John's writing) had different ways of viewing it. Irenaeus (*Against Heresies* 5.30), for example, identified this mysterious number as *Euanthas* (a name that is not identifiable to moderns) *Lateinos* (the Roman Empire), and *Teitan* (the Titans of Greek mythology who rebelled against the gods). Another early conjecture was *arnoume*, a form of the Greek word meaning "to deny" (R. H. Mounce, *Book of Revelation*, 264; W. G. Baines, "The Number of the Beast in Rev. 13:18," *Heythrop Journal* 16:195-196).

The main difficulty with reading it as "Nero Caesar" is that this solution asks us to calculate a Hebrew transliteration of the Greek form of a Latin name and that with a defective spelling! That is quite a complicated procedure! It is worth noting, however, that this defective form of the name (with a missing *yodh*) is attested in a Qumran document dated by a reference to "Nero Caesar." On the other hand, a shift to Hebrew letters is unlikely in that Revelation is written in Greek, and there is no indication in the text itself that the riddle is to be solved by transposing it into another language. How many of John's readers would have been able to understand Hebrew or would have known the numerical equivalents of the letters of the Hebrew alphabet? This question may be difficult to answer definitively, but we would conjecture that in all probability, the answer would be: "not many."

Furthermore, as already noted, the name of Nero was apparently never suggested by the ancient commentators even though his persecut-

"When Will These Things Be?" : Questions on Eschatology

ing zeal was very well known and certainly would have been understood by them to be of such an iconic nature as to make of him a perfect foil for this "beast." Finally, the main problem for those who date the book early is the fact that this beast is not said to be the original persecutor of the church, but a resurrection of the same ("whose death wound was healed," 13:12). This fact changes the whole intentionality of the figure.

Consequently, if the name "Nero Caesar" is really meant by the author to be the proper understanding of the beast's identification, then it is not Nero himself to which he alludes in this mysterious reference, but to his risen self in the form of another to which the writer directs the reader, i.e., the second great persecutor of the church, Domitian. It is as if he has come back from the grave to harass the people of God anew! That is certainly what John intimates in the other figures of the vision, whether the number 666 is meant to suggest that or not.

6. The church at Smyrna did not exist at the time the early date for the Revelation would require. In Revelation 2:8-11, the apostle John addresses a letter to the saints who comprised the congregation in the city of Smyrna. There is one very significant problem with this fact, which makes the early date of Revelation virtually impossible. Not often considered at all by some students of the book, but singularly important is the observation that according to the mid-second-century churchman Polycarp that church did not exist at all in the days of the apostle Paul. For he says that in those days, the congregation there had not yet been established (*Polycarp to the Philippians 11:3* "we had not yet known him [i.e., the Lord]"). This simple statement has enormous evidential value. It implies that when Paul was at work in the region in the late 50s of the Common Era, there were no churches or Christians in the city of Smyrna. Traditionally it is thought that Paul wrote his letter to Titus from Ephesus in Asia Minor in about AD 67. Whether he meant to include that later visit to the area or not, it is hard to determine. Most likely, he wished only to refer to the work Paul had done in Philippi and its environs.

But this is certainly what Polycarp asserts in his letter, which was penned in the year of his martyrdom (155 AD). Although the precise year of Paul's letter to the Philippians is not known with certainty, assuming the imprisonment spoken of there is the one at Caesarea, then the date would range from 56 to 58. This means that the congregation in Smyrna, first mentioned in Revelation 1:11; 2:8, could have been

When Was Revelation Written and Why Does It Matter?

founded no earlier than ca. AD 52-55, and perhaps even as late as 60-64. Moreover, it is possible that during Paul's two-year stay at Ephesus (Acts 19:10), the Christian community at Smyrna saw its beginning (note especially Acts 19:26), though it must be recognized that nothing concrete is known about its actual starting point.

Now it is generally accepted that Paul died in the year AD 67/68. John gives us the impression in Revelation that when he wrote to them, this church had already been tried for a long period of time. So, a pre-AD 70 date for the book simply would not be workable, unless the testimony of the Ante-Nicene father and bishop from Smyrna, the inimitable Polycarp, is to be rejected as unoriginal, unhistorical, or somehow mistaken. In our estimation, this is a view that is utterly without justification and should not, therefore, be taken very seriously.

7. The church at Laodicea is depicted in the letter to them as being rich and well situated (3:17). Historically, however, if we assume that the letter represented the circumstances of the city in the period prior to AD 70, there is very considerable difficulty with this proposition. This absolutely could not have been the case in Laodicea during that time frame. It is well known that the municipality was virtually destroyed by a massive earthquake in AD 60/61. Even though the people of the town were well off enough financially to rebuild their devastated city over time without Imperial support, and proudly wished to show themselves independent of any outside help to do so, it is nevertheless true that it would have taken several years for them to reconstruct its ruined buildings and repair or recreate its demolished infrastructure. To argue that a few short years would permit all of this to take place, to the point where they could again feel extraordinarily secure in their financial well-being, in our estimation, strains the limits of credulity. Yet, that was clearly the case with them. This point alone makes a mid-60s date for the Apocalypse a virtual impossibility.

Too, it is also worth asking, why would John not have made some reference to this very recent and overwhelming tragedy, unless, of course, enough time would have passed when he wrote his book for it to have gradually faded from memory? Yet, there is no reference at all to it or any insinuation about it in the little letter to them. If such a tragic event had happened just a few years before Revelation was penned, why did John fail to mention it? He makes several other easily recognizable references

"When Will These Things Be?" : Questions on Eschatology

to local circumstances in his other letters to the congregations. In their case, he certainly knew that Laodicea was famous for its popular medicinal eye-salve, one of the ways wealth was brought into the city. Why did he not speak of the recent earthquake or the total reconstruction of the city? Perhaps because neither one was very recent.

Now, on the other hand, the later date does not present such a problem. In the mid-90s of the Common Era all of this would have occurred three and one-half decades previous, and so would have been finished long before and thus would have been of no immediate concern. It would have been a distant memory and nothing more. There would have been plenty of time for recovery and rebuilding and ample opportunity for the whole episode to fade into forgetfulness. And that is exactly what had happened.

Consequently, the late date for the letter to the Laodiceans and the book of Revelation generally suits the circumstances of the church at Laodicea much better than dating it in the 60s of the Common Era.

8. *The persecution described in Revelation is one that is said directly to affect the Christians of Asia Minor.* This is a persistent theme throughout the book, beginning with the seven letters to the seven churches. Nero's persecution in AD 64 only affected Christians in Rome. There is no evidence at all that the Christians of Asia Minor were persecuted during that period.

At the same time, it should be noted that this localized event after the conflagration in Rome set a precedent that was eventually followed everywhere (cf. Everett Ferguson, *Church History*, Vol. 1, 64). By the time of Emperor Domitian, some thirty years later, sporadic persecution is known to have been happening all throughout the empire. By that time, the distinction between Christianity and Judaism was widely recognized by Roman authorities, and this had created serious problems for Christians, wherever they lived. So, no such historical challenge can be lodged against the later date as can be for the earlier one.

9. *The imperial cult and its worship in Asia Minor were only enforced as a legal requirement late in the first century and not before.* A very important theme in the book of Revelation is the worship of the image of the emperor (13:4, 8, 12, 15; 14:9, 11; 16:2; 19:20; 20:4; 21:8; 22:15). Worship of the "beast" in the book is all about this, even

When Was Revelation Written and Why Does It Matter?

though, like every other idea presented therein, it is clothed in the mysterious language of figure and symbol. It was a common belief in pagan Roman religion that the dead became deified after their demise. Romans generally venerated their departed ancestors from very early times. The Egyptians worshipped their kings as living gods. The Romans, however, did not follow this practice until later times. In fact, when living rulers attempted to confer deity upon themselves, it was usually met with scorn.

Caligula (37-41), for example, erected a temple to himself in Rome and forced the residents of the city to worship him (Suetonius, *Caligula* 22). In a similar attempt at taking to himself divine glory (ca. 39-40), he tried to have a statue of himself set up in the temple in Jerusalem (Josephus, *Antiquities of the Jews* 18.8.2). In Jewish thought, this represented a serious desecration of the sacred precinct. He ordered the governor of Syria, Petronius, to use whatever military force was necessary to see the deed accomplished. Yet, before Petronius could leave Syria, he was confronted by angry Jews protesting the plan. Philo reported that when Agrippa I heard of what was being planned, he suffered a stroke. He knew it would result in a violent insurrection, ending in much bloodshed. He recovered sufficiently to be able to pen an urgent letter to the emperor, imploring him not to go through with his plan. Petronius, recognizing the danger of starting a revolution by his action, put off his trip to Jerusalem, and in the end, the emperor agreed not to go forward with his decision. Thus, the crisis was averted, and the temple remained unpolluted by pagan idolatry.

Outside the capital, however, veneration of a living emperor was another matter. The first temple dedicated to the "Divine Caesar" was constructed in the city of Pergamum in 29 BC. This could be the reason for John's description of the city as the place "where Satan dwells" (Rev. 2:13). As we noted earlier, Domitian, like Caligula, demanded divine honors, even in the city of Rome. It appears that the region of Asia Minor, where the seven churches found their home, was particularly fond of showing the living emperors divine veneration. Remnants of a temple in Ephesus still stand among the ruins of the ancient metropolis. It seems that it was established for the purpose of worshipping the Flavian dynasty (Vespasian, Titus, and Domitian). The city was granted the honor of being the *neokoros* or "temple-keeper" of the imperial cult. Steven J. Friesen writes:

"When Will These Things Be?" : Questions on Eschatology

> This examination of the temple inscriptions has produced several conclusions about the cult. First, the inscriptions allow us to date the cult precisely since they indicate that the temple was dedicated in 89/90 of the Current Era (CE). This, in turn, leads to the conclusion that the right to establish the provincial cult in Ephesus was granted by Domitian, in the early to mid-eighties of the first century CE (*Twice Neokoros: Ephesus, Asia, and the Cult of the Flavian Imperial Family*, 49).

The importance of the date of the construction and dedication of this shrine cannot be overestimated. As we have seen, veneration of the emperors in the region was an option for residents from very early times. Yet, it was not bound upon them in the provinces until the later period, toward the end of the first century. Certainly, we know, that as the evidence from the Roman governor of Bithynia demonstrates, by the time of the Emperor Trajan (98-117), it had become a capital offense to refuse to participate in the practice (*Letters* 10.96-97; cf. also *Martyrdom of Polycarp* 8; Kyle Pope, *Thinking about AD 70*, 141). It had become a test of allegiance to Rome and the emperor. Further, as we have seen, the Flavian temple was not built until the last decade of the first century. So, the later we move into the first century, the more we may expect to see the requirement, and the more we may expect there to have been persecution on account of Christian resistance to the pagan practice.

It must also be remembered that the persecution under Nero was not about whether Christians were willing to worship at the shrine of the emperor or not. There is no evidence that this represented a matter of any concern at all at the time. Instead, it was about a cruel tyrant who wished to divert public attention away from himself and the burning of the city. As Tacitus noted, "But all human efforts, all the lavish gifts of the emperor, and the propitiations of the gods, did not banish the sinister belief that the conflagration was the result of an order. Consequently, to get rid of the report, Nero fastened the guilt and inflicted the most exquisite tortures on a class hated for their abominations, called Christians by the populace" (Tacitus, *The Annals*, 14.44). At that point in time, worship of the emperor was not required of the citizenry, and it would not be until Domitian pressed the issue, and the provinces, eager to please him, pushed the issue locally. This is a major difficulty for the early date of the book.

When Was Revelation Written and Why Does It Matter?

10. *The literal city of Jerusalem in Palestine could not be the "holy city" of the Revelation*. If the "holy city" is literal Jerusalem in Revelation (11:1-2), and not to be taken as a reference to the church, then there are very serious problems which the prophecies the Revelation predicts. The book predicts the preservation of the "temple of God" and "the altar," and though it says Jerusalem will be trampled underfoot by the nations, it forecasts her ultimate preservation (Erdman, *Revelation of John*, 18-19).

History belies this position as regards the physical city of Jerusalem in the land of Palestine. Literal Jerusalem was, in fact, razed to the ground by Titus and his Roman Legions. It should also be noted that if the temple referred to in the Apocalypse is literal, then the Ark of the Covenant must also be taken as literal. Yet, that presents quite a problem for the interpreter. It is a considerable issue to note that the Ark never came home to Jerusalem after the Babylonian Exile. Therefore, at no time during the New Testament era was there an Ark within the Most Holy Place in the Herodian Temple. The Ark of the Covenant in the Revelation must, therefore, be a purely symbolic reference. It could not be anything else. Does this not suggest that the same thing could be said for the temple that the author spoke about?

If, on the other hand, the temple and city are interpreted in one part of the book to refer to the church, then surely it must be taken to mean the same thing in the rest of the document. The result of this would be that John is predicting the survival of the church in the face of terrible oppression and persecution, and this is, of course, something which proved accurate over the long term. God preserved his spiritual people and so made good on this important promise in the Revelation. And thus, this dating of the work, held by a zealous but very small minority of students and scholars even at the present time, is not only lacking in solid evidence to support it but creates internal inconsistencies which make it almost impossible to justify.

Conclusion

Dating the book of Revelation prior to the fall of Jerusalem is not a viable option on many different fronts. At every turn in the book, there are serious obstacles to that theory. On the other hand, the date for the Apocalypse, which holds that it was written in the latter part of the reign

"When Will These Things Be?" : Questions on Eschatology

of Domitian, is consistent with almost all the evidence from the writings of the early churchmen. Several of these early writers provide solid testimony for its having been written near the end of the first century AD, namely Irenaeus, Clement of Alexandria, Victorinus, and Eusebius. Irenaeus is no doubt the most valuable of the witnesses among the ancient written sources since he wrote very near to the time of the book and seems quite certain of his position on the date and the circumstances of its composition. Writing about AD 180, he declared that the Apocalypse "was seen no long time ago, but almost in our own day, towards the end of Domitian's reign" (*Against Heresies* V. 30.3).

It is difficult to argue with such early evidence, especially given the writer's confidence in the historical accuracy of what he was saying. Being in the unenviable position to have to do so, as is the case with those who argue for the book having been written in the age of Nero, is a most untenable position to be in. To posit that Irenaeus was simply wrong in his assessment of the situation, in spite of his apparent confidence in the matter and relative proximity in time to the events he describes, is a difficult position to defend, especially given the fact that so much of the additional internal evidence seems to fortify and bolster his viewpoint.

Bibliography

Aune, David E. *Revelation 17-22*. Word Biblical Commentary, 52c. Nashville: Thomas Nelson, 1998.

Baines, W. G. "The Number of the Beast in Rev. 13:18." *Heythrop Journal* 16 (1975):195-196

Bettenson, Henry, and Maunder, Chris, eds. *Documents of the Christian Church*. 4th ed. Oxford: University Press, 2011.

Bialik, Hayyim Nahman, et al. *The Book of Legends: Legends from the Talmud and Midrash*. New York: Knopf Doubleday, 1992.

Erdman, Charles R. *The Revelation of John*. Grand Rapids, MI: Baker, 1990.

Ferguson, Everett. *Church History, Volume One: From Christ to the Pre-Reformation: The Rise and Growth of the Church in Its Cultural, Intellectual, and Political Context*. 2nd ed. Grand Rapids, MI: Zondervan Academic, 2013.

When Was Revelation Written and Why Does It Matter?

Fohrer, Georg. *Introduction to the Old Testament.* David E. Green, trans. Nashville: Abingdon Press, 1965.

Friesen, Steven J. *Twice Neokoros: Ephesus, Asia, and the Cult of the Flavian Imperial Family.* Leiden: E. J. Brill, 1993.

Jones, Brian W. *The Emperor Domitian.* London: Routledge, 1992.

King, Daniel H., Sr. *"I Saw the Heaven Opened": A Commentary on Revelation.* Athens, AL: Truth Publications, Inc., 2018.

———. *The Book of Revelation.* Bible Text Books. Athens, AL: Guardian of Truth Foundation, 2010.

Kümmel, Werner Georg. *Introduction to the New Testament.* Nashville, TN: Abingdon, 1973

Mounce, R. H. *The Book of Revelation.* New International Commentary on the New Testament. Grand Rapids: Eerdmans, 1977.

Pope, Kyle. *Thinking about AD 70: Challenging Realized Eschatology.* Athens, AL: Truth Publications, 2019.

Ramsay, William M. *The Church in the Roman Empire.* London: Hodder and Stoughton, 1904.

Rist, Martin. *The Revelation of St. John the Divine.* Vol. 12, The Interpreter's Bible. G. A. Buttrick, ed. New York: Abingdon, 1957.

Wasson, Donald L. "Domitian." *Ancient History Encyclopedia.* www.ancient.eu/domitian/.

Schnelle, Udo, Labahn, Michael, and Lang, Manfred, eds. *Neuer Wettstein: Texte zum Neuen Testament aus Griechentum und Hellenismus.* Corpus Hellensticum. 3 vols. Halle: De Gruyter, 2001.

Personal Eschatology: Men's Track

Where Are the Dead?
    Jesse Flowers

Does the Bible Teach Purgatory?
    Daniel Dow

Does the Bible Teach Reincarnation?
    Steve Wallace

"When Will These Things Be?" Questions on Eschatology

Where Are the Dead?
By Jesse Flowers

Introduction

A subject that many prefer to avoid thinking about, but ultimately is inescapable to one and all is death. The wise man Solomon told us that it is good for men to contemplate death. "Better to go to the house of mourning than to go to the house of feasting, for that is the end of all men; and the living will take it to heart" (Eccl. 7:2). Most people naturally wonder what happens after we die. Do we cease to exist, or is there more than just this earthly realm? And if we do not cease to exist when we die, then where do we go? Do the saved go directly to heaven and the lost to hell? In other words, where are the dead?

The Bible answers these essential questions in both the Old and New Testaments. In the Old Testament, the dead are described as going to a place called "sheol." In the New Testament, the dead are described as

---

Jesse Alan Flowers was born June 21, 1974, in Louisville, KY to Jesse E. Flowers (1941-1992) and Charlotte Flowers. From the age of two, Jesse was raised in Bowling Green, KY where his mother still lives. His father was a gospel preacher throughout his life who was able to hear the younger Jesse preach a few

times before his passing. Jesse has been preaching full-time since 1997 working with congregations in Indiana, Missouri, Texas, and Florida. When Jesse moved to Florida to preach in 2003, he met his wonderful wife, April (Melton). They married in 2005 and have been blessed by the Lord with four precious children, two boys (Jesse and Josiah), and two girls (Anna and Clara). For the past twelve years (2008-present), he has labored with the faithful brethren at the Pruett and Lobit church of Christ in Baytown, TX. The church website is http://www.biblework.com. He can be reached at jafopie@hotmail.com.

going to a place called "hades." The Greek word means "unseen" or the place of departed souls.

When king Hezekiah of Judah was told by the prophet Isaiah to set his house in order, "for you shall die and not live" (Isa. 38:1), he lamented during his sickness, "In the prime of my life I shall go to the gates of sheol; I am deprived of the remainder of my years" (Isa. 38:10). One of the Messianic Psalms of David gives us an essential insight into what part of man goes to sheol following death. "For You will not leave my soul in sheol, nor will You allow Your Holy One to see corruption" (Ps. 16:10).

In Peter's first sermon on Pentecost, he quotes David's prophecy (Acts 2:27), found in Psalm 16:10, and applies it to Jesus Christ. He said that David "spoke concerning the resurrection of the Christ, that His soul was not left in hades, nor did His flesh see corruption" (Acts 2:31). Based on the victorious resurrection of Christ and our future resurrection, Paul declared: "So when this corruptible has put on incorruption, and this mortal has put on immortality, then shall be brought to pass the saying that is written: 'Death is swallowed up in victory.' 'O Death, where is your sting? O hades, where is your victory?'" (1 Cor. 15:54-55). Sheol, or hades, is the unseen realm for the disembodied spirit when it is separated from the body at death. Simply put, hades is the abode of the dead or departed spirits.

Let Us Observe Some Biblical Truths Revealed to Us about Death

All of mankind has an appointment with death (Heb. 9:27; Ps. 89:47-48; Eccl. 8:8; 9:5).

> And as it is appointed for men to die once, but after this, the judgment (Heb. 9:27).

> Remember how short my time is; for what futility have You created all the children of men? What man can live and not see death? Can he deliver his life from the power of the grave? (Ps. 89:47-48).

> No one has power over the spirit to retain the spirit, and no one has power in the day of death. There is no release from that war, and wickedness will not deliver those who are given to it (Eccl. 8:8).

> For the living know that they will die; but the dead know nothing, and they have no more reward, for the memory of them is forgotten (Eccl. 9:5).

Where Are the Dead?

Death spread to all of mankind after Adam sinned (Gen. 2:16-17; Gen. 3:19; Rom. 5:12; 1 Cor. 15:21-22).

And the LORD God commanded the man, saying, "Of every tree of the garden you may freely eat; but of the tree of the knowledge of good and evil you shall not eat, for in the day that you eat of it you shall surely die" (Gen. 2:16-17).

In the sweat of your face you shall eat bread till you return to the ground, for out of it you were taken; for dust you are, and to dust you shall return (Gen. 3:19).

Therefore, just as through one man sin entered the world, and death through sin, and thus death spread to all men, because all sinned (Rom. 5:12).

For since by man came death, by Man also came the resurrection of the dead. For as in Adam all die, even so in Christ all shall be made alive (1 Cor. 15:21-22).

At death, there is a separation between the body and spirit (Jas. 2:26; Eccl. 3:19-21; 12:7).

For as the body without the spirit is dead, so faith without works is dead also (Jas. 2:26).

For what happens to the sons of men also happens to animals; one thing befalls them: as one dies, so dies the other. Surely, they all have one breath; man has no advantage over animals, for all is vanity. All go to one place: all are from the dust, and all return to dust. Who knows the spirit of the sons of men, which goes upward, and the spirit of the animal, which goes down to the earth? (Eccl. 3:19-21).

Then the dust will return to the earth as it was, and the spirit will return to God who gave it (Eccl. 12:7).

Death often comes suddenly and unexpectedly (Eccl. 9:11-12; Jas. 4:13-15).

I returned and saw under the sun that the race is not to the swift, nor the battle to the strong, nor bread to the wise, nor riches to men of understanding, nor favor to men of skill; but time and chance happen to them all. For man also does not know his time: like fish taken in a cruel net, like birds caught in a snare, so the sons of men are snared in an evil time, when it falls suddenly upon them (Eccl. 9:11-12).

"When Will These Things Be?" : Questions on Eschatology

Come now, you who say, "Today or tomorrow we will go to such and such a city, spend a year there, buy and sell, and make a profit;" whereas you do not know what will happen tomorrow. For what is your life? It is even a vapor that appears for a little time and then vanishes away. Instead you ought to say, "If the Lord wills, we shall live and do this or that" (Jas. 4:13-15).

Men fear the bondage of death (Ps. 55:4-5; Heb. 2:14-15).

My heart is severely pained within me, and the terrors of death have fallen upon me. Fearfulness and trembling have come upon me, and horror has overwhelmed me (Ps. 55:4-5).

Inasmuch then as the children have partaken of flesh and blood, He Himself likewise shared in the same, that through death He might destroy him who had the power of death, that is, the devil, and release those who through fear of death were all their lifetime subject to bondage (Heb. 2:14-15).

Death brings sorrow and lamentation (Deut. 34:8; Luke 8:52; John 11:35; 20:11; Acts 8:2).

And the children of Israel wept for Moses in the plains of Moab thirty days. So the days of weeping and mourning for Moses ended (Deut. 34:8).

Now all wept and mourned for her; but He said, "Do not weep; she is not dead, but sleeping" (Luke 8:52).

"Jesus wept" at the grave of His dear friend Lazarus (John 11:35).

But Mary stood outside by the tomb weeping, and as she wept she stooped down and looked into the tomb (John 20:11).

And devout men carried Stephen to his burial, and made great lamentation over him (Acts 8:2).

God has no pleasure in the death of the wicked (Ezek. 33:11; cf. 18:32).

Say to them: "As I live," says the Lord GOD, "I have no pleasure in the death of the wicked, but that the wicked turn from his way and live. Turn, turn from your evil ways! For why should you die, O house of Israel?'" (Ezek. 33:11; cf. 18:32).

Where Are the Dead?

Death is not the end of man's existence (Luke 23:43; Matt. 22:31-32; 2 Cor. 5:1).

As He was dying, Jesus told the repentant thief: "Assuredly, I say to you, today you will be with Me in paradise" (Luke 23:43).

But concerning the resurrection of the dead, have you not read what was spoken to you by God, saying, 'I am the God of Abraham, the God of Isaac, and the God of Jacob'? God is not the God of the dead, but of the living" (Matt. 22:31-32).

For we know that if our earthly house, this tent, is destroyed, we have a building from God, a house not made with hands, eternal in the heavens (2 Cor. 5:1).

Christians do not sorrow over death, as do non-Christians (1 Thess. 4:13).

But I do not want you to be ignorant, brethren, concerning those who have fallen asleep, lest you sorrow as others who have no hope (1 Thess. 4:13).

Those who die in the Lord are blessed (Rev. 14:13).

Then I heard a voice from heaven saying to me, "Write: 'Blessed are the dead who die in the Lord from now on.'" "Yes," says the Spirit, "that they may rest from their labors, and their works follow them" (Rev. 14:13).

The Rich Man and Lazarus

So, since Abel until now, where are the dead? The best and most extensive text in the Bible that provides us with some invaluable insight that can be found in Luke 16:19-31.

There was a certain rich man who was clothed in purple and fine linen and fared sumptuously every day. But there was a certain beggar named Lazarus, full of sores, who was laid at his gate, desiring to be fed with the crumbs which fell from the rich man's table. Moreover the dogs came and licked his sores. So it was that the beggar died, and was carried by the angels to Abraham's bosom. The rich man also died and was buried. And being in torments in hades, he lifted up his eyes and saw Abraham afar off, and Lazarus in his bosom. Then he cried and said, "Father Abraham, have mercy on me, and send Lazarus that he may dip the tip of his finger in water and cool my tongue; for I am tormented in this flame." But Abraham said, "Son, remember that in

"When Will These Things Be?" : Questions on Eschatology

your lifetime you received your good things, and likewise Lazarus evil things; but now he is comforted and you are tormented. And besides all this, between us and you there is a great gulf fixed, so that those who want to pass from here to you cannot, nor can those from there pass to us." Then he said, "I beg you therefore, father, that you would send him to my father's house, for I have five brothers, that he may testify to them, lest they also come to this place of torment." Abraham said to him, "They have Moses and the prophets; let them hear them." And he said, "No, father Abraham; but if one goes to them from the dead, they will repent." But he said to him, "If they do not hear Moses and the prophets, neither will they be persuaded though one rise from the dead."

I am so thankful for these verses that are unique to Luke's gospel. By the inspiration of the Holy Spirit, "the beloved physician" (Col. 4:14) relates to us an incredible story from the teaching of Christ. Our Lord gives us a much better understanding of what happens to us when we pass from this physical life. It is a passage that should provide great comfort and assurance to faithful children of God. However, it is also a passage that should produce great fear and dread among those who live wicked and rebellious lives to the will of God. Furthermore, it effectively answers the question—"where are the dead?"

After the deaths of Lazarus and the rich man, their spirits departed their physical bodies and were transported to hades (16:23), the abode of disembodied spirits. However, we find them in two very separate and distinct compartments in the Hadean realm.

Paradise

Following his death, Lazarus is described in the text as being "carried by the angels to Abraham's bosom" (16:22). On the cross, Jesus refers to this same place as "paradise." Christ spoke words of comfort and reassurance to the repentant thief when He said to him, "Assuredly, I say to you, today you will be with Me in paradise" (Luke 23:43). *Strong's Greek Dictionary of the New Testament* defines "paradise" as "a park, that is, (specifically) an Eden (place of future happiness)" (SECB, 54). We know that "paradise" is not equivalent to heaven, for even after Jesus rose from the grave, He declared to Mary: "Do not cling to Me, for I have not yet ascended to My Father" (John 20:17). Also recall what Peter preached on Pentecost when he quoted and applied David's prophecy (Ps. 16:8-11) to Christ, "that His soul was not left in hades" (Acts 2:31). This portion

Where Are the Dead?

of hades seems to be a place of rest, comfort (16:25), and beauty for the righteous.

Torment

Following his death, the rich man's spirit was "in torments in hades" (16:23). He is pictured as being able to see Lazarus in the bosom of Abraham. He is experiencing tremendous pain and grief, longing for any sort of comfort and reprieve, such as Lazarus being sent to cool, even his tongue, with water (16:24). Yet, his request was denied for two reasons: (1) During his lifetime, he had received good things and Lazarus evil things; now he is comforted, and the rich man is tormented, 16:25. Colly Caldwell writes, "When one's focus is on the things of the world, whatever "good" things he receives in the world will be his reward. He will receive no other "good" in the next life (Matt. 6:1, 2, 5, 6, 16). What he was experiencing now was determined by the way he conducted his life one earth. He had been selfish and uncaring. He was receiving just retribution, i.e., what was due" (Caldwell, 893). (2) Abraham then stated to the rich man: "And besides all this, between us and you there is a great gulf fixed so that those who want to pass from here to you cannot, nor can those from there pass to us" (16:26). Caldwell adds, "This huge spiritual chasm, gorge, or ravine is fixed in the sense that it is permanent, inviolable, and irreversible. Abraham could not change that. God intends that there be a definite distinction between the environment in which the righteous will live and the environment in which the unrighteous will live after death" (Caldwell, 894). This truth taught by Jesus makes it abundantly clear that there will be no more opportunities to change our eternal destiny following death (cf. Heb. 9:27).

This story (or parable) reveals to us that physical death does not end one's existence (16:22-23). There is consciousness after death. (1) We still have sight. The rich man "saw" Abraham afar off (16:23). (2) We still have feelings. Lazarus was "comforted" while the rich man was "tormented" (16:25). (3) We can still communicate. The rich man and Abraham conversed with one another (16:24-31). (4) We still have memory and reasoning abilities. The rich man remembered his five brothers still alive on earth and knew they would end up in torments as well if they did not repent (16:27-28). (5) Another important lesson from this text in Luke is that the word of God, the Scriptures, are all sufficient in instructing mankind in the knowledge of the truth (1 Tim. 2:3-4; 2 Tim. 3:16-17), in bringing them to repentance (Acts 2:38; 3:19; 17:30; 26:18, 20), in order to set them free from their sins (John 8:32).

Where Are the Dead?

The Bible conclusively reveals to us that the dead are in hades. The teaching by our Lord in Luke 16:19-31 serves as a sobering reminder to one and all that it matters how we live our lives before God upon this earth (cf. 2 Cor. 5:10). In death, we will either be in a wonderful place of comfort or a terrible place of torment. Where our spirit will be in hades will all depend on whether we obeyed the gospel (Mark 16:15-16; Rom. 1:16; 2 Thess. 1:8) and remained faithful until death (Rev. 2:10; 1 Cor. 15:58). In death (i.e., in hades), our fate is sealed and cannot be altered. No wonder the psalmist wrote: "Precious in the sight of the LORD is the death of His saints" (Ps. 116:15). No wonder a voice from heaven announced: "Write: 'Blessed are the dead who die in the Lord from now on.' 'Yes,' says the Spirit, 'that they may rest from their labors, and their works follow them'" (Rev. 14:13).

Misunderstandings and Errors about Death
Hades Is Not Hell.

Hades, the realm of the dead or departed spirits, is distinguished in the Scriptures from hell (*gehenna*), the place of eternal punishment following judgment (Matt. 25:41, 46; Mark 9:43-48; 2 Thess. 1:7-9). Jesus taught that hell is the place where "both soul and body" are destroyed by God (Matt. 10:28). Whereas, hades is the realm of departed spirits awaiting the resurrection and judgment.

There Is Separation in Hades.

God does separate the just from the unjust in hades before the final judgment. Our eternal fate is sealed at death (Heb. 9:27). Even in the Hadean realm, Jesus spoke of a great gulf that is fixed (Luke 16:26) separating the good from the evil. One cannot cross over to either side. Although a separation has occurred prior to the judgment day, still following the resurrection of the just and unjust (John 5:28-29), all of mankind must come before the throne of Christ to bow the knee, confess to God, give an account of their earthly life, and receive their eternal reward or condemnation (Matt. 25:31-46; Rom. 2:1-11; 14:10-12; 2 Cor. 5:10).

Where Are the Dead?

Hades Is Not Yet Emptied.
Hades, the realm of departed spirits, has not already been emptied as realized eschatology teaches. *Nelson's New Illustrated Bible Dictionary* defines "Eschatology" as "the study of what will happen when all things are consummated at the end of history, particularly centering on the event known as the Second Coming of Christ. The word comes from two Greek words, *eschatos* (last) and *logos* (study)—thus its definition as 'the study of last things'" (NNIBD, s.v. "Eschatology"). Among the various definitions that are offered for *eschatos*, the latest edition of Bauer's Lexicon says that it "pertains to being the final item in a series, *least, last* in time" (BDAG, 397). The *International Standard Bible Encyclopedia* states: "By 'eschatology,' or doctrine of last things, is meant the ideas entertained at any period on the future life, the end of the world (resurrection, judgment...) and the eternal destinies of mankind" (ISBE, 972). "Realized" signifies accomplishment; therefore, "realized eschatology" (RE) is a doctrine of completed last things. The doctrine claims that all end-time prophecy was fulfilled (realized, accomplished) in AD 70 at the destruction of Jerusalem.

The things that occurred in AD 70, according to realized eschatology: (1) The Second Coming of Jesus Christ. (2) The resurrection of the dead (i.e., hades emptied). (3) Judgment day of the Lord. (4) Establishment of the new covenant. (5) Kingdom fully established. (6) Reception of the eternal inheritance.

This doctrine is blatantly false, has shipwrecked the faith of some (cf. 2 Tim. 2:17-18), and the gospel of Christ is twisted and perverted to reach such conclusions. The fact of the matter is, the Scriptures do not teach that the end of all things has already taken place.

Christ has not returned a second time yet, as proponents of realized eschatology claim. When Christ does return, the New Testament teaches that it will be "the end" (1 Cor. 15:24), the present heavens and earth will be destroyed (2 Pet. 3:7, 10), and all the dead will hear the voice of Christ and come forth (John 5:28-29). This will be the incredible moment when "death and hades delivered up the dead who were in them. And they were judged, each one according to his works. Then death and hades were cast into the lake of fire" (Rev. 20:13-14).

"When Will These Things Be?" : Questions on Eschatology

Mike Willis writes, "Physical evidences demonstrate that the resurrection did not occur in AD 70. If the dead were raised in AD 70, there should be no physical bodies found in tombs that date before AD 70. The existence of Egyptian mummies and other ancient bodies demonstrates that the resurrection did not occur in AD 70" (Willis, 55).

Man Is More than Flesh and Blood
Despite the doctrine of materialism (those who deny humans have an immortal soul that exists beyond death), *the inspired word of God teaches that man is more than just flesh and blood* (Gen. 1:26-27; 2:7; Eccl. 12:7; 1 Thess. 5:23; Jas. 2:26). The prophet Zechariah wrote, "Thus says the LORD, who stretches out the heavens, lays the foundation of the earth, and forms the spirit of man within him" (12:1). In telling the story of the rich man and Lazarus (Luke 16:19-31), Christ completely refutes the error of materialism! These two men both died physically but continue to exist in hades. Joe Price penned, "Man is composed of body and soul, of flesh and spirit... We have an 'outward man' (the flesh) and an 'inward man' (the spirit): the first is temporal, mortal; the second is immortal and continues beyond the death of its body" (Price 76-77, *The Parable of the Rich Man and Lazarus*). Jesus asked the heart-cutting question, "For what profit is it to a man if he gains the whole world, and loses his own soul? Or what will a man give in exchange for his soul?" (Matt. 16:26). When rulers of the Jews were casting stones at him, Stephen called upon the Lord to receive his spirit (Acts 7:59). "The materialist (i.e., Jehovah's Witness, Seventh-Day Adventist, etc.), who claims that man is made of only body and breath, does not believe what Stephen believed. Stephen believed the inward part of man returns to God" (Harkrider, 82-83). Although Abraham, Isaac, and Jacob had been deceased for a good while, Jehovah declared to Moses at the burning bush, "I am the God of Abraham, the God of Isaac, and the God of Jacob," not "I was," but "I am," present tense. God is not the God of the dead, but of the living! "We are more than flesh and bones, and our lives should reflect our understanding of this truth" (Price, 77).

Conclusion

Where are the dead? In other words, where are our deceased fathers, mothers, sons, daughters, brothers, sisters, grandparents, friends, and brethren? Their spirits are dwelling presently in the Hadean realm. If they died in the Lord, they are in comfort. If they died outside of the

Where Are the Dead?

Lord, they are in torment and do not wish for their loved ones on earth to join them there in death. The dead await the voice of the One who is the Judge of the living and the dead (Acts 10:42) to summon them to "come forth—those who have done good, to the resurrection of life, and those who have done evil, to the resurrection of condemnation" (John 5:29).

The apostle John recorded:

> And I saw the dead, small and great, standing before God, and books were opened. And another book was opened, which is the Book of Life. And the dead were judged according to their works, by the things which were written in the books. The sea gave up the dead who were in it, and death and hades delivered up the dead who were in them. And they were judged, each one according to his works. Then death and hades were cast into the lake of fire. This is the second death. And anyone not found written in the Book of Life was cast into the lake of fire (Rev. 20:12-15).

Jesus said, "I am He who lives, and was dead, and behold, I am alive forevermore. Amen. And I have the keys of hades and of death" (Rev. 1:18). Because of Jesus no longer must we have a fear of death (Heb. 2:14-15). Because of Jesus, "then shall be brought to pass the saying that is written: 'Death is swallowed up in victory.' 'O Death, where is your sting? O hades, where is your victory?'" (1 Cor. 15:54-55). Because of Jesus, those who have died can be described as having "fallen asleep" (1 Thess. 4:13). The Son of God declared: "I am the resurrection and the life. He who believes in Me, though he may die, he shall live. And whoever lives and believes in Me shall never die" (John 11:25-26). And so, we exclaim with our brother Paul, "But thanks be to God, who gives us the victory through our Lord Jesus Christ" (1 Cor. 15:57).

Bibliography

BDAG = Arndt, William, F. W. Gingrich, F. W. Danker, and Walter Bauer. *A Greek-English Lexicon of the New Testament and Other Early Christian Literature.* Chicago: University of Chicago Press, 2000.

Caldwell, C. G. "Colly." *Truth Commentaries: Luke.* Bowling Green, KY: Guardian of Truth Foundation, 2011.

Harkrider, Robert. *Acts. Book 1. A Study of Conversions.* Russellville, AL: Impressive Image Production, 1989.

ISBE = *International Standard Bible Encyclopedia*, James Orr, ed. Vol. 2. Peabody, MA: Hendrickson Publishers, 1996.

NKJV = New King James Version. 1996 Update. Nashville, TN: Holman Bible Publishers.

NNIBD = Youngblood, Ronald F., F. F. Bruce, and R. K. Harrison, eds. *Nelson's New Illustrated Bible Dictionary*. Nashville, TN: Thomas Nelson, Inc., 1995.

Price, Joe R. *"The Parable of the Rich Man and Lazarus:" The Parables of Jesus*. Mike Willis, ed., 95-98. Bowling Green, KY: Guardian of Truth Foundation, 2005.

SECB = *Strong's Exhaustive Concordance of the Bible*, 1890.

Willis, Mike. "Realized Eschatology: The AD 70 Doctrine." *"Then Cometh the End. . ." A Study of Eschatology*, 77-82. Bowling Green, KY: Guardian of Truth Foundation, 1999.

Does the Bible Teach Purgatory?
By Daniel and Diana Dow

Introduction
What is purgatory? To fully answer and understand what purgatory is, we must first delve into the Catholic doctrine concerning sin. According to the Roman Catholic catechism, there are two kinds of sin: Mortal and Venial.

Mortal (Deadly) Sins
Mortal (Deadly) Sins are considered to be "grave violation(s) of God's Law. The Catechism teaches that such sins "destroy charity in the heart" and turn man away from God. Pope Gregory I is credited as issuing the first list of seven deadly sins in the late sixth-century. Catholicism

---

Daniel Dow was born July 18, 1960 in Houston, TX where he attended the Bellaire Church of Christ for 20 years. He married Diana Brock of Amarillo, TX on August 26, 1981 (38 yrs.). The Dows have six sons, four daughter-in-laws (Matthew and Sarah, James and Melody, Andrew and Heather, Timothy and Angela, Jonathan, Benjamin) and nine grandchildren: Everlee, Larkyn, Titus, Trace, Arya, Bella, Josiah, Amos, Levi). The Dows also had an infant son, David, who passed away at six days of life. All of their children are faithful servants of the Lord. Daniel attended Tyler Jr. College and Florida College. He has preached the Gospel for 38 years. Daniel trained with W.R. Jones at the Woodland Hills Church of Christ in Conroe, TX. His first full-time work was with the North Jackson St. Church of Christ in Houston, MS (5 years). He has since labored with the Broadway St. Church of Christ in La Porte, TX (9 yrs.—Working again with W.R. Jones and also Robert Goodman.), Caprock Church of Christ in Lubbock, TX (5 yrs.), Huntington Church Christ in Huntington, TX (13 yrs.). Daniel presently preaches for the Borden St. Church of Christ in Sinton, TX (5 yrs.). He can be reached at: dow1960@juno.com.

teaches that a mortal sin involves three things: (1) Its object is a grave or grievous matter (exemplified in the Ten Commandments: murder, theft, adultery, coveting, etc.). (2) It is committed with full knowledge. (3) It is deliberately and freely committed. Mortal sins cut the sinner off from God's saving grace, and he is condemned to eternal damnation in hell unless the sin is confessed and repented.

Venial (Forgivable) Sins

Venial (Forgivable) Sins are considered to be less serious. While these sins weaken the charity in the heart, they do not result in a complete separation from God, nor do they require the consequence of eternal punishment. Venial comes from the Latin word *venia*, which means "pardon." Venial sins can be repaired, and purgatory is the place where these venial sins and their stains are removed.

The Catholic catechism teaches that nothing defiled can enter into heaven. Therefore, anyone less than perfect must first be purified before being admitted in the presence of God. In his book, *The Catholic Catechism, A Contemporary Catechism of the Teachings of the Catholic Church*, Jon A. Hardon explains that this doctrine of purgatory was carved out throughout the centuries by the Church's reflection on revelation. Therefore they concluded, "there exists purgatory, in which the souls of the just who die with the stains of sin are cleansed by expiation before they are admitted to heaven" (273-274).

The Maryknoll Catholic Dictionary defines purgatory as "The state in which souls exist for a time after death to work out the temporal punishment due to venial sins or forgiven mortal sins. The soul is purified in this state to prepare it for its entrance into the delights of heaven" (474).

Purgatory comes from the verb "purge," meaning to purify or cleanse. Note that purgatory is a temporary state.

The History and Origin of the Doctrine of Purgatory

Presently, there are three major religions that believe in purgatory: (1) the Roman Catholic Church (Western), (2) the Greek Orthodox Church (Eastern), and (3) Orthodox Jews. "Purgatory" is never mentioned in the Bible, but is a doctrine that developed over many centuries.

It has been suggested that the Jews of the Babylonian captivity returned to Jerusalem, having been influenced by an ancient Persian reli-

Does the Bible Teach Purgatory?

gion. In his book *Ancient Near Eastern History and Culture*, William H. Striving writes,

> Not only was Zoroastrian eschatology incorporated into early Christianity through Judaism, but also through Mithraism, a Roman religion out of the early Persian faith that became Christianity's chief rival in the first three centuries CE. From Mithraism the church borrowed the concept of purgatory (which is not found in the Bible), as well as December the 25th as the date of Jesus' birthday and the tradition that he was born in a cave (351).

Please note that Zoroastrianism or Mazdayasna is one of the world's oldest continual practicing religions.

Pagan writers and Greek philosophers like Plato and Heraclides Ponticus had their concept of purgatory—an intermediary place where souls would spend an undetermined amount of time after death before moving on to a higher plane of existence. Where was this intermediary place? Various places have been named: beyond the stars, the Milky Way, between the earth and moon, or the backside of the moon, etc.

One might rightly conclude this influence of both Ancient Persian and Hellenistic religions likely perverted the Jewish religion bringing about erroneous thoughts concerning the Hadean realm.

Some of the first signs of this doctrine permeating in the Catholic Church emerged in the sixth century from Pope Gregory I "The Great" (AD 593). Seven hundred years later, in the thirteenth century, Innocent IV (1243-54) writes a letter to believers in Greece trying to unite the Eastern and Western segments of the Catholic Church using the doctrine of purgatory as common ground. Twenty years later (1274), the Second Council of Lyon made a formal declaration on the doctrine of purgatory: henceforth, it was to be considered a formal creed on which both sides should agree. While the East continued to object to the concept of material fire in purgatory, the Council of Lyon pressed two things: (1) The existence of purgatory and (2) the usefulness of prayer and pious works to be offered for the dead. The subject was again addressed in the sixteenth century when the Council of Trent literally ordered: "the bishops to be diligently on guard that the true doctrine of purgatory be preached everywhere, and that Christians be instructed in it, believe it, and adhere to it."

"When Will These Things Be?" : Questions on Eschatology

Does the Bible Teach Purgatory?

While preaching for the Broadway Street church of Christ in La Porte, TX, our family encountered a family who professed to be Catholic in faith. After Diana established a friendship with this woman, they began to talk and casually discuss the Bible. She politely accepted our local bulletin, and Diana kept planting the seed of God's word, which eventually led to doubts and spiritual concerns about her Catholic convictions.

Diana's friend freely acknowledged that she did not know God's word, but before taking any action, sought the counsel of Father Tom, the local priest of the Catholic Church in La Porte. He told her to stop talking about these matters with Diana immediately. He said that she was not knowledgeable and, therefore, unable to discuss the Bible. Such matters were reserved for the Clergy. In her final meeting with Diana, she said Father Tom told her to stop reading and receiving our bulletin. She handed Diana a copy of a lesson booklet entitled *Beginning Apologetics: How to Explain and Defend Catholic Faith*, saying, "Maybe this will help you understand."

Ironically, in a section of this booklet, *"A Beginner's Guide to Apologetics"* (# 8) reads: "Do not accept the Protestant interpretation of a verse when it contradicts Catholic doctrine. Read it yourself—in context—and show the other side how the verse can be interpreted to support the Catholic position. Get them to see how they often get their beliefs from their denomination, and then twist the verses to make them Biblical." Sadly, he pushed her away from true Bible teaching to sow the seeds of Catholicism.

We will approach the subject of purgatory by considering the various "proof texts" used by those who believe in purgatory and examine them in the light of their biblical context.

Matthew 5:25-26

> Agree with thine adversary quickly, while thou art with him in the way; lest haply the adversary deliver thee to the judge, and the judge deliver thee to the officer, and thou be cast into prison. Verily I say unto thee, thou shalt by no means come out thence, till thou have paid the last farthing.

Those who believe in and profess the existence of purgatory see this realm described in the phrase "thou be cast into prison." They also con-

Does the Bible Teach Purgatory?

sider the phrase "thou shalt by no means come out thence, till thou have paid the last farthing" (v. 26) to describe the pains suffered to purify the stained soul.

Contextually, this passage is found in Jesus's Sermon on the Mount, which generally addressed the new way of life in Christ. These attributes define the disciple of Christ. This portion of the sermon addressed the subject of anger and its effect upon our worship of God. It is not a difficult message to digest. Jesus taught that we are to repair strained relationships and make amends with brethren lest we allow the officials and courts of this world to judge us, and we end up in prison for wrongdoing. We are to strive to be at peace with all men (Rom. 12:18-21). However, Jesus said nothing about the afterlife or "purgatory."

Matthew 12:32
> And whosoever shall speak a word against the Son of man, it shall be forgiven him; but whosoever shall speak against the Holy Spirit, it shall not be forgiven him, neither in this world, nor in that which is to come.

Pope Gregory the Great used Matthew 12:32 to defend his belief in purgatory. He wrote,

> We must believe that before the day of judgment there is a purgatory fire for certain small sins: because our Saviour saith, that he which speaketh blasphemy against the holy Ghost, that it shall not be forgiven him, neither in this world, nor in the world to come. Out of which sentence we learn, that some sins are forgiven in this world, and some others may be pardoned in the next. . . as I said, we have not to believe but only concerning little and very small sins, as, for example, daily idle talk, immoderate laughter, negligence in the care of our family. . . ignorant errors in matters of no great weight: all which sins be punished after death, if men procured not pardon and remission for them in their lifetime (*Dialogues* 4:39—AD 594).

In the book, *The Faith of Our Fathers*, James Cardinal Gibbons, wrote that Jesus's teaching "leaves us to infer that there are some sins which will be pardoned in the life to come." He concludes this pardon is in an intermediate state called purgatory (213).

The idea is this: Since sin does not exist in heaven and one cannot receive forgiveness in hell, any remission of sins in the "next world" can only refer to purgatory! However, in the above passage, is Jesus teaching us about a third realm that exists after death?

"When Will These Things Be?" : Questions on Eschatology

In Matthew 12, Jesus demonstrates that He is the Lord of Sabbath (vv. 1-8) by performing miracles (vv. 9-21) and casting out demons (vv. 22-37). This turned into an accusation by the Pharisees that Jesus's miraculous works originated with "Beelzebub, the prince of the demons" (v. 24). Such charges spoke against, not the Son of Man, but instead spoke against and denied the power of the Holy Spirit. For man to defy God's Spirit is unforgivable because it is God's Spirit that guides, directs, and reveals through the Word (John 14:26; 16:13). There is no hope of forgiveness for the one who rejects the work of the Holy Spirit (who reveals and confirms God's word). If a man does not desire or seek after the forgiveness which is offered—there is no forgiveness "*in this world, nor in that which is to come.*"

Jesus is speaking to the seriousness of this blasphemous sin of rejection (Mark 3:29). "The world to come" (12:32) refers to the time when the souls of men will experience an eternal existence, either eternal life or eternal damnation. There is no opportunity to seek forgiveness when one defiantly rejects the Holy Spirit; whether it is right now in "this [present physical] world" or in "that [world] which is to come." It is a far stretch to insert the doctrine and place of purgatory into Matthew 12. There is no implication or inference that such a place exists. This is reading something into the text that simply does not belong. The Bible does not teach purgatory in this text.

1 Corinthians 3:15

> If any man's work shall be burned, he shall suffer loss: but he himself shall be saved; yet so as through fire.

Again Pope Gregory defended the existence of purgatory when he wrote:

> For when St. Paul saith, . . . "if any man's work burn, he shall suffer detriment, but himself shall be saved, yet so as by fire." For although these words may be understood of the fire of tribulation, which men suffer in this world: yet if any will interpret them of the fire of Purgatory, which shall be in the next life: then must he carefully consider, that the apostle said not that he may be saved by fire, that buildeth upon this foundation iron, brass, or lead, that is, the greater sort of sins, and therefore more hard, and consequently not remissible in that place: but wood, hay, stubble, that is, little and very light sins, which the fire doth easily consume. Yet, we have here further to consider, that none can be there purged, no, not for

426

Does the Bible Teach Purgatory?

the least sins that be, unless in his lifetime he deserved by virtuous works to find such favour in that place (*Dialogues* 4:39—AD 594).

Again the idea is promoted that this cannot refer to heaven because there is no suffering in heaven. It cannot refer to hell because no one can be saved, so it must refer to a temporal loss of God and a temporary purifying suffrage, i.e., purgatory. Man's salvation will come by going through the fires of purgatory. Although it is vehemently denied (as in Pope Gregory's dialogue), this has a certain taste of a "second chance" to be saved after death.

The first four chapters of 1 Corinthians address the problems of division. The saints at Corinth had their favorite preachers and rallied around them. Paul was teaching the Corinthian Christians that all of these men were the same. They faithfully worked together and in harmony under God's direction and increase. Paul spoke of the privilege of preaching the gospel and laying a foundation upon which other men, like Cephas or Apollos, could build. Notice the words of Paul:

> But if any man buildeth on the foundation gold, silver, costly stones, wood, hay, stubble; each man's work shall be made manifest: for the day shall declare it, because it is revealed in fire; and the fire itself shall prove each man's work of what sort it is. If any man's work shall abide which he built thereon, he shall receive a reward. If any man's work shall be burned, he shall suffer loss: but he himself shall be saved; yet so as through fire (1 Cor. 3:12-15).

Each teacher's work, that is, the individuals whom he teaches and those who obey the gospel through his influence, will eventually have their faith tested through the fires of trials and persecutions (Jas. 1:2-3 1 Peter 1:6-7; 4:12). Some of these people will prove to be strong and solid (i.e., like gold, silver, and costly stones), but some will show themselves to be weak and unstable (i.e., like hay and stubble). Every individual has the responsibility of standing firm during these tests. Some will emerge stronger and purer; sadly, some will not endure. They will be consumed in the fire, and they will be lost eternally.

In the lesson book *Then Comes The End*—"The Doctrine of Purgatory," Mike Willis wrote,

> The work that a preacher does in teaching others the gospel will be tested. Those who are converted will be tested by the fires of temptation to see if they remain faithful. Some who are lost will be lost because of

"When Will These Things Be?" : Questions on Eschatology

the wrong kind of work that was done by the preacher; others will be lost in spite of the best work that one can do. Those whose works are so destroyed nevertheless will be saved (34).

Even if a teacher loses his weaker converts/students, he will be saved "yet so as through fire." This reminds us of God's warning to Ezekiel: "Yet if thou warn the wicked, and he turn not from his wickedness, nor from his wicked way, he shall die in his iniquity; but thou hast delivered thy soul" (Ezek. 3:19). No doubt, the sad loss of this student (i.e., the destruction of his work) is a part of the fiery trials and tests that the teacher himself must faithfully pass through.

There is absolutely nothing in this text to suggest a place called "purgatory," nor a purging fire that occurs after death. It seems as if Pope Gregory I clearly understood and even acknowledged the text's meaning as "the fire of tribulation" but in the same breath, theorized "*If* any will interpret them of the fire of Purgatory. . ." However, the Bible does not teach of purgatory in this passage.

1 Peter 3:18-20

Because Christ also suffered for sins once, the righteous for the unrighteous, that he might bring us to God; being put to death in the flesh, but made alive in the spirit; in which also he went and preached unto the spirits in prison, that aforetime were disobedient, when the longsuffering of God waited in the days of Noah, while the ark was a preparing, wherein few, that is, eight souls, were saved through water.

The phrase "the spirits in prison, that aforetime were disobedient," is supposedly a reference to purgatory. The Catholic view is that Peter is describing a temporary state for disobedient souls who were eventually saved. The *Beginning Apologetic* workbook said, "At the very least, it proves that a third place can exist between heaven and hell. At the most, it proves the Catholic doctrine of purgatory (32)."

Also thrown into this mix is 1 Peter 4:6, "For unto this end was the gospel preached even to the dead, that they might be judged indeed according to men in the flesh, but live according to God in the spirit." It is taught that "the dead that. . . live according to God in the spirit" are in purgatory, a "prison for disobedient spirits."

When addressing the Hadean territory, the Bible speaks of only two places: (1) Torments (tartarus) (Luke 16:1-13; 2 Pet. 2:4; Jude 6), and

Does the Bible Teach Purgatory?

(2) paradise (Abraham's Bosom) (Luke 16:1-13; 23:43; cf. Acts 2:25-32). The place of torments is described as a place of anguish and fire (Luke 16:24-25). Of these two realms, torment alone would be considered the place of the disobedient spirits or prison to hold the spiritually dead, while they await their final judgment. Purgatory (the third alternative?) is never mentioned.

The Hebrew writer reminds us, "And inasmuch as it is appointed unto men once to die, and after this cometh judgment" (Heb. 9:27). It- would seem that after death, a man (righteous or unrighteous) is judged or separated into one of these two places, and his eternal destiny is sealed. There he awaits his final judgment or sentence rendered by the Great Judge at the Second Coming of Christ Jesus. There is no third chamber for a man to work off or purge himself of the stains of sin. There is no "second chance" to make things right. We either die right, or we are separated from God eternally.

What about Extra-Biblical Sources (2 Macc. 12:44-45)?

> And when he had made a gathering throughout the company to the sum of two thousand drachms of silver, he sent it to Jerusalem to offer a sin offering, doing therein very well and honestly, in that he was mindful of the resurrection: For if he had not hoped that they that were slain should have risen again, it had been superfluous and vain to pray for the dead. And also in that he perceived that there was great favour laid up for those that died godly, it was an holy and good thought. Whereupon he made a reconciliation for the dead, that they might be delivered from sin (2 Macc. 12:44-45)

For many Catholics, the events recorded in 2 Maccabees is the clearest affirmation of the existence of purgatory, although the term "purgatory" is also absent in the Maccabean text. The Catholic booklet, *Beginning Apologetics*, states: "This passage from Maccabees is a *proof text*. It explicitly affirms an intermediate state where the faithful departed make atonement for their sins." Moreover, this is where Catholics find the "authority" for the practice of praying for the dead with a view to their afterlife salvation and purification. Actually, praying for the dead has been a common practice throughout history (Zoroastrianism or Mazdayasna, Chinese Buddhists, Hindus, Muslims, even the Jews pray for the dead at the Wailing Wall.).

This text of 2 Maccabees 12 tells the story about a "noble" Jewish priest, Judas Maccabeus, who led a revolt against the Seleucid Empire.

"When Will These Things Be?" : Questions on Eschatology

After some of his men died heroically in battle, it was discovered that they had in their possession, hidden under their tunics, sacred amulets devoted to the idols of Jamnia. Only in death were their sins discovered. The soldiers gathered a collection and sent it to Jerusalem that a "sin offering" might be offered on the dead's behalf. So, what about this text? Does it offer undeniable proof for the concept of purgatory?

2 Maccabees is an apocryphal book. The term Apocrypha means "hidden things." The Apocrypha is a selection of fifteen books included in the Catholic Bible. Although these books were not found in the Hebrew Bible, they were included in the Latin Vulgate. Throughout history, the divine inspiration of these books has been challenged and called into question. Claims have been made that they should never have been included in the canon in the first place. The Greek Orthodox fathers referred to them as "disputed" books. Martin Luther described the Apocrypha as "books which are not regarded as equal to the Holy Scriptures, and yet are profitable and good to read." In April 1546, after Luther's death and in response to constant challenges concerning their divine authorship, the Council of Trent officially and "infallibly" declared these books to be the sacred second canon (deuterocanonical books). This was sixteen centuries after the truth had been fully and finally revealed (2 Tim. 3:16-17; Jude 3; etc.).

Beginning Apologetics offered this last attempt to convince us to accept the doctrine of purgatory:

> Even if Maccabees is rejected as Scripture, there can be no doubt that, as history, the book accurately reflects the religious character of the Jews of the second century BC. A little more than one hundred years before Christ, Jews prayed for their dead (and still do today). In fact, some of the earliest Christian liturgies (worship services) include prayers for the dead. Ancient Christian tomb inscriptions from the second and third centuries frequently contain an appeal for prayers for the dead. This practice makes sense only if early Christians believed in purgatory even if they did not use that name for it. In fact, the practice of praying for the dead was universal among Christians for fifteen centuries before the Reformation.

First, if "Maccabees is rejected as Scripture," there will always be a doubt, and it must be accepted as fallible. Secondly, just because men "pray for the dead" does not necessarily mean that it is of God. An in-

Does the Bible Teach Purgatory?

scription on a tomb does not determine Bible authority. Making up a place named "purgatory" does not mean it really exists. It doesn't make sense that a "practice" determines God's approval. These are all examples of poor apologetics. These things may explain and defend the Catholic faith, but they are not divinely inspired.

Does the Bible Teach that We Should Offer Prayers for the Dead?

Interestingly, according to Catholic theology, those who die with venial sin must purge themselves of these lesser sins through enduring the fires of purgatory. Yet, the pains of these sins can be relieved, and their time spent in purgatory shortened by their friends who are left in the realm of the living. The 1439 Council of Florence declared:

> If the truly penitent die in the love of God, before they have made satisfaction by worthy fruits of penance for their sins of commission and omission, their souls are purified by purgatorial pains after death; and that for relief from these pains they are benefitted by the suffrages of the faithful in this life, that is, by Masses, prayers, and almsgiving, and by the other offices of piety usually performed by the faithful for one another according to the practice of the Church.

While the Council of Florence may give its approval to praying for and even paying (alms and indulgences) for the deliverance of these sinners, what about the divine word of God? There are at least two passages we are aware of that have been suggested as Bible authority.

2 Timothy 1:16-18

> The Lord grant mercy unto the house of Onesiphorus: for he oft refreshed me, and was not ashamed of my chain; but, when he was in Rome, he sought me diligently, and found me (the Lord grant unto him to find mercy of the Lord in that day); and in how many things he ministered at Ephesus, thou knowest very well.

The text is used to show that Paul prays for his deceased friend Onesiphorus. The Catholic defense is, "[it] makes sense only if he can be helped by prayer." Did Paul pray for the dead? To be honest, this text does not really inform us that Onesiphorus is even dead. Catholics make an assumption without inference or implication, and then irresponsibly and presumptuously insert purgatory into this text. This is a desperate attempt to prove an unprovable doctrine. Attempts to justify praying for the dead and argue for the existence of a place called purgatory make no sense in this text.

1 Corinthians 15:29
> Else what shall they do that are baptized for the dead? If the dead are not raised at all, why then are they baptized for them?

Beginning Apologetics for the defense of the Catholic faith states, "Paul mentions the practice of people having themselves baptized for the dead for the benefit of the dead, who cannot be helped if there is no intermediate state of purification." Admittedly, varied explanations are offered concerning the meaning of this text. Yet, let us consider the overall context of 1 Corinthians 15—our confidence in the resurrection, which has nothing to do with purgatory!

One can no more be baptized for another person than one can believe or repent on behalf of another. Each man is responsible to God for his own life and sins. Solomon said, "This is the end of the matter; all hath been heard: fear God, and keep His commandments; for this is the whole duty of man. For God will bring every work into judgment, with every hidden thing, whether it be good, or whether it be evil" (Eccl. 12:13-14). Paul said, "For we must all be made manifest before the judgment seat of Christ; that each one may receive the things done in the body, according to what he hath done, whether it be good or bad" (2 Cor. 5:10). This means that all the prayers, alms, and even masses offered by others on behalf of my salvation are utterly useless.

Conclusion

While the Bible teaches the existence of an afterlife and the Hadean realm, it does not teach or support the concept of purgatory. The doctrine of "purgatory" does not appear in the first five centuries of the church, and was not made an article of faith until the tenth century. While there are many false tentacles associated with this precept of man (i.e., prayers and alms for the dead, dependence on uninspired doctrines and writings, indulgences, etc. that are absent in the Holy Scriptures), the greatest insult of this doctrine is a blasphemy directed to the Godhead: The Father—Omnipotent and Omniscient; Christ Jesus, the Son of God—the perfect, sinless sacrifice for sin; and the Spirit of God—the giver of all truth, complete and infallible. This doctrine denies the revealed message of the power and efficacy of the blood of Jesus Christ.

Does the Bible Teach Purgatory?

There is no need for a purging purgatory because we have been "justified by His blood... saved from the wrath of God through Him" (Rom. 5:9). The Hebrew writer declared that Christ Jesus, the Son of God, "made purification of sins" and then "sat down on the right hand of the Majesty on high" (Heb. 1:3). In Christ, "we have our redemption through His blood, the forgiveness of our trespasses, according to the riches of His grace" (Eph. 1:7). There is no doubt about the power of Christ's blood to remove (purge) sin from the lives of the obedient believer.

One begins his walk with Christ by dying with Christ. It is in baptism, a likeness to the death, burial, and resurrection of our Lord that we are made alive (Rom. 6:3-11). We arise and walk in a newness of life—spiritually resurrected. As children of God, we always have access to that cleansing blood to remove sin as we confess and repent. "If we walk in the light, as He is in the light, we have fellowship one with another, and the blood of Jesus, His Son, cleanseth us from all sin.... If we confess our sins, He is faithful and righteous to forgive us our sins, and to cleanse us from all unrighteousness" (1 John 1:7-9). Purgatory annuls the previous passages and declares Christ Jesus to be powerless.

Bibliography

ASV = American Standard Version. New York, NY: Thomas Nelson & Sons, 1901.

Catechism of the Catholic Church. Vatican City: Liberia Editrice Vaticana, 1994.

Chacon, Frank and Jim Burnham. *Beginning Apologetics: How To Explain and Defend the Catholic Faith*. Farmington, NM: San Juan Catholic Seminars, 1993.

Gibbons, James Cardinal. *The Faith of Our Fathers: Being a Plain Exposition and Vindication of the Church Founded by Our Lord Jesus Christ*. Baltimore: John Murphy Company, 1917.

Hamilton, Clinton D. *Truth Commentaries: 1 Peter*. Bowling Green, KY: Guardian of Truth Foundation, 1995

Hardon, Jon A. *The Catholic Catechism: A Contemporary Catechism of the Teachings of the Catholic Church*. Garden City, NY: S.J. Double Day & Company, Inc., 1975.

Litmer, Greg. "A Look at Roman Catholicism, (2): Purgatory: Does It Exist?" *Truth Magazine* 24.32 (August 14, 1980): 522-524.

McBrien, Richard P. *The Harper Collins Encyclopedia of Catholicism.* San Francisco, CA: HarperSanFrancisco, 1995.

Mike, Willis. "The Doctrine of Purgatory." *Then Comes the End,* 31-36. Athens, AL: Truth Publications, Inc., 2016.

Nevins, Albert J. *The Maryknoll Catholic Dictionary.* New York: Grossett and Dunlap, 1968.

Patton, Marshall. *Truth Commentaries: 1-2 Timothy, Titus, and Philemon.* Mike Willis, ed. Bowling Green, KY: Guardian of Truth Foundation, 2001.

Pope, Kyle. *Truth Commentaries: Matthew.* Mike Willis, ed. Bowling Green, KY: Guardian of Truth Foundation, 2013.

Salza, John. *The Biblical Basis for Purgatory.* Gastonia NC: 0Saint Benedict Press, 2009.

Striebing, Jr., William H. *Ancient Near Eastern History and Culture.* New York: Longman Publication, 2003.

Willis, Mike. *Truth Commentaries: 1 Corinthians.* Mike Willis, ed. Bowling Green, KY: Guardian of Truth Foundation, 1979.

"Zoroastrianism." *Wikipedia.* Wikimedia Foundation. https://en.wikipedia.org/wiki/Zoroastrianism.

Does the Bible Teach Reincarnation?
By Steve Wallace

Introduction

Childhood includes a make-believe world of stuffed animals that are imagined to be alive, cartoons, and the like. Today, many grownups will tell you about a previous life they have led—and they are not kidding. Their belief in reincarnation has fueled their imagination.

A study of reincarnation takes the student away from many of the Bible dictionaries and encyclopedias. After all, such sources have to do with the *Bible,* and reincarnation is not in the Bible.

Steve Wallace grew up in Dayton, Ohio, and was converted at the Knollwood Church of Christ in 1977. Mike Willis and Ron Halbrook were working there in a two-preacher arrangement, and Steve profited very much from their preaching. He further profited by attending the preacher training classes at the church in Danville, KY, taught by Steve Wolfgang and Kelly Ellis from November 1979 to May 1980. For three years he worked with the church in Burkesville, KY, and then moved to Germany to work with churches consisting of members of U.S. armed forces and their families, mainly the one in Ramstein, Germany near Ramstein Air Force base. There he met and married his wonderful wife Mary. When the former Warsaw pact nations were opened to the west he became involved in part-time work in those countries from 1990-2002, mainly in Lithuania. In this century his part-time foreign work has mainly been in the Philippines and India. In the U.S. his full-time works are churches in Montgomery, AL, (Eastbrook), Fairmont, WV, (Westside), St. Leon, IN, and, presently, the church in Round Lake Beach, IL. Over the years he has contributed some articles to various papers circulated among churches of Christ. He can be reached at: alvincarl1@att.net.

"When Will These Things Be?" : Questions on Eschatology

Reincarnation is the belief that, after death, the soul of a person begins a new life in another body. This doctrine, also known as transmigration, is defined as "the act of transmigrating; especially, the assumed passing of the soul from one body, after death, to another; metempsychosis" (whatdoesthatmean.com, "transmigration"). Additionally, metempsychosis is defined by *Merriam-Webster* as "the passing of the soul at death into another body either human or animal."

McClintock and Strong give us the reason for the repeated passing described above.

> So long, therefore, as the soul has not attained the condition of purity, it must be born again after the dissolution of the body to which it was allied: and the degree of its impurity at one of these various deaths determines the existence which it will assume in a subsequent life.

According to sages of the Far East (whose teaching evolved into Hinduism), rebirth will follow rebirth, and eventually, the soul becomes one with or a part of Brahman.

> In Hinduism, Brahman connotes the highest Universal Principle, the Ultimate Reality in the universe. In major schools of Hindu philosophy, it is the material, efficient, formal and final cause of all that exists. It is the pervasive, genderless, infinite, eternal truth and bliss which does not change, yet is the cause of all changes. Brahman as a metaphysical concept is the single binding unity behind diversity in all that exists in the universe (*Wikipedia*, "Brahman").

During this journey, a soul will not likely be on the same plane. Rebirths may lead to heavens, hells, or different bodies (human, animal, insect). Hence, one may go from being an outcast or a worm to one of higher society (Noss, *Man's Religions*, 106-107).

One might ask if there is anything guiding the journey of the soul, as described above. The answer is, "The law of karma." The *Encyclopedia of Buddhism's* entry on "karma" says it literally means "action," and often appears in context with what might be termed karma's set of guidelines, that is, the belief that one's acts lead to retribution in a future existence (Bronkhorst, 415). Wrong actions will, at length, bring punishment, while refraining from wrong actions, and performing rituals, confessions, and the like, can cause bad karma to be neutralized or expiated (Young, *Encyclopedia of Hinduism*, 458). Karma is thought to direct reincarnation.

Does the Bible Teach Reincarnation?

1. Reincarnation is a testimony to man's innate desire for life beyond this life. Our first parents were tempted when they were told they would not die but would be like God's (Gen. 3:4-5). The Gilgamesh Epic, one of the earliest human writings known to man, records his interest in eternal life (Pritchard, *The Ancient Near East*, v. 1, 79, 88-89). The Egyptians built pyramids and embalmed their nobles because they were looking for life beyond this life. Reincarnation is just another idea of man seeking to meet his own spiritual needs. In our day, one reason for belief in reincarnation in the prosperous West is that people have had good lives and want to come back to earth.

Seeking life beyond this life is the most important pursuit of this life. That said, one must accept that life after death is found in the words of the Bible, not in the whims of mere men. After Jesus died on the cross, He arose from the dead and revealed the way of salvation (Matt. 28; Mark 16; Luke 24; John 20-21). In so doing, He "abolished death and brought life and immortality to light through the gospel" (2 Tim. 1:10; 1 Cor. 15:1-58). The claims of reincarnation are born of another god whose roots are in scriptures that openly commend the most repulsive immorality. The way to life beyond this life is not found in works of mere men but in the words of the only begotten Son of God (John 8:32; 14:6).

2. Reincarnation is built around an entirely different belief system from Christianity. Ephesians 4:4-6 records the seven ones necessary to final salvation:

> There is one body and one Spirit, just as you were called in one hope of your calling; one Lord, one faith, one baptism; one God and Father of all, who is above all, and through all, and in you all.

The doctrine of reincarnation depends upon the acceptance of another god, another set of "holy" books, another way of salvation, and another hope. God has warned of such things in His word (Acts 20:28-30; 1 Tim. 4:1-5; 2 Pet. 2:1). Reincarnation calls for people to believe and trust in a system that mere man has invented. It negates the belief in our Creator and His plan to save man. Looking back on our first point, all men must seek the way of eternal life revealed in God's word, renouncing and ignoring the claims of men (John 3:15; 6:68; 1 Pet. 1:17-19). Reincarnation stands against what the Bible teaches.

"When Will These Things Be?" : Questions on Eschatology

3. The results of the Law of Karma in the Indian caste system. As we noted above, karma is what guides the soul along its journey through a succession of lives. Somewhere around 500 BC, the caste system gradually developed in India. It evolved into five ranks: (a) Brahmins, (b) Kshatriyas, (c) Vaisyas; (d) Shudras; (e) the untouchables.

> Caste is a system of social status and hierarchy characterized not only by social rankings, wealth, and prestige, but also by hereditary occupations and endogamy (*Rationalwiki*, s.v. "Caste").

> Endogamy is the practice of marrying within a specific social group, caste, or ethnic group, rejecting those from others as unsuitable for marriage or other close personal relationships (*Wikipedia*, "Endogamy").

Thus, on one side, we see groups acceptable in society. On the other are the untouchables who are looked upon as outcasts. The caste system was tied to the religious doctrine of karma. According to reincarnation, people continue to be reborn. In all societies, there are people born into poverty or hardship, while others come forth under more favorable conditions. In Indian society, such inequalities imply the workings of the law of karma. If one is born into unfavorable conditions, it is because of sin in a past life. By contrast, a Brahmin could rightly take pride in his situation in life since it speaks well of his works during his previous existence. Further, he could look upon untouchables as sinners in their former lives since the law of karma implicates them. Meanwhile, an untouchable must bear the verdict of the law of karma and accept his outcast status.

As Mike Willis wrote,

> You can understand why one reaches the conclusion that the law of *karma* and reincarnation are not harmless little doctrines for the rich and idle to play with. Here are some of the consequences of the law of *karma*.
>
> **a. The law of *karma* leads to fatalism.** A person must accept his human condition because it is the repayment of how his soul lived in a previous existence. If he is in a lower caste in India, he should accept it rather than trying to improve his station in life. In contrast, the Scriptures teach human initiative: "Whatsoever thy hand findeth to do, do it with thy might" (Eccl. 9:10).
>
> **b. The law of *karma* teaches a faulty responsibility for one's actions.** Every wrong deed will be accounted for, but not before the Judge of all

Does the Bible Teach Reincarnation?

the earth (Rom. 14:12; 2 Cor. 5:10). Rather, it will be accounted for in the next cycle of the soul's existence. A person yet to be born will reap what another sowed.

c. The law of *karma* is a form of legalism. "Salvation" (defined as reaching *nirvana*) is attained through works. There is no concept of forgiveness. In contrast, Paul wrote, "For by grace are ye saved through faith; and that not of yourselves: it is the gift of God: Not of works, lest any man should boast" (Eph. 2:8-9). "Salvation" through works is the concept behind reincarnation and the law of *karma* (Willis, 2).

4. The law of karma is a different way of reckoning human accountability. As opposed to a system of legal works guided by karma, the Bible teaches both law and grace. God's law guides in the ways of righteousness and convicts the sinner of his sins (Ps. 119:104; Acts 2:37; Rom. 1:16-17; 1 Cor. 14:24-25; Titus 2:11-12). God's grace teaches the sinner that forgiveness is possible (Eph. 2:8-10; John 3:16). As Paul's example shows, even the worst sinners can be saved (1 Tim. 1:15). By contrast, there is no forgiveness for the sin of the reincarnate. There is only retribution. The grace manifested in Christ Jesus leads a penitent obedient believer to joy (Acts 8:39; 16:34), but people in eastern religions know only the gloom of strict retribution via karma. They do not know anything about God's grace. Instead, they look ahead to another body in which they will endure the many varied challenges of life on earth again. They will sin again, as "there is no man who does not sin" (1 Kings 8:46). Karma leads them to pay for their sins by their works. In contrast, the Bible teaches that not all accounts of sin are settled on earth (2 Cor. 5:10). The wicked sometimes prosper (see Eccl. 8:9-10; Ps. 73). The Lord's justice will be settled at the judgment, not through an endless cycle of reincarnation. Reincarnation and karma come from the imaginations of men and, hence, they have no hope to offer to the problem of human suffering. In truth, their hope provides no hope. Their writings speak of sin, but they present no way of salvation from it. Karma does change one's morals. It does not tell its followers what must be done. It only brings retribution. (Material from Mike Wills was helpful with numbers 1-4.)

5. Deceit, misleading, and dishonesty are behind claims of reincarnation. While believers in reincarnation may deny the Bible's teaching, there are cases that clearly show that they are wrong in their beliefs. One man wrote of an argument breaking out when two women

"When Will These Things Be?" : Questions on Eschatology

each claimed to be Marie Antoinette in another life. (Someone is either misled, deceived, or lying!) We see a similar example in a man's writing of how many women he had met who claimed to be Cleopatra reincarnated. And, one cannot help but wonder of whom Cleopatra was the reincarnation!

Politics entered into the belief in reincarnation with the choosing of a new Panchen Lama of Tibet. The Tibetan government in exile in India chose a reincarnate Panchen Lama from among likely candidates in that country. However, the government of communist China rules Tibet and claimed the power of making such decisions. Hence, there are now *two* rival Panchen Lamas, one chosen by the government of China and the other by the Dalai Lama with *both claiming to be reincarnates of the same person!*

Can reincarnation be profitable? After the murder of the Romanov family, imposters arose falsely claiming to be survivors of the massacre. Some profited from it. Likewise, a couple might claim their child is the reincarnate of one of their wealthy relatives with the aim of legally acquiring part of their relatives' estate. Or one might say he is the reincarnate of someone else with evidence to be presented in a civil court. These examples are not as farfetched as one might think. Authorities in India have taken the step to bar claims of reincarnation as material evidence or as testimonial evidence in courts (Botelho, *Reincarnation under Scrutiny*, 24-25; Three Indian witnesses known by author). *This action implies that such people are deceived, misled, or lying!*

In the 1980s, Shirley MacLaine became well known for her claims of having lived previous lives. She said that during one of them, she was a court jester in France during the rule of Louis XV. The king decapitated her for her jokes. Author Paul Edwards brought forth some noteworthy facts to bear regarding her claim.

> It may be of some interest to point out that in Voltaire's *Century of Louis XV* there is no mention of any beheading of a woman by the king. Voltaire had the utmost loathing for Louis XV for personal as well as ideological reasons and he would never have suppressed such a juicy royal crime if it had really occurred (Edwards, *Reincarnation: A Critical Examination*, 86).

Though there are many adherents to reincarnation, their divergent views have led to a plethora of different beliefs. Early Buddhists believed

Does the Bible Teach Reincarnation?

that there was no permanent self (soul), which was contrary to the Hindus' teaching of that time. However, there are different theories among Buddhists themselves regarding what returns to life and how it comes about (*Wikipedia*, "Reincarnation"). The dualism of Jainism sets it apart from the Hindus and Buddhists. Beyond this, we find that the *Encyclopedia of Reincarnation and Karma* lists seemingly endless contradicting beliefs that exist among the many people in this world who believe in reincarnation. We see the same chaos in the New Age Movement in the West, which, as a whole, is without a coherent organizational structure (Herbert Fraser, 219). Many reject the idea that humans reincarnate into animals. One group forbids eating beans because they hold departed souls!

We cannot know the motives behind the claims and beliefs listed above. Still, we do know "it is appointed for men to die *once*" (Heb. 9:27) and "the cowardly, unbelieving, abominable, murderers, sexually immoral, sorcerers, idolaters, and *all liars* shall have their part in the lake which burns with fire and brimstone, which is the second death" (Rev. 21:8).

6. The evil surmising and misplaced commending involved in karma. The adherents of karma *must* explain the suffering of Lazarus lying at the rich man's gate in Luke 16 as the results of the wrongs he had done in his past life or lives. Meanwhile, the rich man of that same paragraph *must* implicitly have had "good karma" from his past life or lives. That said, when these two men left this earth, *God* decided the state of both of them regardless of their outward appearances or state on this earth or what people on the earth might have thought of them (Luke 16:19-26). Hence, we cannot help but note the *bad deeds* committed by those who judge by the measure of karma. And let no one forget that, according to their beliefs, evil deeds lead to further reincarnation. If they would just listen to Jesus, they would learn that suffering is not always the result of previous sin (John 9:3).

The workings of karma are inextricably linked with the doctrine of reincarnation. *What has happened in the past life or lives of a person must be assumed!* We have seen in the previous point the deception and dishonesty involved in stories of past lives. Here we note the probable false accusations of karma advocates. Oh, what a mess our karma-powered reincarnated friends make for themselves! And, sadly, how this fits with

"When Will These Things Be?" : Questions on Eschatology

the sinful background out of which the teaching of reincarnation came. May they think about their ways! "For we must all appear before the judgment seat of Christ, that each one may receive the things done in the body, according to what he has done, whether good or bad" (2 Cor. 5:10).

7. Reincarnation and Near Death Experiences (NDE). In some circles, much is said about NDEs in connection with reincarnation. Modern writers tell us that we learn from NDEs that human existence continues after death (Weiss, *Many Lives, Many Masters,* 70-71; Alexander, *Proof of Heaven,* 9).

There are several biblical accounts of the dead miraculously coming back to life (1 Kings 17:17-24; 2 Kings 4:18-37; 13:20-21; Mark 5:35-43; Luke 7:11-16; John 11:1-54). In none of these cases is there an account of a resurrected person telling what he or she experienced while dead. It is interesting to note the recollections of some who have had an NDE.

The memories of a NDE are obviously influenced by what people have seen while living. People have awakened from an NDE and claimed to have seen Jesus, or if they are from a Catholic background, the so-called "Virgin Mary." A man from India might claim to have seen one of their gods. Such deathbed visions are influenced by statues, pictures, and other images seen during life. The same is true for visions seen in a NDE by people who see things they knew during life. Though the following statement is trite, it must be said for the good of those who need to hear it: No one knows the likeness of Jesus, Mary, or other Bible characters, as well as most other ancient people.

While NDEs of many people contain similarities, it must be pointed out that researchers have found differences in almost every story, despite some similarities. Cases have been found where people had negative NDEs in which they imagined themselves in hell or a very unpleasant place. Others have had NDEs that are compatible with the teachings of Hinduism. An atheist reported having an NDE and continued in his unbelief after being resuscitated. In another case, a criminal who confessed to having killed two people had an NDE where he saw himself among saved people. Still, another woman who had an NDE said that she now believes in reincarnation but not in God. Others have switched religions or become more religious. Like the many inconsistent explanations for reincarnation, there is no consistent message from NDEs.

Does the Bible Teach Reincarnation?

The difference between being near death and dead must be emphasized. People who have had NDEs were brought back from being *clinically* dead. They were clearly not dead in the Bible sense of the word (Jas. 2:26; Eccl. 12:7). Biblically, a person only dies once (Heb. 9:27). The Bible teaches that we go to the afterlife *after* death, not when we are *near* death (Luke 16:19-23). Hence, reports from NDEs are similar to someone coming back from a flight in the stratosphere and telling what he saw on the moon.

8. Lazarus and the Rich Man (Luke 16:19-31). When Lazarus and the rich man died, their bodies were buried. They were recognizable in the spirit realm they entered (v. 23). They had *lived* their "life time" (singular; "of life in the physical sense" [Bauer, Arndt, Gingrich, Danker, *A Greek-English Lexicon of the New Testament and Other Early Christian Literature,* 340]; v. 25). It was over. There would be no more lifetimes for either of them. They found themselves in their respective places—"now he is comforted, and you are tormented" (v. 25). "Now" in verse 25 and the "great gulf" of verse 26 mark a transformation that had taken place. They, having died *once*, were no longer free to make choices, move from place to place, or affect matters on earth. All of this is contrary to the many and varied convictions of those who believe in reincarnation. The rich man learned that his brothers were headed for the "place of torment" where he was, and there is no way out of that place (v. 28). He also learned that the word of God was sufficient to bring his brothers to repentance (vv. 29-31). The rich man lived under the Old Testament (v. 29), whereas we live under the New Testament (Matt. 28:18; John 12:48; 2 Thess. 1:8; Eph. 2:14-16; Gal. 3:19). The Scriptures are sufficient to bring people to repentance and lead them in the way that they should go (Mark 16:15,16; Acts 2:38; 2 Tim. 3:16,17; Rom. 1:15-17). One does not earn his salvation via good karma over sequential lifetimes. The Scriptures are sufficient to correct and redirect those who believe in reincarnation.

9. The singular form of the abode of the soul. When referring to the abode of the soul, Paul refers to "our earthly *house*" and "we who are in this *tent*" (2 Cor. 5:1, 4). Why does he not say, "our earthly *houses*" or "we who are in these *tents*," rather than the singular forms he uses? In 2 Corinthians 12:2, 3, if reincarnation is true, Paul should have said, "whether in *a* body I do not know, or whether out of *a* body I do not know," or "whether in *a* body or out of *a* body, I do not know."

"When Will These Things Be?" : Questions on Eschatology

However, he said, "*the* body," indicating one body for one soul. Peter was "in this tent" and said, "shortly I must put off my tent" (1 Pet. 1:13-14). Verse 15 shows that "putting off his tent" was another way to speak of his "decease." There is no hint in these words of a previous or future body.

10. The final judgment and reincarnation. Paul said, "For we must all appear before the judgment seat of Christ, that each one may receive the things done in the body, according to what he has done, whether good or bad" (2 Cor. 5:10). Notice that "each one" and "the body" are singular. Judgment is individual and particular (Matt. 25:14-30). If reincarnation is a reality, then one shall receive for the things done in his *various* "bodies." Further, Hebrews 9:27 reads, "And as it is appointed for men to die *once*, but after this the judgment." The judgment, not life in another body, follows death. There is no room for reincarnation in the Biblical description of the nature and extent of the judgment. "The Lord knows how... to reserve the unjust under punishment for the day of judgment," while the righteous are preserved "for His heavenly kingdom" (2 Pet. 2:9; 2 Tim. 4:18). Also, at the end of time, there will be a judgment based on the works done in the one body which a soul has inhabited (Rom. 14:12; 2 Cor. 5:10; Rev. 20:11-14). Reincarnation and its guide, the law of karma, are inventions of mere men. The words of the Bible are the only hope and guide.

11. The dead who spoke or returned to life. (1) In 1 Samuel 28, we see Samuel's spirit speaking to Saul. Samuel was dead (v. 3), yet his words were his own. His spirit had not entered another body. (2) In 1 Kings 17, a widow's son died, but through Elijah's petition, "the soul of the child came back to him, and he revived" (v. 22). The soul of the child had not gone into another body. If it had, that body would have had to die in order for the soul to be returned. Compare Lazarus in John 11. There is no sign of reincarnation in these texts. (3) At the death of Jesus, His spirit went to the Father, into hades, and not into another body (Luke 23:46; Acts 2:27). (Note: Thoughts in 9, 10, and 11, and also most material therein are from Larry Hafley, 226-227).

12. Reincarnation versus the resurrection. The Bible teaches that, after Jesus's Second Coming, the soul reunites with its body, which will be raised immortal and imperishable (1 Thess. 4:16; John 5:28-29; Phil. 3:21). Unlike the supposed and varied endings of the reincarnate of

Does the Bible Teach Reincarnation?

all stripes, "This corruptible must put on incorruption, and this mortal must put on immortality. So when this corruptible has put on incorruption, and this mortal has put on immortality, then shall be brought to pass the saying that is written: 'Death is swallowed up in victory'" (1 Cor. 15:53-54).

The aim God has put before all men is not a succession of hopeless and imagined reincarnations; it is that we might press forward to "attain to the resurrection from the dead" (Phil. 3:11-12). Rather than an eventual release from a body and our soul going to one of many imagined states, the resurrection is an ultimate state in which the whole person, body and soul, enjoys being in the presence of God, for "we know that when He appears, we will be like Him" (1 John 3:2). In contrast to the many mythological or contrived hopes of people who have turned to fables, we will stand in the presence of the God of all things, "who will transform our lowly body that it may be conformed to His glorious body, according to the working by which He is able even to subdue all things to Himself" (Phil. 3:21). Finally, we will not become part of all created things and beings, or merely be released from suffering, we "shall see His face" (Rev. 22:4; material from Mark Dunagan, "Reincarnation or Resurrection," contributed to this paragraph).

Conclusion

Over hundreds of years, Hinduism was born of its own mythology developed by mere *men*. In Buddhism, which was born out of Hinduism, truth ("enlightenment") comes subjectively through meditation (Chris Reeves, 298). The New Age Movement was born of people who used *their* varied sources as a basis of ideas about the afterlife. Truly did the prophet write,

> Surely you have things turned around! Shall the potter be esteemed as the clay; For shall the thing made say of him who made it, "He did not make me"? Or shall the thing formed say of him who formed it, "He has no understanding"? (Isa. 29:16).

The Bible comes from the eternal God who "inhabits eternity" (Isa. 57:15). "In the beginning God created the heavens and the earth" (Gen. 1:1). He has spoken to man throughout the ages—directly, through Jesus His Son, inspired men and, in our day, the written word they left us.

"When Will These Things Be?" : Questions on Eschatology

Will we be another would be cosmic adventurer born of folklore waiting to pass off into an imagined afterlife? Or, will we leave things in the hands of the one who created and rules all things?

> Now therefore, fear the LORD, serve Him in sincerity and in truth, and put away the gods which your fathers served on the other side of the River and in Egypt. Serve the LORD! And if it seems evil to you to serve the LORD, choose for yourselves this day whom you will serve, whether the gods which your fathers served that were on the other side of the River, or the gods of the Amorites, in whose land you dwell. But as for me and my house, we will serve the LORD (Josh. 24: 14-15).

Bibliography

Alexander, Eben, MD. *Proof of Heaven.* New York: Simon and Schuster, 2012.

Bauer, Walter; Arndt, William F.; Gingrich, F. Wilbur; Danker, Frederick W. *A Greek-English Lexicon of the New Testament and Other Early Christian Literature.* Chicago: University of Chicago Press, 1979.

Botelho, Octavio da Cunha. *Reincarnation under Scrutiny* (booklet). August, 2018. Three sources in India with whom this writer has checked have backed up the words of Mr. Botelho. Two of them spoke to lawyers in India.

"Brahman." *Wikipedia.* Wikimedia Foundation. https://en.wikipedia.org/wiki/Brahman.

Buswell, Robert E., Jr., ed. *Encyclopedia of Buddhism.* New York: Macmillan Reference, 2004

"Caste." *Rational Wiki.* https://rationalwiki.org/wiki/Caste. Accessed Feb. 29, 2020.

Cush, Denise, Catherine Robinson, and Michael York, eds. *Encyclopedia of Hinduism.* New York: Routledge, 2008.

Dunagan, Mark. "Reincarnation or Resurrection." *Fifth Street Church of Christ.* April 8, 2007. https://www.beavertonchurchofchrist.net/sermons/sermons/2007/04/08/reincarnation-or-resurrection.

Edwards, Paul. *Reincarnation: A Critical Examination.* Amherst, NY: Prometheus Books, 1996.

Does the Bible Teach Reincarnation?

McClelland, Norman C. *Encyclopedia of Reincarnation and Karma.* Jefferson, NC: McFarland & Company, Inc., 2010.

"Endogamy." *Wikipedia. Wikimedia Foundation.* https://en.wikipedia.org/wiki/Endogamy.

Fraser, Herbert. "The New Age Movement." *The Preceptor* 40.8 (August 1991): 219-220.

Hafley, Larry Ray. "That's a Good Question." *Truth Magazine* 19.15 (February 20, 1975): 226-227.

"Metempsychosis." *Merriam-Webster.* https://www.merriam-webster.com/dictionary/metempsychosis . Accessed February 26, 2020.

Noss, David S. *Man's Religions.* 7th ed. Collier Macmillan: 1984)

Pritchard, James B., editor. *The Ancient Near East,* Vol. 1. Princeton, NJ: Princeton University Press, 1958.

Reeves, Chris. "Buddhism." *Guardian of Truth* 34.10 (May 17, 1990): 297-300.

"Reincarnation." *Wikipedia. Wikimedia Foundation.* https://en.wikipedia.org/wiki/Reincarnation.

Strong, James and John McClintock,. *Cyclopedia of Biblical, Theological, and Ecclesiastical Literature.* New York: Harper, 1867-1887. Accessed through Ages Software.

"Transmigration." *What Does That Mean?* http://www.whatdoesthatmean.com/dictionary/T/transmigration.html. Accessed February 28, 2020.

Weiss, Bryan L., MD. *Many Lives, Many Masters.* New York: Simon and Schuster, 1988.

Willis, Mike. "Reincarnation." *Guardian of Truth* 39.1 (January 5, 1995): 2.

Personal Eschatology: Women's Track

Where Are the Dead?
   Aleta Samford

Does the Bible Teach Purgatory?
   Diana Dow

Does the Bible Teach Reincarnation?
   Jennifer Maxey

"When Will These Things Be?"
Questions on Eschatology

Where Are the Dead?

By Aleta Samford

Introduction

On March 1, 2002, my first husband of almost 27 years stepped into eternity after losing his battle to very aggressive colon cancer. Steve was only 47 years old. I had not lost anyone so close to me before. By that time, all four of my grandparents had passed away from natural causes of aging. Yet, this was different; this was someone with whom I had become one.

At the end of the week that we buried Steve, folks from the congregation had come over for the evening to sing and pray with me. I remember clearly that evening after everyone left. I remember walking the path through the incredible gifts of plants and flowers, and I vividly remember the loss of connection I felt, of course from losing Steve, but also because I didn't understand where he was. From the time he died, through the funeral preparations and the service itself, I was unsettled: "Where was Steve now?"

I don't mean that I feared he was eternally lost. He lived a faithful life—all his life—and I knew he was with the Lord. Yet, what I am saying

---

Aleta Samford is the wife of Gene Samford who preaches for the church that meets in Kemp, TX. She has taught Bible classes for 45 years, currently teaching teens and the ladies' bible class. She has also developed a series of lessons to help women join the ranks of bible class teaching. The lessons are based on God's Word, The Seven Laws of Teaching, and her own experiences. She may be reached at aletas10@sbcglobal.net.

"When Will These Things Be?" : Questions on Eschatology

is, "Where did Steve's spirit go after he breathed his last breath?" People say, and I had just accepted, that "They're in heaven now." However, having just personally walked with someone to eternity's door, I could not make sense of the fact that he was in heaven—yet.

I didn't remember hearing sermons or lessons or discussions up to that point that could help me with my confusion. How could I have come this far in my faith, and not known where the spirit of my husband now rested?

Then, something happened about which I want to tell you. Let me take your mind back to my home that was so quiet, so full of the scent of flowers. I was turning the lights out to go to bed one night, and while passing through the kitchen near the dining room, I heard a very frightening sound that nearly stopped my heart.

The dining room was an add-on off the kitchen and was suspended a few feet above the ground with the adjoining deck, unlike the rest of the house that was on a concrete slab. What I heard sounded very much like fingers clawing and scratching underneath the dining room floor. I cannot put into words the out-of-reality moment of panic that came over me! I had to do a lot of talking to myself, and a whole lot more with God.

The sound continued at random times for the next several days. Finally, I determined that I needed Pest Control to help me figure this out, which they did: a mother raccoon had found the area under my deck—the perfect place to have her babies, and she was going in and out, providing them with food. She eventually left, but not before traumatizing me in my grieving imagination! Where are the dead? One thing was for sure; I knew where they were *not*!

Where Are They Now?

Answers offered to the question, "Where the dead?" are often filled with confusion, controversy, and even error. Misunderstandings are found inside and outside of the Lord's church. I guess the question we should also ask is, does it matter? Does it affect our salvation? If it doesn't, then is it essential that we discuss it?

Any confusion on spiritual matters has the potential of undermining our faith. So, we must clear up any controversies about the Scriptures that we can, when we can, so that we preserve their integrity and keep

Where Are the Dead?

our trust in God's word strong. This is a subject God has revealed the truth about, so we need to know and understand what He has to say.

The question is this: For those who have ceased to live on this earth, where are their souls or spirits? Where are they now?

Some say that after we die, we will go to a place called purgatory, where there will be another opportunity to have our sins removed. Others say the dead have been reincarnated; that their souls have been reborn in a new body. These topics will be addressed in this series by Diana Dow and Jennifer Maxey, respectively.

Then, others take a materialistic view and say that the dead aren't anywhere, that when a person dies, he or she ceases to exist in any form or fashion. For those who believe the Bible, this is not an acceptable answer, as we will show in this study. Let's begin by looking at what God's word has to say about the nature and the journey of the soul:

> Furthermore, we have had human fathers who corrected us, and we paid them respect. Shall we not much more readily be in subjection to the Father of spirits and live? (Heb. 12:9).

Our souls, our spirits, originated with God. When He said, "Let Us make man in Our image," this had to do with the soul of man (Gen. 1:26).

> And the LORD God formed man of the dust of the ground, and breathed into his nostrils the breath of life; and man became a living being (Gen. 2:7).

> The burden of the word of the LORD against Israel. Thus says the LORD, who stretches out the heavens, lays the foundation of the earth, and forms the spirit of man within him (Zech. 12:1).

At conception, God places a soul within every one of us. The soul dwells within us until we die. When human beings die, the soul separates from the flesh, but continues to exist: "Then the dust will return to the earth as it was, And the spirit will return to God who gave it" (Eccl. 12:7). All go to one place: all are from the dust, and all return to dust. Yet, what about the spirit of man? The soul of Man will go upward, whereas all other animal life simply ceases to exist. No other creature than man possesses the eternal soul.

> The days of our lives are seventy years, and by reason of strength they are eighty years, yet their boast is only labor and sorrow; for it is soon cut off and we fly away (Ps. 90:10).

"When Will These Things Be?" : Questions on Eschatology

Who knows the spirit of the sons of men, which goes upward, and the spirit of the animal, which goes down to the earth? (Eccl. 3:21).

The apostle Paul wrote: "For we know that if our earthly house, this tent, is destroyed, we have a building from God, a house not made with hands, eternal in the heavens" (2 Cor. 5:1). When our body perishes, it ceases to be the dwelling place of the soul, but in the eternal world, God will provide a house fitting for our spirit's new abode.

Let us look at more examples. When the baby died who was conceived in the relationship between David and Bathsheba, David said: "But now he is dead; why should I fast? Can I bring him back again? I shall go to him, but he shall not return to me" (2 Sam. 12:23). For David to be able to go to his dead son, both would need to exist in some way after physical death. Regarding Rachel, the wife of Jacob, when she died: "And so it was, as her soul was departing (for she died), that she called his name Ben-Oni; but his father called him Benjamin" (Gen. 35:18). Without any shadow of a doubt, death is the separation of man's eternal spirit from his earthly body of the flesh. James wrote: "For as the body without the spirit is dead, so faith without works is dead also" (Jas. 2:26).

In determining where the spirit goes, let us consider what Jesus said when He was dying on the cross: "And when Jesus had cried out with a loud voice, He said, 'Father, into Your hands I commit My spirit.' Having said this, He breathed His last" (Luke 23:46). The Scriptures are very clear that the soul goes back into God's care, but let's develop this a little more; let us see just how specific the Scriptures are in helping us understand where, in God's care, the dead are.

With the creation of the world came time. There was the first day, second day, third day, and so on. Man has always lived in time. All humans are born into the world of humankind as innocent, sinless babies. As one grows out of childhood innocence, however, he finds himself in the power of darkness, meaning he is now accountable to God for his sins. Paul wrote: "For all have sinned, and come short of the glory of God" (Rom. 3:23). Nevertheless, there is a way out of darkness into light. We can be delivered from the dominion of Satan into the kingdom of Christ. How? By obeying the New Testament conditions of salvation that God has granted to us through His beloved Son.

He who believes and is baptized will be saved; but he who does not believe will be condemned (Mark 16:16).

Where Are the Dead?

> Then Peter said to them, "Repent, and let every one of you be baptized in the name of Jesus Christ for the remission of sins; and you shall receive the gift of the Holy Spirit" (Acts 2:38).

> If you confess with your mouth the Lord Jesus and believe in your heart that God has raised Him from the dead, you will be saved. For with the heart one believes unto righteousness, and with the mouth confession is made unto salvation (Rom. 10:9-10).

Believing, repenting of sins, confessing Jesus as the Son of God, and being baptized, one is then in the condition Paul spoke of:

> He has delivered us from the power of darkness and conveyed us into the kingdom of the Son of His love (Col. 1:13).

God, in His grace, continues to teach us and help us:

> For the grace of God that brings salvation has appeared to all men, teaching us that, denying ungodliness and worldly lusts, we should live soberly, righteously, and godly in the present age (Titus 2:11-12).

If we faithfully abide in the doctrine of Christ, we are in God's favor and grace. John wrote: "He who abides in the doctrine of Christ has both the Father and the Son" (2 John 9b).

However, should one fall back into sin, he is again under the power of darkness.

> For if, after they have escaped the pollutions of the world through the knowledge of the Lord and Savior Jesus Christ, they are again entangled in them and overcome, the latter end is worse for them than the beginning. For it would have been better for them not to have known the way of righteousness, than having known it, to turn from the holy commandment delivered to them. But it has happened to them according to the true proverb: "A dog returns to his own vomit," and, "a sow, having washed, to her wallowing in the mire" (2 Pet. 2:20-22).

> Whoever transgresses and does not abide in the doctrine of Christ does not have God (2 John 9a).

So, all accountable humanity is either in the kingdom of Christ, or under the power of darkness (lost in sin). This is important to know because we all will die and face certain judgment: "And as it is appointed for men to die once, but after this the judgment" (Heb. 9:27).

"When Will These Things Be?" : Questions on Eschatology

Where Will We Go?

When we die, will we go directly to heaven or hell? Some want to believe that we do, that Aunt Martha is "Up in heaven now, making her famous apple pies!" or that "Old Joe is out in his boat, catching bass in his heavenly home!" You may have heard such things said at funerals. Many hold this view, (and some who would not be so trite as to say their loved one is engaged in an earthly activity), however, I believe the Scriptures indicate differently.

When Jesus died, He committed His spirit into the hands of the Father. Let's go back to when He was on the cross and listen for other clues as to just where that was exactly. To the penitent thief, Jesus said: "And Jesus said to him, 'Assuredly, I say to you, today you will be with Me in paradise'" (Luke 23:43). Where was this paradise? Was it a place on earth, or a place found in another realm? We know it could not have been a place on earth because Jesus was about to die, and we do not doubt that He did die:

> And Jesus cried out again with a loud voice, and yielded up His spirit (Matt. 27:50).

> And when Jesus had cried out with a loud voice, He said, "Father, into Your hands, I commit My spirit." Having said this, He breathed His last (Luke 23:46).

There is no doubt that the penitent thief was about to die, and that he did die:

> Therefore, because it was the Preparation Day, that the bodies should not remain on the cross on the Sabbath (for that Sabbath was a high day), the Jews asked Pilate that their legs might be broken, and that they might be taken away. Then the soldiers came and broke the legs of the first and of the other who was crucified with Him. But when they came to Jesus and saw that He was already dead, they did not break His legs (John 19:31-33).

Since there is no question that they both died, the paradise of which Jesus spoke had to have been in a realm beyond this earthly life, a spiritual realm. Was this paradise of which He spoke the same as heaven? Consider what Jesus said to Mary Magdalene after He died and was resurrected from the dead.

Where Are the Dead?

> Jesus said to her, "Do not cling to Me, for I have not yet ascended to My Father; but go to My brethren and say to them, 'I am ascending to My Father and your Father, and to My God and your God'" (John 20:17).

The paradise Jesus spoke of was not heaven, but forty days after His resurrection, Jesus returned to the Father in heaven:

> Now when He had spoken these things, while they watched, He was taken up, and a cloud received Him out of their sight. And while they looked steadfastly toward heaven as He went up, behold, two men stood by them in white apparel, who also said, "Men of Galilee, why do you stand gazing up into heaven? This same Jesus, who was taken up from you into heaven, will so come in like manner as you saw Him go into heaven" (Acts 1:9-11).

Since Jesus did not ascend into heaven for some days after His death and resurrection, we can conclude that when Jesus died, He went into a realm of the dead called paradise.

In Luke 16, Jesus provided a clear explanation of this realm of the dead in a story familiar to all of us:

> There was a certain rich man who was clothed in purple and fine linen and fared sumptuously every day. But there was a certain beggar named Lazarus, full of sores, who was laid at his gate, desiring to be fed with the crumbs which fell from the rich man's table. Moreover the dogs came and licked his sores. So it was that the beggar died, and was carried by the angels to Abraham's bosom. The rich man also died and was buried. And being in torments in Hades, he lifted up his eyes and saw Abraham afar off, and Lazarus in his bosom. Then he cried and said, "Father Abraham, have mercy on me, and send Lazarus that he may dip the tip of his finger in water and cool my tongue; for I am tormented in this flame." But Abraham said, "Son, remember that in your lifetime you received your good things, and likewise Lazarus evil things; but now he is comforted and you are tormented. And besides all this, between us and you there is a great gulf fixed, so that those who want to pass from here to you cannot, nor can those from there pass to us." Then he said, "I beg you therefore, father, that you would send him to my father's house, for I have five brothers, that he may testify to them, lest they also come to this place of torment." Abraham said to him, They have Moses and the prophets; let them hear them." And he said, "No, father Abraham; but if one goes to them from the dead, they will repent." But he said to him, "If they do not hear Moses and

"When Will These Things Be?" : Questions on Eschatology

the prophets, neither will they be persuaded though one rise from the dead" (Luke 16:19-31, NKJV).

Lazarus and the rich man both experienced death, the separation of the body and the spirit. Yet, where were they? The spirit of Lazarus was carried by the angels to Abraham's bosom, but the rich man was in torments in Hades (hell, KJV). Some say Abraham's bosom is symbolic of eternal heaven, and the torments of Hades are symbolic of eternal hell. In this study, I want us to look at three reasons why this cannot be the case.

1

First, Lazarus was indeed comforted, and the rich man was tormented in flames, but something else is going on here that is not true of hell: the rich man and Abraham are communicating with one another. This is significant because God's word describes a different scenario in hell:

> But the cowardly, unbelieving, abominable, murderers, sexually immoral, sorcerers, idolaters, and all liars shall have their part in the lake which burns with fire and brimstone, *which is the second death*" (Rev. 21:8, emphasis mine).

The second death implies there was a first death. Remember, the rich man and Lazarus have just experienced the first death, i.e., physical death—the separation of the body and the spirit. "Then the dust will return to the earth as it was, And the spirit will return to God who gave it" (Eccl. 12:7). The second death mentioned in Revelation 21 is *another* separation: the *final* separation of the lost from God for all eternity. At that point, God will have nothing to do with them; they will be cut off from all the blessings of the faithful, including all communication with those who were righteous, those who walked in the light. If the rich man were in eternal hell, he could not have had contact with Abraham.

2

Let's turn to Revelation 20:11-15 to develop the second reason this could not have been heaven or hell. Consider this passage from the KJV:

> And I saw a great white throne, and him that sat on it, from whose face the earth and the heaven fled away; and there was found no place for them. And I saw the dead, small and great, stand before God; and the books were opened: and another book was opened, which is the book of life: and the dead were judged out of those things which were written in the books, according to their works (20:11-12).

Where Are the Dead?

Picture this scene of judgment on the day of the Lord, the resurrection day: God is on His throne, the dead are standing before Him, and the books are open. From where did these dead come? Can we know? The text continues:

> And the sea gave up the dead which were in it; and death and hell delivered up the dead which were in them: and they were judged every man according to their works. And death and hell were cast into the lake of fire. This is the second death. And whosoever was not found written in the book of life was cast into the lake of fire (20:13-15).

Were the dead delivered up from hell, and then hell was cast into hell? To help clarify, we must know that the KJV of the New Testament translates three different Greek words into the English word "hell" and that the use of these different words is intentional in helping us understand where the dead are.

The three words are *gehenna*, *tartarus*, and *hades*. Of these three words, *gehenna* (Greek: *geenna*) is the only one that signifies the place of eternal punishment. We see it referred to as hell in these verses of the KJV:

> But I say unto you, That whosoever is angry with his brother without a cause shall be in danger of the judgment: and whosoever shall say to his brother, Raca, shall be in danger of the council: but whosoever shall say, Thou fool, shall be in danger of hell (*gehenna*) fire (Matt. 5:22, KJV).

> And if thy hand offend thee, cut it off: it is better for thee to enter into life maimed, than having two hands to go into hell (*gehenna*), into the fire that never shall be quenched (Mark 9:43, KJV).

> But I will forewarn you whom ye shall fear: Fear him, which after he hath killed hath power to cast into hell (*gehenna*); yea, I say unto you, Fear him (Luke 12:5, KJV).

The second word, *tartarus* (Greek: *tartaros*), is the place of torment for those waiting for the judgment, as were the angels who sinned:

> For if God spared not the angels that sinned, but cast them down to hell (*tartaros*), and delivered them into chains of darkness, to be reserved unto judgment (2 Pet. 2:4).

We will mention *tartarus* again in a moment.

"When Will These Things Be?" : Questions on Eschatology

The third word, *Hades*, is the Greek word that corresponds to the Hebrew word, *sheol*, and refers to the unseen state, the world of the dead, death, or the grave. It occurs in various places in the Bible and is always translated as "hell" by the KJV. Let's look again at Revelation 20:13-14, comparing the KJV with the NKJV. (Other translations reflect the difference, as well).

> And the sea gave up the dead which were in it; and death and hell (*hades,* NKJV). delivered up the dead which were in them: and they were judged every man according to their works. And death and hell (*hades,* NKJV). were cast into the lake of fire. This is the second death (KJV).

To reinforce that the realm of the dead of Luke 16 was indeed Hades, let's look again for further evidence of where Jesus went when He died. On the day of Pentecost, when Peter was reasoning with the crowd, he quoted David from the Psalms: "For You will not leave my soul in Hades, nor will You allow Your Holy One to see corruption" (Acts 2:27, quoting Psa. 16:10). He went on to explain that David could not have been speaking of himself, but was speaking of the Christ: "He, foreseeing this, spoke concerning the resurrection of Christ, that His soul was not left in Hades, nor did his flesh see corruption" (Acts 2:31).

Now, let us look at David's own words in Psalm 16:10 and notice the corresponding Hebrew word for Hades, the realm of the dead: "For you will not leave my soul in sheol (hell, KJV), nor will you allow Your Holy One to see corruption" (Psa. 16:10). When Jesus died, He went into Hades, the waiting place for the dead, and not into *gehenna* hell (though the KJV uses hell). Can we know that the place He went to was not heaven? Again:

> Jesus saith unto her, Touch me not; for I am not yet ascended to my Father: but go to my brethren, and say unto them, I ascend unto my Father, and your Father; and to My God, and your God (John 20:17).

Hades is the term that helps us with our understanding. Jesus went into Hades to await His resurrection by the power of God. Therefore we can only conclude that Hades is, indeed, the place where departed spirits go to await the final resurrection and judgment. Hades is the word used in Luke 16 that describes where the rich man was: "And being in torments in Hades (hell, KJV), he lifted up his eyes and saw Abraham afar off, and Lazarus in his bosom" (Luke 16:23).

Where Are the Dead?

This is (perhaps) the most important of the Scriptures that refer to Hades in that it gives a description of it, which cannot be denied. The rich man found himself in hades—not gehenna hell—and within Hades, he found himself in torment (tartarus). We also know this was before the judgment because the rich man had brothers still alive on the earth.

> Then he said, "I beg you therefore, father, that you would send him to my father's house, for I have five brothers, that he may testify to them, lest they also come to this place of torment." Abraham said to him, "They have Moses and the prophets; let them hear them." And he said, "No, father Abraham; but if one goes to them from the dead, they will repent." But he said to him, "If they do not hear Moses and the prophets, neither will they be persuaded though one rise from the dead" (Luke 16:27-31).

Returning to Revelation 20:12-13, please notice it states that *all* the dead will be raised at the judgment, not just the ones alive when the Lord returns:

> And I saw the dead, small and great, standing before God, and books were opened. And another book was opened, which is the Book of Life. And the dead were judged according to their works, by the things which were written in the books. The sea gave up the dead who were in it, and Death and Hades delivered up the dead who were in them. And they were judged, each one according to his works (Rev. 20:12-13).

If the dead have already gone to heaven or hell, then who will be delivered up from death and Hades? Let's couple this Scripture with what Paul said to the Christians in Thessalonica:

> But I do not want you to be ignorant, brethren, concerning those who have fallen asleep, lest you sorrow as others who have no hope. For if we believe that Jesus died and rose again, even so God will bring with Him those who sleep in Jesus. For this we say to you by the word of the Lord, that we who are alive and remain until the coming of the Lord will by no means precede those who are asleep. For the Lord Himself will descend from heaven with a shout, with the voice of an archangel, and with the trumpet of God. And the dead in Christ will rise first. Then we who are alive and remain shall be caught up together with them in the clouds to meet the Lord in the air. And thus we shall always be with the Lord. Therefore comfort one another with these words (1 Thess. 4:13-18).

"When Will These Things Be?" : Questions on Eschatology

Those who have seen the first death while this earth still stands are in a place (*hades*) awaiting the time when they will rise first; when they will be delivered up. They have not been delivered up yet; no one has been rewarded with heaven, nor punished with hell (*gehenna*). . . yet.

To summarize our second point, would it make sense for eternal hell to deliver up its condemned dead to be judged and then be condemned again back into it? Why would hell be cast into the eternal lake of fire and brimstone, which is hell? By considering contexts and other translations of the word hell, we can conclude that the rich man was in Hades and not eternal hell.

3

Thirdly, and our last point: before we contend that the rich man was already in eternal hell, we need to identify where the beggar Lazarus was in the same scenario.

> So it was that the beggar died, and was carried by the angels to Abraham's bosom. The rich man also died and was buried. And being in torments in Hades, he lifted up his eyes and saw Abraham afar off, and Lazarus in his bosom (Luke 16:22-23).

Lazarus was in Abraham's bosom, a place of comfort. He was in the paradise that Jesus assured the penitent thief about, "Today you will be with Me in paradise" (Luke 23:43). Lazarus found himself in Hades, and within Hades, he found himself in paradise. We can conclude that Hades also describes where the righteous dead await the judgment.

Therefore, the wicked dead wait in the place of torment (*tartarus*), and the righteous dead wait in the place of comfort (i.e., paradise), both parts of the Hadean realm. We know this because the rich man could see Lazarus. Abraham told him that he and Lazarus were separated by a great gulf fixed, which prevented going from one to the other. Lazarus and the rich man were both in Hades, the waiting place of the dead.

What we have discovered in this study is what the Scriptures say happens at death and where the dead are now. Let us review what will happen at the final resurrection (also known as Judgment Day, the Second Coming of Christ, and the Day of the Lord).

> But the day of the Lord will come as a thief in the night, in which the heavens will pass away with a great noise, and the elements will melt

Where Are the Dead?

with fervent heat; both the earth and the works that are in it will be burned up (2 Pet. 3:10).

Those who have already died will rise first:

For the Lord Himself will descend from heaven with a shout, with the voice of the archangel, and with the trumpet of God. And the dead in Christ will rise first (1 Thess. 4:16).

In other words, the Hadean world will give up the souls contained therein. "Then we who are alive and remain shall be caught up together with them in the clouds to meet the Lord in the air. And thus we shall always be with the Lord" (1 Thess. 4:17). Are we told what will happen after all the dead are caught up together with the Lord? "In a moment, in the twinkling of an eye, at the last trumpet. For the trumpet will sound, and the dead will be raised incorruptible, and we shall be changed" (1 Cor. 15:52). The dead will be raised incorruptible, and we will be changed. Why?

Now this I say, brethren, that flesh and blood cannot inherit the kingdom of God; neither does corruption inherit incorruption. Behold, I tell you a mystery; We shall not all sleep, but we shall all be changed. . . . For this corruptible must put on incorruption, and this mortal must put on immortality (1 Cor. 15:50-51, 53).

Let us read again of the view from heaven:

Then I saw a great white throne and Him who sat on it, from whose face the earth and the heaven fled away. And there was found no place for them. And I saw the dead, small and great, standing before God, and books were opened. And another book was opened, which is the Book of Life. And the dead were judged according to their works, by the things which were written in the books. The sea gave up the dead who were in it, and Death and Hades delivered up the dead who were in them. And they were judged, each one according to his works (Rev. 20:11-13).

The final Judgment will be the passing of eternal sentence on the resurrected dead, that is, those given up by death and Hades. Where we find ourselves in Hades will indicate what our eternal destiny will be at the judgment. Whether as the righteous: "His lord said to him, 'Well done, good and faithful servant; you have been faithful over a few things, I will make you ruler over many things. Enter into the joy of your lord'" (Matt. 25:23). Or, whether as the unrighteous:

"When Will These Things Be?" : Questions on Eschatology

> Not everyone who says to Me, "Lord, Lord," shall enter the kingdom of heaven, but he who does the will of My Father in heaven. Many will say to Me in that day, "Lord, Lord, have we not prophesied in Your name, cast out demons in Your name, and done many wonders in Your name?" And then I will declare to them, "I never knew you; depart from Me, you who practice lawlessness!" (Matt. 7:21-23).

> Do not marvel at this; for the hour is coming in which all who are in the graves will hear His voice and come forth—those who have done good, to the resurrection of life, and those who have done evil, to the resurrection of condemnation (John 5:28-29).

The day of judgment is necessary for those still living when Jesus returns. They will face judgment for the first time: "For we must all appear before the judgment seat of Christ, that each one may receive the things done in the body, according to what he has done, whether good or bad" (2 Cor. 5:10). And, finally, death and Hades will be destroyed: "Then Death and Hades were cast into the lake of fire. This is the second death. And anyone not found written in the Book of Life was cast into the lake of fire" (Rev. 20:14-15). Death and Hades will be cast into the eternal lake of fire and brimstone because they will have no further function nor purpose. There will be no need for a waiting place for the dead after the resurrection and judgment because there will be no more physical death.

> The last enemy that shall be destroyed is death (1 Cor. 15:26).

> So when this corruptible has put on incorruption, and this mortal has put on immortality, then shall be brought to pass the saying that is written: "Death is swallowed up in victory." O Death, where is your sting? O Hades, where is your victory? (1 Cor. 15:54-55).

If we do go to heaven after a time, it will be because we obeyed the gospel's conditions of salvation on earth and will have gone on to live faithfully, to die in the Lord.

> Then I heard a voice from heaven saying to me, "Write: 'Blessed are the dead who die in the Lord from now on.' "Yes," says the Spirit, "that they may rest from their labors, and their works follow them" (Rev. 14:13).

Conclusion

Some say that what we've talked about today regarding "Where are the dead?" is all an assumption, but what other explanation can be offered that fits the original language and shows how the Scriptures agree on the truth? Whatever happens at death, whatever you believe or don't

Where Are the Dead?

believe about it, the important thing is the reality and certainty of the judgment.

> The Lord is not slack concerning His promise, as some count slackness, but is longsuffering toward us, not willing that any should perish but that all should come to repentance. But the day of the Lord will come as a thief in the night, in which the heavens will pass away with a great noise, and the elements will melt with fervent heat; both the earth and the works that are in it will be burned up. Therefore, since all these things will be dissolved, what manner of persons ought you to be in holy conduct and godliness, looking for and hastening the coming of the day of God, because of which the heavens will be dissolved, being on fire, and the elements will melt with fervent heat? (2 Pet. 3:9-12).

Does the Bible Teach Purgatory?
By Daniel and Diana Dow

Introduction

What is purgatory? To fully answer and understand what purgatory is, we must first delve into the Catholic doctrine concerning sin. According to the Roman Catholic catechism, there are two kinds of sin: Mortal and Venial.

Mortal (Deadly) Sins

Mortal (Deadly) Sins are considered to be "grave violation(s) of God's Law. The Catechism teaches that such sins "destroy charity in the heart" and turn man away from God. Pope Gregory I is credited as issuing the first list of seven deadly sins in the late sixth-century. Catholicism teaches that a mortal sin involves three things: (1) Its object is a grave or grievous matter (exemplified in the Ten Commandments: murder, theft, adultery, coveting, etc.). (2) It is committed with full knowledge. (3) It is deliberately and freely committed. Mortal sins cut the sinner off from

---

Diana Dow is the wife of Danny Dow who preaches for the Borden Street church of Christ in Sinton, TX. They have six sons, four daughter in-laws, and nine grandchildren. She has spent the past twenty-eight years home-schooling the boys and, with children still at home, will continue a few more years. She teaches private piano and violin lessons as well as conducts and teaches The Coastal Bend Strings, a home school string orchestra. She has taught Bible classes for many years and shares activities, songs and tips on her blog, www.biblesongsandmore.com. She also keeps a more personal blog, *A Keeper at Home*, dedicated to home schooling, family, and writings from her heart: www.dandidow.com. She can be reached at dianaidow@gmail.com.

Does the Bible Teach Purgatory?

God's saving grace, and he is condemned to eternal damnation in hell unless the sin is confessed and repented.

Venial (Forgivable) Sins

Venial (Forgivable) Sins are considered to be less serious. While these sins weaken the charity in the heart, they do not result in a complete separation from God, nor do they require the consequence of eternal punishment. Venial comes from the Latin word *venia,* which means "pardon." Venial sins can be repaired, and purgatory is the place where these venial sins and their stains are removed.

The Catholic catechism teaches that nothing defiled can enter into heaven. Therefore, anyone less than perfect must first be purified before being admitted in the presence of God. In his book, *The Catholic Catechism, A Contemporary Catechism of the Teachings of the Catholic Church*, Jon A. Hardon explains that this doctrine of purgatory was carved out throughout the centuries by the Church's reflection on revelation. Therefore they concluded, "there exists purgatory, in which the souls of the just who die with the stains of sin are cleansed by expiation before they are admitted to heaven" (273-274).

The Maryknoll Catholic Dictionary defines purgatory as "The state in which souls exist for a time after death to work out the temporal punishment due to venial sins or forgiven mortal sins. The soul is purified in this state to prepare it for its entrance into the delights of heaven" (474).

Purgatory comes from the verb "purge," meaning to purify or cleanse. Note that purgatory is a temporary state.

The History and Origin of the Doctrine of Purgatory

Presently, there are three major religions that believe in purgatory: (1) the Roman Catholic Church (Western), (2) the Greek Orthodox Church (Eastern), and (3) Orthodox Jews. "Purgatory" is never mentioned in the Bible, but is a doctrine that developed over many centuries.

It has been suggested that the Jews of the Babylonian captivity returned to Jerusalem, having been influenced by an ancient Persian religion. In his book *Ancient Near Eastern History and Culture*, William H. Striving writes,

> Not only was Zoroastrian eschatology incorporated into early Christianity through Judaism, but also through Mithraism, a Roman

"When Will These Things Be?" : Questions on Eschatology

religion out of the early Persian faith that became Christianity's chief rival in the first three centuries CE. From Mithraism the church borrowed the concept of purgatory (which is not found in the Bible), as well as December the 25th as the date of Jesus' birthday and the tradition that he was born in a cave (351).

Please note that Zoroastrianism or Mazdayasna is one of the world's oldest continual practicing religions.

Pagan writers and Greek philosophers like Plato and Heraclides Ponticus had their concept of purgatory—an intermediary place where souls would spend an undetermined amount of time after death before moving on to a higher plane of existence. Where was this intermediary place? Various places have been named: beyond the stars, the Milky Way, between the earth and moon, or the backside of the moon, etc.

One might rightly conclude this influence of both Ancient Persian and Hellenistic religions likely perverted the Jewish religion bringing about erroneous thoughts concerning the Hadean realm.

Some of the first signs of this doctrine permeating in the Catholic Church emerged in the sixth century from Pope Gregory I "The Great" (AD 593). Seven hundred years later, in the thirteenth century, Innocent IV (1243-54) writes a letter to believers in Greece trying to unite the Eastern and Western segments of the Catholic Church using the doctrine of purgatory as common ground. Twenty years later (1274), the Second Council of Lyon made a formal declaration on the doctrine of purgatory: henceforth, it was to be considered a formal creed on which both sides should agree. While the East continued to object to the concept of material fire in purgatory, the Council of Lyon pressed two things: (1) The existence of purgatory and (2) the usefulness of prayer and pious works to be offered for the dead. The subject was again addressed in the sixteenth century when the Council of Trent literally ordered: "the bishops to be diligently on guard that the true doctrine of purgatory be preached everywhere, and that Christians be instructed in it, believe it, and adhere to it."

Does the Bible Teach Purgatory?

While preaching for the Broadway Street church of Christ in La Porte, TX, our family encountered a family who professed to be Catholic in faith. After Diana established a friendship with this woman, they be-

Does the Bible Teach Purgatory?

gan to talk and casually discuss the Bible. She politely accepted our local bulletin, and Diana kept planting the seed of God's word, which eventually led to doubts and spiritual concerns about her Catholic convictions.

Diana's friend freely acknowledged that she did not know God's word, but before taking any action, sought the counsel of Father Tom, the local priest of the Catholic Church in La Porte. He told her to stop talking about these matters with Diana immediately. He said that she was not knowledgeable and, therefore, unable to discuss the Bible. Such matters were reserved for the Clergy. In her final meeting with Diana, she said Father Tom told her to stop reading and receiving our bulletin. She handed Diana a copy of a lesson booklet entitled *Beginning Apologetics: How to Explain and Defend Catholic Faith*, saying, "Maybe this will help you understand."

Ironically, in a section of this booklet, *"A Beginner's Guide to Apologetics"* (# 8) reads: "Do not accept the Protestant interpretation of a verse when it contradicts Catholic doctrine. Read it yourself—in context—and show the other side how the verse can be interpreted to support the Catholic position. Get them to see how they often get their beliefs from their denomination, and then twist the verses to make them Biblical." Sadly, he pushed her away from true Bible teaching to sow the seeds of Catholicism.

We will approach the subject of purgatory by considering the various "proof texts" used by those who believe in purgatory and examine them in the light of their biblical context.

Matthew 5:25-26

> Agree with thine adversary quickly, while thou art with him in the way; lest haply the adversary deliver thee to the judge, and the judge deliver thee to the officer, and thou be cast into prison. Verily I say unto thee, thou shalt by no means come out thence, till thou have paid the last farthing.

Those who believe in and profess the existence of purgatory see this realm described in the phrase "thou be cast into prison." They also consider the phrase "thou shalt by no means come out thence, till thou have paid the last farthing" (v. 26) to describe the pains suffered to purify the stained soul.

"When Will These Things Be?" : Questions on Eschatology

Contextually, this passage is found in Jesus's Sermon on the Mount, which generally addressed the new way of life in Christ. These attributes define the disciple of Christ. This portion of the sermon addressed the subject of anger and its effect upon our worship of God. It is not a difficult message to digest. Jesus taught that we are to repair strained relationships and make amends with brethren lest we allow the officials and courts of this world to judge us, and we end up in prison for wrongdoing. We are to strive to be at peace with all men (Rom. 12:18-21). However, Jesus said nothing about the afterlife or "purgatory."

Matthew 12:32

> And whosoever shall speak a word against the Son of man, it shall be forgiven him; but whosoever shall speak against the Holy Spirit, it shall not be forgiven him, neither in this world, nor in that which is to come.

Pope Gregory the Great used Matthew 12:32 to defend his belief in purgatory. He wrote,

> We must believe that before the day of judgment there is a purgatory fire for certain small sins: because our Saviour saith, that he which speaketh blasphemy against the holy Ghost, that it shall not be forgiven him, neither in this world, nor in the world to come. Out of which sentence we learn, that some sins are forgiven in this world, and some others may be pardoned in the next. . . as I said, we have not to believe but only concerning little and very small sins, as, for example, daily idle talk, immoderate laughter, negligence in the care of our family. . . ignorant errors in matters of no great weight: all which sins be punished after death, if men procured not pardon and remission for them in their lifetime (*Dialogues* 4:39—AD 594).

In the book, *The Faith of Our Fathers*, James Cardinal Gibbons, wrote that Jesus's teaching "leaves us to infer that there are some sins which will be pardoned in the life to come." He concludes this pardon is in an intermediate state called purgatory (213).

The idea is this: Since sin does not exist in heaven and one cannot receive forgiveness in hell, any remission of sins in the "next world" can only refer to purgatory! However, in the above passage, is Jesus teaching us about a third realm that exists after death?

In Matthew 12, Jesus demonstrates that He is the Lord of Sabbath (vv. 1-8) by performing miracles (vv. 9-21) and casting out demons (vv. 22-37). This turned into an accusation by the Pharisees that Jesus's mi-

Does the Bible Teach Purgatory?

raculous works originated with "Beelzebub, the prince of the demons" (v. 24). Such charges spoke against, not the Son of Man, but instead spoke against and denied the power of the Holy Spirit. For man to defy God's Spirit is unforgivable because it is God's Spirit that guides, directs, and reveals through the Word (John 14:26; 16:13). There is no hope of forgiveness for the one who rejects the work of the Holy Spirit (who reveals and confirms God's word). If a man does not desire or seek after the forgiveness which is offered—there is no forgiveness "*in this world, nor in that which is to come.*"

Jesus is speaking to the seriousness of this blasphemous sin of rejection (Mark 3:29). "The world to come" (12:32) refers to the time when the souls of men will experience an eternal existence, either eternal life or eternal damnation. There is no opportunity to seek forgiveness when one defiantly rejects the Holy Spirit; whether it is right now in "this [present physical] world" or in "that [world] which is to come." It is a far stretch to insert the doctrine and place of purgatory into Matthew 12. There is no implication or inference that such a place exists. This is reading something into the text that simply does not belong. The Bible does not teach purgatory in this text.

1 Corinthians 3:15

> If any man's work shall be burned, he shall suffer loss: but he himself shall be saved; yet so as through fire.

Again Pope Gregory defended the existence of purgatory when he wrote:

> For when St. Paul saith, . . . "if any man's work burn, he shall suffer detriment, but himself shall be saved, yet so as by fire." For although these words may be understood of the fire of tribulation, which men suffer in this world: yet if any will interpret them of the fire of purgatory, which shall be in the next life: then must he carefully consider, that the apostle said not that he may be saved by fire, that buildeth upon this foundation iron, brass, or lead, that is, the greater sort of sins, and therefore more hard, and consequently not remissible in that place: but wood, hay, stubble, that is, little and very light sins, which the fire doth easily consume. Yet, we have here further to consider, that none can be there purged, no, not for the least sins that be, unless in his lifetime he deserved by virtuous works to find such favour in that place (*Dialogues* 4:39—AD 594).

"When Will These Things Be?" : Questions on Eschatology

Again the idea is promoted that this cannot refer to heaven because there is no suffering in heaven. It cannot refer to hell because no one can be saved, so it must refer to a temporal loss of God and a temporary purifying suffrage, i.e., purgatory. Man's salvation will come by going through the fires of purgatory. Although it is vehemently denied (as in Pope Gregory's dialogue), this has a certain taste of a "second chance" to be saved after death.

The first four chapters of 1 Corinthians address the problems of division. The saints at Corinth had their favorite preachers and rallied around them. Paul was teaching the Corinthian Christians that all of these men were the same. They faithfully worked together and in harmony under God's direction and increase. Paul spoke of the privilege of preaching the gospel and laying a foundation upon which other men, like Cephas or Apollos, could build. Notice the words of Paul:

> But if any man buildeth on the foundation gold, silver, costly stones, wood, hay, stubble; each man's work shall be made manifest: for the day shall declare it, because it is revealed in fire; and the fire itself shall prove each man's work of what sort it is. If any man's work shall abide which he built thereon, he shall receive a reward. If any man's work shall be burned, he shall suffer loss: but he himself shall be saved; yet so as through fire (1 Cor. 3:12-15).

Each teacher's work, that is, the individuals whom he teaches and those who obey the gospel through his influence, will eventually have their faith tested through the fires of trials and persecutions (Jas. 1:2-3 1 Peter 1:6-7; 4:12). Some of these people will prove to be strong and solid (i.e., like gold, silver, and costly stones), but some will show themselves to be weak and unstable (i.e., like hay and stubble). Every individual has the responsibility of standing firm during these tests. Some will emerge stronger and purer; sadly, some will not endure. They will be consumed in the fire, and they will be lost eternally.

In the lesson book *Then Comes The End*—"The Doctrine of Purgatory," Mike Willis wrote,

> The work that a preacher does in teaching others the gospel will be tested. Those who are converted will be tested by the fires of temptation to see if they remain faithful. Some who are lost will be lost because of the wrong kind of work that was done by the preacher; others will be

Does the Bible Teach Purgatory?

lost in spite of the best work that one can do. Those whose works are so destroyed nevertheless will be saved (34).

Even if a teacher loses his weaker converts/students, he will be saved "yet so as through fire." This reminds us of God's warning to Ezekiel: "Yet if thou warn the wicked, and he turn not from his wickedness, nor from his wicked way, he shall die in his iniquity; but thou hast delivered thy soul" (Ezek. 3:19). No doubt, the sad loss of this student (i.e., the destruction of his work) is a part of the fiery trials and tests that the teacher himself must faithfully pass through.

There is absolutely nothing in this text to suggest a place called "purgatory," nor a purging fire that occurs after death. It seems as if Pope Gregory I clearly understood and even acknowledged the text's meaning as "the fire of tribulation" but in the same breath, theorized "*If* any will interpret them of the fire of purgatory. . ." However, the Bible does not teach of purgatory in this passage.

1 Peter 3:18-20

> Because Christ also suffered for sins once, the righteous for the unrighteous, that he might bring us to God; being put to death in the flesh, but made alive in the spirit; in which also he went and preached unto the spirits in prison, that aforetime were disobedient, when the longsuffering of God waited in the days of Noah, while the ark was a preparing, wherein few, that is, eight souls, were saved through water.

The phrase "the spirits in prison, that aforetime were disobedient," is supposedly a reference to purgatory. The Catholic view is that Peter is describing a temporary state for disobedient souls who were eventually saved. The *Beginning Apologetic* workbook said, "At the very least, it proves that a third place can exist between heaven and hell. At the most, it proves the Catholic doctrine of purgatory (32)."

Also thrown into this mix is 1 Peter 4:6, "For unto this end was the gospel preached even to the dead, that they might be judged indeed according to men in the flesh, but live according to God in the spirit." It is taught that "the dead that. . . live according to God in the spirit" are in purgatory, a "prison for disobedient spirits."

When addressing the Hadean territory, the Bible speaks of only two places: (1) Torments (tartarus) (Luke 16:1-13; 2 Pet. 2:4; Jude 6), and

"When Will These Things Be?" : Questions on Eschatology

(2) paradise (Abraham's Bosom) (Luke 16:1-13; 23:43; cf. Acts 2:25-32). The place of torments is described as a place of anguish and fire (Luke 16:24-25). Of these two realms, torment alone would be considered the place of the disobedient spirits or prison to hold the spiritually dead, while they await their final judgment. Purgatory (the third alternative?) is never mentioned.

The Hebrew writer reminds us, "And inasmuch as it is appointed unto men once to die, and after this cometh judgment" (Heb. 9:27). It would seem that after death, a man (righteous or unrighteous) is judged or separated into one of these two places, and his eternal destiny is sealed. There he awaits his final judgment or sentence rendered by the Great Judge at the Second Coming of Christ Jesus. There is no third chamber for a man to work off or purge himself of the stains of sin. There is no "second chance" to make things right. We either die right, or we are separated from God eternally.

What about Extra-Biblical Sources (2 Macc. 12:44-45)?

And when he had made a gathering throughout the company to the sum of two thousand drachms of silver, he sent it to Jerusalem to offer a sin offering, doing therein very well and honestly, in that he was mindful of the resurrection: For if he had not hoped that they that were slain should have risen again, it had been superfluous and vain to pray for the dead. And also in that he perceived that there was great favour laid up for those that died godly, it was an holy and good thought. Whereupon he made a reconciliation for the dead, that they might be delivered from sin (2 Macc. 12:44-45)

For many Catholics, the events recorded in 2 Maccabees is the clearest affirmation of the existence of purgatory, although the term "purgatory" is also absent in the Maccabean text. The Catholic booklet, *Beginning Apologetics*, states: "This passage from Maccabees is a *proof text*. It explicitly affirms an intermediate state where the faithful departed make atonement for their sins." Moreover, this is where Catholics find the "authority" for the practice of praying for the dead with a view to their afterlife salvation and purification. Actually, praying for the dead has been a common practice throughout history (Zoroastrianism or Mazdayasna, Chinese Buddhists, Hindus, Muslims, even the Jews pray for the dead at the Wailing Wall.).

This text of 2 Maccabees 12 tells the story about a "noble" Jewish priest, Judas Maccabeus, who led a revolt against the Seleucid Empire.

Does the Bible Teach Purgatory?

After some of his men died heroically in battle, it was discovered that they had in their possession, hidden under their tunics, sacred amulets devoted to the idols of Jamnia. Only in death were their sins discovered. The soldiers gathered a collection and sent it to Jerusalem that a "sin offering" might be offered on the dead's behalf. So, what about this text? Does it offer undeniable proof for the concept of purgatory?

2 Maccabees is an apocryphal book. The term Apocrypha means "hidden things." The Apocrypha is a selection of fifteen books included in the Catholic Bible. Although these books were not found in the Hebrew Bible, they were included in the Latin Vulgate. Throughout history, the divine inspiration of these books has been challenged and called into question. Claims have been made that they should never have been included in the canon in the first place. The Greek Orthodox fathers referred to them as "disputed" books. Martin Luther described the Apocrypha as "books which are not regarded as equal to the Holy Scriptures, and yet are profitable and good to read." In April 1546, after Luther's death and in response to constant challenges concerning their divine authorship, the Council of Trent officially and "infallibly" declared these books to be the sacred second canon (deuterocanonical books). This was sixteen centuries after the truth had been fully and finally revealed (2 Tim. 3:16-17; Jude 3; etc.).

Beginning Apologetics offered this last attempt to convince us to accept the doctrine of purgatory:

> Even if Maccabees is rejected as Scripture, there can be no doubt that, as history, the book accurately reflects the religious character of the Jews of the second century BC. A little more than one hundred years before Christ, Jews prayed for their dead (and still do today). In fact, some of the earliest Christian liturgies (worship services) include prayers for the dead. Ancient Christian tomb inscriptions from the second and third centuries frequently contain an appeal for prayers for the dead. This practice makes sense only if early Christians believed in purgatory even if they did not use that name for it. In fact, the practice of praying for the dead was universal among Christians for fifteen centuries before the Reformation.

First, if "Maccabees is rejected as Scripture," there will always be a doubt, and it must be accepted as fallible. Secondly, just because men "pray for the dead" does not necessarily mean that it is of God. An inscription on a tomb does not determine Bible authority. Making up a place named "purgatory" does not mean it really exists. It doesn't make sense that a "practice" determines God's approval. These are all examples of poor apologetics. These things may explain and defend the Catholic faith, but they are not divinely inspired.

Does the Bible Teach that We Should Offer Prayers for the Dead?

Interestingly, according to Catholic theology, those who die with venial sin must purge themselves of these lesser sins through enduring the fires of purgatory. Yet, the pains of these sins can be relieved, and their time spent in purgatory shortened by their friends who are left in the realm of the living. The 1439 Council of Florence declared:

> If the truly penitent die in the love of God, before they have made satisfaction by worthy fruits of penance for their sins of commission and omission, their souls are purified by purgatorial pains after death; and that for relief from these pains they are benefitted by the suffrages of the faithful in this life, that is, by Masses, prayers, and almsgiving, and by the other offices of piety usually performed by the faithful for one another according to the practice of the Church.

While the Council of Florence may give its approval to praying for and even paying (alms and indulgences) for the deliverance of these sinners, what about the divine word of God? There are at least two passages we are aware of that have been suggested as Bible authority.

2 Timothy 1:16-18

> The Lord grant mercy unto the house of Onesiphorus: for he oft refreshed me, and was not ashamed of my chain; but, when he was in Rome, he sought me diligently, and found me (the Lord grant unto him to find mercy of the Lord in that day); and in how many things he ministered at Ephesus, thou knowest very well.

The text is used to show that Paul prays for his deceased friend Onesiphorus. The Catholic defense is, "[it] makes sense only if he can be helped by prayer." Did Paul pray for the dead? To be honest, this text does not really inform us that Onesiphorus is even dead. Catholics make an assumption without inference or implication, and then irresponsibly and presumptuously insert purgatory into this text. This is a desperate attempt to prove an unprovable doctrine. Attempts to justify praying for the dead and argue for the existence of a place called purgatory make no sense in this text.

Does the Bible Teach Purgatory?

1 Corinthians 15:29
> Else what shall they do that are baptized for the dead? If the dead are not raised at all, why then are they baptized for them?

Beginning Apologetics for the defense of the Catholic faith states, "Paul mentions the practice of people having themselves baptized for the dead for the benefit of the dead, who cannot be helped if there is no intermediate state of purification." Admittedly, varied explanations are offered concerning the meaning of this text. Yet, let us consider the overall context of 1 Corinthians 15—our confidence in the resurrection, which has nothing to do with purgatory!

One can no more be baptized for another person than one can believe or repent on behalf of another. Each man is responsible to God for his own life and sins. Solomon said, "This is the end of the matter; all hath been heard: fear God, and keep His commandments; for this is the whole duty of man. For God will bring every work into judgment, with every hidden thing, whether it be good, or whether it be evil" (Eccl. 12:13-14). Paul said, "For we must all be made manifest before the judgment seat of Christ; that each one may receive the things done in the body, according to what he hath done, whether it be good or bad" (2 Cor. 5:10). This means that all the prayers, alms, and even masses offered by others on behalf of my salvation are utterly useless.

Conclusion

While the Bible teaches the existence of an afterlife and the Hadean realm, it does not teach or support the concept of purgatory. The doctrine of "purgatory" does not appear in the first five centuries of the church, and was not made an article of faith until the tenth century. While there are many false tentacles associated with this precept of man (i.e., prayers and alms for the dead, dependence on uninspired doctrines and writings, indulgences, etc. that are absent in the Holy Scriptures), the greatest insult of this doctrine is a blasphemy directed to the Godhead: The Father—Omnipotent and Omniscient; Christ Jesus, the Son of God—the perfect, sinless sacrifice for sin; and the Spirit of God—the giver of all truth, complete and infallible. This doctrine denies the revealed message of the power and efficacy of the blood of Jesus Christ.

There is no need for a purging purgatory because we have been "justified by His blood... saved from the wrath of God through Him" (Rom.

5:9). The Hebrew writer declared that Christ Jesus, the Son of God, "made purification of sins" and then "sat down on the right hand of the Majesty on high" (Heb. 1:3). In Christ, "we have our redemption through His blood, the forgiveness of our trespasses, according to the riches of His grace" (Eph. 1:7). There is no doubt about the power of Christ's blood to remove (purge) sin from the lives of the obedient believer.

One begins his walk with Christ by dying with Christ. It is in baptism, a likeness to the death, burial, and resurrection of our Lord that we are made alive (Rom. 6:3-11). We arise and walk in a newness of life—spiritually resurrected. As children of God, we always have access to that cleansing blood to remove sin as we confess and repent. "If we walk in the light, as He is in the light, we have fellowship one with another, and the blood of Jesus, His Son, cleanseth us from all sin . . . . If we confess our sins, He is faithful and righteous to forgive us our sins, and to cleanse us from all unrighteousness" (1 John 1:7-9). Purgatory annuls the previous passages and declares Christ Jesus to be powerless.

Bibliography

ASV = American Standard Version. New York, NY: Thomas Nelson & Sons, 1901.

Catechism of the Catholic Church. Vatican City: Liberia Editrice Vaticana, 1994.

Chacon, Frank and Jim Burnham. *Beginning Apologetics: How To Explain and Defend the Catholic Faith.* Farmington, NM: San Juan Catholic Seminars, 1993.

Gibbons, James Cardinal. *The Faith of Our Fathers: Being a Plain Exposition and Vindication of the Church Founded by Our Lord Jesus Christ.* Baltimore: John Murphy Company, 1917.

Hamilton, Clinton D. *Truth Commentaries: 1 Peter.* Bowling Green, KY: Guardian of Truth Foundation, 1995

Hardon, Jon A. *The Catholic Catechism: A Contemporary Catechism of the Teachings of the Catholic Church.* Garden City, NY: S.J. Double Day & Company, Inc., 1975.

Litmer, Greg. "A Look at Roman Catholicism, (2): Purgatory: Does It Exist?" *Truth Magazine* 24.32 (August 14, 1980): 522-524.

Does the Bible Teach Purgatory?

McBrien, Richard P. *The Harper Collins Encyclopedia of Catholicism.* San Francisco, CA: HarperSanFrancisco, 1995.

Mike, Willis. "The Doctrine of Purgatory." *Then Comes the End,* 31-36. Athens, AL: Truth Publications, Inc., 2016.

Nevins, Albert J. *The Maryknoll Catholic Dictionary.* New York: Grossett and Dunlap, 1968.

Patton, Marshall. *Truth Commentaries: 1-2 Timothy, Titus, and Philemon.* Mike Willis, ed. Bowling Green, KY: Guardian of Truth Foundation, 2001.

Pope, Kyle. *Truth Commentaries: Matthew.* Mike Willis, ed. Bowling Green, KY: Guardian of Truth Foundation, 2013.

Salza, John. *The Biblical Basis for Purgatory.* Gastonia NC: 0Saint Benedict Press, 2009.

Striebing, Jr., William H. *Ancient Near Eastern History and Culture.* New York: Longman Publication, 2003.

Willis, Mike. *Truth Commentaries: 1 Corinthians.* Mike Willis, ed. Bowling Green, KY: Guardian of Truth Foundation, 1979.

"Zoroastrianism." *Wikipedia.* Wikimedia Foundation. https://en.wikipedia.org/wiki/Zoroastrianism.

Does the Bible Teach Reincarnation?

By Jennifer Maxey

Introduction

No. The Bible does not teach reincarnation as a viable system of salvation. Thankfully, as women of faith, we never have to fear exploration. We know whom we have believed. We possess the established and confirmed Word. We rest in God's all-sufficiency and provision. With our hearts "rooted and grounded in love," God enables comprehension (Eph. 3:17). With the "eyes of (our) understanding enlightened," God provides clarity and confidence. Our God fearlessly invites all into investigation of His truths, both in creation and His Word. Indeed, it is God's glory to conceal His realities; and it is our honor to search them out (Prov. 25:2).

Jennifer Maxey, daughter of Douglas and Joan Hethcoat, was born in Pascagoula, Mississippi in 1975, and raised in Tennessee. Married for twenty-three years to Kevin Maxey, Jennifer endeavors to fulfill her role as helpmeet to Kevin as he preaches the gospel. Before marriage, Jennifer was blessed to travel, visit, and work with congregations in Brazil and Slovakia. Together, Jennifer and Kevin have been a part of the Lord's work in Germany, Lithuania, Philippines, Arkansas, and Tennessee. Jennifer's education includes an AA from Florida College (95), BA from MTSU (97), ND from Clayton (09), and postgraduate work at Bridgeport University of Connecticut (13). Currently, Jennifer is a full-time Christian, wife, and homemaker; homeschooling mother of five children and director for Classical Conversations; owner and Naturopath at Total Wellness in Columbia, TN, where she runs a part-time practice as a Naturopathic Doctor. Kevin, Jennifer and their family work and worship with the church in Spring Hill, TN. She can be reached at kjjejzemax7@gmail.com.

Does the Bible Teach Reincarnation?

God's Test of Spirits

God's foundational parameters establish the boundaries of our inquiries. "Beloved, do not believe every spirit, but tests the spirits to see whether they are from God" (1 John 4:1). And here is how we scripturally discern between revelation from God's Spirit versus "deceitful spirits and doctrines of demons" (1 Tim. 4:1):

1. "Every spirit that confesses Jesus Christ has come in the flesh is from God" (1 John 4:2).
2. "Every spirit that does not confess Jesus is not from God" (1 John 4:3).
3. "Whoever knows God" listens to the apostles' teaching. This is the Spirit of truth (1 John 4:6).
4. "Whoever is not from God" does not listen to the apostles' teaching. This is the spirit of error (1 John 4:6).

Pass or Fail?

Using God's test of spirits within the dozens of reincarnation religions, here are the results:

- *Most* do believe a man, Jesus Christ, came in the flesh.
- *All* deny that Jesus is THE Christ, the singular, only begotten Son of God.
- *Most* confess a man, Jesus, as "self-realized," "enlightened," and "spiritually evolved" wise teacher and god among many gods.
- *None* confess Jesus as THE singular Way, Truth, and Life of God.
- *Most* listen to Jesus's teaching in the Sermon on the Mount, and general spiritual truisms from apostolic doctrine.
- *None* accept the Bible as THE singular, confirmed, Word of THE Supreme Creator God revealed in the Bible.
- *None* accept the Father, Yahweh, as THE singular, confirmed, sovereign God of all.

Therefore, using God's test of spirits, every woman of faith maintains confident assurance that reincarnation salvation systems are not from God. They are not revealed by the Spirit of Truth. They are revealed by the deceitful spirit of error.

So, does the Bible teach salvation by successive earthly rebirths into various forms of existence (plant, animal, vegetable, rock, or human) based on good or bad karmic accumulation, culminating in eventual self-

"When Will These Things Be?" : Questions on Eschatology

salvation, resulting in elevation to self-realized, enlightened god among many gods, having earned the eternal existence of peace and absence of suffering? No.

"Rightness" is not "Righteousness"

"Well, that's error. It's ridiculous to think humans come back as animals. They're wrong. The end. Now, I'm done." Although women of faith decidedly identify this religious system as error, is it enough for us to just stop there? Do we just stop there, even though more than 6 out of 10 people around us are being led away by this deceitful spirit? Do we just stop there, even though our children and grandchildren encounter this doctrine of demons every single day? Do we just stop there, dismissing all adherents as dishonest seekers?

Certainly, God requires that we investigate the spirits and discern between truth and error, engaging in continual alignment of our steps with His clear teaching. However, God calls us beyond the boundaries of "being right" or "possessing right knowledge." Just "being right" is not righteousness. "For they being ignorant of God's righteousness, and seeking to establish their own righteousness, have not submitted to the righteousness of God" (Rom. 10:3). True righteousness hinges on what you do with what you know. True righteousness involves loving God enough to humbly, purposefully advance the knowledge of His Son, Jesus Christ. "You search the Scriptures, for in them you think you have eternal life; and these are they which testify of Me … But I know you, that you do not have the love of God in you" (John 5:39-42) True righteousness involves loving others enough to engage in difficult conversations, hear other perspectives, and thoughtfully share God's clear, confirmed revelation with them. Yes, reincarnation systems are error. Yes, salvation by reincarnation is wrong. For women of faith, that is the beginning. Now, we reach out.

The Spiritualist Next Door

Reincarnation matters. Representing more than ignorant superstition or religious rebellion, reincarnation viewpoints hold the confidence of 33% of U.S. adults and 26% of culturally designated Christians. When broadened to include associated beliefs of animism, psychics, and astrology, the numbers rise as high as 61% of professed Christians and 78% of general seekers. These numbers include people you know. Many neighbors, friends, family, and—yes, members of local congregations among the churches of Christ—accept reincarnation as spiritual reality.

Does the Bible Teach Reincarnation?

Six-in-ten Christians, 'nones' hold at least one New Age belief

	Believe spiritual energy can be located in physical things	Believe in psychics	Believe in reincarnation	Believe in astrology	NET Believe in at least one
All U.S. adults	42%	41%	33%	29%	**62%**
Christian	37	40	29	26	61
Protestant	32	38	26	24	57
Evangelical	24	33	19	18	47
Mainline	43	44	33	30	67
Historically black	41	43	38	34	72
Catholic	47	46	36	33	70
Unaffiliated	47	40	38	32	62
Atheist	13	10	7	3	22
Agnostic	40	31	28	18	56
Nothing in particular	61	52	51	47	78

Source: Survey conducted Dec. 4-18, 2017, among U.S. adults.

PEW RESEARCH CENTER

In preparation for this study, I sent the following question on my personal Facebook page, and posted in one—*only one*—local group page for our town:

> *"Do you believe in reincarnation? Or know someone who does? I would like to hear an explanation from someone who actually believes it."*

Within the few minutes it was visible in the post feed . . .

- 2 sisters in Christ reached out independently to convey personal convictions in favor of reincarnation
- 1 sister in Christ offered, and subsequently provided, reincarnation literature from a "Christian" perspective
- 4 strangers from my local community shared personal testimonies of past-life regression visions, dreams, and "memories"
- 1 woman detailed her recurring past-life vision memories of being buried alive under rocks on a beach, then watching her parents give up the search because they could not hear her screams from beneath the rubble
- 21 sent screenshots of important passages from reincarnation literature
- 5 recommended books
- 1 self-identified Druid pagan briefly explained the differences between Hinduism, Buddhism, Jainism, and neo-pagan Druid beliefs

"When Will These Things Be?" : Questions on Eschatology

- 1 woman related her visitation encounter from a recently deceased little girl, who arrived in the form of a red cardinal, and directed her to the door of the grieving mother—possibly just in time to prevent suicide due to unfathomable grief
- 4 preachers helpfully directed me towards applicable verses and sound literature on the topic
- 2 sisters in Christ expressed concern about the nature of my question (thanks for watching out for me!)

The inherent claims and assurances of reincarnation captively hold the hearts and minds of people in direct, daily association of women of faith across the globe. That's you. That's me. Should we just ignore them, since this topic feels foreign to us? As vessels in the Master's hand, women of faith mercifully carry the light of God's Word to hearts deceived by darkness. Because Jesus died for them, understanding reincarnation matters.

Why Reincarnation?

As current culture revisits so-called "New Age" belief systems, reincarnation emerges as enduring, logical, scientific "spiritualism." Those who are "self-actualized" embrace an open-minded inquiry of powers, connection, and the journey of souls.

Emotional Appeal. By means of shared emotional vulnerability, and the promise of meaningful connectedness, reincarnation captivates and bonds human hearts. Through sharing within an atmosphere of open inquiry, a particular camaraderie emerges. The cultural conversation regarding each soul's journey is affirming, accepting, allowing. No one judges. No one condemns. No one corrects. Every perspective is honored, considered as important to the continually emerging body of "truth."

Such affinities mirror God's revealed intention for humanity. From the beginning, God created us for spiritual connection on the grandest scale: intimate personal relationship with Him. From the beginning, God fashioned us for participation within the Divine Nature: "So God created man in His own image; in the image of God He created him; male and female He created them" (Gen. 1:27). Furthermore, from the beginning, God shaped us for connection with other humans: "And the Lord God said, '*It is* not good that man should be alone; I will make him a helper comparable to him'" (Gen. 2:18).

Does the Bible Teach Reincarnation?

Reincarnation offers meaningful connection experience, which women particularly recognize as humanity's fundamental need to bond and belong. Ostensibly, a soul's journey through many successive lifetimes creates webs of overlapping, interwoven relationships. In the present, each soul senses and explores possible previous connections in order to discover its own constitution and purpose. Reincarnation appeals on an emotional level through meaningful connection.

Cultural Appeal. Spiritualism and its doctrine of reincarnation impacts the day-to-day existence of every woman of faith. These ancient dogmas, now streamlined and rebranded for modern consumption, meet you at every turn. Do you recognize them? Are your eyes opened?

What are you saying?

Do your words align with God's? Are you ready to give an answer? How about in your everyday conversations?

"Hey Mom, next time I'm born, I hope I'm a butterfly!"	1 John 3:2: "... and it has not yet been revealed what we shall be, but we know that when He is revealed, we shall be like Him."
"You must be channeling Grandma today."	Isaiah 8:19 "And when they say to you, "Seek those who are mediums and wizards, who whisper and mutter," should not a people seek their God? *Should they seek* the dead on behalf of the living?"
"Oh, wow. Deja Vu! We must have known each other in a past life."	Hebrews 9:27 "it is appointed for men to die once, but after this the judgment."
"Looks like that guy has some bad karma!"	Galatians 6:7 "Do not be deceived, God is not mocked; for whatever a man sows, that he will also reap."

What are you reading?

How does such content find its way into daily dialogue, even among Christians? Clearly, reincarnation concepts infiltrate the various forms of media; and Christians consume the media. For example, there are Christians who recommend the two following books, written by proponents of reincarnation salvation:

"When Will These Things Be?" : Questions on Eschatology

1. ***Conversations with God*** by Neale Donald Walsch (New York Times Best-Seller for 137 weeks)

   > **Concepts:**
   > You existed before this life.
   > You chose your own conditions for reincarnation.
   > There is no hell.

2. ***Many Lives, Many Masters*** by Brian L. Weiss, M.D. (New York Times Bestseller)(International Bestseller translated into 30+ languages)

   > **Excerpt:**
   > "Life is endless, so we never die;
   > we were never really born.
   > We just pass through different phases.
   > There is no end."

What's on Your Child's Screen?

Media offers, and the children partake. Beware. Just because it is presented as a cute fluffy puppy, or animated wide-eyed princess does not mean the motives of presentation are innocent. As long as they are in our care, you and I are responsible to guard the hearts and minds of our children and grandchildren. You and I are responsible to navigate life with painstaking effort to teach them the fear of the Lord, not mindless, passive distraction. You and I are responsible to purposefully prepare their heart-soil, not to pollute it by worldly "entertainment" . Pay attention to the AGENDA. Read the reviews. Absolutely no excuse remains. We cannot naively offer the open minds of children and grandchildren on Hollywood's altar.

"Ok, children. Remember: polytheism, reincarnation, and animism are false."

"Ok, children. Run along now, grandma's tired and mommy's at work. Go ahead and choose a movie to watch."

A Few Movie Choices

Choice #1: *Moanna*: Grandma returns as a helpful stingray, then later as a realistic, huggable vision.
Message: Death is not permanent.

Does the Bible Teach Reincarnation?

Choice #2: *Pocahontas*: Mother returns in the leaves, guiding her toward the cliff, drawing her toward John Smith. "The ones you love are still here, still present, still watching over you."
Nature worship: Powhatan's tribe held the natural world as spiritually sacred.
Animism (attribution of a soul to plants, objects, and natural phenomena) present in her song to John Smith. "I know every rock and tree and creature has a life, has a spirit, has a name."
Grandmother Willow (a tree) provides personal spiritual guidance. "You are Spirits' child; they live in the earth, the water, the sky. If you listen, they will guide you."
Message: Physical death is not permanent. We never really separate from those we love. God is nature.
Spiritual guides need not be other-worldly. They can be right here as your backyard tree.
Every natural thing is sacred and holy, deserving reverence.

Choice #3: *Brother Bear*: When a young Inuit hunter needlessly kills a bear, he mystically transforms into a bear himself. His transmigration experience punishes and enlightens his soul.
Message: Life essence, or soul, transmigrates between living entities ever-learning and growing toward an eventual maturity.

Choice #4: *The Princess and the Frog*: Main characters live through 3 life cycles, first as human, then frog, then back to human again. Mama Odie offers wisdom for successful transformation into the next life: "You have to dig a little deeper, to find out who you are. When you find out who you are, you find out what you need."
Message: Answers and help for today emerge from within self. Understanding self more emerges from examination of the past and past lives.

Choice #5: *A Dog's Purpose*: A cute dog died 4 different ways: euthanized, car wreck, old age, natural causes. Each time, the dog experienced rebirth into another cute dog body. In each life, he needed to fulfill his important purpose, impacting human lives.
Message: Reincarnation is real.

Choice #6: *The Lion King*: "Yes, Simba, but let me explain. When we die, our bodies become the grass, and the antelope eat the grass. And so we are all connected in the great *Circle of Life*."

"When Will These Things Be?" : Questions on Eschatology

Message: For millennia, Buddhism presents *the Circle of Life* as six Realms of Existence overseen by Yama, god of death. Were movie makers unaware of the Circle of Life that operates under demonic guard for the last 6000 years or so?

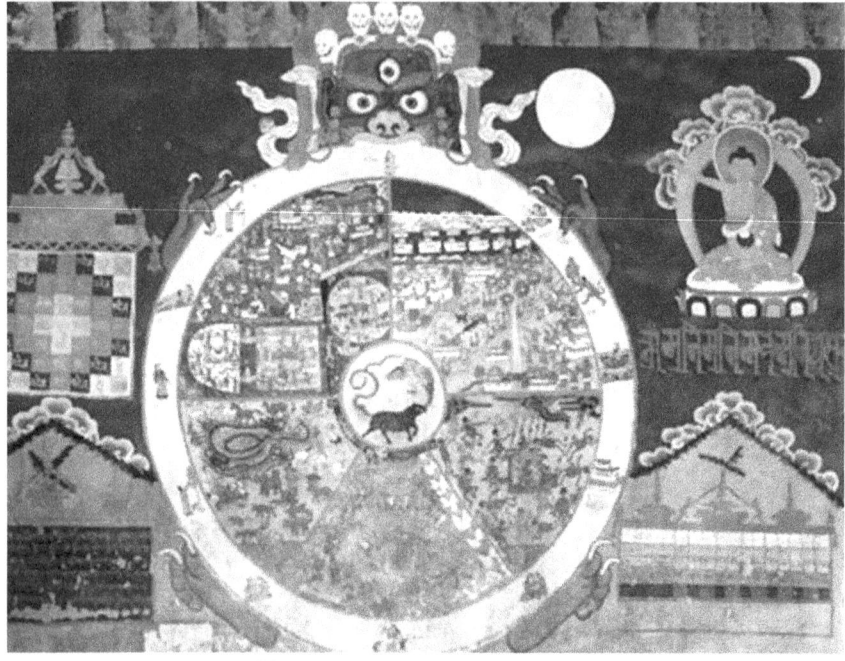

From http://sites.google.com/site/religioninthelionking/circle-of-life. In Buddhism, the circle of life is the belief that humans are reincarnated after death and born again.

Demonstrably, the cultural appeal of reincarnation dogma actively presents in the immediate surroundings of women of faith. In lighthearted conversations, we drop the guards on our mouths, bantering playfully about blatant error. In libraries and bookstores, "New York Times Best-Seller" labels outweigh our better judgement. As frazzled moms, or indulgent grandmas, Hollywood's offer to babysit the children tempts and traps. Conversations, books, and movies provide open highways, delivering doctrines of demons, dressed as cute puppies and princesses, straight into our own hearts and the hearts of our children. "But you be watchful in all things" (2 Tim. 4:5).

Does the Bible Teach Reincarnation?

Behind the Scenes

Who are the reincarnation believers? The only major faiths that reject reincarnation doctrine include Atheism and the Abrahamic religions: Judaism, Christianity, and Islam. Here are a few religions or followings that include reincarnation:

Spiritualism	Judaic mystics	Orphism
Hinduism	(Kabbalah)	Occultism
Buddhism	Spiritism	Satanism
Jainism	Spiritualism	Scientology
Sikkhism	Paganism	Philosopher Pythagoras
Taoism	Neo-paganism	Philosopher Socrates
Confucianism	Gnosticism	Philosopher Plato
Shintoism	Eckkankar	

What is their structure? This "body" of reincarnation believers, even within the individually defined religious systems, represents no particular structure at all. As an ancient, continuously emergent tenet of multiple faith systems, reincarnation resembles an amoebic blob with pseudopods in nearly every corner of religiosity. Surprisingly, adherents accept and celebrate the all-inclusive acceptance of every viewpoint. Lives are built upon the premise that every individual seeks his or her own path through life, toward a loosely defined "salvation," ending eventually as a demi-god, god, Nothing, All, Nirvana, Enlightenment, Self-Actualized, or neverending eternal rebirths. There are innumerable gods. There is no real truth. There is no real death.

In contrast, our understanding of relationship with God emerges from the clear New Testament presentation of the identifiable structure of the church, which is God's house (1 Tim. 3:15):

> Cornerstone + foundation + living stones
> Jesus Christ + apostles and prophets + Christians

"But you are . . . the household of God, built on the foundation of the apostles and prophets, Christ Jesus Himself being the cornerstone, in whom the whole structure, being joined together, grows into a holy temple in the Lord . . . a dwelling place for God in the Spirit" (Eph. 2:19-22). Simply, New Testament Christians accept and celebrate the all-sufficient ability of God to reveal His viewpoint. Lives are built upon faith in Jesus

"When Will These Things Be?" : Questions on Eschatology

Christ, who is the Way, experiencing a clearly defined salvation from the death produced by sin, beginning and ending in eternal fellowship with God. He is One God. He is true God. He is living God.

What are the advantages? Membership in a world religion offers several appealing advantages. Notably, endless do-overs create the possibility of eventual universal salvation for every soul. Every lifetime receives its own judgement, and failure is possible. However, failure only means you have to be reborn and try again. This could seem scary and uncertain, but don't worry. If you have to be reborn, everything is up to you. You decide the best next life to help you grow and develop in your human evolution. You decide the setting, people, challenges, and circumstances of your next life. And actually, you even have the option to forego reincarnation indefinitely and spend some time navigating the spirit realm instead.

It is true that suffering in life presents difficulty, but there is no need to despair. Reincarnation mindset aids detachment from all reality: Nothing is real. Nothing actually exists. Even if self, others, or god exists, nothing should cause stress because each individual is accountable only to their own true, noble self. From the inner depths, the true self leads each seeker through a personal spiritual journey. The answers arise from within, and need not match up or unify with any other standard. The only standard is whatever you decide in your true self. For anyone who prefers to order their own best life with no accountability, no external standards, and no consequences for failure, reincarnation mindset has its advantages.

What's so bad about reincarnation? So far, rebirth religions are presented as somewhat chaotic, with hazy core beliefs, and a tendency toward self-magnification. As women of faith, accustomed to personal relationship with God, continual selfless intercession from Jesus, and constructive revelation from the Spirit, we are not too impressed, but not necessarily bothered either. However, there is more.

There's a Dark Side

In 1866, American Spiritualists held a conference in Providence Rhode Island, at which they passed the following defining resolutions (Rotherham):

1. Resolved, to abandon all Christian ordinances and worship forms.
2. Resolved, to discontinue all Sunday Schools.
3. Resolved, to denounce all forms of sexual tyranny.
4. Resolved, to affirm the non-use of animal foods

Does the Bible Teach Reincarnation?

According to 1 Timothy 4:1-3, these resolutions exactly define Spiritualism as a doctrine of demons.

> Now the Spirit explicitly says that in latter times some will depart from the faith, giving heed to deceiving spirits and doctrines of demons, speaking lies in hypocrisy, having their own conscience seared with a hot iron, forbidding to marry, and commanding to abstain from foods which God created to be received with thanksgiving by those who believe and know the truth.

Over the years since 1866, American Spiritualists refined their system. By their own declarations, Spiritualism, which is the modern uniting umbrella for reincarnation faith systems, bases its science, philosophy, and religion upon the testimony from the dead. Such testimony from the spirit world becomes available on earth through the expertise of mediums. A Spiritualist, then, is "one who believes, as the basis of his or her religion, in the communication between this and the spirit world by means of mediumship and endeavors to mould his or her character and conduct in accordance with the highest teachings derived from such communication." The objective of these religions involves the stated resolve to "protest against every attempt to compel humanity to worship God in any particular or prescribed manner." For clarity, they have included the following denials (nsac.org):

1. Inspiration of the Bible, denied
2. Fall of man, denied
3. Deity of Jesus Christ, denied
4. Atoning death of Jesus Christ, denied
5. Existence of personal devil, denied
6. Differences between demons and angels, denied
7. Existence of heaven, denied
8. Existence of hell, denied

Clearly, the emotionally affirming, universally accepting proponents of good karma reject outright the claims and declarations of Yahweh Elohim, and the authority of His Word.

There's an Agenda

Christian mothers and grandmothers pay attention. We watch out for godless evolutionists. We learn to answer false science. We teach our children about Jesus and God. Just as we become effective in these en-

"When Will These Things Be?" : Questions on Eschatology

deavors, the sleeping giant of reincarnation dogma rises. Suddenly, reincarnation is a legitimized science of souls. Suddenly, spiritualism repackages all God's blessings and benefits. Suddenly, "spirituality" offers all the advantages enjoyed in Christ, without allegiance to God or accountability to standards.

Now There's Justification

"In one fell swoop," every human is his or her own god, and anything goes. Ongoing sin is not my fault; it's just because of residual moral weakness from my past life. Homosexuality is not my fault; it's just because that's who I was before. Transgender preferences are not my fault; it's just that I was female in my last 2 lives, but now my body does not match my true self. Resetting my current body will reset my karma, ensuring that I will be female again in the next life. Adultery is not my fault; it's just that I've reunited with my soul's true match. Envy, hatred, and jealousy are not my fault; it's just that I was so mistreated and unfairly suppressed in a previous existence. Nothing is my fault; it's just that . . . Now there's justification.

Woman of faith, do not wait until your child, grandchild, or Bible class student walks out, justifying all manner of unrighteousness because of his or her past-life identity. God is granting us this precious moment to arm ourselves and our children with God's Infallible Word. Be aware. Reincarnation has a dark side.

Shifting Perspectives

Have you ever tried to think from another religious point of view? I encourage you to take a moment and try out a few perspective shifts, as if you are newly immigrated to the USA:

- Low-born Indian wife and mother, raised in the tradition and values of Hinduism
- High-born Thai woman, raised in the tradition and values of Buddhism
- Alaskan native of Inuit descent, daughter of the tribal chief, raised in tradition of animism
- Middle-class American woman raised in Norway in the tradition of New Age Spiritualism
- Make up your own scenario based upon people you encounter in your world

Does the Bible Teach Reincarnation?

I hope you actually tried this. If you did, what was your experience? What did you notice? In what way does such a shift challenge you? How do you feel about thinking from a different viewpoint? For me, this is difficult. I am uncomfortable even trying to see a different perspective. A part of me immediately begins to defend God and His Word by calling forth all that is wrong with these differing traditions and values. Or, I cannot even begin to understand because I have no idea what an Eskimo believes. Clearly, calling others to consideration of the gospel of Christ, as revealed in the Bible, challenges them, just as it would you or me, if we were in their position.

Sharing God's Gospel

Right now, in 2020, you and I live "at the end of the ages," after the manifestation in flesh of Jesus Christ, Son of the Living God. Because Jesus walked among us, every man and woman with access to a Bible can learn God's definition of "the good." In one confirmed Holy Book, we enjoy direct, unfettered revelations, clarifications, and expectations of the Supreme Creator God. Because God steadily selected and utilized holy men and prophets to record written insights, we receive Divine knowledge of life and death.

Back then, from circa 3500 BC to circa AD 33, the nations had to figure some things out on their own. Since none of these reincarnation religions arose within a setting of an ongoing relationship with Yawheh Elohim, their perspectives challenge those of us carrying around a Bible. Before Jesus walked among us, rulers, thinkers, and philosophers bore the task of defining "the good." Before compilation of God's revelation, pagan priests and "holy men" laboriously sought understanding of Divinity, life, and death. Before Moses or Abraham, perceptions of God arose primarily through trial-and-error observations of this flesh-and-blood realm. Without the confirmed and completed Word, the nations groped, and sometimes partially grasped, spirit-world truths.

The Gospel Is for All

Despite our awareness of Reincarnation's dark side, we recognize that deceptive doctrines beguile, capturing unsuspecting souls. As women of mercy, we reach out to them with God's truth, hoping for receptive hearts. Despite the dark declarations of reincarnation adherents, women of faith discern that the gospel is still for all.

"When Will These Things Be?" : Questions on Eschatology

In his letter to the Romans, Paul assures his audience of "the power of God to salvation for everyone who believes"—not only those from a Jewish heritage, who know about Yahweh Elohim, but also those from among the nations, who may have never heard the name of Yahweh (Rom. 1:16). Peter taught Cornelius, the first Christian from non-Jewish heritage. Then, Paul spoke God's Word at the outskirts of civilized Roman Empire—among the nations. Led by the gospel's power, many turned away "from idols to the living and true God" (1 Thess. 1:9). Throughout the first-century world, faithful men and women shared God's truth with idolatrous pagan worshippers of Mercury, Zeus, Diana, Athena. First-century Christians led sorcerers, temple prostitutes, homosexuals, and demoniacs out of Satan's grip, and into the safety of Christ. Yet, inclusion of Gentiles began way before that.

Leading the nations, or Gentiles, into fellowship with their Creator, is no afterthought. God's intention to include them did not begin on the day Peter wrestled about whether or not to eat unclean things from the sheet in his vision. Indeed, God's intention for the nations preceded the entirety of the Jewish nation and heritage. In His foundational promise to Abraham, who was a non-Jew, (i.e. Gentile), from the nation of Mesopotamia, Yahweh declared His design: "In you all the nations shall be blessed" (Gen. 12:3). Notably, Paul designated this promise as "foreseeing that God would justify the Gentiles by faith" (Gal. 3:8). Not only for Jews, but also for Gentiles, the gospel is for all.

Groping for God

From the beginning, God expected the nations to seek after Him, observing His created world, deducing His power and Supreme Deity. And they did! The Holy Spirit Himself asserts through Paul that the nations "knew God" (Rom. 1:21); and "observed" God clearly—even the invisible attributes of God (His eternal nature, power, and supremacy) (Rom. 1:21). Further, they "knew the righteous judgement of God," clearly discerning that those who practice uncleanness deserve death (Rom. 1:32).

Yahweh Elohim's undeniable renown powerfully prompted investigation among the nations. They were seeking; and the determination of God is "seek, and you shall find" (Matt. 7:7). From the days of antiquity, God assures all who strive toward Him: "If you seek . . . as for silver, and search . . . as for hidden treasure, then you will discern the fear of the LORD and discover the knowledge of God" (Prov. 2:4-5). In his *Study on*

Does the Bible Teach Reincarnation?

the Ritual of the Dead (1860), one man eloquently summarized fundamental discoveries of divinity from ancient times:

> The unity of a Supreme Being, His eternity, His omnipotence, and eternal generation in God; the creation of the world, and of all living things, attributed to this supreme God; the immortality of the soul, completed by the doctrine of penalties and rewards; such is the sublime and abiding substance, in spite of all deviations and mythological embellishment . . ." (Mark)

They discovered so much! They sought, and found! What prompted such purposeful investigation? Specific word choices, declared centuries ago by the mouth of Amos, clarify that it was indeed the "Name," or renowned honor, (*shem* H8034) of God which accosted the attention of the Gentiles. Yahweh's reputation of power and supremacy "called" the Gentiles, causing them to "seek the Lord" (Amos 9:11-12) (Acts 15:16-17). Hearts and minds answered that call, unveiling foundational truths by honest consideration and searching. Admirably, they sensed, sought, and in some cases found.

Common Ground

Reaching out in hope to those "whose minds the god of this age has blinded, who do not believe, lest the light of the gospel . . . should shine on them" (2 Cor. 4:4), women of faith follow the New Testament template seeking common ground. By listening in order to understand, we discern shared points of understanding. Beginning there provides the best chance of true communication and teaching. Inevitably, tension will arise, but we continue patiently in hope of reclaiming a soul by the power of God's gospel.

With 6,000+ years of historical durability, reincarnation and its accompanying religiosity boast undeniable claims of enduring relevance and insight. The ancients approached life objectively. Generally, they considered the known creation as a whole, then constructed a worldview based on observable truths. Foundational to all other considerations, the nations sought out and understood the reality, sovereignty, omnipotence, and omniscience of God. By experience and observation, humanity throughout the ages understood God's "eternal power and godhead" (Rom. 1:20), as attested by the Holy Spirit through Paul, apostle of Jesus Christ.

Further, they participated in and rightly perceived spiritual warfare between "good" and "evil"—among humans, angels, demons, and gods.

Additionally, repeated observance of God's law of sowing and reaping taught the nations inherent justice. They got some things right.

Spiritual reality exists. Almost all the "world religions," inherently assume the reality of a non-physical, spiritual realm populated by spirit-beings.

There is More than Meets the Eye
By seeking, they observed: animating essence separates from the body at death
By faith, we understand: People who are dead on earth are alive in another realm (Luke 16; Matt. 17:3)

There is a God . . . or god . . . or gods
By seeking, they observed: God / Ultimate Reality / Supreme Principle
By faith, we understand: Jehovah is His Name (Psa. 83:18)

- There is a God; He is alive (Exod. 3:14)
- In Him, we live and move and have our being (Acts 17:28)
- A Supreme Creator God knows thoughts and motives of humans (Jer. 17:10)
- Jesus brings resurrection unto eternal life (John 11:25)

There are Powers
By seeking, they observed: spiritual beings / some good / some bad / some powerful
By faith, we understand: angels, demons, principalities and power, rulers of darkness, god of this age

Demons are real, and pervasive
- ***In Jewish places of worship:*** "In the synagogue there was a man possessed by the spirit of an unclean demon" (Luke 4:33)
- ***In Gentile places of worship:*** "The things which the Gentiles sacrifice they sacrifice to demons and not to God" (1 Cor. 10:20)
- ***In Jews:*** "Mary called Magdalene, out of whom had come seven demons" (Luke 8:2)
- ***In Gentiles:*** "A woman whose little daughter had an unclean spirit . . . now the woman was a Gentile" (Matt. 15:22)
- ***In the tombs:*** "immediately there met Him out of the tombs a man with an unclean spirit, who had *his* dwelling among the tombs" (Markk 5:2-3)

Does the Bible Teach Reincarnation?

- *In the heavenly realms:* "For we do not wrestle against flesh and blood, but against principalities, against powers, against the rulers of the darkness of this age, against spiritual *hosts* of wickedness in the heavenly *places*" (Eph. 6:12)
- *In hell (Tartarus):* "For if God did not spare the angels who sinned, but cast *them* down to hell [Gr. *tartarus*] and delivered *them* into chains of darkness, to be reserved for judgment" (2 Pet. 2:4)

Angels are real, and sometimes visit.
- "But the prince of the kingdom of Persia was withstanding me for twenty-one days; then behold, Michael, one of the chief princes, came to help me, for I had been left there with the kings of Persia" (Dan. 10:13).
- "Some have entertained angels without knowing it" (Heb. 13:2)

The Devil (Satan) is real, and active and aware.
- "Be sober. Be on the alert. Your adversary, the devil, prowls around like a roaring lion" (1 Pet. 5:8).

With thousands of years to figure it out, did they get anything right? In several basic observances, God's Book positively affirms the perceptions of the nations. Every world religion (Hinduism, Buddhism, Jainism, Shintoism, Tribal worship, etc.) accurately concluded a few fundamental facts. In privilege, you and I know their conclusions are correct because God's Word says so.

Irreconcilable Differences

As females, we want people to like us. We want to bond and connect. We want to affirm and accept. Sadly, that is not always possible. Although we celebrate common ground, women of faith remember God's warning:

> Do not be unequally yoked together with unbelievers. For what fellowship has righteousness with lawlessness? And what communion has light with darkness? And what accord has Christ with Belial? Or what part has a believer with an unbeliever? And what agreement has the temple of God with idols? For you are the temple of the living God . . . therefore, come out from among them and be separate (2 Cor 6:14-17).

Despite a few areas of agreement, the vast body of reincarnation religion and dogma presents concepts completely outside the borders of God's clearly revealed truth. Indeed, most of their accompanying assertions stand directly opposed to the Word and ways of God. Whether people like us or not, our deepest loyalties rest with the Lord.

Transformed and Resurrected, Not Transmigrated and Reincarnated

Transmigration. Have you ever heard of the "transmigration of souls"? To demonstrate my degree of transmigratory understanding before this project, I will tell you how I reacted when Mark Mayberry approached me about presenting a ladies' lecture on "Reincarnation and the Transmigration of Souls." I started laughing, out loud, and laughed until I lost my breath. So, in case you do not already know: Transmigration, as a religious term, indicates the wanderings of a soul, or life-force, while not united with either a body or a spirit.

Proponents of reincarnation believe that newly dead, disembodied souls transmigrate into another body. It may be a human body. It may be an animal body. It may be a plant body. In a way, transmigration is the soul's way of shopping for a new body.

Transformation. Although my understanding is limited, God's Word teaches me. With God's Word, I am able to read and understand (Eph. 3:3-5). The Bible teaches that one entity dies, and the same entity is raised. Paul expresses that the body "is sown a natural body" (*soma psuchikon*—soul-body) and "it is raised a spiritual body" (*soma pneumatikon*—spirit-body).

The body that is sown will be the same body that is raised. It will have a new form, while still containing remnants of the old form: not that we will "be unclothed, but further clothed, that mortality may be swallowed up by life" (2 Cor. 5:4). Transformation occurs upon one distinct entity or individual that God desires to preserve—"body, soul, and spirit" (1 Thess. 5:23). By God's Word, I know that when I die, God will "transform (my) lowly body" (Phil. 3:21), but my animating life-force will not need to go shopping around for a place to live.

Because of sin, your current body cannot enter the presence of God. That is why He will transform it, just like He transforms a wheatberry into a glorious stalk of golden grain. The wheatberry is sown, but what follows is infinitely more. Right now your body exists in corruption, dishonor, and weakness, but because you have been born again of water and Spirit, God will transform your body to an existence of incorruption, glory, and power (1 Cor. 15: 36, 42, 43). The righteous dead are transformed, not transmigrated.

Does the Bible Teach Reincarnation?

Born Again, Not Re-born ... Again

You and I have already been added to a different body. Do you remember when you submitted to God's will, becoming obedient to death—death of the old you—death of the fleshly you? Then, your old self of flesh was buried with Christ. Someone buried your dead self of flesh into the grave waters of baptism. Neither you, nor your body of flesh remained in that grave, though. And why not? Because you met the cleansing blood of Jesus in that grave! Since His blood powerfully washed away your sins, death could not hold you anymore. So, you rose from that grave to a new life (Rom. 6:1-4). Born again!

In your old life, you consisted only of a flesh-body, animated by soul (*nephesh, psuchē*). When you rose (born of water) to walk in newness of life, you were no longer merely flesh-body + soul. There was something more to the new you. After baptism, you became flesh-body + soul + spirit (born of Spirit) (John 3:5). As a new creature in Christ, you are added to a different body. God adds you to the body of Christ (Acts 2:47; Eph. 1:23).

Superiority of Born Again to Re-Born ... *again*

Born again	vs.	Re-born ... again
Into the heaven-bound body of Christ	**Destination**	Into another earth-bound body
Of water Of spirit	**Nature** "For as many of you as were baptized into Christ have put on Christ" (Gal. 3:27) "That which is born of flesh is flesh; that which is born of spirit is spirit" (John 3:6)	Of flesh
New essential self	**Identity** "... In Christ, he is a new creature; old this are passed away; behold, all things have become new" (2 Cor. 5:17)	Same essential self
Intentional gift of grace now, answered by intentional good words and deed	**Source** " ...The answer of a good conscience toward God " (1 Pet. 3:21)	Inescapable result of karma, earned or lost by "good" or "not good" words and deeds
Reconciled to God	**State** "... You who were once alienated, now He has reconciled in the body of His flesh..." (Col. 1:21-22)	Alienated from "god"
Free-will (active choice)	**Decision** "The Lord ...is longsuffering toward us, not willing that any should perish, but that all should come to repentance" (2 Pet. 3:9)	Fate (passive reception)

"When Will These Things Be?" : Questions on Eschatology

Forgiven : "Enter In"	**Judgement** "In Him, we have redemption through His blood, the forgiveness of sins"(Eph. 1:7)	Condemned : repeat cycle
New birth is salvation	**Result** "Children of God . . . who were born, not of blood, nor of the will of flesh, nor of the will of man, but of God" (John 1:12-13)	Re-birth is defeat
Best possible outcome: fellowship with the fullness of All-Sufficient God	**Hope** "Indeed our fellowship is with the Father, and with His Son Jesus Christ" (1 John 1:3)	Best possible outcome: re-united with universal soul or cessation of suffering
True life as God intended	**Future** "Well done . . . I will put you over many things; enter into the joy of your Master . . . but throw out the worthless servant into outer darkness . . . weeping and gnashing of teeth" (Matt. 25:23,30)	Oblivion when rebirths ended
Look forward and upward for understanding	**Focus** "Say not, 'Why were the former days better than these?'" (Eccl. 7:10) "Trust in the LORD with all your heart, and lean not on your own understanding" (Prov. 3:5)	Look backward and inward for understanding
Foundation of Christ	**Foundation** "Anyone who hears these sayings of mine and does them, I will liken him to a wise man who built his house on the rock" (Matt. 7:24)	Foundation of self
Clear, revealed, answered by God	**Knowledge** "The mystery which has been hidden from ages and from generations, but now has been revealed to His saints" (Col. 1:26)	Vague, mysterious, questioning within self

Jesus Went First

So far, God has only dealt with One Man in the way He intends to deal with all the righteous. And that is Jesus Christ. Jesus is the firstfruits from the dead (1 Cor. 15:20). He is the first one to resurrect to eternal life with the Father. He rose as body + soul + Spirit. He stayed on earth 40 days, proving that He was alive; that it was indeed Him; that He got His body back, and then took it with Him. Although He resurrected, Jesus was "not yet glorified" until He ascended to the Father (John 7:39). We have not seen Him since God glorified His body. We don't know yet what that looks like. But we do know, since He is the firstfruits, that it will also happen to all those who are born again into the body of Christ. What happened to Him will happen to us. Death can only hold those condemned in sin. It could not hold Jesus because He had no sin, so He resurrected. Once you die with Jesus and He cleanses your sins with His blood, you no longer have sin. As long as you remain faithful in Him, Death will not hold you either. Do you believe it? As a part of His body, the church, the gates of hades will not prevail (Matt. 16:18). Because Jesus went first, we can follow.

Jesus is God's Answer

We are so profoundly blessed to know Jesus, and to have access to the revealed, recorded, and confirmed Word of God. Can you even imagine a life based on any foundation except for Him? When I think about the masses of humanity, wandering from religion to religion, grasping and groping for truth, I feel so sad. In past ages, there was a need to look for God, trying to understand His Divinity; trying to search out His creation. "Truly, these times of ignorance God overlooked" (Acts 17:30).

Why are they still looking? About 2000 years ago, God answered everybody's questions. His answer for all people of all ages is Jesus Christ. Jesus explains it like this: "I am the way, the truth, and the life. No one comes to the Father except through Me" (John 14:6). Because Jesus Christ came in the flesh and lived without sin, He is the only viable system of salvation. Because Jesus is the truth, we follow His footsteps, and the teaching of His apostles' and prophets. Because Jesus Christ is the resurrection and the life (John 11:25), God "now commands all men everywhere to repent" (Acts 17:30).

Since God already sent His answer, those who embrace reincarnation theology today have no excuse. God offers a covenant relationship to them. God provides His Word to them. Some rebelliously reject God's offer and provision, but not all. For millions more, they exist as captives to "seducing spirits and doctrines of demons."

Women of Faith, Reach Out

God calls us to reach out to them in hope, listening to their perspectives, finding common ground, and laboring patiently because we understand the tremendous difficulty of shifting one's entire worldview.

"When Will These Things Be?" : Questions on Eschatology

However, do not reach out blindly. Armed with God's truth, beware. Reincarnation has a dark side:

- That rejects Jesus Christ as son of God
- That denies God's claim as Father of all
- That willfully rejects the precious truths upon which you and I have built our lives
- That deceitfully threatens the incipient souls of our children and grandchildren

Even so, in alignment with the righteousness of God, women of faith reach out.

Bibliography

Burley, Mikel. "Believing in Reincarnation." *Philosophy* 87.340 (2012): 261-79. www.jstor.org/stable/41441510. Accessed February 11, 2020.

Carus, Paul. *History of the Devil*. Chicago: Open Court Publishing Co. 1900.

Carelli, Francesco. "The book of death: weighing your heart." *London Journal of Primary Care* 4.1 (2011): 86-7.

Conard, Lætitia Moon. "The Idea of God Held by North American Indians." *The American Journal of Theology* 7.4 (1903): 635-46. www.jstor.org/stable/3153757. Accessed March 7, 2020.

"Defining Spiritualism." *National Spiritualist Association of Churches*. https://nsac.org/what-we-believe/definining-spiritualism/. Accessed February 2020.

Faber, Roland. "The Healing and Poisonous Fruits of the Unity of Religions." *The Ocean of God: On the Transreligious Future of Religions*. New York, NY: Anthem Press, 2019. www.jstor.org/stable/j.ctvjsf6hs.5. Accessed March 3, 2020.

Gellman, Marc. "Lord, please don't make me a cockroach." *Press-Republican* (July 12, 2018) https://www.pressrepublican.com/opinion/columns/lord-please-don-t-make-me-a-cockroach/article_4dc719b9-889d-5a52-a132-961a72cf510f.html

Harper, Douglas. *Online Etymological Dictionary*. https://www.etymonline.com/.

Does the Bible Teach Reincarnation?

Kerry Brown, ed. *The Essential Teachings of Hinduism: Daily Readings from the Sacred Texts.* London: Arrow Books Ltd., 1990.

MacDonald, John. "Paradise." *Islamic Studies* 5.4 (1966): 331-83. www.jstor.org/stable/20832856. Accessed March 3, 2020.

Mark, Joshua J. "Religion in the Ancient World." *Ancient History Encyclopedia.* https://www.ancient.eu/religion/. Last modified March 23, 2018.

Martin, Luther W. "Reincarnation and Transmigration." *Guardian of Truth* 34.17, (September 6, 1990): 528-529.

Mead, G. R. S. "The Doctrine of Reincarnation Ethically Considered." *International Journal of Ethics* 22.2 (1912): 158-79. www.jstor.org/stable/2376756. Accessed February 11, 2020.

Nitobe, Inazo. "The Religious Sense of the Japanese People." *Pacific Affairs* 2.2 (1929): 58-64.

Pang, You-Yuan; Lu, Rita .-H.; Chen, Pao-Yang. 2019. "Behavioral Epigenetics: Perspectives Based on Experience-Dependent Epigenetic Inheritance." *Epigenomes* 3.18 (August 22, 2019): 1-13.

Pierret, Paul. "The Dogma of the Resurrection among the Ancient Egyptians." *The Old Testament Student* 4.6 (1885): 267-75. www.jstor.org/stable/3156772. Accessed March 3, 2020.

Rotherham, Joseph Bryant. *Familiar Spirits, Past and Present: A Warning against Spiritualism.* London: Morgan and Chase, 1868.

Stambaugh, J. Death before Sin? *Acts and Facts* 18.5 (May 1,1989) https://www.icr.org/article/295.

Webster, Merriam. https://www.merriam-webster.com/ 2020

Appendix: General Studies

Premillennialism
  Mike Willis

Postmillennialism
  David Dann

Amillennialism
  Sean Cavender

The New Heavens and New Earth
  Jim McDonald

The AD 70 Doctrine
  Don McClain

Eco-Eschatology
  Mat Bassford

What Does the Bible Teach about Hades and Sheol?
  Kyle Pope

"When Will These Things Be?"
Questions on Eschatology

Premillennialism
By Mike Willis

Many who believe in the inspiration of the Bible also embrace a view of the end times identified as "premillennialism" or "dispensationalism." Because every premillennial teacher has some different or unique twist, one expects that certain details of their doctrine will vary from one premillennialist to another.

Definition of Significant Terms

To understand millennialism, one must know some terms that are frequently used in these discussions. Here is a summary of some of the different beliefs that have been advanced:

Postmillennialism is "the belief that the Second Coming of Christ will follow the millennium" (Webster). "An optimistic type of theology which predicts a 'golden age,' a Christianized millennium of predominantly human achievement before the Second Advent and the subsequent, eternal reign" (Douglas, 794). Some of our religious ancestors, such as Alexander Campbell, who published a paper entitled *Millennial Harbinger*, held this view of the end times. Although he was mistaken in his belief, his position did not undermine the biblical doctrine of the church, as is the case with other millennial theories.

Premillennialism is "the doctrine that the reappearance of Christ on earth will precede the millennium" (Webster). "The view which asserts that Christ will come a second time before the 1,000 years of His millennial rule, upholds a general chiliastic theology of Millennialism, and places the rapture of the saints, the first resurrection, the tribulation, and the Second Advent before the Millennium in prophetic time sequence, with the brief release of bound Satan, the second resurrection, and Last Judgment afterward" (Douglas, 798-799).

Amillennialism "denies such a thousand-year reign . . . stresses that the Apocalypse normally treats numbers symbolically. The binding of

"When Will These Things Be?" : Questions on Eschatology

Satan for a thousand years simply means that he is completely bound; this has been effected through the victory of Calvary" (Douglas, 36). We are amillennialists in our convictions about the end times.

The Theory of Premillennialism

The theory of premillennialism may be summarized as follows: When Jesus came to the earth, He came intending to establish an earthly kingdom. The Jews rejected Jesus and crucified Him. God instituted an alternative plan to establish a spiritual kingdom, the church. The church age will last until Christ establishes His earthly kingdom. Sometime soon, Jesus will come back and silently raise the righteous dead and rapture the living saints from the earth. Seven years of tribulation will be experienced on earth when Satan is loosed for a little season. Jesus will return to earth, bringing His saints with Him. The battle of Armageddon will occur. Satan will be defeated. Jesus will establish an earthly kingdom over which He will reign for 1000 years. At the end of the 1000-year reign, the wicked dead will be raised, and all men will be judged. The righteous will then be welcomed into heaven, and the wicked will be cast into hell.

What Is Wrong with Premillennialism

It teaches that Christ came to establish an earthly kingdom.

The kingdom Christ came to establish was spiritual (Luke 17:20-21; John 18:36-37; 3:3-5; Rom. 14:17). The kingdom is the church (Matt. 16:16-18). It was established on Pentecost (Mark 9:1; Acts 1:8; 2:1-4, 47). In this respect, the kingdom has come (Acts 8:12; 28:23; Col. 1:13-14; Heb. 12:28; Rev. 1:9). The doctrine that Jesus came to establish an earthly kingdom is wrong. Jesus did not come in His first coming and will not come in His Second Coming to establish an earthly kingdom.

It teaches that Jesus failed in what he set out to do—to establish an earthly kingdom.

The Bible teaches that Christ would not fail in His mission (Ps. 2). If Jesus failed when He came to establish the kingdom on His first coming, what guarantee would we have that He would be able to accomplish at His Second Coming what He failed to do the first time? The very idea that the Son of God failed in what He purposed to accomplish is blasphemous.

Premillennialism

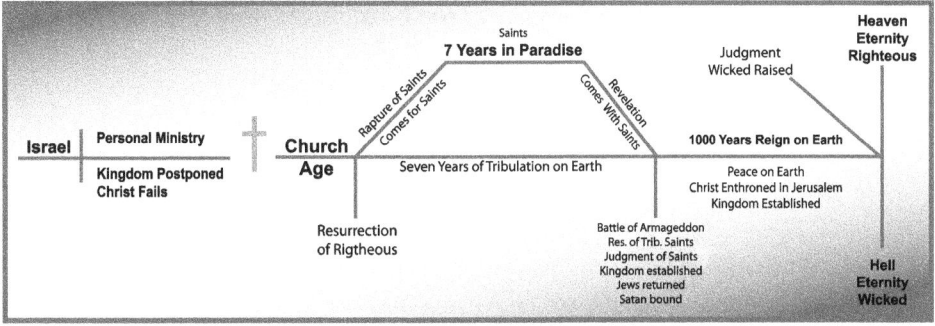

It teaches, by logical implication, that Christ is not presently reigning as King, by denying that the kingdom is presently established.

If there is no kingdom, how could there be a king over that kingdom? Hence, the theory implies that Jesus is not presently King of kings and Lord of lords (1 Tim. 6:15). If there is no kingdom, how could one be a citizen of it (John 3:3-5)? Yet, the Bible repeatedly affirms that Jesus is presently reigning (Heb. 10:10-13; 1:3, 13; 1 Cor. 15:26-26; 1 Tim. 6:15; Acts 2:29-36; Rev. 3:21). (Note the implications of the fact that Jesus is presently reigning for the 1000-year reign of Christ in Revelation 20.) Sacred Scripture shows that: (a) Jesus is reigning on the throne of David (Isa. 9:6-7; Luke 1:32-33; Acts 2:29-31); (b) He has the key of David (Isa. 22:22; Rev. 3:7); (c) He rules in the midst of His enemies (Ps. 110). His is not a reign in total utopia; (d) Jesus has all authority (Matt. 28:18; Eph. 1:19-22; Col. 2:16).

It teaches that Jesus's death on the cross was not Christ's intended purpose for coming to the earth.

Jesus expressed that He came to save the lost (Luke 19:10) and prophesied of His death (Matt. 16:21). God's plan to save humanity through the death of His Son was purposed before the creation of the world (Rev. 13:8).

It teaches that the church, instead of being a part of God's eternal purpose, is an accident (cf. Eph. 3:8-11).

The church age was necessary because the Jews rejected Jesus as the Christ. Yet, this was not unexpected but foreshadowed in Old Testament prophecy (Ps. 22; Isa. 53; etc.).

"When Will These Things Be?" : Questions on Eschatology

It teaches an imminent coming of the Lord based on a misinterpretation of Matthew 24.

For as long as I can remember, premillennialists have been preaching that the Second Coming is near. Prophetic speculation is part of denominational history. William G. Miller predicted the Lord's coming on March 23, 1843, and on March 23, 1844, and a third time on October 22, 1844. Ellen G. White reinterpreted Miller's predictions to make them refer to activities in heaven. Thus was founded the Seventh Day Adventists. Charles Taze Russell (Jehovah's Witnesses) predicted the Lord's coming in 1914. Edgar C. Whisenant mailed out a book to every church in the U.S. announcing *88 Reasons Why the Rapture Could Be in 1988*. Billy Graham preached that the Second Coming was imminent when I was a boy growing up. Attempting to find evidence of the imminent return of Christ through a misinterpretation of Matthew 24 is a key feature of premillennialism. The truth is that no one knows when Christ will come again (Matt. 24:36).

Premillennialism has many problems of correct Bible exegesis.

It demands several resurrections, including at the rapture, after the tribulation period, and after the millennium (the general resurrection). In contrast, the Scriptures teach that there is but one resurrection (John 5:28-29; 2 Thess. 1:6-9; Acts 24:15).

It teaches more than one "Second Coming." Premillennialists believe in the following comings: (1) A secret coming at the rapture. At this time, the saints will be taken to heaven, where they will stay for seven years and then return to this earth. Have you seen the bumper sticker that reads: "In case of rapture, this car will be unmanned"? (2) A coming to establish His earthly kingdom. Yet, how many "Second Comings" are there?

It gives the "last day" a new meaning. Resurrection (John 11:24; 6:39-40) and judgment (John 12:48) are to occur on the last day. Premillennialism believes that there is a thousand-year reign of Christ between resurrection and judgment. That would demand 365,000 "last days"!

It offers salvation to people after the Second Coming. The day of grace is over when Christ comes again (Matt. 25:6-10; Luke 17:26-30). Christ's Second Coming will be for judgment (Heb. 9:27-28).

Conclusion

Premillennialism is a speculative approach to Bible prophecy that contradicts many plain statements of Scripture, and should, therefore, be rejected.

Bibliography

Douglas, J.D., ed. *The New International Dictionary of the Christian Church*. Grand Rapids, MI: Zondervan, 1978.

Postmillennialism
By David Dann

The apostle Paul instructed Timothy, saying, "Be diligent to present yourself approved to God, a worker who does not need to be ashamed, rightly dividing the word of truth" (2 Tim. 2:15, NKJV). The doctrinal system of "Postmillennialism" is an example of men failing to rightly divide the word of truth.

What Is Postmillennialism?

According to this view, "Increasing gospel success will gradually produce a time in history prior to Christ's return in which faith, righteousness, peace, and prosperity will prevail in the affairs of people and of nations. After an extensive era of such conditions the Lord will return visibly, bodily, and in great glory, ending history with the general resurrection and the great judgment of all humankind" (Gentry, 13-14). Postmillennialists anticipate "the world-as-a-system returning to God" in "a massive, systemic conversion of the vast majority of humankind" (Gentry, 42). Thus, postmillennialism is the term applied to the belief that Christ will come again only after this golden millennial age has run its course in history. Some proponents believe that the golden age will last for one thousand literal years.

In contrast, many others view the golden age as merely a long and full period, rather than a literal one thousand years. While various millennial theories have circulated for centuries, Thomas Brightman (1562-1607), the English Presbyterian, is considered the modern formulator of the postmillennial view (Gentry, 16-17). According to one writer, "It comes as a surprise to many that for most of the nineteenth century, postmillennialism was 'the commonly received doctrine' among American Protestants, as one minister put it in 1859. Postmillennialism dominated the religious press, the leading seminaries, and most of the Protestant clergy, and it was ingrained in the popular mind" (Pointer). In fact, many preachers who sought a restoration of the New Testament order in the nineteenth century,

Postmillennialism

including Alexander Campbell, promoted a postmillennial view in which they anticipated conversion to Christ taking place on a scale so grand that it would inevitably usher in the Second Coming of Christ (Wolfgang, 54). Some argue that this unrealistic and mistaken view of a future conversion of the majority of mankind is what led Campbell to adopt unscriptural innovations, such as the missionary society, as his frustration mounted in trying to accomplish this perceived goal. While many religious people continue to hold to the classical postmillennial view, others have more recently taken it a step further. Postmillennialists who subscribe to the form of the doctrine known as "Christian Reconstructionism," "Dominion Theology," or "Theonomic Postmillennialism" look for the rise of a theocratic form of government in which the civil laws and punishments of the Law of Moses will be implemented and carried out in society (Riddlebarger, 30-31; Strimple, 58-59).

What Is Wrong with Postmillennialism?
It misapplies Old Testament prophecy.

In unfolding His plan to redeem man from sin through Jesus Christ, God made three significant promises to Abraham (Gen. 12:1-3). Postmillennialists go beyond what the New Testament offers as the fulfillment of God's promises and claim that, for the third promise to be fulfilled, the vast majority of all nations must be converted to Christ (Kik, 22). Passages such as Habakkuk 2:14, which states, "For the earth will be filled with the knowledge of the glory of the LORD, as the waters cover the sea," are misused to teach that the majority of mankind will become Christians. The problem with postmillennialism is that it claims that Old Testament prophecies must be fulfilled in a manner that is beyond the scope of what the Scriptures teach.

It makes the reign of Christ a current failure.

Jesus Christ has been reigning as King in heaven ever since His ascension to the Father following His resurrection from the dead (cf. Acts 2:32-33). Interpreting the millennium as non-literal, many postmillennialists believe that this period extends from Jesus's first coming all the way to His Second Coming. However, since there is no widespread evidence of the world-as-a-system turning to Christ, postmillennial expectations can lead to a dismal view of His reign. As one writer puts it, "Postmillennialism was a widely accepted eschatological position among American evangelicals in the period of unprecedented technological growth between 1870

"When Will These Things Be?" : Questions on Eschatology

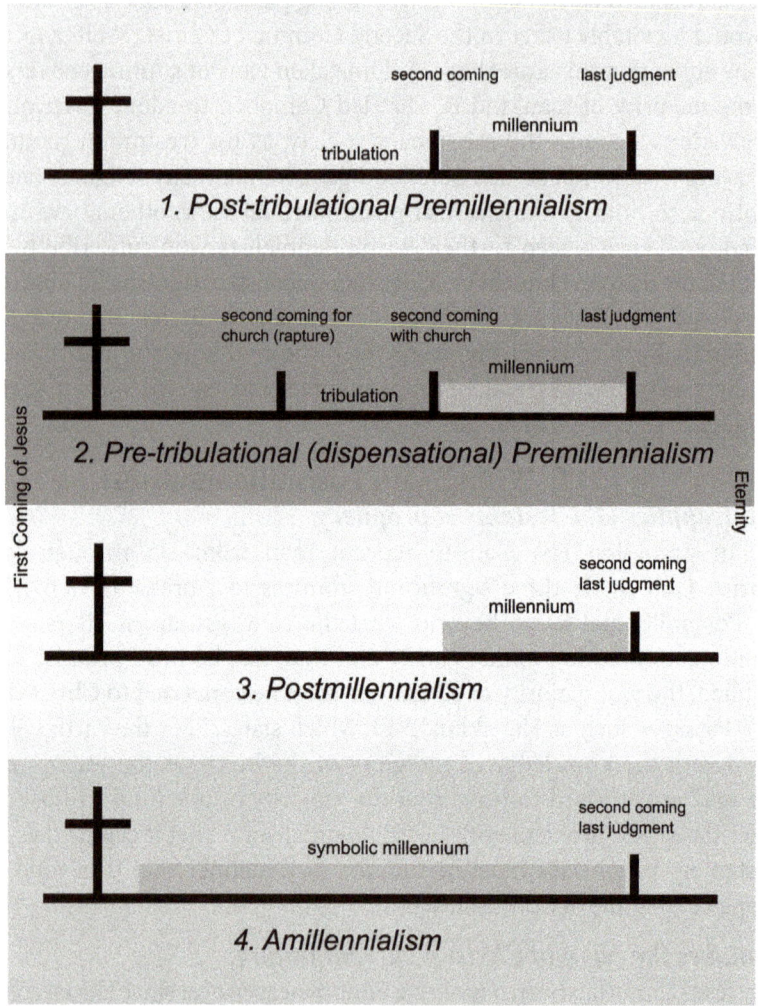

Comparison of Christian Millennial Teachings

and 1915. But with the coming of the 'war to end all wars' (World War I), the Great Depression, and the horrors of Auschwitz and Hiroshima, optimism gave way to pessimism" (Riddlebarger, 30). The problem with postmillennialism is that it demands things of Christ's reign that the Bible does not teach and cannot be harmonized with what is witnessed in the world.

Postmillennialism

It ignores New Testament warnings concerning opposition to the gospel.

Jesus warned His apostles, saying, "If the world hates you, you know that it hated Me before it hated you" (John 15:18; cf. 1 John 3:13). Rather than promising the saints a golden age of worldwide acceptance of the gospel, Christ and His apostles continually warned that the Christian's journey through this world involves suffering that ultimately will be relieved beyond this earthly life (cf. Rom. 8:18). The problem with postmillennialism is that it ignores these warnings in favor of constructing a view of earthly life that does not harmonize with what the Bible teaches.

It changes the focus of the Christian's hope.

The "one hope" of the child of God is not that of living in a perfectly righteous and just environment on earth, but is, instead, based on anticipation of the coming of Christ at the end of time (cf. Eph. 4:4; Titus 2:11-13; Col. 1:3-5). Encouraging suffering saints to remain faithful despite the prospect of losing their earthly lives in the face of persecution, John writes:

> And I saw thrones, and they sat on them, and judgment was committed to them. Then I saw the souls of those who had been beheaded for their witness to Jesus and for the word of God, who had not worshiped the beast or his image, and had not received his mark on their foreheads or on their hands. And they lived and reigned with Christ for a thousand years" (Rev. 20:4).

This passage, which supposedly discusses the millennial golden age, makes no mention of peace and justice on earth or the mass conversion of the world to Christ but looks beyond this earthly life for the fulfillment of the Christian's longing. The problem with postmillennialism is that it offers an earthly hope to the people of God in addition to the one heavenly hope that is revealed in His word.

How Does Postmillennialism Differ from a Biblical View of the Future?

The majority will not be converted to Christ.

Notice that in the Parable of the Sower, only one out of the four types of soil is considered "good ground" (Matt. 13:23). Rather than promising that the majority would eventually travel the narrow way, Jesus states plainly: "there are few who find it" (Matt. 7:13-14). In contrast with the teachings of postmillennialists, there will never come a time when the vast majority of humanity chooses to travel the narrow way that leads to eternal life.

Opposition to the gospel will increase.

Rather than heralding the arrival of a golden age of righteousness on earth, Paul writes, "Yes, and all who desire to live godly in Christ Jesus will suffer persecution. But evil men and impostors will grow worse and worse, deceiving and being deceived" (2 Tim. 3:12-13; cf. 2 Pet. 3:3). Even the very passage which supposedly predicts the millennial golden age places the coming of Christ at a time of opposition rather than a time of great peace and righteousness (cf. Rev. 20:7-8). Contrary to what postmillennialists teach, opposition to the gospel will continue right up until Christ returns in judgment.

Wickedness will be defeated at the Second Coming of Christ.

In his second letter to the church in Thessalonica, the apostle Paul indicates that the Second Coming of Christ is the point at which wickedness and justice will be eradicated (cf. 2 Thess. 1:6-10). Contrary to the picture painted by postmillennialists, the world will still be populated with "those who do not know God" and those "who do not obey the gospel" when Jesus comes again in judgment.

Perfect peace and righteousness will be found beyond the judgment.

The faithful will find peace and rest from wickedness and unrighteousness in the dwelling place of God in eternity, rather than in this world (cf. John 14:1-3; 2 Pet. 3:13-14). This present world is destined to be burned up without ever arriving at a worldwide golden age of righteousness. Contrary to what postmillennialists teach, the faithful will not find perfect peace and righteousness here on earth but will find it beyond the resurrection and judgment.

Conclusion

The postmillennial view of this world and its future is vastly different from the perspective presented in Scripture. The problem, of course, is that postmillennialism adds to what is stated in God's word while seeking to diminish clear pronouncements of Scripture (cf. Rev. 22:18-19). When it comes to what lies ahead, why not simply trust the word of the Lord, instead of the speculative theories of men?

Postmillennialism

Bibliography

"Amillennialism." *Wikipedia.com.* https://en.wikipedia.org/wiki/Amillennialism.

Gentry, Kenneth L., Jr. "Postmillennialism." *Three Views on the Millennium and Beyond.* Darrell L. Bock, ed., 11-57. Grand Rapids, MI: Zondervan, 1999.

Kik, J. Marcellus. *An Eschatology of Victory.* Phillipsburg, NJ: Presbyterian and Reformed, 1971.

Pointer, Steven R. "American Postmillennialism: Seeing the Glory." *Christian History* 61 (January, 1999): www.christianitytoday.com/history/issues/issue-61/american-postmillennialism-seeing-glory.html.

Riddlebarger, Kim. *A Case for Amillennialism.* Grand Rapids, MI: Baker, 2003.

Strimple, Robert B. "An Amillennial Response to Kenneth L. Gentry, Jr." *Three Views on the Millennium and Beyond.* Darrell L. Bock, ed. 58-71. Grand Rapids, MI: Zondervan, 1999.

Wolfgang, Steve. "Millennialism and the American Political Dream." *Guardian of Truth.* 26.4 (January 28, 1982): 54-58. www.truthmagazine.com/archives/volume26/GOT026016.html.

Amillennialism
By Sean Cavender

Introduction

People are often captivated by various teachings about the end of time, the return of Christ, and the kingdom of God. Many people expect that God still needs to complete His promises regarding the land that He would give to Israel, as well as the establishment of the kingdom of God on earth. Millennial doctrines often assert that the kingdom of God will be established in Jerusalem. They also interpret the 1,000 years of Revelation 20 in a literal way, expecting Jesus will reign on the throne of David in Jerusalem for a literal 1,000 years.

Famous authors like Hal Lindsey, Tim LaHaye, and Jerry B. Jenkins have sensationalized the "end times." The popularity these authors have may give the appearance that amillennialism is a fringe theory. However, amillennialism has been the dominant way to understand Revelation 20 and other passages throughout much of "church history," with Origen, Augustine, Luther, and Calvin all taking an amillennial interpretation of the book of Revelation (Elwell and Yarborough, 361).

Defining Amillennialism

Both *pre-* and *post-*millennial theories argue for an earthly kingdom of God. The amillennial view, and the teaching of Scripture, denies an earthly kingdom. Instead, amillennialism emphasizes the nature of the millennial kingdom. *Baker's Encyclopedia* defines amillennialism as: "The amillennial (*no* millennium, at least of a visible, earthly nature) interpretation stresses the symbolism of Revelation and holds that now, during the present age, Satan is bound and the church is experiencing the millennium" (Elwell and Beitzel, 1460). Koester offers this brief comment: "Amillennialism describes theological systems that do not include an explicit thousand year period…" (Koester, 180). So, we see that an amillennial interpretation of the book of Revelation opposes millennial concepts of an earthly and nationalistic Messianic kingdom that will exist for a literal 1,000 years.

Amillennialism

Various interpretations about the 1,000-year reign are derived from the text of Revelation 20:1-6. Amillennialism denies assertions of a literal 1,000-year reign of Jesus on the earth because Jesus affirmed that His kingdom was not of this world (John 18:36). Christ did not teach that His kingdom would be established in Jerusalem after His Second Coming, where He would reign for 1,000 years on the earth. Jesus said that His kingdom would exist, i.e., "come with power" within the lifetime of His generation (Mark 9:1). In the preaching of the apostles, they make it clear that Jesus was reigning as king over His kingdom (Acts 2:33, 36; 8:12, 35). They announced that Jesus is seated in heaven at the right hand of God. He is king over His kingdom, and He established His kingdom after His earthly ministry (cf. Matt. 16:18). The kingdom of God is not something that will be established on earth at the Second Coming of Christ because it has already been established. All who are saved by the blood of Christ are citizens of His kingdom (Col. 1:13).

Figurative Language in Revelation

One of the first keys to an amillennial interpretation is first understanding the literary context in Revelation. The book of Revelation is from the apocalyptic literary genre. Apocalyptic literature frequently used various signs, symbols, and numbers that represent real circumstances experienced by the original audience. The figurative imagery and symbols used are not to be interpreted as if they would literally come to pass. Apocalyptic writing also gives a glimpse into things that would shortly come to pass (Rev. 1:3). While apocalyptic books, like Revelation, can and do at times provide insight into the future, final judgment, that is only secondary to its purposes. Its primary function was to explain the present reality to whom the message was initially given.

Explaining Revelation Chapter 20

Revelation 20 is used by those who argue for a literal 1,000-year reign of Christ on the earth. However, we want to examine Revelation 20 in light of what the Bible teaches. We must remember that we must allow clear and straightforward passages of Scripture to explain more difficult and figurative passages of Scripture.

Satan Bound (Rev. 20:1-3)

Revelation 20 opens with the devil cast into the bottomless pit, or the abyss, and bound for 1,000 years. Readers must identify the abundant use of figures in the chapter. Satan is described as a "dragon," "the serpent of old," and "the devil" (Rev. 20:2). This is a reminder of the terrible things that Satan did in waging war against Christ and the church through the violent persecutions against Christians (Rev. 6:9-11). Revelation 20 reminded the suffering saints that the devil has been judged and defeated by Jesus.

Christ came to earth to bind the devil and to destroy sin and death (Mark 3:27; 1 John 3:8; Heb. 2:14). Since the devil has been defeated, the kingdom of God has come and has been established (Matt. 12:28). Satan's defeat is associated with the inauguration of the kingdom of God. Revelation 20 describes God's judgment and the binding of Satan. This has been accomplished through the work of Jesus.

Saints Reign with Christ (Rev. 20:4-6)

Revelation 20 not only considers Satan's defeat but also describes the victory given to faithful Christians! Brother Dan King makes the point that Revelation 20 does not depict the so-called "1,000-year reign of Christ"; the chapter actually describes the reign of the martyred saints *with* Christ for 1,000 years (King, 319).

Jesus is presently reigning as King and has been since He ascended to be at the right hand of the Father (Acts 2:33-36; Eph. 1:20-23; Rev. 3:7, 21). Revelation 20 offers vindication and hope to those who have been loyal and devoted servants to King Jesus, even at the cost of their lives. The martyred saints have hope because they have taken part in the "first resurrection," having been raised in newness of life (John 5:25-27; Rom. 6:3-6). This "first resurrection" is associated with salvation; it does not refer to the bodily resurrection at the end of the age. Those who have taken part in the "first resurrection" have nothing to fear in eternity since "the second death has no power" over them (Rev. 20:6).

The 1,000 Years: Literal or Figurative? (Rev. 20:1-6)

Numbers in the book of Revelation are highly symbolic. Large numbers appear in Revelation to describe something vast and innumerable (Rev. 5:11; 7:4, 9). The number 1,000 is used throughout Scripture to be inclusive and exhaustive of particular items. In Psalm 50:10, the parallel statements, "every beast of the field" and the "cattle on a thousand hills," emphasize that every creature belongs to God. The use of 1,000 is not meant to limit the number of cattle that belong to God to only those on a thousand hills. Rather, it is used in a fuller sense to describe all creatures

Amillennialism

that belong to God. Also, God assured Israel that He would bless them to the thousandth generation if they would be faithful to His covenant (Deut. 7:9). The number 1,000 depicts the defeat of Satan. By contrast, the 1,000 years is a symbol to faithful saints, assured of total victory for being loyal to Christ.

Conclusion

Amillennialism looks to the Scriptures to see how God has been faithful to His covenants and has established the kingdom of promise by setting His Son, Jesus Christ, upon the throne of David to rule over the everlasting kingdom. Praise to God that the kingdom has been inaugurated, the New Covenant established, and that King Jesus offers forgiveness of sins and citizenship in His kingdom (Col. 1:13).

Bibliography

Elwell, Walter A. and Barry J. Beitzel. *Baker Encyclopedia of the Bible.* Vol. 3. Grand Rapids, MI: Baker Book House, 1988.

Elwell, Walter A. and Robert W. Yarbrough. *Encountering the New Testament: A Historical and Theological Survey.* Grand Rapids, MI: Baker Academic, 2013.

King, Sr., Daniel H. *"I Saw the Heaven Opened" : A Commentary on Revelation.* Athens, AL: Truth Publications, Inc., 2018.

Koester, Craig R. *Revelation and the End of All Things.* Grand Rapids, MI: Eerdmans, 2018.

The New Heavens and New Earth
By Jim McDonald

> And I saw a new heaven and a new earth, for the first heaven and the first earth are passed away, and the sea is no more . . . (Rev. 21:1).

Various individuals, including some brethren, see this passage as literal and conclude that the eternal dwelling place of the redeemed, resurrected souls will be planet earth.[1] Before we accept this position as truth, let us examine what inspired writers meant by the expression, *"a new heavens and a new earth."* John is not the only biblical writer to use the phrase. Yes, considering the nature of Revelation, one should be extremely cautious in making Revelation 21:1 literal when the expression is surrounded by highly symbolic language. For example, John saw four horses in the first four seals of the seven seals (Rev. 6:1-8); the sealing of 12,000 out of each of the twelve tribes of Israel (Rev. 7:5-8); the plagues of the seven trumpets (Rev. 8, 9); an angel who stood with one foot on the sea, the other on land (Rev. 10:2); the measuring of the temple (Rev. 11:1-2); the great red dragon who, with one sweep of his tail, brought one-third of the stars of heaven crashing onto the earth (Rev. 12:4). Who regards these visions as literal? One should do a second take on literalizing the phrase "new heavens and a new earth" when the book overall is so highly symbolic and figurative.

There are four passages in the Bible where the expression "new heavens and a new earth" is found. Two appear in the Old Testament writings of

---

1   **Editors' Note:** In asserting that Revelation 21:1 is not "literal" the reader will note from points made latter in this study that brother McDonald is not denying that the first heaven and first earth will literally *pass away*. Nor is he asserting that the heavens and earth referenced in 2 Peter 3:7-13 are merely figurative references to the replacement of the Jewish system with the kingdom of Christ—as proponents of the AD 70 Doctrine assert. Throughout this study, brother McDonald uses the term "figurative" to refute the false concept that the "new heaven" and "new earth" of eternal life describe the present universe rejuvenated. He later writes, "He will literally burn up and dissolve the earth by His word. It's that simple."

The New Heavens and New Earth

the prophet Isaiah (65:17; 66:22). The expression occurs twice in the New Testament (2 Pet. 3:13; Rev. 21:1). It is clear that Isaiah's promise of a "new heavens and a new earth" was not intended to be understood in a literal sense. Instead, the writer is promising, in the era of the Messiah, a new order of things: the church and salvation offered to all men without respect of persons. The church, God's promised kingdom (Dan. 2:44), and the redemption one finds in Christ are Isaiah's "new heavens and a new earth." Isaiah's "new heavens and a new earth" are here, but not literally so. The fact that Isaiah used the same expression as John and Peter (but intended to suggest a new literal earth) should cause men to question, "Since the expressions in Isaiah were figurative, is it not possible that the appearance of the expressions in both Peter and John's writing is also figurative?"

The apostle Peter affirms that in the last days, mockers would come and say, "Where is the promise of His coming, for from the days the fathers fell asleep all things continue as they were from the beginning of the creation" (2 Pet. 3:3-4). These mockers questioned the veracity of the Lord's words that He would come again, and Peter reminded them that they willfully forgot an important truth. The heavens from old, and an earth, compacted out of water and amidst water by the word of God, was overflowed with water and perished—by the word of God. Yet, the heavens that now are, and the earth by the same word, are stored up for fire, being reserved against the day of judgment and destruction of ungodly men (2 Pet. 3:5-7).

Jehovah's Witnesses argue that symbolism is here: that the world *"perished"* but wasn't destroyed—it's still here! That's what will happen when Jesus comes again. That, although the world overflowed with water, *it* didn't perish. It was cleansed, and Noah and his family continued to live on it, and that in like manner, when the earth is *"destroyed"* at Jesus's Second Coming, it will be purified and made suitable for God's redeemed ones to live here—a new earth, so to speak. There is a huge problem with this explanation: Peter uses two words to describe two different things, not one. Peter speaks of the world, then he speaks of the earth, but *he is not using two different words to describe the same thing.* The *"world"* refers to the people of Noah's day; the *"earth"* is our planet. True, the *"earth"* of Noah's day is still here, but the *"world"* of Noah's day is gone. It did perish.

Having discussed the *"world"* of Noah's day, Peter next turned his attention to the *"earth"* of Noah's day. What will happen to that earth? Let

"When Will These Things Be?" : Questions on Eschatology

Peter tell us: "But the heavens that now are, and the earth, by the same word have been stored up for fire, being reserved against the day of judgment and destruction of ungodly men" (2 Pet. 3:7). Again, "The day of the Lord will come as a thief, in the which the heavens shall pass away with a great noise and the elements shall be dissolved with fervent heat, and the earth and the works that are therein shall be burned up" (2 Pet. 3:10). "The earth is stored up for fire," i.e., it will be "burned up" and "dissolved" (2 Pet. 3:11). Is this symbolism? If it is, then the Second Coming of Christ is symbolism as well.

The thrust of Peter's argument is to show that God keeps His word. Scoffers had derided and denied it, but Peter showed that God keeps His word. The world came into existence *by the word of God*. The world of Noah's day perished *by the word of God*. The heavens and earth *were* created by the same word of God, and they are destined to be destroyed by the same word. There is no symbolism there. If God does not burn up and dissolve the earth, then we cannot believe His word. God literally created the world by His word. He will literally burn up and dissolve the earth by His word. It's that simple.

After admonishing his readers to live soberly and godly in view of the truth that the heavens and earth will be dissolved (2 Pet. 3:11), Peter then adds, "according to His promise, we look for new heavens and a new earth wherein dwelleth righteousness" (2 Pet. 3:13).

Scoffers mock Jesus's promise to return to the earth, but God keeps His word, just as He will keep His promise to provide "a new heavens and a new earth wherein dwelleth righteousness." Where did Jesus ever mention a new heavens and a new earth? Read all the gospels, and you will find no reference anywhere by Jesus to "new heavens and a new earth," yet Peter said that "according to His promise, we look for new heavens and a new earth wherein dwelleth righteousness."

Still, there is something you *will* find connected with the promise Jesus made about His coming again. In John 14:1-4, Jesus said, "Let not your heart be troubled: ye believe in God, believe also in me. In my Father's house are many mansions: if it were not so, I would have told you. I go to prepare a place for you. And if I go and prepare a place for you, I will come again, and receive you unto myself; that where I am, there ye may be also. And whither I go ye know, and the way ye know." Clearly, Jesus did

The New Heavens and New Earth

not intend to return to the earth to remain; He planned to return to the earth to get those who served Him and then carry them with Him to His Father's house. When Jesus prayed in John 17, He prayed to the Father that those whom the Father had given Him would be with Him where He was to behold His glory (John 17:24). Once again, we see Jesus's intent was not to come back to live on the earth with the redeemed. His intention was to carry those whom the Father gave Him to where He was going when He said in John 14 that He was going away.

There are two things in John 14 we must not forget. There is the promise of Jesus's return; the return the scoffers questioned. However, coupled with that was Jesus's promise that He was going to His Father's house to prepare many mansions for His own. He does not mention in the passage "new heavens and a new earth," but He does mention a new order of things: God's children being carried to heaven. Friends, the inspired apostle Peter said, "According to His promise, we look for new heavens and new earth." Jesus's promise to go and prepare a place for His redeemed ones, then come back for them and carry them to that place so they can behold His glory is the new heavens and new earth—a wondrous new order of things!

Isaiah's "new heavens and a new earth" in chapters 65 and 66 were not literal; they were the church that Jesus bought with His blood. Peter's "new heavens and a new earth" are not literal either. He tells us that the first earth and heavens will be dissolved and burned up. Our earth will be destroyed; it will not be "revamped" for the redeemed to dwell on. Who doubts that the new heavens and earth John wrote about are the same new heavens and earth Peter wrote about? Peter's new heavens and earth are not literal, and neither are the new heavens and earth of which John wrote. Using symbolic language, John described a new order of things: God's redeemed, through all the ages, at home in heaven with Him.

The AD 70 Doctrine
By Don McClain

The AD 70 Doctrine is a systematic view of the "end times" that embraces full-preterism. The term "preterism" comes from the Latin *praeter*, meaning *past*. Full-preterism deems all biblical prophecies as past or already fulfilled. This doctrine is also known as—"realized eschatology" (C. H. Dodd in the 1930s), "covenant eschatology" (Max King in the 1980s), and "Transmillennialism" (Tim King in the 2000s).

What Is the AD 70 Doctrine?

The doctrine asserts that the second and final coming of Jesus, the resurrection of the dead, and the final judgment, all occurred in AD 70, nearly 2,000 years ago. They believe and teach that, in correlation with these events, the eternal kingdom was established in all its power and glory, the body of Christ was actually redeemed, saints were forgiven, death was conquered (i.e., spiritual death), the end of the world occurred (the Jewish dispensation ended), the Law of Moses was brought to its end, the New Covenant was completed, and the hope of the new heavens and new earth was fully realized.

Some of this sounds very odd to many of us, and we may be tempted quickly to dismiss it, thinking it is either inconsequential or unbelievable. However, Full-preterism is growing, even among churches of Christ. Therefore, we need to be aware of its teachings and its devastating consequences.

General Refutation of the AD 70 Doctrine

Space does not permit an in-depth refutation of these things. My prayer is that what is presented will be substantive enough to increase the reader's understanding of the doctrine and why it is false. If someone is leaning towards this doctrine, hopefully, this will help awaken him to its error and steer him away from it. I would also direct you to Kyle Pope's book, *Thinking About 70 AD*, and Bruce Reeves' study on this subject earlier in the book for a much fuller treatment of this doctrine.

The AD 70 Doctrine

The AD 70 Doctrine asserts that Jesus came for the second and final time when the Romans destroyed Jerusalem and the temple in AD 70. This was indeed a historical event to which some of the Old Testament prophets pointed (Dan. 9:26-27), and Jesus Himself foretold (Matt. 24:1-35; Mark 13:1-31; Luke 21:5-33). AD 70 advocates seldom miss an opportunity to force a passage referring to a coming of the Lord into this one historical event.

Nevertheless, the Bible teaches Jesus will come again in our future—visibly, audibly, personally, and bodily (Acts 1:9-11; 1 Thess. 4:13-18; 2 Thess. 1:7-10). Luke's description of Jesus's ascension in Acts 1:9-11 is a straightforward historical narrative with emphasis on the presence of eyewitnesses. As the Lord ascended out of their *sight*, the disciples were literally "looking at Him" (v. 9) The angel said, "This Jesus, who has been taken up from you into heaven, will come in just the same way as you have *watched Him go into heaven*" (v. 11, emphasis mine).

Paul describes Jesus's future return in 1 Thessalonians 4:16-17, where he says, "The Lord Himself will descend from heaven with a shout, with the voice of the archangel and with the trumpet of God." Also, in 2 Thessalonians 1:7-9, Paul affirms, "You who are troubled rest with us when the Lord Jesus is revealed from heaven with His mighty angels . . . ."

Full Preterists assert that the above descriptions of Jesus's future coming are all "figurative" and should not be taken literally. Did the apostles "figuratively" see Jesus ascend? Would those who were "alive" and remain" when Jesus "figuratively" descended "figuratively" meet Him in the air to "figuratively" be with Him forever? How would the destruction of Jerusalem provide comfort for Christians suffering in Thessalonica? Would the "figurative" punishment of their persecutors provide them actual relief or just "figurative" relief?

The argument that "this is figurative language" simply does not work because of the context of these passages.

Full Preterists also deny any future personal, bodily resurrection. They assert that "the resurrection" of John 5:28-29, 1 Corinthians 15, and Philippians 3:10, 21, etc., occurred in AD 70.

As with any false doctrine, terms must be redefined, and their applications changed. To sustain this doctrine, they are forced to define "resurrection" as being (1) purely spiritual or (2) only figurative such as in Ezekiel 37 or Colossians 2:13. They fail to recognize that figurative language is rooted in known reality. For the Scriptures to use the concept of resurrection figuratively, there must be a basic understanding of its literal reality (cf. Acts 24:15-21; 26:6-8).

AD 70 proponents exercise extreme mental gymnastics when it comes to 1 Corinthians 15. They assert Paul is speaking of a "corporate" raising of "Old Testament saints" and the "gathering" of the pre-AD 70 "divided church" (Jews & Gentiles) into one body. Adherents are forced to conclude that (1) the death under consideration is spiritual and cannot be physical, (2) Jesus's resurrection ("firstfruits"), and the resurrection in the text (the harvest), are different in kind, (3) Christians were not made spiritually alive until AD 70, and (4) the church was "corruptible, perishable, and mortal" before AD 70.

The denial of a personal bodily resurrection of the believer logically results in the denial of Jesus's resurrection (1 Cor. 15:12-19). To teach the resurrection of 1 Corinthians 15 as being different in kind than Jesus's resurrection destroys Paul's firstfruits analogy, (1 Cor. 15:20, 23). If baptized believers were to be made spiritually alive in AD 70, they must have been spiritually dead before AD 70. Was Paul spiritually dead when he wrote the epistle? The truth is, Christians were alive spiritually in Christ before AD 70, not merely in a proleptic sense (cf. Rom. 6:3-6; Eph. 1:3-16; Col. 2:12-13; 2 Cor. 5:17; etc.). The pre-AD 70 church was indeed washed, purified, made alive, enjoying every spiritual blessing in Christ that anyone could enjoy while on this side of eternity. They were complete in Him (Eph. 1:3-16; Col. 2:9-10).

Consequences of the AD 70 Doctrine

This false teaching leads to further error. Whenever one holds to an erroneous view of a particular biblical doctrine, by necessity, other teachings of Scripture must also be changed to support and defend it. To quote Edward E. Stevens, an AD 70 proponent: "Indeed, the preterist view does 'change our views on a lot of things.' It has implications for many doctrines . . . . Do we completely grasp the full impact of the preterist worldview upon all other biblical doctrines besides eschatology (i.e., ecclesiology, soteriology, sacramentology, et al.)?" ("Doctrinal Implications of Preterist Eschatology").

The AD 70 Doctrine

Error does not exist in a vacuum! One cannot alter one aspect of truth and not alter others. Just think of the effects this teaching has on the application of biblical teaching today. Why partake of the Lord's Supper? Why be baptized? Why assemble with the saints? Is there any biblical instruction applicable today?

More problems: How could there be concurrent covenants, concurrent priesthoods, and concurrent sacrificial systems? If Christians could not be forgiven of their sins before AD 70, was the sacrifice of Christ insufficient?

Since AD 70 advocates affirm that hope has been realized and we already have our eternal inheritance, what do we have to look forward to or anticipate? If spiritual death has been finally and fully destroyed, how can a Christian sin today? For that matter, how can *anyone* sin or be separated from God? Max King followed this doctrine to its logical end and embraced universalism.

Conclusion

Paul marked Hymenaeus and Philetus as false teachers because they "strayed concerning the truth, saying that the resurrection is already past; and they overthrow the faith of some" (2 Tim. 2:16-18). Their heresy was not just a matter of timing, as the Preterists insist, (they were only off about three years). No, their error also involved the nature of the resurrection and negated the faith and hope of those who were thus deceived. Full-preterism still makes shipwreck of the faith! Do not be deceived.

Bibliography

Stevens, Edward E. "Doctrinal Implications of Preterist Eschatology: Introduction to the Series." *Kingdom Counsel* (newsletter) Sept.-Oct., 1991. Bradford, PA: International Preterist Association.

Eco-Eschatology
By Matthew Bassford

In 2019, a teenage activist named Greta Thunberg burst onto the world political scene. Like a sandwich-board-wearing prophet of catastrophe, she predicted disaster if the people of the world did not repent—in this case, of the sin of abusing the environment. In a speech at the 2019 U.N. Climate Action Summit, she warned, "People are dying. Entire ecosystems are collapsing. We are in the beginning of a mass extinction."

Though shrill, Thunberg expresses the fears of millions. A steady drumbeat of scientific studies over the past several decades has foretold a dramatic change in the earth's climate as a result of the burning of fossil fuels. Proponents of this view foresee apocalyptic consequences: coastal cities flooding, continents being scourged by superstorms and drought, and possibly even the end of the human race.

As others have observed, these premonitions of doom have distinctly religious and even biblical overtones. Judgment is coming! Unless we repent, we will all surely perish! This is even more ironic because most diehard environmentalists are materialists. They believe in sin, but they don't believe in God. In His place, they have turned to a reverence for the planet and the environment. This fragile jewel's fate is in our hands, and unless we act soon, it will be everlastingly too late!

Three Problems

Though this appeal is compelling to many, it has three serious problems. First, it elevates the situation on earth right now to privileged status. If the climate changes, if species die, it's an unthinkable tragedy.

However, according to scientists' and materialists' own convictions, this is nothing more than planetary business as usual. They believe that the history of the earth is replete with dramatic climate changes and mass extinctions. If the spotted owl and the snail darter go the way of the dinosaur, what makes that particularly tragic? Given time, something else will evolve to take their place (or so we are told).

Eco-Eschatology

Second, this way of thinking elevates humankind to an illogically privileged position. Its adherents set up a dichotomy between nature on the one hand (beautiful, delicate, pristine) and man on the other hand (corrupting, befouling, destroying). They think we're something different.

Again, though, this is not something that their philosophy allows. They affirm that we are animals. We are part of nature. We evolved up from the primordial slime like the bears and the wombats, and in our essence, we are the same as they.

If people are part of nature, their works are part of nature also. A bulldozer is just as much an instrument of Darwinian triumph as more powerful legs, or more efficient lungs are. Survival of the fittest, baby! Why does the wolf have a moral obligation not to prey upon the sheep?

Third, it presumes that humankind can predict the future and is in control of its own destiny. The materialist conception of the universe leaves no room for any powers greater than us. We must act to protect the planet because both our salvation and our uttermost destruction lie in our own hands.

This, too, is silly. Even the godless must admit that the human race isn't that wise or that powerful. As anyone who pays attention to weather forecasts knows, we can't predict, with more than coin-flip accuracy, whether it's going to rain next Tuesday. Yet, these folks are dead certain about what the climate is going to be like 50 years from now.

One of the great internal proofs of the inspiration of Scripture is biblical prophets' ability to foretell the future accurately. Outside of the Bible, the record of fortune-tellers is demonstrably and uniformly lousy. Thunberg et al. want us to believe that "Things Are Different" when it comes to climate change. I'm guessing that it's not.

Additionally, even if people expend every effort to turn the climate clock back, there are no guarantees of success. If the Yellowstone supervolcano erupts, or a sufficiently large asteroid comes crashing into the planet, it doesn't matter whether various nations hit their emissions-reduction targets or not. We're all doomed anyway.

Man's Role in God's Creation

An appropriately biblical view of the relationship between man, God, and His creation addresses all these problems. First, we have reason to understand ourselves as different from all other living creatures. God did not breathe His Spirit into the nostrils of the bears and wombats. As Genesis 2:7 reports, that dignity is unique to man.

We stand apart from the rest of the physical world. Indeed, we stand above it because God has put us above it. According to Psalm 8:6, God has given us dominion over His handiwork. When we impose order on the planet, it is because we have the right to do so.

As with all of God's other grants of authority, we should exercise this one with restraint and wisdom. It is not godly for us to wantonly destroy and despoil the beauty that He has made. If herds must be slaughtered and forests must be felled so that humanity may be fed and housed, so be it. We are worth more than many sparrows, after all. However, when we act from greed rather than need, the ugliness we create only mirrors the ugliness already existing in our hearts. A good Christian is a good steward of the creation.

Indeed, there is great spiritual value in leaving portions of that creation untouched and unspoiled. My family and I enjoy traveling around the state and the country to visit various parks, and we all feel that the majesty of nature brings us closer to God.

There is a sublimity to a mighty waterfall or a grove of old-growth redwoods or the shattered ruins of a volcano that cannot be captured by words or photographs or videos. In their presence, we are reminded that we are, indeed, very small. Our hearts are provoked to cry out, "What is man, that You are mindful of Him?" (Psa. 8:4). Without these reminders, we are prone to forget.

God's Role in His Creation

Most of all, though, the eco-eschatologists err in forgetting precisely this; we are not great and in control. God is. Though we do not know the day nor the hour, God has promised us that He, and no other, will seal the fate of this present creation. The heavens and the earth are reserved for His fire, and until that day comes, no other force in the universe can destroy them.

In this, we can find assurance. Though I regard the environmentalist narrative with considerable skepticism, I do believe that we can harm ourselves and the planet significantly through foolishness and evil.

Eco-Eschatology

However, we should not think that we can extinguish life that God does not want to be extinguished, and especially not that we can destroy ourselves. We are sustained by His will, and as long as the earth continues, so will we.

Conclusion

Mankind was created to desire and search for meaning. The drive to matter exists in each one of us, and it obviously animates Thunberg and her ilk. We all want to imagine that we are the heroes of our own stories, that our actions will spell the difference between triumph and disaster.

In reality, though, we are not and cannot be the great Mover of creation and fate. God is, and when we behave as though the future depends on us, we arrogate His role to ourselves. If we want to find meaning, then we can't do so by preserving the planet from harm. Instead, we find it by devoting the short season that we spend on this planet to Him.

Bibliography

Thumberg, Greta. "Transcript: Greta Thunberg's Speech at the U.N. Climate Action Summit." *NPR.org*. September 9, 2019. https://www.npr.org/2019/09/23/763452863/transcript-greta-thunbergs-speech-at-the-u-n-climate-action-summit.

What Does the Bible Teach about Hades and Sheol?
By Kyle Pope

Introduction

The Greek word *hadēs* occurs eleven times in the New Testament. When quoting Old Testament passages, this word is consistently used to translate the Hebrew word *sheōl* (cf. Acts 2:27, 31; Ps. 16:10; 1 Cor. 15:55; Hos. 13:14). *Sheōl* occurs sixty-five times in the Old Testament. In the Septuagint (LXX), the Greek Old Testament translated before the time of Christ, sixty of these instances are rendered with the word *hadēs*.

The King James Version (KJV) in many cases translated both words "hell," in keeping with the Old English meaning of the word *helle* as the "nether world, abode of the dead, infernal regions" in addition to being the "place of torment for the wicked after death" (*Online Etymology Dictionary*). Since modern English now uses both the word "hell" and the word "hades" almost exclusively in reference to the place of final punishment for the wicked, this has led many to apply Scriptures referring to *sheōl* or *hadēs* to the place of final punishment. What does the Bible teach about this place referred to in Scripture as *sheōl* or *hadēs*? In this study, we will seek an answer by surveying the use of both words.

References to Sheol in the Old Testament

The KJV translated *sheōl* in the following ways: "grave" (31x); "hell" (31x); "pit" (3x). In spite of this, unlike some of the synonyms for *sheōl*, we will consider later, it does not seem that *sheōl* is ever used simply of a physical pit or grave. We will test this assertion by considering what is said about sheol in general.

First, it is clear that the living are said to go to the dead in sheol (Gen. 37:35). A man's death is described as being "gathered to his people" (Gen. 25:8, 17; 35:29; 49:33; Num. 20:24; Deut. 32:50). This is reflected in David's words at the death of his son: "I shall go to him, but he shall not return to

What Does the Bible Teach about Hades and Sheol?

me" (2 Sam. 12:23). Sheol is where one is said to go when he dies (Gen. 42:38; 44:29, 31). Sheol is the place of the dead. One does not generally go "alive" into sheol (Num. 16:28-33 [30, 33 "pit"= *sheōl*]; cf. Ps. 55:15), because it is the house of the dead (Job 17:13). All the dead go there (Ps. 89:48; 141:7). This includes the wicked (Ps. 9:17), the wealthy (Job 21:13), the mighty (Isa. 14:9-15), and even the righteous (Ps. 16:10).

Some hyperbolic language is used in connection with sheol. For example, those spared from death and delivered from danger are said to be "brought up" from Sheol (Ps. 30:3; 86:13; Jonah 2:2). In trials, one is said to be near Sheol (Ps. 88:3). Discipline delivers one from sheol (Prov. 23:14), but adultery is the path to sheol (Prov. 5:5; 7:27). One should not conclude from this that sheol is not a real place. This use of hyperbole describes the actual result that can come from sin and certain dangers.

Although this is a spiritual condition, there are spatial descriptions given to it. For example, it is said to be deep (Job 11:7-8). It has "lowest" parts (Deut. 32:22; Ps. 86:13; Prov. 9:18). In this vein, it is the Lord who brings people down to (or up from) sheol (1 Sam. 2:1-10 [6 "grave" = *sheōl*]). It is said to be "beneath" (Prov. 15:24; Isa. 14:9). We should note that this is a spiritual condition and should not be confused with pagan concepts of a physical place located somewhere underground. Just as the abode of God is said to be "above," the abode of the dead is said to be "below."

Some of these spatial descriptions may be given to explain some facts about its nature that are personified. For example, it is never satisfied (Prov. 27:20; 30:16; Hab. 2:5). It is never full (Isa. 5:14). It is cruel (Song of Sol. 8:6). Sorrows are associated with it—either sorrow in going there or sorrow in being there (Gen. 43:38; 44:29, 31; 2 Sam. 22:6; Ps. 18:5; 116:3).

A key theme to which references to sheol often relate is the fact that it is a place hidden from the things of life (Job 7:9; 14:13; Ps. 6:5), even though God sees all those who are there (Job 26:6; Ps. 139:8; Prov. 15:11). One cannot hide from God in sheol (Amos 9:2), and the wicked are silenced in that realm (Ps. 31:17). Those "under the sun" cannot see activity in sheol (Eccl. 9:10). While this text has led some to argue that the state of the soul in sheol is one of unconsciousness, we should note that the focus of Ecclesiastes is on things as they appear "under the sun" (Eccl. 1:3, 9, 14; 2:11, 17, 18, 19, 20, 22; 3:16; 4:1, 3, 7, 15; 5:13, 18; 6:1, 12; 8:9, 15,

"When Will These Things Be?" : Questions on Eschatology

17; 9:3, 6, 9, 11, 13; 10:5). Solomon addresses things as they appear, not as they necessarily are. "Under the sun," one can see nothing that the dead do. Because of this, the dead cannot praise God in the company of the living (Ps. 30:9).

Sheol is said to "swallow" people up (Prov. 1:12). It has a "mouth" or entrance (Ps. 141:7; Isa. 5:14) that consumes the sinful (Job 24:19; Prov. 9:18). Bars enclose it (Job 17:16), and gates guard access to it (Isa. 38:10). These descriptions will be important when we see New Testament references to this place and its nature. In general, those who have gone there do "not come up" (Job 7:9). Yet, a promise is made of the time when God will "ransom" or "redeem" souls from sheol (Hos. 13:14; Ps. 49:15).

Words Used in Synonymous Parallelism

At least two Old Testament words are used prominently in synonymous parallelism with *sheōl*: (1) *shachath* and (2) *bowr*. Considering the use of these words further demonstrates biblical teaching on the realm of the dead.

1. Shachath is used twenty-three times in the Old Testament and translated in the KJV in the following ways: "corruption" (4x); "pit" (14x); "destruction" (2x); "ditch" (2x); "grave" (1x). Unlike *sheōl*, there are many cases in which it is clear that only a literal physical pit is being described (Job 9:31; Ps. 7:15; 9:15; 35:7; 94:13; Prov. 26:27; Isa. 51:14; Ezek. 19:4, 8). However, in several cases, its association with *sheōl* makes it clear that a spiritual sense is being described. For example, one of the most important Messianic texts declares, "For You will not leave my soul in sheol (*sheōl*), nor will You allow Your Holy One to see corruption (*shachath*)" (Ps. 16:10, NKJV). Jonah uses hyperbole in speaking of his deliverance, saying, "I went down to the moorings of the mountains; the earth with its bars closed behind me forever; yet You have brought up my life from the pit (*shachath*), O LORD, my God" (Jonah 2:6; cf. 2:2 "Out of the belly of sheol (*sheōl*) I cried"). Job says in sorrow, "If I say to corruption (*shachath*), 'You are my father,' And to the worm, 'You are my mother and my sister,' Where then is my hope? As for my hope, who can see it? Will they go down to the gates of sheol (*sheōl*)? Shall we have rest together in the dust?" (Job 17:14-16).

As we saw with the word *sheōl*, one who is delivered from danger is kept from *shachath* (Job 33:18, 22, 24, 28; Isa. 38:17). Redemption from

What Does the Bible Teach about Hades and Sheol?

shachath to the "light of the living" is similarly foreshadowed (Job 33:30; Ps. 103:4). The wicked shall be brought down to *shachath* (Ps. 55:23; Ezek. 28:8). In all of these texts, it is clear that *shachath* is being used to describe the place of the dead, generally called sheol.

2. Bowr is used sixty-nine times in the Old Testament and translated in the King James Version in the following ways: "pit" (42x), "cistern" (4x), "dungeon" (12x), "well" (9x), and "fountain" (1x). Similar to *shachath* (but unlike *sheōl*), in most cases in which it is used, it is clear that only a literal physical pit is being described (Gen. 37:20, 22, 24, 28, 29; 40:15; 41:14; et al.). Yet, also like *shachath* in several cases, its association with *sheōl* makes it clear that a spiritual sense is being described. The psalmist writes, "O LORD, You brought my soul up from the grave (*sheōl*); You have kept me alive, that I should not go down to the pit (*bowr*)" (Ps. 30:3, NKJV; cf. 28:1). Further, "For my soul is full of troubles, and my life draws near to the grave (*sheōl*). I am counted with those who go down to the pit (*bowr*); I am like a man who has no strength, adrift among the dead, like the slain who lie in the grave (*qeber*), whom You remember no more, and who are cut off from Your hand. You have laid me in the lowest pit (*bowr*), in darkness, in the depths" (Ps. 88:3-6; cf. 143:7). Solomon speaks of the plotting of the wicked, who say, "Let us swallow them alive like sheol (*sheōl*), and whole, like those who go down to the Pit (*bowr*)" (Prov. 1:12, NKJV).

As was said of *sheōl*, the proud will be brought down to *bowr*. For example, Lucifer (Isa. 14:12), used in Scripture to identify, not Satan, but the king of Babylon (Isa. 13:1), is told, "You shall be brought down to sheol (*sheōl*), to the lowest depths of the Pit (*bowr*)" (Isa. 14:15, NKJV).

Just as *sheōl* is a place hidden from the sight of the living, Isaiah declares, "For the grave (*sheōl*) cannot praise thee, death cannot celebrate thee: they that go down into the pit (*bowr*) cannot hope for thy truth. The living, the living, he shall praise thee, as I do this day: the father to the children shall make known thy truth" (Isa. 38:18-19, NKJV). We should note, the point here is that the dead cannot hope to learn the truth, thus changing their fate, as opposed to stating that they are incapable of perceiving truth.

Tyre is told, "I will bring you down with those who descend into the Pit (*bowr*), to the people of old, and I will make you dwell in the lowest part of the earth, in places desolate from antiquity, with those who go down to the Pit (*bowr*), so that you may never be inhabited; and I shall establish glory in the land of the living" (Ezek. 26:20, NKJV). Here we see "the Pit," like sheol in a spiritual sense, is said to be in "the lowest part of the earth" that houses the "people of old."

Assyria, like a "cedar of Lebanon" (Ezek. 31:3) is said to have been cut down (Ezek. 31:12) and "delivered to death, to the depths of the earth, among the children of men who go down to the Pit (*bowr*)" (Ezek. 31:14). In this judgment, God declares, "In the day when it went down to hell (*sheōl*), I caused mourning" (Ezek. 31:15, NKJV), explaining, "I made the nations shake at the sound of its fall, when I cast it down to hell (*sheōl*) together with those who descend into the Pit (*bowr*)" (Ezek. 31:16a). In this text, other "trees" (likely referring to other nations) are said to be "comforted" by this in the "depths of the earth" (Ezek. 31:16b), for "they also went down to hell (*sheōl*) with it, with those slain by the sword; and those who were its strong arm dwelt in its shadows among the nations" (Ezek. 31:17, NKJV). In each of these texts, *bowr*, like *shachath*, is being used to describe more fully the place of the dead called sheol.

Two Important Old Testament Passages

Having considered most of the Old Testament references, the question arises as to whether we should understand the realm of sheol as a conscious or unconscious condition. Two significant passages help us answer this question.

1. Psalm 49. The focus of this Psalm is a contrast between "those who trust in their wealth" (49:6) and the "upright" (49:14). Even the rich cannot "redeem his brother" (49:7a) to give "to God a ransom for him" (49:7b) in the hope that he might "continue to live eternally, and not see the Pit (*shachath*)" (49:9). The fact is that the wise and the fool all die (49:10a), leaving their wealth (49:10b), houses (49:11), and honor to others (49:12a). In this, the one who trusts in wealth "is like the beasts that perish" (49:12b).

The psalmist explains that this is "the way of those who are foolish" and those who follow them (49:13)—"like sheep they are laid in the grave (*sheōl*)" (49:14a) and their beauty is "consumed in the grave (*sheōl*)" (49:14c)—but, "The upright shall have dominion over them in the morning" (49:14b). The term "morning" here may have an eschatological meaning because the psalmist confidently asserts, "God will redeem my soul from the power of the grave (*sheōl*), for He shall receive me" (49:15). This clearly reflects confidence in a conscious reception by God.

What Does the Bible Teach about Hades and Sheol?

This Psalm ends with encouragement not to fear the rich (49:16) because, in death, the rich man takes nothing with him (49:17) when he goes to the "generation of his fathers" (49:19). Again, the one who "does not understand" this "is like the beasts that perish" (49:20). The psalmist here affirms (at the very least for the "upright"—with whom he identifies) a conscious state whereby God will "receive" him. If not, there is no contrast.

2. Ezekiel 32. After pronouncing judgment on Ammon, Moab, and Edom (25:1-17), Tyre and Sidon (26:1-27:36; 28:1-26), and Egypt (29:1-31:18), the prophet is commanded to pronounce a lament of judgment on Pharaoh (32:2). This lamentation calls Pharaoh to consider his future contact with "those who go down to the Pit (*bowr*)" (32:18). While this language is certainly poetic, it offers some profound facts about the afterlife.

Referring to Pharaoh, Ezekiel is told, "The strong among the mighty shall speak to him out of the midst of sheol (*sheōl*)" (32:21a, ASV). We might take this to mean that the dead speak to him through their example—they were powerful, but now lie in shame—but this is referring to what Pharaoh and his multitudes will see and hear after death. The Lord promises him, "I will lay your flesh on the mountains, and fill the valleys with your carcass" (32:5, NKJV).

Pharaoh is then told who will be in sheol. These include Assyria (32:22-23), Elam (32:24-25), Meshach and Tubal (32:26-28), Edom (32:29), and the Sidonians (32:30). Although these, like Pharaoh, "caused terror in the land of the living" (32:25; cf. 32:24, 26-27, 32), when Pharaoh is said to see them "bear their shame with those who go down to the Pit (*bowr*)" (32:24-25, 30)—Ezekiel is told, "Pharaoh will see them and be comforted over all his multitude"—that is, he is consoled to see they have died as his multitudes have died—"Pharaoh and all his army, slain by the sword" (32:31). If the condition of the soul in sheol is not conscious, there would be no way that Pharaoh could "see" those listed here. If these sinful souls pass out of existence, they do not "bear their shame" and could not "speak to him out of the midst of sheol" (ASV).

References to Hades in the New Testament

The Greek word *hadēs* is used only eleven times in the New Testament. As mentioned above, in New Testament quotations from the Old Testament, New Testament authors consistently translate the Hebrew word *sheōl* with the Greek word *hadēs*. We should not imagine from this

"When Will These Things Be?" : Questions on Eschatology

that New Testament writers were thus affirming pagan Greek concepts and mythology that they associated with a fanciful land of the dead, which was literally in the heart of the earth, also called "hades." New Testament usage builds upon the earlier translation of the Old Testament into Greek, in which sixty out of sixty-five times *sheōl* was translated *hadēs*. So, when the New Testament refers to hades, it is describing the same place identified in the Old Testament as sheol.

Old Testament Quotations. In three passages, *hadēs* is used in quotations from the Old Testament to translate *sheōl*. In Acts 2:27 and 31, Luke quotes Psalm 16:10. Verse 27, quite literally quotes, "For You will not leave my soul in hades (*hadēs*), nor will You allow Your Holy One to see corruption" (NKJV). In verse 31, Peter explains that David, "foreseeing this, spoke concerning the resurrection of the Christ, that His soul was not left in hades (*hadēs*), nor did His flesh see corruption" (NKJV). Peter asserts that Jesus went to hades in His death and came out of hades in His resurrection.

In 1 Corinthians 15, Paul addresses the general resurrection of the dead. After describing what will happen at the Lord's "coming (*parousia*)" (15:23), when "the trumpet will sound, and the dead will be raised incorruptible, and we shall be changed" (15:52), Paul explains that "when this corruptible has put on incorruption, and this mortal has put on immortality, then shall be brought to pass the saying that is written" (15:54a), paraphrasing Hosea 13:14, "Death is swallowed up in victory. O Death, where is your sting? O hades, where is your victory?" (15:54b-55). As noted above, Hosea 13:14 is one of the important Old Testament texts promising a time when souls will be *ransomed* from sheol. Its application in 1 Corinthians 15:55 demonstrates when this will happen. It is when the "corruptible" has put on "incorruption" that hades will be robbed of its power.

Independent Uses. Similar to the pronouncements of judgment we saw in our Old Testament studies concerning Tyre (Ezek. 26:20) or the king of Babylon (Isa. 14:15), Jesus declares that Capernaum (where Jesus spent much of His public ministry) would be "brought down to hades (*hadēs*)" (Matt. 11:23; Luke 10:15). After Peter's confession that Jesus is "the Christ, the Son of the living God" (Matt. 16:16), Jesus proclaimed that, upon this bedrock of faith which Peter just confessed, "On this rock I will

What Does the Bible Teach about Hades and Sheol?

build My church, and the gates of hades (*hadēs*) shall not prevail against it" (Matt. 16:18, NKJV). We are reminded of Old Testament descriptions of the "bars" (Job 17:16) and "gates" (Isa. 38:10) of sheol. The imagery is not that of the church storming the gates of hades, but Christ conquering the stronghold of death leading forth His redeemed church in liberty from the realm of the dead.

The most extensive treatment of hades in the New Testament is found in Luke 16:19-31. It describes the death of a rich man and a beggar named Lazarus (vv. 19-22). When they both die, the beggar is said to be carried by angels to "Abraham's bosom" (v. 22a) while the rich man is simply said to be buried (16:22b) then found "in torments in hades" (v. 23a). In Jewish rabbinical literature, the phrase "Abraham's bosom (or lap)" is used of the abode of the righteous after death (*Kiddushin* 72b). In Luke, it appears to be within hades, yet "afar off" from the "torments" of the rich man and within sight and speaking range of Abraham and Lazarus (v. 23b). When the rich man begs to change his condition, Abraham tells him "a great chasm" (v. 26, NASB) separates the two realms preventing anyone from crossing over.

Many have tried to dismiss this as parabolic, fictitious, figurative, or even drawn from pagan concepts; however, it reflects the same principles we found in Old Testament teaching on sheol. Namely: (1) all the dead go to sheol (Ps. 89:48; 141:7); (2) the wicked bear shame there (Ezek. 32:24, 25, 30); (3) but the upright are received by God (Ps. 49:15b) in the hopes of one day being redeemed from sheol (Ps. 49:15a; cf. Hos. 13:14); (4) it has different parts (Deut. 32:22; Ps. 86:13; Prov. 9:18); and (5) once there, none can change his fate (2 Sam. 12:23; Job 7:9; Isa. 38:18-19). In many respects, Jesus's words simply illustrate in specific terms the theme of Psalm 49: "those who trust in riches" perish, but God receives the "upright."

Another independent use comes at the beginning of John's vision in the book of Revelation. Jesus identifies Himself to John, saying, "I am He who lives, and was dead, and behold, I am alive forevermore. Amen. And I have the keys of hades (*hadēs*) and of Death" (Rev. 1:18). This text becomes vital in consideration of identifying when hades was actually to be universally overcome. Further, during the vision in Revelation, when the fourth seal is opened (Rev. 6:7), John sees, "a pale horse. And the name of him who sat on it was death, and hades (*hadēs*) followed with him. And power was given to them over a fourth of the earth, to kill with sword, with hunger, with death, and by the beasts of the earth" (Rev. 6:8, NKJV). Hades is here figuratively used to describe the power of death over events upon the earth. Finally, near the end of Revelation, after the judgment before the "Great White Throne," "death and hades" (*hadēs*) will deliver up all their dead (Rev. 20:13) and both will be cast into the "lake of fire" identified as the "second death" (Rev. 20:14).

Synonymous Parallels. Similar to what we saw of *sheōl* in the Old Testament, at least three words may be used synonymously with *hadēs* (or some part of it): (1) *paradeisos*; (2) *abussos*; and (3) *tartaroō*. These words help us further understand the biblical teaching on this realm of the dead.

1. *Paradeisos* is used three times in the New Testament and translated "paradise" each time. Properly, it is a Persian word that means "garden" or "park." The Greek Old Testament used it in this sense of the "garden of the Lord" (Gen. 16:10, "garden of Eden" (Joel 2:3), or garden generally (Isa. 1:30). In 2 Corinthians 12:4, it is used in Paul's description of his vision of being caught up to the "third heaven" (12:2) "into paradise" (*paradeisos*). In Jewish thought, heaven was conceived in three realms: (1) where the clouds are; (2) where the stars are; and (3) where God is. In Revelation 2:7, one who "overcomes" is promised the right to "eat from the tree of life, which is in the midst of the paradise (*paradeisos*) of God." Both of these seem to apply to the heavenly realm of God. In Luke 23:43, Jesus promises the thief on the cross, "today you will be with Me in paradise (*paradeisos*)." We noted above that, upon death, Jesus was said to go into hades (Acts 2:27, 31). This makes it clear that Jesus was using *paradeisos* (like "Abraham's bosom") of the part of hades reserved for the righteous.

2. *Abussos* is used in the New Testament nine times, seven of which are found in Revelation of the "bottomless pit" in which Satan and his angels are said to be bound (Rev. 20:1, 3) or to ascend from (Rev. 9:1-2, 11; 11:7; 17:8). This former sense seems to be the idea used by the evil spirits who beg Jesus not to "command them to go out into the Abyss (*abbussos*)" (Luke 8:31), which may relate to the use of *tartaroō* below. The final use comes in Romans 10:7, as Jesus is comparing the wording of Deuteronomy 30:12-14 to illustrate the "word of faith"(10:8), Paul paraphrases, "Who will descend into the Abyss (*abbussos*)?" He then explains that to ask this

What Does the Bible Teach about Hades and Sheol?

would "bring Christ up from the dead." This equates the Abyss (or part of it) with hades.

3. *Tartaroō* is used only once in the New Testament. Unfortunately, almost all translations continue to translate this word "hell." Alexander Campbell's *Living Oracles* is an exception to this, putting it, "For God, indeed, did not spare the angels who sinned, but with chains of darkness confining them in tartarus (*tartaroō*), delivered them over to be kept for judgment" (2 Pet. 3:4, LO). Jude parallels this writing, "And the angels who did not keep their proper domain, but left their own abode, He has reserved in everlasting chains under darkness for the judgment of the great day" (6, NKJV). Like *abussos* above, this applies to a realm where sinful angels are bound awaiting "the judgment of the great day." Is this part of hades (as *abussos* was applied to hades—Rom. 10:7)? The Greek Old Testament uses *tartaros* in at least one passage synonymously with hades. Proverbs 30:16 reads, "hades; and the eros of a woman; and tartarus and the earth that is not filled with water; and the water and fire never says, 'enough'" (Pope). In 2 Peter, the apostle uses sinful angels as one example to show, "the Lord knows how to deliver the godly out of temptations and to reserve the unjust under punishment for the day of judgment" (3:9). This indicates that, like sinful angels, in hades, God reserves "the unjust under punishment for the day of judgment."

Conclusion

Having surveyed the biblical teaching on sheol and hades, let's close with some questions that may arise as we consider this biblical doctrine.

Is Hades Purgatory? No. Purgatory is a concept taught by the Roman Catholic Church that is not found in Scripture. It holds that some who are not yet worthy to enter eternal life go to a place where they can be purified from some sins and then, eventually, enter heaven. We have seen that once a soul is assigned a condition of punishment or comfort in hades, he cannot change that condition (Luke 16:26; Isa. 38:18-19). Souls in hades await the day of judgment (2 Pet. 3:9) in the hope that God will "redeem" their souls from it (Hos. 13:14; Ps. 49:15). Souls who are delivered from hades will either go into the "lake of fire" (Rev. 20:14) or into the heavenly "paradise of God" (Rev. 2:7).

Is Hades Annihilation? No. Although many passages emphasize that sheol and hades are hidden from the view of the living (Job 7:9; 14:13; Ps.

"When Will These Things Be?" : Questions on Eschatology

6:5; Eccl. 9:10), it is clear that the wicked and the righteous continue to live (cf. Matt. 22:32) and can see (Luke 16:23; Ezek. 32:31), hear (Luke 16:25), speak (Luke 16:24-25; Ezek. 32:21), bear shame (Ezek. 32:24), experience comfort (Luke 16:22; Ps. 49:15), or torment (Luke 16:23). These things could not be said of souls who pass out of existence.

Is Hades Hell? No. Hades will be emptied, then cast into the "lake of fire" where the wicked are also cast (Rev. 20:14). Scripture describes this as "everlasting punishment" (Matt. 25:46). When Jesus spoke of the place of final punishment after judgment, He consistently used the Greek word *gehenna* (Matt. 5:22, 29, 30; 10:28; 18:9; 23:15, 33; Mark 9:43, 45, 47; Luke 12:5; Jas. 3:6). Although some Jews conceived of this as the place of punishment in hades after death (*Genesis Rabbah* 48), this is not biblical terminology. In Scripture, all the dead go to sheol or hades (Ps. 49:15; 89:48; 141:7; Luke 16:23; Rev. 20:13), only the wicked go to gehenna.

When Will Hades Be Emptied? Several answers have been offered to this question. Some say...

1. At the resurrection of Christ. It is true that in His death and resurrection, Jesus was said to destroy "him who had the power of death, that is, the devil" (Heb. 2:14). However, at the beginning of Revelation, He was still said to hold the "keys of hades and of death" (Rev. 1:18). If hades had already been opened, no keys would be needed. Additionally, Jesus promised that the "gates of hades" would not prevail against His church (Matt. 16:18). Properly, Christ's church would not begin until Pentecost, leaving no victory to be won. In writing 1 Corinthians, Paul foresaw the time when death, as the last enemy, would be conquered (15:26). If this had occurred at Christ's resurrection, it would have been a past (not a future) event.

2. At the destruction of Jerusalem. The destruction of Jerusalem was undoubtedly an act of Divine judgment upon Israel, but to draw this conclusion, we would have to apply all promises of a "Day of Judgment" to AD 70 (cf. 2 Pet. 3:9). We saw above that Paul said Hosea 13:14 would be fulfilled when the "corruptible" has put on "incorruption" (1 Cor. 15:54-55). It is at that time when hades is said to be robbed of its victory. Death (spiritual and physical) and corruption (spiritual and physical) have continued after AD 70. Revelation 20:11-15 describe events that must precede death and hades giving up "the dead that are in them" (v. 13).

What Does the Bible Teach about Hades and Sheol?

Namely: (1) Christ sitting on His throne of judgment (v. 11); (2) heaven and earth fleeing away (v. 11); (3) all being judged (v. 13). Then, after hades is emptied, "death and hades" are cast into the "lake of fire" (v. 14). If hades was emptied at AD 70, then Death (spiritual and physical) must also have ended. It did not.

3. At the Final Judgment. Only at the final judgment upon Christ's return will all the scriptural conditions described be met, for hades to be emptied, and the souls residing therein be cast into the "lake of fire" (Rev. 20:14) or enter the heavenly "paradise of God" (Rev. 2:7). May we all anticipate that glorious day and live in such a way as to prepare for it.

Bibliography

"Hell," *Online Etymology Dictionary.* https://www.etymonline.com/search?q=hell.

www.ingramcontent.com/pod-product-compliance
Lightning Source LLC
Chambersburg PA
CBHW050846160426
43194CB00011B/2053